Developing Online Help
for Windows 95™

Copyright © 1996 International Thomson Computer Press

I(T)P™   A division of International Thomson Publishing Inc.
The ITP Logo is a trademark under license.

Printed in the United States of America.

For more information, contact:

International Thomson Computer Press
20 Park Plaza, Suite 1001
Boston, MA 02116
USA

International Thomson Publishing GmbH
Königswinterer Strasse 418
53227 Bonn
Germany

International Thomson Publishing Europe
Berkshire House 168-173
High Holborn
London WCIV 7AA
England

International Thomson Publishing Asia
221 Henderson Road #05-10
Henderson Building
Singapore 0315

Thomas Nelson Australia
102 Dodds Street
South Melbourne, 3205
Victoria, Australia

International Thomson Publishing Japan
Hirakawacho Kyowa Building, 3F
2-2-1 Hirakawacho
Chiyoda-ku, 102 Tokyo
Japan

Nelson Canada
1120 Birchmount Road
Scarborough, Ontario
Canada M1K 5G4

International Thomson Editores
Campos Eliseos 385, Piso 7
Col. Polanco
11560 Mexico D.F. Mexico

International Thomson Publishing Southern Africa
Bldg. 19, Constantia Park
239 Old Pretoria Road, P.O. Box 2459
Halfway House, 1685 South Africa

International Thomson Publishing France
1, rue st. Georges
75 009 Paris France

1 2 3 4 5 6 7 8 9 10 QEBFF 01 00 99 98 97 96
Library of Congress Cataloging-in-Publication Data
(available upon request)

ISBN: 185032-211-2

Publisher/Vice President: Jim DeWolf, ITCP/Boston
Project Director: Chris Grisonich, ITCP/Boston
Marketing Manager: Kathleen Raftery, ITCP/Boston
Production: Jo-Ann Campbell • mle design • 562 Milford Point Rd. • Milford, CT 06460 • 203-878-3793

Developing Online Help for Windows 95™

Scott Boggan

David Farkas

Joe Welinske

INTERNATIONAL THOMSON COMPUTER PRESS

I⟨T⟩P™ An International Thomson Publishing Company

London • Bonn • Boston • Johannesburg • Madrid • Melbourne • Mexico City • New York • Paris
Singapore • Tokyo • Toronto • Albany, NY • Belmont, CA • Cincinnati, OH • Detroit, MI

ACKNOWLEDGEMENTS

Editing and Production

Py Bateman, Editor, Indexer, Project Manager
Jen Brandon, Editorial Assistant
Jo-Ann Campbell, *mle design*, Production

Reviewers and Experts

Tami Beutel, Technical Consultant

Gary Benson
Angie Burlingame
Carl Chatfield
Jean Farkas
Raymond Lee
Kathy MacLean
Steve Pruitt
Faith Sohl

Writing Contributions

Lin Laurie, WinPro Online Press
Frank Elley, BTC Productions
Jon Yonsky, Bristol Software

Programming

David Stidolph, Imagine That!
Jeff Kovitz, Touch Send Corporation

Scott—

Thanks to Lesley and Sally for their patience and support. And yes Sally, the book is now "over."

Dave—

For Jean and Eva

Joe—

For my dad, Joe

Contents

Chapter 4   **General Issues for Writing Help**   **41**

Chapter 5   **Writing Procedure Topics**   **53**

Chapter 22   Authoring Tools   503

Introduction

WHO THIS BOOK IS FOR

This book is a comprehensive guide to creating online Help using the Microsoft Windows Help compiler. The book focuses on WinHelp 4, the version of Windows Help that is used in Windows 95 and Windows NT 3.51 and later. This book was written for technical writers, programmers, trainers, and anyone else who works on Windows Help systems or is about to. Much of the information will be useful for those who develop Help systems in environments other than Windows. Increasingly, Windows Help is being used not simply for computer documentation but as a general online publishing tool for distributing policy and procedure manuals, online books and periodicals, and many other kinds of information. Almost all of the material in this book dealing with the construction of Help systems applies to general publishing as well as documentation.

WINDOWS 3.1 HELP DEVELOPERS

Those who are developing Windows 3.1 Help may want to see the first edition of this book, *Developing Online Help for Windows*. Originally published by Prentice Hall/SAMS, the first edition is available in its second printing from International Thomson ISBN: 1-85032-219-8 (1-800-842-3636).

WHAT KIND OF INFORMATION IS IN THIS BOOK

This book covers both the design and the construction aspect of Windows Help. By "design" we mean the writing, graphics, navigation, and related aspects of Help. Chapters on these topics plus a chapter on the design process make up the first nine chapters of this book. By "construction" we mean coding topic files for the Help compiler, incorporating graphics and multimedia, customizing the Help interface, creating the project file, and using the compiler to build a Help file. This is the technical side of Help. Chapters on these topics plus a chapter on managing Help development follow the design chapters. Separating the design material from the construction material worked well in the first edition of this book, so we retained this organizing principle. We believe that when people are thinking about design problems, they do not need to be thinking about construction and *vice versa*.

WHAT WE PROVIDE AND WHAT YOU WILL NEED

In addition to about 600 pages of printed information, this book includes a CD-ROM disc. The disc provides some valuable resources that you'll need in order to develop Windows Help files.

- The WinHelp 4 Help compiler.

- HCW.HLP, a Help file from Microsoft that provides good technical information, especially detailed syntax for Help macros.

- WINHELP4.DOT, a Microsoft Word template for authoring Help.

Since many of the examples in this book assume you've got the following files, now would be a good time to install them if you haven't already done so. The first five items in the following table are available on the disc included with this book.

Item	Filename	Description
Windows Help	WINHLP32.EXE	The Windows Help engine is used to run your compiled Help file. This file is included with every copy of Windows.
Help Workshop	HCW.EXE and HCRTF.EXE	Help Workshop is composed of two files. The Help compiler (HCRTF.EXE) converts your topic (.RTF) files, graphics and multimedia files, and project file into a binary file that is readable by Windows Help. HCW.EXE provides a graphical front end that lets you create project files, contents files, and run the Help compiler.

Item	Filename	Description
		There are different versions of the compiler: HCW.EXE is used to build WinHelp 4.0 files; HCP.EXE and HC31.EXE build Windows 3.1 Help files.
Help Author's Guide	HCW.HLP	An online Help file that provides a variety of technical information (including syntax for Help macros and .RTF files) about building Help.
Hotspot Editor	SHED.EXE or SHED2.EXE	The Hotspot Editor lets you create graphic images that contain multiple hotspots, each of which can include a jump or a pop-up, or run a Help macro.
Multiple Resolution Bitmap Compiler	MRBC.EXE	The Multiple Resolution Bitmap Compiler lets you create bitmaps for various display resolutions and combine them into one file.
Word processor or standalone Help authoring tool		A word processor is used to create the rich-text format (.RTF) files used by the Help compiler. Although you can use any word processor that supports .RTF files (including Ami Pro and WordPerfect), Microsoft Word is preferred by most Help authors because it includes many features that simplify the process of authoring Help.
		Some authoring tools, such as ForeHelp, contain their own word processors. If you have one of these tools, you do not need a separate word processor.

TYPOGRAPHICAL CONVENTIONS

The typographical conventions used in this book are listed below.

Convention	What it Describes...
Bold	Help macro names (**ExecFile**) and statements (**bmc** or **mci**) appear in bold, as do user interface components including buttons and text boxes (**Help Filename** box).
Italics	Placeholders for text you provide (*item-name*).
`monospace type`	Sample code and other Help examples; for example, `EnableItem( item_tutorial )`.
CAPS	File names (SHED.EXE).
SMALL CAPS	Key names (ENTER).
...	An ellipsis indicates that the item can be repeated several times. For example, **MRBC** *file1.bmp [file2.bmp file3.bmp ...]*
[ ]	Square brackets indicate that an item is optional. When you're authoring, don't type the brackets themselves.

A word about Microsoft and its influence

The Microsoft Corporation exerts an enormous influence in the world of online Help. First, as the architects of the Windows Help compiler, they control the feature set of WinHelp. WinHelp has steadily improved since Windows 3.0 and is one of the best hypertext publishing tools available. Second, Microsoft's own Help systems are highly influential because they are usually high in quality and very often exhibit new and progressive thinking.

We can and should try to leverage the progressive designs that we see from Microsoft and in the work of other software vendors. At the same time, we need to think independently, examining a broad range of Help designs from Microsoft and others, but never following anyone slavishly. Remember that a software vendor's decisions may be based on factors specific to their software products, the tools they use, the people they employ, and other factors that have nothing to do with your situation. Yes, follow the best practices in the industry, but don't let what you see override your own good judgment and talent.

Other sources of information on Help

Since the release of WinHelp in Windows 3.0, there has been surprisingly little information about Windows Help. Technical writers and software developers have often had to struggle to learn about the process of developing Help.

This situation has changed dramatically since we wrote the first edition of our book. For starters, Microsoft has dramatically improved the documentation included with Help Workshop. Furthermore, there are now several resources available on Windows Help:

- The Microsoft Windows SDK Forum on CompuServe (Library 16) is a great way to reach Microsoft's Developer Support staff and fellow Help authors. You can reach the SDK Forum by typing **go winsdk** at any prompt.

- Another good resource is the WinHelp list server on the Internet. You can subscribe by sending mail to the following address:

  Address: **listserv@Admin.HumberC.ON.CA**
  Message: **sub Winhlp-L** *Your Name*

  For example,

  ```
  sub Winhlp-L Sigmund Freud
  ```

- Check out the USENET newsgroup on the Internet:

  ```
  comp.os.ms-windows.programmer.winhelp
  ```

- There are many good resources available on the World Wide Web. To keep up with the latest Web sites, use a search tool such as Yahoo, Lycos, or the Web Crawler and search for "WinHelp" or "Windows Help."

About the authors

Scott, Dave, and Joe work together on a variety of consulting services, including professional seminars on Windows Help.

SCOTT BOGGAN

Scott Boggan is the documentation manager for the Internet division of CompuServe. Scott has ten years experience in both print and online documentation since the early days of Windows 3.0. Prior to joining the computer industry, he was a rock musician who was part of the early "Seattle Sound." Scott earned a Political Science degree from Western Washington University and has taken advanced courses in computer documentation and technical communication at the University of Washington. Scott wrote chapters 10-16. His CompuServe ID is 70003,7270.

DAVE FARKAS

David K. Farkas is a professor in the Department of Technical Communication at the University of Washington. His educational background includes a Ph.D. in British literature from the University of Minnesota. At the University of Washington he teaches graduate and undergraduate courses in computer documentation, information design, and multimedia. He also supervises graduate theses, publishes research articles, and gives conference presentations. Dave regularly stares at his monitor thinking how much he'd like to be on a river with his canoe. Dave wrote chapters 1-9. His Internet address is farkas@u.washington.edu and his home page is at http://www.uwtc.washington.edu/tc/farkas.html.

JOE WELINSKE

Joseph Welinske is president of WinWriters, a Seattle company that specializes in Windows Help training and consulting. Joe has a B.S. in computer engineering from the University of Illinois and an M.S. in Instructional Design from Loyola University in Chicago. Joe teaches Publications Project Management in the Technical Communication Certificate Program at the University of Washington. Joe founded and manages the WinHelp Journal and hosts the annual WinHelp Conference. He spends his spare time at candle-light bowling and pub crawls with good buds John Waters, Lani Guinier, and Travis Bickle. Joe wrote Chapters 17-23. His CompuServe ID is 71640,3260. Internet: 71640.3260@compuserve.com.

1

Help and the Documentation Set

This chapter provides a broad understanding of online Help. We define Help, distinguish several different forms of Help, and identify one broad category—standard Help—that is the focus of this book. We also compare the features of WinHelp 4 to WinHelp 3.1 and, for Help newcomers, provide a very brief introduction to Help construction.

What is Help?

Help is online computer documentation designed primarily to support the user's ongoing work. A direct contrast to Help is tutorial documentation. Most tutorials ask users to work on "canned" tasks that have been created by the tutorial author. Users learn from the tutorial and, when finished, apply this knowledge to their work.

Some forms of Help can serve an additional role: supporting computer users in learning about something not related to the work they are currently doing. In serving this role, however, Help does not provide the hand-holding that tutorials do.

Kinds of Help

Most of this book is about "standard" Help. This is our term for the Help systems we see all around us in Windows 3.1 and Windows 95 software products. But other kinds of Help are also discussed.

STANDARD HELP

Standard Help consists of Help topics—chunks of Help information—that are in many ways similar to the sections of a print manual. A great many of the topics are procedure topics: numbered steps preceded by some kind of conceptual introduction. Other kinds of standard Help topics include command topics, overview topics, and screen region topics. These kinds of standard Help topics are all coded in the same way. Also, they are treated identically by the Help compiler. Their appearance and content, however, as well as the roles they play in supporting users, are very different. If you are totally unfamiliar with procedure topics and standard Help, you should jump ahead for a moment and take a look at Chapter 5, *Writing Procedure Topics*.

The structure of standard Help systems is also similar to the structure of manuals (and to printed books in general)—there is a table of contents, an index, and hypertext jumps (the equivalent of print cross references).

Standard Help most frequently supports ongoing work by performing a quick reference function. The user goes to Help with a problem, finds the appropriate Help topic, uses that Help topic to solve the problem, and returns to work as quickly as possible. Standard Help, however, is versatile and can be used apart from any current work. Users interested in learning about an unfamiliar feature of a software product can browse through a succession of Help topics as though reading a chapter of a user's guide, or treat the Help system as a hypertext document and navigate among the Help topics.

Starting with Apple's balloon Help, a new kind of Help has gradually become well accepted in the computer industry. In this model, the user clicks on an element of the interface and displays a brief Help topic that appears right next to the element of interest. This form of Help is simple but highly useful. In WinHelp 4, it primarily takes the form of *What's This? Help*.

What's This? Help, shown below in Figure 1.1, is destined to play a major role in many Help systems. Because What's This? Help is part of WinHelp and because it fits the standard Help paradigm of letting users quickly access Help information and return to their work, we include What's This? Help as a special form of standard Help.

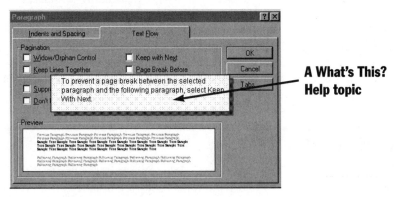

Figure 1.1. *What's This? Help.*

Related to What's This? Help is *status line Help*. Status line messages appear when the user clicks an element of the interface, but they appear at the bottom of a window. For an example of a status line Help message, see Figure 1.2. Status line messages are convenient and unobtrusive, but they are necessarily very brief and, in addition, are easy to overlook. Although not part of WinHelp, status line messages can be readily programmed into Windows 95 software applications. Status line Help can be considered a minor form of standard Help.

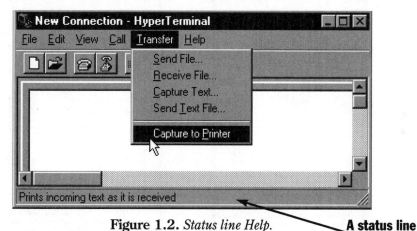

Figure 1.2. *Status line Help.*   **A status line
Help message**

WIZARDS AND COACHES: PERFORMANCE SUPPORT HELP

Another form of Help, fundamentally different from standard Help, is performance support Help. Whereas the primary role of standard Help is reference, performance support Help maintains a dialog with the user and guides the user step by step through the completion of the task.

In some respects, performance support Help resembles online tutorials. But there is a crucial difference. With online tutorials, users follow scenarios created by the tutorial author and therefore create "pretend" products, such as an imaginary database for an imaginary wine cellar. With performance support Help, you perform actual work; within certain limits you are prompted to create the database that you really need. Notice, however, that performance support Help systems are not well suited for learning computer tasks apart from ongoing work. Users rarely browse through a performance support Help system.

The two main kinds of performance support Help are *wizards* and *coaches*. Wizards replace the product's regular interface. Coaches assist the user in working with the product's regular interface. Wizards must be tightly integrated with the software application. Such integration is often implemented in coaches. So, for example, the coaching Help system shown below in Figure 1.3 can monitor user actions and respond to user errors with a special "Oops!" topic that assists the user in trying that action again. Wizards and coaches are discussed in Chapter 7, *Performance Support Help: Wizards and Coaches.*

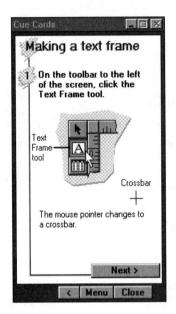 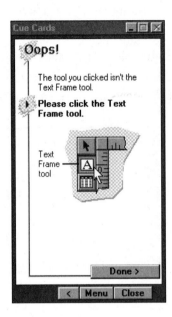

Figure 1.3. *Coach Help prompting the user and responding to an error.*

INTELLIGENT HELP

The ultimate form of user assistance is an expert and extremely patient human being who stands over the user's shoulder watching everything he or she does. This human being can answer any question and will volunteer comments as necessary. Help aspires to simulate this kind of assistance by combining two capabilities: First, monitoring user actions to infer both the user's goals and the reasons the user is having difficulty. Second, engaging in a natural language dialog with the user, so that, for instance, the user can type in questions and receive answers. Success thus far has been limited. Intelligent Help is beyond the scope of this book.

An introduction to Windows Help

Here is a brief account of the relationship between Help and Windows; it will be useful for those who are new to Help development in the Windows operating system.

THE WINDOWS HELP APPLICATION

Every copy of Windows includes an application that "runs" the Help systems we author. In Windows 95 (and Windows NT) this application is WinHlp32.EXE. It resides in the Windows 95 folder WINDOWS. In Windows 3.1 this application is WinHelp.EXE. In Windows 95 there is still a WinHelp.EXE application for running WinHelp 3.1 Help systems.

The features of the Help systems we create are largely determined by this component, although external add-ons—such as Windows DLLs—can provide extra functionality. If you have never examined a Windows Help system, you should choose Help from the Start button in the Windows 95 task bar, explore the Windows 95 Help system, and pay particular attention to the topics on how to use Help. See Table 1.1 for a list of the most important enhancements introduced in WinHelp 4.0.

THE WINDOWS HELP COMPILER

In order to create a Windows Help system, you must have a copy of the Windows Help compiler. There are several slightly different compilers for WinHelp 3.1 and currently one compiler for WinHelp 4. One or more of these compilers are included with most Windows development products. In addition, many of the commercial Help authoring tools such as Doc-To-Help, ForeHelp, and RoboHELP license and include a Help compiler. The Help compiler for WinHelp 4 is HCRTF.EXE. The file HCW.EXE is a utility needed for authoring WinHelp 4 Help systems. HCRTF.EXE and HCW.EXE are collectively known as "Help Workshop." Help Workshop is included on the CD that comes with this book.

Once you have the Help compiler and Help Workshop, all you need is a word processor that can save files in rich-text format, the format which the Help compiler reads. Many Help authors use Microsoft Word; some of the Help authoring tools *must* be used in conjunction with Word. The basic procedure is very simple. Using the word processor or a Help authoring tool, you create the topic file for the Help compiler to run. You also create an .HPJ (project) file, an auxiliary file that gives the Help compiler certain information it requires. Finally, you can create a .CNT file (contents file), new in WinHelp 4, which will provide a table of contents for your Help system in an expandable and collapsible "outliner" format. The .HPJ file is not shipped; it is used only during the compilation process. The .CNT file is shipped with your compiled .HLP file. Under some circumstances, you will ship some other files with the compiled Help file. The authoring process is not technically difficult, especially if you stick with the basic features and use a Help authoring tool.

WINHELP 3.1 AND WINHELP 4 FEATURES

WinHelp 4.0 incorporates a variety of enhancements over WinHelp 3.1. No particular enhancement is overwhelmingly important, but collectively they are very significant. All of the differences are fully explained in Parts 2 and 3 of this book. But here is a brief preview of the most important changes. For brief explanations of all the WinHelp commands, look ahead to Tables 3.1 and 3.2.

Table 1.1. *Major WinHelp 4 enhancements*

Feature	WinHelp 4	WinHelp 3.1
Window behavior	You can create 255 different types of secondary windows and display 9 at a time. Secondary windows will automatically size themselves to fit their content. You have complete control over the buttons you add to secondary and main windows.	You can create only 6 types of secondary windows and display only one secondary window at a time. You must fake buttons on secondary windows.
Online table of contents	The new table of contents (Contents tab on the Help Topics dialog box) uses an outliner metaphor. For the first time, the information in multiple Help files can be seamlessly combined.	You must create your contents using hypertext jumps. Faking an outline structure is very time consuming.
Printing and copying	Users can print clusters of topics at a time from the Contents tab. Users can easily drag the pointer across a Help topic to copy the text and graphics.	Unless special add-on modules are included with the Help file, users must print one topic at a time. Copying is slow and awkward.
Online index and Find	The Index tab of the Help Topics dialog box looks like an index.	The Topics Found dialog box is inefficient and confuses users.

Table 1.1. *(continued)*

Feature	WinHelp 4	WinHelp 3.1
	For the first time, the keywords from multiple Help files can be seamlessly combined. The index is now supplemented by a full-text search feature.	
Graphics	Bitmaps may now contain up to 16 million colors. For the first time multimedia support, in the form of AVI files, is built into Windows Help. For the first time WinHelp supports bitmaps of various color depths. For the first time, transparent bitmap graphics are supported.	Bitmaps can contain only 16 colors. High-resolution graphics require an external DLL.
Jumps	In addition to specifying a specific destination for a jump, you can use the ALink and KLink macros to send out a special "broadcast message" for any topics with certain associated keywords.	You must specify a specific destination for a jump. If that destination topic is unavailable, the user receives a broken jump error message. This creates problems for modular products in which different customers receive different sets of Help files and problems when users don't install all the Help files they receive.
Shortcut Help buttons	You can add to a Help topic special Shortcut buttons that use a Help macro to operate the software product. For example, the user could click a button and open a dialog box.	There is no standard means of operating the software from Help.
What's This? Help	"What's This?" pop-up windows can now be attached directly to the interface.	

Table 1.1. *(continued)*

Feature	WinHelp 4	WinHelp 3.1
Better authoring	WinHelp provides a more complete environment for compiling a Help system. Help Workshop is faster and more robust then the WinHelp 3.1 compilers, with better debugging and better support for customizing the Help interface. Many other authoring improvements have been made, including a variety of new macros.	Each of the WinHelp 3.1 compilers is a simple DOS program.
Training Cards	A collection of special Training Cards macros have been added so that Help authors can establish interactivity between Help and the software product. They are intended to support the development of wizard and coach type Help systems and even online tutorials.	Interactive Help such as wizards and coaches, as well as online tutorials, require special tools and development environments.

The transition from print to online documentation

We have thus far considered standard Help and other forms of Help. Now we turn to the print medium. Until fairly recently the main components of most documentation sets were print manuals, including an installation guide, a tutorial, a comprehensive user's guide, a command reference, and a quick reference card. One reason for the dominance of print was that online Help systems were poorly designed, often just afterthoughts. Usually they contained limited kinds of information, such as command syntax, and provided only rudimentary access to this information.

Now online Help, in its various forms, is far more complete, far better designed, and in most software products is at least as important if not more important than the print components. Indeed, the balance is rapidly shifting toward documentation sets in which print components play a limited role. To fully understand the causes and implications of this transition, we should consider the perspective of software vendors, businesses, users, and documentors.

SOFTWARE VENDORS

The transition to online documentation has been driven largely by the desire of software vendors to cut costs. Thick manuals and other print pieces cost far more to manufacture and ship than does a floppy disk or CD-ROM. Very likely we will soon see complete electronic distribution of both documentation and the product.

Software companies benefit in another key respect. A difficult problem in the software development cycle is the considerable delay that occurs while manuals are at the printer. If any changes in the interface are made during this time, Read Me files become necessary. In contrast, late changes in online documentation can be made along with late changes in the software product.

The major drawback of online documentation for software vendors is that it facilitates software piracy. When someone illegally copies the application, they just can as easily copy the documentation; there is no need to photocopy a thick manual.

BUSINESSES

Large organizations typically buy site licenses for commercial software, and they are reluctant to bear the very considerable cost of providing printed manuals for each user. Without manuals, however, organizations face high training costs and reduced productivity. This dilemma is largely resolved by online documentation. Furthermore, online documentation is extremely convenient for organizations because it can be distributed and readily updated over networks.

USERS

At this time, the primary advantage of Help over print for users is superior information access. Online tables of contents and indexes are faster and more capable than their print equivalents, and hypertext jumps are far more convenient than print cross references. Other powerful forms of access, such as full-text search and various forms of context sensitivity have no equivalent in print. Online Help has other advantages over print, including saving shelf space. Significant drawbacks of online Help from the user's point of view are the following:

- Help systems are not available without a computer.

- Help systems sometimes require significant amounts of space on the user's hard disk.

- Help systems are inferior to print in terms of information display.

- Help systems, in contrast to books, are not familiar from childhood (although this is changing).

- Help systems are intangible and do not provide the comfortable tangibility and heft of printed books.

Regarding tangibility and heft, we note that fans of printed books always assume a pleasant, medium-sized manual. Tangibility and heft become burdensome in the case of a multi-volume documentation set.

The strongest argument for print is superior information display. A well-printed book is more legible than any screen and can present more text in a given amount of space. Because Help systems must share valuable screen space with the software application, Help information is usually viewed in a smaller-than-ideal display area and often requires scrolling. Books do not compete for screen real estate. Because users cannot resize the dimensions of printed pages and because of their superior resolution, printed books can offer highly refined multi-column layouts, screening, reverse-outs, and highly detailed graphics. On the other hand, Help makes possible such electronic display features as pop-up text, hotspot graphics, and multimedia. Ultimately Help will surpass print in regard to information display as well as information access.

DOCUMENTORS

The documentation community, we believe, has gained much from the transition to online Help. Online documentation offers vistas of creative design that are impossible in print. In our experience, few documentors who become adept with online Help ever wish to return to print documentation. Furthermore, because Help systems, in contrast to manuals, are integrated with and often inseparable from the product, documentors are themselves becoming more fully integrated into the product development team. The main drawback for documentors is the need to learn new design skills and development technologies. Another drawback is that we have not yet worked out fully adequate methods for reviewing and editing online documents.

The print components of the documentation set

We believe that the increased reliance on online document is one of those rare situations: a "win" for all parties concerned. Nevertheless, we need to recognize that print has its place and should not be swept away in an over-enthusiastic commitment to online documentation. Many users forego their reliance on print only when convinced that a software product offers first-rate Help. Furthermore, there remains a shrinking but still significant minority of the total user base that rejects online documentation altogether. With these considerations in mind, we should examine the role of various forms of print documentation in the contemporary documentation set.

DOCUMENTATION FOR INSTALLATION AND FAILURE RECOVERY

Help systems generally cannot be used until the software is running or when the software has crashed. Thus, documentation for installation and failure recovery are two niches for print.

TUTORIALS

Online tutorials (or "computer-based training") are more capable than print tutorials. They are usually more graphical, can block user errors, and can monitor and adapt to the user's success in learning. On the other hand, print tutorials can be written more quickly and do not require a special online authoring tool. Thus low-budget projects create a niche for print tutorials.

QUICK REFERENCE CARDS AND QUICK START CARDS

Quick reference cards present various kinds of shortcut information, such as keyboard combinations. They are handy and relatively cheap, and so are worth providing, even though the same information can easily be made available in Help. *Quick start guides* enable aggressive users to install the software product and begin performing basic tasks immediately. They are also cheap, handy, and worth providing.

DEEP-LEVEL REFERENCE

Deep-level reference includes theory and technical notes. Often a subject covered in deep-reference documentation requires several pages. Whenever a user would need to read an extensive amount of text, print should be considered. On the other hand, many collections of deep-level reference documentation consist of thousands of pages—making the documentation difficult to transport and making information access tedious. A good approach to deep reference is to put it online but provide good facilities for on-demand printing of individual sections. Much deep-level documentation is migrating to sites on the World Wide Web. Banyan Systems, to name just one company, maintains an extensive collection of technical notes on the Banyan web site.

COMMAND REFERENCE

Command reference manuals are a traditional print component; however, the advantages of integrating command information with the software product (for example, with context sensitivity) are sufficiently compelling that command references have largely been replaced by command topics. Command topics may themselves be replaced in many software products by What's This? Help topics.

USER'S GUIDE

Before the ascendance of Help, the *user's guide* was the central piece in the documentation set. A user's guide explains all of the tasks that can be performed with the software. It consists of procedures introduced by just enough conceptual information to explain the purpose and context of each procedure. User's guides are, therefore, fairly similar to the procedure topics in a Help system—the main difference is that user's guides usually contain more detailed text than Help and more refined layout. The overlapping role of these two components is one of the major issues facing documentors today.

One solution is to continue to provide a traditional user's guide. To defray this expense, some software vendors now charge extra for print manuals. Another solution is to design a much slimmer user's guide that focuses on concepts and strategies and omits all procedures except those the user needs to get started. The design rationale here is that procedures are more accessible online while the print medium is superior for presenting paragraphs of conceptual material.

2

The Design Process

This chapter deals with designing a Help system. It presents the model of the Help design process that we advocate. The model consists of successive cycles of these three activities: (1) Designing, (2) Building, and (3) Evaluating. In the context of this chapter, "building" means writing Help topics, adding graphics, and constructing some sort of working .HLP file, even if it consists only of a handful of sample topics.

This chapter is specific in its focus. It does not discuss the roles of various team members, Help construction, schedules, or budgets. These topics are discussed in Chapter 23, *Managing Help Projects*. For a thorough guide to publications project management, see JoAnn Hackos' book *Managing Your Documentation Projects* and for a highly practical book emphasizing the "people and process" side of documentation, see Price and Korman, *How to Communicate Technical Information: A Handbook of Software and Hardware Documentation*.

Design in cycles

The idea underlying our model of the design process is to design, build, and evaluate in successive cycles, each cycle more complete and "final" than the previous one. This is illustrated in Figure 2.1.

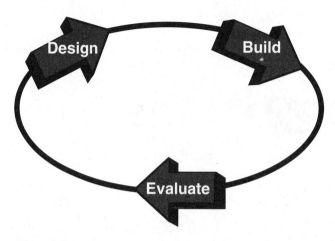

Figure 2.1. *Cycles of designing, building, and evaluating.*

The complete model is shown in Table 2.1. The table shows three cycles of designing, building, and evaluating, but more cycles are certainly possible.

Table 2.1. *The Help design process*

	Design	Build	Evaluate
Cycle 1	Analyze the design context. Answer key design questions.	Build sample topics.	Conduct internal review. Perform early user testing.
Cycle 2	Develop a detailed design.	Build a prototype.	Evaluate the prototype.
Cycle 3	Make necessary design changes.	Write, review, and edit your Help system.	Conduct the summative evaluation.

The great benefit of this model is that the Help author (or Help team) invests a relatively small amount of time in writing Help information and building Help until the Help author knows that he or she has the best possible design.

The opposite of this model is a one-cycle process that works like this: completely design the Help system, write and construct the entire Help system, and then evaluate it at the end. The one-cycle process is dangerous, because you don't really find out how good your design is until it is too late to correct faults. Companies in many different industries prefer multiple cycles of designing, building, and evaluating. An automobile maker will make preliminary models of a new car, evaluate the models to the fullest extent possible, make a prototype and fully evaluate the prototype, and then and only then re-tool a factory to manufacture the new car.

The specifics of this Help design process differ greatly in different settings. At a large software company a single Help system may involve 25 or more people plus a separate usability testing department. More typically, the process is carried out by a small team or even just one person. This process works regardless of the setting. Below we look at the various activities that make up this process.

Analyze the design context

The design context is the "big picture," and the very first part of designing Help is to make sure you understand the big picture. This requires gathering and analyzing a lot of information. Usually you will need to talk to programmers, interface designers, marketers, customers, and others. These are the main considerations that make up the design context.

THE PRODUCT

You must know the product well and think about it from many angles. How large and complex is the product? Are there many features to document? Is the product difficult, with a steep learning curve? How straightforward is the user interface? What are the major deficiencies of the interface that you must compensate for in the documentation?

THE INTENDED USERS

Nothing is more important than gaining information and insight about your users and their needs. Who are they? What are their backgrounds and jobs? Can you divide them into distinct categories? Sometimes you will inherit good information from your organization's marketers and interface designers. Often you will need to seek this information yourself. Surveys and systematic studies are ideal, but not often feasible; however, you can get extremely valuable information if you can just find time to visit (or even telephone) two or three representative customer sites. Often you can get valuable information relatively easily by talking to your company's technical support staff.

THE COMPLETE DOCUMENTATION SET

Help must be designed to work with whatever print components your documentation department is writing and possibly with such other online components as an online tutorial or demo. The ultimate goal, of course, is to create a documentation set with well-designed and carefully coordinated components, a documentation set that will support the entire user base from the moment they open the box, through the initial learning curve, to proficiency, to mastery, and after they return to the product after long periods of non-use.

CONSTRAINTS

You can write your novel any way you please. Documentation, unfortunately, is always subject to constraints in the form of schedules, limited staff and budgets, less-than-ideal tools, disk space restrictions, and the need to follow the design of earlier versions or related products. You must carefully consider such constraints.

Answer key design questions

Very closely related to understanding the design context is asking key design questions. The design questions posed below pertain to standard Help. Other forms of Help will require corresponding design questions.

WHAT KINDS OF HELP TOPICS WILL YOU WRITE?

In most Help systems, procedure topics are the most prevalent. But in addition to procedure topics, you may want to write What's This? topics, overview topics, shortcut topics, error-message topics, and other kinds as well.

ABOUT HOW MANY HELP TOPICS WILL YOU WRITE?

You should have an early estimate of the number of Help topics that you will write. This estimate is extremely useful in scheduling and negotiating for resources. It also affects certain design decisions.

The number of topics depends on the size and complexity of the software product and on the design of your Help system. You can develop a "guesstimate" by studying the interface of your software product and working out your own rough measures along these lines:

- For every command in the product that does not display a dialog box, figure on one procedure topic.

- For every command that displays a simple dialog box, figure on three procedure topics.

- For complex dialog boxes, figure on six procedure topics.

You can also develop a guesstimate by examining the Help system in an existing product that is similar to yours.

WHAT WILL BE THE FEATURES OF THE HELP SYSTEM?

Decisions must be made at an early stage about the features and capabilities of your Help system. Will you implement a browse sequence? Will you include a lot of graphics and hotspot graphics? Will you use several different window types? As you work out your overall design, you will also begin to see how much work lies ahead and whether you are in danger of violating a constraint such as your deadline or a restriction on the maximum size of the Help file.

Build some sample topics and evaluate

After you have analyzed the design context and answered key design questions, create a few sample topics. Ideally, these will be representative topics: at least one of each kind of Help topic you will be writing and topics that illustrate special problems or design ideas. These topics are too few in number to be called a prototype, but they are enough for an early evaluation.

The most frequently performed evaluation at this stage is an internal review. This review can be a formal process or you can ask someone down the hall to look at your sample topics and offer comments.

In addition, even a few sample Help topics are enough for certain kinds of usability testing. Are your topics properly geared to your users or do they assume too much expertise? Do users distinguish among the various kinds of Help topics you have written and use them appropriately? Does your layout make your Help topics easier to understand and do users find it attractive?

Develop a detailed design

After the first evaluation, you move from high-level design to detailed design. As Table 2.1 shows, this is the beginning of the second cycle. The detailed design process should culminate with a fully specified Help design with no issues left undecided. One part of the detailed design, the task analysis, cannot be undertaken without a good *alpha* version or a good prototype of the software or—at the least—a very good set of specs. But all aspects of the detailed design will come out better if the Help author has a clear picture of the appearance and function of the software product. Detailed design consists of the following design tasks.

PLANNING SCREEN LAYOUT AND GRAPHICS

You must work out the layouts for your Help topics. Not only does each kind of Help topic have a distinctive layout, but even a single kind of topic has a surprising number of variations. Let us consider procedure topics. Some procedure topics will include graphics; others will include tables of various sizes and kinds. Some will consist of only a single step. Some procedure topics will contain several short procedures. Steps themselves differ: a step that shows two ways to carry out the step is laid out differently from a simple step. All these differences must be recognized and planned for at the beginning, and all the variations in your layout should be accounted for in your template. If you start improvising layouts in the middle of the writing process, you will add major inconsistencies to the appearance of your Help system.

DETERMINING WRITING CONVENTIONS AND TERMINOLOGY

Now you make specific decisions about writing. How often will you use examples and how long will they be? Will you explain more than one way to carry out an action? In addition, terminology must be handled consistently and should follow any applicable industry standards.

This book is not a style guide but it can help you make many writing decisions. Also, many of Microsoft's style and screen layout guidelines are provided on the disc accompanying this book in a file called Guidelines.HLP. In addition, Microsoft's *The Windows Interface Guidelines for Software Design* will answer a great many terminology questions. *The Microsoft Publications Style Guide,* (Version 1) is an unreleased document that has circulated widely in the documentation community. This style guide is now too old to be useful, but we can hope that Microsoft will choose to publish the revised version.

Adhering to writing conventions and terminology standards is difficult whenever more than one writer is working on a project. The members of the Help team should meet early in the project to compare their earliest topics, paying special attention to matters that are not specified in style guides. Perhaps one writer's topics are a lot more detailed than another writer's or entail different assumptions about the product's users. Another writer is using many more graphics than the rest. These differences must be worked out.

CONDUCTING A TASK ANALYSIS

A task analysis is a logical breakdown of the tasks users can perform with the product. Broadly speaking, the task analysis corresponds to your hierarchy of procedure topics because those topics reflect user tasks. In theory, you should inherit a task analysis from the product planners and interface designers, and then adapt it for your own needs. Help authors, however, often inherit little or nothing of value. You may need to develop your own task analysis from the specs, by studying the interface, and by thinking through all the task scenarios.

A perfect interface would clearly reveal the complete functionality of the product and serve as the basis of a complete task analysis. But you need to mentally separate yourself from the product's user interface in order to identify meaningful tasks that are obscurely revealed on the interface (for example, tasks that depend on a combination of dialog boxes). You may even identify useful tasks that, through some oversight, the software product cannot do at all. (This is when you ask for a raise!) Whether you inherit it, devise it, or something in between, a task analysis is necessary to write a complete Help system. For more information on task analysis, see Carlisle, *Analyzing Jobs and Tasks*; Rubenstein and Hersh, *The Human Factor: Designing Computer Systems for People*; and Holtzblatt and Beyer's journal article, "Making Customer-Centered Design Work for Teams."

G THE STRUCTURE OF YOUR

ly create the procedures branch of your Help table
lop the hierarchy for the other branches of the con-
in the outline view of your word processor, or, with
file, the actual working table of contents for your

e software product will require you to add, change,
erarchy up-to-date. You may even want a more com-
ncludes jumps and browse sequences. Unless your
navigational structure of your Help system is diffi-
of paper. Updating this large and complex diagram
lopment tools, such as ForeHelp, can display useful
you choose not to represent the full navigational
sketch will help you envision your design.

NHANCEMENT AND FOR K

he time or other resources to create their ideal Help
nt Help system for a subsequent release of the soft-
the current Help system so that it can be readily
to add "Demo" buttons on certain topics that will
exactly where these buttons will be located and how
they will function. Better yet, prototype at least one current topic with the Demo button.

Sometimes Help developers face unexpected problems. An important team member quits or is re-assigned. Your schedule is compressed. To protect yourself from such emergencies, devise a plan for scaling back the scope of the Help system. Are there components of the Help system you can omit without destroying the integrity of the design? You might, for example, hold off on making the screen region topics until it is clear that there will be time for them. You can also omit or compress certain stages of the development process, such as the final edit.

A TIP: BORROW FROM OTHERS

Throughout the entire design process, it's smart to borrow ideas from existing Help systems. You can borrow clever design ideas, such as navigation and windowing techniques. You can also save yourself many hours of work by studying Help topics in other systems. Also, look at the structure of the contents hierarchy, the browse sequences, and the index entries.

```
        Borders Books * Music * Cafe
  1629 Orrington Avenue Evanston, IL 60201
                (847) 733-8852
3398    144/0002/02  000031            SALE
ITEM        TX RETAIL DISC  SPEC     EXTND
1 Sidelines  1   3.50                 3.50
   TIGERLILY
1 CD 1007678 1  16.99 29%  11.99     11.99
  BEST TOP 50 CD - 0098037007
   DEVELOPING ONLINE HELP
1 SO 0000055 1  46.95                46.95
                 SUBTOTAL            62.44
    8.000%       TAX1                 5.00
3 Items          AMOUNT DUE          67.44
                 VISA                67.44
   4271382003886773 1197 657864  4986
                 CHANGE DUE            .00
      06/27/96          01:31 PM
Borders is happy to be here in Evanston!
```

Look at numerous Help systems, especially very good ones, innovative ones, and ones that document a product similar to yours. Don't copy material "wholesale"; you will violate someone's intellectual property rights. Don't borrow ideas mechanically; you will probably make your own design worse. But innovations and design practices flow freely through the documentation community, and advancements in the state of the art often come about as each Help author borrows and improves upon previous designs.

Build a prototype

After the detailed design, build a prototype of your Help system. The prototype will enable you to conduct a more realistic and more extensive evaluation of the design. In the world of online Help a prototype is usually a small subset of the entire Help system. For example, you might prototype all the Help topics (command and overview topics as well as procedure topics) pertaining to a single functional area, such as printing. The prototype topics represent the finished Help system, so they must be fully written and constructed. If possible, link these topics in the table of contents and with jumps, so you can more completely evaluate how users will navigate among them.

If you prototype a larger subset, so much the better. Your evaluation will be still more realistic. A prototype, however, is something you are willing to throw away: don't build such a large prototype that you become committed to it.

Many Help writers go beyond building a prototype. They build the complete Help system in skeletal form. Every topic is created and linked, but (with the exception of the prototyped topics) these topics may contain nothing more than the *topic heading*. A skeletal version is very useful. You get a feel for the finished Help system early in the development process. A skeletal version is especially useful for understanding the structure of your Help system and designing the various forms of information access.

Evaluate the prototype

A prototype will provide you with a better understanding of your Help system, even if your evaluation consists of nothing more than studying your prototype. But a prototype enables you to conduct other forms of evaluation and formulate more detailed questions than you could when you just had sample topics. This is the time, therefore, for the main evaluation.

FORMS OF EVALUATION

There are numerous forms of evaluation. Some of the most important are listed here:

- **Careful analysis**. Just take the time to really study your prototype. Often, Help authors get too swept up in the need to get work done to thoughtfully assess their designs.

- **Design guidelines.** Adopt the best set of design guidelines you can find and determine whether your Help system follows them.

- **Comparison with existing systems.** See how other designers have solved the same problems you are facing.

- **Expert opinion.** Get the opinions of people who have made many Help systems, conducted usability tests on their Help systems, examined many Help systems, and studied the literature.

- **Usability testing.** Observe typical users working with your Help system and, especially, working with it as they try to accomplish tasks with the software product.

USABILITY TESTING

Usability testing is the most reliable way to learn how successful your Help system will be in the hands of your users. Usability testing does not have to be an elaborate, extremely time-consuming process. "Quick and dirty" tests conducted on prototypes are fine.

Create scenarios that require usability subjects to perform tasks with the software using the Help system to guide them. Observe users' success in finding the Help information and performing the tasks. Through observation and by polling your subjects, determine whether the Help information is complete enough, whether they understand it, and whether they are comfortable using your Help system.

If you have a working table of contents or even just an outline of the table of contents in a word processing file, you can describe a task and ask subjects to tell you what branch of the hierarchy they would explore to find the relevant Help topic. Two good books on usability testing are Dumas and Redish, *A Practical Guide to Usability Testing*, and Rubin, *Handbook of Usability Testing: How to Plan, Design, and Conduct Effective Tests*.

Make necessary design changes

You may find that your Help design meets all requirements. If so, you can set to work writing and constructing Help topics. Very possibly, however, your evaluation will uncover problems, and you will need to modify your design to reflect what you have learned.

When you modify your design, especially if the modifications are considerable, you may want to update your prototype and conduct another round of usability testing, or another form of evaluation, to confirm that the design problem has been solved and that no new problems have been introduced. This follow-up evaluation will be different from the main evaluation because it will focus on the things that were changed in the re-design. Given typical constraints of time and budget, however, an extra cycle of prototyping, evaluation, and possible re-design is often not feasible.

Write Help in drafts

Once the last evaluation and the last design changes have been completed, the design process ends and the writing and construction starts.

WRITING, REVIEWING, AND EDITING

It is possible to write and perfect each Help topic in one sitting. In most documentation projects, however, writers produce several drafts. In the first draft the key information should be present, but the text need not be highly polished—especially if the software product is still undergoing significant change. This draft should be reviewed by developers for technical accuracy and completeness. Some developers go further and take an interest in the clarity of the Help topics. If you are puzzling over how to explain an especially difficult procedure, talk to your technical support staff about their success in explaining it on the phone. The draft should then be revised and edited for clarity, correctness, and consistency.

TRACKING YOUR PROGRESS

For small Help systems you can track your progress simply by scanning your topic files and periodically compiling a Help file. When projects get larger, however, and especially when a team of people are working together, a more formal tracking system is needed. You will need a system that will tell you how many topics still need to be written, who is writing which ones, and how far along the various topics are. This kind of information can be kept and updated in a spreadsheet. In some organizations, a complete database system is used to track the progress of the Help project.

Quality testing

Quality testing (or "QA"—quality and assurance testing) does not really pertain to the design process, the subject of this chapter. Still it is so important that we mention it here anyway.

It is absolutely necessary to test the entire Help system for a very broad range of quality considerations. These include the following:

- Do all jumps work and go to the correct topics?
- Is context sensitivity correctly implemented?
- Do graphics display properly?
- Is the text properly aligned and spaced?
- Do topics come up in the correct windows and do windows display properly?
- Do the text and graphics reflect any last-minute changes in the interface?

The summative evaluation

The very last stage of evaluation comes after the software product and its Help system have been completed and shipped. This is the "summative evaluation" or "post mortem." (All the evaluations conducted before completion of the project are called "formative.") Summative evaluations can be frustrating because you can't use what you've learned until the next version of the Help system. Still, certain design problems, especially those involving access and navigation, can be hard to uncover until all the topics are written and all the forms of navigation and information access have been fully implemented.

Furthermore, it is impossible to conduct some of the best forms of user evaluation until the product is in use. These include customer-response tear-off forms, on-site visits, feedback from tech support calls, and reviews in the trade press. Assuming that there will be another release of the product and a revised Help system, the summative evaluation simply feeds back into the next design effort.

3

Window Types, Screen Layout, Graphics, and Multimedia

WinHelp 4 is a full-featured application for presenting online information. It offers many options regarding window types and behavior, screen layout, and the inclusion of traditional graphics, hotspot graphics, and multimedia. In this chapter, we examine these options.

This chapter and the other chapters in Part 1 focus on design issues. The subsequent parts cover all aspects of construction. We have chosen not to clutter the design chapters will continual cross references back to the construction chapters. But the book's extensive index will direct you from the design to the construction of any aspect of WinHelp.

Windowing in WinHelp 4

WinHelp provides three kinds of Help windows: main windows, secondary windows, and pop-up windows. WinHelp 4 provides more flexibility and control in the use of windows than does WinHelp 3.1.

MAIN WINDOWS

Main Windows in WinHelp 4 can be configured in any way by the Help author but normally feature a menu bar and, below the menu bar, a toolbar. A typical menu bar includes the menus File, Edit, Bookmark, Options, and Help. Figure 3.1 shows a typical main window; this window also displays a pop-up window. Table 3.1 lists the commands under each of these menus and provides capsule explanations of their functions.

The toolbar normally features the Help Topics, Back, and Print command buttons and, often, the two browse buttons. These are explained in Table 3.2.

The Help author chooses a single default size and position for all the main windows in the Help system, though, of course, users can freely re-size and move main windows (and secondary windows as well). Setting this default entails a trade-off. On the one hand, you don't want to cover up too much of the software product with a large Help window. On the other hand, small Help windows increase the number of topics the users will have to scroll. In the case of tables, it is especially desirable to prevent horizontal scrolling; in the case of graphics, it is highly desirable to prevent any scrolling.

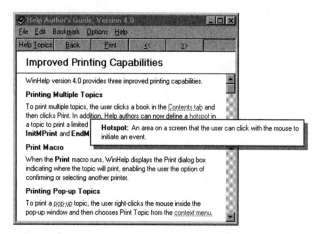

Figure 3.1. *A typical main Help window with a pop-up window.*

Only one main Help window can be displayed at one time. Thus, navigating from one main window to the next means replacing the first window with the second. There is an appealing simplicity to this windowing style. On the other hand, it is often useful to display more than one window at a time—something you can do with secondary windows.

Table 3.1. *The menus and commands in main Help windows*

Menus	Commands	Comments
File	Open	Opens other .HLP files.
	Print Topic	Prints the current Help topic.
	Exit	Closes the Help system.
Edit	Copy	Copies selected text and graphics onto the Clipboard.
	Annotate	Opens a text area in which you can annotate the current Help topic.

Table 3.1. *(continued)*

Menus	Commands	Comments
Bookmark	Define [Bookmark]	Adds the current topic to a bookmark list. The user can quickly return to any topic on the list by clicking it.
Options	Keep Help on Top	Determines whether the Help system will appear on top of other windows.
	Display History Window	Displays a list of previously visited Help topics.
	Font	Allows you to increase or decrease the point size of the Help font by two points.
	Use System Colors	Allows you to override the assigned background color of your Help topics with the Microsoft Windows background color setting.
Help	Version	Displays the version of the Winhelp.EXE application that is displaying these Help topics.

Table 3.2. *The command buttons in main Help windows*

Command	Function
Help Topics	Displays the Help Topics dialog box with the most recently used page active.
Back	Displays the previously displayed Help topic.
Print	Prints the current Help topic.
Previous (≤ <) and Next (≥ >) browse sequence buttons	Display the previous and next Help topics in a sequence established by the Help author.

POP-UP WINDOWS

Pop-up windows are a very prevalent, highly convenient window type. Pop-up windows have no buttons or other controls. They appear over, but do not replace, their parent window when users click hotspot text or a hotspot graphic. They disappear with the next mouse click.

Pop-up windows usually display definitions of unfamiliar terms. Help authors also use pop-up windows to display a list of related topics the user can jump to. It is possible for pop-up windows to contain jumps to other topics, but this technique makes Help confusing, and its use should be restricted to *glossary topics*. The fundamental role of pop-up windows is to serve as "satellites" to main and secondary windows.

SECONDARY WINDOWS

Originally secondary windows were used to supplement main windows. They were envisioned as something akin to pop-up windows, and lacked much of the functionality of main windows. Their special trait was to remain on the screen after their parent main window was dismissed. This trait has proven very useful, especially for information such as code examples, reference tables, and other content that users might want to view for a period of time even as they display new topics in the main window.

In the later years of WinHelp 3.1, Microsoft expanded the role of secondary windows in certain Help systems. Notably in Microsoft Word 6.0 Help and Excel 5.0 Help, most procedure topics are displayed in secondary windows. These secondary windows are sized tall and narrow and can be set to stay on top. This design, however, presented some problems in WinHelp 3.1 because secondary windows lacked some key features. Secondary windows could not contain true toolbar buttons, secondary window topics did not appear in the History list, and secondary window topics could not be displayed with the Back button or Browse Sequence buttons—although Help authors often found workarounds to make up for these deficiencies.

This basic design continues in Office 95 Help, but now secondary windows are more capable. In WinHelp 4, a secondary window can contain a complete button bar, and most of the main window's menu commands are available from a floating menu that the user can access by right-clicking. Secondary windows, however, still lack the Bookmark and History features. A WinHelp 4 secondary window is shown in Figure 3.2.

One new feature of secondary windows is that the Help author can specify "size to fit." In other words, each secondary window can size itself to fit the length of its topic, developing scroll bars only if the amount of material is too large for the screen to display. This feature serves to reduce the amount of screen real estate required by the Help system. Another new feature is the ability to display multiple secondary windows (up to nine) at one time. Because Help authors can define different types of secondary windows, each with its own dimensions, Help authors can define a secondary window type with larger dimensions when they want to prevent scrolling, as they would in topics with tables or graphics.

Especially with the functionality added in WinHelp 4, secondary windows are now well suited for displaying Help topics. Generally speaking, Help authors favor secondary windows when they want narrow windows with few controls and plan on writing brief topics with only small graphics or tables. They can, however, define a different secondary window type with greater dimensions to accommodate a large graphic or a table. Help authors favor main windows when they want larger windows, a full set of controls (in particular the Bookmark), and plan to write more substantial topics.

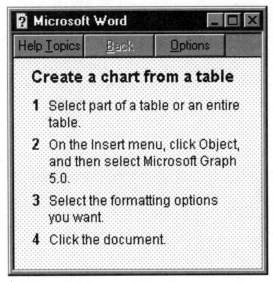

Figure 3.2. *A WinHelp 4 secondary window.*

Screen layout

As William Horton has noted in his book *Designing and Writing Online Documentation*, the screen is not the page. Among the significant differences between the two media are the superior resolution of print and the difference in aspect ratio (proportion of height and width) between most print documents and most screens. On the other hand, many traditional guidelines for page design translate to the screen. Some general principles for screen layout appear below. Although these principles are certainly useful, almost any screen layout is a unique combination of design elements. Help authors, therefore, should rely ultimately on their own experience and talent as designers.

OVERALL SIMPLICITY

Probably the main principle of screen design is the need for simplicity. Print manuals employ such refined layout elements as multiple columns, reverse outs, screening, page bleeds, and multiple thumbnail-size graphics. These must be used very cautiously in Help because (1) screen resolution is limited in comparison with print; (2) users display Help on monitors with different sizes, dimensions, and other characteristics; and (3) Help authors don't know how users will choose to size Help windows.

BLANK SPACE

A general screen design principle is to provide ample blank space. No one likes long blocks of text on the computer screen. Ample blank space makes Help information more appealing and easier to read. It is difficult, however, to reconcile this principle with the need to document complex software products. If you have a lot of information to convey and you leave generous amounts of blank space, the user may have to scroll through a very long topic. Thus you are taking away with one hand what you are giving the user with the other. The Help topic shown in Figure 3.3 follows sound design principles but reaches the limit of acceptability as far as the amount of text it includes.

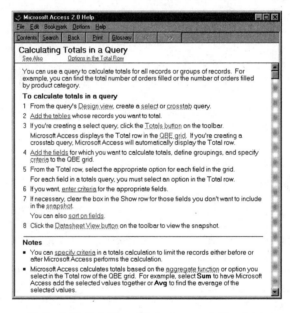

Figure 3.3. *A Help topic with just enough blank space.*

VERTICAL SPACING AND INDENTATION

Related to the amount of text you include are vertical spacing and the indentation of text blocks. The goal is to not only provide adequate blank space but to use the blank space to visually suggest how the content is organized. Figure 3.4 is part of a Help topic from Solitaire Help in Windows 3.0. Notice the jarring inconsistency in indentation between the procedures "Moving a Card" and "Canceling Your Last Move." Figure 3.5 shows a revised version of this topic in Windows 3.1 and Windows 95. Notice how the indentation has been greatly simplified. Notice also how vertical space has been added to visually separate the individual procedures. We see here that some of the principles writers have used for generations in print serve well in Help.

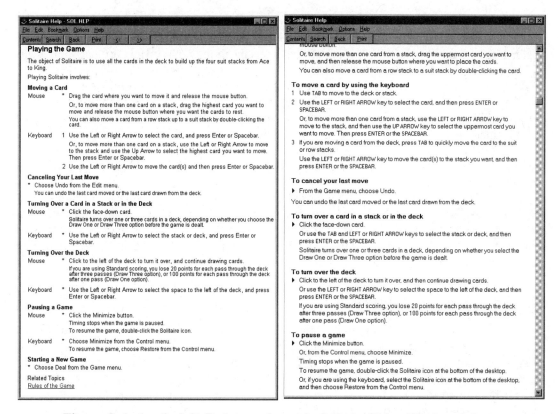

Figure 3.4. *(on the left) Bad screen layout in Solitaire Help—Windows 3.0.*

Figure 3.5. *(on the right) Much improved screen layout in Solitaire Help—Windows 95.*

FONTS

A font is apt to be a good screen font if it is made up of fairly thick strokes and doesn't have very small and delicate design elements. Both serif and sans serif fonts can work well as screen fonts, although Help authors generally prefer sans serif fonts. Before settling on a font, check to see how it displays on different monitors (especially monitors with different resolutions), in different font sizes, and with the line spacing and other variables that you are using in your Help system.

Help authors very often limit themselves to standard Windows fonts to be sure the fonts are available on the user's system. By far the most common choices are MS Sans Serif and its close relative Arial—two very good screen fonts. But MS Serif and its close relative Times New Roman—also good screen fonts—are used frequently.

Microsoft's type specifications for WinHelp 4 stipulate 8 point MS Sans Serif. Bold is used for headings; regular for text. Few would ask for a size smaller than 8 points, and some people prefer larger, 9 or 10 points. The complete type specifications for WinHelp are part of the file MS Style.HLP, which can be found on the disc that accompanies this book.

As originally planned, WinHelp 4 would have allowed software vendors to ship any TrueType font with their Help systems in Help's baggage file system. Although this feature was cancelled, the Help community is apt to see it eventually. This feature adds some extra complexities to installing Help files, and software vendors must obtain the copyright to the fonts they ship. Despite these drawbacks, some software vendors would like to ship specialized symbol fonts with their Help systems, and others are interested in shipping special fonts for aesthetic reasons.

Leading (or "line spacing") is an important variable related to fonts. A rule of thumb is for leading to be 120 percent of the text size—for example a 10 point font might be set with 12 points of leading. Microsoft's type specification of 8 point Sans Serif also stipulates 12 points of leading. This ample amount of leading enhances the legibility of the MS Sans Serif font. For further information on WinHelp font issues, see Chapter 12, *Formatting Topics*.

SCREEN RESOLUTION

A complicating factor in regard to fonts, graphics, windows, and all other visual aspects of Help is the user's screen resolution. The standard resolution remains VGA (640 x 480 pixels), but many users can display higher resolutions (800 x 600 and 1024 x 768), which make everything on the screen smaller. Help authors can choose to have their Help windows adjust their size and position in relation to the user's screen resolution (relative positioning) or to maintain absolute size and position regardless of the user's screen resolution (absolute positioning). Because of the differences among monitors and the very different settings for color and screen resolution that users choose, Help authors must check the appearance and behavior of their Help systems across a broad range of monitors and settings.

COLOR FOR TEXT AND BACKGROUNDS

As the Help author you can assign any colors you want to your Help system. You can assign the text color, the color of the main background area (or "client" area), and if you create a special "nonscrolling region" (explained below), you can assign a color to that. Despite this freedom, however, it is best to be conservative in your use of color. Using garish colors, incompatible colors, or too many colors will tire, distract, and confuse users—especially when color is the background for text. A sound decision is to set the color of the window client area (the window background) to white or near white.

Microsoft has chosen a soft yellow as the background color for their secondary windows. This color is very readable and has the advantage of making the Help system look different from the main work area of the software application. The RGB color values for this soft yellow are red 255, green 255, and blue 225. Because of the WinHelp 4 Use System Colors command, the user can override any colors you have set in favor of the system's background color as set by the user.

TEXT EMPHASIS

In print documents italics, boldface, and upper-case type are used—sparingly—to emphasize specific words or phrases. These devices can also be used in Help, although italics are especially hard to read on the screen and should be used even more sparingly than in print. In Help, however, you can emphasize a word or phrase by assigning it a color, a design technique that in print is usually too costly.

NONSCROLLING REGIONS

Nonscrolling regions (sometimes called "banners") are special areas at the top of Help topics that remain in place as the rest of the topic scrolls. A Help topic with a nonscrolling region appears in Figure 3.3 above. The most typical role of nonscrolling regions is allowing users to view the topic heading even as they scroll through the topic. Similarly, if jumps to related topics are placed in the nonscrolling region, the user can choose these jumps regardless of where they have scrolled to in the topic. Some further uses of nonscrolling regions are these:

- If a Help topic contains a long table, the nonscrolling region can be used for column headings.

- In glossary topics and other topics with alphabetical entries, the nonscrolling region often contains an alphabetical array of hot graphics so that if the user clicks, say, the "M" button, the topic scrolls (using the "mid-topic jump" technique) to the beginning of the "M" entries. This kind of nonscrolling region is shown in Figure 6.9.

- The nonscrolling region is an appropriate place for special Help buttons such as Overview and Print Topic.

- Hotspot graphics can be placed in the nonscrolling region of a group of Help topics to simulate dialog-box functionality. Figure 3.6 shows a very effective use of this technique. Clicking on one of the option buttons changes the content of the Help window. Dialog-box functionality can also be achieved using an add-on module available from ForeHelp.

Very often, Help designers assign a colored background to nonscrolling regions. The background color visually distinguishes the nonscrolling region from the rest of the topic, and is often aesthetically appealing. Because there is almost always text in nonscrolling regions, you should choose a background color that allows the text to be read easily. You need adequate contrast but want to avoid overpowering or garish backgrounds. The desirability of a particular combination of text color and background depends on numerous factors including the font size of the text, the size of the nonscrolling region, the color of the client area of the Help topic, and the overall effect you are trying to achieve. Assuming black or dark blue text, light gray is a reliable and attractive color for the nonscrolling region. Yellow and dark cyan are more adventuresome choices that will work well in some situations. Assuming white or yellow text, blue and dark blue—among others—become possible. Light green, light blue, light cream, and medium gray (the bottom row on the standard Windows 95 color palette), are good background colors for dark text, except that they will appear as dithered colors on systems that are set to display only 16 colors. For more on the use of color in WinHelp, see "Formatting Text," in Chapter 12, *Formatting Topics.*

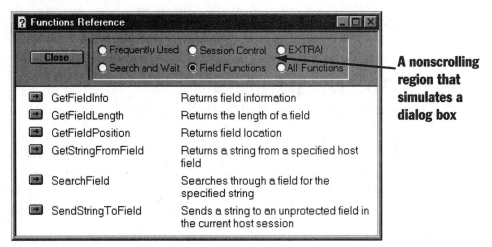

A nonscrolling region that simulates a dialog box

Figure 3.6. *Simulated dialog box functionality in a nonscrolling region.*

RULES

Another element of screen layout is the use of rules (or "score lines"). Used in moderation, rules help organize the content of Help topics. For example, in Figure 3.3 above, a rule sets off the notes from the rest of the Help topic. If you use a nonscrolling region, a rule will appear at the bottom of the nonscrolling region even if the color of the nonscrolling region is the same as that of the main Help topic background area. Rules often fit nicely into a color scheme for Help topics. For instance, you might assign the same color to step numbers and to a rule.

TABLES

Tables are used in Help topics for the same reasons they are used in print: to show relationships among items of information. A simple but useful table is shown in Figure 3.6 above. As explained in Chapter 12, *Formatting Topics,* WinHelp 4 poses certain complications for table construction, especially in regard to adding table rules.

Graphic elements in Help

There are three kinds of graphic elements in WinHelp:

Static graphics	Bitmapped or vector images that serve as illustrations but are not active.
Hotspot graphics (or "hypergraphics")	Bitmapped images that exhibit special behavior when clicked. They can display a pop-up window, jump the user to a new topic, or trigger a macro.
	There are single-hotspot graphics and graphics with multiple hotspots.
Multimedia	AVI files (and other file types) that display animation sequences and, at times, sound and video sequences.

Each kind of Help graphic, as we shall see, can greatly improve a Help system. Help graphics, however, present authors with significant difficulties:

- Graphic elements (and especially hotspot graphics and animation sequences) take time to create and incorporate into Help. Often there are technical issues in regard to file type (bitmap images with different bit depths vs. vector graphics), resizing, positioning with text, and so forth.

- Graphics, especially color graphics and multimedia, add considerably to the size of the compiled Help file, possibly requiring you to ship an extra disk and tempting users not to install the Help system.

- Multimedia makes demands in regard to computer hardware and software that not all users can meet.

There are two fundamental principles of graphic design that both benefit users and lessen the number and size of the graphics in a Help system.

1. Use a graphic only when it serves a definite purpose. Don't use a graphic to show what would be obvious without a graphic. Only rarely do we use a graphic for decoration.

2. Show as little as possible. If you are explaining a toolbar, don't show an entire window. If you use a multimedia sequence, keep it short. When there is extraneous information, users find it hard to focus on what is really relevant to them.

Below we describe the major reasons for using static graphics, hotspot graphics, and multimedia in Help. For a good general treatment of graphics, see William Horton's *Illustrating Computer Documentation*.

STATIC GRAPHICS

In the most general terms, graphics show the appearance, structure, and context of real or imaginary objects. In Help, we use static graphics to:

1. Show an element to be acted upon.

2. Show feedback.

3. Introduce a region of the screen.

4. Represent abstract relationships.

5. Categorize Help information with pictographs.

6. Enhance the appearance of the Help system.

Showing interface elements to be acted upon

In contemporary graphical user interfaces, there are many interface controls that use graphic symbols rather than text. In such instances, the best way to identify these controls to users is with graphics. Indicating what interface element the user is supposed to act upon is the most prevalent form of graphic in Help systems. Such a graphic is shown below:

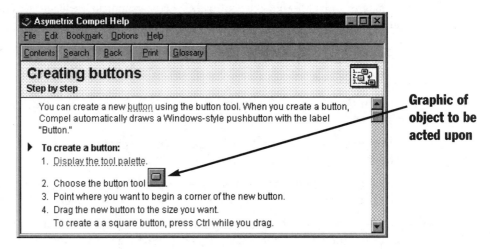

Figure 3.7. *Showing an interface element to be acted upon.*

In WinHelp 4, this use of graphics is partly supplanted by special Shortcut buttons, shown in Figure 3.8, that operate the software product from Help topics. If the interface element is hard to find and not used often, it is usually better to add the Shortcut button rather than to merely show users how to find it.

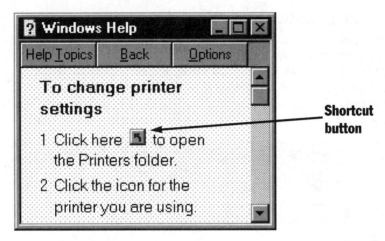

Figure 3.8. *A Help Shortcut button.*

Showing feedback

As we will see in the next chapter, procedure steps sometimes include feedback statements that show the user the system's response to the user's action. A visual display of this feedback may be appropriate, especially when the response to an action is hard to notice or unusual. In Figure 3.9, the first graphic shows the user the interface element to act upon and the second graphic provides feedback, showing the somewhat atypical way in which the system responds to that action.

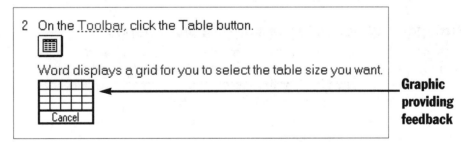

Figure 3.9. *A graphic showing feedback.*

Introducing a region of the screen

Graphics can help introduce a group of interface elements such as a toolbar, palette, or even an entire window. Each interface element can be identified with callout labels. This function, however, can usually be performed more effectively using hotspot graphics.

Representing abstract relationships

When you explain abstract concepts, you may need graphics that are diagrams of entities that don't exist at all rather than screen captures of the software product's interface. The Help topic from MathCad shown in Figure 3.10 nicely illustrates how abstractions can be made clear graphically. Conceptual diagrams such as this one are not used as often as they should be. This is because diagrams often require more work than screen captures and because sophisticated visual thinking is needed to represent an abstraction as a graphic.

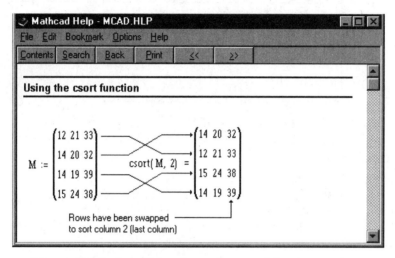

Figure 3.10. *A graphic representing an abstract concept.*

Categorizing Help information with pictographs

Pictographs are graphics that convey a specific word or idea. When a user knows the meaning of a pictograph, the pictograph communicates more quickly and requires less mental effort than reading text. Often Help systems incorporate pictographs to categorize Help information. Here are the most important uses of pictographs in Help:

- A pictograph located at the top of each Help topic can indicate whether the topic is a procedure topic, a command topic, or some other kind of Help topic. Very often, as in Figure 3.7 (in the nonscrolling region), the numbers 1, 2, 3 are used to indicate procedure topics. Stair steps are also used. A graphic showing a menu with a command selected can be used for command topics, and a globe can be used for overview topics.

- In software products made up of separate modules or other distinct groupings, a pictograph located at the top of each Help topic can visually indicate which module or grouping the Help topic belongs to. In the example shown in Figure 3.11, the software product includes three distinct editors. Therefore, a distinctive pictograph is used in the Help topics pertaining to each editor.

- Within a particular topic, pictographs can categorize blocks of text as overview information, tips, etc. Pictographs can also distinguish mouse vs. keyboard actions. Such pictographs enable users to quickly find the information they seek on a Help topic.

Sometimes pictographs are immediately self-disclosing, but usually users need to be shown the pictograph at least once with some kind of identifying label in order to learn what it stands for.

How to maintain the district calendar

You can use District Table Editor to add, change, or delete a specific date or a range of dates in your District Calendar table.

Figure 3.11. *Help pictographs indicating the module or grouping a topic belongs to.*

Adding visual appeal

Another purpose of graphics in Help is to lend visual appeal to a Help system and to suggest that the software company does high-budget, high-quality work. Very rarely should a graphic be added simply for decoration. But it is a plus when graphics lend visual appeal and prestige to a Help system, at the same time they are serving more substantive roles.

HOTSPOT GRAPHICS

The distinctive function of hotspot graphics is to display an extra level of detail. For example:

- At times the pictographs discussed above are coded as hotspot graphics to display specific kinds of Help information such as overviews and tips. This technique is illustrated in Figures 4.5 and 4.6.

- When a Help topic introduces users to a toolbar, palette, or other region of the screen, hotspot graphics can be used to display pop-up windows that explain each interface element in the graphic. This use of hotspot graphics is shown in Figure 3.12 and later in Figure 6.3.

- Along similar lines, a graphic of an item of computer hardware or some other object in the physical world can employ hotspots that display pop-up windows to show an exploded view of the object.

Users should not wonder whether a particular graphic employs hotspots or have to test the graphic with the mouse pointer. Text labels can tell users to click on a graphic to display more information, and visual cues—such as green border lines—can be used to signal the presence of hotspots. Better yet, the logical and consistent use of hotspot graphics will enable users to predict which graphics are hot.

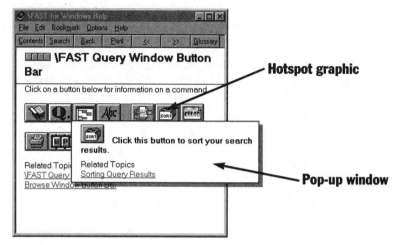

Figure 3.12. *Using hotspot graphics to introduce a region of the screen.*

MULTIMEDIA

Multimedia can add real value to Help, or it can be useless, glitzy decoration. Below we describe appropriate uses for the various forms of multimedia.

Animation

A series of static graphics can show change over time, but animation sequences do this far more effectively. Animation sequences are especially good for showing non-routine interface actions such as manipulating the handles in a drawing package to create complex curves.

Animation can also help explain abstract processes. For example, the graphic that explains MathCad's CSORT function would be still more effective if the numbers could dynamically change positions in the two arrays.

Video and Audio

In contrast to animation, video has few uses in software documentation. Graphical user interfaces do not have the visual complexity of the world beyond software, and the ability of video to create a realistic record of actions and events is not needed. Video might be used, however, in hardware documentation, for example, to show a user assembling components.

Audio is potentially very useful: if users can hear rather than read procedure steps, they can keep their eyes on the software product's interface and carry out the actions as they hear them. Users, however, must have rapid and precise control of the audio procedures. This represents a significant technical challenge.

4

General Issues for Writing Help

Above all else computer documentation is about writing. This chapter discusses these key writing issues:

- Task orientation.

- The kinds of information we write.

- Examples and analogies.

- International audiences.

- The amount of information we write.

The last issue is an introduction to minimalist documentation, an area of intense interest in the documentation community. After looking at these general writing issues, we will, in the next three chapters, closely examine how to write procedure topics, the mainstay of standard Help; how to write other kinds of standard Help topics; and how to design and write wizard and coach Help.

Task orientation

A basic principle of computer documentation is task orientation. The idea is that people use computers to get their work done. They are not interested in learning or thinking about the technology for its own sake—at least not until their work is finished. Because users see the computer simply as a tool, they want to interact with computers using their own terms and concepts rather than the computer's. They want the computer and computer documentation to—as much as possible—reach out into their world rather than to force them to reach into the world of the computer. Table 4.1 illustrates task orientation by contrasting the task view of an alarm clock to an engineer's "system" view. The user sees the alarm clock in terms of how alarm clocks are used. The engineer sees the alarm clock from the perspective of its internal organization. The task view forms the basis of good documentation; the system view does not. The principle of task orientation will serve you well in almost every aspect of writing computer documentation, from deciding what Help topics need to be written to choosing specific words and phrases.

Table 4.1. *Task orientation vs. system orientation*

Task view of an alarm clock	System view of an alarm clock

Getting it unpacked and plugged in
    Removing the shipping tie-downs
    Plugging in the power cord
	Packaging
	    Shipping tie-downs

Using it as a clock
    Viewing the time
    Setting the time
    Adjusting the brightness of the clock face
	Power
	    AC (power cord)
	    DC (battery)

Using it as an alarm clock
    Setting the alarm time
    Setting the alarm to ring
    Turning off the alarm
    Activating the snooze feature
	Internal electronics
	    processor
	    peripheral electronics/circuits

Getting protection from a power outage
    Installing a battery
    Monitoring the no-battery installed indicator
    Monitoring the battery power-on indicator
	Display
	    Time display
	    Alarm-set display
	    No-battery display
	    AM/PM display

	Controls
	    Hour button
	    Minute button
	    Alarm button
	    Minute button
	    Alarm button
	    Time button
	    Alarm on/off switch
	    Snooze lever
	    Illumination adjustment knob

The kinds of information we write

Essays and narratives are as diverse as the world we live in. In contrast, computer documentation is a highly focused form of writing that is restricted in the kinds of information it contains. Thus it is possible to usefully classify Help information. In fact, almost all the information we provide—in procedure topics, in the other standard help topics, and in entirely different models of online Help—falls into one of the seven categories shown in Table 4.2.

Table 4.2. *Seven categories of Help information*

1.	Purpose	The main reason the user is performing a task, the intended result.
2.	Actions	Actions that will achieve this result.
3.	Feedback	Information that lets the user know he or she has acted correctly and that the system has responded properly.
4.	User options	Variations on the purpose of the procedure that are being suggested to the user.
5.	Secondary results	By-products of the purpose. They are usually routine but may be harmful.
6.	Conditions	Special circumstances or problems that, when they apply to a user, call for some action.
7.	System description	Descriptive information about the nature and behavior of the system.

You can use this classification as a brainstorming tool so that you don't overlook information you might want to include. Also, if you understand the nature and role of each category of Help information, you are better equipped to decide which items of candidate information to include or leave out. We continue to refer to this classification in the next three chapters.

PURPOSE AND ACTIONS

Of the seven kinds of Help information, *purpose* and *actions* are the two most important. Users need to understand the purpose before they will take an action; no one likes to jump off into the darkness. Help topics, therefore, must include purpose and action information, unless this information can be readily inferred. Every procedure topic begins with a topic heading, which is a brief statement of purpose—for example "Downloading files." Procedure topics also contain two other components whose main role is to convey purpose information. These are the *conceptual element* and the *infinitive subheading*. (You can preview these components and the other components of procedure topics by looking ahead to Figure 5.1.) Once the user understands the purpose of the procedure and decides that the purpose matches his or her goals, the user wants to carry out the actions. An action may be as simple as "Click the Download button." Many action statements, however, are augmented with one or more modifiers, for example: "When the connection has been established, click the Download button."

THE FIVE OTHER KINDS OF HELP INFORMATION

Our interactions with computers are too complex for us to document software (and hardware) products with only purpose and action information. Five other kinds of information are also necessary.

Feedback

Feedback appears directly after action information. We provide feedback to give users assurance that they have performed the correct action and that the system has responded properly. This step shows feedback information in its simplest form:

1 Click the vertex whose position you want to change.
  The vertex turns magenta, and the pointer changes to a four-headed arrow.

Computer users, however, do not necessarily need explicit feedback statements like the one above to tell them that they are on track. Other kinds of Help information can provide feedback. In the following example, the action statement in Step 2 includes a modifier that shows the location of the action in Step 2. But this modifier does double-duty, for it provides feedback for the action statement in Step 1:

1 On the Options menu, choose Resources and Costs.

2 In the Resources and Costs dialog box, choose Assign Workloads.

As we will see below, secondary results can also provide feedback. Occasionally Help authors provide negative feedback information that helps users recognize a problem.

User options

Software products are often very complex and allow users to perform a great many tasks. Documentors could treat each task as a distinct procedure, but this would lead to an enormous number of largely redundant procedures. Instead, we routinely treat certain tasks as user options, as optional variations on the main purpose of the procedure we are documenting. User options are very often presented as steps.

To download your files in compressed form, click Compression.

This step is simply an optional variation on the main purpose of the procedure, downloading files. If an option concerns relatively few users, it is apt to be presented as a note.

Whenever documentation contains phrases like "If you want to" or "You can," the writer is presenting a user option.

Secondary results

Users carry out computer tasks to achieve a purpose. But because of the complexity of computer systems, there are often secondary results that occur along with the main purpose of the procedure. Secondary results are usually routine: they may be too unimportant, too obvious, or even too deeply buried in the internal operations of the system to mention. On the other hand, documenting them may give the user a richer understanding of how the task at hand fits the broader context. For example, in this conceptual element for the procedure topic "Inserting a manual page break," users benefit from this statement of a secondary result:

> When you insert a manual page break, QuickWriter automatically adjusts the automatic page breaks that follow.

Notice, however, in Figure 4.1 how another Help author is using the same secondary result to provide the user with feedback after the action statement in Step 3.

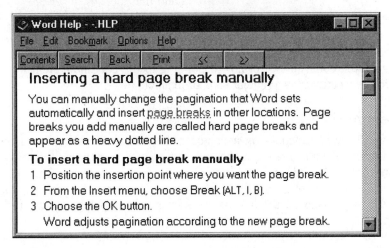

Figure 4.1. *Using a secondary result to provide feedback.*

Conditions

Conditions are special circumstances or problems that apply to some of the users of the software product. Each user determines whether the condition applies to his or her situation and, if it does, takes the specified action.

For example:

> If you are in the Transactions module, switch to the Report
> module to format and print the report.

Often if a condition is not addressed, it is impossible for the procedure to go forward. There is no way to print a report from the Transactions module.

In other cases, the procedure can go forward, but the result is not fully successful:

If the edges of the scanned graphic are blurry, choose Sharpen Edges.

If the user ignores the corrective action and proceeds with the task, the scan will not come out well.

Sometimes leaving a condition unaddressed results in an undesirable secondary result. In the following example, the condition is that the user has an existing file with the same name as the file being archived. The unwelcome secondary result of archiving the new file is losing the existing file:

Caution
If you archive a file into a folder that already contains a file with the same name as the file being archived, the existing file will be replaced automatically by the new one.

Notice that this condition does not apply to users unless they have an existing file with the same name as the new one. Furthermore, even when the condition applies, the user may want to overwrite the existing file.

Depending on the consequence of not responding to the condition, Help writers may present a condition as a caution, as a regular step, or in a note.

System description

Task oriented information focuses on user goals, the results users want to achieve. System description information concerns the make-up or function of a software (or hardware) product. It may pertain to either the internal workings of the product or to its user interface. Task orientation is an important principle in documentation; and, indeed, much of the bad documentation written in the past focused on the internals workings of computer systems rather than the goals of users.

Some types of system description, however, can be very useful. Although telling a user that input is stored in a particular buffer is probably unwarranted, telling a user that a certain field can accept only numbers is very useful system description.

What's This? and command topics provide functional descriptions of some aspect of the interface. Users easily infer the connection between the system description and their own purposes. For example, the What's This? topic shown below identifies an interface element and describes its function:

Formats the selected text as boldface.

The user, however, can mentally transform this functional description into a purpose and action statement: "To format the selected text as boldface, all I need to do is click this checkbox."

Because of the endless complexity of language, this classification scheme could be expanded to cover exceptions and variations. We think, however, that it serves well in this relatively simple form as an aid to Help authors.

Examples and analogies

Examples and analogies are important rhetorical devices that can be used in writing any kind of Help information. They are especially prevalent in writing purpose, action, and feedback information. People learn from examples and analogies more readily than from abstract explanations and technically oriented definitions. Below we see the conceptual element from a procedure topic. The two examples add some length to the conceptual element, but they make clear why the user might want to add users to groups:

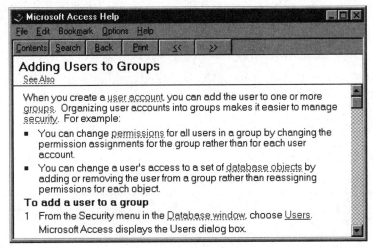

Figure 4.2. *Using examples in a conceptual element.*

In the procedure step shown below, the brief example makes clear the kind of suffix that the user must type.

> If you select the 24-hour format, type a suffix, for example PST for Pacific Standard Time.

When we use analogies, we explain something unfamiliar by comparing it to something that is familiar. Analogies usually appear in overview topics or in the conceptual element of procedure topics, as we see below. This procedure topic is from Microsoft Publisher, a product geared for entry-level users. For these users, the simple desk analogy works well:

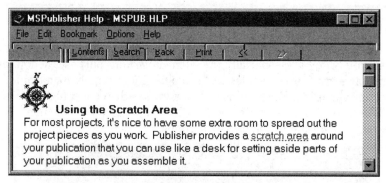

Figure 4.3. *Using an analogy in the conceptual element.*

Every analogy has at least one point of similarity and multiple points of dissimilarity with the thing it explains. A scratch area and a desktop are similar in one respect but totally dissimilar in many respects. Analogies are worthwhile only when the point or points of similarity are meaningful, the points of dissimilarity do not add confusion (the fact that desks are made of wood is not a problem in this analogy), and when the analogy as a whole is not too complex and lengthy.

Writing for international audiences

Many software products are sold around the world, and so the documentation, and the interface as well, must be translated and made culturally appropriate for other nations. This is called "localizing." Ensuring that the original version can be easily localized is called "internationalizing." Internationalizing has become an important part of writing Help.

The major ways of internationalizing are these:

- Avoiding highly idiomatic phrasing and terms that do not lend themselves to translation.

- Carefully scrutinizing documentation for examples that might give offense or cause other cultural collisions. For example, kinds of food and ways of eating that are routine in North America are highly inappropriate in certain cultures.

- Compensating for the expansion of text that takes place when some languages are translated into others. For example, English text expands by about 30 per cent when translated into German or Spanish.

For a detailed treatment of this subject, see Nancy Hoft's book *International Technical Communication.*

How much information do we write?

One of the most difficult issues in documentation is how much information to provide. Computer users are impatient. They want to get their work done, and they don't like to read. On the other hand, they are frustrated and even angry whenever a Help system doesn't explain an issue in enough depth to be clear to them or when there is no mention of the particular option they want to pursue or condition that applies to them—no matter how obscure or little-used these may be. A very difficult problem, therefore, is how much depth to provide in our explanations and how far we can go in cluttering up Help topics with special issues.

MINIMALIST DOCUMENTATION

Minimalism is an approach to computer documentation that directly addresses the issue of how much information we should provide. Minimalism was conceived by John Carroll; Carroll's thinking and research on minimalism are summed up in his book, *The Nurnberg Funnel: Designing Minimalist Instruction for Practical Computer Skill*, and in the recent article published by van der Meij and Carroll in the journal *Technical Communication*, "Principles and Heuristics for Designing Minimalist Instruction."

Carroll observed that users are impatient with verbose, slow-paced documentation and very often prefer to exercise their own problem-solving skills. Minimalism has numerous facets, but in the context of Help the minimalist approach entails highly streamlined procedures that provide only information that users will truly need. Explanations of both concepts and actions should be "bare bones" to encourage users to infer concepts and discover the correct actions by working with the interface. To prevent users from being bogged down in the documentation, information on unusual user options and unusual conditions is kept to an absolute minimum. Here too users are encouraged to find what they need to know by exploring and reasoning about the interface.

The promise of minimalism is brief Help topics that users will like and really use. In addition, users will better remember procedures for having exercised their problem-solving skills. The potential pitfalls in minimalism are that users will not be able to achieve their goals, that they will achieve their goals but expend more effort doing so than they really wanted to, and that by figuring things out for themselves they will learn inefficient methods or develop faulty mental models of the product that will get them in trouble later on. Because minimalist documentation must be so carefully attuned to the audience, extensive usability testing is required. Furthermore, when audiences are diverse, minimalism becomes more difficult to achieve. Microsoft and Lotus are two software vendors that have recently shifted toward minimalism in their Help designs. We take a closer look at minimalism in the next chapter.

LAYERING

Layering is a prevalent strategy in all forms of technical communication. It consists of giving users clear choices regarding what information they will read. In print documents, we layer information by providing headings, appendices, cross references, and explanatory footnotes.

The extreme opposite of layering is a document consisting of page after page of undifferentiated text; readers have no way to efficiently choose what parts they want to skip.

Help systems are often layered to a significant degree. Jumps and pop-ups are just two forms of layering in Help. Layering is perhaps our best approach to resolve users' contradictory demands for complete and comprehensive and yet very brief Help information. With layering, the minimalist strategy becomes less risky. When users have trouble with a minimalist Help topic, they can access more complete information.

Microsoft Works (4.0) Help, shown below as Figure 4.4, is a good example of layering. Users initially access procedure topics (labeled "Step by Step"), but can click the More Info tab to display a topic that lists further choices. These choices typically include an overview topic and topics presenting user options and conditions.

A more thoroughgoing example of layering is shown in Figures 4.5 and 4.6. The concept here is "minimalism with a safety net." The user is first presented with a minimalist Help topic. This topic, however, is part of a cluster of topics; thus the brief and unintimidating minimalist topic is backed up with more complete information for those who need it. By clicking on the pictographs, the user can display pop-up windows containing overview information, examples, complete steps, what if's (user options and conditions), tips (another kind of user option), and related topics. These various forms of supplementary information are made available to the user in a consistent, predictable design.

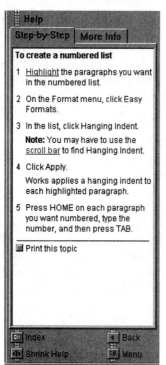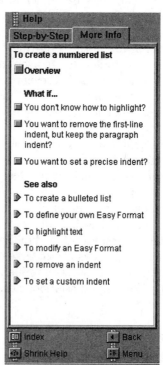

Figure 4.4. *Layering in Microsoft Works.*

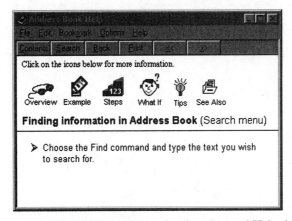

Figure 4.5. *Minimalist information in a layered Help design.*

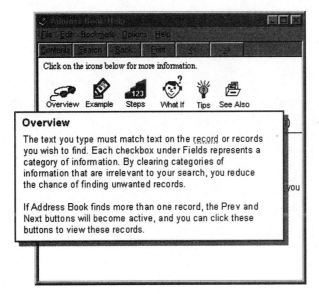

Figure 4.6. *More detailed information in a layered Help design.*

One drawback of extensive layering is that Help systems necessarily become more complex for users. There are more hotspot objects, more places to go, and more things to understand about navigating the Help system. Furthermore, layering generally increases the total amount of information in the Help system. Finally, the complexity entailed in layering (like other forms of complexity) tends to cause other problems. For example, in the prototype shown above, users can print only the content of the main Help window. Despite these drawbacks, however, layering is a very good way to address the difficult issue of how much information to provide in Help.

5

Writing Procedure Topics

Standard Help is the most prevalent and important form of Help. Procedure topics are the most prevalent and important kind of topic in standard Help. They serve the central role in documentation: explaining the purpose of tasks, how to carry them out, and what the special issues are. Because procedure topics are so prevalent and important, they receive a full chapter in this book.

Our approach is to explain procedure topics as a set of components—some required, some optional, each serving certain roles. For each component we present the key design issues and design recommendations.

Table 5.1 introduces each component. Figure 5.1 shows each component identified in a procedure topic.

Table 5.1. *The components of procedure topics*

Component	Description	Kinds of information conveyed
Topic heading	Introduces the topic as a whole.	Purpose
Conceptual element	Elaborates on the topic heading.	Purpose, other information
Infinitive subheading	Introduces individual procedures when multiple procedures appear in one procedure topic.	Purpose

Table 5.1. *(continued)*

Component	Description	Kinds of information conveyed
Steps	Contains an action statement, often with a modifier. Sometimes contains a feedback statement.	Actions, feedback, user options, conditions, other information
Notes	Contains information that does not fit comfortably in the rest of the topic.	User options, conditions

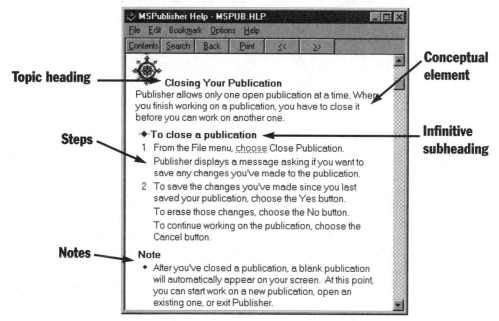

Figure 5.1. *The components of procedure topics.*

The topic heading

The topic heading briefly states the purpose of the procedure topic. The user, in a single glance, tries to determine whether this procedure matches his or her purpose. If it appears to, the user will read more of the topic.

CONVEYING ADEQUATE INFORMATION

Users see topic headings listed in the contents, index, and other places besides the procedure topic itself. Thus, they often make the decision whether to access the entire topic on the basis of the relatively few words in the topic heading. For this reason especially the Help author must pack a lot of meaning in these few words.

Writing really effective, really meaningful topic headings is a challenge. Each topic heading must be task oriented. It must reach out and communicate with users in terms of their backgrounds and the tasks they need to perform.

To achieve this goal, Help authors should, when appropriate, write topic headings that are longer than the traditional three or four words (as in "Deleting a file"). Often a prepositional phrase is enough to greatly enhance the heading. For example, the topic heading "Using macros" will be meaningless to novices. The topic heading "Automating your work" is too general. Experienced users know lots of ways to automate their work. The longer topic heading "Automating your work with macros" satisfies all users.

Very long headings, however, can become cumbersome, especially when they appear in narrow secondary windows. Also, long headings can be a problem if they appear as entries in the Help contents; for, if they extend beyond the right edge of the scrolling list, they will cause the contents to develop a horizontal scroll bar. Finally, when Help systems are localized into such languages as German and Spanish, these headings will become still longer. For these reasons, a reasonable guideline is to keep most topic headings below seven or eight words. Th relationship between topic headings and contents entries is discussed further in Chapter 8, *Designing the Contents, Browse Sequences, and Jumps.*

PHRASING

There are three ways to phrase topic headings of procedure topics. These are shown in Table 5.2.

Table 5.2. *The phrasing of topic headings*

Gerunds	Automating your work with macros
Roots	Automate your work with macros
Infinitives	To automate your work with macros

Traditionally Help authors have used *gerunds*. Gerunds have a strong "introductory" quality and work well when they precede a conceptual element, infinitive subheadings, or steps. *Root forms*, such as "Print one or more mailing labels for a single address," have a more abrupt quality, but they are similarly flexible. Microsoft and Apple use root forms in Help systems in which jumps to topics are listed as answers to questions, as shown in Figure 5.2.

Infinitives make for highly focused statements of purpose; they strongly suggest that steps (command verbs) will follow. Consequently, infinitive topic headings work best in a model in which the conceptual element and infinitive subheading are eliminated and the user goes directly from the title to the steps. A list of infinitives in the contents is repetitious; consequently, when Help authors choose infinitives for the topic headings, they use gerunds or roots for the contents entries.

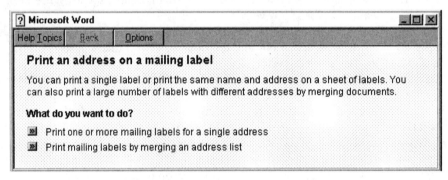

Figure 5.2. *Root forms as answers to questions.*

The conceptual element

The conceptual element is an expansion of the topic heading. It provides more detailed purpose information and, very often, other kinds of information as well.

In writing the conceptual element, you must decide how much purpose information your users need. For example, consider this conceptual element:

> **Applying a filter to view serials by category**
> Often the Holdings window will display more serials than you can easily scan. You can choose which serial categories will be displayed by applying one or more filters.

The topic heading, while relatively detailed, will probably not suffice for all users of this software product. Of the two sentences in the conceptual element, the second would be enough for many users. This Help author, however, has also included the first sentence, which reaches out into the world of the user by making explicit the problem that the filters solve. A good idea is for

Help authors to ask themselves questions such as these: "What problem does this procedure solve for users?" "How does this procedure fit into their work?" "Why is it in our software product?" The answer to these questions often becomes a valuable part of the conceptual element.

The following is a conceptual element that does not reach out to the user and does not provide a clear understanding of the purpose of the procedure:

> **Setting preferences for the current editing session**
> While you can create and apply preferences using named preference sets and files, you can also access the Preference Sets and Files dialog box and apply preferences while you edit without storing the information as a default or named set.

This conceptual element focuses on how the software product operates, but never explains how this relates to the needs of users. The underlying idea here is that users do not need to save preference sets they won't be using in the future.

PROCEDURE TOPICS WITHOUT A CONCEPTUAL ELEMENT

Traditionally, procedure topics always included a conceptual element, even when none was needed. In fact, Help authors often struggled to find something to say when writing conceptual elements that were mere placeholders.

One could certainly argue, for example, that the conceptual element is unnecessary in this procedure topic:

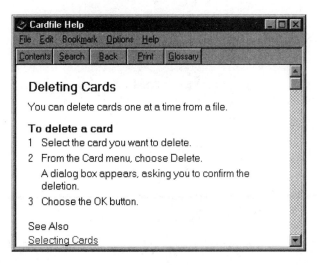

Figure 5.3. *A simple procedure topic in which the conceptual element is of marginal value.*

The concept "deleting" is extremely simple: even children understand the idea of discarding what is no longer needed. Because the concept underlying this procedure is so simple, the topic heading tells the story pretty fully. About the only information the conceptual element contributes is that cards can be deleted only one at a time. The value of the infinitive subheading in this Help topic is also highly questionable, an issue we discuss shortly.

These days, we often see Help topics without conceptual elements. Help writers decide whether to include them on a case-by-case basis. We believe that this is a sound practice, a good way to accommodate users' desire for brief Help topics—as long as Help writers do not omit necessary conceptual elements.

Some Help systems, including Microsoft's Help system for Windows 95, are aggressively minimalist. As shown below, most procedure topics in Windows 95 Help provide no conceptual information other than the topic heading. Although there are overview topics (for example, the topic, "If you've used Windows before"), this information is brief indeed, and—in contrast to the layered Help topics shown in Figures 4.4 to 4.6—there are few direct links from the procedure topics to these overview topics. On the one hand, few users will complain about being overwhelmed with text. On the other hand, users who rely on this Help system to learn Windows 95 will need to exercise their problem-solving skills.

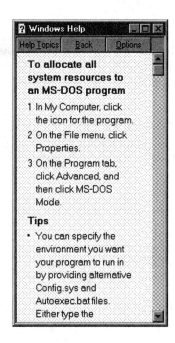

Figure 5.4. *A minimalist procedure topic from the Windows 95 Help system.*

Help authors should adopt this model cautiously. First, because this Help system does not attempt to fully document the Windows 95 operating system, the Microsoft Help authors did not have to address many conceptually difficult issues and tasks. Second, in accordance with minimalist principles, Microsoft conducted many cycles of usability testing to fine tune these Help topics. Without extensive testing, the odds of providing very little but just the right information diminishes. Finally, even if this Help system fails certain users, Windows 95 is supported by an online tour as well as many third-party books and training seminars.

The infinitive subheading

In the past the infinitive subheading has been customary in procedure topics. But this component is worthwhile only when two or more procedures appear in one procedure topic, as shown in Figure 5.5.

In this topic, the two procedures are sufficiently similar in their purpose that the topic heading and the conceptual element can properly introduce both of them. The infinitive subheading functions as a more specific purpose component than either the topic heading or the conceptual element. It differentiates the purposes of the two procedures. In topics with one procedure, the infinitive subheading simply re-states the topic heading and is unnecessary.

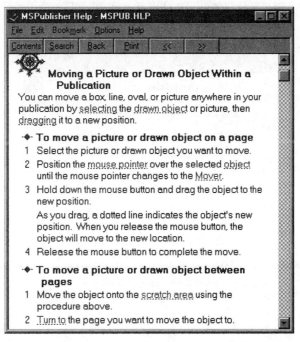

Figure 5.5. *Two procedures in one procedure topic.*

PROCEDURE TOPICS WITHOUT AN INFINITIVE SUBHEADING

In the Windows 95 Help system and in the Help model for the Office 95 products, Microsoft avoids topics with multiple procedures and, hence, does not utilize infinitive subheadings. Their model utilizes a great many short, narrowly sized secondary windows that contain relatively little text. If two or more procedures were included in one topic, this topic could not be short. (In Help systems in which the topic headings are expressed as infinitives, there is a further barrier to using infinitive subheadings.)

We believe that topics with two procedures are sometimes useful. Often two short, closely related procedures make their meanings clearer in juxtaposition with each other. Also, the use of multiple-procedure topics greatly cuts down the total number of topics, making the contents much simpler to create and easier for users to work with. Certainly, multiple-procedure topics with infinitive subheadings make sense when procedure topics will be displayed in traditionally sized main windows. Even in narrow secondary windows, procedure topics made up of two short procedures can still be used. These topics will generally be long enough that a vertical scroll bar appears and the infinitive subheading that begins the second procedure may not be visible. Users, however, will know that there is a second procedure in the topic when they see the infinitive subheading of the first procedure (as well as the scroll bar). Assuming that there is no conceptual element, a two-procedure topic in a secondary window would look like this:

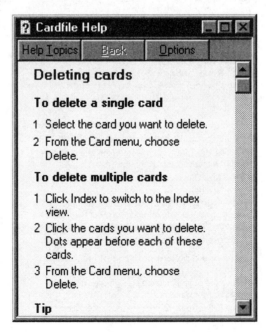

Figure 5.6. *A two-procedure topic in a secondary window.*

Steps

The steps tell users how to get their work done. Looking at steps superficially, one might think they are very simple to write. In fact, there is considerable craft involved, and well-crafted steps are necessary for users to carry out procedures efficiently.

Steps are a special component of procedure topics in that they consist of subcomponents. Figure 5.7 shows a step with the subcomponents labeled; Figure 5.8 shows a logical breakdown of the subcomponents of steps.

Each step contains an action statement. With only rare exceptions, each action statement consists of a command verb plus *a direct object*: "Drag the icon." The subject of the command verb is an implied "You." We can think of the command verb plus object as the *core* of the action statement. In addition, one or more modifiers may be present to add to the meaning of the core in various ways.

Although most steps are only one sentence long, we sometimes add a sentence other than the feedback statement, as explained below. Thus three-sentence steps are possible.

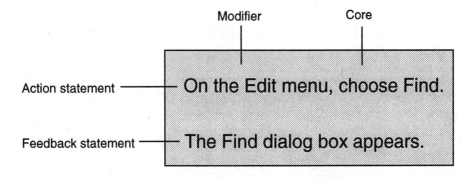

Figure 5.7. *A step with the components labeled.*

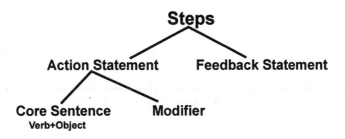

Figure 5.8. *A logical breakdown of the components of steps.*

ACTION STATEMENTS

We now look at design issues regarding action statements. Later we consider the various kinds of modifiers and how they affect action statements.

Keep action statements short and simple

Most action statements consist of a single action, a single command verb. There are times, however, when more elaborate action statements are efficient. Two successive actions can be included in one action statement:

> Click Add and then click Browse.

Two short, closely related user options can be written as one action statement:

> To select a single file, click on the file name. To select multiple files, drag the mouse pointer over the files in the list.

Brief items of relevant information, such as relevant system description or an example, can also be included:

> In the Drive Name text box, type in a new Drive name. The name may consist of up to seven characters.

> Click any cell under the column that shows the field you want to search. For example, to locate a specific option number in the Option Selection table, click any cell in the Option Number column.

But avoid paragraph-length action statements. Furthermore, avoid logically complex action statements such as this one:

> To sort by date, click the Date in the Type box, then click the Ascending or Descending option button. Repeat Steps 2-4 to sort by Text or Number and click a different item in the Type box.

Limit the number of steps in a procedure

It is important to limit the number of steps in your procedures. Too many steps intimidate users and cause them to get lost in the middle of a procedure. Whenever a procedure has more than five or six steps, try to divide the procedure into two shorter ones. If you cannot break up a lengthy procedure, there is probably a problem in the software product's user interface, and you may want to speak to the programmer or user interface designer about simplifying this part of the interface.

Consider showing only one way to carry out an action

Many Help writers routinely show two (or even more) actions that achieve the same result:

> On the File menu, choose Open.
> Or -
> Click the New Image command button.

Writers who follow a minimalist strategy often choose, however, to simplify procedure topics by documenting only one way. This is usually the "standard" way, the one users can understand and learn most easily. Shortcuts can be presented in a separate group of shortcut topics.

Consider leaving out "obvious" actions

One way to simplify procedures is to omit the "Click OK" step that concludes many procedures. On the one hand, this short step provides closure for the procedure. On the other hand, the step is probably unnecessary for all but novice users. We don't, after all, document the Cancel button that is paired with the OK button on most dialog boxes. If your product is used by novices, explain the OK and Cancel buttons in the introductory documentation. In general, consider leaving out obvious steps and obvious information in steps.

Consider providing both high-level and detailed steps

As we have seen, one dilemma in documentation is deciding how much detail to provide. You can effectively layer action statements by writing a high-level action statement for more sophisticated users and backing this up with a "how" button that takes the user to more detailed action information:

A less effective version of this technique used in print documentation is to elaborate on the action statement with a "by" prepositional phrase:

> Select the graphic you wish to resize by clicking the button at the top of the column and then clicking the graphic.

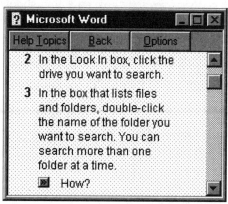

Figure 5.9. *A step with a "how" button.*

Consider referring users to What's This? Help

If you have implemented What's This? Help, you may want to shorten your procedure topics by referring users to the What's This? topics:

> Make selections from the dialog box. Consult What's This? Help as necessary.

> Make selections from the dialog box. If you want more information about any part of the dialog box, right click that part to display a What's This? Help topic.

MODIFIERS IN ACTION STATEMENTS

The main purpose of steps is to convey actions. But modifiers add important meaning to action statements. Here are the most important modifiers and some issues regarding their use.

Location modifiers

The location modifier directs the user's action by making clear where on the interface an interface element is located:

> From the Insert menu, choose Date and Time.

When an interface element will be hard for the user to find, consider adding a Shortcut button to display that element for the user.

Time modifiers

When users need to wait before taking an action, time modifiers let them know when to act:

> When the Transactions window is displayed, click Next.

Manner modifiers

Occasionally, it is necessary to specify exactly how an action should be carried out. This situation usually occurs in software products, such as graphics applications, in which user actions are often more complex than choosing from menus and dialog boxes:

> Drag the handles so that they extend beyond the borders of the rectangle.

Notice that the word "until," which we associate with time, is often used to explain manner:

> Press the tab key until the pointer is in the field where you wish to type.

When an action is particularly hard to describe, consider adding one or more graphics or, ideally, an animation sequence.

User option modifiers

The user option modifier appears often in procedures. It indicates an optional variation on the main purpose of the procedure:

> To set the speed at which the tones will be emitted, type a value between 1 and 10 in the Speed box.

> If you want to open the document so that it can be viewed but not changed in any way, click Read Only.

Most often, this modifier begins with "To." You can emphasize that the action is optional with the expanded phrase "If you want to."

When a procedure contains a series of closely related steps with user option modifiers, a good design choice is a two-column table. The first column lists the options with a column heading such as, "To accomplish this." The second column lists the actions with a column heading such as, "Do the following."

Modifiers that explain a step's purpose

The purpose of the procedure as a whole is conveyed in these components: (1) the topic heading, (2) the conceptual element, and (3) the infinitive subheading. But in certain instances users are more smoothly guided through a procedure when they are shown the purpose of an individual step. Usually this step concludes an action presented in several previous steps:

> Click the bottom edge of the border model to complete the box.

> Choose Do It to return to your document.

In contrast to the user option modifier, the purpose modifiers describe actions that are required. The user cannot move forward in the procedure without carrying them out. There is potential confusion for users because the purpose modifier begins with "to" and the user option modifier very often begins with "To." Purpose modifiers, however, normally follow the core of the action statement (the verb plus object), whereas the user option modifier normally precedes the core. The Help writer can also make any user option unambiguous by using "If you want to."

Condition modifiers

Some steps present a condition that applies to all or some users. The user determines whether he or she is subject to the condition and, if so, takes the specified action:

> If your view of the tape is not expanded, double click on the icon to display its tape volumes.

The placement of multiple modifiers

You may have noticed that most modifiers precede the core sentence. At times, however, an action statement requires more than one modifier, and so it may be necessary to move a modifier to the end of the sentence. Very often it is the location modifier that is moved:

> If you want to work with the Ribbon, click Ribbon on the View menu.

FEEDBACK STATEMENTS

At times it is helpful to provide a feedback statement after an action statement to indicate the visible result of the action. Feedback enables users to confirm that they have done the right thing, that the system has responded appropriately, and that they are on track. Here is a step that provides very direct and explicit feedback:

> On the Edit menu, choose Find. The Find dialog box appears.

In tutorial documentation especially, writers provide feedback statements after almost all action statements. In Help, however, explicit feedback statements, such as the one above, are used sparingly for reasons of brevity. Explicit feedback statements are reserved for instances in which the system response is hard to notice or unusual.

As noted in Chapter 4, *General Issues for Writing Help*, various kinds of information can work as feedback. In the next example, the location modifier in the second step serves as "implicit feedback" for the action in the first step.

> 1 On the Options menu, choose Resources and Costs.
>
> 2 In the Resources and Costs dialog box, choose Assign Workloads.

Similarly, time modifiers such as "When the Transactions window is displayed," can serve as implicit feedback. Users will certainly realize that if the Transactions window does not appear, something has gone wrong.

Feedback can become complex. Below we see a step in which explicit feedback is followed by a condition. This level of complexity will not greatly tax most users, but it should not appear regularly:

> On the File menu, choose Open. The Open dialog box will generally appear.
>
> If the Drawing Modification alert box appears, click Save Changes or Discard Changes.

Notes

The note component sets items of Help information outside the main flow of a Help topic. The information in the note is usually less important than the rest of the topic. The information in warning notes, however, is more important.

Often Help authors are not careful with notes; they use notes as a dumping ground for information that, with more care, could be worked into the main flow of a Help topic. This is an unfortunate practice because the handling of notes has a significant effect on the overall quality of a topic.

KINDS OF NOTES

Notes can convey a broad range of information. Often they convey user options that do not concern enough users to be included as a step:

> **Note:** To add text to the page number (for example, the word "Page"), place the insertion point before or after the page-number mark. Type the text you want to appear with each page number.

They may be tips, better ways to do something:

> **Tip:** When naming pages, it's helpful to use the default names provided by Visio. By using default page names, you can rearrange pages more easily.

Often notes address conditions that apply only to a few users.

> **What if**
> If you have files saved in Version 1.0 format, they must be updated to at least Version 4.0 before they can be included in a broadcast message. To update these files, open them in Version 4.0 and then save them.

They may be secondary results that concern only certain users of the software product:

> **Note**
> When you disconnect two frames that appear in the middle of a chain, you break only that single connection and the result is two chains. The first chain contains all the text of the story, although some may be contained in the overflow area. There is no text in the second series of frames, but they remain connected, and you can add text to them or connect them to other frames at any time.

NOTE SUBHEADINGS

As the examples above show, notes are typically introduced by subheadings. The all-purpose subheading "Note" is the most prevalent, but more precise subheadings, such as "Tip" are desirable because they help users decide whether they want to read the note. It is bad practice to write one giant note in which the individual note items are not even separated from one another.

NOTES THAT WARN USERS

Users are usually highly selective about reading notes. Therefore, when necessary, use subheadings that demand the user's attention. Notes with the subheadings "Danger," "Warning," and "Caution" warn users of injury to persons, damage to software or hardware, or potential loss of data. The subheading "Important" is used for information that will prevent the completion of a task or forestall significant problems:

Important
In order for your computer's hard drive to be included in the weekly back-up, you must close the network mail service on your computer before midnight on Friday evening.

Any irrevocable action with significant consequences is a candidate for a "Caution" or "Important" subheading:

IMPORTANT
Once transactions have been entered, they can no longer be recalled.

PLACEMENT OF NOTES

Notes normally appear at the end of a Help topic. If a note pertains to a particular step of a procedure topic, it is often advisable to place it directly after that step. Occasionally a note with broad relevance appears in the conceptual element. Notes expressing danger, warning, or caution must appear before the user would take the action that might lead to the unwanted result. So too with some notes labeled "Important."

USING NOTES EFFECTIVELY

It is a sound strategy—a form of layering—to keep the steps and conceptual element short and uncluttered by moving less important information to notes. Even so, users are intimidated when they see numerous notes at the bottom of a Help topic, and they face the nagging question, "Should I look at that note?" Placing less important information in notes is certainly not a complete solution to the problem of having a great deal of information that we need to convey to users.

Some Help authors simplify Help topics by bringing the conceptual element to the bottom of the topic in the form of a note. If the Help author wishes to do this, he or she should use a distinctive subheading such as "Explanation" so users who want conceptual information can readily find it.

CONCLUSION

In conclusion, even though procedure topics are composed of standard components that convey prescribed kinds of information, there is craft and creativity in the writing of procedure topics. Moreover, good writing matters. Without it we frustrate users and turn them away from both the Help system and the software product. With it, we reduce their level of stress and enable them to go back to the software product ready to get their work done.

6

Writing Other Standard Help Topics

Although procedure topics are the most prevalent kind in standard Help systems, almost all standard Help systems include other kinds as well. This chapter describes the most important kinds of standard Help topics other than procedure topics and explains how they are used. These topics are previewed in the following table. If you wish to see how some of these kinds of Help information appear in WinHelp 4's online table of contents, look ahead to Figures 8.6, 8.7, and 8.8.

Table 6.1. *Topics other than procedure topics in standard Help*

Kind of Help topic	Make-up and function
What's This? topic	A brief explanation of a part of the interface which the user has clicked.
Command topic	An explanation of a command and, very often, the elements on the command's dialog box.
Screen region topic	A graphic of a major element of the interface with brief explanations of the smaller elements on the major one.
Overview topic	A conceptually oriented explanation of an aspect of the software product.
List topic	A list of jumps directing users to other topics in the Help system.

Table 6.1. *(continued)*

Kind of Help topic	Make-up and function
Keyboard shortcut topic	A list of keyboard combinations (and mouse actions) that enable users to work more quickly. (Not to be confused with the Shortcut buttons in WinHelp 4 procedure topics.)
Pop-up definition topic	Normally a brief explanation of an unfamiliar term. Displays when the user clicks hotspot text on a "parent" Help topic.
Glossary topic	Consists of one lengthy topic with an alphabetical list of all the pop-up definition topics. Users can click entries on this list to display the desired pop-up definition.
Error message topic	An explanation and corrective action for some difficulty the user is encountering.
Troubleshooting topic Diagnostic topic Recommendation topic	Lists of problems that users may have encountered. Procedures and recommendations for solving the user's problem.

What's This? Help topics

What's This? Help is, in effect, a WinHelp 4 feature, although the capability existed in WinHelp 3.1. These topics appear in pop-up windows but, as we see in the next figure, they display directly from the software product's interface.

The ways in which What's This? Help topics can be displayed depends on how this feature has been programmed. The main ways are these:

1. Right clicking the element of interest. (If standard programming practice has been followed, users right-click and then left-click the What's This? command to display the topic.)

2. Clicking the Help button found in the title bar of many windows and then clicking the element of interest.

3. Clicking an element of interest (or otherwise putting the input focus on the element) and then (if it has been implemented) pressing the F1 key.

4. Pressing the SHIFT+F1 key and then clicking a menu command or command button.

In all of these cases the user is essentially pointing at an interface element and querying it for a brief explanation.

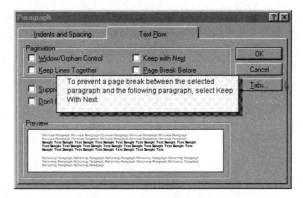

Figure 6.1. *A What's This? Help topic.*

THE VALUE OF WHAT'S THIS? HELP

What's This? Help is simple but highly useful; it is a major addition to standard Help. Let's consider the value of What's This? Help in documenting dialog boxes. The labels that appear on option buttons, checkboxes, and many other dialog box elements are necessarily very brief—rarely more than three or four words. Consequently, many users will be puzzled by the phrases such as "Keep with Next." The user wonders what is being kept with what. With What's This? Help, the user can very quickly and directly display a brief but generally adequate description of this feature. This is minimalist documentation at its best: users are encouraged to solve their problems with the least amount of documentation.

DRAWBACKS

As good as it is, there are drawbacks to What's This? Help:

1. Users must find the element of the interface that is relevant to their goal before they can display the What's This? Help topic.

2. These topics are suited only for relatively brief explanations.

3. To establish the context-sensitivity between these topics and the interface elements that trigger them is not simple and requires the participation of a programmer.

Because of the first two drawbacks, What's This? Help does not work as the sole means of documenting a software product but rather is effective only in conjunction with a complete standard Help system. Because of the third drawback, some software vendors may reject What's This? Help altogether.

Microsoft has developed a technique that eliminates the first drawback and expands the usefulness of What's This? topics: When the user chooses certain procedure topics from the contents, (1) the appropriate menu drops and the appropriate command is selected from the menu (a kind of animation sequence), (2) the relevant dialog box is displayed, and (3) the relevant What's This? topic is displayed. See for example the contents entry for the topic "Type over existing text" in Word 7.0 Help. This technique gets the user effortlessly to the relevant part of the interface. As a result, What's This? Help topics can replace procedure topics for tasks that require only a brief explanation. You can view the contents file statements that achieve this effect; for example, you can open the WinWord.CNT file in a word processor and find the contents file statement "3 Type over existing text =!fDoTheISAction(hwndApp, 5166)."

WRITING WHAT'S THIS? HELP

The role of What's This? Help topics is to explain the purpose of an interface element. There are several ways to write What's This? Help. In this example, the purpose of the interface element is made clear by a functional description of the element:

> Saves the contents of the active window.

Note that the user must infer the necessary action.

In the next example, purpose is conveyed by a purpose modifier (to save…) and the necessary action is stated explicitly:

> Click this to save the contents of the active window.

When you are confident that your users understand how to perform the necessary action, you can simplify the What's This? topic by writing only the functional description.

Some What's This? topics are more complex. In the next example, the first sentence is a general functional description of the "trail" feature. The "which" clause is admirably task oriented because it reaches out into the user's world and makes clear why the user should care about the tail of a mouse pointer. The second sentence is a *purpose modifier* that makes clear that the length of the tail can be changed, and the *core sentence* explains how to perform the action. Because sliders are not the most familiar of interface elements, it is appropriate to include the explanation of the action.

> Adds a trail to the mouse pointer, which makes it easier to see on LCD screens. To change the length of the pointer trail, drag the slider below.

What's This? Help topics pose a challenge to command topics, the kind of Help topic we look at now.

Command topics

Command topics provide a functional description of a command and its dialog box elements. In terms of content, therefore, command topics are very much like What's This? topics, except that for many dialog box elements the What's This? topic is longer than the descriptions in a command topic. This is because Help authors tend to provide a little more information when they know that this information makes up a single very short topic rather than being just one portion of a command topic. A See Figure 6.2 for a typical command topic.

There are also similarities in how the two kinds of Help topics are accessed by users. Although in most Help systems command topics are accessible from the contents and in other ways, command topics are most often accessed from the command topic's dialog box when the user presses the F1 key or clicks a special Help command button that can be added to a dialog box. Both What's This? and command topic Help, therefore, provide the benefit of context sensitivity. When the user invokes Help, no searching is necessary, for the appropriate Help topic appears.

The big difference is that What's This? Help is more focused; it displays only information about the specific interface element the user has queried at that moment. In contrast, when a user displays a command topic, the user must scan the entire topic for the heading that matches the label of the element the user is interested in. This pinpoint specificity of What's This? Help can be viewed as a compelling advantage over command topics.

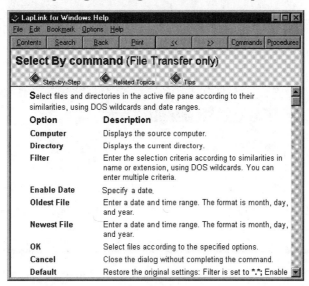

Figure 6.2. *A typical command topic.*

On the other hand, there is sometimes value in grouping the functional descriptions of all the dialog box elements on one topic. Furthermore, users benefit from the explanation of the overall purpose of the command that appears at the top of command topics. Finally, the Help author can include a graphic or some other element that pertains to the dialog box as a whole.

It is possible to document a dialog box with both a command topic and What's This? Help; in fact, much of the text would be the same. However, it is difficult to justify the effort necessary to create all these extra Help topics. Finally, we will argue the benefit of implementing What's This? Help rather than command topics so that the Help command button (and the F1 key) can serve as a pathway to procedure and overview topics.

Screen region topics

Screen region topics consist mainly of a graphic of a major interface element such as an application's main workspace, a palette, a dialog box, or a toolbar. Typically this graphic is composed of multiple hotspots, each of which, when clicked, displays a pop-up that identifies and explains a particular command button, check box or other smaller interface element on the major one. The text usually consists of functional descriptions along the lines of What's This? and command topics. A screen region topic is shown in Figure 6.3.

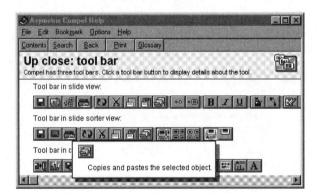

Figure 6.3. *A screen region topic using pop-up windows.*

Some screen region topics employ a static graphic with callouts consisting of hotspot text that offer more detailed information. This design is an effective form of layering: the user who simply wants to find out what the part of the graphic is called can just read the callout but does not have to click on it.

On the surface it appears that the function of screen region topics is better served by What's This? topics. Screen region topics are clearly less direct and, we might say, less efficient. Why create a graphic of a component of the interface and then add pop-ups to explain the graphic, when you can directly annotate the interface? But screen region topics justify themselves, for they often serve an introductory function. We create screen region topics for key parts of the interface, feature these topics prominently in the Help contents, and invite users to introduce themselves to the software product in this way. What's This? Help topics do not lend themselves to this role.

Overview topics

As we have seen, procedure topics have components that explain the purpose of the task and provide related information. There is always a topic heading and there may be a conceptual element and infinitive subheadings. Some tasks, however, demand conceptual knowledge which some users do not possess and which requires more explanation than belongs on a procedure topic. For documenting such tasks, an overview topic is very effective.

Some overview topics provide a conceptual overview for a single procedure topic, particularly if that topic contains no conceptual element. More frequently, however, overview topics provide the conceptual background for a group of procedure topics (and, often, the associated command topic) pertaining to some complex feature. So, for example, the overview topic shown in Figure 6.4 provides the conceptual background for a group of procedure topics that explain specific procedures pertaining to charts. Notice the button in the nonscrolling region of the procedure topic that displays the overview topic and that another button (labeled "Example and demo") initiates a brief online tutorial.

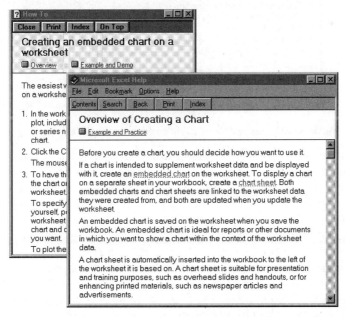

Figure 6.4. *An overview topic and one of its related procedure topics.*

Many software products require users to have subject-matter knowledge—a background in music theory, accounting, project management, or some other discipline related to the software product. Because users often lack appropriate subject-matter knowledge, Help authors sometimes provide it in overview topics. As shown in Figure 6.5, the Help system for Paint Shop Pro includes overview topics that explain color theory.

Overview topics are very similar to the introductory sections that very often appear in print user's guides. In other words, in a user's guide, a chapter on creating charts will very likely begin with a brief conceptually oriented overview that provides background for the particular procedures pertaining to charts. Users with "top down" learning style will read the overview section first. Users with a more aggressive, bottom-up learning style will go immediately to the procedure topic of interest and will consult the introductory section only if necessary.

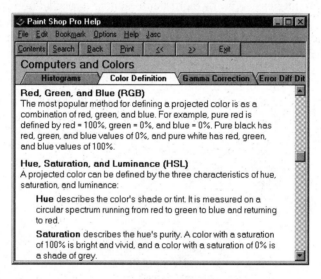

Figure 6.5. *An overview topic conveying domain knowledge.*

These two patterns of user behavior suggest that Help systems should provide both top-down and bottom-up access to overview topics. Top-down access means access from the Help contents, the index, and other places where users might go to read up on a feature before they try to work with that feature in the software. Bottom-up access means supporting users who have begun to work with the feature, may have accessed a procedure topic, and now want overview information. In a system with bottom-up access, users should be able to display overview topics directly from procedure topics, and there should be a short pathway to overview topics from dialog boxes and other interface elements. In a moment we will consider how this bottom-up access can be provided.

Overview topics very often consist of several paragraphs of text. Because some users are reluctant to read extended text on the computer screen, we may choose to provide this kind of information in both Help and print manuals.

List topics

List topics, such as the one shown in Figure 6.6, are basically lists of jumps to other Help topics. Thus, they are very simple in their content and appearance. In many Help systems, however, list topics are an important form of navigation. Some list topics also contain a paragraph of conceptual information located above the list of jumps. Such list topics are hybrids of list and overview topics, but our focus now will be on list topics that consist solely of jumps.

How do list topics typically work? In many Help systems, a user who is having difficulty with a dialog box (or another interface element) can click a Help button on that interface element (or press the F1 key) to display a Help topic that has been associated with that dialog box using context sensitivity. This topic is usually either a command topic or a list topic that provides jumps to all the procedure topics associated with the dialog box as well as to the associated overview topic. If command topics are replaced by What's This? Help topics, Help buttons can be made to display list topics, giving users excellent bottom-up support while they work.

List topics have other uses, too. For example, the hotspot text or graphic that directs users to related topics often does so by displaying a list topic. Also, when the online contents is so large that some entries would cause the Contents dialog box to develop a horizontal scroll bar, a list topic can be used as a kind of extra level in the contents hierarchy.

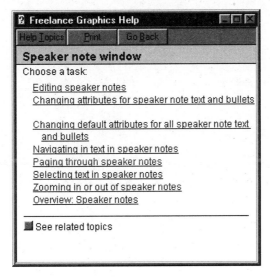

Figure 6.6. *A list topic.*

Keyboard shortcut topics

A common category of Help information consists of shortcuts for performing various computer actions, especially executing commands. Most shortcuts are keyboard combinations, but there are mouse shortcuts as well. It is usually not worthwhile to document the standard accelerator key combinations (The ALT key plus the underlined letters of menus and commands), because these are visible, as underlined letters, on the software product's interface. But many software products provide other key combinations, and these shortcuts, along with mouse shortcuts, should be documented. In software products with relatively few shortcuts, shortcut topics are often organized around the nature of the input, for example, a topic for mouse actions, a topic for function key actions, and a topic for CRTL key actions. When there are numerous shortcuts, shortcut topics are usually organized by function: a topic for text-selection shortcuts, a topic for navigation shortcuts, and so forth—as shown in Figure 6.7:

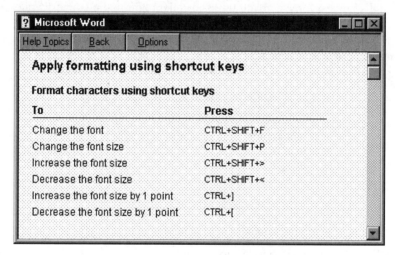

Figure 6.7. *A keyboard shortcut topic.*

Definition topics and the glossary

When writing procedure topics, overview topics, and other kinds of topics, Help authors often feel the need to explain terms that will be unfamiliar to some of their users. In online Help, these terms are routinely explained by definition topics. Definition topics are displayed in pop-up windows.

Help authors should think of definition topics as explanations rather than definitions. "Explanation" suggests an attempt to really reach out to the user, whereas "definition" suggests an interest in making precise distinctions. Topics conceived as definitions enable knowledgeable individuals to sharpen their understanding of an idea, but individuals who are unfamiliar with pop-up windows will do better with the second of the two definition topics that appear below as Figure 6.8.

Because a definition topic may be accessed from any one of a number of Help topics, these topics must be written as independent modules that make sense in any context in which they appear.

Definition topics are not usually included in the index. However, a glossary topic, usually one lengthy Help topic, provides a central location for displaying all the definition topics in the Help system. Clearly users benefit when they can readily access any definition topic.

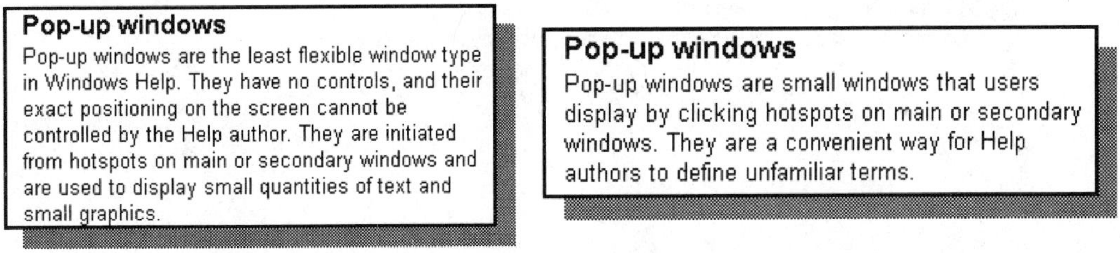

Pop-up windows
Pop-up windows are the least flexible window type in Windows Help. They have no controls, and their exact positioning on the screen cannot be controlled by the Help author. They are initiated from hotspots on main or secondary windows and are used to display small quantities of text and small graphics.

Pop-up windows
Pop-up windows are small windows that users display by clicking hotspots on main or secondary windows. They are a convenient way for Help authors to define unfamiliar terms.

Figure 6.8. *A definition style and an explanation style definition topic.*

Figure 6.9, shows a glossary with the definition topic "Report icon." Glossaries can be quite sophisticated. This glossary employs an array of alphabetical buttons in the topic's non-scrolling region. These buttons use the mid-topic jump macro to take the user immediately to any portion of the glossary topic. Note as well that a special Definitions button has been added to this Help system's button bar, a good idea if you believe your users will want to use the glossary frequently. Finally, note that the Report icon definition topic includes hotspot text that displays definition topics some users may need to fully understand the Report icon definition topic.

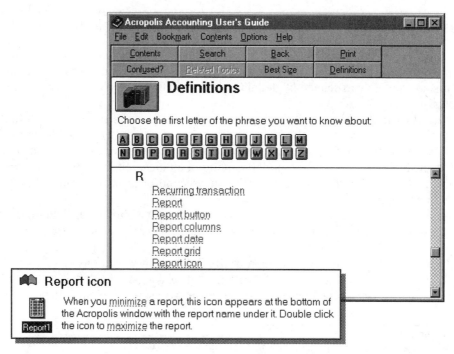

Figure 6.9. *A glossary with a definition topic.*

Error-message topics

When error-message topics are included in Help, they generally supplement the system messages that appear in message boxes on the software product's interface. These topics are displayed by a Help button that is added to the message box. A message box and Help topic are shown in Figures 6.10 and 6.11 below:

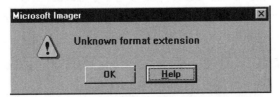

Figure 6.10. *A message box with a Help button.*

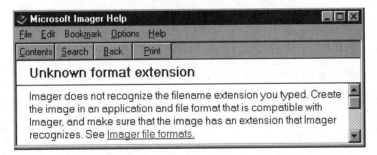

Figure 6.11. *An error-message Help topic.*

The error-message topics should also be listed in the contents and included in the index. There are compelling reasons to include error-message topics in a Help system:

1. They are a form of layering. They provide more detail about the problem or issue; users who do not need the detail can ignore the Help button.

2. They enable users to copy the message. Users often want a printed copy of an error message or want to email the message to a system administrator or a technical support technician. WinHelp error messages can be easily copied into a word processor or mail program.

3. They are usually written by Help authors and will be more clearly written than system messages, which are very often left in the hands of programmers.

Of course, not all system messages need error-message Help topics. A good plan is to limit system messages to one or two sentences. If some users will need more detailed information, write a Help topic.

Because error message topics are so closely related to system messages, the section on message boxes in Microsoft's *Windows 95 Interface Guidelines for Software Design* is useful reading. Conversely, because of this close relationship, this section on error-message topics can help programmers write better system messages.

KINDS OF ERROR-MESSAGE TOPICS

Many error-message topics stem from user errors. Here the system is ready to carry out the user's purpose, but the user has not performed a prerequisite action:

"No editor specified. Choose Edit/Select Editor to select your default editor."

You chose Edit/Editor and no default editor is specified.

You may start a DOS or Windows-based word processor or text editor from ViewBuilder, but you must first select the application as your default editor. Choose Edit/Select Editor and specify the pathname for the application's executable file.

Other error-message topics pertain to problems with the system:

"Cannot build due to insufficient space on your disk."

You were building or restoring a document and there is not enough available space on your hard drive to complete the task.

Move or delete files on your disk until you have space available equal to twice the size of the combined source files, or copy the document to another disk which has sufficient space using File/Copy.

At times, the system message is a confirmation message, a chance for the user to reconsider before taking an action with far-reaching implications. The role of the error-message topic is to ensure that the user fully understands the situation. This is the case of the system message and error-message topic shown in Figures 6.12 and 6.13.

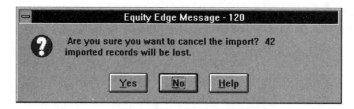

Figure 6.12. *A system message that asks for confirmation.*

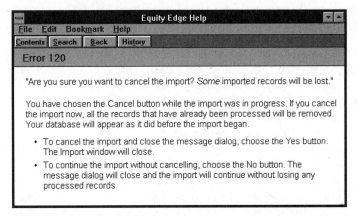

Figure 6.13. *An error-message topic used for confirmation.*

ERROR-MESSAGE INFORMATION

In all cases, the role of error messages is to explain the problem or issue, and to make clear either the corrective action that is required or the user's choices. Sometimes it is necessary to explicitly state how to avoid repeating the error. This error-message topic contains three sentences. The first explains the problem, the second states the necessary course of action, and the third helps the user avoid repeating the error.

> **Cannot create hash table**
> You were including or removing source files from a document, and there was not enough system memory available. Close all unneeded applications currently running and try again. If this error occurs frequently consider installing additional memory in your computer.

Tone is an important consideration in error messages. Ominous and accusatory phrasing should be avoided. Avoid "fatal," "aborted," "illegal," "violation," and even "error." Nothing is wrong with "invalid."

Phrases that use "Cannot" work well, but extreme personification, shown in the body of the following topic, is silly and should be avoided:

> **Cannot carry out query**
> You really have me stumped. Please type a new query.

Also avoid humor and, especially, offensive humor:

> **Error!** Take another shot in the dark, bozo.

Troubleshooting topics

Users go to standard procedure topics to learn how to do something. If a problem arises, an error message may prescribe the appropriate action. Often, however, users encounter problems that for one reason or another are not addressed or appropriately addressed by error messages. In such cases troubleshooting topics are invaluable.

Broadly speaking, the troubleshooting topics in any Help system belong to two categories: (1) *Diagnostic topics* and (2) *Recommendation topics.*

Diagnostic topics are simply lists of problems (or symptoms of problems) that users are known to encounter. Users click on the item that most closely resembles the problem they face. When the list of problems is short, a single diagnostic topic may suffice. Typically, however, there is a hierarchy of diagnostic topics that lead the user from a general statement of a problem to a more specific statement, and, finally, to the recommendation topic. Although diagnostic topics are simple in appearance, much work must be done to work out the troubleshooting logic. Figure 6.14 shows a top-level diagnostic topic and one of its branches.

From the user's point of view, the recommendation topics are the "payoff." They enable users to solve their problems. Recommendation topics often look like procedure topics. There is often a topic heading that either states the problem or states the nature of the corrective action. There may be a conceptual element to elaborate on the topic heading. Usually there are steps for correcting the problem. If there is no clear-cut solution for the problem, there will be hints and suggestions rather than a specific procedure.

A recommendation topic is shown in Figure 6.15. Notice that this recommendation topic includes further troubleshooting logic. If the procedure doesn't fix the user's problem, the user can follow a jump to a deeper-level recommendation topic. Such jumps can also take users to diagnostic topics so they can continue the troubleshooting process.

 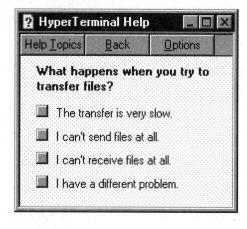

Figure 6.14. *A top-level diagnostic topic and one of its branches.*

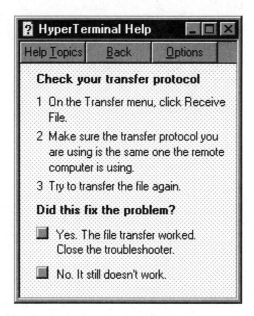

Figure 6.15. *A recommendation topic.*

Standard Help follows a reference model. When a user consults standard Help to solve a problem, the user expects to access a single Help topic, use this topic to solve the problem, and then leave the Help system. Troubleshooting topics are more like a guide than a source of information. There is a kind of intelligence embedded in the troubleshooting logic of the diagnostic topics and, to some degree, a sequence of diagnostic topics conduct a dialog with the user. Troubleshooting Help, therefore, resides at the border between standard Help and a different model, the prompt model represented by wizards and coaches. We now turn to this model.

7

Performance Support Help: Wizards and Coaches

Performance support Help is a fundamentally different model from standard Help. In contrast to standard Help, which functions as an online reference, performance support Help engages the user in a dialogue. It stays with the user as the user works, and provides a series of prompts. The user responds to these prompts, clicks to receive another prompt, and then acts again. Often, extensive programming underlies this dialogue. Some of the most sophisticated user assistance technology now available is found in performance support Help. For both these reasons, performance support can provide users with a high level of user assistance and a high level of comfort. For certain purposes, it is the most effective form of documentation we have. On the other hand, performance support Help has some major limitations and potential pitfalls.

Performance support Help, we believe, will become more sophisticated and more prevalent, but it will serve as an important adjunct to standard Help rather than as a replacement. As we will see, performance support Help cannot be used to document many portions of a software product, and even where it can be used effectively, users will often want more control over learning about and using the software than performance support Help allows. Note that the performance support model does not accord with the minimalist idea of giving users the least amount of documentation and encouraging them to exercise their problem-solving skills.

Performance support Help can be divided into two fairly distinct families. The first category we call *wizards*. The second category we call *coaches*. These are explained in Table 7.1.

Table 7.1. *Two kinds of performance support Help*

Wizards	Provide a simplified interface for performing the task. This interface may be an alternative to the software product's regular interface or may be the sole means of performing the task.
Coaches	Guide the user in working with the regular interface.

Unfortunately, the terminology surrounding performance support Help is confusing. For the first category, most software vendors use the term "wizards," although Microsoft, which introduced the term, has now added a similar term, "answer wizard," for other kinds of user assistance. For the second category, such terms as "guides," "interviewers," and "cue cards," are used—in addition to coaches.

The term "wizard" is apt because when we go to wizards, they ask us questions and do something for us. The term "coaches" is fairly apt because human coaches shout instructions as we do the kicking and throwing. But, as we shall see, Help coaches behave differently than human coaches because they may step in and perform actions themselves.

Wizards are more prevalent than coaches. Most software is installed using wizards, and many software products offer users a selection of wizards for achieving various tasks. Wizards are even familiar outside the world of computer applications. ATM (automated banking) machines are wizards. They walk the user through banking tasks by means of an interactive dialogue.

Coaches exist only within software products, are less prevalent than wizards, and offer more design challenges and risks.

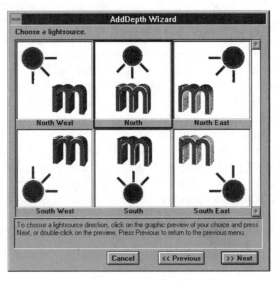

Figure 7.1. *Add Depth's Wizard Help.*

Examples of wizard and coach Help appear in Figure 7.1 and 7.2. Add Depth is a software product that enables users to create 3-D text and import this 3-D text into their documents. The Add Depth wizard (Figure 7.1) enables a user to work productively with a subset of Add Depth's features with virtually no investment in time. Salsa, a database product, includes a coach (Figure 7.2) that teaches the user how to use Salsa while he or she builds a useful database.

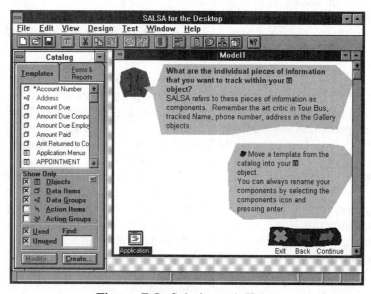

Figure 7.2. *Salsa's coach Help.*

The relationship between performance support Help and WinHelp is complex and varies from product to product. Both wizards and coaches pre-date WinHelp 4 and are often developed entirely or largely independent of WinHelp. Wizards can be written in the same code as the software product itself or in the product's macro language or using supplemental products such as Visual Basic. Coaches, however, are often created using regular WinHelp topics. Finally the Training Cards features included in WinHelp 4 are intended as a means of creating coaches—although we have not heard of any development work, other than experiments, with Training Cards either within or outside Microsoft. Because this chapter focuses on design issues, it applies to wizards and coaches regardless of how they are created. In this chapter, we look first at wizards and then at coaches.

Wizards

Wizards provide a simplified user interface that enables a user to make a succession of easy-to-understand choices in order to complete a task. Because many of these choices trigger a significant effect, wizards seem to perform tasks almost automatically. It is impressive that a novice computer user can effortlessly format a newsletter with the Word Newsletter wizard. Without the wizard, such a newsletter might require an hour's work on the part of a proficient user of Word. Furthermore, this wizard embodies graphic design knowledge that many users do not possess. The first and second panels of this wizard are shown below in Figures 7.3 and 7.4.

Wizards do have two major shortcomings, however. The first is rigidity. To a great extent, the outcomes of a wizard-supported task must be programmed in advance. The Word Newsletter wizard restricts the user to 32 design variations. The Add Depth wizard allows permutations of six special-effects variables.

Even though outcomes are programmed, wizards can leave certain options open-ended. The Add Depth wizard adds its special effects to any text the user types. Similarly, the Word Newsletter wizard doesn't constrain the content of the newsletter or the number of pages in the newsletter. The Word Calendar wizard, while offering only 12 variations in the calendar's design, allows users to create calendars for any year within a 450-year range. Even where a wizard does constrain the user, the user can often take the result of a wizard and customize it using the regular interface and full feature set of the software product.

Wizards are not only rigid in terms of their outcomes, they are rigid in that they structure the user's work agenda. For example, the Add Depth wizard and the Word Newsletter wizard determine the sequence in which the user encounters the choices that complete the task. The designers of the wizard will presumably work out an appropriate sequence, and in many cases this sequence is inherently constrained by the nature of the task. But many users want as much freedom as possible in structuring their work.

The second shortcoming is the slow pace. This is the flipside of the dialogic nature of wizards—and coaches as well. In contrast to such elements of graphical user interfaces as dialog boxes, in which users make numerous choices, wizard panels ask the user to make one choice from a set of mutually exclusive options. (Occasionally, a wizard will ask the user to choose an option and, in addition, take a further step, such as typing text or a value.)

In much the same way, ATMs provide users with single choices—as in "Do you want to make a withdrawal from Checking Account 1 or Checking Account 2?"

Slow pacing tends to limit the complexity of the tasks for which wizards are used. Complex tasks require users to work their way through many panels and require a considerable programming effort. Even so, the payoff may justify creating such a wizard. For example, the Eagle Hardware store chain has a wizard that enables homeowners to plan a deck. Here the value of the wizard to the homeowner and Eagle Hardware justifies the time the wizard demands.

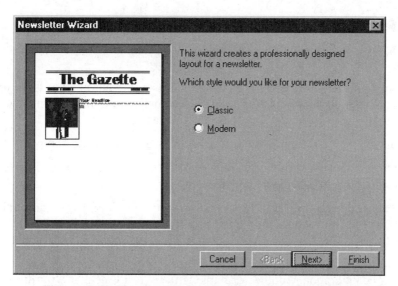

Figure 7.3. *The first panel of the Word Newsletter wizard.*

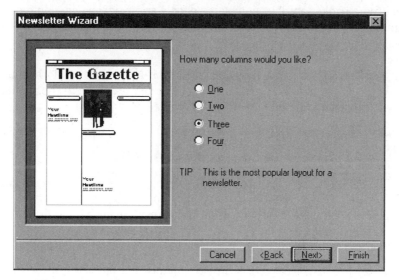

Figure 7.4. *The second panel of the Word Newsletter wizard.*

APPROPRIATE USES OF WIZARDS

Given the strengths and limitations of wizards, what kinds of tasks are they suited for? We suggest using wizards for these four purposes:

1. To automate infrequently performed tasks that users do not need to learn or tasks that are difficult or even impossible for users to accomplish or on their own. Here the wizard is likely to be the sole means of carrying out the task.

2. To enable experienced users to get a head start on accomplishing complex tasks.

3. To enable casual users of the software to produce useful end products. Here the wizard is only an alternative to the regular interface.

4. To give users a successful first experience with the product, help them understand the capabilities of the product, and encourage them to graduate to the product's regular interface.

In regard to the first purpose, we create wizards to perform such functions as software installation and configuration. Another example is the Word Calendar wizard; few would format a calendar and calculate the dates on their own.

The third purpose evokes an objection: some people argue against shielding users from the product's regular interface. Such wizards, they say, become "crutches." Many users, however, are fully satisfied with the results they achieve with a good wizard. They are quite willing to accept the wizard's limitations.

The fourth purpose answers the objection to the third. Users often do become impatient with the slow pace and constrained results of a wizard and graduate to the regular interface. Furthermore, we can encourage them to do so.

DESIGNING AND WRITING WIZARDS

Below are guidelines for designing and writing wizards.

1. Because you generally present only one choice on a wizard panel, there is usually room for a graphic. The graphic should make clear the result of each option. Note how the Add Depth wizard provides graphics on an array of large command buttons, whereas the Word Newsletter wizard changes the graphic to match the currently selected option.

2. Phrase wizard text in simple terms. In general, present options to users in the form of questions: "Which style would you like for your newsletter?" "How many columns would you like?" Provide brief conceptual information and tips so that users will understand the implications of the option they are considering.

3. When relevant to the task, each graphic as well as the explanatory text should reflect the previous choices. So, for example, the second Word Newsletter wizard panel, shown in Figure 7.4 above, previews a two-column layout in the "Classic" style that the user chose in the previous panel. In this way, the user sees the wizard's end product emerging step by step.

4. When appropriate, include panels that simply present information rather than offering a choice, as shown in Figure 7.5.

5. Carefully consider the wizard's controls. The typical controls are presented in Table 7.2.

6. When appropriate, suggest what actions the user might take after completing the wizard. Encourage the user to customize the wizard's end product using the software's regular interface. Point to the likely next task in the user's workflow. Suggest the use of an appropriate coach. Remind the user of the availability of standard Help or provide a jump to a useful Help topic.

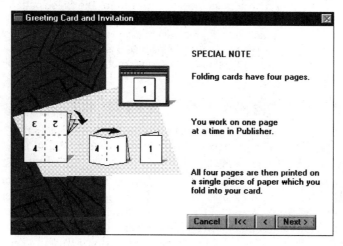

Figure 7.5. *A wizard panel that presents only information.*

Table 7.2. *Typical controls for wizards*

Option buttons	The most common means for letting users select the desired option for each panel.
Text box	Allows the user to add text that will appear in the wizard's end product, or to type a value that will be used by the wizard.
Next button	Allows the user to confirm the option he or she has selected and advances the wizard to the next panel.
Back or Previous button	Allows the user to return to a previous panel and reconsider previous choices.
Cancel button	Allows the user to cancel the wizard and all actions that the wizard has taken.
Finish button	Completes the action of the wizard. The Finish button should be the final wizard command. This button can also be placed on other wizard panels to allow the user to immediately produce a final result using the wizard's defaults. In some cases, it is not advisable to allow users to generate a result without making explicit choices.

WHO SHOULD DESIGN AND WRITE WIZARDS?

Wizards are, in part, a learning tool, but they are primarily a productivity tool. Also, wizards are not created using WinHelp. They are programmed in the software product's own code or programmed in development environments such as Borland's Delphi or Microsoft's Visual Basic and are incorporated into the product's code. For these reasons, the questions may arise: (1) Are wizards truly Help or are they part of the software product's user interface? (2) Which members of the product team should take responsibility for designing wizards?

Our response is that documentation of all kinds is a part of the user interface and that those who write manuals, write standard Help systems, and design and write coaches and wizards are specialists in the advisory aspect of the user interface. Wizards, WinHelp Shortcut buttons (buttons in Help topics that operate the interface), and other new forms of user assistance are beginning to dissolve the artificial distinction between documentation and interface. Help writers—experts in the advisory interface—are ideally qualified to work with *other* kinds of interface designers and programmers in the creation of wizards.

Useful information regarding wizards can be found in Microsoft's *Windows Interface Guidelines for Software Design*. In addition, a book on wizards by Carolyn Snyder and Jared Spool is scheduled for publication in 1996. The performance support model has become important in the corporate training community as well as in computer documentation. For a collection of interesting articles on performance support systems written from a training perspective, see *Performance Improvement Quarterly*, volume 8, no. 1 (1995), a special issue edited by Gloria Gery.

Coaches

Coach Help consists of sequences of Help topics that "walk" the user through the steps that make up a task or through a series of tasks. The defining feature of coaches is that users work with the product's regular interface.

Coaches are intended to provide a high level of user support and comfort. The topics are short, and with each step or task the user completes, the user is shown a new topic focusing on the next action or decision the user must make. The typical "rhythm" is this: read a coach Help topic, perform an action with the product's regular interface, click the coach Help topic's Next button or choose from a set of options, read the next coach Help topic, and continue.

Wizards, of course, must be tightly integrated with the software product. Integration with the software product is often implemented in coaches. When this integration is relatively sophisticated and comprehensive, the coach is more successful. One of the capabilities that can be achieved through integration with the software product is detecting and correcting user errors. An example, from Microsoft Publisher (2.0), is shown in Figure 7.6. If the user fails to click the Text Frame tool, the cue card will detect this error when the user clicks the Next button. Then, a special error correction (or "Oops!") topic will display instead of the topic that is normally next in the sequence.

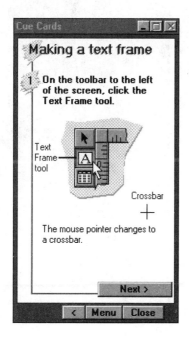 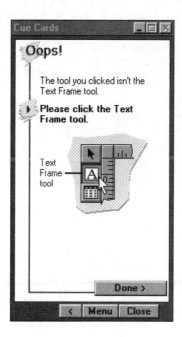

Figure 7.6. *A procedure topic and an error correction topic in a coach.*

Coach Help does not require this kind of integration, however. In fact, much coach Help in the Windows environment is created using only the basic WinHelp features. Despite the benefits of integration with the product, the essence of coach Help lies in the logical branching among the coach Help topics. This logical branching is carried out partly with navigation commands, in particular the Next (or Continue) button found on many coach topics. It is also carried out by means of jumps, often in the form of hotspot buttons, located on the topics.

The logical branching of coach Help takes the following forms:

1. Displaying lists of coach-supported tasks that the user can branch to, as shown in Figure 7.7.

2. Directing the user to continue the task by advancing, in a linear manner to the next topic, as shown in Figure 7.8.

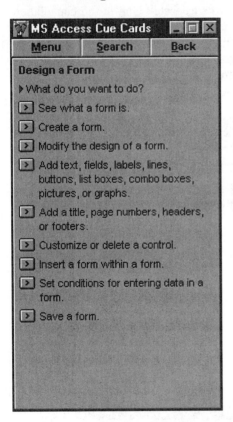
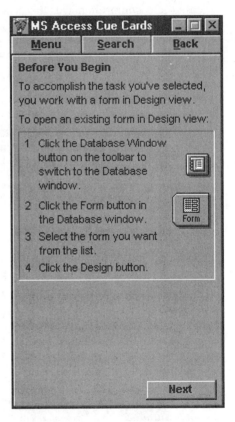

Figure 7.7. *(at left) A topic listing coach-supported tasks.*

Figure 7.8. *(at right) A topic that is part of a linear sequence.*

3. Offering appropriate options within a given task, as shown in Figure 7.9.

4. Offering further information about the task in the form of tips, examples, and overviews. See, for example, the first jump listed in Figure 7.7.

5. Directing the user, after the completion of the task, to other coach supported-tasks, to other forms of user assistance, or back to the software product's user interface, as shown in Figure 7.10.

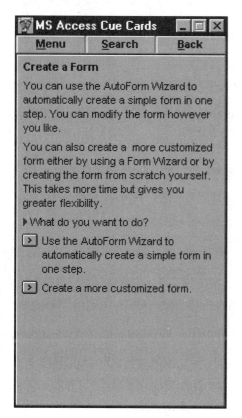
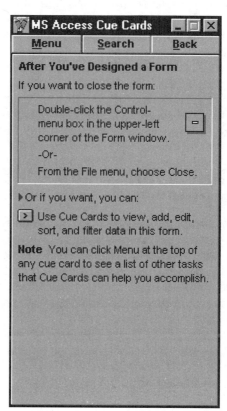

Figure 7.9. *(at left) A topic with options.*

Figure 7.10. *(at right) A topic that concludes a task.*

Coach Help also is much akin to troubleshooting Help topics, discussed in Chapter 6, *Writing Other Standard Help Topics*. This is because troubleshooting topics step the user with careful logical branching through a carefully worked out sequence of topics (the diagnostic topics) and finally to a recommendation topic.

COACH HELP AND ONLINE TUTORIALS

Coach Help is also closely related to online tutorials, and the similarities and differences do much to explain coach Help.

Like coach Help systems, online tutorials provide slow pacing and a high level of user support and comfort. Online tutorials always detect and correct user errors, and they very often complete tasks for users if the user fails in several attempts. When such capabilities are implemented in coach Help through tight integration with the software product, the similarity between the coach Help system and an online tutorial is still greater.

There is one great drawback to tutorial documentation, both print and online. Tutorials are a learning tool, but not a productivity tool. The user works on "canned" examples and does not get actual work done. Given the impatience of users and the increasing pressures of the workplace, many users bypass tutorial documentation. Coach Help can provide the high level of support characteristic of tutorials while allowing users to accomplish real work.

There are some trade-offs, however, in giving users a free reign in the product's regular interface. These issues are discussed on the following pages.

INTEGRATION OF COACHES AND THE SOFTWARE PRODUCT

As noted above, many coach Help systems are integrated with the software application. This integration takes a variety of forms, but the basic idea is always the same. When a user chooses a task, typically from a list of choices, the coach, in effect, "knows" the actions the user will need to perform. Otherwise, the coach could not display the appropriate topics when the user clicks the Next buttons and other controls. If the coach system knows the actions the user is supposed to perform, it can also display error correction ("Oops!") topics when the user fails to perform the correct action.

But there are other possibilities as well. Apple's Guide Help for System 7.5 places bright red circles, called "Coachmarks," around the interface element that the user is supposed to click next. If the user performs the wrong action repeatedly, the coach "steps onto the field" and performs the action for the user.

COACH TECHNOLOGIES

The technology for integrating coach Help systems with the software product takes several forms. Salsa's Interviewer was coded in Visual Basic and then compiled with the product's core code. Coaches created in regular WinHelp topics are often integrated with the product with DLLs. WinHelp 4 Training Cards promise to perform this integration as well.

Microsoft Project includes a Word template (CUECARDS.DOT) for making cue cards. This template does not in any way support the integration of cue cards with the software, but it gives Help developers a head start in achieving the look and feel of cue cards.

PROBLEMS WITH COACHES

Coaches pose three significant problems: (1) error detection and correction, when implemented, is often inadequate, (2) users lose their place in complex coach Help systems, and (3) coaches have difficulty sharing the screen with the software application.

Limited error detection

Even in those coach Help systems that are integrated with the product, error detection and correction is often quite limited. Often, the system can detect only blatant errors such as the user's failure to choose the command specified on the coach topic or the user's attempt to carry out an action before a prerequisite action has been carried out. Users trying to both learn and accomplish work in an unfamiliar software product are bound to commit errors, and coach Help is only partly equipped to handle these errors.

The tendency of users to get lost in coach Help

The second and related problem is that users tend to get lost when using complex coach systems. Users make incorrect choices in the software product's interface and in the coach system, and get "out of synch" with the coach topics. As noted above, error recognition and correction tends to be limited, and consequently does not fully control this tendency. Moreover, even when a coach system displays an "Oops!" message, a confused user may not respond to it properly and so may continue in the wrong direction.

It is certainly possible to make relatively simple, straightforward coaches. Apple's very successful Guide Help for System 7.5 supports numerous tasks, such as changing a system setting, that are relatively linear in structure and distinct from one another. Many coaching systems, however, are more ambitious; they support much larger, more open-ended, and more interrelated tasks such as creating a full-scale database. Here the logical branching structure is truly complex, and the prospect of users getting lost is very real.

Difficulties sharing the screen with the interface

A final challenge is that, unlike wizards, coach Help must share the screen with the software product's interface. This is also true of standard Help, but standard Help does not display a succession of Help topics that stay on the screen and guide users step by step through tasks.

Because they share the screen with the software product, coach Help topics must be limited in size. Consequently, unless the coach Help topics are written for individual steps, as shown above in Figures 7.2 and 7.6, there will be less opportunity for graphics and explanations.

In addition, even though limited in size, coach topics physically may cover the software product's responses to user actions. including dialog boxes and system messages. This competition for screen space must be worked out. Sometimes coach Help topics include steps instructing users to move or minimize the coach topic, but this is an awkward interaction between the user and the coach system. Ideally, coach topics will be programmed to move elsewhere on the screen rather than to cover active elements of the interface.

Approaching coach Help cautiously

The promise of coach Help is to guide users with a high level of comfort through the process of learning about the software and achieving productive work. We see, however, that there are major challenges in fulfilling this promise, whether or not the coach Help system is integrated with the software.

Because of these challenges, Help authors should create and evaluate coaches for smaller, more constrained tasks before attempting a comprehensive coach Help system. In fact, Help authors might give a second thought to strengths online tutorials.

One reasonable strategy is not to regard a complex open-ended coach as an introductory piece of documentation. In other words, indicate to users that they should begin with an online demo (or "tour"), an online tutorial, or a wizard before undertaking tasks with coach Help.

DESIGNING COACH TOPICS

Below we present some design considerations and recommendations for coach Help. Because individual coach Help systems vary greatly, you must carefully assess how these guidelines apply to the coach Help system you are planning.

1. Decide the scope of your coach Help topics. Some coach Help systems, such as Salsa's Interviewer and Publisher's cue cards, provide separate topics for individual steps. This slows the pacing but enables the coach topic to provide more complete explanations and graphics. It also makes possible step-by-step error detection and correction. Alternatively, many coach Help systems, such as Access cue cards, present complete procedures, enabling users to move more quickly through their tasks.

2. Plan out the logical branching of your coach system. Build a flow chart or a similar diagram to map the branching relationships among your topics. Pay attention to the interrelationships among various coach-supported tasks. Try to keep the branching as clear to users as possible.

3. Keep coach Help topics short enough to prevent scrolling; if users will be clicking from one topic to the next, they should have to scroll topics as well.

4. Write coach Help topics like brief procedure topics. You can apply your experience writing standard Help procedure topics to writing coach Help. As shown in Figure 7.8, coach Help topics contain many of the same components as procedure topics do. To keep coach topics short, use *layering* extensively. Provide jumps for displaying overviews, examples, tips, and other necessary information.

6. When the coach system does not provide error correction, use more feedback statements in the coach topics. Tell users what the result of an action should be, so they can recognize and correct errors themselves.

7. Make coach Help topics visually distinct from the software product's interface. Raymond Lee, a Microsoft designer, notes that users see the various hotspot buttons and other controls on coach topics and confuse Help topics with the product's interface. Lee stresses the importance of giving coach topics adequate margins and making coach topics visually distinct from the interface.

8. Provide an adequate set of navigation controls. Raymond Lee suggests the use of these controls:

   - Lists of hypertext jumps that let users choose tasks they want to perform.
   - A Next button to allow users to advance to the next topic.
   - A Back button to allow users to return to the previous topic.
   - A "Menu" button that allows users to return to the list of tasks supported by the coaches.
   - A Help button that provides the user with direct access to all the information in the software product's Help system.

CONCLUSION

In this chapter we examined performance support Help and considered how this Help model fits in with standard Help and the rest of the documentation set. Now we change directions. We are still dealing with Help design rather than construction, but we will now look at the design of information access, in particular the Help contents and index. These are covered in Chapter 8, *Designing the Contents, Browse Sequences, and Jumps*, and Chapter 9, *Creating the Index*.

When we design the information access in Help systems, we certainly consider wizards and coaches. The Help contents and index, therefore, as well as jumps and other forms of information access can take users to wizards and coaches as well as to standard Help topics. But because there are so many more standard Help topics than wizard or coach topics, our chapters on information access focus on standard Help.

8

Designing the Contents, Browse Sequences, and Jumps

The importance of information access is self-evident: the best Help information is of little value unless users can find exactly what they need without undue effort. WinHelp 4 is impressive in its access features, and with good design information access can be a major strength of your Help system. All the forms of access in WinHelp 4 are presented in Table 8.1. This chapter focuses on the WinHelp contents, the online table of contents. We will also consider browse sequences and hypertext jumps.

Table 8.1. *Forms of access in WinHelp 4*

Form of Access	Function	Comments
Contents	Provides hierarchical access to Help topics.	Equivalent to a print table of contents.
Index	Users select from an alphabetized list of index entries.	Equivalent to a print index.
Full-text search	Users type a word or phrase that represents the information they are looking for. The Full-text search feature displays all the Help topics containing the word or phrase.	No equivalent in the world of print.

Table 8.1. *(continued)*

Form of Access	Function	Comments
Jumps ("Hypertext jumps")	Users navigate electronically to related topics.	Equivalent to print cross references, but much faster and more acceptable to users.
Browse sequence buttons and other browse features	Users can navigate through a sequence of Help topics defined by the Help author.	Equivalent to paging forward and backward through a printed book.
The Back button and History list	Users can easily return to topics they have recently displayed.	No equivalent in the world of print. The History list is available only in main windows and tracks only main windows.
The Bookmark command	Users mark topics they may want to return to. They can then return to these topics quickly.	Equivalent to physical bookmarks in the world of print. Bookmarks are available only in main windows and can return users only to main windows.
Context-sensitive access for the following: What's This? Help, Help buttons on dialog boxes, the F1 and SHIFT+F1 keys, and status line Help	The Help information that is displayed depends on what interface element the user is pointing to (or has given the input focus to).	No equivalent in the world of print.
Natural language input	Users query the Help system by typing normal sentences.	No equivalent in the world of print. Not part of WinHelp 4, but implemented in Windows applications by some software vendors.

The Contents

The WinHelp contents, just like a print table of contents, is a hierarchical breakdown of all the topics included in the Help system. This hierarchy consists of "branches" for the various kinds of Help information. So, for example, there is apt to be a branch for the shortcut topics, although this will be a very small branch. If the product is a language reference, there may be a very large branch for commands. In the case of software applications, the largest branch is usually the procedure topics, along with topics such as overview topics that usually appear with the procedures topics. Often, instead of one procedures branch, there are multiple procedures branches—one for printing topics, one for formatting topics, and so forth.

Users search these branches conceptually. They compare their goals with the entries they see at the top of the hierarchy and focus on the most promising branch. Level by level they navigate down to the bottom of the hierarchy to the Help topic of their choice. Figure 8.1 presents such a scenario.

Searching a Contents Hierarchy

A novice user of a word processor has seen documents with hanging indents and wants to know how to create them. Not having any phrases in mind that describe this kind of layout, this user shies away from the index. Nonetheless, he will probably be able to find the appropriate topic in the contents.

Looking at the main groupings of the procedure topic branch, he decides that his goal is unrelated to creating and saving documents, unrelated to printing, possibly related to entering text, but—yes!—probably falls under the category "Formatting Text." So exploring the formatting branch of the hierarchy, this user chooses formatting paragraphs and then encounters a procedure topic "Formatting numbered and bulleted paragraphs with hanging indents." Recognizing the match between the topic heading and his goals, the user chooses to access this Help topic.

Figure 8.1. *A scenario: Searching a contents hierarchy.*

Users also use the contents to familiarize themselves with the software product. They learn a lot when they see how the Help topics are grouped in the hierarchy. The procedure branch—or branches—is especially important for it provides a task-oriented breakdown of the product's features.

THE WINHELP 4 CONTENTS

As we see in Figure 8.2, the WinHelp 4 contents is a "page" on the Help Topics dialog box and uses an expandable/collapsible outline format, akin to the outline view in a word processor, the Windows 3.1 File Manager, and the Windows 95 Explorer. Users display Help topics by double clicking on book icons and page icons—note how the right corners of these Help "pages" are turned down. Book icons are "containers" for other (lower-level) book icons and for page icons. They are akin to chapter and section titles in the print world. Page icons represent individual Help topics. Thus, the top level of any hierarchy will consist solely or mostly of book icons, and the very bottom level of the hierarchy must consist entirely of page icons.

Figure 8.2. *The Contents page of the Help Topics dialog box.*

Help designers do not have to use the new contents, but there is much to be said in its favor:

- The outliner format provides a graphical view of the hierarchy and clearly shows the user's place in the hierarchy.

- Users benefit from the clear differentiation of the topic groups (the book icons) and the Help topics (the page icons).

- In contrast to WinHelp 3.1 contents topics, the WinHelp contents holds its place—when a user returns to it after navigating through the Help system, the hierarchy appears just as it did when the user left it.

- The contents allows users to print Help topics in groups.

- The contents allows Help authors to create merged contents from several HLP files.

- The contents brings uniformity to the hierarchical access in Windows Help. WinHelp 3.1 contents topics are often sufficiently different from one another to require significant extra effort from users.

The WinHelp 4 contents does have limitations; we consider these limitations and some superior designs later in this chapter.

THE WINHELP 3.1 CONTENTS TOPICS

In WinHelp 3.1 there is no special contents functionality. An online table of contents consists simply of standard Help topics (or possibly a single topic) with lists of jumps that users click to move downward in the information hierarchy. These topics are usually called "contents topics." Figures 8.3 and 8.4 show a portion of a typical WinHelp 3.1 contents hierarchy. Figure 8.3 shows the top level contents topic; the entries (jumps) on this topic are the topic heading of the second-level contents topics—among them, "Starting, Saving, and Closing a Publication." Figure 8.4 shows this particular second-level contents topic. The entries on this topic are topic headings of procedure topics—for example "Starting a Publication" and "Starting with a PageWizard." These topics make up the third and last level in this hierarchy. Indeed, whatever the size of the hierarchy the bottom level consists of the procedure topics, command topics, and all the other topics that contain the information users are trying to find.

The major drawback of the standard WinHelp 3.1 format for the contents hierarchy is that there is no graphical depiction of the depth of the hierarchy. Rather, users must mentally construct this hierarchy and recognize their location in the hierarchy when all they can see are the various lists. Users, therefore, often have trouble recognizing where they are in the Help hierarchy—on what branch and at what level—especially in larger Help systems. Help designers often provide some visual cues to help users distinguish the levels—for example, the jumps to the bottom level might be preceded by bullets. But these cues are only modestly effective.

The strength of the 3.1 contents topics is that designers have considerable freedom and flexibility. Because the contents topics are actual Help topics rather than just containers in a graphical browser, Help authors can add text and graphics. For example, in Figures 8.3 and 8.4, we see *pictographs* that distinguish procedure topics from reference topics, and in Figure 8.4, we see the headings ("Starting a Publication" and "Naming, Saving, and Closing Your Publication") that subdivide the entries into two groups—in effect creating an extra, "virtual" level in the information hierarchy. Another popular design choice is the use of graphical contents topics made up of hotspot pictographs, as shown in Figure 8.5. Some Help authors even create outliner-style contents topics in WinHelp 3.1, a task which requires much effort.

Help designers may even now prefer to use WinHelp 3.1 contents topics. They may have a special design goal that requires the flexibility these topics provide. Also, for small hierarchies, WinHelp 3.1 contents topics are simpler and more convenient than the WinHelp 4 Contents page.

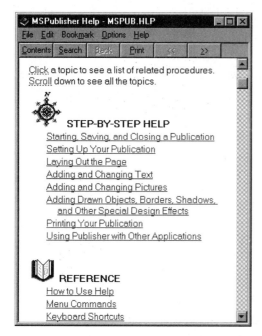

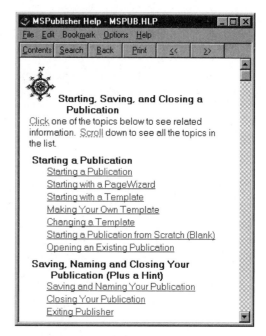

Figure 8.3. *(at left) The first level of a Windows 3.1 contents hierarchy.*

Figure 8.4. *(at right) The second level of a WinHelp 3.1 contents hierarchy.*

Figure 8.5. *A top-level WinHelp 3.1 contents topic using hotspot pictographs.*

DEPTH AND BREADTH OF WINHELP 4 CONTENTS HIERARCHIES

Every hierarchy, whether print or online, has a certain shape, certain proportions of depth and breadth. In WinHelp 4 contents, as in other information hierarchies, depth and breadth are important design variables. The deeper the hierarchy, the more clicking (actually double-clicking) is necessary to reach a Help topic. In addition, even with the outline view, deep hierarchies cause users to lose track of their location. For all these reasons, even with 500 topics in your hierarchy, you should try very hard to limit each branch to three levels (three double-clicks displays the Help information). Furthermore, even with a much larger Help system, you should try very hard not to exceed four levels.

The number of icons that display when a user opens a book icon is the breadth of that part of the hierarchy. The breadth of all the parts of the hierarchy make up the total breadth. Naturally, breadth tends to decrease depth and *vice versa*. Within limits, users do better scanning a list than descending to deeper levels; thus, moderately broad hierarchies, say 8 to 10 icons, are desirable. On the other hand, no one wants to scan a list of 20 or 30 icons, even though such broad hierarchies might enable the Help author to keep the depth to two levels.

MANAGING THE HIERARCHY

Now we turn to specific issues regarding the design of the WinHelp 4 contents.

Managing the proportions of the hierarchy

Help authors, of course, cannot simply choose the ideal proportions for their contents hierarchy. The breadth and depth necessarily reflect the software product. If a software product has an unusual number of print features, and documenting these features requires 30 procedure topics, the print part of the hierarchy is apt to be broad, perhaps excessively so. Furthermore, the proportions of the hierarchy reflect various Help design decisions. For example, if a Help author has chosen to create a glossary topic, this topic may well appear as a single page icon (a one-level, one-topic branch) at the top level of the hierarchy. The decision whether to group all troubleshooting topics as a single branch or to integrate them with particular functions (placing the printing troubleshooting topics with the printing procedure topics, and so forth) will significantly effect the proportions of the hierarchy.

Although constrained in many ways, Help authors can still exercise significant control over the dimensions of their hierarchies by subdividing large lists into groups or combining two small groups. Perhaps the Help author will recognize that the 30 print topics fall naturally into two or three groups. As long as this grouping will be meaningful to users as they search the hierarchy, it is probably wise to add some depth to the hierarchy but eliminate the objectionable breadth. Similarly, a Help author might notice that the book icon "Creating Graphics" has only three page icons under it and that the book icon "Importing Graphics" has only five page icons under it. Not liking the inadequate breadth, the Help author might create a new book icon "Creating and Importing Graphics" that contains eight page icons.

Managing the top level of the hierarchy

Some of the most important decisions concern the top level of the hierarchy. One of these decisions is whether to group all the procedure topics under a single top-level book icon, labeled "How to... "or "Procedures" or whether to place the main branches of the procedure topics at the topic level. The difference is shown in Figures 8.6 and 8.7. The second design option shortens the pathway to the Help information and is preferable, unless the sum total of these procedure-topic icons plus the non-procedure icons makes the top level too long—as is the case in Figure 8.7. One solution is this: create a top-level book icon called "Reference" and place the appropriate non-procedure icons under it. This design option is shown in Figure 8.8.

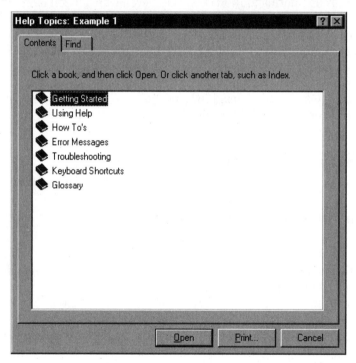

Figure 8.6. *Grouping all the procedure-topic branches under a single top-level book icon.*

Figure 8.7. *Placing the main procedure-topic branches at the top level in the hierarchy.*

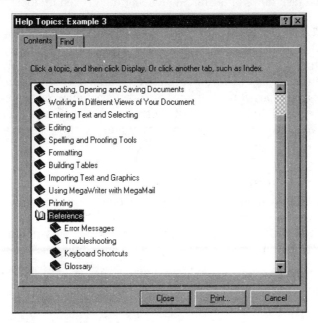

Figure 8.8. *Grouping certain branches under a Reference book icon.*

Sequencing icons

In addition to grouping all the book and page icons, you must also sequence the icons that are displayed from a single book icon and, thus, appear in one list. The sequence should both help users search the contents efficiently and help users develop a good mental model of the software product. The hierarchy of procedure topics is especially important because it reflects the task structure of the product. In fact, a good procedure topic hierarchy teaches users as much about the product as the menu structure does. Because it is so important, we focus on the procedures part of the contents here.

The main principles for sequencing procedure topic icons are these:

- Sequence tasks according to the user's task flow—the order in which tasks are usually performed.

- Sequence frequently performed tasks before infrequently performed tasks.

- Sequence simple tasks before complex tasks.

- Place closely related topics next to one another.

These principles do not account for all the sequencing issues Help authors face, and these principles conflict with one another. For example, a task that is infrequently performed may come early in the user's task flow whenever it *is* performed. Also, many tasks do not have an obvious place in the task flows of users. Sequencing the procedure-topic icons is very much a matter of compromise and judgment.

A limitation in the current release of the contents also affects sequencing. If you will be listing both book and page icons inside a book, the page icons must appear first in the list of icons. Very often the page icon for an overview topic appears first, which is fully appropriate. But if the list includes a page icon for a relatively minor issue, this icon must also appear before all the book icons (possibly right after the overview topic), even though the Help author would have preferred to place this icon at the bottom of the list. From one perspective, this limitation has a positive aspect: it enforces visual orderliness in the sequencing of book and page icons.

Phrasing page-icon labels

Because the labels on page icons represent topic headings, the phrasing of these labels should be identical or reasonably similar to the topic headings. Users are surprised and puzzled when they click a page icon and view a topic with a heading that is very different from the label on the page icon. There are, however, good reasons for minor differences in phrasing.

- When topic headings are very long, Help authors may want to shorten the corresponding page icon labels to make the labels easier for users to scan.

- When topic headings are very long, the corresponding page-icon labels may extend beyond the right edge of the list box. This situation causes the contents to develop a horizontal scroll bar to enable users to read the complete label. The appearance of a horizontal scroll bar is not highly dysfunctional, but Help designers try to avoid it. Whether a label will extend beyond the right edge depends in part on how far down it is located in the contents hierarchy. At times, Help authors must count individual characters to see if a particular label will cause a scroll bar to appear.

- When topic headings are phrased as infinitives, page labels must be rephrased (typically as gerunds) to prevent a repetitious list of infinitives from appearing in the contents.

Clearly, now that there is more variation in the phrasing of topic headings, the phrasing of topic headings and the entries in the contents must be carefully coordinated.

DEFICIENCIES OF THE CONTENTS—AND POSSIBLE ALTERNATIVES

The WinHelp 4 contents is not ideal. A surprising limitation is the lack of a "Collapse All" button. Such a button and, to a lesser extent, an "Expand All" button would make the contents significantly easier to use. Another desirable capability is for the contents to automatically update its display of the hierarchy as the user navigates from one topic to another. The Doc-To-Help navigator is an add-on module that replaces the standard WinHelp 4 Contents page and provides this and other enhancements. The WinHelp 3.1 version of the Navigator is shown below as Figure 8.9.

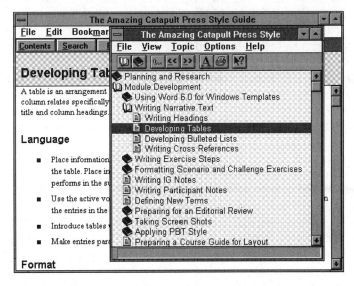

Figure 8.9. *The Doc-To-Help Navigator.*

Browse sequences

At times, users consult standard Help not to solve an immediate problem but to read a group of Help topics that will teach them about an unfamiliar feature. For this purpose users generally prefer to read these topics in the sequence the Help author considers most logical and helpful. Browse sequences are the traditional way to support this use of standard Help.

When browse buttons are included, they appear as Previous topic and Next topic buttons (<< and >>) on the button bar of main or secondary windows. Browse buttons are shown in Figure 8.10. Whenever the user displays a topic that is not part of the browse sequence, the browse buttons are grayed out; if the user displays a topic at the beginning or the end of a browse sequence, the Previous or the Next button (respectively) is grayed out.

Figure 8.10. *Previous and Next buttons on the button bar of a main window.*

The simplest way to design and implement a browse sequence is to create one giant chain of Help topics. Good designers, however, usually create separate browse sequences for all the topics pertaining to a particular feature—for example, the styles feature of a word processing application. This browse sequence might begin with the styles overview topic, followed by all the styles topics in the best reading order. Sometimes Help authors will add a custom "First" button to the button bar that jumps the user to the first topic in whatever browse sequence they are in. See the file First.HLP, on the disc included with this book, for an example of a First button and instructions for making one.

Because of the significant effort involved in designing and implementing browse sequences, many software developers choose not to provide them. Without browse sequences, however, users will find reading a succession of topics a chore—or impossible. If the user accesses a topic from the index, via a hypertext jump, or in any other way besides the contents, there is no practical way to read through the group of topics that this topic belongs to. If the user accesses a topic through the WinHelp 4 contents (and assuming the group of topics is sequenced in the best reading order), the user will have to read the first topic in the sequence, re-display the contents, double-click the page icon for the next topic, read the topic, re-display the contents, and so forth. A synchronized contents, such as the Doc-To-Help Navigator, is a very adequate equivalent to browse sequences.

Omitting browse sequences is especially undesirable when software vendors choose not to provide a comprehensive *user's guide*. A key role of the user's guide is to let users learn about a feature by reading a succession of sections. If there is no user's guide and no browse sequence feature (or equivalent) in Help, our users' information needs go partly unmet.

Jumps to related topics

Hypertext jumps to related topics are analogous to cross references in print documents, but are much faster and more convenient, and so are more likely to be used. A topic may be considered a related topic for one or more of the reasons shown in Table 8.2 below:

Table 8.2. *Criteria for listing a topic as a related topic*

Closely associated tasks	This is the most common reason for listing a related topic. If the user of a communication package is choosing a particular form of terminal emulation, the user will likely be choosing other communications settings as well. These other settings should be related topics.
Reversals or opposites	Users may be interested in the opposite or reversal of the task they are reading about—for example, installing fonts and its opposite, removing fonts. In this case, a topic about a related task, deleting fonts, would also be relevant.
Near misses	A user could easily access "Sending many fax messages automatically" when the user really wants the topic "Sending one fax message to many recipients." Related topics serve the valuable role of pointing users in the right direction.
Other kinds of Help information about the topic	The list of related topics is one pathway for directing users to an overview topic or other kinds of Help information pertaining to the current topic.

For some Help topics, few or no related topics need be listed. For others, numerous related topics seem plausible. To avoid overburdening the user, most Help topics should list no more than four or five jumps to related topics. A potential related topic may meet more than one of these criteria: for example it is both a closely associated task and a possible near miss. Such topics are stronger candidates for inclusion.

The criterion of closely associated tasks can generate a very large number of related topics. For example, for any formatting task, there are many other formatting tasks that the user might be interested in performing. One solution to this problem is to include only the most important of the associated tasks as related topics and then include a *list topic* as a pathway to the rest of the associated tasks.

KINDS OF JUMPS TO RELATED TOPICS

In WinHelp 4 there are three ways to create jumps to related topics: standard "topic" jumps, ALink macro jumps, and KLink macro jumps. Each is discussed below from the perspective of design. Construction issues are covered in Chapter 11, *Creating Hypertext Links.*

Standard "topic" jumps

Topic jumps are familiar to Help authors from WinHelp 3.1. Jumps often take the form of hotspot jump text formatted with green underlining. When the user clicks the hotspot text, say "Deleting files," that topic is displayed. Lists of these jumps appear at the bottom of Help topics under the subheadings "See Also" or "Related Topics." Another alternative is to list related topics in a pop-up window that displays when the user clicks the "See also" hotspot text in the topic's nonscrolling region. Alternatively, when a related topic is closely associated with a particular step, it may appear right within that step. Figure 8.11 shows jumps listed in a pop-up window and within steps.

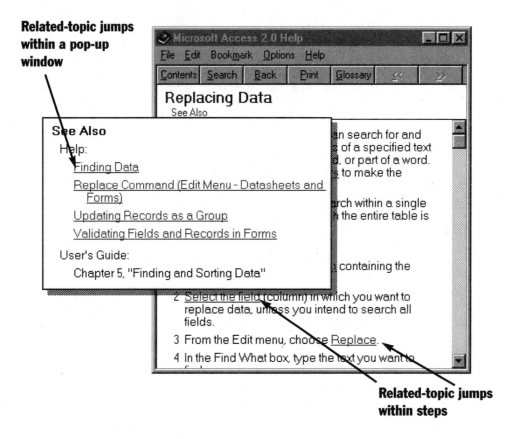

Figure 8.11. *Related topics in a pop-up window and within steps.*

Jumps to related topics can also appear beside hotspot buttons, as shown in Figure 8.12.

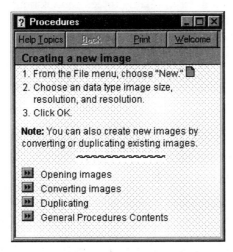

Figure 8.12. *A list of related topics with their hotspot buttons.*

ALink macro jumps

ALink macro jumps are usually initiated from a Related Topics or See Also button. A *Topics Found box* appears, and one or more related topics will be listed, as shown in Figure 8.13.

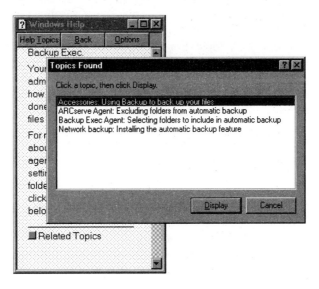

Figure 8.13. *An ALink jump and Topics Found box.*

Both **ALink** macro jumps and standard topic jumps listed in pop-up windows require two steps: users click first to view a list of related topics and click again to display a related topic. This difference is a reason to place related topic jumps directly in main and secondary windows when there are no more than three or four jumps.

The main benefit of **ALink** jumps pertains to jumps between .HLP files. With **ALink** jumps, there are no error messages if the user chooses not to install all the related .HLP files. If the file is not installed, the topic is simply not listed in the Topics Found box.

KLink macro jumps

To users, **KLink** jumps look just like **ALink** jumps. The difference is that the related topics that appear in the Topics Found box are based on the index. So, for example, if a Help topic about printing has a related topic coded with the K keyword "printing," the Topics Found box will display every Help topic for which the K footnote "printing" was assigned as part of the process of creating the index.

This method provides an easy way to generate related topics. The drawback is that the Help author gives up the chance to individually choose the related topics. The number and kind of related topics depend on how the index is constructed. **KLink** macros also cause difficulty during localization, for the macro text must be translated to match the index terms in each language.

Mid-topic jumps

Mid-topic jumps take users to different locations in a single, lengthy Help topic. They are very useful in certain situations. The use of mid-topic jumps in glossary topics is explained in Chapter 6, *Writing Other Standard Help Topics*. Mid-topic jumps can also serve as a miniature online contents within a lengthy topic. For example, let us consider a lengthy overview topic consisting of a brief introduction and four distinct sections, each explaining a different aspect of color theory. By adding mid-topic jumps to the introduction, a Help author enables users who don't want to read the entire topic to jump directly to the section they care about. Furthermore, if the Help author intends to provide related topic jumps from several procedure topics to this overview topic, he or she can code these related-topic jumps as mid-topic jumps. Through this technique, a user can jump from the current procedure topic to the portion of the overview topic that is most pertinent.

9

Creating the Index

The contents supports users who want to search conceptually. The index supports users who can formulate a word or phrase to describe the information being sought. If the user thinks of an apt word or phrase for the information he or she seeks and if this word or phrase has been assigned as an index entry to the appropriate Help topic, the index provides rapid access to the desired information. The index is especially suited to knowledgeable users, but a really good index with a rich set of index entries is highly valued by almost all users.

Unfortunately, the index is by far the weakest part of a great many Windows Help systems. Skimpy, inconsistent indexes abound. Indexing is a specialized activity and many Help teams do not have someone who is fully qualified (or willing) to create the index. Also, Help teams often fail to allocate enough time to create a quality index.

This chapter covers the basic principles of WinHelp 4 indexing. It will prepare you to create a solid, useful index. In addition, Help indexers will benefit from such books on back-of-book indexing as Larry Bonura's *The Art of Indexing* and Hans Wellisch's *Indexing from A to Z*. If you are an experienced print indexer, you have an excellent background for Help indexing, and some of the material in this chapter will be familiar—but much will be new.

WinHelp 4 also includes a full-text search feature. This enables users to display desired topics by typing words that appear in these topics. The strengths and limitations of this feature will be discussed. Finally, we will briefly discuss the more advanced forms of information access such as Lotus's Ask the Expert and Microsoft's Answer Wizard.

A review of the WinHelp 3.1 and 4 indexes

This section reviews the operation of the WinHelp 3.1 index (called the Search dialog box) and the WinHelp 4 index and briefly explains how index entries—or "keywords"—are associated with Help topics in the topic file using the K footnote. This section can be skipped by those who understand the features and operation of the WinHelp indexes and know the basics of index construction.

THE WINHELP 3.1 INDEX

The WinHelp 3.1 index is shown in Figure 9.1. The user types a word or phrase in the text box, which dynamically scrolls the keyword list. Alternatively, the user can directly scroll the keyword list. When the user selects a keyword in the keyword list, the topics (or single topic) associated with that keyword appear in the Topics Found box. The user clicks one of these topics to display the topic.

Many users are confused by this interface. For example, they do not understand the relationship between the keyword list and the Topics Found box. For this reason and others the index was redesigned in WinHelp 4.

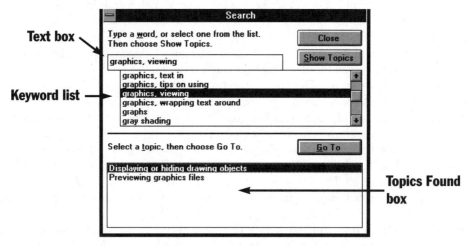

Figure 9.1. *The WinHelp 3.1 index.*

THE WINHELP 4 INDEX

In WinHelp 4 the index, shown in Figure 9.2, is more usable because subentries are indented under main entries. Also, its operation is more familiar to users because its user interface resembles a traditional print index.

Because of this similarity, "index entry" rather than "keyword" is used in this chapter to make the discussion easier to follow. "Keyword" is used in Chapter 10, *Creating Help Topics*, which deals with construction rather than design.

In the WinHelp 4 index, the user types a word or phrase in the text box or scrolls the list of index entries. Then he or she double-clicks the most promising entry. If there is one Help topic associated with that entry, that topic immediately appears. If there are multiple topics, they appear in a Topics Found box, and the user chooses the desired topic.

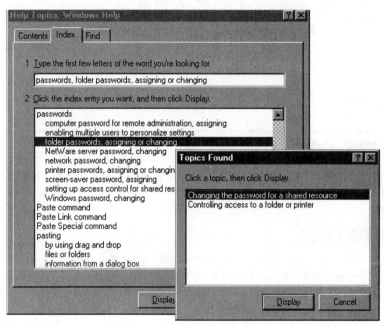

Figure 9.2. *The WinHelp 4 online index with the Topics Found box.*

CONSTRUCTING AN INDEX: A PREVIEW

A brief preview of the procedure for constructing a WinHelp 4 index is helpful in understanding the design issues, and is provided here.

We create an index entry for a topic by assigning a "K" footnote to that topic and then listing one or more index entries (or "keywords") in the footnote. The procedure is largely unchanged from WinHelp 3.1.

For example, as shown (in simplified form) in Figure 9.3, the Help topic "Copying records" has three index entries assigned to it: "copying records," "duplicating records," and "records, copying." The last of these entries is an entry with a *qualifier*, akin to a modifier. If the compiled index has more than one qualifier for the entry "records," each of these qualifiers will be displayed as an indented subentry.

$#K**Copying records**

1   Select the record you want to copy.

2   From the Edit menu, choose Copy.

$Copying records

#proCopyingRecords

Kcopying records; duplicating records; records, copying

Figure 9.3. *A topic file showing the K footnote with index entries.*

Indexing concepts

We now cover two fundamental concepts: rich indexing and audience analysis in indexing. Later, we cover the indexing process and present a method for generating index entries.

RICH INDEXING

An index is considered rich when Help topics have an ample number of index entries. Rich indexing is the fundamental guideline for creating a quality index. The goal of the indexer is to reach out to the user with a variety of relevant index entries so that the user stands the best possible chance of finding the desired topic.

If the index contains only one entry per topic, the indexer is, in effect, saying to the user: "Either make the right guess or you're out of luck." Users who fail to find the desired information in an index react poorly.

Consider the range of terms that might occur to someone looking for a Help topic on passwording files:

- passwording or password

- files, passwording

- encryption

- security

- protecting documents

- locking documents

There are others as well.

Avoid farfetched entries. You do not want to clutter your index with entries, such as "intruder protection," which are unlikely to be used. There is no reason to add unnecessary index entries for those topics that genuinely require only one or two. The typical problem, however, is too few rather than too many entries.

AUDIENCE ANALYSIS

Creating an index is a form of communication and, like all other forms of communication, it requires analyzing the audience. By analyzing our audience, we think of entries we might otherwise miss. A Help author, for example, might realize that the product's customers include former mainframe users and so would remember to generate mainframe-oriented index entries. For example, as a synonym for the index entry "opening documents," the writer might add "loading documents." Similarly, for an entry-level word processing application, the writer would remember to include entries drawn from the world outside computers, such as "erasing text" and "discarding documents."

Audience analysis also helps us recognize index entries that are unlikely to be used. For example, we can expect mainstream computer users to know that "delete" is the standard term in the computer industry, and for this audience we would not include entries such as "erasing text" and "discarding documents."

The indexing process

An index must be planned systematically from the outset of the project. Here are the stages of this process and the issues that must be considered.

WHO SHOULD CREATE THE INDEX—AND WHEN?

The dedicated indexer

If your publications department supports numerous products, you may be able to employ a full-time professional indexer to index both Help systems and print books. Alternatively, consider hiring a contractor. This person should have an extensive indexing background, WinHelp indexing experience, and an acquaintance with software products similar to yours.

In either case, the cost may be somewhat greater than having writers and editors index as they write and edit, but the quality of the indexing will be much higher.

The best time for the professional indexer to begin working on a WinHelp index is after the Help topics have been edited. The indexer can also index while the Help topics are being edited (in parallel with the editing) but extensive editing changes in the Help topics may require further changes in the index.

The editor as indexer

Editors can also index as they edit. If multiple editors are contributing to the index, one editor should coordinate the effort in order to minimize the inevitable inconsistency that occurs whenever more than one individual creates an index. This person should also take sole responsibility for the final edit of the index.

Writers as indexers

In smaller documentation groups especially, Help writers may need to index their own Help topics. It is highly desirable for one person—very possibly an editor—to coordinate this effort and take sole responsibility for the final edit of the index.

Even when writers are not indexing, they should add K footnotes for any good index entries they think of that will not be obvious to the indexer. Also, depending on the Help tools being used, it may be necessary for the writers to create one index entry for each topic (a match or near match of the topic heading) so that the index can be used to access topics in the compiled Help system during the Help development process.

In very small documentation groups, one individual may be responsible for every aspect of a Help system. This individual can do most of the indexing while writing and editing, or save most of the job for a dedicated indexing pass through the topic file. In any case, he or she must at least allocate a period of time to carefully edit the index.

ESTIMATING THE SIZE OF THE INDEX

A rough rule of thumb, applicable to medium and large software products, is that the total number of index entries assigned to Help topics should be four or five times the number of the procedure topics and other major topics in the Help system. (The number of index entries that appear in the compiled index will be smaller because many entries are assigned to multiple Help topics.) Different products will require greater or fewer index entries in their Help systems, but if your index departs greatly from this ratio, you should determine the reasons why this is so.

ESTIMATING THE TIME REQUIRED

It is very difficult to estimate the time required for an index, even when you have an idea of its size. Indexers vary in productivity, and more careful indexing will clearly require more time. The "quick and dirty" approach to indexing is to generate index entries entirely or largely from reading the topic headings. This approach, however, results in low quality.

Here are some rough but useful guidelines for estimating time:

- High-quality indexes for large Help systems often require three to five person-months.

- High-quality indexes require about 8-10 percent of the total time allocated to the entire Help project.

- Editing an index is a larger job than it may first appear. Editing often takes 20 percent of the total amount of time allocated for the index. Because editing comes at the end of the project, there is often pressure to shorten the editing process in order to meet a ship date.

Publications departments should consider maintaining some sort of record of the time required for indexing various Help systems.

USABILITY TESTING

Chapter 2, *The Design Process*, emphasized the enormous value of testing your Help system on potential users. If you can find the extra time, index entries can be easily and effectively tested. Your subjects can watch you perform a task on the computer, perhaps with a beta version of the software product, and then report the words they would use to describe what they have seen. With some ingenuity, this kind of testing can be performed with nothing beyond rough drawings of the relevant portions of the software's interface. You can also ask subjects to tell you whether your entries seem appropriate ("Are these terms you would use?") and to suggest alternatives. Unlike many other kinds of usability testing in which you must work with subjects individually, here you can work with an entire group of subjects. This cuts down the time you need to spend. While not exactly usability testing, a very worthwhile activity is to look at the index entries in competing products.

RE-USING INDEX ENTRIES

In the Microsoft Windows environment, certain Help topics are common to many software products. You may be able to re-use parts of your topic files, including the index entries in the K footnotes. Or, you may maintain some kind of database record of the index entries for particular topics.

ESTABLISHING CONVENTIONS: PHRASING, CAPITALIZATION AND PUNCTUATION

There are several mechanical issues that must be resolved before you begin generating your index. These are discussed below.

The syntax of entries

Many index entries are verb forms that express the verb-plus-object relationship. For these index entries, use gerunds ("deleting files"). Many other entries, of course, are simply noun phrases ("overtype mode").

Singular or plural index entries

Index entries can be singular or plural. Plural forms are shorter and simpler and should be used when feasible. Generally there will be no problem expressing gerund entries as plurals ("deleting files"). Nouns can often be expressed as plurals, especially when we can envision the user working with several of them, as in "arcs" or "balanced columns." Other nouns are singular, because they are concepts ("alignment" or "parity"). In the case of interface elements, the plural is used when there are more than one of them ("toolbars"); singular is used when there is one ("ruler").

Capitalization

Use lower case for most index entries, but use upper case for interface elements that are normally upper case in documentation. These include commands ("Open command") and such interface objects as "Standard tool palette" and "Date field." Upper case should also be used for terms that are normally upper case, such as "ASCII."

Punctuation

Commas are used to create subentries that are indented under the main entry or to reverse the word order in a main entry. This issue is discussed in more detail below.

COORDINATION AND EDITING

As noted above, when several individuals (probably writers and editors) work together on an index inconsistency in indexing styles becomes a major problem. One good technique is this: periodically an indexer should begin indexing a topic by first looking at a comparable topic in the Help system that has already been indexed. So, for example, if an indexer is about to index the topic "Previewing a form," this person might first look at a colleague's comparable topic, "Previewing a report."

The coordinator of the indexing effort has a major role in controlling inconsistency as well as ensuring overall quality. The coordinator should set forth indexing guidelines at the outset, should periodically review each individual's indexing, and should perhaps schedule occasional meetings in which the individual indexers compare notes on what they are doing.

With indexing, as with writing, the time spent in coordination is recouped later, because there are fewer inconsistencies and other problems to reconcile in the editing phase.

These are the main problems that are identified and corrected in the editing phase:

- "Holes" in the index. For example, there are no index entries for particular topics.

- Unintentional duplications and variations. For example, there are entries for both "date" and "dates" and entries for both "adding record entries" and "adding records."

- Inconsistent indexing of similar topics. For example, the topic "Previewing a form" has the four entries "previewing forms," "forms, previewing," "print preview," and "zoom view," while the topic "Previewing a report" has the three entries "previewing reports," "reports, previewing," and "print preview."

As noted, be prepared to devote 20 percent of the total indexing effort to editing.

USEFUL WAYS TO LOOK AT THE INDEX

Indexers need to review index entries and their associated topics in two different ways. You need to scan the list of index entries and check the topic titles associated with them. In addition, you need to look at a list of *topic titles* with their associated index entries.

The Entries with Topics report

The Entries with Topics report, shown in Table 9.1, is an alphabetical list of index entries with their corresponding topics. Although the compiled Help system provides precisely this view, it is not feasible to double-click through the hundreds or thousands of index entries to display the corresponding topics. Fortunately, Help Workshop includes a tool that generates an Entry with Topics report. Furthermore, this report can be imported into a spreadsheet that can be sorted into the Topics with Entries report. Some of the Help authoring tools also provide both reports. The Entries with Topics report is especially useful in editing the index for inconsistent phrasing or unintentional duplications.

Table 9.1. *The Entries with Topics report*

Index Entries	Topic Title
adding cards	Adding cards
adding cards	Duplicating cards
cards, adding	Adding cards
cards, adding	Duplicating cards
cards, deleting	Deleting cards
deleting cards	Deleting cards
duplicating cards	Duplicating cards
new records	Adding cards

The Topics with Entries report

The Topics with Entries report, shown in Table 9.2, is an alphabetical list of topics with their assigned index entries. This information is available by scrolling through the topic file and viewing the index entries in the footnote window. It is difficult, however, to get an overview of the relationship among numerous topics and their index entries when you must scroll through multiple topics. Fortunately, as explained above, there are ways to get a useful Topics with Entries report. This report is especially useful in finding holes in the index and inconsistent indexing of similar topics.

Table 9.2. *The Topics with Entries report*

Topic Title	Index Entries
Adding cards	adding cards
Adding cards	cards, adding
Adding cards	new records
Deleting cards	cards, deleting
Deleting cards	deleting cards
Duplicating cards	adding cards
Duplicating cards	cards, adding
Duplicating cards	duplicating cards

A method for generating index entries

Taken in the right spirit, generating index entries is intellectually challenging and creative. It entails getting inside the minds of your users, seeing the product the way they do, and anticipating the words and phrases they will think of. Furthermore, it requires an excellent command of language.

In this section, we present a method for generating a rich set of index entries. We focus first on procedure topics, then command topics, and then on other categories of Help information.

INDEXING PROCEDURE TOPICS

When choosing index entries for procedure topics, look for (1) matches and near matches of topic headings; (2) inversions of the topic headings; (3) synonyms; and (4) associated terms.

Matches and near matches of the topic heading

The topic heading of a procedure topic is usually a very good index entry. Often minor modifications are necessary, particularly re-phrasing a topic heading so that it alphabetizes under the appropriate letter. For example, the topic "Working in print preview" will become "print preview." If you have decided on plural index entries, you may have to pluralize some singular topic headings. For example "Deleting a file" might become "deleting files." In the case of very long topic headings, you will need to generate shorter index entries. When necessary, a five or six word index entry is acceptable, but most entries should be much shorter.

In a large index, certain gerunds, such as "creating," "adding," and "changing" can appear so many times that their value to users diminishes. Users are not likely to scan thirty "creating" entries. Help authors may choose to limit the number of entries for such gerunds to the most common user tasks and use broad entries such as "adding records" rather than "adding names," "adding addresses," and "adding phone numbers."

Inversions of the match or near match entries

Users often formulate their index queries around the object rather than the action, so inversions of the match or near match index entry are valuable. So for example the index entry "deleting files" becomes "files, deleting" and "creating polygons" becomes "polygons, creating." Inversions (or "reversals" or "flipped entries") are easy to generate and add a lot of value to the index.

Synonyms

You have no guarantee that users will search your index using the words that appear in your topic headings. Synonyms, therefore, are a very important kind of index entry. You open a welcome safety net under your users when you add synonyms to your index.

For example, for the topic "Passwording documents" you should add the synonyms "locking documents" and "encryption."

Many good synonyms will come directly to mind as you consider the words that make up the topic heading. Other good synonyms come to mind as you read the body of the topic. For example, somewhere in the body of the topic the Help writer may have written "This protects..."—and at that moment you may well think of one more synonym, "protecting documents." Sometimes it is necessary to focus on the overall purpose of the task in order to generate a good synonym. For example, an indexer who was having trouble finding a synonym for the topic "Sending many fax messages automatically" thought broadly about the task and came up with "batch transmission." This immediately suggested another good synonym, "broadcast transmission," for the topic "Sending one fax message to many recipients."

Associated terms

Whereas synonyms reflect the purpose of the task being documented, associated terms have a broader or narrower focus. They are words and phrases that are likely to come to the user's mind as he or she is trying to formulate an appropriate index entry.

Very often associated terms are highly specific. For example, a user looking for information about choosing communications settings for connecting to a remote computer, might think of "baud rate," "modem," or even "CompuServe"—if CompuServe is the service the user wishes to connect to. Occasionally, important and distinctive dialog box titles or the labels of specific controls are included as associated terms—for example, the checkbox label "Keep with Next" is a possibility.

Associated terms may also be general. A user looking for a Help topic on passwording a document, might think of "security." A user looking to connect to a remote computer might think of "settings." Indexers cannot, of course, include every word that might come into the minds of thousands of users; the law of diminishing returns does apply. One of the challenges of indexing, therefore, is to decide which potential entries are the most likely to be used.

COMMAND TOPICS

Some capable indexers omit command topics from the index. They do so if users will be able to access command topics readily using the contents, the SHIFT+F1 and F1 keys, and Help buttons on dialog boxes. We believe, however, that command-topic index entries add value to an index.

Indexing command topics is easier than indexing procedure topics. There are fewer decisions to make and fewer index entries to assign. When choosing index entries for command topics, look for (1) exact matches of the topic title and (2) associated terms.

Exact matches

When entries for commands are included in the index ("Copy command"), there is rarely any need to modify the command name.

Associated terms

There are not likely to be synonyms for command topics, but there may be associated terms. Many of these will be the same as the associated terms in the corresponding procedure topics. So, for example, the associated terms "baud rate" and "settings," would be assigned both to the Communications Settings command topic and to the procedure topics that document the Communications Settings dialog box.

GENERATING INDEX ENTRIES FOR OTHER CATEGORIES OF HELP INFORMATION

Index entries should be assigned to certain other kinds of Help topics, notably overview topics and screen region topics. We offer no systematic method for generating these index entries, but some illustrations will prove helpful.

Overview topics will usually have concepts as index entries. For example, an overview topic dealing with color theory might have the index entries "RGB color model," "hue," "saturation," and "luminescence." Screen region topics should be assigned index entries that match the various interface elements. It is desirable to assign the index entry "shortcuts" to all the shortcut topics.

Although What's This? Help topics may replace command topics in many software products, they should not be indexed. They contain only a small amount of information and are usually designed to be read while the interface element they explain is displayed. Pop-up definitions are written to stand alone, so they can be indexed if they contain significant information not found in other Help topics.

Special problems: Managing entries and subentries

When a user chooses an entry in the index, one of two things occurs. If the index entry was assigned to one topic only, that topic is immediately displayed. If the index entry was assigned to multiple topics, the topic headings of all the topics are displayed in the Topics Found box, shown above in Figure 9.2, and the user chooses from this list. (To be more precise, the entries in the Topics Found window are topic titles—$ footnotes in the topic file—but these footnotes are usually identical or similar to the topic heading.)

Users cannot efficiently scan a large number of topics in the Topics Found box. Furthermore, if there are more than ten entries, this window will develop a vertical scrollbar, making the scanning task more burdensome. Therefore, if a Topics Found list will display more than eight or ten topic headings, the indexer should divide the main entry into more specific entries. You can do this in two ways: (1) by using indented subentries as qualifiers or (2) by using qualifiers in the main entry. Qualifiers logically divide or limit the main entries they pertain to.

When the main entry is a noun, you typically use indented subentries to divide a broad entry into more specific entries:

```
cards
        adding
        deleting
        editing
        formatting
```

You can also see the use of subentries in Figure 9.2.

When the main entry is a gerund, there is a choice. You can use indented subentries as qualifiers, or you can use a qualifier in the main entry itself. These two options are shown below, respectively.

```
numbering
        footnotes
        pages
        paragraphs

numbering footnotes
numbering pages
numbering paragraphs
```

If you are likely to have more than three or four qualified entries, it is usually best to use indented subentries. The user can more easily scan a list of indented subentries than a list of phrases consisting of gerunds with nouns.

There is one advantage to using gerunds with nouns, however. You can have subentries for each phrase, which allows for even more detail and specificity in the index.

```
numbering footnotes
numbering pages
        automatically
        troubleshooting problems with
numbering paragraphs
```

This technique is equivalent to a three-level index, which WinHelp 4 does not support but which can be found in many book indexes. In print a three-level index would look like this (though with the addition of page numbers):

```
numbering
        footnotes
        pages
                automatically
                troubleshooting problems with
        paragraphs
```

In WinHelp 3.1 indexers use punctuation (a comma or a colon) to imply a subentry, because they cannot format index entries as indented subentries. For an example, see the graphics entries in Figure 9.1.

THE NEED FOR STUB ENTRIES

The need for stub entries is a construction issue with an implication for design that needs to be considered here. At least in the initial release of WinHelp 4, the first subentry will not appear indented under the main entry. This is appropriate for a single entry that is inverted ("ASCII characters, listed"). But if there will be a list of subentries, the first should align with the rest and not appear on the same line as the main heading, as we see below:

> cards, adding
> > deleting
> > editing
> > formatting

The solution is to create a stub entry by coding at least one entry with a blank subentry, In this case, you would code an entry for one of your Help topics associated with cards as "cards, <space>" as shown below:

> Kcards, ; cards, adding;

This technique creates a stub entry and forces the first true subentry to indent.

STUB ENTRIES AS "UMBRELLA" ENTRIES

But what happens if the user clicks the stub entry? One possibility is for the stub entry to display a single topic, whatever topic the stub entry was arbitrarily assigned to. Users may wonder why a seemingly random topic appeared.

A better alternative is to assign the stub entry to every topic that will be a subentry of the main entry. So, for example, we could assign the stub entry to all topics pertaining to cards. (The entry "cards," of course, still appears only once in the index.) When the user clicks the stub entry "cards," he or she will see a complete list of the card topics.

This practice does not accord with traditional indexing. In a print index, you don't add page numbers to an entry that is divided into subentries. But some users may benefit from an "umbrella"-type entry, and it does prevent the display of an arbitrary Help topic.

The use of authoring tools for indexing

Many of the third-party authoring tools let Help authors add index entries more easily, and some provide the Entries with Topics report and the Topics with Entries report. Some authoring tools also automatically add index entries to topics. Currently, however, they add an entry based only on the topic title, which does not result in even a minimally acceptable index. For example, the topic "The Clipboard" would appear in the index among the "T" entries. We see that while Help authoring tools make indexing easier, they do not perform any of the intellectual work of indexing.

Merged indexes

WinHelp 4 allows you to merge index entries from multiple Help files, provided these Help files are specified in the contents file. Merged indexes require considerably more planning and editing than a normal index. If the merged Help files contain topics similar to one another, there are likely to be index entries that are illogical when merged together. For example,

```
formatting
        paragraphs ----------------------(assigned to topics in Help file A)
        text       ---------------------(assigned to topics in Help file A)
formatting text ---------------------(assigned to topics in Help file B)
```

The index entry "formatting text" should have been edited to fit into the subentry "text" under the main entry "formatting" instead of appearing as a unique entry.

Alternatives to the index

There are other forms of information access that function somewhat like online indexes. Below we discuss the WinHelp 4 full-text search feature and the natural-language type of indexing seen in Microsoft's Answer Wizard and Lotus's Ask the Expert.

THE FULL-TEXT SEARCH FEATURE

The WinHelp 4 full-text search feature appears as a page in the Help Topics dialog box. With this feature, the user can type a word or phrase in a text box, and WinHelp will display the titles of any topics that contain these characters. Users can also employ Boolean logic to enter multiple search terms and broaden or narrow their searches. Because full-text search is clearly a powerful feature and one that Help developers have long sought, these questions arise: How useful is full-text search? Does it replace the index?

The answers, we think, are that full-text search is primarily useful for savvy computer users and that it is no substitute for the index. There are several reasons:

1. The interface for the full-text search feature is complex and not intuitive, and so many users will not use full-text search.

2. Many users who learn to use this feature will still not formulate successful searches. They will, for example, often type overly broad search terms, such as "formatting," which will result in too many found topics. They will have difficulty constructing effective Boolean searches.

3. Even for proficient users the full-text search feature has significant limitations. Whereas a good indexer generates synonyms, associated terms, and other forms of rich indexing, the full-text search feature can only find a topic if the user's search terms appear in the topic.

NATURAL LANGUAGE INPUT

In Chapter 1, *Help and the Documentation Set*, we discussed the possibility of intelligent Help that would monitor the user's actions, infer the user's needs, and understand and respond to the user's natural language queries. This capability does not yet exist, but certain software vendors—notably Lotus (in Word Pro), Apple (in System 7.5), and Microsoft (in the Office 95 applications) have enhanced the online indexes of their Help systems so that they mimic natural language understanding. In these advanced indexes, users type questions in their own words.

Allowing users this kind of flexibility in entering index terms is a significant advance in online Help. We can hope that Help authors outside Lotus, Apple, and Microsoft will soon have the tools to create this kind of index. This powerful form of indexing, however, is no escape from the arduous task of creating a quality index. Indeed, this form of indexing requires significantly more effort and sophistication on the part of the indexer.

10

Creating Help Topics

Now that you're familiar with design principles and strategies for online Help, the second part of this book turns to the nuts and bolts of building a Windows Help system. This section explains everything you need to know in order to build a Help file, including how to create the help topic and project files, customize Help's interface, integrate graphics and multimedia, work with Help macros, design Help topic access, add context sensitive links, and build and debug the Help file.

Most of your Help development work will be spent creating Help topics. Each topic contains a discrete chunk of information, such as an explanation of a procedure or a pop-up definition of a key term.

This chapter covers:

- Organizing your topic files.

- Choosing a word processor.

- Creating a topic file.

- Defining Help topic properties.

Make sure you have planned both the organization and content of your Help system before you begin creating topic files. See Chapters 1 through 9, for more information about content and organizational strategies. For information on several software tools that help automate the process of creating topic files, see Chapter 22.

At a glance Help topic files

WinHelp 4.0	WinHelp 3.1
New window type footnote (>) lets you assign a default window to a topic; this window type is honored from the Index and Find tabs, and the new **ALink** and **KLink** macros.	All topics accessed through the keyword list default to the main window.
New A-keyword footnote lets you create special keywords for linking topics using the **ALink** macro.	All links must be created manually using hotspot formatting, or one of the Jump macros.
K-keyword footnotes (K) can be used to link topics using the **KLink** macro.	K-keywords used only for search keyword list.
Topic IDs (known as "context strings" in WinHelp 3.1) may contain spaces.	Spaces are invalid characters in "context strings."

Topic file overview

The topics in a Help system are stored in "topic files." A topic file is simply a rich-text format (.RTF) file containing the Help information as it appears to the user, plus *control codes*—footnotes and special formatting attributes (such as underline, double underline, and hidden text) that the Help compiler uses to build a Help file.

Most Help authors create their topic files in a word processor, as shown in Figure 10.1. Figure 10.2 shows the portion of the topic file that appears to the user once it is compiled into a Help file.

**Hard page break—
separates one
topic from another**

**Topic heading
and custom
footnote markers
(see below)**

Topic text

**Reference to a
bitmap graphic**

**Formatted hotspot
jump**

**Topic footnotes—
define topic ID,
title, keyword and
browse code**

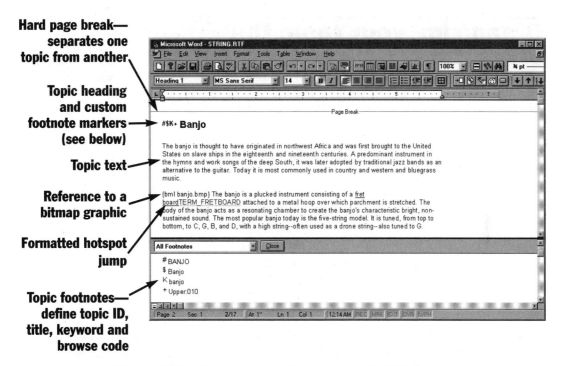

Figure 10.1. *How a sample topic appears to the Help author.*

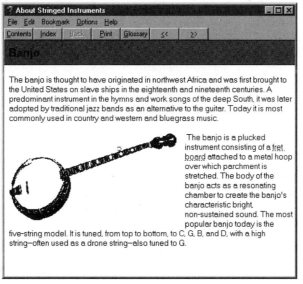

Figure 10.2. *How the same topic appears to the Help user.*

Organizing your topic files

Before you start building your Help system, you should plan how you are going to organize your topic files. A Help project may include one or more topic files. These topic files can be compiled into one Help file, or multiple Help files. This can be confusing to beginning Help authors who are trying to organize a Help project, but it's really no different than organizing the source files that make up a printed document.

With a small printed document, it usually makes sense to have the entire project in one file. Likewise, for a small Help project it's practical to place all of your topics in one topic file. This single topic file is compiled into one Help file.

Figure 10.3. *One topic file compiled into one Help file.*

Once a printed document gets to a certain size (perhaps six or eight chapters), most authors divide each chapter into a separate document. Similarly, many Help projects are organized into multiple topic files. These topic files are then compiled into one Help file (just as an average-sized book is bound into a single volume).

Figure 10.4. *Multiple topic files compiled into one Help file.*

Very large printed documents are not only divided into separate files, but they may be bound into separate volumes (reference guide, user guide, getting started, and so on). And so it is with large-scale Help projects: the separate topic files are compiled into multiple Help files. Under WinHelp 4, many Help authors also employ this modular design strategy for products that are composed of many different components.

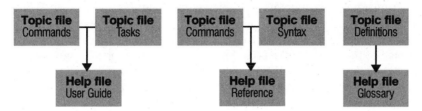

Figure 10.5. *Multiple topic files compiled into multiple Help files.*

The benefits of splitting a project into multiple topic files are many:

• Your word processor works faster when dealing with small files.

• Splitting a project minimizes source control problems on projects using multiple authors. You can assign topic files to individual authors and they can work on them concurrently.

• It is easier to find a particular topic for editing and debugging purposes. For example, you might place task-oriented topics in one file (TASK.RTF), commands in another (COMMANDS.RTF) and dialog boxes in a third (DIALOG.RTF).

• When testing interim builds, you can easily exclude individual topic files in order to speed up compilation time (just remove the topic file from the [FILES] section of the project file).

Choosing a word processor

You can use any word processor (or integrated Help authoring tool such as ForeHelp) that supports rich-text format files to create your topic files. Since rich-text formatting is stored as plain text, you can create topic files in *any* text editor. This is far from desirable, however, because rich-text formatting is represented with arcane .RTF "tokens."

```
\par \pard\plain \s1\sb120\sa120\keepn \b\f7\fs28 \page {\cs17\fs20\up6 #{\footnote \pard\plain \f7\fs20
{\cs17\b\f5\up6 #}{\b\f5 BANJO}}${\footnote \pard\plain \f7\fs20 {\cs17\b\f5\up6 $} {\b\f5
Banjo}}K{\footnote \pard\plain \f7\fs20 {\cs17\b\f5\up6 K}{
\b\f5 banjo}}+{\footnote \pard\plain \s18 \f7\fs20 {\cs17\f5\up6 +}{\f5 Upper:010}}} Banjo
\par \pard\plain \sb240\sa240 \f7\fs20 The banjo is thought to have originated in northwest Africa and wa
s first brought to the United States on slave ships in the eighteenth and nineteenth centuries. A
predominant instrument in the hymns and work songs of the deep South, it was later adopted by
traditional jazz bands as an alternative to the guitar. Today i
t is most commonly used in country and western and bluegrass music.
\par \pard \sa240 \{\bml banjo.bmp\} The banjo is a plucked instrument consisting of a {\ul fret
board}{\v\cfl1 TERM_FRETBOARD} attached to a metal hoop over which parchment is stretched. The
body of the banjo acts as a resona
ting chamber to create the banjo's characteristic bright, non-sustained sound. The most popular banjo
today is the five-string model. It is tuned, from top to bottom, to C, G, B, and D, with a high string--often
used as a drone string--also tuned to G.
```

Figure 10.6. *Topic files are simple text files marked up with obscure codes.*

If you're curious, you can open an .RTF file as text (see Figure 10.6): in Word, just check the Confirm Conversions box in the File Open dialog box and open any .RTF file. When prompted by the Convert File dialog box, highlight Text Only and click OK.

Making sense of these .RTF tokens is difficult, and a waste of time unless you're an .RTF hacker trying to achieve some special effect or troubleshoot a problem. If you're serious about developing Help and don't currently own a word processor, get one!

> **NOTE** *Although the WordPad accessory included with Windows 95 supports .RTF files, it does not support all of the .RTF formatting used in Help topic files. If you save a topic file using WordPad, you will lose all footnote information and hidden text will be converted to non-hidden text.*

Nearly all word processors support .RTF files, but most Help authors use Microsoft Word because it supports a wide variety of Help authoring tools. Another reason for Word's popularity is that some of the formatting and codes used to create Help topic files (such as custom footnote markers) are more easily accessible in Word than in other word processors.

Most word processors can work with their native file format (.DOC files in Word, for example) much more efficiently than they can rich-text format. Therefore, if you're working on a large project you may want to maintain two versions of your topic file—one in your editor's native format, and one in rich-text format. If you're using Word, for example, you could do your work in the .DOC file, and prior to each build use the Save As command from the File menu to save the file in the .RTF format.

Creating a topic file

Before you can build a Help topic, you must create a topic file. Of course, the actual steps will vary, depending on the type of topics you are creating.

To create a topic file:

1. Create a new document in your word processor.

2. Type one or more of the custom footnotes recognized by the Help compiler to define the properties for the Help topic. Each topic must include a pound sign (#) footnote (a topic ID); the other footnotes will vary, depending on the topic. See Table 10.1 for the various footnotes recognized by the Help compiler.

3. Type a topic heading. In the finished Help file this heading will appear at the beginning of the topic, just beneath Help's menu and/or button bar.

4. Insert the topic text. You can type the text, paste it from the Clipboard, or import it from an existing document.

5. Enter a hard page break to separate the topic from the others in the topic files. Each topic in the topic file must be preceded with a hard page break (an exception is the first topic in the file).

The procedure for creating a hard page break depends on your word processor; in Microsoft Word, for example, press CTRL+ENTER. The next figure illustrates a hard page break separating the topics named "Guitar" and "Acoustic Guitar."

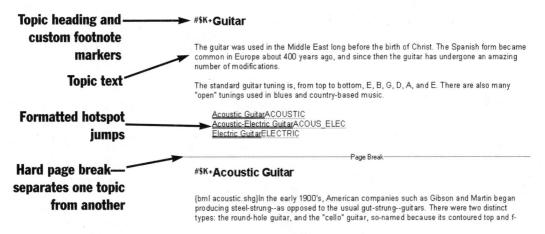

Figure 10.7. *Two Help topics separated by a hard page break.*

6. Repeat steps 2–5 for each topic you want to include in the topic file.

7. Save the file as rich-text format (.RTF file extension).

For simple Help systems, you may want to give your topic file the same basename (identical, except for the file extension) as that used for the project file. On larger Help systems containing multiple topic files, you should adopt a naming convention (for example, the topic file containing task information may be named TASKS.RTF, the overview topic file named OVERVIEW.RTF, and so on).

Help topic footnotes

The properties for each Help topic are defined by footnotes. When you build the Help file, the compiler either converts the footnotes into things the Help user can access (for example, keywords or topic titles), or uses them internally to manage the Help system (for example, topic IDs or topic entry macros).

The Help compiler recognizes nine footnotes, each of which is described in Table 10.1. All of the footnotes are optional except one: each topic must contain a topic ID.

Table 10.1. *Topic file control codes*

Footnote	What it creates	Description	Notes
Pound sign (#)	Topic ID	Uniquely identifies a topic.	Required for each topic. Known as "context strings" in WinHelp 3.1.
Dollar sign ($)	Title	Determines the title for the topic, as displayed in the Topics Found dialog box, the Bookmark dialog box, and the History window.	Generally used for most topics. Can be omitted for pop-up topics.
Plus sign (+)	Browse code	Determines the order of a topic within a browse sequence.	Used only if you add browse buttons to the button bar. Can be omitted for pop-up topics.
Letter "K" (K)	K-keyword	Creates keyword (s) used in the index.	Used for most topics, except pop-ups. Aside from their indexing value, K-keywords let you link topics using the **KLink** macro.
Letter "A" (A)	A-keyword	Creates special keyword(s) that don't appear in the index.	Used for topics that you want to access via the **ALink** macro.
Greater than symbol (>)	Default window type	Associates the topic with a Help window you define. Honored from the Index and Find tabs, and the linking macros.	Necessary only if your Help system uses secondary windows.
Asterisk (*)	Build-tag indicator	Determines which topics are included when the compiler builds the Help file.	Used only if you want to omit certain topics from the build. Rarely used by most Help authors.

Table 10.1. *(continued)*

Footnote	What it creates	Description	Notes
Exclamation point (!))	Topic entry macro	Runs a Help macro each time the user displays the topic.	Used to access Help's more advanced features.
At sign (@) or any other nonreserved footnote marker	Comment	Adds a comment to the topic.	Your comments are not visible to the Help user.

ASSIGNING HELP TOPIC FOOTNOTES

The footnotes you create for each Help topic will vary, depending on the type of topic you are creating. Most of your topics will include at least three footnotes—a topic ID (#), a topic title ($), and a search keyword (K). If you implement a browse sequence (a useful navigational aid for most Help systems), you will also add a browse code (+).

If you're creating a topic that will be accessed through a pop-up (such as a glossary entry), you need only assign a topic ID footnote (#).

To assign a footnote to a Help topic:

1. Place the insertion point at the very beginning of the first line in the topic heading and insert a footnote.

   In Word, click the Insert menu and click Footnote. The Footnote dialog box appears.

2. Type the appropriate symbol from Table 10.1 as a custom footnote marker. For example, to create a search keyword type an uppercase K (K).

   In Word, type the desired footnote marker in the **Custom Mark** box and click OK. The footnote marker will appear in the document window and the footnote pane will open.

3. Type the appropriate text to the right of the footnote marker in the footnote pane.

   For example, to create a search keyword you would type the text as you want it to appear in the keyword list.

4. When you're finished working in the footnote pane, move the insertion point back into the document window.

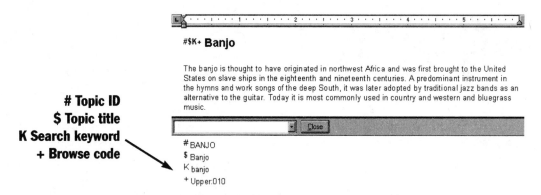

 # Topic ID
$ Topic title
K Search keyword
+ Browse code

Figure 10.8. *Topic properties for the Banjo topic.*

The following sections give specific information about how to create each of the footnotes in Word.

CREATING TOPIC IDs

The Help compiler requires a topic ID—a text string used to identify a topic—for each topic in your topic file. You will reference a topic ID each time you create a hypertext jump or pop-up. Topic IDs are used internally by Help Workshop and are never seen by the Help user.

You create a topic ID by inserting a #footnote marker. Each topic ID must be unique; that is, you can't use the same topic ID to refer to more than one topic in a Help file, even if the topics are in different .RTF files.

To create a topic ID:

1. Place the insertion point at the very beginning of the first line in the topic heading and insert a footnote.

   In Word, click the Insert menu and click Footnote. The Footnote dialog box appears.

2. Type a pound sign (#) as a custom footnote marker.

   In Word, type the footnote marker in the **Custom Mark** box and click OK. A superscript pound sign (#) appears in the text window and the insertion point moves to the footnote pane.

3. Type the topic ID to the right of the pound sign in the footnote pane.

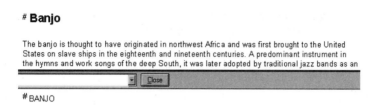

Figure 10.9. *Topic ID #BANJO identifies the topic named "Banjo."*

Notes on topic IDs

- Topic IDs may contain any character, except those reserved for other footnotes (# = > @ ! %). Topic IDs should not include leading or trailing spaces.

- Topic IDs are not case-sensitive; that is, the Help compiler treats "FILEOPEN," "FileOpen," and "fileopen" identically.

- A topic can have more than one topic ID. This is commonly used on long topics (such as glossary topics) to create a midtopic jump. For more information, see "Creating a mid-topic jump" in Chapter 11, *Creating Hypertext Links*.

- You may want to prefix the topic IDs for context-sensitive topics with IDH_. Help Workshop recognizes these as context-sensitive topics and displays information during the build that will help you troubleshoot any problems in your context-sensitive links (see Chapter 19, *Programming Calls to Help* for more information on context-sensitive Help). Don't begin context-sensitive topic IDs with a number.

- Although there are few naming restrictions for topic IDs, you should adopt a naming convention and stick with it. This is especially important if you're working on a large Help project with several authors.

  Create meaningful prefixes or suffixes. For example, you might prefix topics describing task-oriented procedures with TASK_, pop-up definitions with TERM_, overview topics with OVER_ and so forth.

  Be succinct yet descriptive. Extremely short names may be easy to type, but you will have a tough time remembering the contents of a topic if you haven't used it for a while.

- Unlike previous versions, WinHelp 4 now permits you to include spaces in a topic ID. However, you shouldn't include spaces in topic IDs that you will include in the [MAP] section of your project file.

  When the Help compiler encounters a space in mapped topic ID, it gets confused and displays an error message complaining about an invalid context ID. For example, the Help compiler recognizes "IDH_ELVIS" as a valid topic ID in a file included in the [MAP] section, but "IDH ELVIS" generates a compiler error. See Chapter 19 for more information.

- Keep in mind that if your Help project has multiple topic files, each topic ID in the entire project must be unique. For example, if your project has three topic files and one of them contains a topic ID called FILEOPEN, then you can't use that topic ID in either of the other two files (sometimes difficult to avoid if you're implementing What's This? Help in WinHelp 4).

- Devise a tracking system for your topic IDs. Using a database or a spreadsheet will help immensely, particularly on a large project. See Chapter 23, *Managing Help Projects* for more information on managing Help projects. The disc included with this book includes a macro called HelpTracker that will help you manage topic IDs.

CREATING TOPIC TITLES

Don't confuse topic titles with topic headings. The topic heading appears beneath the menu and button bars in the Help window.

Topic titles appear in four primary instances: in the Topics Found dialog box (Figure 10.10), the Find dialog box, the History list, and on the Bookmark menu. They also appear if the Find Similar option is used in the Find tab.

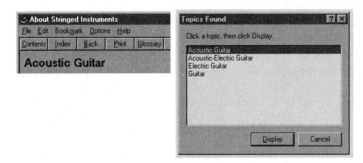

Figure 10.10. *Topic heading (left) and topic titles (right).*

You create a topic title by inserting a $ footnote marker.

To create a topic title:

1. Place the insertion point at the very beginning of the first line in the topic heading and insert a footnote.

   In Word, click the Insert menu and click Footnote. The Footnote dialog box appears.

2. Type a dollar sign ($) as a custom footnote marker.

   In Word, type the footnote marker in the **Custom Mark** box and click OK.

3. Type the topic title to the right of the dollar sign in the footnote pane.

#$Acoustic Guitar

{bml acoustic.shg}In the early 1900's, American companies such as Gibson and Martin began
producing steel-strung--as opposed to the usual gut-strung--guitars. There were two distinct
types: the round-hole guitar, and the "cello" guitar, so-named because its contoured top and f-

All Footnotes   Close

\# ACOUSTIC
$ Acoustic Guitar

Figure 10.11. *Topic title "Acoustic Guitar" matches the topic heading "Acoustic Guitar."*

Notes on topic titles

- Although they are not required, nearly all of your topics should have titles. Topic titles
  are mandatory for each topic that contains a keyword because such topics are frequently
  identified using their topic titles. Topics that don't have titles appear as (untitled #n), as
  shown in the next figure. This makes it difficult for the user to keep track of the Help topics that have been accessed.

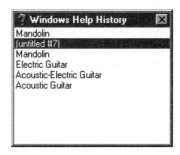

Figure 10.12. *How an untitled topic appears in the History list.*

- In general, the topic title should match the heading that appears in the topic—a user who
  double-clicks a topic title named "Creating a style sheet" may be confused if it displays a
  topic whose heading is something different, like "Working with style sheets."

- Many Help authors omit titles from their pop-up topics because they aren't accessible
  from the Topics Found dialog box or History list and can't be added to the Bookmark
  menu.

  WinHelp 4.0's full-text search may change this habit. By default, WinHelp's full text
  search index omits topics without titles. Therefore, you may elect to include a topic title
  for pop-up topics (such as a glossary definitions) that you want to be accessible via full
  text search. Other pop-ups—such as WinHelp 4's "What's This?" topics—are meaningless out of context and should not include topic titles.

- During the development of your Help project, heading names frequently change. Each time you change a heading, remember to open the footnote pane and change the topic title as well.

BUILDING KEYWORDS

Topic keywords are words (or phrases) associated with a topic, usually for indexing purposes. There are three kinds of keywords:

- K-keywords are primarily used to create search keyword entries. They are also used to create links using the **KLink** macro. With the exception of pop-ups, nearly all of your topics should have K-keywords.

- A-keywords are used to create links using the **ALink** macro. Together, they make it easy to create links to related topics, especially in a modular system that contains a variable number of Help files.

- Multi-index keywords let you create more than one keyword list for your Help file. These are seldom used by most Help authors.

Usability studies show that the keyword list is the first place most users turn for a quick answer to a specific problem. Unfortunately, keyword lists are often poorly implemented in Help systems. Developing a keyword list is a tedious and highly specialized skill, and is usually one of the last tasks in the project (which often means there is not enough time to do a proper job). Budget adequate time and resources in your Help development project to build a respectable keyword list!

A common misconception is that the addition of full-text search in WinHelp 4 reduces or even eliminates the need for a keyword list. This is simply untrue. As explained in Chapter 9, *Creating the Index*, full-text search serves the user well only if the user knows the exact text he or she is looking for.

K-keywords

K-keywords serve two purposes. First, and most important, they allow the user to quickly find information, much like index entries in a printed book. The user accesses K-keyword entries from the Index tab, illustrated in Figure 10.13. When the user selects a keyword and clicks Display, the topic appears, unless more than one topic matches the selected keyword, in which case the Topics Found dialog box appears (see Figure 10.14).

Figure 10.13. *How K-keywords appear to the Help user.*

K-keywords are also used by the **KLink** macro to create dynamic links to other Help topics. When the user accesses a link created using the **KLink** macro, WinHelp dynamically builds a list of every topic containing the K-keyword referenced in the macro and displays the list in the Topics Found dialog box.

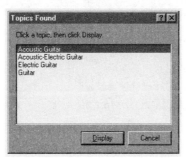

Figure 10.14. *A list of topics containing a specific keyword.*

Building links with K-keywords is especially useful for cross-referencing related (or "See Also") topics. Instead of building a list of hard-coded jumps, you can simply reference the **KLink** macro with the appropriate keyword. Using the **KLink** macro is invaluable if you're shipping a modular system that contains a variety of .HLP files. For more information on the KLink macro, see "Dynamic links: The ALink and **KLink** macros" in Chapter 11.

You create a K-keyword by inserting a K footnote marker.

To create a K-keyword:

1. Place the insertion point at the very beginning of the first line in the topic heading and insert a footnote.

   In Word, click the Insert menu and click Footnote. The Footnote dialog box appears.

2. Type an uppercase K (K) as a custom footnote marker.

   In Word, type the footnote marker in the **Custom Mark** box and click OK.

3. Type the keyword to the right of the uppercase K in the footnote pane. To enter more than one keyword, separate them with a semicolon (;). See "Notes on keywords" later in this section for more information.

K _{guitar}

Figure 10.15. *A K-keyword named "guitar."*

Multiple-level index entries

In WinHelp 4 you can create an index that is two levels deep. This depth makes your keywords very easy to read.

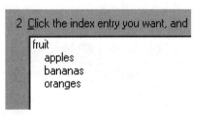

Figure 10.16. *Multiple-level index entries.*

To create a multiple-level index entry:

1. When you're entering your K-footnote, type the first-level keyword entry, then a comma and a semicolon (;).The first level keyword looks just like a single-level entry.

2. After the semicolon, type the first-level entry again, followed by a comma (,) or a colon (:).

3. Type a space and the second-level entry, followed by another space and a semicolon. This action results in the second-level keyword, indented beneath the first level.

For example, the three entries under "fruit" in Figure 10.16 were created with the following K footnotes in the appropriate topics:

```
fruit,;fruit, apples,;
fruit,;fruit, bananas,;
fruit,;fruit, oranges,;
```

The first keyword—**fruit,**—creates the first level of the index. Because you added this keyword to each of the topics associated with fruit, all of those topics will appear in the Topics Found dialog box when the user clicks the keyword **fruit**. It may be tempting to cut corners and add the **fruit** keyword to only one topic—that's all you have to do to have **fruit** appear in the keyword list. But then, the keyword **fruit** would be appear on a line by itself in the index and would not show apples, bananas, and oranges as subordinate entries.

Sorting keyword phrases

If you're building a fairly sophisticated index, it probably contains keyword phrases (keyword entries that contain more than one word, such as **fruit juice**). If your index contains keyword phrases, make sure you insert a comma before the semicolon or WinHelp will sort your index incorrectly.

For example, consider the two groups of keywords illustrated in Table 10.2. Both groups contain keyword phrases (**fruit juice** and **vegetable juice**). Notice however, that the fruit entries contain a comma before the semicolon, but that the vegetable entries do not.

Now look at how WinHelp sorts the entries. Because the second level entries for fruit contain a comma, they look fine. The vegetable entries, however, are a mess. If your index contains keyword phrases, make sure to add a comma before the semicolon!

Table 10.2. *Keyword phrases (left) and how they are sorted in WinHelp*

```
fruit,;fruit, apples,;              fruit juice
fruit,;fruit, bananas,;             fruit
fruit,;fruit, oranges,;               apples
fruit juice;                          bananas
vegetable;                            oranges
vegetable;vegetable, tomatoes;      vegetable
vegetable;vegetable, carrots;       vegetable juice
vegetable;vegetable, potatoes;      vegetable, carrots
vegetable juice;                      potatoes
                                      tomatoes
```

A couple of idiosyncrasies. First, notice that "fruit juice" appears before "fruit" since WinHelp sorts "fruit " (that is, "fruit" and a space) before "fruit, " ("fruit" and a comma). Also, notice that the comma is omitted before the semicolon in the keyword "fruit juice" since WinHelp will include the comma and display the keyword as **fruit juice,**.

Converting WinHelp 3.1 keyword lists

If you're converting a WinHelp 3.1 project, this new feature will affect your existing keywords. Although WinHelp 3.1 supports only a single-level index entry, many Help authors group their entries by entering the first-level "keyword," a comma, and the second-level keyword entry.

For example, the WinHelp 3.1 keywords for the three fruit topics would look like:

```
fruit, apples
fruit, bananas
fruit, oranges
```

Such keywords will certainly work when displayed by WinHelp 4, but they will look like this:

Figure 10.17. *WinHelp 3.1 keywords that simulate*
multiple levels look like this under WinHelp 4.

To take advantage of the new two-level keyword index in WinHelp 4, you must add the footnote **fruit,**; to each of the appropriate topics. When planning your WinHelp 3.1 conversion, you should probably set aside some time to revise your search keywords.

A-keywords

A-keywords are very similar to K-keywords, except that they are invisible to the user (that is, they don't appear in the Help index). Thus they have one valuable purpose: they enable *associative* links between topics. If you want to suggest that the user look at some other topics that are related to the topic at hand, but not related so strongly that they would share K-keywords, you can use the **ALink** macro. When the user accesses a link created using the **ALink** macro, WinHelp dynamically looks for all of the topics containing the A-keyword referenced in the macro and displays the list in the Topics Found dialog box.

Like K-keywords, A-keywords are useful for building links to related topics, especially if you're shipping a modular Help system and aren't sure which Help files are installed. In fact, the **ALink** macro has several advantages over the **KLink** macro—they are easier to localize, and often take less coordination with other Help authors (See "Dynamic links: The ALink and KLink macros" in Chapter 11).

You create an A-keyword by inserting an "A" footnote marker.

To create an A-keyword:

1. Place the insertion point at the very beginning of the first line in the topic heading and insert a footnote.

   In Word, click the Insert menu and click Footnote. The Footnote dialog box appears.

2. Type an uppercase A (A) as a custom footnote marker.

   In Word, type the footnote marker in the **Custom Mark** box and click OK.

3. Type the keyword to the right of the uppercase A in the footnote pane. Separate multiple keywords with semicolons (;).

ᴬ allguitars

Figure 10.18. *An A-keyword named "allguitars."*

Notes on keywords

- Keywords are not case-sensitive and may contain spaces and punctuation. Most authors create keywords using lowercase letters (unless the keyword is a proper noun), just like in a printed index.

- You can add more than one keyword to a topic; this is usually done by separating the keywords with a semicolon. Figure 10.19, for example, contains two keywords separated by a semicolon (guitar;acoustic guitar). If you want to use a semicolon within one of your keywords, you can define an alternate separator character (see Chapter 18, *Creating the Project File*).

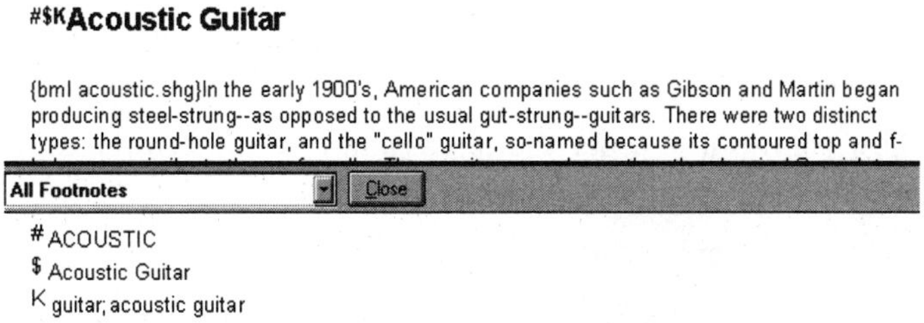

#$ᴷ**Acoustic Guitar**

{bml acoustic.shg}In the early 1900's, American companies such as Gibson and Martin began producing steel-strung--as opposed to the usual gut-strung--guitars. There were two distinct types: the round-hole guitar, and the "cello" guitar, so-named because its contoured top and f-

| All Footnotes | ▾ | Close |

\# ACOUSTIC
\$ Acoustic Guitar
ᴷ guitar; acoustic guitar

Figure 10.19. *Adding multiple keywords to a topic.*

- Remember that the user selects a topic from the Topics Found dialog box using its topic title. Therefore, it is essential that each topic containing a keyword also contain a title. For complete information on topic titles, see the previous section "Creating topic titles."

- If you enter two or more keywords that are identical except for case (such as "Opening a File" and "opening a file"), Help Workshop will change the keywords so they are consistent and display a warning message.

- You can assign a keyword footnote to a specific paragraph in the topic. Such a keyword enables you to jump to a specific point in the topic from the search keyword list (see "Creating a midtopic jump" in Chapter 11).

- You can also associate a Help macro with a keyword, so that when the user clicks the keyword WinHelp runs the macro. For example, you might use this to access specific tasks in a tutorial from your Help index. For more information, see "Running Help macros" in Chapter 16.

Multi-index keywords

Windows Help also supports multiple keyword tables. Though not widely used, this can be a valuable feature if you're documenting an application that has commands or terms corresponding to those in a similar application. For complete information on multiple keyword tables, see the topic on the MULTIKEY option in the online *Help Author's Guide*.

CREATING BROWSE SEQUENCE CODES

Browse codes are used to build "browse sequences," navigational aids that enable a user to leaf back and forth through related Help information, much like in a printed book. Browse sequences can help add structure to a nonlinear medium that can be confusing. Although many Help systems don't include browse sequences—Microsoft's are prime examples—they are a valuable addition to almost any Help file.

Browse sequences are accessed by two buttons on Help's button bar: the button labeled >> (called the "Next" button) moves forward, and the << button (or "Previous") moves back. At the beginning of a browse sequence, the << button is disabled; at the end of a sequence, the >> button is disabled. If there is no browse sequence defined, both browse buttons are disabled.

The order of the topics in a browse sequence is established by the Help author. Creating a browse sequence is a three-step process:

1. Think about how you want to order the topics and plan the browse sequence. There are two types of browse sequences: single-level and multiple-level.

2. Implement the browse sequence using browse codes.

3. Use the Help project file (.HPJ) to add the browse buttons to the button bar. See "Creating a button bar" in Chapter 15 for complete information.

Planning a browse sequence

There are two main types of browse sequences: single-level and multiple-level. Single-level browse sequences are like a giant chain, with the topics ordered sequentially from start to finish. Multiple-level browse sequences contain branches, much like a web.

Suppose you're documenting the menu commands for an application. You might order the commands alphabetically, from A to Z, in a single-level browse sequence.

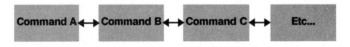

Figure 10.20. *A single-level browse sequence.*

Alternatively, you could create one browse sequence that accesses the various menus (File, Edit, View, and so on), and another that accesses the menu commands. This would be a multiple-level browse sequence.

For example, one browse sequence could move through the menu topics (File, Edit, View, and so on). However, once the user accesses a command topic (say, the New command on the File menu), the sequence would browse to the next command on that menu (Open, Save, Save As, and so on through Exit).

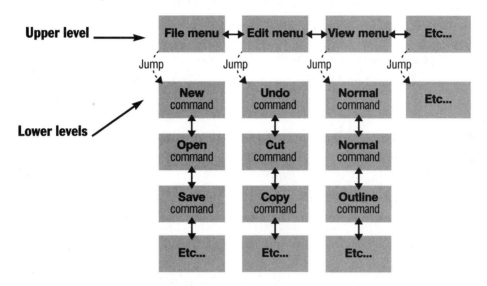

Figure 10.21. *A multiple-level browse sequence.*

Your Help file can contain any number of browse sequences, but each topic may appear in only one browse sequence. Before you begin coding a browse sequence, it's a good idea to sketch out a diagram detailing how you want to order each topic. If you want to display a topic in more than one browse sequence, you can create a duplicate or "dummy" topic.

How browse codes are sorted

To create a browse sequence, you assign a plus sign (+) footnote marker to each topic. As it builds the Help file, the Help compiler sorts the browse codes. There are three approaches to entering browse codes; the method you use will usually depend on the size of your Help project.

- **Sorting topics in the order of appearance.** If you want the Help compiler to sort the topics sequentially using the order in which they appear in the topic file, type an identical browse code footnote for each of your topics (for example, leave the footnote text blank or type **auto**). If your Help project contains multiple topic files, Help will sort the topics in each file beginning with the first file listed in the [FILES] section of the project file.

This approach is practical for small projects, but can quickly become unmanageable as a project grows.

> **TIP** *You can quickly re-order your topics by using the outline mode in your word processor.*

- **Sorting topics alphabetically**. To order a browse sequence alphabetically by topic title, simply type the topic title in the footnote pane. For example, the browse code for a topic titled "Copy command" topic might be "Copy command"; it would appear before "Delete command" in the browse sequence.

  This approach works well for reference information.

- **Sorting topics numerically**. For medium to large projects, you probably want to assign numeric codes and sort topics numerically. You should use the same number of characters for each browse code. For example, although the number 15 is higher than 5, topic 15 will come before topic 5 since the compiler sorts the codes alphabetically (comparing "1" to "5"). To correct the problem, enter your browse codes using two- or three-digit numbers (for example, 05 or 005).

\# BANJO
\$ Banjo
K banjo
+ Upper:010

\# GUITAR
\$ Guitar
A guitar
+ Upper:015

Figure 10.22. *Numeric browse codes.*

It's a good idea to begin your browse sequence at 010 and enter numbers in increments of 10 (020, 030, and so on). This makes it easy for you to insert a topic in the middle of the sequence if it is necessary to do so later in the project. The Help compiler ignores skipped numbers.

Adding a browse code

Browse codes are implemented using a plus sign (+) footnote marker. You can define browse code footnotes as either numbers or characters; browse codes are not case sensitive.

To add a browse code:

1. Place the insertion point at the very beginning of the first line in the topic heading and insert a footnote.

   In Word, click the Insert menu and click Footnote. The Footnote dialog box appears.

2. Type a plus sign (+) as a custom footnote marker.

   In Word, type the footnote marker in the **Custom Mark** box and click OK.

3. Type the browse code to the right of the plus sign in the footnote pane.

+ 005

Figure 10.23. A numeric browse code.

Creating a multiple level browse sequence

The footnotes for a multiple-level browse sequence will typically contain a group name, which identifies the browse-sequence level, and a sequence number, separated by a colon: **menu:005**. For example, to create the multiple-level browse sequence illustrated previously in Figure 10.21, you might enter the browse codes listed in the following table.

Table 10.2. *Multiple-level browse codes*

Menu	Topic	Browse code
File Menu		main:010
	New	file:010
	Open	file:020
	Save	file:030
	Save As	file:040
	Quit	file:050
Edit Menu		main:020
	Undo	edit:010
	Cut	edit:020
	Copy	edit:030
	Paste	edit:040
	Paste Special	edit:050
View Menu		main:030
	Normal	view:010
	Outline	view:020
	Page Layout	view:030
	Draft	view:040

Notes on browse codes

- If you want to exclude a topic from a browse sequence, simply omit the footnote marker. For example, you don't need to include browse codes for topics that appear only in pop-ups, or in Help windows that don't include browse buttons.

- To quickly add browse codes, copy the + footnote reference marker and paste it into each topic, then open the footnote pane and edit the code.

- If you create a multiple-level browse sequence, you should probably create an "Up" button that jumps to the top level in the browse sequence. Otherwise, in order to get back to the menu topics, the user would need to access the Contents tab, the Back button, or the History list. For information on creating an Up button, see "Conditionally modifying the Help interface" in Chapter 16.

SPECIFYING A WINDOW TYPE FOR A TOPIC

WinHelp 3.1 doesn't provide much control over the window used to display a Help topic. Topics accessed from the search keyword list, for instance, always appear in the main window.

WinHelp 4.0 gives you the ability to associate a topic with a particular window type. This window type will then be the default window for the topic. This makes it easy to consistently control the presentation of your Help information; for example, "How To" topics can appear in small auto-sized windows, reference information in a larger main window, code samples in another, and so on. If a default window is not specified, topics appear in either the main or current Help window.

A topic will appear in this default window each time the user opens it from:

- The Index and Find tabs.

- An **ALink** or **KLink** macro.

The default window type is specified using a greater than symbol (>) footnote marker.

To specify a window type for a topic:

1. Place the insertion point at the very beginning of the first line in the topic heading and insert a footnote.

   In Word, click the Insert menu and click Footnote. The Footnote dialog box appears.

2. Type a greater than symbol (>) as a custom footnote marker.

   In Word, type the footnote marker in the **Custom Mark** box and click OK.

3. Type the name of the window to the right of the greater than symbol in the footnote pane. The window type must be defined in your project (.HPJ).

```
>proc
```

Figure 10.24. *A default window type named "proc."*

When this topic is displayed from the Find or Index tabs, or from an **ALink** or **KLink** macro, it will appear in the window type "proc."

The default window is honored in most cases, but what about standard hotspot jumps? These will require you to append the ">windowname" to the end of the topic ID, just as you do under WinHelp 3.1. Similarly, the default window type is not honored from the contents file, so you will need to append ">windowname" to topic statements (or type the window type in the **Window Type** box of Help Workshop). For more information on jumping to a topic in a secondary window, see "Special types of links" in Chapter 11.

This inconsistency is guaranteed to create all kinds of confusion. In fact, the Microsoft team that built WinHelp wanted to honor the default window type for all jumps, but ran out of time and thought honoring it in some cases (that is, Index and Find tab, plus the **ALink** and **KLink** macros) was better than dropping the default window feature altogether.

ADDING CONDITIONAL BUILD TAGS

From time to time in the course of your Help development, you may want to exclude topics from a Help system. For example, you may want to temporarily exclude incomplete topics from a test build, or create different builds using the same topic files.

Build tags let you control which topics are included in your Help system. Build tags are completely optional; any topics without build tags will always be included in your build.

Implementing a conditional build tag is a two-step process:

1. Insert the build tags into the topic file.

2. Use the project file to instruct the Help compiler which topics you wish to include or exclude. For information on specifying which topics are built, see "Controlling which topics are compiled" in Chapter 20.

You create a build tag by inserting an asterisk (*) footnote marker. The build tag footnote must be the first footnote in the topic, or it is ignored by the Help compiler. A topic can have one or more build tags.

To create a build tag:

1. Place the insertion point at the very beginning of the first line in the topic heading and insert a footnote. Make sure the build tag is the first footnote in the topic.

   In Word, click the Insert menu and click Footnote. The Footnote dialog box appears.

2. Type an asterisk (*) as a custom footnote marker.

   In Word, type the footnote marker in the **Custom Mark** box and click OK.

3. Type the build tag to the right of the asterisk in the footnote pane.

* Incomplete

Figure 10.25. *A sample build tag used to denote a topic that is incomplete.*

Notes on build tags

- Build tags can include both letters and numbers, and are not case-sensitive. The tag cannot include any spaces. If you want to create multiple build tags, use a semicolon to separate them.

- A major limitation of build tags is that excluding a topic from your build will cause errors in any other topics that include a link to that topic. For instance, if topic B is a destination for jumps contained in topic A, excluding topic B from the build will create an error in topic A.

  You can work around the problem by creating dummy topics that remove any jumps that are broken by the build tags (duplicate topic A as topic C, remove the links to B in topic C, and then add build tags so that Help builds topics B and C instead of A and B). This approach quickly becomes unwieldy, particularly on "web-like" Help systems with an abundance of links. For this reason, most Help authors give up on "single sourcing" their projects with build tags and maintain separate topic files for each Help project.

CREATING TOPIC ENTRY MACROS

WinHelp 4 contains over 85 macros that let you customize the appearance and behavior of your Help files. For example, you can use macros to customize Help's button bar and menus, manage windows, or run other Windows programs.

If you place a macro in a topic footnote, it is executed when the user first displays the topic. These so-called "topic entry" macros are ideal for customizing a specific topic—perhaps you want to add a button to the button bar, add a menu item, or run another program.

You create a topic entry macro by inserting an exclamation point (!) as the footnote marker.

To create a topic entry macro:

1. Place the insertion point at the very beginning of the first line in the topic heading and insert a footnote.

   In Word, click the Insert menu and click Footnote. The Footnote dialog box appears.

2. Type an exclamation mark (!) as a custom footnote marker.

   In Word, type the footnote marker in the **Custom Mark** box and click OK.

3. Type the macro to the right of the exclamation point in the footnote pane. The following example adds a button named WIN.INI to the button bar when the user displays the topic. The button runs the **ExecFile** macro to open the WIN.INI file.

```
! CreateButton(btn_ini, WIN.INI, ExecFile(win.ini))
```

Figure 10.26. *Topic entry macro that creates a button named WIN.INI when the user displays the topic.*

If you want to run more than one macro when the Help topic is opened, separate the macros with colons or semicolons. For more information on macros, see Chapter 16: Working with Help Macros.

> **TIP** *If you want to customize all of the topics in a Help file, add a macro to the [CONFIG] section of the project file. See "Running Help macros" in Chapter 16 for more information.*

ADDING AUTHOR COMMENTS

You might want to enter a comment to document a tricky macro, flag an unfinished topic, or write a note to a coworker on the project. Your comments are not visible to the Help user and don't increase the size of your finished Help file.

You add a comment to a topic by inserting an at sign (@) footnote marker.

To add an author comment:

1. Place the insertion point at the very beginning of the first line in the topic heading and insert a footnote.

   In Word, click the Insert menu and click Footnote. The Footnote dialog box appears.

2. Type an at symbol (@) as a custom footnote marker.

   In Word, type the footnote marker in the Custom Mark box and click OK.

3. Type the comment to the right of the at symbol in the footnote pane.

```
@ don't forget to update this before shipping
```

Figure 10.27. *An author comment.*

WORKING WITH HELP TOPIC FOOTNOTES

Adding and editing multiple topics can be very repetitious, even in an authoring tool. Oftentimes, the quickest way to add topics or edit the properties for a Help topic is to use the footnote pane. To edit a footnote, you can simply open the footnote pane and edit the footnote text.

When creating Help topics, it is often convenient to copy an existing footnote, paste it into the desired topic, and then edit the footnote as necessary. To copy a footnote, select the footnote marker in the document window and press CTRL+C. You can then move the insertion point to another topic and paste the footnote by pressing CTRL+V.

To delete a footnote, open the document window and select the footnote mark you want to delete and press BACKSPACE or DELETE. Note that you cannot delete a footnote from within the footnote pane.

11

Creating Hypertext Links

The ability to create electronic cross-references, or "hypertext links," is one of the biggest strengths of a system like Windows Help. Links provide the user with several paths to information, each path accessible with just a click of the mouse. For the author, hypertext can simplify the organization of documents, breaking the linear restrictions of traditional print media.

This chapter explains how to add hypertext links to your Help topic files. For information on how to add links to other parts of a Help system (such as the Contents or Index tabs), see Chapter 17, *Help Topic Access*. For information on how to add hypertext links to a graphic image, see Chapter 13, *Creating Help Graphics*.

This chapter covers:

- Creating basic jumps and pop-ups.

- Creating links using Help macros, including the **ALink** and **KLink** macros.

- Creating special links, including interfile jumps to topics in other Help files, jumps to a topic in another window, and midtopic jumps.

Since hypertext links contain hidden text, it's a good idea to set your word processor to display hidden characters while you edit your topic file. In Word, choose Options from the Tools menu, click the View tab, and make sure the Hidden Text option is checked. Word displays hidden text with a dotted underline.

At a glance Hypertext link support

WinHelp 4.0	WinHelp 3.1
New **ALink** and **KLink** macros enable you to build dynamic links that are created when the user runs the Help file.	All links must be created when you compile the Help file.
Can jump to a topic from the contents file.	

Creating basic links

There are two basic ways to create a link: you can use character formatting in your word processor, or you can use Help macros. This section explains how to create basic links using character formatting in your word processor.

CREATING A JUMP

Jumps are used to connect topics in your Help system. When the mouse pointer moves over a jump (called "hotspot text"), the pointer changes shape to a hand. When the user clicks the hotspot text, WinHelp displays the topic specified by the topic ID.

> The mandolin has eight steel strings tuned in four pairs to the notes G, D, A, and E. Like the violin and the <u>banjo</u>, the mandolin is tuned to open fifths. This tuning provides a different set of chords than is available on the <u>guitar</u>.

Figure 11.1. *How jumps appears to the Help user.*

Figure 11.2 illustrates how a standard jump appears to the Help author.

Jump text formatted with a double underline → jump texttopicID ← Topic ID formatted with hidden text

Figure 11.2. *Anatomy of a standard jump.*

Jump text—what the user sees in the compiled Help file—can be any series of characters. By default, WinHelp 4 displays jumps using green text with a single underline; WinHelp 3.1 uses a double underline. For information on how to control the appearance of the jump, see "Customizing the appearance of links" later in this chapter.

TopicID specifies the topic ID of the destination topic. The user does not see this text in the finished Help file. When the user clicks the jump text, Help displays the specified topic in the current window type. See "Jumping to a topic and displaying it in another window type" later in this chapter for more information on how to specify the window type used to display a topic. To jump to a topic contained in another Help file, see "Linking to a topic in another Help file" later in this chapter.

> **TIP** *To make it easy to identify hotspots while working in the topic file, many Help authors format the hotspot using green text. The color you use in your word processor does not affect the appearance of the finished Help file (unless you type an asterisk or percent sign before the topic ID; see "Customizing the appearance of links" later in this chapter).*

To create a jump:

1. Place the insertion point directly after the text or bitmap you want to be the jump.

2. Type the topic ID associated with the destination topic (the topic to which you want to jump). You must not leave any spaces between the jump text and the topic ID.

   The topic ID will not be visible to the Help user; it simply tells Help which topic to display when the user clicks the jump text.

3. Select the jump text and change its character formatting to double underline.

4. Select the topic ID. Turn off the double underline and change the character formatting to hidden.

5. Be sure to change the character formatting back to non-hidden before typing any new text.

   This avoids formatting additional characters as hidden text, which would cause text to disappear, or, in the case of paragraph markers, create errors in your Help file. The disc included with this book includes a WordBasic macro named "FixHiddenParagraphs" that will unhide hidden paragraph markers.

The following example creates hotspot text reading "Getting Started" that jumps to the topic with the topic ID "getstart."

```
Getting Startedgetstart
```

After you've compiled your Help file, you'll want to test your jumps to be sure they go to the correct topics. For information on debugging strategies, see Chapter 20, *Compiling, Debugging, and Testing.*

CREATING A POP-UP

Pop-ups are similar to jumps, except that instead of switching to another topic, they display a small box over the current topic. Pop-ups are most commonly used to define key terms, but they are well-suited for any information that is brief (such as short tips or shortcuts). You can also include a graphic image in a pop-up, a useful way to illustrate toolbar buttons or other small screen images. Last, but not least, under WinHelp 4 pop-ups are used for What's This? topics.

> The banjo is a plucked instrument
> consisting of a fret board attached
> to a metal hoop over which
> parchment is stretched. The body

Figure 11.3. *How a pop-up appears to the Help user.*

The syntax used to create a pop-up is identical to that used for a jump, except that you format the hotspot text using a single underline. Figure 11.4 illustrates how a standard pop-up appears to the Help author.

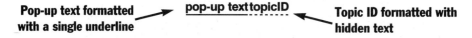

Figure 11.4. *Anatomy of a pop-up.*

Pop-up text can be any series of characters. This is what the user sees in the compiled Help file. By default, WinHelp displays pop-ups using green text with a dotted underline; the color you use in your word processor does not affect the appearance of the finished Help file. For information on how to control the appearance of the jump, see "Customizing the appearance of links" later in this chapter.

TopicID specifies the topic ID of the destination topic. The user does not see this text in the finished Help file. When the user clicks the pop-up text, Help displays the specified topic in a pop-up window. The following example creates pop-up text reading "Windows Help" that displays the topic "term_winhelp" in a pop-up window.

```
Windows Helpterm_winhelp
```

For information on how to pop up a topic from another Help file, see "Linking to a topic in another Help file" later in this chapter.

To create a pop-up:

1. Place the insertion point directly after the text or bitmap you want to be the pop-up.

2. Type the topic ID associated with the topic you want to pop-up. You must not leave any spaces between the pop-up text and the topic ID.

   The topic ID will not be visible to the Help user; it simply tells Help which topic to display when the user clicks the pop-up text.

3. Select the pop-up text and change its character formatting to single underline.

4. Select the topic ID. Turn off the single underline and change the character formatting to hidden.

5. Be sure to change the character formatting back to non-hidden before typing any new text.

   This avoids formatting additional characters as hidden text, which would cause text to disappear, or, in the case of paragraph markers, create errors in your Help file. The disk included with this book includes a WordBasic macro named "FixHiddenParagraphs" that will unhide hidden paragraph markers.

Creating links with macros

Although most jumps are created using standard character formatting in your word processor, you can also link topics using Help macros. While creating links with Help macros is a little more difficult than using hotspot formatting, macros are essential if you want to:

- Create a link that is not activated by a hotspot. For example, if you want to link a topic through a menu item, a button on the button bar or whenever the user enters a topic, you need to use a macro. You must also use a macro when creating a link using an authorable button. For information on creating menu items and buttons see Chapter 15: *Creating the Help Interface*. To learn how to create a topic entry macro, see Chapter 16: *Working with Help Macros*.

- Link a topic and perform another action (such as close a window or run another application) all in one step. Macros can be chained to perform several actions at once.

- Create a link to a topic in another .HLP file that is resolved dynamically when the user accesses a hotspot. This lets you design Help files that are modular (you can link to optional Help files that may not be installed on the user's system without causing an error) and extensible (you can link to topics in Help files that don't yet exist, but might be installed at a later date).

Help macros offer a very powerful and flexible way to create hypertext links, but at a price. Consider the following tradeoffs as you decide whether to create links using macros or standard hotspot formatting:

- Standard hotspots are easier to debug than Help macros because the Help compiler checks each jump hotspot to make sure you entered a valid topic ID. This checking is not performed on macro hotspots.

- Standard hotspots are a little easier to create since you don't have to remember the macro syntax. Granted, the macro syntax in WinHelp 4 is simpler than it was in WinHelp 3.1, but standard hotspots are still the easiest way to go.

- Pop-ups created using the **PopupID** macro will appear in the compiled Help file with a single underline rather than a dotted underline. This inconsistency may confuse your users since they won't be able to tell the difference between a jump and a pop-up.

The formatting used to create a macro hotspot is identical to that used for a jump, except that the hotspot text is followed by an exclamation mark and the appropriate macro syntax. Figure 11.5 illustrates how a macro hotspot appears to the Help author.

Hotspot text formatted with a double underline → hotspot text!Helpmacro ← **Macro syntax, preceded with an exclamation point and formatted with hidden text**

Figure 11.5. *Anatomy of a macro hotspot.*

Hotspot text can be any series of characters. This is what the user sees in the compiled Help file. *Helpmacro* is the macro you want to run when the user clicks the hotspot. It must be preceded with an exclamation point. For example, the following macro hotspot runs the **KLink** macro and displays a list of the topics containing the keyword "printing."

```
Related Topics!KLink(printing)
```

To create a hotspot using a macro:

1. Place the insertion point directly after the text or bitmap you want to be the hotspot.

2. Type an exclamation mark (!) followed by the Help macro. You must not leave any spaces between the hotspot text, the exclamation mark, and the macro.

3. Change the character formatting of the hotspot text or graphic to double underline.

4. Change the character formatting of the exclamation mark and Help macro to hidden.

5. Be sure to change the character formatting back to non-hidden before typing any new text. This will help you avoid formatting characters as hidden text.

DYNAMIC LINKS: THE ALINK AND KLINK MACROS

Creating and maintaining standard topic links is a very time-consuming process. Entering the proper topic ID and testing the hotspots is tedious work, especially on a large Help project. Furthermore, standard links are very finite: each link displays one topic and one topic only.

Two new macros in WinHelp 4—**ALink** and **KLink**—let you create dynamic links to topics in other .HLP files. Links created using these macros are automatically updated as you add or delete .HLP files to your Help system.

When the user accesses a jump created using the **ALink** or **KLink** macro, WinHelp searches the current Help file (plus any others in the family of Help files, as defined in the contents file) for any topics containing that keyword. It quickly builds a list of those topics and displays them in the Topics Found dialog box, from which the user can select a destination.

Figure 11.6. *Topics Found dialog box.*

Implementing these macros is a two-step process:

1. When you build a topic, you add a topic footnote using either the standard K-keyword, or the new A-keyword ("associative" keyword). The only difference between the two is that the A-keyword will not appear in Help's keyword search list. See "Building keywords" in Chapter 10 for more information on adding keywords to your topic files.

2. Create a jump by referencing the appropriate keyword in an **ALink** or **KLink** macro hotspot.

ALink and **KLink** will certainly prove to be two of the most useful additions to WinHelp 4. Because they let WinHelp resolve the jumps at runtime, instead of when the Help file is built, these macros let you build Help systems that are:

- **Modular** You can link to optional Help files that may or may not be present on the user's system. When WinHelp builds the list of linked topics, it looks for all of the .HLP files listed in the contents file for the project. If an .HLP file is on the user's system, the link will be accessible to the user; if one of the specified .HLP files is not available, WinHelp skips it without displaying an error message.

- **Extensible** You can add links today that access tomorrow's Help files. As more .HLP files are installed on the user's system, more topics will appear in the Topics Found dialog box.

An example

Let's look at an example. Consider the Help author who wants to build a list of "See Also" cross-references for each topic explaining how to print. Under WinHelp 3.1, the author must manually create a link for each related topic, carefully entering each topic ID.

Setting up your printerPrinter_setup
Printing multiple pagesPrinting_multiple_pages
Printing an envelopePrinting_an_envelope
Printing an outlinePrinting_an_outline

Figure 11.7. *A SeeAlso list built using standard jumps.*

Under WinHelp 4, the task is made much simpler by the **KLink** macro. Assuming that each topic has a K footnote named "printing" (a fair assumption, since each topic is probably referenced in the keyword list under "printing"), the author creates a single link:

See Also!KLink(printing)

Figure 11.8. *Building a SeeAlso list using a* **KLink** *macro.*

When the user clicks the hotspot, WinHelp instantly builds a list of all related topics. If the user installed the .HLP for the whizbang new print spooler utility (referenced in a **:Link** or **:Index** command in the contents file), any of its related topics will appear in the Topics Found dialog box. If the .HLP file is not installed on the user's system, no problem: WinHelp will not display an error message.

Choosing between ALink and KLink

How do you decide whether to use **ALink** or **KLink**? Implementing **KLink** macros takes less work initially—you can use existing K-keywords without adding new A-keywords to your topic files—but they alone are impractical for many projects. Of course, you can mix and match the **ALink** and **KLink** macros.

Here are some issues to consider before choosing the **KLink** macro:

- **Is the keyword list complete at the time you create the links?** Many times, the keyword list is done at the end of the development project and is not ready at the time the links are made. This is especially true if you have a separate team producing the keyword list. If the keyword list is not fairly solid when you begin linking topics, you probably want to use the **ALink** macro.

- **Will you be localizing your product?** If you are localizing your product, you should avoid using the **KLink** macro: translating your K-keywords will break all of your jumps. Remember that your A-keywords are not visible to the user and therefore do not need to be translated.

- **Can you build effective links using K-keywords?** General index terms may not be useful for creating meaningful links. For example, you may want to create links to a few specific topics—perhaps a subset of the printing topics—that may not be associated with specific K-keywords.

- **Do you want users to see the keywords used to link the topics?** Since all of your K-keywords will appear in the keyword list, you will need to use A-keywords if you don't want users to see the keywords used to link your topics.

ALink and KLink macro syntax

The syntax for the **ALink** and **Klink** macros is as follows.

ALink (*keyword* [; *keyword*] [, *type*[, *topicID* [, *window-name*]]])
KLink (*keyword* [; *keyword*] [, *type*[, *topicID* [, *window-name*]]])

Parameter	Description
keyword	Specifies one or more keywords to search for. You must enter the keyword exactly as it appears in the footnote pane, including any punctuation (such as commas). Multiple keywords must be separated by a semicolon. If any keyword contains a comma or a space, the entire keyword string must be enclosed in quotation marks.
type	Specifies the action to perform if one or more keywords are found. If this parameter is not specified or is zero, the default action is always to display the Topics Found dialog box containing the topic title. This parameter may specify one or more of the following values, separated by spaces:

Value	Meaning
JUMP (1)	Specifies that if only one topic matches any of the keywords, WinHelp should jump directly to that topic.
TITLE (2)	Specifies that if a keyword is found in more than one Help file, WinHelp should display the title of the Help file (as specified in the .CNT file) beside the topic title in the Topics Found dialog box.
TEST (4)	Specifies that the macro should return a value indicating whether or not there is at least one match.

Parameter	Description
topicID	Specifies the topic to display in a pop-up window if no matches are found. To specify a topic in a different Help file, the topic ID should end with an at sign (@) and the name of the Help file.
window-name	Specifies the window type in which to display the topic. If this parameter is not specified, the window type that is specified for a topic (if one is defined) is used, or the default or current window is used. If this macro results in an inter-file jump, the window type must be defined in the project file for the Help file that is being jumped to.

In addition to the keyword, the **KLink** and **ALink** macros also let you specify three parameters: *type, topic-ID,* and *window-name.* Many of your linking macros will simply include a keyword, but if you want to specify any of the parameters appearing after *type* you must include the commas that separate the parameters, even if you don't specify the parameter itself.

For example, if you want to use the *topicID* parameter, you must precede it with a comma, even if you don't specify the *type* parameter:

```
Related Topics!ALink(keyword1;keyword2, ,topicID)
```

Similarly, if you want to use the *window-name* parameter, you must precede it with a comma, even if you don't specify the *type* or *topicID* parameters:

```
Related Topics!ALink(keyword1;keyword2, , ,window-name)
```

Examples

The following macro hotspot runs the **KLink** macro and displays all of the topics containing the K-keyword "printing":

```
Related Topics!KLink(printing)
```

The next example displays all of the topics containing the A-keyword "printing"; if only one topic exists, it jumps directly to the topic:

```
Related Topics!ALink(sample,jump)
```

The last example displays all of the topics containing the A-keyword "customizing" and "options"; if neither topic exists, WinHelp displays the topic "error_msg":

```
Related Topics!ALink(customizing;options, ,error_msg)
```

Linking macro bugs

At the time of this writing, there are a few bugs in the linking macros that you should be aware of.

- **KLink** macros containing more than one keyword won't work correctly if the contents file references only one .HLP file. If two keywords are specified with **KLink**, only the first keyword will be found and WinHelp ignores any that follow.

  For example, if you reference multiple K footnotes in a **KLink** macro, such as **KLink (one;two;three)**, the Topics Found dialog box will display only the first footnote entry. Also, it will display the current topic if it matches the first footnote.

  You can fix the **KLink** bug as explained below.

  1. Add at least one **:Link** or **:Index** statement to the contents file. You can reference any filename you want, and WinHelp will ignore it if it doesn't exist. For example,

     ```
     :Link=foo.hlp
     :Index title=dingo.hlp
     ```

     If you use the **:Link** statement to link two Help files, you should also use the **:Index** statement to reference the other filename, or the Index page in the Help Topics dialog box disappears.

  2. Add a **:Base** statement to the contents file. WinHelp will first look in this file to find topics listed in the contents file.

     ```
     :Base filename.hlp
     ```

  Another alternative to correcting this bug is to stick with **ALink:** the bug does not occur with links created using the **ALink** macro.

- Under some circumstance, **KLink** and **ALink** will show the same topic multiple times in the Topics Found dialog box. If a single topic contains more than one keyword and more than one of the keywords are specified in the **KLink** or **ALink** macro, the topic will appear more than once.

Enabling ALink and KLink jumps to other Help files

By default, the **ALink** and **KLink** macros limit their searches to keyword matches in the current .HLP file. If your Help system comprises multiple .HLP files and contains a contents file, you can have WinHelp search other .HLP files for A- or K- keywords.

There are two ways to enable **ALink** and **KLink** jumps to other .HLP files. The method you choose depends on whether you want to merge the keyword lists for your .HLP files:

- Use the **:Index** option in the contents file. The keywords in the additional .HLP files are included in a combined index, and WinHelp will search all of the .HLP files for A- or K- keywords.

- Use the **:Link** option in the contents file. The keywords in the additional .HLP files do not appear in the combined index, but WinHelp will search the .HLP files for A- or K-keywords.

To enable ALink and KLink jumps to other Help files:

1. In Help Workshop, open the contents file.

2. Click either the Index Files button or the Link Files button.

3. Click Add, and then type the name of the Help file(s) that you want to search when an **ALink** or **KLink** macro is run.

   Help Workshop adds either an **:Index** or a **:Link** command for the Help file(s) you add.

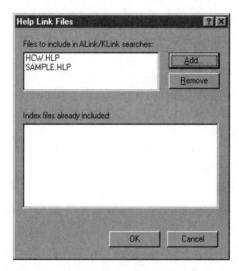

Figure 11.9. *Linking the keywords from multiple .HLP files.*

Listing the keywords from a compiled .HLP file

What if you want to use the **ALink** and **KLink** macros to create a link to an .HLP file, but don't have the source code and don't know the names of its keywords? Fortunately, Help Workshop will let you create a report listing all of the A- or K-keywords contained in any compiled .HLP file.

To create a report listing the keywords from another .HLP file:

1. Open Help Workshop.

2. From the File menu, click Report.

3. In the **Help Filename** box, specify the name of the .HLP file for which you want to create a report.

4. Specify the name of the report in the **Output Filename** box.

5. Under the Display area, click either A-keywords or K-keywords.

6. Click **Report** to begin the report.

Help Workshop will display the report as it writes the information to the specified file.

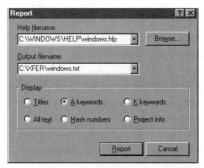

Figure 11.10. *Getting a report of the keywords in an .HLP file.*

Figure 11.11. *Help Workshop creates a keyword report.*

Creating a "Related Topics" button

Take a look at the cross references in Microsoft's Windows 95 Help files, and you'll see they are accessed by clicking a small gray "authorable button." Together with the **ALink** and **KLink** macros, authorable buttons make it very easy to build slick cross-referencing into your Help system.

Figure 11.12. *A small authorable button that accesses a linking macro.*

Authorable buttons are created using the **{button }** statement; for complete information, see "Creating an authorable button" in Chapter 15.

To create a "Related Topics" button:

1. Place the insertion point at the spot in the topic file where you want the button to appear.

2. Type the **{button }** statement in your topic file.

3. Type the label you want to appear on the button, followed by a comma. To create a blank label, leave a blank space before the comma.

4. Type the appropriate **ALink** or **KLink** macro.

5. Type the text you want to appear next to the button.

If you want to omit the label, and leave a space before the first comma, the button appears as a small square. To create the unlabeled button illustrated in Figure 11.9, type:

```
{button , KLink(printing)} Related Topics
```

If you want to label the button, type the label text before the comma. To create a button labeled "Related Topics," type:

```
{button Related Topics, KLink(printing)}
```

▨ Related Topics

Figure 11.13. *An authorable button with text that accesses a linking macro.*

LINKING AND PERFORMING ANOTHER ACTION IN ONE STEP

One of the advantages to creating a link with a macro is that you can perform more than one operation from a single hotspot. This is possible because you can run several macros at once. Just write them in one after the other, separating each with a colon or semicolon.

For instance, suppose you want to create a jump that displays a topic in a particular secondary window type, and then closes the main window. This is impossible with a standard jump, but is easily accomplished with a hotspot that runs two macros:

```
Click here!JI(>code,example);CloseWindow(main)
```

The example displays the "example" topic in a secondary window type named "code," and then closes the main Help window.

Special types of links

Many of your links will likely be simple jumps and pop-ups, but there are several other types of links possible in Help. If you're building even a moderately sophisticated Help file, you may want to take advantage of midtopic jumps, secondary window jumps, and interfile jumps.

JUMPING TO A TOPIC AND DISPLAYING IT IN ANOTHER WINDOW TYPE

With the new focus on secondary windows in Windows 95, some of your links will likely jump to a topic and display it in a different window type. This is easily accomplished using either a standard hotspot jump, or a macro hotspot.

As you may recall from Chapter 10, one of WinHelp 4's highly touted new features lets you specify the default window type for a topic using the > footnote marker. It would seem logical that the default window type would be honored by all jumps.

Unfortunately, WinHelp honors only the default window type from the Index and Find tabs and from the **ALink** and **KLink** macros. By default, all other jumps will display the destination topic in the current window type, even if you've specified a default window type for the destination topic using a > footnote!

For instance, if the user is viewing topic A in the main window and clicks a standard hotspot jump to topic B, Help will also display topic B in the main window—even if topic B contains a > footnote specifying "proc" as the default window type.

This inconsistency is bound to create all kinds of confusion. Just remember: if you're creating a jump using anything other than the **ALink** or **KLink** macro, you must specify the window type.

For more information on specifying a default window type, see "Specifying a window type for a topic" in Chapter 10.

Hotspot jumps

One way to jump between windows is with the tried and true hotspot jump. A hotspot jump to a topic in a secondary window is created just like any other jump, except that the topic ID is followed by a greater than symbol (>) and the name of the window:

hotspot text topicID>windowname

Figure 11.14. *Jumping to a topic in another window.*

```
Code samplesample01>code
```

The example creates a hotspot called "Code sample" that jumps to the "sample01" topic and displays it in a secondary window named "code."

Macro jumps

You can also use one of the **Jump** macros (including **JumpId, JumpKeyword, JumpHash,** or **JumpContext**) to jump to a topic and display it in another window. Notice that if the destination topic is in the current Help file, you can omit the filename:

JumpId*(>windowname, topic-ID)*

```
Code sample!JumpId(>code, sample01)
```

The example jumps to topic "sample01" in the current file and displays it in a secondary window named "code."

LINKING TO A TOPIC IN ANOTHER HELP FILE

With WinHelp's new support for modular Help systems, you will likely need to create a jump to a topic stored in another Help file. These "interfile" links are created by inserting an at sign (@) and the name of a Help file at the end of the topic ID.

hotspot text topicID@filename

Figure 11.15. *Jumping to a topic in another Help file.*

```
Terms you should knowdefinitions@glossary.hlp
```

The example jumps to the "definitions" topic in GLOSSARY.HLP. You can also use the same technique to pop up a topic stored in another Help file: just use a single underline instead of a double-underline.

Should you need them, both the **JumpID** and **PopupID** macros also support interfile links. The following example displays the "definitions" topic in GLOSSARY.HLP.

```
Terms you should know!JumpId(glossary.hlp,definitions)
```

Keep in mind that pop-ups created using the **PopupID** macro will appear in the compiled Help file with a solid underline rather than a dotted underline. This inconsistency may confuse your users; you're probably better off creating pop-ups using a standard hotspot rather than the **PopupID** macro.

An interfile jump to a topic in another window

To create a jump to a topic in another file and display it in a particular window type, type a greater than symbol (>) and the name of the window immediately after the topic ID:

hotspot text topicID>windowname@filename

Figure 11.16. *Jumping to a topic in another Help file and displaying it in another window.*

The following example jumps to the "definitions" topic in GLOSSARY.HLP and displays it in a secondary window named "glossary."

```
Terms you should knowdefinitions>glossary@glossary.hlp
```

Of course, you can also use a *Jump* macro:

JumpId*(filename>windowname, topic-ID)*

```
Terms you should know!JumpId(glossary.hlp>glossary,definitions)
```

Notice here one of Help's little idiosyncrasies: a standard hotspot looks for the window name after the *topic-ID*, but a **Jump** macro requires the window name to appear after the *filename*. Go figure.

Important note! If you are performing an interfile jump and displaying it in a secondary window, you must define the secondary window in the project file for the *destination* topic, not the *source* topic. For example, if you're jumping from SAMPLE.HLP to GLOSSARY.HLP and displaying the topic in a window named "glossary," "glossary" must be defined in the [WINDOWS] section of the project file for GLOSSARY.HLP.

How WinHelp finds other files

If you're creating interfile links, you should be aware of how WinHelp looks for files. WinHelp searches for files (including Help files, contents files, external programs, and DLLs) in the following locations:

- If a path is specified, WinHelp first searches for the file in the path. (If not found, the path is removed and the following locations are searched.)

- The folder that contains the current Help file.

- The current folder.

- The System subfolder in the Windows folder.

- The Windows folder.

- The folders listed in the PATH environment.

- The location specified in WINHELP.INI.
- The registry.

Setting the registry

There are two methods for ensuring that WinHelp can find files it needs. The preferred method is to have your setup program list a Help file in the registry. For more information on this technique, see "How WinHelp finds a file" in the *Help Author's Guide*.

Updating WINHELP.INI

If you're installing .HLP files over a network, are shipping on removable media such as a CD-ROM, or if WinHelp can't find a file, you should probably specify the path in the WINHELP.INI file. This will ensure that WinHelp can find your Help file and even display an error message. Like other "initialization" files, WINHELP.INI is a text file stored in the Windows folder. The syntax is:

```
[FILES]
HLP-filename=path, message
```

Here are some sample entries from a WINHELP.INI file.

```
[FILES]
FWTUTOR.DLL=F:\FONTWORK
SCRNCAMP.EXE=C:\WINDOWS\SCRNCAM
SAMPLE.HLP=F:\DATA\, Unable to find the file. Please insert the CD
into drive F.
```

If you're shipping a software product, you can have your setup program modify (or create, if necessary) the WINHELP.INI file to include the filename and location.

CREATING A MIDTOPIC JUMP

Midtopic jumps are commonly used on long topics to make accessing specific information easier for the user. For example, many Help systems contain a series of alphabetic buttons in the non-scrolling region, with each button jumping to the index entries corresponding with the letter. Of course, even midtopic jumps will not make up for overly long, poorly organized Help topics. Always "chunk" Help information into relatively small topics.

Midtopic jumps are possible because Help topics can contain more than one topic ID. By assigning a topic ID to a particular paragraph, you can create a jump to that paragraph. Note that midtopic jumps are ignored in secondary windows that are set to auto-size.

To create a midtopic jump:

1. Place the insertion point at the very beginning of the first line in the paragraph you want to jump to.

2. Insert the pound footnote marker (#).

3. Type the topic ID in the footnote pane.

Figure 11.17. *Multiple topic IDs in a single topic.*

4. Place the insertion point in the paragraph that will contain the jump and create a jump that references the topic ID you typed in Step 3.

You can use a similar technique to access a particular paragraph from the search keyword list: just assign multiple keyword entries (K footnote) to a topic.

Customizing the appearance of links

You may occasionally want to change the appearance of links in your Help file. By default, links are indicated using character formatting, both color (green) and underline (single underline for jumps, dotted underline for pop-ups), but you can change either or both settings.

Why would you want to do this? One possibility: if you're creating a glossary of terms, you may find the green hotspot color too overwhelming (the dreaded "green screen") and want to change the hotspots to black. Or, if you're documenting a programming API that uses underlines, you may want to hide the WinHelp's underline so you can see those used in the programming syntax.

Since Help users are accustomed to the standard hotspot format, make sure you've got a good reason to change the defaults. You may want to tell users that they can override the custom color formatting by entering **Colors=None** in the [Windows Help] section of WIN.INI. This setting tells WinHelp to ignore custom colors and use the system defaults for foreground and background colors. This is a global setting and will override the custom color formatting specified in all .HLP files.

CHANGING THE COLOR OF A LINK

You can change the color of a link by inserting an asterisk (*) before the topic ID. WinHelp will still indicate the hotspot with a solid or dashed underline.

To change the color of a link:

1. Position the cursor in the main window and insert an asterisk (*) at the beginning of the topic ID. Make sure the asterisk is formatted as hidden text. The asterisk prevents WinHelp from displaying the link using the default green color.

2. Select the hotspot and use the character formatting feature in your word processor to specify the color you want to use. If you want WinHelp to display links in the user's default text color (usually black), set the hotspot color to "Auto."

hotspot text *topicID

Figure 11.18. *Customizing the color of a link.*

HIDING A LINK

To hide a link, insert a percent sign (%) before the topic ID. Users can still locate hotspots by pressing CTRL+TAB.

To hide a link:

- Position the cursor in the main window and insert a percent sign (%) at the beginning of the topic ID. Make sure the percent sign is formatted as hidden text.

hotspot text %topicID

Figure 11.19. *Hiding a link.*

If you've formatted the hotspot color as "Auto," WinHelp will display the link in the user's default text color (usually black). If you don't want the hotspot to be entirely invisible, you can use the character formatting in your word processor to choose a hotspot color. For example, if you format the hotspot text in blue, WinHelp will display the hotspot in blue.

SPECIAL HOTSPOT CHARACTERS

The following table summarizes the special characters used to create special types of links and to customize the appearance of hotspots.

Character	Name	Purpose
Asterisk (*)	Underlined hotspot	Removes the default green color from the hotspot, and displays it using only an underline.
At sign (@)	Interfile jump	Specifies that the jump is to a topic located in a different .HLP file from the current file.
Exclamation point (!)	Macro hotspot	Specifies that the hotspot contains a Help macro.
Percent sign (%)	Invisible hotspot	Removes the default green color and underlining from the hotspot, making it invisible.
Greater than symbol (>)	Window type	Specifies that the topic is to be displayed in the specified window, either the main Help window or a secondary window.

Linking topics with graphics

Don't forget that you can also create links with graphic files. See "Creating a single hotspot graphic" and "Creating a multiple hotspot graphic" in Chapter 13 for complete information.

12

Formatting Topics

Design and layout is important in any kind of technical documentation, but is especially critical in online documents. You will encounter several challenges when designing online Help. For starters, the relatively small size and poor resolution of the computer screen limits your choices in terms of design and layout.

Other challenges are unique to Windows Help. Many of the character attributes—including superscript and subscript, and all capitals—aren't supported by the Help compiler. Some of the paragraph formatting options supported in your word processor—such as table borders and shading—are ignored by the Help compiler. Finally, unless you include fonts with your Help system, you're limited to those that ship with Windows.

This chapter addresses specific formatting problems and also contains general advice that will help you work more efficiently.

This chapter covers:

- Choosing fonts.

- Character formatting, including text color and unsupported formats.

- Paragraph formatting, including indents, line spacing, tabs, unsupported options, borders, and controlling line breaks.

- Creating tables using tab stops, hanging indents, table formatting, and graphics.

- Creating fixed- and relative-width tables.

- Creating a nonscrolling region.

- Formatting pop-up topics.

At a glance Formatting support

WinHelp 4.0	WinHelp 3.1
Supports fonts like Wingdings, Script, and various international fonts.	Supports only ANSI fonts and the Symbol font.
Full support for bullets, smart quotes, em-dashes, and en-dashes.	Bitmaps are used for special characters, or the .RTF file is processed to accommodate special characters.
Automatic localization of quotation marks (for example, "text" will be automatically translated to «text» in French).	Help authors must manually localize quotation marks.

Using style sheets

Not to state the obvious, but don't forget to format your topic files using style sheets! Style sheets are essential for you to maintain consistency in your online documentation.

- If you use a Help authoring tool, take a look at its style sheets and edit them as necessary to comply with the principles discussed in this chapter and your own aesthetics. For example, if you use RoboHELP you will want to edit ROBOHELP.DOT and ROBORTF.DOT.

- If you're working on a project with other Help authors, set up a network directory to store the latest version of your style sheets. Then, configure your word processor so everyone shares the version stored on the network. In Word, choose Options from the Tools menu, click the File Locations tab, and modify the Workgroup Templates option so it points to the directory containing the shared templates.

  If you develop Help for both Windows 3.1 and Windows 95/NT, you may want to develop separate style sheets for each platform. To achieve a consistent look with the Windows 95 user interface, some WinHelp 4.0 systems use a smaller font (8 point MS Sans Serif, instead of 10 point) for the body text. Although small type sizes are difficult to read, 8 point type is practical for Windows 95 since the context menu (activated by right-clicking the mouse) provides the user with the option of enlarging the font.

- If you don't use an authoring tool, take a look at the styles in the sample Word template included on the disc in the back of this book.

- If you want to create a non-scrolling region for your Help topics, create a Heading1 style using the "Keep with Next" attribute. This will ensure that your topics consistently have a non-scrolling region. Keep in mind, however, that you shouldn't use the "Keep with Next" option with your pop-up topics (see "Creating a nonscrolling region" later in this chapter for more information).

Choosing fonts

Font selection is critical in producing Help that is legible on the screen, and there is certainly no shortage of fonts available on the market. Why, then, do all the Help files you see use the same font?

The main issue is the availability of fonts on the user's system. If you author a Help system with a font that is not available on the user's system, Windows will substitute a different font (usually Times New Roman or Arial). This can significantly change the appearance and layout of your Help file, especially if you use tables or hanging indents.

While it is possible to ship fonts with your Help system, a variety of cost, licensing, and distribution issues make that option impractical. Of course, in a corporate environment you can probably predict your user's font configuration (especially if you have a standard software suite or corporate fonts). But since it's usually impossible to predict which fonts are available on the user's system, you should probably stick with the fonts that ship with Windows (Table 12.1).

Table 12.1. *Standard Windows Fonts*

Font	Design	Format
Arial, Bold, Italic, Bold Italic	Sans serif	TrueType
MS Sans Serif, Bold	Sans serif	Bitmap
MS Serif, Bold	Serif	Bitmap
Symbol	Symbol	TrueType
Times New Roman, Bold, Italic, Bold Italic	Serif	TrueType
Wingdings	Dingbat	TrueType

The dingbats and symbol fonts aside, you have basically four choices: two serif fonts (Times New Roman and MS Serif) and two sans serif (Arial and MS Sans Serif) fonts. Although the visual design of these fonts is certainly a factor in your decision, they look so similar that the font's format—TrueType versus bitmap—usually plays a larger role. Here are some points to consider when choosing between TrueType (Arial and Times New Roman) or bitmap (MS Sans Serif and MS Serif).

- **Onscreen legibility**. Microsoft spent a great deal of effort tuning all of the Windows fonts for onscreen legibility at small sizes (they literally spent years on Arial and Times New Roman) and it shows: their screen quality is unrivaled. Screen quality varies somewhat depending on the font size, so be sure to test font quality at the point sizes you plan to use in your Help file.

- **Serif versus sans serif**. Small serifs are sometimes difficult to read on screen. Therefore, most Help systems use a sans serif font (either MS Sans Serif or Arial) for both body text and headings.

- **Italics versus obliques**. True italics aren't just slanted: they have different letterforms than their roman counterparts. Most TrueType fonts, including Arial and Times New Roman, have true italics (compare the lowercase "e" in Times New Roman regular and italic). Bitmap fonts, however, don't have true italics: Windows simulates an italic by slanting or "obliquing" the type.

Arial Regular	*Arial Italic*
MS Sans Serif Regular	*MS Sans Serif Oblique*
Times New Roman Regular	*Times New Roman Italic*
MS Serif Regular	*MS Serif Oblique*

Figure 12.1. *Italics vs. obliques (shown at actual screen resolution of 96dpi).*

Italics are difficult to read onscreen, but obliqued fonts are nearly illegible. If your Help systems include italic text, you should use Arial and Times New Roman.

- **Ease of authoring**. Many word processors (including Word) suppress the display of bitmap fonts (typically substituting Arial or Times New Roman), so you won't have true WYSIWYG when you're formatting tables, hanging indents, and the like.

- **Character set.** Arial and Times New Roman both have a full ANSI character set; MS Sans Serif and MS Serif are non-ANSI fonts and have fewer characters (they don't include smart quotes, em-dashes or en-dashes, or bullets). If you use a bitmap font, you can format the missing characters using TrueType fonts or create a graphic file for special characters. To view a font's character set, run the Windows Character Map utility from the Accessories menu.

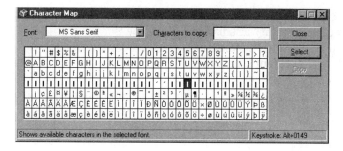

Figure 12.2. *The Windows Character Map. Notice this bitmap font is missing several characters (including those in the fourth row).*

- **Design preference.** Although the TrueType and bitmap font designs are visually quite similar, there are slight differences.

Looking at the sans serif fonts, you'll notice the characters in Arial are slightly wider than those in MS Sans Serif, which means Arial will fit fewer characters on a line. Furthermore, since Arial has a taller x-height than MS Sans Serif, you will need to add more line spacing (or "leading") to Arial to enhance readability. The bottom line: you'll be able to fit more characters on the screen using MS Sans Serif (which is probably why the Windows 95 Help system uses 8 point MS Sans Serif).

Comparing the serif fonts, you'll notice the reverse is true: Times New Roman is more compact (has narrower characters and shorter x-height) than MS Serif.

In addition, remember that while TrueType fonts can be scaled to any size, bitmap fonts look very ragged at 18 points and up. If you need to use large point sizes, you're better off using TrueType fonts.

Formatting text

Since most of your Help content is comprised of words, text formatting is obviously a critical component of your Help file design. With some care and planning, it's easy to design Help topics that look good and work around some of the limitations of the Help compiler.

SPECIAL CHARACTERS

One of the limitations of the WinHelp 3.1 compiler is the way it handles special characters such as bullets, typographers ("smart") quotes, em-dashes and en-dashes, and bullets. RTF files use special codes to represent these characters, but unfortunately, the 3.1 Help compiler doesn't recognize the standard RTF codes and ignores them, leaving a blank space in place of the original character.

Since the Help compiler does recognize other codes for these special characters, many of the help-authoring tools provide some type of post-processor to edit the RTF file before compiling. Other WinHelp 3.1 authors work around this limitation by creating their own macros (see FixSpecialChars on the disc in the back of this book) or substituting bitmaps for the affected special characters.

Fortunately, WinHelp 4 provides full support for bullets, smart quotes, em-dashes, and en-dashes without any conversion or other work. Note that Help Workshop will automatically localize quotation marks (for example, "text" will be automatically translated to «text» when compiled for the French language).

TEXT COLOR

For the best legibility on the screen, you must format your text with a color that has high contrast against the window background. Since the highest contrast is achieved with dark text on a light background, many Help authors format their text using black and choose a white or light yellow window background.

If you format your text using the "Auto" setting, WinHelp will display text using the color specified by the user. To set the text color, start the Windows Control Panel and click the Display icon. Next, click the Appearance tab in the Window Properties dialog box and click the Window Text option. Similarly, the user's default window background settings are specified using the Colors tab in the Window Properties dialog box. In general, it's a good practice to honor the user's preferences and format your topic file text using the Auto setting.

If you format your Help text using a specific color (that is, anything but Auto), the user can always override the text (and background window) color by right-clicking a topic with the mouse, and then clicking Use System Colors. The user can also override your color settings by using the Control Panel's Display Properties.

You should never use light colors (such as cyan or yellow) against a light background or dark colors (dark blue, dark magenta) against a dark background.

AUTO-NUMBERING

Many Help authors use the auto-numbering feature in their word processor to create procedure topics. While this technique works fine using the WinHelp 3.1 compiler, autonumbering is not supported by the WinHelp 4 compiler. This limitation may be corrected in a future release, but until then you must manually number lists.

UNSUPPORTED TEXT FORMATTING

The Help compiler supports most of the text formatting options available in your word processor, including bold, italic, underline, and small capitals. A few text formatting options are ignored by the Help compiler; these are listed in Table 12.2 along with some suggested workarounds.

Table 12.2. *Unsupported character formatting*

Unsupported character format	Workaround
Superscript and subscript text.	Create graphics for the desired characters.
All capitals text.	Type the text with the SHIFT key down instead of using the All Caps attribute.
Mathematical equations and formulas.	Create a graphic.
Expanded and condensed letter spacing.	Expanded letterspacing can be simulated by inserting an extra space between each character. To achieve other special letterspacing effects, create a graphic.
Single-underlining, double-underlining, and hidden text.	Create a graphic (these formatting attributes are reserved for use by the Help compiler).

Formatting paragraphs

Most of the standard paragraph formatting options available in popular word processors are supported by the Help compiler. This means your word processor will usually display your topics as they will appear in Help. This section discusses paragraph formatting and the differences between WinHelp and your word processor.

- **Text alignment** The Help compiler supports left, right, and center text alignment. The Help compiler does not support justified text.

- **Indents** The Help compiler supports left, right, first-line, and hanging indents. You can position text relative to the Help window by adjusting the left and right indentation values. To add white space relative to the left and right edges of the Help window, try setting your left margin to 0.08" and the right margin to 0.09".

- **Tabs** The Help compiler supports left-, right-, and center-aligned tab stops. It does not support leader tabs (such as dots or lines) or decimal tabs.

- **Line spacing** You can use either automatic line spacing, or specify exact spacing. If you format a paragraph using automatic or single line spacing, the Help compiler will adjust the spacing to accommodate the tallest character (or graphic) placed on the line. The Help compiler also preserves the 1.5 and double line spacing options, increasing the line height by 50% and 100%, respectively.

  Automatic line spacing works well most of the time, but you can control the line spacing precisely by specifying an exact value in your word processor. This is generally a good idea for fonts that have a fairly tall x-height (such as Arial). For example, if you use

9 point Arial, you should probably increase the line spacing from 12 to 13 points in order to create more white space on the screen and improve readability.

- **Paragraph spacing** The Help compiler supports the standard "space before" and "space after" paragraph attributes. As with any document created in a word processor, you should use paragraph spacing instead of extra carriage returns to add space between paragraphs.

- **Paragraph borders** The Help compiler's support for paragraph borders is limited. It does support any combination of left, right, top, and bottom borders, including boxed paragraphs. You can include thin (1 pixel) and thick (2 pixel) single lines, or double lines.

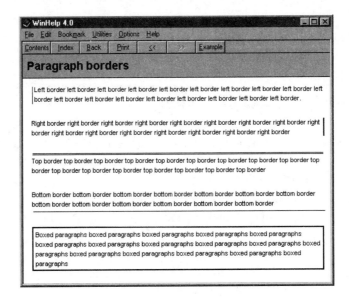

Figure 12.3. *The Help compiler supports a variety of paragraph borders.*

The Help compiler does not support colored borders (all borders are displayed in black), shadows, paragraph shading, or coloring. It also ignores any space you specify between the text and the border.

If you format consecutive paragraphs using borders, your word processor will display the paragraphs with one large box, but the WinHelp will draw an individual box around each paragraph.

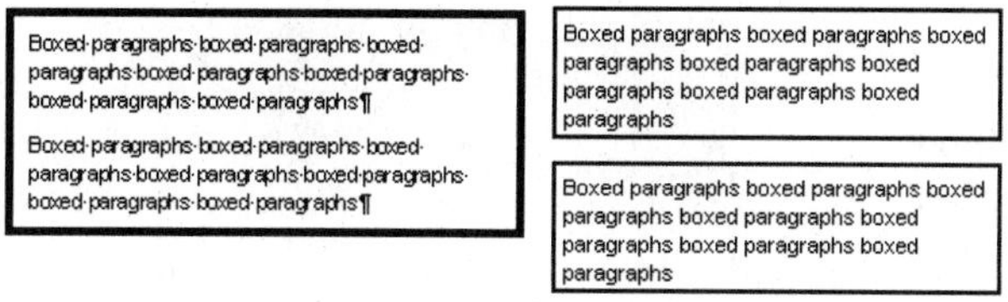

Figure 12.4. *Word processing programs (left) let you box consecutive paragraphs, but the Help compiler (right) creates a separate box for each paragraph.*

To create a box around multiple paragraphs, simply enter a soft carriage return (in Word, press SHIFT+ENTER) between each paragraph.

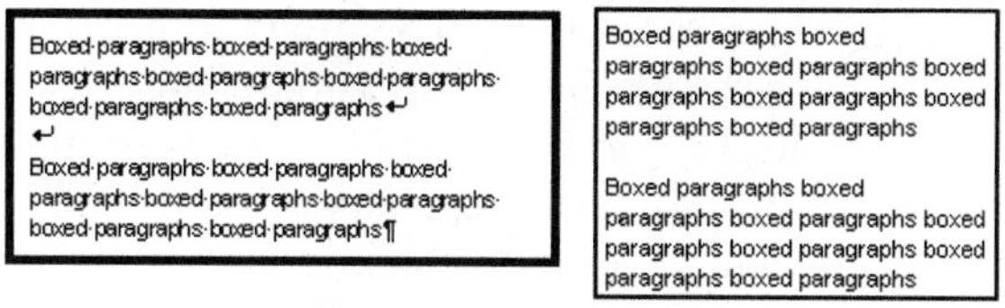

Figure 12.5. *If you separate consecutive boxed paragraphs with soft carriage returns (left), Help will display them all in one box.*

CONTROLLING WORD-WRAPPING AND LINE BREAKS

You may occasionally want to prevent WinHelp from word-wrapping a paragraph as the user resizes the Help window. If you prevent word-wrapping, WinHelp will display a horizontal scroll bar if the user sizes the window smaller than the paragraph width.

To prevent word-wrapping in Word, you can use the Keep Lines Together setting (click Paragraph from the Format menu, click the Text Flow tab, and check the Keep Lines Together box).

One of WinHelp's anomalies is that punctuation characters (including periods, commas, and smart quotes) will wrap to the next line if formatted differently than the preceding text. For example, if you have a period after a jump or a pop-up, WinHelp will sometimes wrap the period to the next line as the user sizes the Help window (Figure 12.6).

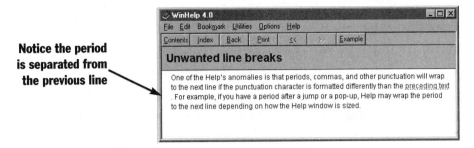

**Notice the period
is separated from
the previous line**

Figure 12.6. *Help will break punctuation to the next line if it is formatted
differently than the preceding text.*

When deciding how to break a line, WinHelp looks at any font or character formatting (bold, italic, underline, hidden, and so forth) changes. Naturally, this means that a period formatted as normal text following a hotspot (formatted as hidden text) will trigger a line break. Therefore, to prevent unwanted line breaks, format the punctuation using the same character attributes as the hotspot text that precedes it (Figure 12.7). (Note that it's the same as the text, not the topic ID.) In the example below, you would format the period as single underline text, just like the pop-up text.

this period may break to the next line_{popup_text}.

this period will always stay with the hotspot._{popup_text}

Figure 12.7. *To prevent unwanted line breaks, format punctuation
using the same attributes as the hotspot text.*

Creating tables

Tables are useful in all types of technical documentation, but they are especially valuable in the online medium because they take up very little space and are easily scanned by the reader. They also provide a convenient way to arrange text next to a graphic.

There are four ways to produce tables in Help, each with its own advantages and disadvantages.

Table 12.3. *Four techniques used to produce a table*

Technique	Works best for	Comments
Use standard tab stops.	Simple tables with one line of text per cell.	
Create a hanging indent.	Small two or three column tables.	Works well if the left most column(s) contain only one line of text; right cell may contain multiple lines.
Use the table feature in your word processor.	Tables containing more than three columns, or table with lots of text in the left column.	Some table formatting options are ignored by the Help compiler.
Create a graphic.	Highly designed visuals.	Increases size of compiled .HLP file. Text in table will not appear in Find tab when user performs a full-text search, nor can it be copied onto the Clipboard by pressing CTRL+C.

USING TAB STOPS

You can use tab stops instead of a table to arrange columns of numbers and text. This approach works best for creating small two or three column tables, provided the text in each column is confined to one line (otherwise, you must divide the text in each column into separate paragraphs). Figure 12.8 illustrates a three column table creating using tab stops.

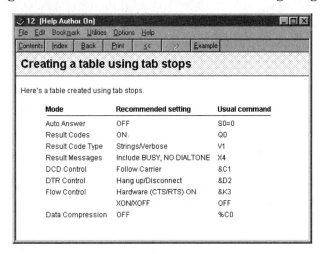

Figure 12.8. *A table created using tab stops.*

USING A HANGING INDENT

You can also create a table using a hanging indent. This technique works best if the text in the left column fits on one line. Unlike tables created using standard tabs, a hanging indent can accommodate several lines of text in the right column.

In general, tables created using a hanging indent work better than tables created using standard table formatting, since the text in the right column wraps well as the user resizes the window. Although you can create a variable-width table using standard table formatting (see later in this chapter), it requires you to center the table, which looks odd if the rest of your text is left-aligned.

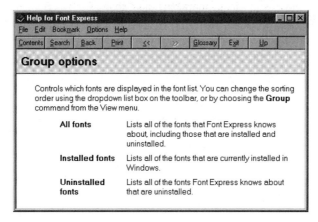

Figure 12.9. *A table created using a hanging indent.*

To create a hanging indent, set the left indent where you want the left column to begin, and set the value for the hanging indent where you want the rightmost column positioned. You should also set a tab stop at the same position as the hanging indent.

Figure 12.10. *A hanging indent in Word.*

Hanging indents are typically used for two-column tables. You can also use a hanging indent for a three-column table, provided the text in the first two columns fits on one line.

Column1   **Column2**   Here is the text in Column 3. This text will wrap as necessary to fit the width of the Help window.

USING TABLE FORMATTING

The most obvious way to create a table, of course, is to use the table formatting features in your word processor. This is the best option if the cells in your table contain text that wraps to more than one line.

Creating a table using standard table formatting has two limitations. First, these tables are less flexible than hanging indents for creating a relative-width table. Furthermore, the Help compiler ignores some of the formatting options, including shading, cell borders, right-aligned text, and centered text. If you create a table using these unsupported table features, Help Workshop displays a "Table cell borders are not supported" error message (HC1012). To format a table using these features, create the table as a graphic (discussed in the following section).

Although you cannot place a rule across the entire table, you can add a border to the text within a cell. To do so, simply select the text within the cell (not the entire cell itself) and apply border formatting.

Recommended setting	Usual command
OFF	S0=0
ON	Q0

Figure 12.11. *Adding a border to a cell.*

Another way to add a rule to a table is to split the table in order to create a paragraph. You can then format the paragraph to include a border. You will probably want to format the paragraph using a small font size (such as 4 points) so the paragraph appears to be part of the table.

CREATING A TABLE AS A GRAPHIC

If you want to format a table using options unsupported by the compiler, you can create a graphic. Since spreadsheets are convenient for handling tabular data, many authors create a table in a spreadsheet program and then save it as a bitmap or metafile. This technique can provide attractive results without much effort. The table in Figure 12.12 was created in Excel, formatted using the AutoFormat feature (the "3D Effects 2" option), and displayed against a gray Help background.

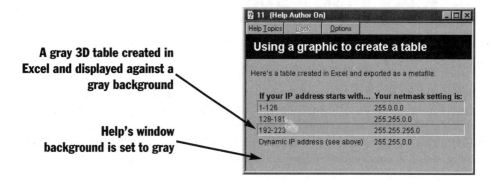

A gray 3D table created in
Excel and displayed against a
gray background

Help's window
background is set to gray

Figure 12.12. *A table saved as a graphic.*

WinHelp 4.0's full-text search capability complicates the use of graphics for tables: none of the text in a graphic will appear when the user performs a search. If you're producing a catalog, directory, or a similar document that requires full-text search, you should stick with standard tables or hanging indents as outlined earlier in this chapter. Also, remember that the information in a table cannot be copied onto the Clipboard.

If you have Excel, follow the steps below to create a table as a graphic.

To create a table as a graphic:

1. Type the table text in a spreadsheet program.

2. Format the table as you want it to appear in Help.

   In some cases, you may want to hide the gridlines. In Excel, click the Options command on the Tools menu. Click the View tab, and under Window Options clear the Gridlines check box.

   Using Excel's AutoFormat feature (click AutoFormat on the Format menu) can provide attractive results with minimal effort.

3. Highlight the table, press the SHIFT key and click Copy Picture from the Edit menu. The Copy Picture dialog box appears.

4. Choose a file format. You have a choice of exporting as a metafile or as a bitmap. The metafile will display better at various resolutions and provide better print quality.

   To export a metafile, click **As Shown when Printed**.

   To export a bitmap, click **As Shown on Screen** and click **Bitmap**.

Figure 12.13. *Exporting information from Excel as a metafile*

5. Click OK to copy the image onto the Clipboard.

6. Paste the image directly into your topic file.

- OR -

If your Help file contains several graphics, you may decide to place the image by reference in your topic file. This requires a drawing program that can export metafiles. Paste the image from the Clipboard into the drawing program and save it as a Windows metafile. Then place it by reference in your topic file. For more information on metafiles, see "Help graphics overview" in Chapter 13.

CONTROLLING THE WIDTH OF A TABLE

When you create a table, you must consider how it will appear when the user sizes the width of the Help window. In some cases, you will want to fix the width of the table so it remains the same size regardless of the Help window size. Other times, you may want the table to resize as the user sizes the Help window.

Be sure to examine all your tables at various screen resolutions. In general, try to keep tables as narrow as possible—a table that looks good at 1024x768 can overwhelm the screen on a 640x480 display. Also, as part of your testing you should resize the width of the Help window and make sure that the table text wraps correctly.

Creating a fixed-width table

If the user sizes the width of the window too narrow, the line breaks can change and cause alignment problems, depending on how you created your table (Figure 12.14).

Text wrapping problems such as this usually occur with tables created with hanging indents or tab stops. By default, these are variable-width tables: Help will adjust the width of each column as the window is sized. It's easy, though, to fix the width of hanging indents and tabs to prevent them from wrapping.

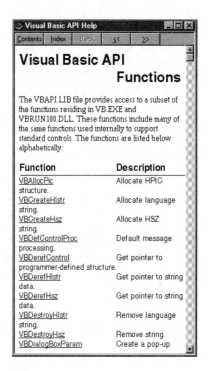

Figure 12.14. *Alignment problems can occur in variable-width tables when the user sizes the Help window.*

To fix the width of a table created with a hanging indent or tab stop:

1. Open your topic file and select the table.

2. Use your word processor's paragraph formatting options to prevent a page break within the paragraph.

   In Word, click Paragraph on the Format menu. Click the **Text Flow** tab. Under Pagination, check the **Keep Lines Together** box.

By default, tables created using the table feature in your word processor are fixed width—if the Help window isn't wide enough to display the table, WinHelp adds a horizontal scroll bar to the bottom of the window.

Creating a variable-width table

In some cases, you will want to create a variable-width table. When WinHelp displays such a table, it adjusts the width of the columns as the user sizes the window. The columns will maintain their relative width until the window reaches the table's minimum size, then Help will display a horizontal scroll bar.

This technique is useful for tables created with table formatting, since they are fixed-width unless you specify otherwise. If you use Word, follow the steps below to create a variable-width table. (By default, tables created using hanging indents and tab stops are variable-width.)

To create a variable-width table:

1. Open your topic file and select the table.

2. Click Cell Height and Width from the Table menu.

3. Click the **Row** tab, and under Alignment, click the **Center** button.

The minimum size is determined by the actual width of the cell you create. When WinHelp displays the table, it will enlarge the width of the cell as the user widens the Help window, but it will not shrink the cell less than its minimum width. You should set the width of each cell to the narrowest width you want it to appear.

This technique works fairly well, but it is not foolproof. For starters, it takes a lot of trial and error to get satisfactory results. Also, variable-width tables appear centered in the Help window, and can look out of place if the rest of the Help text is left-aligned.

Creating a nonscrolling region

Readers in complex online documents can sometimes lose track of their place, particularly in long topics. This is often referred to as being "lost in hyperspace."

To minimize this problem, you can define the area just below Help's button bar as a "nonscrolling region" (sometimes called a "banner"). As the user scrolls through the Help topic, the nonscrolling region remains visible.

A nonscrolling region is frequently used to display the name of the current topic, similar to a header on a printed page. In addition to text, the nonscrolling region can include graphics. For example, some Help systems include bitmaps that pop up related topics or a brief overview of the current topic.

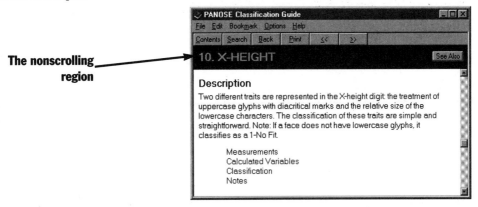

Figure 12.15. *A nonscrolling region.*

To create a nonscrolling region:

1. Select the paragraph(s) you want to appear in the nonscrolling region.

   The text or graphics you want to appear in the nonscrolling region must be at the beginning of the topic (that is, immediately following the hard page break separating the current topic from the previous topic).

2. Use your word processor's paragraph formatting options to prevent a page break between the current paragraph and the next paragraph.

   In Word, click Paragraph on the Format menu. Click the Text Flow tab. Under Pagination, check the **Keep with Next** box.

You can define only one nonscrolling region per topic. Within a topic, if you format more than one group of paragraphs to be nonscrolling, the compiler will generate a "Nonscrolling region is defined after scrolling region" error message (HC3048).

Don't forget that you can control the background color of a nonscrolling region (see "Customizing the window color" in Chapter 15). You can also add buttons to the nonscrolling region (see "Adding a button to the nonscrolling region" in Chapter 13).

TIP *Don't define a nonscrolling region for topics that will be used as pop-ups. If you do, when the pop-up is displayed, only the nonscrolling region will be visible. See the next section for more information.*

Formatting pop-up topics

Pop-up topics, such as glossary terms, have two special formatting considerations.

DON'T ASSIGN A NONSCROLLING REGION

First, and most important, don't use a nonscrolling region for a pop-up. If you do, when the pop-up is displayed, only the nonscrolling region will be visible (see Figure 12.16).

To avoid formatting a pop-up with a nonscrolling region, create a specific style for the pop-up heading (the Word template included with this book uses "PopupHeading").

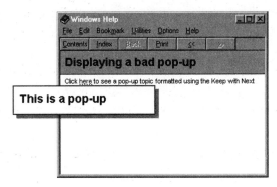

Figure 12.16. *A pop-up topic formatted with a nonscrolling region.*

CONTROLLING THE WIDTH OF A POP-UP

When Help displays a pop-up, it bases the width of the pop-up window on the width of the primary Help window. If the Help window is wide, the line length of the pop-up text increases accordingly. Long line lengths often affect readability.

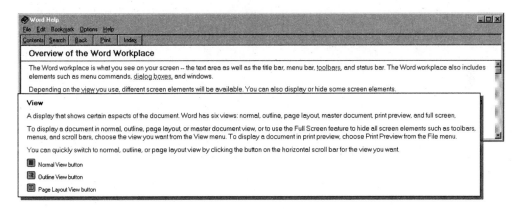

Figure 12.17. *A pop-up window's width based on the width of the primary Help window.*

To control the width of a pop-up window, simply place the pop-up text in a table. A width of about four inches works well at various screen resolutions and window sizes.

#**Pop-up heading**

> Placing pop-up text in a table lets you control the width of the pop-up. This will improve readability if the user sizes the width of the Help window.

Figure 12.18. *A pop-up placed in a table.*

13

Creating Help Graphics

The old adage about a picture being worth a thousand words carries added significance in the online medium, where there just isn't room for a thousand words. Graphic images are *de rigeur* in any Help system, and WinHelp 4 brings many graphics enhancements.

You may want to review Chapter 3 for a summary of the uses for graphics.

This chapter covers:

- An overview of Help graphics formats, including a look at issues surrounding color depth, resolution, and file size.

- Creating and preparing graphics.

- Creating hotspot graphics.

- Placing graphics into a topic file.

- Miscellaneous graphic techniques.

At a glance Graphic support

WinHelp 4	WinHelp 3.1
Supports up to 16 million colors.	Supports up to 16 colors; high resolution images require an external DLL.
Several common bitmaps (bullets, dashes, symbols, etc.) built into compiler.	All graphics must be created by Help author.
Transparent bitmap support built into compiler; allows background window color to show through graphics.	All graphics are opaque (that is, the background window color does not show through the graphic).
Better support for multiple color depth graphics: can reference multiple files in a single {bmx} statement and Help will determine the most appropriate image for the user's display.	Help author must choose one color depth, which is used on all systems regardless of the video display capabilities of the user's system.
WinHelp will not distort BMP or SHG files if you create the file at a different resolution or with a different video driver than the user is running.	Many Help authors process their graphics through a utility such as MRBC or ShgRez to fix their resolution and prevent distortion.

Help graphics overview

This section covers the basics of graphic file formats, color, and resolution issues. If you are an experienced graphic artist, you may want to skip ahead to "Creating hotspot graphics."

This chapter uses a few key terms to describe the different types of Help graphics:

- **Static graphic**. Like a graphic in a printed manual, a *static* graphic is for illustration purposes only and doesn't do anything when it is clicked by the user.

- **Hotspot graphic**. A *hotspot* graphic performs an action when clicked, such as displaying a pop-up or jumping to a topic.

- **Multiple hotspot graphic**. A *multiple hotspot graphic* (or hypergraphic) contains more than one hotspot region. Each hotspot performs a different action—perhaps jumping to a topic, displaying a pop-up, or running a Help macro—when clicked.

FILE FORMATS FOR HELP GRAPHICS

There are several different file formats involved in developing graphics for Help. Help uses standard Windows graphics such as bitmaps and metafiles, plus a few proprietary formats.

Bitmap file

A bitmap graphic breaks an image into a grid of equally-sized pieces, called "pixels." Bitmap graphics are typically created in paint programs (including Paintbrush, PhotoShop, and others), which treat images as collections of dots rather than shapes.

Help supports two kinds of *bitmap* files: Windows bitmap (.BMP extension) and device-independent bitmap (.DIB extension, a bitmap format that offers no advantage over standard .BMP files and is very rarely used in Help).

Bitmap graphics are ideal for capturing software screens, and they are very good for reproducing photo-realistic images. Bitmap graphics also have the advantage of being very easy to create and modify.

Metafile

Help also supports Windows *metafiles*, which have a .WMF extension. Metafiles are a type of vector graphic, which store an image as a collection of geometric points and shapes. Vector graphics are created using drawing programs such as CorelDRAW, FreeHand, and Illustrator.

Metafiles have two advantages over bitmap data: they can be resized without distortion (the "jaggies" that come with re-sizing a bitmap), and they produce much smaller files.

Unlike most vector graphics, however, Windows metafiles often contain more than just vector data. For example, a metafile might use vector information to describe an image outline, a bitmap to provide the fill, and text as a caption.

Multiple hotspot graphic file

Multiple hotspot graphics are created using the Hotspot Editor, a program that comes with most of the Help development tools. Multiple hotspot graphic files have an .SHG extension.

To create a multiple hotspot graphic, you simply import a bitmap or metafile into the Hotspot Editor, (optionally) assign a few hotspots, and save it as an .SHG file (see "The Hotspot Editor" later in this chapter).

Other file formats

I will mention two other formats in passing. Icon files, which have an .ICO file extension, are small (32x32 pixels) bitmaps that appear when an application is minimized.

WinHelp 3.1 lets you specify an icon in the project file, but WinHelp 4 dropped this feature. Any references to icons in the project file are ignored by Help Workshop, and WinHelp 4 represents the main Help window with a purple book icon, and secondary windows with a page icon containing a question mark.

The Help compiler also supports a graphic format called a "multiple resolution bitmap," which has an .MRB extension. This graphic format is rarely used these days (see "Multiple resolution bitmaps: worth the trouble?" later in this chapter).

Figure 13.1. *WinHelp icons for the main window (left) and for secondary windows.*

COLOR DEPTH

When dealing with graphics, you will need to think about *color depth*, or how many colors to include. Color depth greatly affects the size of your graphics, and also raises compatibility issues.

Monochrome graphics

With the exception of a few older laptops that use monochrome displays, nearly all desktop PCs can display at least 16 colors, Therefore, most Help authors don't limit themselves to monochrome (two colors, black and white) graphics unless disk space is extremely tight. As illustrated in Table 13.5, monochrome graphics offer big savings (they are one-fourth the size of 16 color images, and one-seventh the size of 256-color images) and are definitely better than no graphics at all.

> **TIP** *You can enhance monochrome graphics by filling them with a pattern of black and white pixels, much like a printed halftone. For example, you can approximate a light gray using a 10% to 20% black pattern.*

Color graphics

Computers produce color by increasing the number of bits displayed for each pixel on the screen. The more information that is recorded for each pixel, the more shades and hues can be displayed in the image. The following table lists the number of bits per pixel used to create various color depths (for example, when you hear someone say "8-bit graphic," they mean it contains 256 colors).

Table 13.1. *Color depths for PCs*

Bits per pixel	Number of colors
1	2
4	16
8	256
16 (high color)	32,768 or 65,536 (depending on format)
24 (true color)	16,777,216

16-color graphics

Despite the growth of multimedia PCs containing 256-color graphics capabilities, there is still a very large installed base of computers that can display only 16 colors. Because of this (plus limited disk space availability) many Help authors have traditionally played it safe and used colors from the standard Windows 16-color palette.

The standard sixteen colors and their red-green-blue (RGB) values are presented in the following table. If you're creating graphics for a 16-color display, you must stick with these color values; any other colors will be changed to the closest solid color in the Windows 16-color palette.

If you are reducing a 256 color image to 16 colors, make sure to have your paint program reduce the image using the colors in the Windows palette, not an "optimized" (or "adaptive") palette. When displaying an image on a 16 color system, WinHelp will ignore an optimized palette and substitute the nearest color in the Windows 16 color palette. When you reduce an image using the Windows 16-color palette, try using a diffuse dither (it usually provides better results than a patterned dither).

Table 13.2. *The Windows 16-color palette*

Color	RGB value	Color	RGB value
Black	0, 0, 0	Dark blue	0, 0, 128
Blue	0, 0, 255	Dark cyan	0, 128, 128
Cyan	0, 255, 255	Dark green	0, 128, 0
Green	0, 255, 0	Dark magenta	128, 0, 128
Magenta	192, 0, 192	Dark red	128, 0, 0
Red	255, 0, 0	Dark yellow	192, 192, 0
Yellow	255, 255, 0	Light gray	192, 192, 192
White	255, 255, 255	Dark gray	128, 128, 128

256-color graphics and beyond

More and more Help systems will feature high color graphics now that WinHelp 4 supports high resolution images containing up to 16 million colors.

This trend is due partially to the increased popularity of high-capacity distribution media like CD-ROMs. Another key development is WinHelp 4's support for multiple-color depth graphics. With this feature you can place several versions of a graphic in a Help file, each with a different color depth. When Help displays the graphic, it chooses the image that will look best on the user's system. If you choose to build Help with graphics containing 256 or more colors, you should probably also include graphics containing fewer colors for the benefit of users who can't display 8-bit images. For information on configuring your Help file for multiple color depths, see "Placing a graphic for multiple color depths" later in this chapter.

On a 256-color system, Windows actually reserves 20 colors for the system palette. Therefore, if you are designing for a 256 color system, your palette can contain only 236 custom colors. You can use any of the following colors (in addition to the colors from the 16-color palette) without palette conflict or any other color mapping problems. Note that these four additional colors will appeared dithered when displayed on a 16-color system.

Table 13.3. *Four additional colors in the Windows 256-color palette*

Color	RGB value	Color	RGB value
Light green	192, 220, 192	Light cream	255,251,240
Light blue	166, 202, 240	Medium gray	160, 160, 164

For more information on color palettes, see "Editing color palettes" later in this chapter.

SCREEN RESOLUTION

Screen resolution refers to the number of pixels on a screen. Numerous video standards have been introduced as the PC has evolved, each with a different screen resolution. The following table summarizes the most common video standards.

Table 13.4. *PC video standards*

Video standard	Resolution	Windows support
CGA	640x200	3.1 only
EGA	640x350	3.1 only
VGA	640x480	3.1 and Windows 95
Super VGA	800x600	3.1 and Windows 95
8514	1024x768	3.1 and Windows 95

Screen resolution is important to Help authors for a couple of reasons. Most important, you'll need to consider screen resolution in order to determine the dimensions of your graphics. At the time of this writing, various sources estimate that nearly 70 percent of Windows 3.1 systems are running at resolutions of 640x480 or 800x600. Therefore, most Help authors design for the lowest common denominator and size their graphics to fit on a 640x480 screen. Remember to leave room for Help's title, menu, and button bars.

Screen resolution is also a consideration because bitmaps include information about the resolution of the video driver. Some programs—including WinHelp 3.1—will try to maintain the size of the graphic by stretching it on systems with different resolution.

Screen resolution has been a big problem for Help authors and users running "large fonts" video drivers. Fortunately, version 4.0 of the Help compiler solves this problem: Help files compiled using Help Workshop will look fine on most systems (but files built using the 3.1 compiler will not improve when displayed under WinHelp 4). Furthermore, most of the *hardware* issues related to screen resolution have disappeared. CGA and EGA are virtually obsolete—and unsupported in Windows 95—and there is no noticeable stretching with VGA, Super VGA, and 8514 graphics.

For information on how to process graphics so they won't stretch or shrink under WinHelp 3.1, see "Avoiding resolution problems with ShgRez" later in this chapter. In addition, there is a tool called MRBC (multiple resolution bitmap compiler) that can be used to correct resolution problems, but is now largely obsolete (see "Multiple resolution bitmaps: Worth the trouble?" later in this chapter).

EFFECT OF GRAPHICS ON FILE SIZE

For most Help developers, the largest constraint surrounding graphics has been their enormous size. This constraint will vanish as the industry gradually moves away from distributing software on floppy disks in favor of high capacity media like CD-ROMs. But Help graphics are still often considered a luxury when push comes to shove in the battle for space on the distribution media.

Color depth and file format

The color depth and file format both make a big difference in the size of your graphics. The following table illustrates the relative file sizes for various graphics formats. The figures were derived by creating an average-sized graphic (258x288 pixels) and exporting it as a metafile and as a bitmap at various color depths.

Table 13.5. *File size comparison for a metafile and various bitmaps*

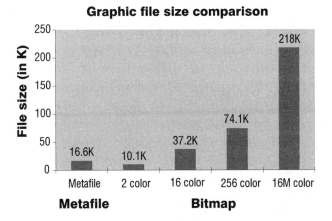

Here are some observations.

- Monochrome graphics are about one-quarter the size of 16-color bitmaps.

- Increasing from 16 to 256 colors roughly doubles the file size, and increasing to 16 million colors creates a file nearly six times the size of a 16-color bitmap.

- Metafiles are about the same size as a monochrome bitmap, roughly half as large as 16-color bitmaps, and nearly 4.5 times smaller than 256-color bitmaps.

Compressing graphics

The Help compiler does offer significant compression, especially for certain types of bitmaps. The compression ratio varies widely from about 10–60 percent, depending on the size of the graphic and the number of colors it contains.

Of course, the highest compression ratios are achieved on large graphics containing very few colors. Compressing a typical 16 or 256 color Help graphic generally achieves savings of 30-50 percent, depending on the size of the image and the number of colors it contains.

Don't expect metafiles to compress as efficiently as bitmaps. Informal testing results show that compressing a 20K .WMF creates a file that is actually 13 bytes larger than the original. Compressing a 106K metafile shaves about 5K from the file size.

Of course, you should always enable compression when you build the final version of your Help file (see Chapter 20, *Compiling, Debugging, and Testing,* for more information). During interim builds, however, most authors disable compression to shorten the build time.

Note that using the Hotspot Editor to estimate the compression ratios (a popular WinHelp 3.1 technique) is no longer an accurate technique under WinHelp 4. The Hotspot Editor always compresses graphics using Zeck compression; Help Workshop chooses the most efficient compression scheme (Zeck, RLE, or a combination of the two) for each graphic. Therefore, Help Workshop usually achieves better compression ratios than the Hotspot Editor.

CHOOSING A GRAPHIC FILE FORMAT

Which is the best format to use—bitmap or metafile? Here are some recommendations, which are summarized in the table below.

- Bitmaps are the best choice if you need to reproduce a photo-realistic image or a software screen shot. On the downside, however, bitmaps tend to be quite large and are difficult to resize.

- Metafiles are very effective for graphics containing a lot of text because they scale better at various screen resolutions. They are also great for black and white line art, such as technical illustrations, especially if the original art is created in a vector drawing program.

- Because Windows-based metafiles are not compatible with the Macintosh, you should stick with bitmaps if you want to ensure cross-platform compatibility.

At a glance Choosing a graphic file format

File format	Ability to resize	B&W line art	Text-intensive graphics	Screen shots	Photo graphic images	Porta-bility	File size (com-pressed)
Raster (.BMP, .DIB)	○	⊙	⊙	●	●	◉	⊙
Vector (.WMF)	●	●	●	○	○	○	●

● Excellent   ◉ Good   ⊙ Fair   ○ Poor

Notes on metafiles

- Many paint programs can read vector data, but cannot write vector data. If you open a metafile in a paint program, it displays a bitmap image based on the vector data. Therefore, if you use a paint program to open a metafile and then save the image, it is converted to a bitmap—even if the file extension is .WMF. Create your metafiles in a drawing package such as FreeHand, Illustrator, or Visio.

- Be careful which fonts you use when creating metafiles. Since metafiles store text using TrueType fonts, the graphic will look strange on a user's system that doesn't have the correct font.

  Some paint programs (including CorelDRAW) give you the option to convert text to curves when you export a metafile. If your drawing package doesn't provide this feature, you should stick with the Windows core fonts (Arial and Times New Roman are your best bets) when creating graphics.

Creating and preparing graphics

There are many fine books on creating computer graphics, but here are a few tips for creating and preparing Help graphics.

CAPTURING SCREENS

If you're documenting a software product, you'll probably need to capture a few screen shots. There are several good Windows screen capture utilities available, including Hijaak, Paint Shop Pro, RoboHELP's PaintIt, and SnapIt. Most of these utilities include features that make capturing screens a snap (excuse the pun): you can auto-increment file names, precisely define the area you want to capture, convert files between various formats, and even edit files.

If you don't have a screen capture program, you can use the PrintScreen function built into Windows.

To copy the entire Windows screen onto the Clipboard:

- Press the PRINT SCREEN key.

To capture the active window only:

- Press ALT+PRINT SCREEN.

In some cases, you may want to capture open menus. Because the Windows menu manager uses the ALT key, this is a little more difficult.

To capture a screenshot with an open menu:

1. Activate the program you want to capture and hold down the ALT key.

2. Without releasing the ALT key, press the keyboard accelerator for the menu you want to capture.

3. Move the selection with the arrow keys (make sure ALT is still down).

4. Press the PRINT SCREEN key.

CROPPING GRAPHICS

Graphics with extra white space cause alignment problems when placed in topic files. This is particularly noticeable when you place a graphic in the nonscrolling region or align a graphic on the baseline with the Help text, as illustrated in Figure 13.2.

Figure 13.2. *Alignment problems (top) due to white space.*

In most paint programs you can easily crop a graphic image. For example, if you use Windows Paint, you can carefully select the bitmap (including the last pixel on each of the four sides) and use the Copy To command from the Edit menu to create a new bitmap file.

RESIZING GRAPHICS

Many times you will want to resize a graphic image. Of course, word processing programs let you scale a graphic image, but the Help compiler ignores this information and displays all images at full size. Therefore, in order to resize a Help graphic you will need to use a graphics program.

As mentioned earlier, you can usually resize a metafile with good results. When you resize a bitmap, however, the paint program simply duplicates or removes pixels as necessary to fill the new image dimensions. This process visibly distorts the image.

WexTech Systems, the developers of Doc-To-Help, have a product called Smooth Scaling that takes a different approach to resizing a bitmap. It uses an anti-aliasing technique that makes graphics slightly fuzzy but leaves many small details (including text) fairly legible.

The figure below compares two 70 percent reductions, one from Smooth Scaling and the other from Paint Shop Pro. Notice that the text in the image on the left is legible, whereas that in the image on the right is not. Smooth Scaling is not suited for all graphics—photographic images are one example—but it works very well for screen shots.

Figure 13.3. *A 70 percent reduction created using SmoothScaling (left), and using Paint Shop Pro (right).*

Never use a graphic scaled for Help in your print document: you'll get much better results scaling the image in your word processor or page layout program. Therefore, you must maintain two separate copies of your images: one for Help and one for print.

> **TIP** *If you're having problems with the color palette in SmoothScaling, try switching out of 256-color mode when you scale the image.*

EDITING COLOR PALETTES

When Windows is running in 256-color mode, it is capable of displaying only 256 colors at once. Each 256-color bitmap image has its own palette containing the colors in the image. When an image is displayed, its palette becomes the active palette for all other images.

If you display two 256-color images at once and the images use different color palettes, color flashing and other undesirable results (or "palette conflict") will occur. This happens because Windows tries to display both images using the closest colors in the active palette. Palette conflict is illustrated in Figure 13.4; notice that Magritte's "Son of Man" (left) looks even stranger than Dali!

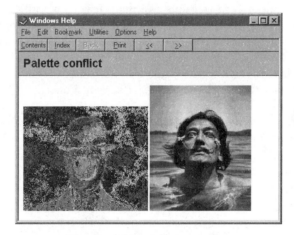

Figure 13.4. *Palette conflict.*

To avoid palette conflict when displaying more than one 256 color graphic at once, make sure images that will be displayed together are created using the same palette. As long as your graphic images use the same color palette or collectively use fewer than 236 colors (256 minus the 20 system colors used by Windows in 256-color mode), you can display two or more graphics at the same time without palette conflict.

You can view and edit a bitmap's palette using any decent paint program, or use the BitEdit and PalEdit tools included on Microsoft's JumpStart CD, part of their Multimedia Development Kit.

Placing graphics into a topic file

There are two ways to insert a graphic into your topic file:

- If the graphic is a bitmap or metafile, you can include it directly by copying it onto the Clipboard from your graphics program, and then pasting it into your topic file. This technique works only for .BMP, .DIB, and .WMF files.

- You can place a graphic by reference using one of four reference commands. This technique works for all Help graphics, including .SHG and .MRB files.

PASTING A GRAPHIC

Pasting a bitmap or metafile directly into your topic file gives you a WYSIWYG view of your topics in your word processor. Pasting a graphic directly into a topic file can cause the WinHelp 3.1 compiler to run out of memory, but creates no problems under WinHelp 4 thanks to the compiler's efficient use of system memory. This technique is practical as long as the graphic appears only once within the Help file.

To paste a graphic:

1. In your paint or drawing package, select the image and copy it onto the Clipboard.

2. Open a topic file and position the insertion point where you want to display the image.

3. Paste the image from the Clipboard.

PLACING A GRAPHIC BY REFERENCE

To place a graphic file by reference, you type a bitmap statement in the topic file to tell the Help compiler how you want the graphic to appear. Placing a graphic by reference creates a link to the graphic file.

Most Help authors place their graphics by reference. The advantages are many:

- You have more flexibility in the appearance of the graphic: you can wrap text along its left or right margin, or align the graphic on the baseline of the text.

- If you are including a graphic more than once within your Help file, placing the graphic by reference reduces the size of your Help file. Since graphic references create a link to the graphic file, Help Workshop includes only one copy of the image in the .HLP file.

- You can use .SHG files created with the Hotspot Editor (and .MRB files created with the Multiple Resolution Bitmap Compiler).

- You can make your bitmaps transparent, so that the background window color appears in place of any white pixels in the graphic.

- You can edit the graphic without having to update the reference in the topic file.

- Your word processor will work faster on large topic files since it doesn't have to display graphic images.

To place a graphic by reference:

1. Open a topic file and position the insertion point where you want to display the image.
2. Create a link to the graphic file by typing the following syntax:

   {bmx[t] *filename***}**

Parameter	Description
x	Specifies how the graphic appears in the topic. You can specify the following characters:

Value	Meaning
c	Aligns the bitmap as a text character on the baseline of the text in exactly the same place in the paragraph where the reference occurs. Because the bitmap is treated as text, any paragraph formatting properties assigned to the paragraph also apply to the bitmap.
l	Aligns the bitmap along the left margin. Text is aligned with the upper right corner of the bitmap and wraps along the right edge of the image.
r	Aligns the bitmap along the right margin. Text is aligned with the upper left corner of the bitmap and wraps along the left edge of the image.

Parameter	Description
t	Specifies that the white background of the graphic should be replaced by the background color of a Help topic. This character can be used only with 16-color bitmaps.
filename	Specifies the name of the graphic file to include.
	You can specify multiple files representing different color depths for the same graphic by separating the filenames with a semicolon (see "Placing a graphic for multiple color depths" later in this chapter).

For example, **{bmct banjo.bmp}** places a file named BANJO.BMP. The letter "c" in the command signifies the bitmap will be aligned as a character and "t" means all of its white pixels will be transparent.

Left-aligning a graphic

To ensure that the text wraps properly around the right edge of the graphic, you should place **bml** references at the beginning of a paragraph. Don't include a space between the reference and the text that follows it unless you want to indent the first line of text.

#$K+ **Banjo**

The banjo is thought to have originated in northwest Africa and was first brought to the United States on slave ships in the eighteenth and nineteenth centuries. A predominant instrument in the hymns and work songs of the deep South, it was later adopted by traditional jazz bands as an alternative to the guitar. Today it is most commonly used in country and western and bluegrass music.

{bml banjo.bmp} The banjo is a plucked instrument consisting of a fret boardTERM_FRETBOARD attached to a metal hoop over which parchment is stretched. The body of the banjo acts as a resonating chamber to create the banjo's characteristic bright, non-sustained sound. The most popular banjo today is the five-string model. It is tuned, from top to bottom, to C, G, B, and D, with a high string--often used as a drone string--also tuned to G.

Figure 13.5. *A left-aligned graphic reference in the topic file.*

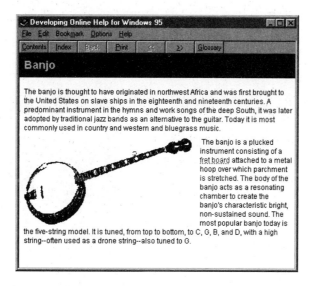

Figure 13.6. *A left-aligned graphic as it appears to the Help user.*

Right-aligning a graphic

To ensure that the text wraps properly around the left edge of the graphic, you should place **bmr** references at the beginning of a paragraph.

Note the use of soft carriage returns (or "line breaks") in Figure 13.7. Using a hard carriage return would align the first line of the second paragraph ("The mandolin has...") with the bottom edge of the mandolin graphic, leaving a very large space between the two paragraphs. Using a soft return (entered in Word by pressing SHIFT+ENTER) treats the lines as one paragraph, giving you more control over the appearance of both the text and graphic.

#$K+·**Mandolin**¶

{bmr·mandolin.bmp}The·mandolin·is·a·member·of·the·lute·family.·It·is·perhaps·best·known·for·its·
tremelando·effect,·which·was·developed·in·Southern·Italy·for·playing·a·type·of·serenade.·In·the·1940's·Bill·
Monroe·introduced·the·mandolin·to·pop·music·by·cross-breeding·it·with·old-time·dance·and·country·songs.·
It·has·remained·popular·ever·since,·its·brilliant·sound·making·it·well-suited·to·rock,·bluegrass,·and·country·
music.↵
↵
The·mandolin·has·eight·steel·strings·tuned·in·four·pairs·to·the·notes·G,·D,·A,·and·E.·Like·the·violin·and·the·
banjoBANJO,·the·mandolin·is·tuned·to·open·fifths.·This·tuning·provides·a·different·set·of·chords·than·is·
available·on·the·guitarGUITAR.¶

Figure 13.7. *A right-aligned graphic reference in the topic file.*

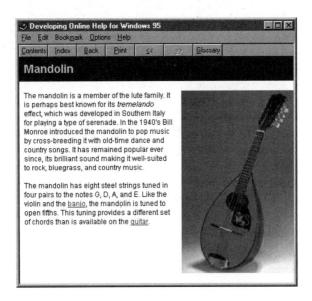

Figure 13.8. *A right-aligned graphic as it appears to the Help user.*

Aligning a graphic as a character

Help formats a **bmc** graphic just like a text character, aligning the graphic along the baseline of the text. Since the graphic is treated like text, it inherits the paragraph formatting properties for the current paragraph. Therefore, don't specify negative line spacing for a paragraph with a **bmc** graphic reference.

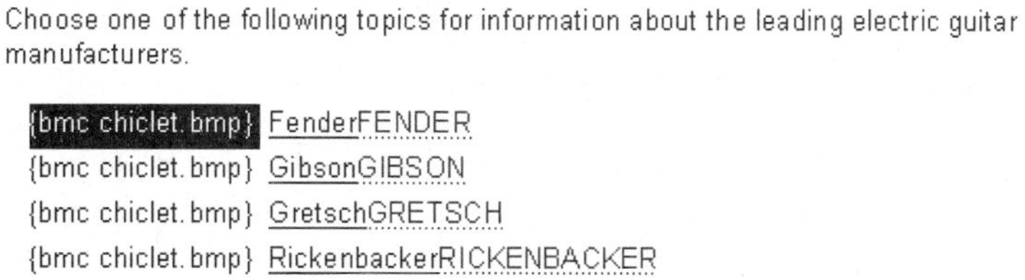

Choose one of the following topics for information about the leading electric guitar manufacturers.

{bmc chiclet.bmp} FenderFENDER
{bmc chiclet.bmp} GibsonGIBSON
{bmc chiclet.bmp} GretschGRETSCH
{bmc chiclet.bmp} RickenbackerRICKENBACKER

Figure 13.9. *A character-aligned graphic reference in the topic file.*

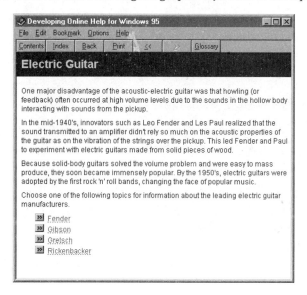

Figure 13.10. *A character-aligned graphic as it appears to the Help user.*

As mentioned previously in "Cropping graphics," a graphic with extra white space surrounding its live image area will often have alignment problems when placed in text. This is particularly critical when placing a graphic using the **bmc** command. Be sure to trim any white space along the bottom of the graphic image, or it won't align properly with the text baseline.

Creating hotspot graphics

Help is not limited to static pictures. The Help compiler enables you to create "hotspot" graphics that display pop-up windows, jump to other topics, or run Help macros.

There are two types of hotspot graphics. A *single hotspot* graphic has one "hot" region encompassing the entire image. You create a single hotspot within your word processor, using the same process you would to create a jump or pop-up, or to run a Help macro.

A *multiple hotspot* image is one that has several "hot" regions, each one containing a different pop-up, jump, or macro. You create these so-called "hypergraphics" using the Hotspot Editor, a utility included with most Help authoring and software development tools.

Hotspots have many applications: you're limited only by your imagination. You can create a button that jumps to a particular topic. You can display a dialog box from your application with pop-up windows that describe its various elements. You can even create a bitmap that executes a Windows application. You can use hotspot graphics in pop-up windows, nonscrolling regions, and secondary windows.

> **TIP** *You can display all of the hotspots within a topic by opening a Help file and pressing CTRL+TAB.*

CREATING A SINGLE HOTSPOT GRAPHIC

You create a single hotspot graphic in your topic file, using the same basic procedure you would to create a jump or a pop-up, or to run a macro.

To create a single hotspot graphic:

1. Open your topic file and type a bitmap reference (using either the **bmc**, **bml**, or **bmr** statement) where you want the hotspot to appear. Don't forget to include the curly brackets before and after the statement.

2. If you are creating a jump or displaying a pop-up, type the topic ID associated with the topic. You must not leave any spaces between the graphic reference and the topic ID.

   -OR-

   If you are running a Help macro, type an exclamation mark (!) followed by the macro. You must not leave any spaces between the graphic reference, the exclamation mark, and the macro.

3. To create a jump or run a macro, select the entire bitmap reference (including both curly brackets) and change its character formatting to double underline. To create a pop-up, change its character formatting to single underline.

4. Select the topic ID or macro (including the exclamation mark). Turn off the single- or double-underline format, and change the character formatting to hidden.

5. Be sure to change the character formatting back to non-hidden. This avoids formatting additional characters as hidden text.

The following example makes "chiclet.bmp" a pop-up hotspot that displays the topic associated with the topic ID "fender."

{bmc chiclet. bmp}FENDER

Figure 13.11. *A single hotspot graphic.*

MULTIPLE HOTSPOT GRAPHICS

To create multiple hotspots within a single bitmap, you must use the Hotspot Editor, as described next.

The Hotspot Editor

The Hotspot Editor (SHED.EXE) lets you create a multiple hotspot graphic that can display pop-up windows, jump to other topics, and/or run Help macros. It is included with the Windows SDK and most third-party Help authoring tools.

Two versions of the Hotspot Editor are widely available at the time of this writing. The Win32 SDK comes with version 3.10, but you may want to track down version 2.0. Version 2.0 originally shipped with Microsoft's Multimedia Viewer and is available from Microsoft JumpStart CD or their ftp file server on the Internet.

Version 2.0 (SHED2.EXE) offers two advantages over version 3.10. First, you can easily import and export graphic files with its Import Bitmap and Export Graphic commands. Version 3.10 has no export facility and uses an awkward Replace command to import images. Second, version 2.0 correctly displays images containing more than 16 colors; version 3.10 does not (this is more a nuisance than a limitation, since the image looks fine once it's compiled into an .HLP file).

Since version 2.0 of the Hotspot Editor creates .SHG files that can't be opened with version 1.0 of the Hotspot Editor, you should stick with one version or the other. Note that .SHG files created with version 2.0 cannot be processed using ShgRez (see later in this chapter), but this step is not necessary for files built using the 4.0 Help compiler.

CREATING A MULTIPLE HOTSPOT GRAPHIC

To create a multiple hotspot graphic, open a graphic image in the Hotspot Editor and define the hotspot areas. Use the Hotspot Editor to save the file using a .SHG extension, and place it in your topic file just as you would any other graphic image.

Creating the graphic

Since you can't create graphics using the Hotspot Editor, you must first create the image using a paint or drawing program. The Hotspot Editor accepts .BMP, .DIB, and .WMF files.

Unlike previous versions, WinHelp 4 will support graphic images containing up to 16 million colors. When you open a graphic containing 256 or more colors in version 1.0 of the Hotspot Editor, the color palette will be inaccurate, but the image will look fine once it is compiled into Help.

Defining hotspot attributes

After you've created a graphic, you're ready to define your hotspot attributes. These attributes determine:

- The size of the hotspot areas.
- The location of the hotspot areas.
- Whether or not the hotspot areas are visible to the Help user.
- The type of hotspots (jump, pop-up, or Help macro).

To open a graphic image, click the Open command from the File menu. The image will appear in the Hotspot Editor's window as shown in Figure 13.12.

Figure 13.12. *The Hotspot Editor.*

Creating the hotspots

Once you've opened a graphic image in the Hotspot Editor, you can define the hotspot regions. Each region is simply a rectangular area in the graphic. Defining the region is much like drawing a rectangle in a graphics program: click and hold down the left mouse button and drag the mouse, releasing the button when the area is the size you want. A selection rectangle (or "bounding box") will appear, similar to the one in Figure 13.13.

A rectangle with sizing handles displays the hotspot region. You can use the sizing handles to resize the region, or—for more precise sizing control—double-click the rectangle with the left mouse button to display the Attributes dialog box. The Attributes dialog box is illustrated in Figure 13.14.

Figure 13.13. *The Hotspot Editor with a selection rectangle.*

TIP *To create a hotspot region and automatically display the Attributes dialog box, draw the rectangle using the right mouse button instead of the left.*

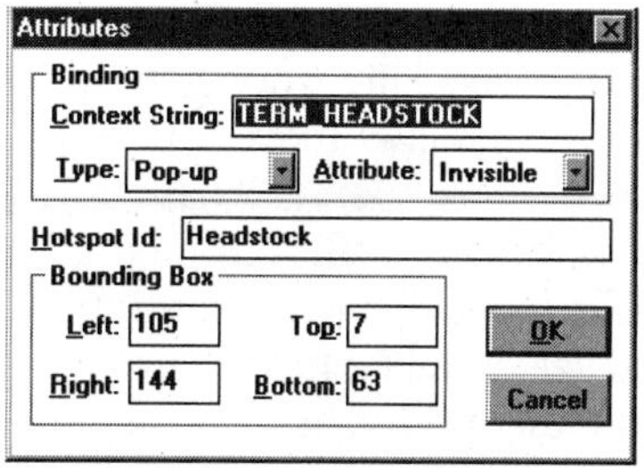

Figure 13.14. *The Attributes dialog box.*

The Attributes dialog box lets you define a hotspot's attributes:

- Use the **Context string** box to determine which topic or macro is associated with the hotspot. To display a pop-up window or jump to a topic, type the topic ID with which it is associated. To run a macro, type the macro string (see Chapter 16 for information on working with Help macros).

- Use the **Type** box to specify what type of hotspot you want to create: a jump, a pop-up, or a macro.

- Use the **Attribute** box to determine whether the hotspot is visible or invisible to the user when it is displayed in Help. Visible pop-up regions are surrounded by a dotted green line, while visible jumps and macros are indicated by a solid green line.

  Invisible jumps and pop-ups do not contain lines; if you create a graphic containing invisible hotspots, you may want to tell the user that the graphic contains a hotspot.

- Use the boxes in the Bounding Box area to change the left, right, top, and bottom boundaries of a hotspot region. The coordinates are measured in pixels. These controls are useful for precisely controlling hotspot placement.

- Use the **Hotspot ID** box to specify a name for the hotspot. By default, the Hotspot Editor creates a unique name for each hotspot region. As illustrated in Figure 13.15, assigning meaningful Hotspot IDs makes it much easier for you to select a specific hotspot (especially if the graphic is crowded or the hotspots are small) while you create and edit .SHG files.

- You can set the preferences for the Context String, Type, Attribute, and Hotspot ID by clicking the Preferences command from the Edit menu.

Editing a hotspot

Once you've created a hotspot, you may need to go back and perform minor adjustments. There are several techniques that simplify the process of editing hotspot attributes: selecting hotspots, cutting, copying, and pasting hotspots, moving hotspots, and resizing hotspots.

Selecting a hotspot

Selecting a hotspot can be difficult, especially when you're working with graphics that contain many hotspots. Frequently, you accidentally move a hotspot, or unintentionally create a new hotspot.

If you've created Hotspot IDs, the most efficient method to select a hotspot is by clicking the Select command from the Edit menu. This displays the Select dialog box (shown in Figure 13.15), which makes it simple to select hotspots from even the most complex graphic. You can select a hotspot by clicking it with the mouse, or by pressing TAB or SHIFT+TAB.

Cutting, copying, and pasting a hotspot

The Hotspot Editor includes full support for the Clipboard. This feature is particularly useful if you're creating several hotspots of the same size within a graphic. Create a hotspot that includes the attributes you want, then copy it onto the Clipboard. You can then simply paste the hotspot, editing the topic ID and other settings as needed.

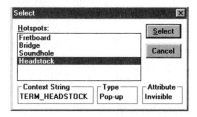

Figure 13.15. *The Select dialog box.*

Defining default hotspot properties

Many of your hotspots share the same basic properties for type (jump, pop-up, or macro) and attribute (visible or invisible). Rather than define these anew for each hotspot, you can click Preferences on the Edit menu and define the default hotspot properties.

Replacing the graphic image

You can't directly edit graphic images in the Hotspot Editor. Because no graphics programs can open .SHG files, you can't edit a graphic image in a .SHG file. However, you can replace a graphic using the following procedure.

To replace the image in a .SHG file:

1. Open the new graphic file in a graphics program and copy it onto the Clipboard.

2. Open the .SHG file containing the image you want to change.

3. From the Edit menu, click Replace.

> **TIP** *If you're running SHED2.EXE, you can simply use the Import command on the File menu to import a graphic.*

Moving a hotspot

Moving a hotspot is much like moving an element in a graphics program: click in the center of the hotspot and hold down the left mouse button, then drag the mouse, releasing the button when the hotspot is in the proper location.

Resizing a hotspot

To resize a hotspot, select the hotspot and move one of the eight sizing handles. For more precise control, select the hotspot and right-click the mouse or press ENTER to display the Select dialog box, illustrated in Figure 13.15. This method provides precise control over the pixel coordinates of the hotspot area.

Changing the tabbing order

Multiple hotspot graphics have something called a *tabbing order*. When the Help user presses the TAB key, the hotspots are displayed in a particular sequence. The order in which you create the hotspots determines the tabbing order: the first hotspot you create is first in the tabbing order, the second hotspot is second, and so on.

You should always test your graphics to make sure the tabbing order is correct. On toolbar buttons, for example, most users will expect the tabbing order to move from left to right. To test the tabbing order in Help, just press the TAB key. To view the tabbing order in the Hotspot Editor, click Select from the Edit menu; the Hotspots list box displays the hotspots according to their tabbing order.

To change the tabbing order:

1. From the Hotspots list, select the hotspot you want to move to the top of the order.

2. Press DELETE or click Delete from the Edit menu.

3. Click Undo from the Edit menu. This restores the hotspot and moves it to the top of the tabbing order.

4. Repeat steps 1–3 for as many hotspots as necessary.

This process can get confusing if you're reversing several hotspots. To reverse a tabbing order that mistakenly moves from right to left, you would select the rightmost button first and work your way left (that is, delete and undo each button in *reverse* order).

Saving a multiple hotspot graphic file

Once you've created a multiple hotspot graphic, save it by clicking the Save As command from the File menu. You should save hotspot graphic files using an .SHG ("segmented hypergraphic") file extension.

If you're using version 3.10 of the Hotspot Editor, make sure you use the Save As command when you first save a multiple hotspot file—if you use the Save command, the Hotspot Editor will try to overwrite the file using the original filename, and display the following prompt:

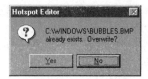

Figure 13.16. *Be careful not to overwrite your bitmap files with an .SHG file extension.*

Clicking Yes to this prompt will create an .SHG file with a .BMP file extension, which is guaranteed to cause confusion.

Placing a multiple hotspot graphic

You place a multiple hotspot graphic in your topic file just as you would any other graphic image. Unlike other graphics, however, multiple hotspot graphics must be included by reference using one of the **bmc**, **bml**, or **bmr** commands. For complete information, see the section "Placing a graphic by reference" earlier in this chapter.

AVOIDING RESOLUTION PROBLEMS WITH SHGREZ

Substantial stretching and distortion problems occur in WinHelp 3.1 if you and the Help user are running different display drivers.

Most high resolution video cards (that is, 1024x768 and up) include software video drivers with a mode called "Large fonts." Many users running high video resolutions install these drivers to enlarge fonts so they're easier to see on screen. A standard video driver (or "small fonts") uses 96 dots on the screen to represent one inch (a so-called "logical inch"); by comparison, a large fonts driver uses 120 pixels to display the same inch.

When WinHelp 3.1 detects a system running a large fonts video driver, it tries to maintain the logical inch by enlarging the bitmap from 96 pixels per inch to 120 pixels per inch. Figure 13.17 illustrates the result of stretching.

To avoid stretching in files built using the WinHelp 3.1 compiler, you can use the Hotspot Editor together with a freeware utility called ShgRez. ShgRez can strip out the resolution information in a .SHG file, so the graphic will not be scaled, regardless of the display resolution or video driver. ShgRez is included on the disc in the back of this book.

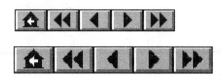

Figure 13.17. *Original graphic (top) and how it looks in WinHelp 3.1 when displayed using a large fonts video driver.*

There is one tradeoff with stripping resolution information from a graphic: if the Help user prints the topic containing the graphic, it will appear very, very small. Also, ShgRez works only on .SHG files that were created from bitmaps, not Windows metafiles (but since metafiles generally scale without distorting, they generally don't need to be processed with ShgRez anyway).

To fix the resolution of a .SHG graphic using ShgRez:

1. Run the Hotspot Editor and save the graphic as a .SHG file.

2. Run ShgRez.

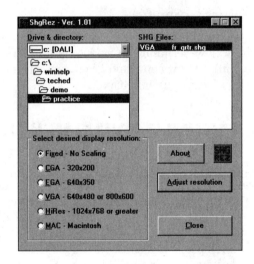

Figure 13.18. *The ShgRez utility.*

3. Select the .SHG file(s) you want to adjust. The current resolution of each file is displayed next to its file name.

4. Under Select Desired Display Resolution, select the resolution you want to use for the file(s). Select **Fixed-No Scaling** to prevent the graphic from being scaled.

5. Click the **Adjust Resolution** button. The .SHG Files list is updated to indicate the new resolution information.

Of course, if you open the .SHG file in the Hotspot Editor and make any changes, you'll have to use ShgRez again to save the resolution information.

Multiple resolution bitmaps: worth the trouble?

The multiple resolution bitmap compiler (MRBC) was created to avoid many of the distortion problems that occur when bitmap images are displayed on a video display resolution that is different from the one you were running when you created the graphics.

The idea behind MRBC is that you create bitmap files for each display resolution (CGA, EGA, VGA, and 8514) and then combine the files into one bitmap image. When it needs to display a multiple-resolution bitmap, WinHelp checks the video display type for the computer and chooses the bitmap that most closely matches its resolution, aspect ratio, and color support.

The MRBC was valuable in resolving incompatibilities with CGA and EGA systems, but most people don't use it much anymore. With MRBC you can prevent the stretching problems that occur under WinHelp 3.1 due to large fonts video display drivers. It's a simple technique: take two identical copies of a bitmap, and combine them as an .MRB file, declaring one as a VGA resolution and the other as 8514 resolution. This solves the same problem as does ShgRez (see the previous section), but since MRBC is storing two copies of the bitmap, it doubles the disk space requirement for the graphic.

The following example shows how to create an .MRB file containing graphics for 640x480 and 1024x768 resolutions.

To create a multiple resolution bitmap:

1. Create a VGA resolution bitmap.

2. Open the bitmap in a paint program, and click the Save As command from the File menu to rename the file using an .854 file extension.

3. Run the multiple resolution bitmap compiler by typing the following command at the DOS prompt:

```
mrbc /s example.vga example.854
```

where EXAMPLE.VGA and EXAMPLE.854 are the names of your bitmap files.

You place an .MRB file just as you would any other graphic image:

```
{bmc example.mrb}
```

See the online *Help Author's Guide* for complete information on the syntax for using MRBC.

USING HELP WORKSHOP'S BUILT-IN BITMAPS

In WinHelp 4, Help Workshop provides ten default bitmaps. You place these bitmaps in your topic file just as you would a bitmap that you created. The following lists the names of the bitmaps and shows how they appear:

Figure 13.19. *The bitmaps built into Help Workshop.*

If you place a bitmap that has the same name as one of Help Workshop's ten built-in bitmaps, it will build your Help file using your image instead of its own bitmap.

Creating a transparent graphic

WinHelp 4 gives you the option of making a bitmap transparent against the window background. When the image is displayed in Help, the background is colored with the background color from the current Help window. This technique is especially useful for designs that aren't rectangular, since the image will not appear within a square boundary.

To create a transparent graphic:

1. Open a topic file and position the insertion point where you want to display the image.

2. Type **{bmct** *filename***}**. (**t** indicates a transparent bitmap.)

```
{bmct winhelp.bmp}
```

Figure 13.20. *A transparent bitmap reference in the topic file.*

Figure 13.21 illustrates a Help graphic as it appears to the user. The same graphic is placed two ways: once using the **bmc** command, and once using the **bmct** command.

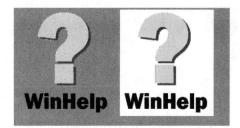

Figure 13.21. *Two bitmaps in a compiled Help file: one is transparent (left), the other is not.*

Notes on transparent bitmaps

There are several issues to consider when implementing transparent bitmaps.

- If you use transparent bitmaps, you may elect to choose a background window color from the standard 16-color Windows palette. If you choose a dithered color for the background window, any white pixels in the graphic will appear in the nearest solid color. For example, if your window background uses the light yellow color (255,255,226) favored by Microsoft, the white pixels in your transparent bitmap will remain white because that is the closest solid color.

- Transparent bitmaps may contain only 16 colors. Unfortunately, the compiler doesn't tell you this if you try to make a 256-color image transparent. If your graphics don't appear transparent in Help, make sure they contain only 16 colors. Monochrome graphics always appear transparent in WinHelp.

- Because Help stores only one copy of each bitmap, you can't reference the same bitmap as transparent in one topic and normal in another topic. If you attempt to do so, Help Workshop displays an error message.

- WinHelp makes the white pixels transparent the first time the bitmap is displayed. If you display the bitmap in another window with a different color, Help will not change the color of white pixels.

- If you use a transparent bitmap in both the nonscrolling region and the topic area (or scrolling region) of the same topic, WinHelp displays the transparent pixels using the background color of the main topic area. For example, if you define a dark gray nonscrolling region and a white topic area, a transparent bitmap in the nonscrolling region will have a white background (not gray).

Placing a graphic for multiple color depths

Many WinHelp 3.1 authors are reluctant to include high resolution color images in their Help file because the images don't look good on low resolution devices.

One of the biggest improvements to graphics in WinHelp 4 is its support for multiple color depths. You can include more than one version of a graphic within a single bitmap reference statement. When the Help file is opened on the user's system, Help checks the video display settings and uses the most appropriate bitmap file.

By placing multiple graphics at various color depths, you are guaranteed that your Help file will look attractive regardless of the user's hardware capabilities. This removes yet another barrier to using high quality graphics in Help (the last barrier, of course, being disk space). Keep in mind that each graphic you include will increase the size of the .HLP file.

To place a graphic for multiple color depths:

1. Open a topic file and position the insertion point where you want to display the image.

2. Type **{bm**x *filename; filename; filename; filename***}**, where *filename* indicates a bitmap. The filenames must be separated by semicolons.

{bmc banjo_16.bmp;banjo_256.bmp}

Figure 13.22. *Referencing multiple color-depth bitmaps in a topic file.*

Notes on multiple color depths

- If you reference the same bitmaps in multiple topics, make sure you list the bitmaps in the same order for each topic. WinHelp looks at the first name in the bitmap statement; if it is different, WinHelp will store separate copies for each of the bitmaps, a process which could dramatically increase the size of your Help file.

  For example, if you reference **{bmc banjo_16.bmp;banjo_256.bmp}** in one topic and **{bmc banjo_256.bmp;banjo_16.bmp}** in another, Help will store separate copies of all four bitmap files.

- Multiple-file bitmap references take precedence over single-file bitmap references. For example, if you have several instances of **{bmc banjo_16.bmp}**, changing any one of them to **{bmc banjo_16.bmp;banjo_256.bmp}** will change all instances. WinHelp will then automatically display the most appropriate of the two graphic files, even in topics where only one is specified.

- The first occurrence of a multiple-file bitmap command takes precedence over all subsequent commands, regardless of how many files they specify. For example, if Help Workshop finds **{bmc banjo_16.bmp; banjo_256.bmp}** first when you compile, it will ignore both **{bmc banjo_16.bmp}** and **{bmc banjo_16.bmp; banjo_256.bmp; banjo_2.bmp}**.

Miscellaneous graphic techniques

Here are several specialized graphic techniques that you may use from time to time.

PLACING GRAPHICS IN TABLES

It is usually difficult to precisely control the alignment of graphics using the {bmc }, {bml } and {bmr} graphic references. If you're having a tough time with your screen design, try placing the graphic reference in a table. Here are three examples of how to apply this technique.

Placing a graphic in a pop-up

One of the problems with placing a graphic using the **bmc** command is that it increases the line spacing of the line of text as necessary to accommodate the height of the graphic. You can use the **bml** or **bmr** commands, but the text wrap may be undesirable, especially for a small graphic in a pop-up window.

If you want to precisely control the placement of a graphic and how the text wraps around it, consider using a two-column table.

[#] **Install font button**

{bmc BTNI NST. SHG}	Installs the selected font(s) into Windows, adding them to application font menus.

Figure 13.23. *Controlling the placement of a graphic in a pop-up topic.*

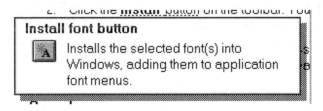

Figure 13.24. *How it appears in Help.*

Layering text over a bitmap

Another table technique enables you to layer text over a bitmap. This technique is useful for creating a watermark effect or for creating a multi-column grid in a Help topic.

Figure 13.25 illustrates a topic containing text over a bitmap and a two column grid.

- Format the left column so it is very narrow. Place the background graphic by reference using a **{bmx}** command. A negative line indent causes the graphic to bleed off the left edge of the Help window. (Even though the column containing the bitmap is very small, Help will display the entire image.)

- The center column includes text and graphics that appear on top of the background. The center column width matches the width of the graphic.

- The right column contains the text you want to display in the rightmost column of the two-column grid.

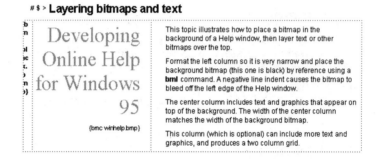

Figure 13.25. *Layering text over a bitmap.*

When WinHelp displays the topic, it paints the screen from left to right, beginning with the bitmap referenced in the left column. Since the width of the bitmap is much wider than the left column, the contents of the center column are displayed on top of the bitmap.

This technique requires some trial and error work with the width of your tables and the size of the bitmap, but it provides a nice effect. If you use this technique, you'll probably want to size the Help window in pixels so the bitmap bleeds off the bottom of the Help window regardless of the user's display resolution (see "Absolute vs. relative window sizing" in Chapter 15 for more information). See the sample file for Chapter 13 on the disc included with this book for help on layering text over a bitmap.

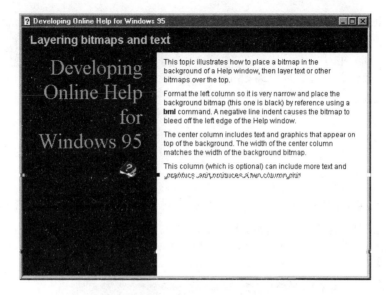

Figure 13.26. *How it looks in WinHelp.*

Adding a button to the nonscrolling region

Some Help systems use a "See Also" or other button in the right side of the nonscrolling region. It seems natural to place an image in the nonscrolling region using a right-aligned tab stop, but this approach causes the image to disappear off the right side of the window if the user sizes the window smaller than the width of the tab stop.

You can use tables to format a button so that it appears on the right side of a window and moves when the Help window is resized. This ensures that the button remains visible regardless of the window size. Here are some tips:

To add a button to the nonscrolling region:

1. Place a section break after the previous topic (it can be before or after the current topic's page break). Without a section break, there's no way to place a table in the first paragraph of a topic.

2. Create a two column table.

3. Place the topic footnotes and the topic heading in the left column. Adjust the width of the left column just wide enough to display the topic heading.

4. Place the graphic image in the right cell. Set the width of the right column just wide enough to accommodate the graphic, and right-align the graphic reference.

5. Format the table so it uses a variable width (that is, the width of its columns will adjust as the user sizes the window).

In Word, click the Table menu and click the Cell Height and Width command. Then click the Row tab and set the table Alignment to **Center**.

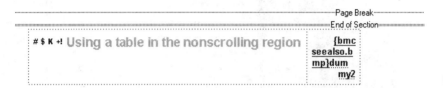

Figure 13.27. *Using a table to place a button in the nonscrolling region.*

The table should look like the example in Figure 13.27 when displayed in your word processor. As Figure 13.28 shows, as the user widens the Help window, the button in the nonscrolling region moves.

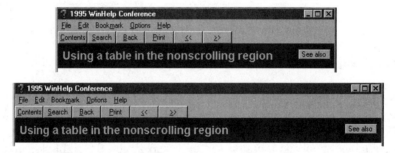

Figure 13.28. *As the window is widened, the button in the nonscrolling region moves.*

BLEEDING GRAPHICS

Filling the Help window with a graphic is a technique you can use to create a stronger visual impact for your Help systems.

By default, Help leaves an eight pixel left margin on the edge of its window, preventing graphics from filling the screen. Negative indents let you overcome this restriction.

To place a graphic (or text) to the left edge of the window without bleeding it, specify a negative line indent of seven points. To bleed a graphic over the left edge of the window, increase the negative indent more than seven points. To specify a negative line indent in Word, click Paragraph from the Format menu, click the Indents and Spacing tab, and specify a value in the **Left** box under Indentation.

Bleeding a graphic off the top, bottom, or right margin requires no special formatting. Help leaves a top margin of three pixels for text, but if you place a graphic in the first paragraph of a Help topic it will appear directly beneath the button bar with no white space showing.

If you want to size the window to match the dimensions of a graphic, make sure the window is configured to size in pixels (see "Absolute vs relative window sizing" in Chapter 15).

HELP WATERMARKS

Many third party development tools—including Doc-To-Help and RoboHelp—provide DLLs that enable you to display a bitmap in the window background and to place text on top, much like a watermark on a sheet of paper. Check CompuServe for sample files that demonstrate watermarks.

It's a challenge to design a watermark that doesn't render the text illegible. You should use very light colors when designing watermarks, and you may want to display them only in specific topics (like a contents topic).

14

Creating Multimedia Help

If you're looking to add a little sizzle to your Help files, nothing beats multimedia. Today's savvy computer users aren't satisfied with plain text and boring graphics. Adding video, animation, and sound is one way to make a striking impression that makes your work stand out in the crowd.

Not that multimedia is simply gratuitous entertainment. Sound and motion can help you communicate difficult concepts and procedures with an economy and grace that words can't match.

WinHelp 4 provides solid multimedia support, largely because of the multimedia enhancements built into Windows 95.

This chapter covers:

- An overview of multimedia formats.

- Playing standard Windows video files (.AVI) and Lotus ScreenCam files.

- Playing audio files, including wave and MIDI.

- Playing multimedia using MCI strings.

- Other multimedia authoring options from Microsoft.

At a glance Multimedia support

WinHelp 4	WinHelp 3.1
Support for Video for Windows (AVI) built into Help using new {mci } statement; no additional files required.	No direct multimedia support; third-party DLLs required.
Multimedia support for audio (WAV, MIDI) to be provided in upcoming maintenance release. Can use sound functionality built into Windows API.	Can use the sound functionality built into the Windows API.

Multimedia overview

The term "multimedia" refers to a variety of file formats that play audio and video files on a computer. This section provides an overview of multimedia file formats and how WinHelp stores multimedia files.

AUDIO FILE FORMATS

Windows uses two types of audio files: waveform audio and MIDI.

- Waveform audio (or "wave") files are digitally sampled sound clips. Wave files are perfect for playing realistic sound effects, spoken voice, and music. These files tend to be of very high quality, but are very large (even when compressed). Wave files have the .WAV file extension.

  Wave files are typically created using a microphone and other output device (like a cassette deck or CD) and utilities included with your computer's sound card. These utilities range from the Sound Recorder (SNDREC32.EXE) included with Windows to the professional WAVE for Windows from Turtle Beach Systems.

- MIDI files contain musical notes and other information necessary for a synthesizer to play a song. MIDI—which stands for "musical instrument digital interface"—controls which notes are played, the duration of each note, the instrument used to play the note, and various effects that modify the sound.

  Any computer with a sound card can play MIDI information, but sound cards that feature wavetable synthesis provide the most realistic audio for MIDI files. MIDI files have the .MID file extension.

MIDI files are created using a MIDI-compatible keyboard and an editing package called a "sequencer." There is a wide range of MIDI keyboards available, ranging from $100 models from Casio and Yamaha to high-end offerings from Roland and Kurzweil. Midisoft makes a solid line of entry-level sequencing software; high-end packages include Vision from Opcode and Cakewalk from Twelve Tone Systems.

In order to play either type of audio file from Help, the user must have a sound card and the appropriate software drivers installed, and have speakers or headphones connected to the computer.

If you're using music in your Help file, keep in mind that wave files require much more disk space than MIDI files. For example, an average quality (16 bit 22kHz sample) monophonic wave file that is one-half second long requires about 20K of disk space—enough room to hold a two minute MIDI file!

Of course, MIDI files don't provide you with much control over the playback quality (a MIDI file that sounds great on a wavetable synthesizer will sound unrealistic and unconvincing on a cheap FM synthesis sound card), but they are practical for adding a basic music soundtrack to your WinHelp file. For reproducing sound effects, spoken voice, or music soundtracks demanding realistic instrumentation and high quality sound fidelity, you'll want to stick with wave files.

VIDEO AND ANIMATION FILE FORMATS

There are many video file formats, but the most common formats used in Help are Video for Windows (.AVI) and Lotus ScreenCam. Video files typically include sounds that play while the video is being shown.

Microsoft Video for Windows

Video for Windows files offer full motion computer video and audio without special hardware. Video for Windows files have the .AVI (audio video interleaved) file extension. By interleaving the image and sound data, .AVI files provide reasonable performance when read from devices with relatively slow data transfer rates, such as CD-ROM drives.

.AVI files are usually created using a video camera and then converted to the PC using a video capture card (such as Creative Lab's VideoBlaster or Intel's Smart Video Recorder Pro). Once digitized on the PC, videos are manipulated using editing software like Adobe's Premiere.

Another way to create an .AVI file is to capture video images directly from the computer screen. You can add audio explanations at the same time by using a microphone. This works well for software training videos.

To capture movement on the screen as an .AVI file, you can use a utility called CapScrn included with RoboHELP and available for free from Microsoft's Multimedia JumpStart program (see "Playing multimedia using MCI strings" later in this chapter). CapScrn version 1.1

won't work under Windows 95 unless you obtain the updated 32-bit drivers, or add the following line to the [DRIVERS] section of the SYSTEM.INI file:

```
msvideo8=scrncap.drv
```

Lotus ScreenCam

ScreenCam is a video format created by Lotus that enables you to capture images from your computer screen and include voice-over audio. ScreenCam files aren't suitable for traditional video (such as input from a video camera), but they provide a few advantages over .AVI files for capturing images from a computer screen.

Because ScreenCam files are screen-based—not frame-based like .AVI files—they require much less memory and a less sophisticated computer system for playback. In fact, ScreenCam files can be played back on 386-based systems in full motion, full screen format with no loss of resolution, at speeds approaching 30 frames-per-second.

ScreenCam files require less than one-half of the disk space used by .AVI files. For example, a 20-second ScreenCam file captured at 640x480 resolution requires about 345K of disk space. By comparison, a 20 second .AVI file captured at 640x480 using a 20 frames-per-second frame rate requires about 895K. Of course, ScreenCam also requires you to ship a runtime player that is about 600K in size, so ScreenCam's disk savings may not pay off unless you ship several video files.

As of this writing, ScreenCam 2.0 is incompatible with Windows 95, but Lotus Development Corp. is reportedly planning an upgrade. Lotus can be reached toll-free in the U.S. at 1-800-343-5414.

Apple QuickTime

QuickTime is the video format used on the Apple Macintosh. There are several players available for Windows that can play QuickTime files, but it's generally much simpler to convert QuickTime files to the AVI format since support for AVI is built into Windows.

If you have existing QuickTime files, there are several utilities available that can convert them to .AVI files. Some QuickTime files translate well, but others increase in size or fail to convert properly. If you plant to convert QuickTime to .AVI, you should perform some test conversions early in your development cycle.

Animation files

Animation files are typically used for displaying a variety of moving images, from simple cartoons to complex computer-generated images. Animation files are similar to video files, except that they usually are smaller and often have better color and resolution.

One approach to creating animation files is to define an object, a starting point, and an end point, and then let the computer create the intermediate frames. Another approach is to draw an image and then erase it and redraw it in a different position on the screen. There are several tools available for creating animation files, including AutoDesk Animator Pro and Gold Disk Animator.

If your animation utility has an external player, you can use it to play your animation files from WinHelp. If the animation program includes an MCI driver, you can use MCI strings to play the animation (see "Playing multimedia using MCI strings" later in this chapter).

HOW HELP STORES MULTIMEDIA FILES

Unless you specify otherwise, Help Workshop stores multimedia files within the .HLP file's internal file system, called "baggage."

Storing multimedia files in baggage is generally the best option since it prevents the user from unintentionally deleting or losing the multimedia file. If the file contains material protected by copyright, this option also makes it more difficult for the user to copy the file.

Shipping your multimedia files separately is an attractive option in some cases. If you're installing your Help file on the user's hard disk, shipping the multimedia files separately gives the user the flexibility to delete them but still have access to your Help content. This option is advantageous if the multimedia file is being accessed from both the Help file and your application. And finally, your Help file will compile much more quickly if you don't store multimedia files in baggage.

If you elect not to include the multimedia file in WinHelp's baggage, you must ship the file along with your .HLP file. In most cases, you'll want to install the multimedia files in the same folder with your Help file.

See "Placing a file in baggage" in Chapter 16 for more information on baggage.

Playing video files

Video files can be included in any Help topic, including pop-ups. When displaying a video file, WinHelp creates an embedded window and automatically sizes the window to accommodate the image or controller (if any). If the window is too small to display the controller, WinHelp crops the right and bottom edges; the user can resize the window, if necessary.

By default, WinHelp provides the user with control over the playback of the .AVI file by including a controller and a menu. You can tell WinHelp to play the .AVI file when the topic is entered, and configure the user control by omitting the default video controller, the menu, or both.

{MCI } STATEMENT SYNTAX

{mci[_left | _right] [options,] *filename*}

Parameter	Description
_left or **_right**	Aligns the embedded multimedia window to the left or right side of the Help window.
options	Specifies various options for the multimedia control window. To specify more than one option, separate the options with spaces (not commas).
	If you don't specify any options, the standard controller appears and the file is not played until the user clicks the Play button.

Value	Description
EXTERNAL	Stores the multimedia file outside of the Help file (that is, it is not placed in Help's baggage).
NOPLAYBAR	Hides the multimedia controller. This is useful for auto-play and repeat.
NOMENU	If there is a video controller, this hides the menu button.
REPEAT	The file automatically repeats (or "loops") until the user stops it or displays another topic.
PLAY	The file automatically plays when the topic is displayed.

filename	Specifies the name of the multimedia file to include in the topic.

EXAMPLES

Here are several examples illustrating how to play multimedia files.

NOTE *Once WinHelp 4 adds support for MCI audio files, you can use any of the following examples with audio files: just substitute the appropriate file extension (.WAV or .MID) in place of the .AVI extension. See "Playing sound files" later in this chapter for more information.*

Playing a video file

The following command creates an embedded window and displays the first frame of the video. When the user clicks the Play button, the remaining frames in the video clip play.

To play a video:

1. Open your topic file and move the insertion point to the place where you want the video to appear.

2. Type the **{mci }** statement, specifying the name of an .AVI file.

   The following command creates a multimedia control window that displays the first frame of the file SAMPLE.AVI when the topic is shown:

   ```
   {mci SAMPLE.AVI}
   ```

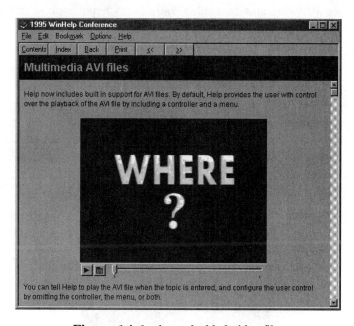

Figure 14.1. *An embedded video file.*

Playing a video upon topic entry

Unlike Help's macros, the **{mci }** statement does not require you to enter a topic entry macro footnote to play a video when the user enters a topic. Instead, you include the PLAY option within the **{mci }** statement.

To play a video upon topic entry:

1. Open your topic file and move the insertion point to the place where you want the video to appear.

2. Type the **{mci }** statement followed by the **PLAY** option and one comma.

3. After the comma, specify the name of an .AVI file.

   The following command creates a multimedia control window that automatically plays the file SAMPLE.AVI when the topic is shown:

   ```
   {mci PLAY, SAMPLE.AVI}
   ```

Customizing the video controller

By default, Windows displays a standard video controller when it displays an .AVI file. The controller contains a slider bar and two buttons. The button on the left plays the video. The button on the right displays a menu that lets the user:

- Adjust the size of the video window to 50 percent, 100 percent, or 200 percent. Reducing the window may be necessary to improve performance on older systems.

- Adjust the playback speed. Once again, this gives the user the flexibility to optimize performance; for example, on a fast system the user may want to slow the video playback rate.

- Copy the video onto the Clipboard.

- Send MCI strings to precisely control the video playback (a feature most users will never touch).

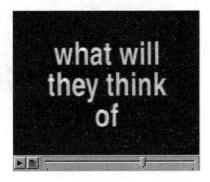

Figure 14.2. *The standard video controller.*

You have three options for customizing the video controller:

- **Use the default.** This is usually the best option, since the controller provides options that some users may need to optimize performance.

- **Delete only the menu.** This leaves the user with only two options—start and stop. Because it disables the copy command, you may want to use this option if you're distributing video clips protected by copyright and you're concerned about piracy.

  The following example deletes the menu:

  ```
  {mci NOMENU, SAMPLE.AVI}
  ```

- Remove the controller altogether. If you don't want to provide the user with any control over the video playback, you can remove the controller altogether. This will frustrate some users, especially if the video clip is long, so don't delete the controller unless you have a good reason to do so.

  The following example deletes the entire controller:

  ```
  {mci NOPLAYBAR, SAMPLE.AVI}
  ```

Playing a video in a different window

You may want to play a video file in a pop-up or secondary Help window, or in a special .AVI window used for multimedia files.

> **IMPORTANT** *If you're displaying an .AVI in a secondary or pop-up window, you'll need to stick with the PLAY option: REPEAT won't work.*

Playing a video in a pop-up window

One of the advantages to placing an .AVI file in a pop-up window is that it doesn't take up valuable real estate in the Help window until the user accesses the pop-up.

To place a video in a pop-up window:

1. Open your topic file and create a pop-up topic. You probably don't want to include a topic heading for the pop-up window; it will detract from the video.

2. Add an **{mci }** statement to the topic. Because the user must click on a hotspot to display the pop-up window (and therefore presumably wants to see the video), you should probably set the .AVI to play automatically when the pop-up is displayed:

   ```
   {mci PLAY, SAMPLE.AVI}
   ```

   You may also want to remove the playbar, since the user can stop viewing the video by simply clicking outside the pop-up window.

   ```
   {mci PLAY NOPLAYBAR, SAMPLE.AVI}
   ```

A well-designed pop-up topic might look like that shown in Figure 14.3.

Help usually leaves a little extra room around the video image in the pop-up window. Therefore, you may want to set the background color of the pop-up to match the border color in your .AVI file. For example, if your .AVI file has a black border, you could set the pop-up color to black using the **SetPopupColor** macro:

```
SetPopupColor(0,0,0)
```

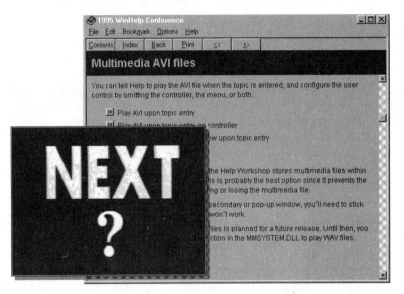

Figure 14.3. *A pop-up topic that plays an .AVI file.*

Playing a video in a secondary Help window

Playing a video in a secondary Help window may be desirable if you want to keep the Help topic visible while playing the video. This technique requires that you carefully configure the secondary window properties.

To play a video in a secondary Help window:

1. Create the secondary window type. You should probably set the size of the secondary window to match the size of the video file. This is done by setting the window to auto-size and sizing the window in pixels.

   First, set the window to auto-size: check the **Auto-size height** box on the General tab of the Window Properties dialog box.

Then, carefully size the width of the Help window (which involves some trial and error) to match the width of the video file. Finally, set the Help window so it sizes in pixels: clear the **Adjust for user's screen resolution box** on the Position tab of the Window Properties dialog box.

2. Open your topic file and add a new topic. If the topic will be accessed from the Index or Find tabs or from one of the linking macros, be sure to include a default window type footnote (>) containing the window name you used in Step 1.

3. Add an **{mci }** statement. You should probably set the video to autoplay when the window is opened:

```
{mci PLAY NOPLAYBAR, SAMPLE.AVI}
```

Your topic might look like that shown in Figure 14.4.

Figure 14.4. *A topic that plays an .AVI file in a secondary window.*

Playing a video in an external window

Another option for playing AVI is to use an external video player, such as the Media Player included with Windows. Like playing a video in a secondary window, this technique lets the user display a Help topic and video at the same time.

Using an external window to play a video is a little easier than using a secondary window since you don't have to configure the window yourself. However, using an external player requires that the .AVI files are stored on the disk, not in Help's baggage system. Also, this approach will affect performance slightly, since it takes extra time to run the external program.

To play a video in an external window:

1. Open your topic file and create a hotspot jump.

2. Use the **ExecFile** macro in the hotspot to run Media Player and pass it the name of an .AVI file. If you want to begin playing the video file automatically when the user clicks the hotspot and close the video window when the file is finished playing, include the **/play** and **/close** options.

The following example illustrates a sample hotspot.

```
Run Media Player!ExecFile(mplayer.exe, /play /close
c:\windows\media\sample.avi)
```

Figure 14.5. *A topic that plays an .AVI file in Media Player.*

If you don't include the **/play** option, Media Player displays two windows: one for the video clip, and one for a controller. This controller provides the user with even more flexibility for directing the video playback than does the standard WinHelp video controller.

Figure 14.6. *Media Player will display a controller if you don't specify the /play option.*

Playing Lotus ScreenCam files

In order to play Lotus ScreenCam movies, you must either ship the runtime player (about 600K in size) or export the movie as a standalone player.

If you want to ship more than one movie, you should include the movies and the runtime player (this saves space since you won't including the player along with each standalone movie). The following example runs a ScreenCam movie from a hotspot. The **/sc** parameters hide the title and product information screens and close the movie when it has finished playing.

```
Click here!ExecFile(scrncamp.exe, foo.scm /sc)
```

You should always avoid copying files to the Windows folder, and the ScreenCam player is no exception. One approach is to install the player in the folder containing your Help file: that way, you won't need to include a pathname in the macro you use to run the player. Otherwise, copy the ScreenCam player to a directory on the path, or specify the pathname in the command used to play the movie. You can also update the WINHELP.INI to specify the path to the ScreenCam player:

```
[Files]
scrncamp.exe=C:\WINDOWS\SCRNCAM
```

If you're shipping a single tutorial file, you can create a "standalone movie" containing both the ScreenCam player and the movie. The following example plays a file named TUTORIAL.EXE; the **/sc** parameters hide the title and product information screens and close the movie as soon as it completes.

```
Click here!EF(tutorial.exe /sc)
```

Playing sound files

The first release of WinHelp 4 does not reliably support using the MCI interface to play wave and MIDI sound files. Compatibility issues forced Microsoft to remove MCI audio support, but this feature is planned for a future release. Keep your eyes on the online resources for WinHelp (including CompuServe and the Internet) to find out about the status of a maintenance release providing MCI audio support.

At the time of this writing, there are two options for playing sound from WinHelp. The simplest method is to use the sound support built into the MMSYSTEM.DLL included with Windows 3.1 or the WINMM.DLL included with Windows 95. Alternatively, you can use a custom DLL.

MODIFYING THE PROJECT FILE

In order to play a .WAV or .MID file from WinHelp, you'll need to provide the project file with some information about WINMM.DLL or MMSYSTEM.DLL. Adding the **RegisterRoutine** macro to the project file tells WinHelp about the audio function in the DLL and how to pass it information.

To add audio support to a project file:

1. Open the project file in Help Workshop.

2. Click the **Config** button.

3. Click the **Add** button.

4. Type the following line in the **Macro** box:

```
RegisterRoutine(MMSYSTEM.DLL, sndPlaySound, Su)
```

The line tells WinHelp to look in the MMSYSTEM.DLL for a function named **sndPlaySound**, and that the function parameter types are a string and an unsigned short integer.

Or, type the following line:

```
RegisterRoutine(WINMM.DLL,sndPlaySoundA, U=SU)
```

This tells WinHelp to look in the WINMM.DLL for a function named **sndPlaySoundA**, and that the function parameter types are a string and an unsigned long integer.

PLAYING A WAVE FILE

Once you register the audio function in MMSYSTEM.DLL, you can use it just as you would one of the WinHelp macros. As explained in Chapter 16, there are several options for running a Help macro, including when the user opens the Help file, enters a topic, clicks a hotspot or button, and more.

sndPlaySound(*filename*,flag) or **sndPlaySoundA**(*filename*,flag)

Parameter	Description
filename	Specifies the name of the audio file to play. Help first looks for the audio file in the current folder, then in the Windows SYSTEM folder; the HELP folder in the Windows folder; the Windows folder; the folder specified in WINHELP.INI (if any); and the PATH environment. If it can't find the audio file, Help uses the system default sound; if there is no default, it does not play the sound.

Parameter	Description
flag	Specifies various options for the audio playback. You can sum the values, if you want. For example, entering 10 continuously loops a sound file, and would not play the default if the specified file can't be found.

Value	Description
0	Returns control to Help once the sound is finished.
1	Returns control to Help immediately. You can stop the sound by playing the same sound or another sound with the flag set to 0.
2	If the sound file can't be found, does not play the default sound.
8	Sound repeats until it is stopped. You must also specify the 1 flag.
16	If a previous sound is currently playing, returns control to Help immediately without playing the new sound.

The flag returns **True** if the sound (or default) is played; otherwise it returns **False.**

The following example plays the file named SAMPLE.WAV. Be sure to include the quotation marks around the filename, or the command won't work. You can use double quotation marks (") or opening and closing single quotation marks (` ').

```
Play a WAV file!SndPlaySound("SAMPLE.WAV",1)
```

PLAYING A MIDI FILE

The procedure for playing a MIDI file is identical to that used to play a .WAV file, except that you type the name of the MIDI file you want to use.

The following command plays a file named SAMPLE.MID. Be sure to include the quotation marks around the filename. You can use double quotation marks (") or opening and closing single quotation marks (` ').

```
Play a MIDI file!SndPlaySound("SAMPLE.MID",1)
```

STORING AUDIO FILES

You can't use **sndPlaySound** or **sndPlaySoundA** to play wave or MIDI files from baggage because they do not recognize the exclamation point that identifies a baggage file. You can either install your audio files in the same folder as your Help file, or store them in baggage and use a custom DLL (such as HYPRO.DLL, available from 76443.3232@compuserve.com) to play them from WinHelp.

Playing multimedia using MCI strings

Yet another way to playback multimedia files is with the MCI (media control interface) interface built into the Windows API. So-called MCI "strings" are valuable if you need more precise control over the playback of your video or audio files. You can also use MCI strings to playback any multimedia file that includes MCI drivers (such as Autodesk Animator Pro or Gold Disk Animator files).

There are several MCI strings available, but those most useful to Help developers—**play**, **pause**, **resume**, and **stop**—let you play a specific portion of a multimedia file. For instance, these commands enable you to play specific frames of an .AVI file. There are also several commands that let you configure the video playback. For complete information on the various MCI strings, see the Help file MCISTRWH.HLP that is included with the Windows SDK and many compilers.

The extra control comes at a price. Using MCI strings is considerably more work than just playing a multimedia file using the **{mci}** statement or **sndPlaySound** function. If you're playing a video file, it appears in a separate window that cannot be stopped, paused, or otherwise controlled by the user.

In order to use MCI strings, you must register the **mciSendString** function from the MMSYSTEM.DLL in the [CONFIG] section of your project file. You can open the project file in a text editor and add the following line, or enter it using Help Workshop as explained in "Modifying the project file" earlier in this chapter.

```
[CONFIG]
RegisterRoutine("MMSYSTEM.DLL","mciSendString","SIuu")
```

The first example below, which plays an .AVI file, illustrates the unique nature of the MCI string syntax. First, each MCI string is treated as a separate macro command; multiple strings are separated with semicolons. The double-backslashes in the **open** command are necessary to represent a single backslash in a pathname. The **alias** parameter in the open command specifies an alias that is referenced in the remaining MCI strings. The **wait** command prevents the movie from closing before it plays. Note that the last three parameters of each command are always zero.

```
Play an AVI file!mciSendString("open
c:\\windows\\media\\skiing.avi alias
movie",0,0,0);mciSendString("play movie
wait",0,0,0);mciSendString("close movie",0,0,0)
```

The next example disables the audio portion of an .AVI file, sets the window title, and plays frames 15 through 26 of the .AVI file.

```
Play selected frames of an AVI!mciSendString("open
c:\\windows\\media\\skiing.avi alias movie",0,0,0);
mciSendString("set movie audio all off",0,0,0);
mciSendString("window movie text Your title
here",0,0,0);mciSendString("play movie from 15 to 26
wait",0,0,0);mciSendString("close movie",0,0,0)
```

The last example plays a MIDI file.

```
Play a MIDI file!mciSendString("open
c:\\windows\\media\\canyon.mid alias song",0,0,0);
mciSendString("play song wait",0,0,0);mciSendString("close
song",0,0,0)
```

Microsoft's Multimedia Viewer and MediaView

Windows Help is not Microsoft's only entry into the world of multimedia. There are two other technologies—Multimedia Viewer and MediaView—that enable you to create and publish multimedia and hypertext systems. This section briefly describes Viewer and MediaView (some of this information has been adapted from a Microsoft positioning paper on these technologies).

MULTIMEDIA VIEWER

Microsoft's Multimedia Viewer is an authoring system designed for multimedia titles and hypertext publications. Viewer evolved from Windows Help, and the latest release—version 2.0—is based on the WinHelp 3.1 core technology. Because of these origins, authoring a Viewer title is basically identical to authoring a WinHelp title, with a few additional features.

Viewer 2.0 provides a superset of the WinHelp 3.1 functionality including full-text search, multimedia display of video, audio, and animation files; and a customizable user interface. The first versions of Encarta, Bookshelf, and Cinemania were authored in Viewer and provide a good example of its capabilities. Microsoft has announced that they have stopped Multimedia Viewer development and will not release any updates.

Since WinHelp 4 incorporates most of Viewer's functionality, why would you choose to author a title in Viewer instead of WinHelp 4? Viewer offers a few advantages over WinHelp 4.0:

- If you want sophisticated layout options, you can use Viewer's panes (sections of a window) to control the placement of text and graphics within the user interface.

- Its search and indexing features offer more advanced features such as search categories, aliases, and fuzzy searching. (Note that Viewer uses a different full-text search technology than WinHelp 4.)

- Viewer provides more flexible authoring features (such as topic groups and topic exit macros).

There are a few downsides to using Viewer. If you ship a Viewer title, you must include about two megabytes of runtime files for the user to view your title. Also, Viewer titles are not directly compatible with WinHelp 3.1 or 4.0; specifically, WinHelp 4 does not support panes, topic groups, or search fields, and uses a different full-text search indexer and user interface. Finally, you should consider the long term prospects for Viewer, especially the lack of support and continued development.

Viewer was once a commercial product, but Microsoft now provides it at no cost on the JumpStart CD-ROM and on its Internet FTP server. Viewer is also available on the Microsoft Developer Network (MSDN) Level 2 CD-ROM.

The Multimedia Viewer forum on CompuServe is a valuable resource for learning more. From any CompuServe **go** prompt, type **winmm** and then visit Forum 6 for Multimedia Viewer.

MEDIAVIEW

MediaView has now assumed the throne as Microsoft's high-end multimedia authoring tool. MediaView uses Viewer's basic layout engine, index and search engine, file system, navigation services, and multimedia rendering, but provides C, C++, and Visual Basic programmers with the flexibility to design their own user interface.

The process used to author a MediaView title is basically identical to that used to author a WinHelp or Viewer title. The real difference is that a programmer must design a user interface and program a custom application to play the MediaView title. This customization allows for a truly spectacular user interface (the 1995 versions of Encarta, Cinemania, and Bookshelf were all created using MediaView), but adds significant development time and expense to your multimedia project.

MediaView is available on the Microsoft Developer Network (MSDN) Level 2 CD-ROM and on the JumpStart CD-ROM.

Note that many MediaView developers have complained about the sparse documentation available from Microsoft. One of the best places for help with MediaView is the MediaView forum on CompuServe. From any CompuServe **go** prompt, type **winmm** and then visit Forum 3 for MediaView.

Learning more about multimedia

Here are some valuable sources for information on multimedia.

- Burger, Jeff. *The Desktop Multimedia Bible*: Addison-Wesley, 1993.

- *Multimedia Demystified*. Cupertino, CA: Apple Press, 1993.

- Pruitt, Stephen. *Viewer How-To CD*. Corte Madera, CA: The Waite Group Press, 1994.

Microsoft has several multimedia tools that are useful for Help authors.

- Microsoft's JumpStart CD is available from Microsoft's Multimedia Development Group. At the time of this writing, you can get a free copy by sending an email message to **mmd-info@microsoft.com.**

- Microsoft's FTP server on the Internet provides the latest versions of various Help development tools and utilities. Point your Web browser or FTP program to:

  ```
  ftp://ftp.microsoft.com/
  ```

  For example, to get the latest multimedia utilities, open the following folder:

  ```
  ftp://ftp.microsoft.com/developr/drg/multimedia/jumpstart/
  ```

15

Creating the Help Interface

One of the reasons for WinHelp's amazing popularity has been its customizable interface. Under WinHelp 3.1 most of this customization requires DLLs and arcane macros (along with a healthy bit of sweat and elbow grease), but WinHelp 4.0 provides a flexible interface with minimal effort right out of the box. In particular, it provides several new interface options for working with Help windows, buttons, menus, and keyboard shortcuts.

This chapter explains how to work with:

- Help windows, including the main window and secondary windows.
- Help buttons, including the button bar, authorable buttons, and shortcut buttons.
- Help menus, including the menu bar and floating menu.
- Help's keyboard interface.

This section discusses many of the Help macros used to create the Help interface. If you're not familiar with how to create a macro, see Chapter 16, *Working with Help Macros*. In particular, see the section called "Running Help macros" so that you understand the various ways in which a macro can be executed.

At a glance Interface customizations

WinHelp 4.0	WinHelp 3.1
Secondary windows have button bars, just like the main window.	Hotspot bitmaps are placed in the nonscrolling region of a secondary window to simulate a button.
Secondary window height can be set to "auto-size" based on the length of the topic.	Window size must be hardcoded in the project file.
A window type footnote (>) lets you assign a default window to a topic; this window type is honored from the Index and Find tabs, and the new **ALink** and **KLink** macros.	All topics accessed through the keyword list default to the main window.
A macro can be set to run each time a particular window type opens.	Macros are copied to each topic that appears in a particular window type.
A window can be sized in pixels, in addition to Help "units" that size the window as a percentage of screen size.	A DLL is required to specify the size of a window in pixels.
Three-dimensional "authorable" buttons containing text can be added to topics.	Hotspot bitmaps are used to simulate a button.
Buttons can easily be removed from the button bar in the main window.	
Submenus can be added to a menu using the **ExtInsertMenu** macro.	The macro exists, but is undocumented by Microsoft.

Working with Help windows

Help includes three types of windows: main windows, secondary windows, and pop-up windows.

- The "main" window is Help's default window. It includes a menu bar and a button bar.

- A secondary window is virtually identical to the main window, except it doesn't include a menu bar. Note that WinHelp 3.1 secondary windows are second-class citizens, the largest complaint being their lack of a button bar.

- A pop-up window appears when the user clicks on dotted-underline text.

Pop-up windows are so basic that, aside from explaining how to set the color of a pop-up window, this section focuses on the customization options available for main and secondary windows. Throughout this chapter, the generic term "window" refers either to a main or a secondary window.

There are only a few differences between main and secondary windows in WinHelp 4.0; these differences are summarized below:

Table 15.1. *Feature differences between the main window and secondary Help window*

Help feature	Main window	Secondary window
Menu bar	✓	
History window	✓	
Bookmark feature	✓	
Window height can be automatically sized to fit the topic length.		✓

In WinHelp 4, you can define up to 255 secondary windows. Each window can have its own size, position, color, and title. Any nine of the 255 secondary windows can be open at the same time as the main window.

Before you begin designing a windowing strategy for your Help system, think about the type of information you want to present. You may want to refer back to Chapter 3, *Window Types*, *Screen Layout*, *Graphics*, and *Multimedia*, for design guidelines on Help windows.

CREATING A WINDOW

Help Workshop makes it easy to create main or secondary Help windows. As you work with Help Workshop, it writes your window settings to the [WINDOWS] section of the project file.

Note that in order to customize the main window, you must first "create" it using Help Workshop. This isn't technically accurate: if you build a Help file without explicitly creating a main window, your Help system will by default appear in the main window. (Odd that Help Workshop doesn't include a default "main" window type.)

To create a window:

1. Open a project file in Help Workshop. (See Figure 15.1.)

2. Click Windows, the Windows Properties dialog box appears.

3. Click General, then Add. The Add a New Window Type dialog box appears.

   In the **Create a window named** box, type the name of the window. The name may contain eight or fewer characters. If you are going to customize the main window, you'll need to "create" it by typing **main**.

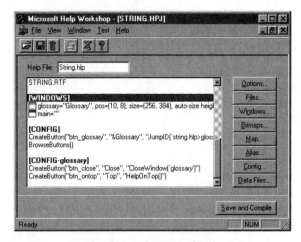

Figure 15.1. *Help Workshop.*

Figure 15.2. *The Add a New Window Type dialog box.*

4. Choose one of the window types from the **Based on this standard window** list. This list contains three window "templates"—Procedure, Reference, and Error Message—that will help you quickly define secondary window attributes. The three templates are described in Table 15.2.

Table 15.2. *Basic characteristics for the three secondary window "templates"*

Template	Suggested use	Characteristics
Procedure	Displaying procedures.	Auto-sizing. Three buttons (Help Topics, Back, Options). Positioned in the upper right corner of the screen.

Table 15.2. *(continued)*

Template	Suggested use	Characteristics
Reference	Displaying reference material.	Auto-sizing. Three buttons (Help Topics, Back, Options). Positioned on the left side of the screen and fills about two thirds of the width of the screen.
Error message	Displaying error messages.	Auto-sizing. No buttons. Lets WinHelp determine the position (upper right corner of the screen unless the user changes the position).

5. Click OK to return to the Windows Properties dialog box.

6. Click one of the tabs and specify the rest of the window settings. The various settings are explained throughout this chapter.

SETTING THE WINDOW TITLE

You can set the text that appears in a Help window's title bar and on its taskbar button. The title you specify will be used for any Help topics that appear in the specified window. For example, if you display procedural topics in a secondary window named "proc," you might want to title the window "How To."

The window title can be up to 50 characters in length, but you should try to keep it as short as possible.

To set the window title:

1. Open a project file in Help Workshop.

2. Click Windows then General.

3. In the **Window Type** list, select the window type.

4. In the **Title bar text** box, type the title. You can also type a comment in the Comment box (comments are ignored by Help Workshop and don't increase the size of your Help file).

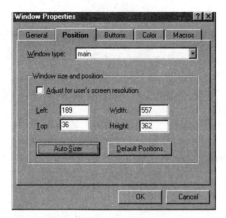

Figure 15.3. *The General properties sheet.*

Sorting out Help's titling

There are three different places where you can specify the text appearing in Help's title bar. Figuring out which title will be used by WinHelp can get confusing. Here's the order WinHelp uses to decide which title to use:

1. The title for the current window type (specified in the **Title Bar Text** box). This appears in the [WINDOWS] section for each window. You probably want to assign a title for each window type.

2. The :TITLE option in the contents file. In Help Workshop, this is specified in the **Default Title** box when you edit the contents file. This is the best place to set the title for your Help files. Most Help authors assign a title in the contents file for every Help file.

   If you're building a modular system containing more than one .HLP file, the title specified in the :TITLE option of the base contents file will be displayed regardless of which Help file is open. This feature helps you integrate the various .HLP files by providing a consistent title.

   For example, suppose you're building a modular Help system for American League baseball that includes a file named AL.HLP and a separate .HLP file for each team. If you define the title in the main contents file (AL.CNT) to read "AL Baseball," that text will appear in the title bar for each Help file (MARINERS.HLP, INDIAN.HLP, and so forth), regardless of the title specified in the individual .CNT files.

   A title specified in an individual .CNT file (MARINERS.CNT might contain the title "Seattle Mariners") will only be used if the Help file is run standalone (for example, if its icon is double-clicked).

3. The TITLE option in the [OPTIONS] section of the project file. This is specified using the **Help title** box in Help Workshop's Options dialog box (click the Options button, then the General tab). This option is primarily used for .HLP files that don't include contents files.

If none of these options specifies a title, Help will use the title "Windows Help" for the main window, and leave the title bar blank for any secondary windows.

SETTING THE WINDOW SIZE AND POSITION

WinHelp 4.0 provides you a great degree of control over the size and position of a Help window. This is accomplished using the Auto-Sizer, one of the slickest components in Help Workshop. Unlike the sizing component of third-party Help authoring tools, which simulate a window within a cramped dialog box, the Auto-Sizer displays an actual window that you can size and position at will on the desktop.

> **NOTE** *Microsoft confusingly has two "auto-size" components in Help Workshop: the Auto-Sizer that lets you manually size the window, and the "auto-size" feature that tells Help to automatically size the window. (Apparently, Microsoft's usability lab was overbooked when they were naming the user interface!) See "Automatically sizing a Help window" next for information on how to automatically size a window.*

To set the window size and position:

1. Open a project file in Help Workshop.

2. Click Windows, then Position.

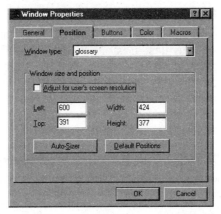

Figure 15.4. *The Position properties sheet.*

3. In the **Window Type** list, select the window type.

4. Choose one of the following options:

   - To size the window as a percentage of the screen size (that is, in 1024x1024 Help units), check the **Adjust for user's screen resolution** box. This is the best setting for most Help windows.

   - To size the window in pixels, clear the **Adjust for user's screen resolution** box. This is the best setting if you want to precisely control the layout of your topic text or graphics.

     (For more details on the two sizing options, see "Absolute versus relative window sizing" later in this chapter.)

5. Click the **Auto-Sizer** button. The Help Window Auto-Sizer window appears.

Figure 15.5. *Sizing a window with the "Auto Sizer."*

6. Position and size the window as you want it to appear.

Automatically sizing a secondary window

Part of Microsoft's Help model for Windows 95 is short, task-oriented topics in small secondary windows. In large part, this design is practical because WinHelp 4 can automatically size a window to fit the length of a topic. Whether the rest of the world adopts the Microsoft model remains to be seen, but the "auto-size" feature is so easy that it will tempt most authors.

Auto-sizing frees you from making tough decisions at design time, and instead lets Help decide how large to make a secondary window. (You cannot auto-size the main Help window.) When Help displays the topic, it automatically adjusts the height of the window to fit the topic length.

The auto-size feature changes only the height of the window; it does not alter the width of the window. Also, you will not be able to implement midtopic jumps in windows that are set to auto-size: nothing happens when the user clicks on the jump.

To automatically size a secondary window:

1. Open a project file in Help Workshop.

2. Click the Windows button.

3. Select a window in the Window type list.

4. Under Window Attributes, check the **Auto-size height** box.

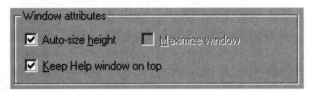

Figure 15.6. *Automatically sizing a window.*

Absolute versus relative window sizing

There are two ways to define the window size: as a percentage of screen size, and in pixels.

- **As a percentage of screen size**. Under this "relative" sizing scheme, WinHelp sizes its window in device-independent "Help units." WinHelp defines the screen as 1024 units wide by 1024 units tall.

  If you create a window that is 512x512 Help units, it will always occupy one-half of the screen, regardless of whether it is displayed at VGA resolution (640x480 pixels) or 8514 resolution (1024x768). This is the only way to size a Help topic using WinHelp 3.1 (unless you use an external DLL).

  To size a window as a percentage of screen size, check the **Adjust for user's screen resolution** box on the Position page in the Window Properties dialog box. This setting is usually best for most Help windows.

- **In pixels**. You can size a window in "absolute" terms by using pixels. If you create a window that is 640x480 pixels, it will take up a full screen at VGA resolution, but only one-half of the screen at 8514 resolution. This feature is new for WinHelp 4.0.

  To size a window in pixels, clear the **Adjust for user's screen resolution** box. Use this setting if you need to precisely control the layout of a particular topic. Suppose you build a heavily formatted table at 1024x768. The table looks great on your system, but the lines of text will re-wrap when the Help file is displayed at any other screen resolution. Similarly, this option is the only way you can size the window to match the dimensions of a bitmap at all screen resolutions.

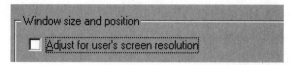

Figure 15.7. *Clear the Adjust for user's screen resolution box to have Help size a window in pixels.*

As an example, say you design an online tutorial to fill the screen on a 640x480 display. You size the Help system to take up the entire screen (that is, 1024x1024 Help units), and check Adjust for user's screen resolution. When displayed on a system at 640x480 resolution, the Help topic will look fine.

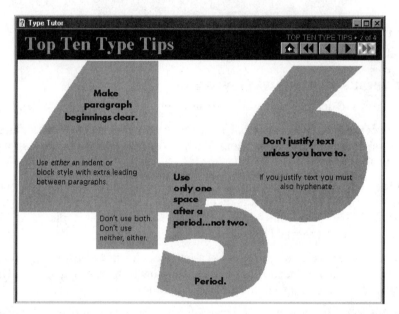

Figure 15.8. *A Help topic sized at 1024x1024 Help units at a resolution of 640x480.*

However, when you display the Help system at a higher resolution, it contains extra white space. Help adjusts the size of the window for the high resolution display, making the screen much too large for the bitmap.

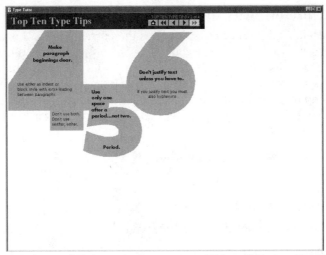

Figure 15.9. *The same Help topic (1024x1024 Help units) at 1024x768 resolution.*

Clearing the **Adjust for user's screen resolution** box and setting the window size to 640x480 will force Help to size the window in pixels, ensuring that the Help system will look good at all resolutions.

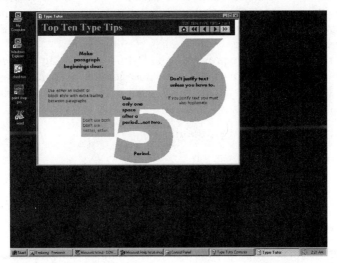

Figure 15.10. *A Help topic with the Adjust for user's screen resolution box cleared and the window sized in pixels (640x480), viewed at a resolution of 1024x768.*

Help's default window size and position

Each time the WinHelp application closes, it writes the current size and position for the main window to the user's WIN.INI file. When you define the properties for the main window, you can instruct Help to use this window size and position as the "default." The next time you run WinHelp, the main window will appear exactly as it was last sized and positioned by the user.

Help does not keep track of the size and position for a secondary window. If you specify the "default" setting for a secondary window, Help positions it at the top right-hand side of the user's screen.

To use the default window size and position:

1. Open a project file in Help Workshop.

2. Click Windows, then Position.

3. In the **Window Type** list, select the window type.

4. Check the **Default Positions** button.

CREATING AN "ONTOP" WINDOW

Another feature that makes the minimalist Help model practical is the ability to keep a window on top of other windows, even when the user switches to another program. Combined with auto-sizing, this feature is perfect for task-oriented topics because it lets the user simultaneously read and carry out the procedure.

If you're documenting a software program, you should avoid using this setting unnecessarily (especially with large-sized Help windows) because it takes over the screen. Of course, the user can always change the ontop state by right-clicking the Help window with the mouse, and then pointing to Keep Help On Top.

To make a window stay on top by default:

1. Open a project file in Help Workshop.

2. Click Windows. The Windows Properties dialog box appears.

3. In the Window Type list, select the name of the window you want to modify.

4. In the Window Attributes area, check **Keep Help window on top**.

You can change the state of the window during a Help session by using the **HelpOnTop** macro. **HelpOnTop** toggles the current state of the window from on top to not on top, However, since it provides no way to verify the command status before toggling, **HelpOnTop** cannot be used reliably.

If you want to set a window's ontop state, you can use the **Generate** macro to control the ontop state, regardless of its current state. The following macro sets the current window to stay On Top:

```
Generate(273, 1471, 0)
```

To set a window to Not On Top, specify a value of **1472** as the second parameter in the **Generate** macro. To set the window to Default, specify a value of **1470**.

CUSTOMIZING THE WINDOW COLOR

Each Help window contains two main areas: the primary topic area, and the nonscrolling region. Help Workshop lets you customize the color for either region. Remember that the nonscrolling region will appear only on topics for which you've marked the opening paragraph(s) with the "Keep with next" setting. For information on how to create a nonscrolling region, see "Creating a nonscrolling region" in Chapter 12.

When customizing the window color, most Help authors stick with the standard 16 colors in the Windows palette. Colors from the 256 color palette look great when displayed on systems running 256 or more colors, but appear dithered on 16 color systems. This dithering makes the text very difficult to read. For more information on color, see "Color depth" in Chapter 13.

To customize the window color:

1. Open a project file in Help Workshop.

2. Click Windows. The Windows Properties dialog box appears.

3. Click the Color tab.

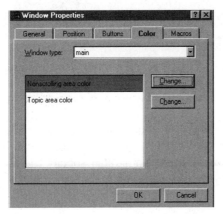

Figure 15.11. *The Color tab in Help Workshop.*

4. In the **Window Type** list, select the name of the window you want to modify.

5. Click the **Change** button for either the Nonscrolling area or Topic area.

6. In the Color dialog box, select the color you want to use.

> **TIP** *To create a window with the light yellow color used by Microsoft's Help files, specify the RGB value 255,255,226.*

SPECIFYING A WINDOW TYPE FOR A TOPIC

WinHelp 3.1 doesn't provide much control over the window used to display a Help topic. Topics accessed from the Search keyword list, for instance, always appear in the main window.

WinHelp 4 gives you the ability to associate a topic with a particular window type. You might use this technique, for example, to display a "How To" topic in a particular secondary window. A topic will appear in this default window each time it is accessed from the Index or Find tabs, or from an **ALink** or **KLink** macro.

Note that the default window type is *not* honored from standard jumps (whether created by standard hotspot formatting or using one of the **Jump** macros) or from a contents file. This inconsistency is guaranteed to confuse; don't forget that you must still specify the window type in standard jumps and in the contents (.CNT) file!

For more information on specifying a default window, see "Specifying a window type for a topic" in Chapter 10. See Chapter 17 for information on specifying a window type in the contents file, and see Chapter 11 for information on how to jump to a topic and display it in another window.

SPECIFYING A DEFAULT WINDOW TYPE FOR ALL TOPICS

You can easily define a window type that will be used for all topics when they are opened from the Contents, Index, and Find tabs. The default type is honored for all topics unless you override it either by specifying a default window type in a topic footnote (>), or by specifying a window type in a contents file entry.

To specify a default window type for all topics, open your contents file in Help Workshop and click the Edit button. In the Default Help Information dialog box, type the default window type in the **Default Window** box. You must also specify the filename of the Help file (and optionally, a default title). If you open your contents file in a text editor, you'll see the following entry:

```
:Base filename.hlp>window
```

MANAGING HELP WINDOWS

Managing windows—closing, sizing and positioning, setting the focus—is accomplished using Help macros. Complete macro syntax information is available in the online *Help Author's Guide* (HCW.HLP), but several common techniques are presented here.

The following examples use hotspots to run the macros; of course, you can run a Help macro when the user opens the Help file, enters a topic, clicks a menu item or button, and so forth. If you haven't already done so, you may want to see Chapter 16 to familiarize yourself with how to use macros.

See Chapter 11 for complete information on creating hypertext links between topics in different windows.

Closing a window

Closing a window is pretty simple:

CloseWindow(*window-name*)

```
Close window!CloseWindow(main)
```

Help ignores the macro if the specified window is not currently open.

Closing all secondary windows

If you've got several secondary windows open and want to close all but the current secondary window, you can use the **CloseSecondarys** macro. This makes it easy to clean up the screen if your Help system uses several different secondary windows.

CloseSecondarys()

```
Close secondary windows!CloseSecondarys()
```

Jumping to a topic and closing a window

Simple hotspots are quick and easy for basic jumps, but you may want to get creative. Suppose you want to provide a way to jump from a topic in a secondary window to a topic in the main window, and then close the secondary window.

Here's where the **Jump** macros are valuable. Since Help lets you run multiple macros if you separate them with semicolons (or colons), you can run a **Jump** macro followed by a **CloseWindow** macro:

JumpId(*filename>window-name, topic-ID*) ; **CloseWindow** (*window-name*)

```
Back to the main window!JumpId(foo.hlp>main, sample01) ;
CloseWindow(code)
```

In the example, the hotspot uses the **JumpId** macro to jump to the "sample01" topic in FOO.HLP and display it in the main window. **CloseWindow** then closes the secondary window named "code."

The *filename* parameter is optional; if you want to jump to a topic in the current Help file, leave it blank:

```
Back to the main window!JumpId(>main, sample01) ;
CloseWindow(code)
```

Sizing and positioning a window

You may want to size and position a window during a Help session (that is, without requiring the user to close and restart WinHelp). The **PositionWindow** macro lets you reset the size and position of a window. Unlike Help Workshop, this macro lets you size a window using only "Help units" (that is, as a percentage of the screen size).

PositionWindow(*x, y, width, height, display-state, window-name*)

```
Size and position window!PositionWindow(200,200,400,400, 5,
"main")
```

Changing the window focus

There may be times when you want to activate, or set the "focus," to a particular Help window. This is done using the **FocusWindow** macro.

FocusWindow(*window-name*)

```
Set window focus!FocusWindow(main)
```

Updating a window

You may want to display a topic in a particular window, and then return the focus to the window that called the macro. This macro is often used as a topic entry macro to update a secondary window whenever the topic is shown.

For example, consider a Help system that displays most of its content in the main window, but uses a small secondary window to display supplementary information (such as examples). Rather than force the user to keep re-activating the main window, you could use **UpdateWindow** to display the topic in a secondary window and keep the focus on the main window.

The following example displays the "topic1" topic in a secondary window named "example," and then restores the focus to the window that ran the macro.

UpdateWindow(*[filename>]window-name, topic-ID*)

```
UpdateWindow(example, topic1)
```

Jumping to the previous topic

You may occasionally want to allow the user to jump back to the previous topic and display it in the appropriate window. This is easily accomplished using marker macros. In the current topic, use the **SaveMark** macro to save a marker that keeps track of the topic location and the window it is displayed in. You can then jump to the topic in that window by using the **GoToMark** macro.

For example, suppose you're in a topic in the main window that explains macro syntax, and that you want to create a jump to a topic displaying example code in a secondary window. By saving a marker called "current" before the jump, you can easily allow the user to get back to the main window. The following macro saves the marker, jumps to another topic in a secondary window named "second" and closes the main window:

```
SaveMark(current);JumpID(>second,code);CloseWindow(main)
```

You can easily create a jump from the example code window back to the previous topic (and close the secondary window) using the following macro:

```
GotoMark(current);CloseWindow(second)
```

If you specify the same marker text again in another topic, WinHelp will display the topic in which you most recently set the marker.

RUNNING A MACRO EACH TIME A WINDOW OPENS

You can associate a macro with a particular window type so that each time the user opens a topic displayed in that window, Help runs the macro. This feature is useful for customizing a particular window type; for example, you might:

- Add a menu or menu item to the menu bar.

- Add a custom button to the button bar, or change a button definition.

- Close any secondary windows that are open with the **CloseSecondarys** macro.

- Reset the color of the pop-up window using **SetPopupColor**.

To run a macro each time a window type opens:

1. Open a project file in Help Workshop.

2. Click Windows. The Windows Properties dialog box appears.

3. Click the Macros tab.

4. In the **Window Type** list, select the name of the window you want to modify.

5. Click Add.

6. In the **Macro** box, type the macro you want to run when the window is opened.

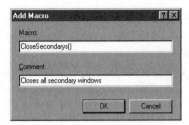

Figure 15.12. *Associating a macro with a window type.*

Macros you add to a secondary window will appear in a special [CONFIG] section for that window type. Any macros you assign to a secondary window apply only to that window type.

If you add a macro to the main window, it will appear in the [CONFIG] section of the project file along with any macros that apply to the entire Help file. This can get confusingóone might expect Help Workshop would create a separate [CONFIG] section for the main window.

What if there is a conflict between a macro associated with the entire Help file and one associated with the main window? In that case, the macro assigned to the main window will take priority over macros assigned to the entire Help file.

CREATING A SPLASH SCREEN

Many Help authors want to create a "splash" screen that appears when the user first opens the Help file. This is fairly easy to do in WinHelp 3.1, but is complicated somewhat in WinHelp 4.0 since the Help Contents dialog box automatically appears if a contents file is present.

WinHelp 3.1

Setting a splash screen is pretty simple in WinHelp 3.1, since WinHelp will always display the "contents" (as specified using the CONTENTS option in the project file) topic when a Help file is first opened. To display the splash screen, you set the contents topic to point to the splash screen, and then change the Contents button so it displays the "real" contents topic.

To create a WinHelp 3.1 splash screen:

1. In the [OPTIONS] section of the project file, set the CONTENTS option to point to the topic you want to use as a splash screen.

   For example, the CONTENTS option might look like this:

   ```
   CONTENTS=splash
   ```

2. Add a macro to the [CONFIG] section of the project file to change the Contents button so it points to the "real" contents topic:

   ```
   CBB("BTN_CONTENTS",JumpID(`MYHELP.HLP',`the_real_contents')")
   ```

This macro uses the **ChangeButtonBinding** (or **CBB**) macro to change the contents button to jump to the topic "the_real_contents" in the MYHELP.HLP file.

WinHelp 4.0

WinHelp 4.0 complicates the task of creating a splash screen: if a contents file is associated with the Help file, WinHelp automatically displays the Help Topics dialog box when the Help file is opened. You could omit the contents file in favor of a splash screen, but excluding such an important navigational aid just to implement a splash screen may not make sense.

One approach is to build two .HLP files: one containing the splash screen, and one containing the main Help information. The splash screen .HLP file (which, of course, doesn't include a contents file) displays the splash topic and runs the main .HLP file. This technique lets you include a contents file with your Help system. (The file names SPLASH.HLP and MAIN.HLP are simply examples; you can name the files whatever you want.)

To create a WinHelp 4 splash screen:

1. Create a topic file and define the splash screen topic.

   You probably want to add an OK button in this topic that will run the main .HLP file, and a Cancel button that exits Help. This is a perfect use for WinHelp 4's authorable buttons. The extra spaces surrounding the "OK" text (five spaces before and three spaces after) will set the width of the OK button to match that of the Cancel button.

   ```
   {button     OK   , EF(main.hlp);CloseWindow(splash)} {button
   Cancel, CloseWindow(splash)}
   ```

   Clicking OK will run the **ExecFile** (or **EF**) macro to open MAIN.HLP and close the window named "splash." Clicking Cancel also closes the window named "splash."

   > **NOTE** *The splash screen topic uses the **ExecFile** macro to run the main .HLP file. Here's another of WinHelp's idiosyncrasies: if you use a simple **JumpID** macro to jump from a Help file that doesn't include a contents file, WinHelp ignores the contents file associated with the destination Help file.*

2. Create a project file for SPLASH.HLP and define a secondary window named "splash" that contains no buttons. You probably want to create the window so it is auto-sized based on the topic length.

3. Configure the splash Help file so it displays the topic in a secondary window. Add the following macro to the [CONFIG] section of the project file.

   ```
   CloseWindow(main);JI(>splash,contents)
   ```

   When the splash screen file is opened, the **CloseWindow** macro closes the main window, and the **JumpId** (or **JI**) macro displays the splash screen topic ("contents") in a secondary window named "splash."

4. Compile the splash screen topic in a .HLP file. Do not build a contents file for the file.

5. Create the main Help file. You can include a contents file for the main file.

6. The SPLASH.HLP file should be run first; if the user clicks OK, the MAIN.HLP file will appear.

   Therefore, if the Help system will be run standalone (that is, as a double-clicked file icon), you should create an Explorer icon for the SPLASH.HLP file. Likewise, if the Help file will be invoked from a program, make sure to call the SPLASH.HLP file in the application code.

You can modify the secondary window flags with functions built into the Windows API. This disguises the fact that the splash screen is WinHelp, providing you with a truly custom look. Notice in Figure 15.13, for example, that the Help window resembles a modal dialog box (it does not contain a system menu, or the standard minimize, maximize, and close buttons). See the sample Help file included on the disc in the back of this book for more information (thanks to Michael Cessna for this one).

Figure 15.13. *A WinHelp 4 splash screen.*

CUSTOMIZING THE COLOR OF POP-UPS

By default, Help displays pop-up colors using the background color of the current window. Running the **SetPopupColor** macro lets you customize the color used for all pop-up windows. This macro sets the color for all pop-ups in the file until you exit the file or re-run the macro.

You will probably want to run **SetPopupColor** when the Help file is opened by adding it to the [CONFIG] section in the project file, or you might use it as a topic entry macro to set the color on a topic-by-topic basis.

To customize the pop-up window color:

1. Open a project file in Help Workshop.

2. Click Config. The Configuration Macros dialog box appears.

3. Click Add. The Add Macro dialog box appears.

4. Type the **SetPopupColor** macro in the **Macro** box. **SetPopupColor** takes three integers from 0 to 255, representing a red-green-blue (RGB) color value.

   SetPopupColor(*red,green,blue*)

   The following macro sets the pop-up color to yellow.

   ```
   SetPopupColor(255,255,0)
   ```

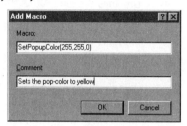

Figure 15.14. *Setting the pop-up color.*

5. Type a comment in the **Comment** box, if you want. Comments are not visible to the Help user and will not affect the size of the compiled Help file.

Working with Help buttons

WinHelp 4 includes button bar support for both the main and secondary Help window, plus so-called "authorable" buttons that behave like standard three-dimensional Windows pushbuttons.

CREATING A BUTTON BAR

Help lets you customize the button bar in both the main and secondary windows. Each window can display up to 22 buttons.

By default, the main window includes four buttons (Contents, Index, Back, and Print). The default secondary window buttons vary, depending on the default window type used to create the window (see "Creating a window" earlier in this chapter). Secondary windows based on the "Procedure" and "Reference" window types include three buttons (Help Topics, Back, and Options), and windows based on "Error Message" include no buttons.

Help Workshop lets you add standard buttons, or you can add your own custom buttons using the **CreateButton** macro. Help includes eight standard buttons, which are listed in the following table along with brief descriptions. The table also lists the button ID, which you'll need to reference if you change the button definition or disable the button.

Button	Button ID	Description
Contents	btn_contents	If a contents file is present, this button displays the Contents tab in the Help Topics dialog box. If no contents file is available, it displays the default topic or the first topic in the file.
Index	btn_search	Displays the Index tab in the Help Topics dialog box.
Find	btn_find	Displays the Find tab in the Help Topics dialog box.
Help Topics	btn_topics	If a contents file is present, the first time this button is pressed it displays the Contents tab in the Help Topics dialog box; after that, it displays the tab most recently used. If no contents file is available, it displays the Index and Find tabs in the Help Topics dialog box.
Print	btn_print	Displays the Print dialog box and prints the current topic.
Back	btn_back	Displays the previously viewed topic in the current window.
Options	btn_menu	Displays a menu containing six commands: Annotate, Copy, Print Topic, Font, Keep Help on Top, and Use System Colors.
Browse	btn_previous, btn_next	Adds browse buttons to the button bar. You must define browse codes in your topic files to build a browse sequence.

Adding a standard button

Help Workshop makes it easy to add any of the eight standard Help buttons to a main or secondary window.

To add a standard button to a window:

1. Open a project file in Help Workshop.

2. Click Windows, then Buttons.

3. Select a window in the **Window type** list. (See Figure 15.15.)

4. Check the boxes in the Buttons area that correspond with those you want to have appear on the button bar.

For example, if you check the **Browse** box under the Buttons area, Help Workshop will add browse buttons to the button bar.

Figure 15.15. *Adding a standard Help button to a window.*

Adding a custom button

You can add a custom button to a Help window using the **CreateButton** macro. Help equally sizes all of the buttons on the button bar according to the length of the longest button text; therefore, try to keep the button text short. Buttons cannot include graphics.

Note that you must have one standard button on the button bar in order to add a custom button (otherwise, the Help compiler ignores the custom button).

To add a custom button to a window:

1. Open a project file in Help Workshop.

2. Click Windows, then Macros.

3. Select a window in the **Window type** list.

4. Click Add. The Add Macros dialog box appears:

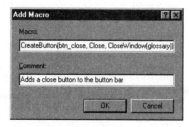

Figure 15.16. *Adding a custom button to a window.*

5. Type a **CreateButton** macro in the **Macro** box.

   CreateButton(*button-ID, name, macro*)

   For example, to create a button that closes a window named glossary, you might type:

```
CreateButton(btn_close, Close, CloseWindow(glossary))
```

In the compiled Help file, custom buttons are added to the right of the standard buttons, and appear in the order in which they appear in the project file. In the following example, the Tutorial button would appear on the left of the See Also button.

```
[CONFIG]
CreateButton(btn_tutor, Tutorial, JumpId(tutorial.hlp, contents))
CreateButton(btn_seealso, SeeAlso, ALink(topic1))
```

Figure 15.17. *Buttons added to the button bar in the order they appear in the project file.*

You can specify a keyboard shortcut for a button by entering an ampersand before the letter in the button text that you want to use as the shortcut. The following example makes the letter "o" the shortcut, which activates the button when the user presses ALT+O:

```
CreateButton(btn_close, Cl&ose, CloseWindow(glossary))
```

If no shortcut is specified, WinHelp automatically chooses the first letter that does not conflict with any other button. If WinHelp cannot find a unique keyboard shortcut, it uses the first letter of the button text and displays a dialog box containing all of the duplicate shortcuts for the user to choose one.

Removing the standard buttons

By default, Help's main window includes four standard buttons: Contents, Index, Back, and Print. You can remove all or some of the standard buttons from your Help file.

To remove all of the standard buttons from the main window:

1. Open a project file in Help Workshop.

2. Click Windows, then Buttons.

3. Select "main" from the **Window type** list.

   If "main" does not appear, you will need to create a main window by clicking the General tab, clicking the **Add** button, and typing "main."

4. Click **No default buttons**.

Figure 15.18. *Removing all standard buttons from the main window.*

You can remove a custom button during a Help session with the **DestroyButton** macro; see "Conditionally modifying the Help interface" later in this chapter for more details.

Disabling or enabling a button

You can disable or enable buttons during a Help session using the **DisableButton** and **EnableButton** macros. Help lets you disable custom buttons or standard buttons.

> **DisableButton**(*button-ID*)

For example, the following macro disables the Print button:

```
DisableButton(btn_print)
```

Once you disable a button, it will be unavailable to the user until it is re-enabled with the **EnableButton** macro or re-activated through a user action (for example, the Print button will be enabled if the user jumps to a topic in another Help file). Help's marker macros are probably the easiest way to conditionally enable or disable a button for a particular topic; see "Conditionally modifying the Help interface" later in this chapter for information on this technique.

Changing a button definition

You can change the definition for a button during a Help session using the **ChangeButtonBinding** macro. Help lets you change the button definition for a custom button or a standard button.

> **ChangeButtonBinding**(*button-ID, button-macro*)

For example, if you add a "See Also" button to the button bar, you will probably need to change the button definition for each topic so that it always references the appropriate topics.

The following macro changes the button so that it searches for A-keywords with the text "topic1."

```
ChangeButtonBinding(btn_seealso,ALink(topic1))
```

If you need to change the button for only a few specific topics, you should use Help's marker macros; see "Conditionally modifying the Help interface" later in this chapter for information on this technique.

If you need to change the button definition for a button that is disabled, remember WinHelp 4's new **ChangeEnable** macro. It lets you change the button binding and enable the button all in one step, rather than running both the **ChangeButtonBinding** and **EnableButton** macros. The following example enables the Up button and changes the button binding to jump to the topic associated with the topic ID "section1."

ChangeEnable (*button-ID, button-macro*)

```
ChangeEnable(Up, JumpId(section1))
```

Destroying a button

To destroy a button you added to the button bar using the **CreateButton** macro, you can use the **DestroyButton** macro. The following example deletes the button with the button ID "btn_orderform."

DestroyButton (*button-ID*)

```
DestroyButton(btn_orderform)
```

Note that you once you add a standard button to the button bar, you cannot remove it using the **DestroyButton** macro. Also, Help will display an error message if you attempt to use **DestroyButton** to remove a button that hasn't been added to the button bar.

CREATING AN AUTHORABLE BUTTON

You can add a real three-dimensional push button containing text to a Help topic using the new **{button }** statement. These so-called "authorable" buttons can be added to a main or secondary window, or to the nonscrolling region.

The width of the button depends on the length of the text you assign to it. You cannot assign a keyboard shortcut to an authorable button, nor can you change the font (8 point MS Sans Serif) or add a graphic to the button.

The syntax used to create an authorable button is as follows:

{button [label], *macro1[: macro2: ...: macroN]***}**

Parameter	Description
label	The name appearing on the button. This is optional; if you omit the label, the button will appear as a small square.
macro1	The name of the macro you want to run when the button is pressed. You can run more than one macro by separating them with colons. If the specified macros is a DLL function, you must surround it with quotes when using it in an authorable button.

To create an authorable button:

1. Open a topic file and position the insertion point where you want to display the button.

2. Type the {button} statement.

   For example, the following statement creates the button shown below. The button uses the **ExecFile** macro to open the WIN.INI file.

   ```
   {button WIN.INI, EF(win.ini)}
   ```

Figure 15.19. *An authorable button with text.*

If you omit the label and leave a space before the first comma, the button appears as a small square.

Figure 15.20. *An authorable button without label text.*

The syntax for creating this button is shown below.

```
{button , EF(win.ini)}
```

Don't confuse the button statement with a macro hotspot—the button statement does not require an exclamation point.

Creating rolodex-style buttons

At first blush, it would seem logical that you might use authorable buttons to create a rolodex-style alphabetic group of buttons. Unfortunately, there's one problem: the width of each button varies according to the width of the letter used for a label. This results in a pretty ragtag group of buttons:

Figure 15.21. *A rolodex-style button bar created using authorable buttons.*

The buttons don't look so bad if the window is wide enough to display the entire alphabet in one row. Otherwise, you're probably better off using either a multiple hotspot graphic or a series of individual hotspot bitmaps. Using individual hotspot bitmaps is perhaps the most flexible solution, since the buttons will wrap when the user resizes the window.

CREATING SHORTCUT BUTTONS

WinHelp 4 also features new shortcut buttons. These buttons, which usually appear in "How To" topics, don't just tell a user what to do, they help the user accomplish their task. Shortcut buttons let you run or activate an application and send it WM_COMMAND messages. For example, the following topic from the Windows 95 Help system runs the Control Panel so the user can change the screen resolution.

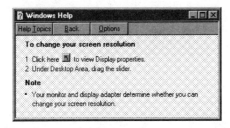

Figure 15.22. *A shortcut button in a Help topic.*

Shortcut buttons are created with the new **Shortcut** macro and the shortcut bitmap (SHORTCUT.BMP) built into Help Workshop. The **Shortcut** macro is similar to **ExecFile**, except that in addition to running an application it can also pass standard WM_COMMAND messages to a Windows application.

To create a shortcut button:

1. Open a topic file and position the insertion point at the spot where you want to display the shortcut.

2. Place the SHORTCUT.BMP reference. For example, to align the shortcut button on the baseline, you would type {bmc shortcut.bmp}.

3. Type an exclamation mark, followed by the Shortcut macro:

    ShortCut(*window-class, program***[, *wParam***[, *lParam***[,*topic-ID*]]])**

For example, the following macro copies the current topic to the Clipboard, runs or activates WordPad, and pastes the text into a document.

```
CopyTopic();ShortCut(WordPadClass, wordpad, 0xE125)
```

4. Select the bitmap reference (including the curly brackets), and apply the double-under-line character formatting.

5. Select the exclamation mark and the shortcut macro, and apply the hidden character format.

```
{bmc shortcut.bmp}!CopyTopic():ShortCut(notepad, notepad, 0x0302)
```

For more information about the **Shortcut** macro, see Chapter 16.

Working with Help menus

Help's main window includes five standard menus: File, Edit, Bookmark, Options, and Help. Unlike with the buttons on the button bar, you cannot remove or modify the standard Help menus or menu items using standard Help macros. You can, however, add additional menu items to the standard menus, or create new menus.

The standard menus are listed in the following table. The table lists the menu ID, which you'll need to reference if you add a menu item to a menu.

Menu	Menu ID	Description
File menu	mnu_file	Access the File menu.
Edit	mnu_edit	Access the Edit menu.
Options	mnu_options	Access the Options menu.
Help	mnu_help	Access the Help menu.
Floating menu	mnu_floating	Appears when you right-click a topic.

Don't forget that secondary Help windows cannot include menu bars; with the exception of the floating menu, menu macros are ignored if they are run from a secondary window.

There are several different ways to run a menu macro. For example, you might alter the menu when the user opens a Help file, opens a particular window type, clicks a hotspot, or enters a particular topic. Since most Help systems set the menu when the user opens the Help file, the following examples explain how to use Help Workshop to edit the menu. The syntax for the macros remains the same regardless of how you run them; see Chapter 16 for complete information on macros.

ADDING A MENU

You add a custom menu to Help using the **InsertMenu** macro. Once you define a menu, you can add menu items to it using any of the three macros described in the next section, "Adding a menu item."

To add a custom menu:

1. Open a project file in Help Workshop.

2. Click Config, then Add.

3. Type an **InsertMenu** macro in the **Macro** box.

    InsertMenu(*menu-ID*, *menu-name*, *menu-position***)**

    For example, to create a menu named "Tools" as the fourth item on the menu bar, you might type:

    ```
    InsertMenu(mnu_tools, &Tools, 3)
    ```

ADDING A SUBMENU

You can also add a submenu to an existing menu using the new **ExtInsertMenu** macro. This is a convenient way to group several menu items that are similar in function.

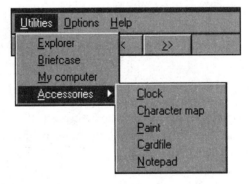

Figure 15.23. *A submenu in Help.*

The syntax in the initial release of the online *Help Author's Guide* is incorrect; here is the correct syntax:

ExtInsertMenu(*parent-ID*, *menu-ID*, *menu-name*, *menu-position*, *display-state***)**

Notice that the *display-state* parameter is not optional: without it, the Help compiler interprets the closing parenthesis as the last parameter and doesn't add the menu. In addition to the documented CHECKED and GRAYED *display-state* parameter values, you can also use **0** to enable the menu item, and **1** to disable it.

The following macro adds a submenu named Find to the Tools menu:

```
ExtInsertMenu(mnu_tools, mnu_find, &Find, 1, 0)
```

ADDING A MENU ITEM

There are three Help macros that you can use to add an item (or command) to a menu. Each of the macros lets you add an item to any of the standard Help menus, or to a custom menu that you've already created using the **InsertMenu** macro. The following table describes the three macros.

Macro	Description
AppendItem	Appends a menu item to the end of a menu.
InsertItem	Inserts a menu item at a given position on a menu.
ExtInsertItem	Inserts a menu item at a given position on a menu, in a given state.

To add a custom menu item:

1. Open a project file in Help Workshop.

2. Click Config, then Add.

3. Type one of the menu item macros in the **Macro** box.

- To simply add a menu item at the end of a menu, use the **AppendItem** macro. If you're adding several menu items, add them in the order you want the menu items to appear.

    AppendItem(*menu-ID, item-ID, item-name, macro***)**

    ```
    AppendItem(mnu_file, itm_calc, &Calculator, ExecFile(calc.exe))
    ```

- To more precisely control the position of the menu item, use the **InsertItem** macro. It lets you specify the menu position for the item. The first position is specified by entering **0**.

    InsertItem(*menu-ID, item-ID, item-name, macro, position***)**

    For example, to create a command named "Calculator" as the fourth item on Help's File menu, you would type:

    ```
    InsertItem(mnu_file, itm_calc, &Calculator, ExecFile(calc.exe),3)
    ```

- To add a menu item and set the state of the item, use the **ExtInsertItem** macro. This macro is identical to **InsertItem**, except it allows you to specify the display state (enabled or disabled) of the item.

    ExtInsertItem(*menu-ID, item-ID, item-name, macro, position, display-state***)**

    The following macro adds a Calculator command to Help's File menu and disables the menu item: **0** enables the item, and **1** disables it. (Note that the *Help Author's Guide* incorrectly documents the *display-state* values, and that the parameter is not optional.)

    ```
    ExtInsertItem(mnu_file, itm_calc, &Calculator,
    ExecFile(calc.exe), 3,1)
    ```

CHANGING A MENU ITEM

You can change a menu item during a Help session using the **ChangeItemBinding** macro. Help only lets you change custom menu items; you cannot edit the standard items.

> **ChangeItemBinding(***item-ID*, *item-macro***)**

The following macro changes the Calculator menu item so that it runs a custom calculator program.

```
ChangeItemBinding(itm_calc, EF(mycalc.exe))
```

ADDING A SEPARATOR BAR

You can also use **ExtInsertItem** to add a separator bar to a menu. The following macro adds a separator bar to a menu named "mnu_words."

```
ExtInsertItem(mnu_words,separator, , , 1, 2048)
```

REMOVING A MENU ITEM

You can remove any custom menu item created using the **AppendItem**, **ExtInsertItem**, or **InsertItem** macros. This macro cannot be used to delete a standard menu item.

> **DeleteItem(***item-ID***)**

The following macro deletes the Calculator menu item:

```
DeleteItem(itm_calc)
```

DISABLING A MENU ITEM

You can disable or enable a menu item during a Help session using the **DisableItem** and **EnableItem** macros. Help only lets you disable custom menu items; you cannot change the state of the standard items. For example, the following macro disables the Calculator menu item:

> **DisableItem(***item-ID***)**

```
DisableItem(itm_calc)
```

Once you disable a menu item, it will be unavailable to the user until it is re-enabled with the **EnableItem** or **ExtAbleItem** macro.

> *EnableItem* (*item-ID*)

```
EnableItem(itm_calc)
```

The **ExtAbleItem** macro is a hybrid of **EnableItem** and **DisableItem**: it lets you enable or disable a menu item. The syntax for **ExtAbleItem** is shown below.

>**ExtAbleItem**(*item-ID, display-state*)

To enable an item, specify a **display-state** of **0**; to disable an item, specify a *display-state* of **1**. (Note that the *Help Author's Guide* incorrectly documents the display-state values.)

```
ExtAbleItem(itm_calc, 1)
```

Help's marker macros are probably the easiest way to conditionally enable or disable a menu item for particular topics; see "Conditionally modifying the Help interface" later in this chapter for information on this technique.

RESETTING A MENU

If you've made any changes to Help's menus, you can quickly restore the menu to its original state using the **ResetMenu** macro. This macro deletes all custom menus and menu items, enables all standard menu items, and restores the item bindings of the menu items to their default settings.

>**ResetMenu()**

```
ResetMenu()
```

CREATING A FLOATING MENU

One of the more interesting "new" macros (actually, it is available in WinHelp 3.1 but is undocumented) is **FloatingMenu**. The floating menu, or "context" menu appears when the user right-clicks, and displays six standard Help commands (Annotate, Copy, Print Topic, Font, Keep Help on Top, and Use System Colors).

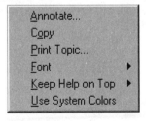

Figure 15.24. *Help's floating menu (or "context" menu).*

You can add menu items to the bottom of the floating menu using the **AppendItem** macro. For example, you might use Help Workshop to add the following macro to the [CONFIG] section:

```
AppendItem(mnu_floating, itm_clock, C&lock, EF(clock))
```

In addition to the right mouse button, you might allow the user to access the floating menu by clicking a hotspot. This is done using the **FloatingMenu** macro.

> **FloatingMenu()**
>
> ```
> Click here!FloatingMenu()
> ```

There is no way to disable an item on a floating menu.

Working with keyboard shortcuts

Unlike the Macintosh, early versions of Windows did not require a mouse. As part of this heritage, most applications and Windows itself feature a very usable keyboard interface, with a keyboard equivalent for every command displayed on menus or a button bar.

Although you can specify the keyboard shortcut for custom menu items and buttons, these are usually accessed through awkward ALT+key combinations (for example, to display the History window the user must press ALT,O,D). You may want to add simpler keyboard shortcuts to your Help file for commands that are frequently used.

ADDING A KEYBOARD SHORTCUT

You add a keyboard shortcut using the **AddAccelerator** macro. Most of the time, you'll want to set the keyboard shortcuts when the user opens the Help file; this is done by placing an **AddAccelerator** macro in the [CONFIG] section of the project file.

To add a keyboard shortcut:

1. Open a project file in Help Workshop.

2. Click Config, then Add.

3. Type an **AddAccelerator** macro in the **Macro** box.

   AddAccelerator(key, shift-state, macro**)**

   In order to define the *key* and *shift-state* parameters, you will need to know the virtual key codes used by Windows for the various keys. These are listed in topic explaining **AddAccelerator** in the online *Help Author's Guide* file.

   For example, here are several macros that create a keyboard interface for a Help file:

   ```
   AddAccelerator(VK_HOME, NONE, "Finder()")
   AddAccelerator(VK_RIGHT, NONE, "Next()")
   AddAccelerator(VK_LEFT, NONE, "Prev()")
   AddAccelerator(VK_BACK, NONE, "Back()")
   ```

The first macro will display the Help Topics dialog box when the user presses HOME. Lines two and three enable the RIGHT and LEFT ARROW keys to access the next and previous topics, respectively, in the browse sequence. Finally, the fourth macro displays the previous topic in the history list when the user presses the BACKSPACE key.

REMOVING A KEYBOARD SHORTCUT

You remove a keyboard shortcut using the **RemoveAccelerator** macro. Most keyboard shortcuts are global, but you may occasionally want to remove a keyboard shortcut when the user opens a particular Help topic or performs an action (like clicking a button).

> **RemoveAccelerator***(key, shift-state)*

The following macro removes the HOME keyboard shortcut (assigned in the previous example).

```
RemoveAccelerator((VK_HOME, NONE)
```

Conditionally modifying the Help interface

One of the advantages of Help is that you can dynamically modify its interface during a Help session. You might want to add or remove a menu item for a specific topic, or you might want to disable a button. You might even want to change the action performed by a button or menu; for example, if you place a See Also button on the button bar, you could change the button for each topic.

To conditionally modify Help's interface, you use Help's "marker" macros. These macros let you save or delete a mark, and then test whether or not a mark exists. Like the conditional **IfThen** and **IfThenElse** statements in languages such as WordBasic, you can then perform an action—such as run a Help macro—depending on the result.

If this sounds moderately difficult, you're right. Do you need to mess with marker macros? If you want to conditionally modify the Help interface for particular topics—creating, deleting or disabling buttons or menus, or creating or deleting keyboard shortcuts—the answer is yes. This type of Help file design adds a fair amount of overhead to your project, since you will likely end up adding marker macros to nearly all of the topics in your project. Consider the trade-offs before designing a system that conditionally modifies the Help interface.

The following example illustrates how to modify the button bar, but the same principle applies if you want to modify the menu or keyboard interface.

Suppose you want to add a button to the button bar in topic A in a Help file, but delete the button in all other topics. It seems logical that you could use the **CreateButton** macro to add the button to topic A, and add the **DestroyButton** macro to the remaining topics.

Unfortunately, it's not that easy: if you run **DestroyButton** in a topic which never contained the button, Help displays an unfriendly error message (Figure 15.25). (Of course, you could avoid this problem by preventing users from randomly accessing topics—that is, forcing the user to go from topic A to B, whereupon you could confidently delete the button in topic B— but that is not typical of most hypertext systems.)

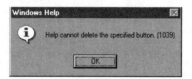

Figure 15.25. *The error message that appears if you try to delete a button or menu item that is not defined in the current topic.*

Here's where the marker macros earn their keep. In topic A, create a marker called "button" and add the button to the button bar.

```
IfThen(IsNotMark("button"), SaveMark(button):
CreateButton(sample_btn, &Tutorial,
JumpContents(tutorial.hlp))
```

This example uses the **IfThen** macro to test whether or not there is a text marker called "button." If the marker does not exist, it creates a marker using **SaveMark**, and then runs the **CreateButton** macro to create a button that jumps to the Contents topic in the TUTORIAL.HLP file. If the marker exists (that is, if the button were already on the button bar), the macro does nothing.

In the other topics, add the following macro:

```
IfThen(IsMark("button"), DeleteMark(button) :
DestroyButton(sample_btn))
```

This macro uses **IfThen** to test whether or not there is a text marker called "button." If the marker exists, it uses the **DeleteMark** macro to delete the marker and then runs **DestroyButton** to remove the button. If the marker does not exist (that is, there is no button on the button bar), the macro does nothing.

We may not need to mess with marker macros much longer. Help already supports topic entry macros, that run a macro when the user enters a topic. We hope that future versions of Help will include "topic exit" macros. Topic exit macros will make it possible to customize Help's interface when the user exits a particular topic: in the previous example, Topic A would simply contain a topic exit macro that deletes the button.

16

Working with Help Macros

Windows Help includes over 85 commands, or "macros" that let you customize Help's interface and manage the behavior of your Help files. These built-in macros let you customize Help's interface and manage its behavior, including:

- Customize Help's button bar and menus.
- Access Help's standard buttons and menu items.
- Jump to or display a topic in a pop-up window.
- Manage Help windows.
- Create custom keyboard shortcuts (or "accelerators").
- Conditionally perform actions using Help "markers."
- Run Windows programs.
- Extend the power of Help by using a custom Dynamic Link Library (DLL) like a Help macro.

This chapter is not intended as a comprehensive reference to the macro syntax—that information is contained in the online *Help Author's Guide* (HCW.HLP) included on the disc in the back of this book. Instead, this chapter focuses on:

- How to run a Help macro.
- The rules for creating a Help macro.

- A quick reference to the Help macros.
- A variety of macro tips and techniques.

At a glance Help macros

WinHelp4.0	WinHelp 3.1
Quotation marks are not required for macros (unless the macro is used in a contents file).	Quotation marks are required for all macros.
You can use the long form of a macro in your topic file to enhance readability and Help Workshop will convert it to the short form.	Help compiler uses the macro syntax you specified.
If the final parameter for a macro is 0 or " ", the parameter can be omitted.	All macro parameters must be specified.
You can use descriptive string values instead of numeric arguments for macros.	Macros that use numeric arguments require numerals.
29 new macros, including new macros for linking (**ALink** and **KLink**), debugging (such as **Test**), printing, running programs (**ExecFile** and **Shortcut**), and more.	
Macro hotspots can contain 4096 bytes.	512-byte limit for macro hotspots.

Before you begin

Working with Help macros is probably the most technically demanding aspect of Help development. Although implementing Help macros can be somewhat difficult at times, the results can be very impressive.

Although it's not essential, some experience in programming may prove helpful in working with macros. Even if you're an experienced programmer, be prepared for some trial and error in creating and debugging some of your macros.

If you run into problems or have questions about Help macros (or any other WinHelp-related issue, for that matter), check out one of the online WinHelp forums:

- The Microsoft Windows SDK Forum on CompuServe (Library 16) is a great way to reach Microsoft's Developer Support staff and fellow Help authors. You can reach the SDK Forum by typing **winsdk** at any go prompt.

- Another good resource is the WinHelp list server on the Internet. You can subscribe by sending mail to the following address:

Address: **listserv@Admin.HumberC.ON.CA**
Message: **sub Winhlp-L** *Your Name*

For example,

```
sub Winhlp-L Sigmund Freud
```

- Check out the USENET newsgroup on the Internet:

```
comp.os.ms-windows.programmer.winhelp
```

You might also consult your development staff—depending on their schedule, most developers are happy to help solve a technical problem.

Help macro rules

Help macros contain a macro name, followed by one or more parameters enclosed in parentheses, as shown below.

MacroName(*parameter1, parameter2, ...*)

There are several rules that govern the use of Help macros:

- Macro names are not case sensitive; therefore, you can enter them using any combination of upper- and lower-case letters.

Each macro name has a long and a short version—for example, **JumpID** and **JI**. You can use either version in your topic files, but most Help authors use the long form to enhance readability. If you use the long form, Help Workshop will reduce it internally to its short form to reduce the size of the .HLP file.

NOTE: If you use a Help macro in your contents file, you must use the long form.

- Macro parameters must be separated by commas.

```
InsertMenu(mnu_options, &Options, 3)
```

Note that if you want to specify some but not all of a macro's parameters, you must type any commas that precede the parameter, even if you don't specify every parameter:

```
ShortCut(SciCalc,calc.exe, , ,ERROR_MSG)
```

- Parameters can be either text strings or numbers, and are separated by commas. If the final parameter for a macro is 0 or "", the parameter can be omitted.

```
PositionWindow(100, 100, 500, 500, NORMAL, "Samples")
```

Help Workshop will accept either decimal or hexadecimal numbers. If you want to specify a number in hexadecimal, use a prefix of 0x. For example, you can represent the decimal number 666 as **666** or **0x29A**.

NOTE: If you use a Help macro in your contents file, numeric parameters must use a number.

- Some macros don't accept parameters; if so, you must still include parentheses after the macro name:

```
BrowseButtons()
```

- You can include more than one macro in a string by separating them with a colon or semicolon. WinHelp will run the macros sequentially in the order in which they are listed.

```
CloseSecondarys();JumpId(>task, topic_ID)
```

- If you want to include a special character in a macro string, you must precede that character with a backslash (\). Special characters include double quotation marks ("), opening and closing single quotation marks (` '), and backslashes (\). For example,

```
ExecFile(myapp.exe \"special characters\")
```

Since .RTF files use backslashes to mark the beginning of certain formatting, you must double the backslashes for every level of nested macros that you use:

```
CreateButton(button-ID, name, ExecFile(myapp.exe \\"special char-
acters\\"))
```

- If you need to specify a path within a macro, use a forward slash instead of a backslash.

```
ExecFile(c:/folder/sample/myapp.exe)
```

You can also use a forward slash in a nested macro:

```
CreateButton(button-ID, name,
ExecFile(c:/folder/sample/myapp.exe))
```

A double backslash can also be used to specify a path.

```
ExecFile(c:\\folder\\sample\\myapp.exe)
```

Calling a macro from a contents file, program, or index entry

If you are running a macro from a contents (.CNT) file or calling a macro from a Windows program, the macro is not processed by Help Workshop; therefore the macro syntax rules are slightly different. These rules also apply if you are running a macro from an index entry. Here are the special rules:

- You must use the short name for the macro. For example, instead of **ExecFile,** you would use **EF**.

- You must enclose all string parameters within quotation marks. Quotation marks can be either matching double quotation marks (" and "), or a matched set of single open and single closed quotation marks (` and '):

```
InsertMenu("menu_example","&Example", 3)
```

If a string is enclosed in double quotation marks, any nested strings (that is, strings enclosed within the string) must be enclosed in opening and closing single quotation marks:

```
CreateButton("button_setup", "&Setup", ExecFile(`setup', 0))
```

In the example, the (`**setup**', **0**) parameters for the **ExecFile** macro must use the opening and closing single quotation marks since they're nested within the parameters for the **CreateButton** macro. If you get in the habit of using the single quotation marks, you'll avoid any confusion that may arise when you're working with nested macro strings.

NOTE: The single open quotation mark (`) is different from the single closed quotation mark ('), or apostrophe. The former is on the same key as the tilde (~), while the latter is on the same key as the double quotation mark (").

When typing macros in your word processor, you may want to disable smart quotes to avoid compilation errors. In Word, click Auto Correct from the Tools menu and clear the **Change Straight Quotes to Smart Quotes** box.

- You must use numeric values for all numeric parameters. For example, instead of **KLink(printing, TITLE)** you would type **KLink(printing, 2)**.

- You must supply all the parameters for a macro. The only parameters you can omit are trailing arguments that would have a value of 0 or "".

Running Help macros

There are many ways to run a Help macro. The various methods are summarized in Table 16.1, and explained in detail throughout this section.

Macros that affect the Help buttons, menus, or menu items remain in effect until the user chooses a new topic, quits Help, or opens a new Help file. Also, some of the macros won't work from secondary or pop-up windows.

Table 16.1. *Different ways to run a Help macro*

To run a macro when the user:	Type the macro in:
Opens a Help file.	The [CONFIG] section of the Help project file (.HPJ).
Opens a particular Help window.	In the [MACROS] section for the Help window.

Table 16.1. *(continued)*

To run a macro when the user:	Type the macro in:
Displays a topic.	A topic entry footnote (! marker).
Clicks a hotspot.	A hotspot jump.
Clicks a keyword in the Index tab.	The [MACROS] section for the Help project.
Clicks an item in the Contents tab.	The contents file.

WHEN THE USER OPENS A HELP FILE

If a macro appears in the [CONFIG] section of the project file, Help executes the macro when the user opens the Help file. Use this method any time you want to customize the entire Help file, such as creating the browse buttons on Help's button bar.

To run a macro when the user opens a Help file:

1. Open a project file in Help Workshop.

2. Click Config. The Configuration Macros dialog box appears.

3. Click Add. The Add Macro dialog box appears.

4. Type the macro in the **Macro** box. For example, to add browse buttons to Help's button bar, you would type:

```
BrowseButtons()
```

5. Type a comment in the **Comment** box, if you want. Comments are not visible to the Help user and do not affect the size of the compiled Help file.

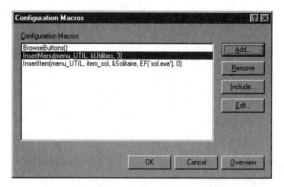

Figure 16.1. *Macros in the [CONFIG] section of the project file are run when the user opens the Help file.*

If you open the project file in a text editor, your configuration macros will be listed in the [CONFIG] section:

```
[CONFIG]
BrowseButtons()
InsertMenu(menu_UTIL, &Utilities, 3)
InsertItem(menu_UTIL, item_sol, &Solitaire, EF(`sol.exe'), 0)
```

If more than one macro is listed in the [CONFIG] section, they are executed in the order in which they are listed. For example, if you place one or more **CreateButton** macros before the **BrowseButtons** macro in the [CONFIG] section, the browse buttons will appear to the right of the custom button(s) on the button bar.

WHEN THE USER OPENS A HELP TOPIC

If a macro is authored in a topic footnote, it is executed when the user first displays that topic. You use an exclamation point (!) as the footnote marker for topic macros.

To run a macro when the user opens a Help topic:

1. Place the insertion point at the beginning of the first line in the topic, and insert a footnote.

   In Word, click Footnote from the Insert menu. The Footnote dialog box appears.

2. Create a custom footnote marker using an exclamation point (!).

   In Word, type the exclamation point in the **Custom Mark** box and click OK. The footnote marker will appear next to the heading and the footnote pane will open.

3. Type the macro to the right of the exclamation point in the footnote window. If you want to run more than one macro when the Help topic is opened, separate them with colons or semicolons.

The **DisableButton** macro shown in the following figure causes WinHelp to disable a button on Help's button bar when the user opens the topic.

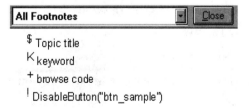

Figure 16.2. *Topic entry macros (! footnote) are run when the user opens the Help topic.*

WHEN THE USER CLICKS A HOTSPOT

If a macro is defined in a hotspot, it is executed when the user clicks the hotspot. You might do this to create hotspot text that runs one of the linking macros (**ALink** or **KLink**).

Macro hotspots are formatted using the same method as regular hotspots: the text or bitmap for the hotspot is formatted as double-underlined text, and the macro—preceded by an exclamation point (!)—is formatted as hidden text.

To create a hotspot that runs a macro:

1. Place the insertion point directly after the text or bitmap you want to be the hotspot.

2. Type an exclamation mark (!) followed by the Help macro. You must not leave any spaces between the hotspot text, the exclamation mark, and the macro.

3. Change the character formatting of the hotspot text or graphic to double underline.

4. Change the character formatting of the exclamation mark and Help macro to hidden.

5. Be sure to change the character formatting back to non-hidden to avoid formatting additional characters as hidden text.

The following macro hotspot runs the printing macros to print the Help topics containing the topic ID "Printing" and "EF_Paths." (For more information on the print macros, see later in this chapter.)

Print topics!InitMPrint():MPrintId(Printing):MPrintId(EF_Paths):EndMPrint()

Figure 16.3. *A macro that is run when the user clicks the hotspot.*

WHEN A PARTICULAR WINDOW TYPE IS OPENED

You can associate a macro with a particular window type, so that when the user opens the window, the macro runs. This technique is useful if you want to customize a menu or a button bar. Keep in mind that the macro will run each time a topic appears in the window.

To run a macro each time a window type is opened:

1. Open the project file in Help Workshop.

2. Click Windows, then the Macros tab.

3. In the **Window Type** list, select the name of the window you want to modify.

4. Click Add.

5. Type the macro you want to run when the window is opened.

   When the "proc" window type is opened, the following macro will close all secondary windows (except the one that is currently open).

Figure 16.4. *A macro for a particular window type is run
when a topic is displayed in the window.*

If you open the project file in a text editor, any macros associated with a window type will
appear in a special [CONFIG] section that references the specified window type:

```
[CONFIG-proc]
CloseSecondarys()
```

WHEN THE USER ACCESSES AN INDEX ENTRY

You can associate a macro with a particular keyword, so that when the user double-clicks an
index entry, the macro runs. You can run any macro, but this feature might be particularly useful for starting a utility program, a wizard or DLL.

The macro syntax rules for running a macro from an index entry are the same as those used
for running a macro from a contents file or Windows program. See "Calling a macro from a
contents file, program, or index entry" earlier in this chapter for more information.

To run a macro when an index entry is accessed:

1. Open the project file in Help Workshop.

2. Click Options, then the Macros tab.

3. Click Add, and the Keyword Macros dialog box appears.

4. Type the appropriate keyword(s) in the **Keyword(s) to associate with macro(s)** box.
   Separate multiple keywords with semicolons.

   If you specify a keyword that already appears as a K-keyword footnote in one of your
   topic files, the Topics Found dialog box will appear and let the user choose a topic title. If
   you specify a keyword that does not appear as a K-keyword footnote in a topic file, Help
   will run a macro when the user double-clicks the keyword in the index.

5. Type the appropriate macro(s) in the **Macro(s) to associate with keyword(s)** box. Separate multiple macros with semicolons.

   The specified macro(s) will run whenever a user double-clicks any of the keywords specified above in Step 4.

6. If the keyword you entered above in Step 4 appears in more than one topic, use the **Title that appears in the Topics Found dialog box** box to type the topic title for the keyword.

   The title you specify will appear in the Topics Found dialog box only if the keyword is linked to both a macro and to one or more topics. In this case, double-clicking the title in the Topics Found dialog box runs the macro.

The macro illustrated in Figure 16.5 creates a keyword that runs an application called TUTORIAL.EXE.

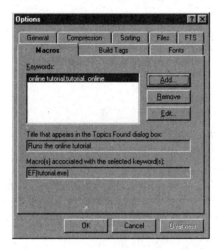

Figure 16.5. *Any macros in the [MACROS] section are run when the user double-clicks the associated keyword.*

If you open the project file in a text editor, any macros associated with keywords appear in the [MACROS] section:

```
[MACROS]
online tutorial;tutorial, online
EF(`tutorial.exe')
```

WHEN THE USER CLICKS A PAGE IN THE CONTENTS FILE

You can associate a macro with a particular page icon in the contents (CNT) file, so that double-clicking the book icon will run the macro. This might be useful for starting a program or wizard, or calling a DLL.

To run a macro when a user clicks a page in the contents file:

1. Open the contents (.CNT) file in Help Workshop.

2. Click **Add Above** or **Add Below** to create a new page icon, or click **Edit** to edit an existing page icon. The Edit Contents Tab Entry box appears.

3. Type the title that will appear in the contents in the **Title** box.

4. In the **Topic ID** box, type the name of the macro(s) you want to run. Separate multiple macros with colons.

   For example, to bring up the Control Panel so the user can change the desktop settings, you would type:

   ```
   EF(`Desk.cpl',`Display, 2')
   ```

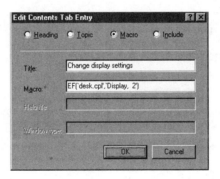

Figure 16.6. *A macro in the contents file is run when the user double-clicks an icon.*

If you opened a contents file in a text editor, the syntax for the command might look like this:

```
2 Change display settings=!EF(`desk.cpl',`Display,  2')
```

> **NOTE** *The syntax used to call a macro from a contents file is different from the format used in your topic and project files. For example, in a contents file you must use the macro's short name, quotation marks around all string parameters, numeric values for numeric parameters, and you must supply all the parameters for a macro. For more information, see "Calling a macro from a contents file" earlier in this chapter.*

FROM A SOFTWARE PROGRAM

You can run a macro from a software program by sending a HELP_COMMAND parameter in the WinHelp API call. This syntax for calling WinHelp looks like this:

```
WinHelp(hwndProgram, "HelpFile[>WindowName]", HELP_COMMAND,
"macro");
```

The following example uses the **ALink** macro to jump to any topics containing the keyword **get_start** in the TUTORIAL.HLP file:

```
case IDM_HELP_KEYBOARD:
WinHelp (hwnd, "sample.hlp", HELP_COMMAND, (DWORD)
"AL(`GET_START\')");
return 0;
```

> **NOTE** *The syntax used to call a macro from a software program is different from the format used in your topic and project files. For example, if you're calling a macro from a program, you must use the macro's short name, quotation marks around all string parameters, numeric values for numeric parameters, and you must supply all the parameters for a macro. For more information, see "Calling a macro from a contents file" earlier in this chapter.*

Help macro functional reference

This section summarizes each of the standard Windows Help macros, grouped alphabetically according to their functions. An asterisk indicates the macro is new in WinHelp 4.

Table 16.2. *Windows Help macros*

Macro/Abbreviation	Description
Accessing Help's menus and buttons	
Back	Displays the previous topic in the history list.
BrowseButtons	Adds browse buttons (>> and <<) to the button bar.
ChangeButtonBinding CBB	Changes the Help macro assigned to a button on Help's button bar.
ChangeEnable* CE	Enables a button on the button bar and changes the macro assigned to the button.
Contents	Displays the contents topic in the current Help file.
CreateButton CB	Adds a new button to the button bar.
DestroyButton	Removes a button added with the **CreateButton** macro.
DisableButton DB	Disables a button added with the **CreateButton** macro.
EnableButton EB	Re-enables a button added with the **CreateButton** macro.
Find*	Displays the Find tab of the Help Topics dialog box.

Table 16.2. *(continued)*

Macro/Abbreviation	Description
Accessing Help's built-in menu items	
Finder* FD	Displays the Help Topics dialog box in its last state.
History	Displays the history list.
Menu* MU	Displays the context menu, which is typically accessed by right-clicking the mouse.
Next	Displays the next topic in the browse sequence.
Prev	Displays the previous topic in the browse sequence.
Search	Displays the Search dialog box, allowing the user to search for a keyword.
SetContents	Designates a specific topic as the contents topic.
About	Displays Help's About dialog box.
Annotate	Displays the Annotation dialog box from Help's Edit menu.
BookmarkDefine	Displays the Define dialog box from Help's Bookmark menu.
BookmarkMore	Displays the More dialog from the Bookmark menu. This command appears if the menu lists more than nine bookmarks.
CopyTopic CT	Copies the current topic to the Clipboard.
Exit	Exits Windows Help.
FileOpen FO	Displays the Open dialog box from Help's File menu.
HelpOn	Displays the Help file that explains how to use Windows Help (equivalent to choosing the How to Use Help command from the Help menu).
Printing macros	
EndMPrint*	Dismisses the printing message box and stops the printing of multiple topics.
InitMPrint*	Displays the Print dialog box to prepare WinHelp for printing multiple topics.
MPrintHash*	Prints a topic identified by a hash number (must be used in conjunction with the **InitMPrint** and **EndMPrint** macros).
MPrintID*	Prints a topic (must be used in conjunction with the **InitMPrint** and **EndMPrint** macros).
Print	Prints the current topic.
Customizing Help's menus	
AppendItem AI	Appends a menu item to the end of a custom menu.

Table 16.2. *(continued)*

Macro/Abbreviation	Description
Customizing Help's menus	
ChangeItemBinding CIB	Changes the macro assigned to a custom menu item.
CheckItem CI	Places a checkmark beside a menu item.
DeleteItem	Deletes a custom menu item.
DisableItem DI	Disables a custom menu item.
EnableItem EI	Re-enables a custom menu item.
ExtAbleItem	Enables or disables a menu item.
ExtInsertItem	Inserts a menu item at a given position on a menu, in a given state.
ExtInsertMenu	Inserts a submenu in a previously defined menu.
FloatingMenu	Displays the context (floating) menu at the current mouse pointer position.
InsertItem	Inserts a menu item on a menu.
InsertMenu	Adds a new menu to the menu bar.
ResetMenu	Resets the Help menu bar and menus to their default states.
UncheckItem UI	Removes a checkmark beside a menu item.
Creating hypertext links	
ALink* AL	Jumps to the topics that contain the specified A-keyword.
JumpContents	Jumps to the contents topic of a specified Help file.
JumpContext JC	Jumps to a specified context number within a Help file.
JumpHash JH	Jumps to a specified hash number within a Help file.
JumpHelpOn	Jumps to the contents topic of the How to Use Help file.
JumpID JI	Jumps to a specified context string within a Help file.
JumpKeyword JK	Opens a Help file, searches through the keyword table, and displays the first topic containing a specified keyword.
KLink*	Jumps to the topics that contain the specified K-keywords.
PopupContext PC	Displays the topic with a specific context number in a pop-up window.
PopupHash	Displays the topic with a specific hash number in a pop-up window.
PopupId PI	Displays the topic with a specific context string in a pop-up window.

Table 16.2. *(continued)*

Macro/Abbreviation	Description
Working with other programs	
ControlPanel* EF	Opens a specific tab in a Control Panel dialog box.
ExecFile* EF	Runs a program or opens a file and runs the program associated with that file.
RegisterRoutine RR	Registers a Dynamic Link Library (DLL) function as a Help macro.
ShellExecute* SE	Opens, prints, or runs a file or program.
ShortCut* SH	Runs or activates a program and sends it a WM_COMMAND message.
TCard*	Sends a message to a program that is invoking WinHelp as a training card.
Managing Help windows	
CloseSecondarys* CS	Closes all Help windows except the current secondary window.
CloseWindow CW	Closes either a secondary or main Help window.
FocusWindow	Changes the focus to the specified window.
HelpOnTop	Toggles the ontop state of Help (equivalent to checking or unchecking Help's Always on Top command).
NoShow*	Prevents a Help window from being displayed.
PositionWindow PW	Sets the size and position of a Help window.
SetPopupColor* SPC	Sets the background color of a pop-up window.
UpdateWindow* UW	Jumps to the specified topic in the specified window, and then returns the focus to the window that called the macro.
Help markers	
DeleteMark	Deletes a text marker added with the **SaveMark** macro.
FileExist* FE	Checks to see whether the specified file or program exists.
GotoMark	Jumps to a marker set with the **SaveMark** macro.
IfThen IF	Tests the condition of the **IsMark** macro and executes a Help macro if the specified marker exists.
IfThenElse IE	Tests the condition of the **IsMark** macro and executes one of two Help macros, depending on whether or not the specified marker exists.
IsBook*	Determines whether WinHelp is running as a standalone system (a double-clicked book icon), or if it is being run from a program.
IsMark	Tests whether or not a marker set by the **SaveMark** macro exists. This macro is used as a parameter for the **IfThen** and **IfThenElse** macros.

Table 16.2. *(continued)*

Macro/Abbreviation	Description
Help markers	
IsNotMark* NM	Tests whether a marker set by the SaveMark macro does not exist.
Not	Reverses the condition returned by the **IsMark** macro. This macro is used as a parameter for the **IfThen** and **IfThenElse** macros.
SaveMark	Saves the location of the current topic and file and associates a text marker with the location. You can then use the **GoToMark** macro to jump to this location.
Working with keyboard shortcuts	
AddAccelerator AA	Assigns a Help macro to an accelerator key (or key combination) so the macro is run when the user presses the accelerator.
RemoveAccelerator RA	Removes an accelerator key assignment.
Testing and debugging	
Compare*	Displays a Help file in a second instance of WinHelp; useful for testing a localized Help file.
Test*	Provides various options for testing the topics in a Help file.
TestALink*	Tests whether an **ALink** macro has a link to at least one topic.
TestKLink*	Tests whether a **KLink** macro has a link to at least one topic.
Miscellaneous	
Flush* FH	Forces WinHelp to process any pending messages, including previously called macros.
BackFlush* BF	Removes the back history list from the current window. This macro does not affect the list displayed in the History window.
Generate*	Posts a message to the currently active Help window.

Help macro alphabetical reference

This section summarizes each of the standard Windows Help macros, grouped alphabetically.

Table 16.3. *Alphabetical reference to the Windows Help macros*

Macro	Syntax	Description
About	About()	Displays Help's About dialog box.
AddAccelerator AA	AddAccelerator(*key, shift-state, macro*)	Assigns a Help macro to an accelerator key (or key combination) so the macro is run when the user presses the accelerator.
ALink* AL	ALink(*keyword[; keyword]* [, type[, topic-ID [, window-name]]])	Jumps to the topics that contain the specified A-keyword.
Annotate	Annotate()	Displays the Annotation dialog box from Help's Edit menu.
AppendItem AI	AppendItem(*menu-ID, item-ID, item-name, macro*)	Appends a menu item to the end of a custom menu.
Back	Back()	Displays the previous topic in the History list.
BackFlush* BF	BackFlush()	Removes the back History list from the current window. This macro does not affect the History list displayed in the History window.
BookmarkDefine	BookmarkDefine()	Displays the Define dialog box from Help's Bookmark menu.
BookmarkMore	BookmarkMore()	Displays the More dialog from the Bookmark menu. This command appears if the menu lists more than nine bookmarks.
BrowseButtons	BrowseButtons()	Adds browse buttons (>> and <<) to the button bar.
ChangeButtonBinding CBB	ChangeButtonBinding(*button-ID, button-macro*)	Changes the Help macro assigned to a button on Help's button bar.

Table 16.3. *(continued)*

Macro	Syntax	Description
ChangeEnable* CE	**ChangeEnable(** *button-ID, button-macro* **)**	Enables a button on the button bar and changes the macro assigned to the button.
ChangeItemBinding	**CIBChangeItemBinding** (*item-ID, item-macro*)	Changes the macro assigned to a custom menu item.
CheckItem CI	**CheckItem(** *item-ID* **)**	Places a checkmark beside a menu item.
CloseSecondarys* CS	**CloseSecondarys()**	Closes all Help windows except the current secondary window.
CloseWindow CW	**CloseWindow(** *[window-name]* **)**	Closes either a secondary or main Help window.
Compare*	**Compare(** *HLP-filename* **)**	Displays a Help file in a second instance of WinHelp; useful for testing a localized Help file.
Contents	**Contents()**	Displays the contents topic in the current Help file.
ControlPanel*EF	**ControlPanel(** *CPL_name[, panel_name, tabnum]* **)**	Opens a specific tab in a Control Panel dialog box.
CopyTopic CT	**CopyTopic()**	Copies the current topic to the Clipboard.
CreateButton CB	**CreateButton(** *button-ID, name, macro* **)**	Adds a new button to the button bar.
DeleteItem	**DeleteItem(** *item-ID* **)**	Deletes a custom menu item.
DeleteMark	**DeleteMark(** *marker-text* **)**	Deletes a text marker added with the **SaveMark** macro.
DestroyButton	**DestroyButton(** *button-ID* **)**	Removes a button added with the **CreateButton** macro.
DisableButton DB	**DisableButton(** *button-ID* **)**	Disables a button added with the **CreateButton** macro.
DisableItem DI	**DisableItem(** *item-ID* **)**	Disables a custom menu item.
EnableButton EB	**EnableButton(** *button-ID* **)**	Re-enables a button added with the **CreateButton** macro.
EnableItem EI	**EnableItem(** *item-ID* **)**	Re-enables a custom menu item.

Table 16.3. *(continued)*

Macro	Syntax	Description
EndMPrint*	EndMPrint()	Dismisses the printing message box and stops the printing of multiple topics.
ExecFile* EF	ExecFile(**program**[, *arguments* [, *display-state*[, *topic-ID*]]])	Runs a program or opens a file and runs the program associated with that file.
Exit	Exit()	Exits Windows Help.
ExtAbleItem	ExtAbleItem(*item-ID, display-state*)	Enables or disables a menu item.
ExtInsertItem	ExtInsertItem(*menu-ID, item-ID, item-name, macro, position, display-state*)	Inserts a menu item at a given position on a menu, in a given state.
ExtInsertMenu	ExtInsertMenu(*parent-ID, menu-ID, menu-name, menu-position, display-state*)	Inserts a submenu in a previously defined menu.
FileExist* FE	FileExist(*filename*)	Checks to see whether the specified file or program exists.
FileOpen FO	FileOpen()	Displays the Open dialog box from Help's File menu.
Find*	Find()	Displays the Find tab of the Help Topics dialog box.
Finder* FD	Finder()	Displays the Help Topics dialog box in its last state.
FloatingMenu	FloatingMenu()	Displays the context (floating) menu at the current mouse pointer position.
Flush* FH	Flush()	Forces WinHelp to process any pending messages, including previously called macros.
FocusWindow	FocusWindow(*window-name*)	Changes the focus to the specified window.
Generate	Generate(*message, wParam, lParam*)	Posts a message to the currently active Help window.
GotoMark	GotoMark(*marker-text*)	Jumps to a marker set with the **SaveMark** macro.

Table 16.3. *(continued)*

Macro	Syntax	Description
HelpOn	HelpOn()	Displays the Help file explaining how to use Windows Help (equivalent to choosing the How to Use Help command from the Help menu).
HelpOnTop	HelpOnTop()	Toggles the ontop state of Help (equivalent to checking or unchecking Help's Always on Top command).
History	History()	Displays the History list.
IfThen IF	IfThen("*marker*"/*macro, macro*)	Tests the condition of the **IsMark** macro and executes a Help macro if the specified marker exists.
IfThenElse IE	IfThenElse("*marker*"/*macro, macro1, macro2*)	Tests the condition of the **IsMark** macro and executes one of two Help macros depending on whether the specified marker exists.
InitMPrint*	InitMPrint()	Displays the Print dialog box to prepare WinHelp for printing multiple topics.
InsertItem	InsertItem(*menu-ID, item-ID, item-name, macro, position*)	Inserts a menu item on a menu.
InsertMenu	InsertMenu(*menu-ID, menu-name, menu-position*)	Adds a new menu to the menu bar.
IsBook	IsBook()	Determines whether WinHelp is running as a standalone system (a double-clicked book icon), or if it is being run from a program.
IsMark	IsMark(*marker-text*)	Tests whether or not a marker set by the **SaveMark** macro exists. This macro is used as a parameter for the **IfThen** and **IfThenElse** macros.
IsNotMark* NM	IsNotMark("*marker-text*")	Tests whether a marker set by the **SaveMark** macro does not exist.

Table 16.3. *(continued)*

Macro	Syntax	Description
JumpContents	JumpContents(*filename*)	Jumps to the contents topic of a specified Help file.
JumpContext JC	JumpContext(*[filename,window-name,] context-number*)	Jumps to a specified context number within a Help file.
JumpHash JH	JumpHash(*[filename,window-name,] hash-code*)	Jumps to a specified hash number within a Help file.
JumpHelpOn	JumpHelpOn()	Jumps to the contents topic of the How to Use Help file.
JumpID JI	JumpId(*[filename,window-name,] topic-ID*)	Jumps to a specified context string within a Help file.
JumpKeyword JK	JumpKeyword(*[filename,] keyword*)	Opens a Help file, searches through the keyword table, and displays the first topic containing a specified keyword.
KLink*	KLink("*keyword[; keyword]*" [, *type[,* "*topic-ID*"[, *window-name]]]*)	Jumps to the topics that contain the specified K-keywords.
Menu* MU	Menu()	Displays the context menu, which is typically accessed by right-clicking the mouse.
MPrintHash*	MPrintHash(*hash-code*)	Prints a topic identified by a hash number (must be used in conjunction with the **InitMPrint** and **EndMPrint** macros).
MPrintID*	MPrintID(*topic-ID*)	Prints a topic (must be used in conjunction with the **InitMPrint** and **EndMPrint** macros).
Next	Next()	Displays the next topic in the browse sequence.
NoShow*	NoShow()	Prevents a Help window from being displayed.
Not	Not("*marker*" /*macro*)	Reverses the condition returned by the **IsMark** macro. This macro is used as a parameter for the **IfThen** and **IfThenElse** macros.

Table 16.3. *(continued)*

Macro	Syntax	Description
PopupContext PC	**PopupContext(***[filename,] context-number***)**	Displays the topic with a specific context number in a pop-up window.
PopupHash	**PopupHash(***[filename,] hash-code***)**	Displays the topic with a specific hash number in a pop-up window.
PopupId PI	**PopupId(***[filename,] topic-ID***)**	Displays the topic with a specific context string in a pop-up window.
PositionWindow PW	**PositionWindow(***x, y, width, height, display-state, window-name***)**	Sets the size and position of a Help window.
Prev	**Prev()**	Displays the previous topic in the browse sequence.
Print	**Print()**	Prints the current topic.
RegisterRoutine RR	**RegisterRoutine(***DLL-name, function-name, format-spec***)**	Registers a Dynamic Link Library (DLL) function as a Help macro.
RemoveAccelerator RA	**RemoveAccelerator(***key, shift-state***)**	Removes an accelerator key assignment.
ResetMenu	**ResetMenu()**	Resets the Help menu bar and menus to their default states.
SaveMark	**SaveMark(***marker-text***)**	Saves the location of the current topic and file and associates a text marker with the location. You can then use the **GoToMark** macro to jump to this location.
Search	**Search()**	Displays the Search dialog box, allowing the user to search for a keyword.
SetContents	**SetContents(***filename, context-number***)**	Designates a specific topic as the contents topic.
SetPopupColor* SPC	**SetPopupColor(***r, g, b***)**	Sets the background color of a pop-up window.
ShellExecute* SE	**ShellExecute(***filename, [options [, show-flag[, operation[, path [, topic-id]]]]]***)**	Opens, prints or runs a file or program.

Table 16.3. *(continued)*

Macro	Syntax	Description
ShortCut* SH	**ShortCut(***window-class, program [, wParam[, lParam[, topic-ID]]]***)**	Runs or activates a program and sends it a WM_COMMAND message.
TCard*	**TCard(***command***)**	Sends a message to a program that is invoking WinHelp as a training card.
Test*	**Test(***test-num***)**	Provides various options for testing the topics in a Help file.
TestALink*	**TestALink(***keyword[; keyword]***)**	Tests whether an **ALink** macro has a link to at least one topic.
TestKLink*	**TestKLink(** "*keyword[; keyword]*" **)**	Tests whether a **KLink** macro has a link to at least one topic.
UncheckItem UI	**UncheckItem(***item-ID***)**	Removes a checkmark beside a menu item.
UpdateWindow* UW	**UpdateWindow(***[filename,] window-name, topic-ID***)**	Jumps to the specified topic in the specified window, and then returns the focus to the window that called the macro.

Macro tips and techniques

This section describes several tips and tricks for using macros. As mentioned earlier in this chapter, this is not meant as a comprehensive macro reference, but as a hands-on workshop on using macros in your Help file. For reference information on the macro syntax, see the online *Help Author's Guide* (HCW.HLP) included on the disc in the back of this book.

Two other chapters in this book focus on putting Help macros to work:

- See Chapter 15 for techniques on modifying windows, the menu and button bar, and creating a keyboard interface.

- See Chapter 11 for techniques on creating hypertext links.

RUNNING EXTERNAL PROGRAMS

There are four WinHelp macros to run external programs from a Help file. The macro you choose will depend on how much control you need over the program, and which program you're trying to run.

- **ExecFile** is the simplest macro to create and is probably the one most Help authors will use. This macro offers many enhancements over its WinHelp 3.1 predecessor, **ExecProgram** (which is unsupported in WinHelp 4).

- If you need to print a file, **ShellExecute** is the one to use. Unfortunately, it doesn't work with version 4.00 or 4.01 of the Help compiler.

- **Shortcut** is especially valuable if you want to prevent WinHelp from running a new instance of a program that is already running, and provides the ability to send WM_COMMAND messages to an application.

- **ControlPanel** is the simplest way to run Control Panel programs (or "applets").

The following table covers the key differences among the macros used to run external programs.

Table 16.4. *Choosing which Help macro to use for running a Windows program*

To:	Use this macro
Run a Windows program or open a file. This gives more flexibility than **ShellExecute** over the program's display.	**ExecFile**
Print a file. Note that this macro is broken in version 4 and 4.01 of the Help compiler.	**ShellExecute**
Run a Windows program and pass it information using a WM_COMMAND message. This macro has one primary advantage: if the program is already running, WinHelp will simply activate it instead of running a new instance.	**Shortcut**
Open a program from the Windows Control Panel.	**ControlPanel**

ExecFile

ExecFile is the simplest method for running an external program. Although similar to **ShellExecute**, the **ExecFile** macro syntax is a little simpler and offers greater control over how the external program's window is displayed. The syntax is as follows:

> **ExecFile(***program[, arguments[, display-state[, topic-ID]]]***)**

At its most basic form, you can simply specify a program's filename:

```
ExecFile(sol.exe)
```

To specify the path for a filename, be sure to use a forward slash rather than a backslash. You can also use double backslashes.

```
ExecFile(c:/example/test.exe)
ExecFile(c:\\example\\test.exe)
```

You can also specify parameters for an application. The following example runs Word and tells it not to open a new document.

```
ExecFile(winword.exe /n)
```

The following example runs Paint and minimizes its window.

```
ExecFile(paint.exe, , SW_MINIMIZE)
```

As with all macros, if you want to specify a parameter, you must include all of the commas that separate any parameters that precede it. In the case of **ExecFile**, however, you cannot specify the *topic-ID* parameter unless you also specify the *display-state* parameter. The following macro tells WinHelp to display the topic associated with the topic ID "error_msg" if it can't find the DEMO.EXE program.

```
ExecFile(demo.exe, , SW_SHOW, error_msg)
```

ShellExecute

In theory, **ShellExecute** has one big advantage over **EF**: it can be used to print a file. Unfortunately, as of this writing the macro doesn't work. Look for an interim release of the Help compiler (perhaps version 4.02) to fix the **ShellExecute** macro.

A function named **ShellExecute** was available under WinHelp 3.1 as part of the Windows API, but its syntax is different than WinHelp's **ShellExecute** macro. Help files compiled under WinHelp 3.1 will run fine under Windows 95, but if you're converting a WinHelp 3.1 project you'll need to change each occurrence of the macro to **ExecFile** (or edit each occurrence to match WinHelp's **ShellExecute** macro syntax when it is fixed).

Shortcut

The **Shortcut** macro is especially valuable if you want to prevent WinHelp from running a new instance of a program that is already running. It also provides the ability to send WM_COM-MAND messages to an application.

Using **Shortcut** requires some technical information about the program, including the *window-class*. Depending on how you're using **Shortcut**, you may also need to know the *wParam* and *lParam* arguments. You can get this information from your development staff, or by running the Spy (or Spy++) application included with the Windows SDK and most Windows compilers.

ShortCut(*window-class, program[, wParam[, lParam[, topic-ID]]]*)

There are a couple of uses for the **Shortcut** macro.

Instance control

Instance control is a big advantage for Help developers. Many applications support multiple instances. For example, if you run the Calculator applet—perhaps using **EF(CALC.EXE)**—while Calculator is already running, you will have two copies of Calculator open at once. This isn't a very courteous thing to do, since the user must clean up after your Help file.

The following **Shortcut** macro will run Calculator, unless a copy of the program is already running, in which case WinHelp will activate it.

```
ShortCut(SciCalc,calc.exe)
```

If you want to include some error handling in case WinHelp can't find the specified program, you can specify a topic ID in the **Shortcut** macro. In the following example, the ERROR_MSG topic ID will pop up if the program cannot be found.

```
ShortCut(SciCalc,calc.exe, , ,ERROR_MSG)
```

Notice that since the above macro doesn't send a message to the application, it excludes the *wParam* and *lParam* parameters (but leaves the commas).

Sending messages to an application

The other advantage to the **Shortcut** macro is its ability to send messages to a Windows application. Messaging is the lifeblood of Windows, and sending a message to a program allows you to control its menu commands and keyboard accelerators.

The beauty of the **Shortcut** macro is that instead of instructing a user how to accomplish a task, you can do it for them. For example, the following macro runs Help Workshop and enables the View Messages command.

```
ShortCut(hcw_class, hcw, 0x802D)
```

You can also use **Shortcut** in other interesting ways. For example, suppose you want to copy the current Help topic and then run WordPad and paste it into a document.

```
CopyTopic();ShortCut(WordPadClass, wordpad, 0xE125)
```

You can also send more than one message to the application. The following macro copies the current Help topic, runs WordPad and pastes the Clipboard contents into the document. It then moves to the next Help topic, copies it, and pastes it into the same WordPad document.

```
CopyTopic();ShortCut(WordPadClass, wordpad,
0xE125);Next();CopyTopic();ShortCut(WordPadClass, wordpad,
0xE125)
```

ControlPanel

If you want to run one of the applets from the Control Panel so users can verify or change their Windows configuration, the new **ControlPanel** macro is the one to use. The syntax for Control Panel is as follows:

ControlPanel(*CPL_name[, panel_name, tabnum]***)**

The *CPL_name* and *panel_name* parameters for the standard Windows control panel applets are listed in the following table. Note that some of the control panels don't recognize parameters; if so, the *panel_name* and *tabnum* parameters are not listed.

Table 16.5. *Parameters used in the ControlPanel macro*

Description	CPL_name	panel_name	tabnum
Sets up programs and creates shortcuts.	APPWIZ.CPL		
Changes display settings.	DESK.CPL	Display	0=Background 1=Screen Saver 2=Appearance 3=Settings
Changes how numbers, currencies, dates, and times are displayed.	INTL.CPL	Regional Settings	0=Regional Settings 1=Number 2=Currency 3=Time 4=Date
Changes joystick settings.	JOY.CPL	Joystick	0=Joystick
Changes mouse settings.	MAIN.CPL		
Changes settings for multimedia devices.	MMSYS.CPL	Multimedia	0=Audio 1=MIDI 2=CD Music 3=Video 4=Advanced
Installs a new modem and changes modem properties.	MODEM.CPL		
Configures network hardware and software.	NETCPL.CPL		
Changes passwords and sets security options.	PASSWORD.CPL	Passwords	0=Change Passwords 1=Remote Administration 2=User Profiles
Provides system information and changes advanced settings.	SYSDM.CPL	System	0=General 1=Device Manager 2=Hardware Profiles 3=Performance
Changes date, time, and time zone information.	TIMEDATE.CPL	Date/Time	0=Date & Time 1=Time Zone

Here are some examples of how to run various control panel applets:

```
ControlPanel(MMSYS.CPL,Multimedia,1)
ControlPanel(NETCPL.CPL)
ControlPanel(SYSDM.CPL,System,1)
```

Running a control panel applet from a contents file

You can't run the **ControlPanel** macro from a contents file: WinHelp doesn't recognize it. (In fact, Help Workshop automatically converts all **ControlPanel** macros into the **ExecFile** macro, which is in turn converted to **EF**.)

Instead, you'll need to use the **EF** macro to run a control panel applet from a contents file. Note that the **EF** syntax is a little different when running a control panel applet. In particular, the *panel_name* and *tabnum* parameters must both be enclosed within the same set of quotation marks:

EF(`cpl_name'[,`panel_name,tabnum'])

Thus, this works:

```
EF(`Desk.cpl', `Display,2')
```

but this does not work:

```
EF(`Desk.cpl', `Display', `2')
```

Running other applets

Two other items appearing in the Control Panel—the Fonts and Printers folders—are not actually applets, but shortcuts to internal Windows functions. Since these are not CPL devices, you must use the **ExecFile** macro.

To run the Fonts folder from WinHelp, enter the following macro:

```
EF("rundll", "SHELL32.DLL,SHHelpShortcuts_RunDLL FontsFolder",0)
```

To run the Printers folder from WinHelp, enter the following macro:

```
EF("rundll", "SHELL32.DLL,SHHelpShortcuts_RunDLL
PrintersFolder",0)
```

How WinHelp locates files

One of the challenges in launching an external program is making sure that WinHelp can find it. Because most installation programs allow the user to specify the installation folder, your Help macro cannot always reliably specify a pathname for the external program.

WinHelp searches for external programs and DLLs (and other files) in the following locations:

- If a path is specified, WinHelp first searches for the file in the path. (If not found, the path is removed and the following locations are searched.)

- The folder that contains the current Help file.

- The current folder.

- The SYSTEM subfolder in the Windows folder.

- The Windows folder.

- The folders listed in the PATH environment.

- The location specified in WINHELP.INI.

- The Help portion of the registry.

Updating WINHELP.INI

If you suspect WinHelp won't be able to find an external program you are running from a macro, you can have your installation program update the WINHELP.INI file. For more information, see "Updating WINHELP.INI" in Chapter 11.

Using relative pathnames

Another option is to specify a relative path to the program or file you want to run. For example, while it's usually impossible to determine the drive letter or folder used to install your application, most setup programs automatically create the subfolders created within the main folder.

Suppose that, by default, your setup program creates a folder named YOURAPP on the C drive (C:\YOURAPP), and that you want to run a program named APP.EXE installed in a folder named \UTILITY. You could run the program using the following macro, provided the user accepted the default setup folder:

```
EF(c:/yourapp/utility/test.exe)
```

This is a very dangerous assumption, however, since the user may very well specify a different drive or folder in which to install your product. Your macro will be much more bulletproof if you specify a pathname that is relative to the \YOURAPP folder. As long as the user doesn't rename or delete the folder or the application, WinHelp will find the specified program:

```
EF(utility/test.exe)
```

Similarly, if you know that TEST.EXE is located in a parent folder (that is, up one level toward the root), you could type:

```
EF(../test.exe)
```

Checking to see if a file or program exists

If you're documenting a modular product that includes optional components, you may want to check to see whether a specified file or program exists before running it. Enter the **FileExist** macro. **FileExist** looks to see whether a specified file or program exists. If the file or program exists, **FileExist** returns TRUE; otherwise, it returns FALSE. The macro syntax is very simple:

> **FileExist**(*filename*)

By itself, **FileExist** is of little value. But you can use **FileExist** to look for a file or program and then use the **IfThenElse** macro to determine whether to run the file or take some other action. For example, the following macro checks to see if SAMPLE.EXE has been installed. If the file is present, WinHelp uses **ExecFile** to run it. If the file is not present, WinHelp uses **PopupId** to display the topic associated with the topic ID "app_not_installed."

```
IfThenElse(FileExist(sample.exe), ExecFile(sample.exe),
PopupId(app_not_installed))
```

CONDITIONALLY PERFORMING AN ACTION

Chapter 15 introduced the marker macros and explained how to use them to dynamically modify the interface of a Help file during a Help session. You might want to add or remove a menu item for a specific topic, or you might want to disable a button. You might even want to change the action performed by a button or menu. For example, if you place a See Also button on the button bar, you could change the button for each topic.

Here's another example of using marker macros to conditionally perform an action. You may want to play a sound effect each time the user loads the Help file. By using a marker macro, you guarantee that the sound is not played if the user jumps to another Help file, and then back again.

To run a macro when the user opens a Help file, that you place the macro in the [CONFIG] section of the project file. See "Running Help macros" earlier in this chapter for information on the various options you can choose from to run a macro.

The example uses the **IfThen** macro to test whether or not there is a marker called "first_time." The first time the user opens the Help file, the marker does not exist, so Help creates one using **SaveMark.** Help then runs the **sndPlaySound** function to play a wave file. If the marker already exists (that is, if the user had already opened the Help file), the macro does nothing.

```
IfThen(IsNotMark("first_time"), SaveMark("first_time");
sndPlaySound("welcome.wav",1))
```

You might consider adding this macro to the splash screen topic mentioned in Chapter 15.

PRINTING GROUPS OF HELP TOPICS

Another major improvement in WinHelp 4 is the printing capability. Using the four new print macros—**InitMPrint, MPrintId, MPrintHash,** and **EndMPrint**—you can create predefined groups of topics that can be printed by the user.

The printing macros are used in conjunction to prepare the printer, specify the topics you want to print, and dismiss the print job. **InitMPrint** must always appear at the beginning of the topic group to initialize the printer. Likewise, **EndMPrint** must always be used at the end of the group to dismiss the Print Topic dialog box and terminate the print job.

Sandwiched in the middle of the **InitMPrint** and **EndMPrint** macros, you will use **MPrintId** or **MPrintHash** to specify the topics you want to send to the printer. The two macros are identical, except that **MPrintId** identifies a topic using a topic ID, and **MPrintHash** identifies a topic using a hash number. If you want to print a topic from a Help system but don't know its topic ID and can't access the source files, you can use the Report command in Help Workshop to get the hash numbers of all the topics and use **MPrintHash** to identify the topics you want to print. Otherwise, it's easier to use the **MPrintId** macro.

There are several ways you can let the user print a group of topics. Here are some ideas:

- Create a hotspot in the topic that the user can click to print a group of topics:

```
Print
topics!InitMPrint();MPrintId(topic_1);MPrintId(topic_2);EndMPrint()
```

- Create an authorable button in the topic:

```
{button Print topics,
InitMPrint();MPrintId(topic_1);MPrintId(topic_2);EndMPrint()}
```

- Add a keyword to the index:

```
InitMPrint();MPrintId(topic_1);MPrintId(topic_2);EndMPrint()
```

When the user runs the macro to print the group of topics, Help displays the Print dialog box. If the user clicks OK, Help jumps to each topic specified and sends it to the printer. Once the print job is complete, the last topic specified in the macro will be displayed in WinHelp. Make sure the last topic specified in the topic printing group is the same one used to start the print job; otherwise, you force the hapless user to backtrack to return to the original spot in the Help file.

If a topic you specified in the macro does not exist, WinHelp prints the default topic (as specified in the CONTENTS setting in the [OPTIONS] section of the project file).

PLACING A FILE IN BAGGAGE

WinHelp has its own internal file system, called "baggage." Once a file is stored in baggage, you can retrieve it using a DLL (such as Paul Arnote's EW256BMP.DLL).

To store data files in Help's own file system, you list them in the [BAGGAGE] section of the project file. You can store up to one thousand data files. In the list, use paths relative to the project file's ROOT option; if there is no ROOT option, specify the path relative to the project folder.

To store a file in baggage:

1. Open a project file in Help Workshop.

2. Click Data Files, then Add. The Files Used by Help DLLs dialog box appears.

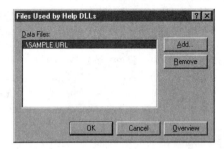

Figure 16.7. *A file stored in baggage.*

3. Locate the file you want to add to baggage and click OK.

If you opened your project file in a text editor, the [BAGGAGE] section would look like this:

```
[BAGGAGE]
.\SAMPLE.URL
```

In the topic file, references to files stored in baggage must be immediately preceded by an exclamation mark. Files listed in baggage are case-sensitive, so your topic file must reference the filename exactly as it appears in the [BAGGAGE] section.

Notes about baggage

- Under WinHelp 4, the **{mci}** statement automatically places multimedia files in baggage unless you specify otherwise. If you are building a WinHelp 3.1 file, you must manually place multimedia files in the [BAGGAGE] section of your project file.

- You cannot store MIDI files in baggage. Also, the **sndPlaySound** and **sndPlaySoundA** functions will not accept the exclamation mark required for playing a file stored in baggage. Use another DLL (such as HYPRO.DLL) to extract and play a .WAV file stored in baggage.

REGISTERING A DLL FUNCTION

If you need to extend your Help system with a feature not included in WinHelp, you can write a custom DLL (dynamic-link library) and access it just as you would an internal WinHelp macro.

In order to use a function built into a DLL, you must tell WinHelp about the name of the DLL and the format for the parameters it accepts. This is accomplished using the **RegisterRoutine** macro.

RegisterRoutine *(DLL-name, function-name, format-spec)*

The following example shows how to register two routines. The first command registers the **sndPlaySound** function in the MMSYSTEM.DLL. The second registers the **MessageBox** function built into Windows.

```
[CONFIG]
RegisterRoutine("mmsystem.dll", "sndPlaySound", "Su")
RegisterRoutine("user32.dll", "MessageBox", "USSU")
```

Of course, once you register a function, you can access it like a macro. The following command displays a message box and plays a wave file.

```
MessageBox(hwndContext, "Nice work, you did it!", "Developing
Online Help for Windows 95", 0); sndPlaySound("CHIMES.WAV",1)
```

MACRO BUGS

As with any software product, there are a few macro bugs and documentation inaccuracies in the first version (4.00.0950) of Help Workshop. Keep your eyes open for the latest versions of HCW.EXE, HCRTF.EXE, WINHLP32.EXE, and FTSRCH.DLL.

- There are several bugs associated with the **KLink** and **ALink** macros; see Chapter 11, *Creating Hypertext Links* for more information.

- **NoShow()** could be used in early versions of Help Workshop to prevent a topic from displaying, but does not appear to work in the first release.

- The **Compare** macro does not work, which in turn breaks the **Test** macro when you specify a value of **7** for the *test-num* parameter.

- **ExtInsertMenu** is incorrectly documented in the *Help Author's Guide*. The correct syntax is as follows:

    ExtInsertMenu *(parent-ID, menu-ID, menu-name, menu-position, display-state)*

Note that the display-state parameter is not optional. Furthermore, the acceptable values for display-state are **0** for normal, and **1** for grayed.

The following command adds a submenu named "Find" to the Tools menu:

```
ExtInsertMenu(mnu_tools, mnu_find, &Find, 1, 0)
```

For more information, see "Adding a menu" in Chapter 15.

17

Help Topic Access

The most visible changes in WinHelp 4 are certainly the new methods for accessing topics. In WinHelp 3.1 the most common points of entry to topics have been the contents topic and the search keyword list. The former is best suited for exploring and the latter for targeting specific topics quickly. Both of those entry points have undergone a significant facelift in WinHelp 4.0. To further enhance topic access, the much requested full-text search capability is also now provided.

The new topic access features are WinHelp enhancements, not required functions. Therefore you can choose to continue shipping your Help system without these features and not have any compatibility problems in Windows 95. However, if the new features are embraced by a broad base of users, you may find it necessary to include them in your Help system to meet user expectations. Since Microsoft is championing the use of the new features through their own Help systems, it is likely that they will become a standard.

The topic access features are: the Contents page, the Index page, and the Find page. These "pages" appear to the user in the Help Topics browser box. The Help author enables the pages and the browser through the use of the "contents file." This chapter describes each of the topic access components and explains how to implement them.

The Help Topics browser and contents file greatly improve the linking of modular Help files through the Contents, Index, and Find pages. This feature is described in the last section of this chapter.

The Help Topics browser

The centerpiece of topic access in WinHelp 4 is the Help Topics browser box shown in Figure 17.1. This box is a standard Windows 95 dialog box which can contain tabs for the Contents, Index, and Find pages. A user can click the tabs to quickly change pages. The Help Topics browser becomes the common point from which the user can quickly navigate to different topics of the Help system.

This browser is not part of the compiled Help file but instead is generated by WinHelp when the Help file is launched. In order for WinHelp to display the browser, a special file called the contents file must be shipped along with the Help file. The contents file, described in the next section, also controls the appearance of the Contents, Index, and Find pages. The general appearance and operation of the Help Topics browser is the same for all Help systems that use it.

Figure 17.1. *The Help Topics browser showing the Contents page on top.*

The user can display the browser at any time as long as you have provided the necessary buttons in the Help file. One of these buttons is a holdover from WinHelp 3.1 and three new buttons are available with WinHelp 4. The old one is the Contents button. If you elect to link your Help file to a contents file, the Contents button displays the browser with the Contents page on top.

The Index button, which replaces Search, displays the browser with the Index page on top. The Find button places the full-text search interface on top. Finally, the Help Topics button displays either the Contents page or whatever page was last selected in the current Help session. These buttons can be selectively added to the button bars of the main and secondary windows as shown in Figure 17.2.

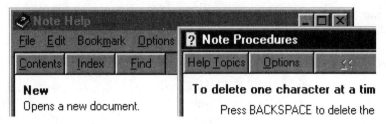

Figure 17.2. *Buttons can be used to display the Help Topics browser with various pages on top.*

THE CONTENTS

The Help Topics browser is generated by WinHelp whenever a user launches a Help file that has a contents file with it. The contents file is simply an initialization file that WinHelp reads when launching your Help file. The contents file has a .CNT extension and must be shipped along with your Help file. Figure 17.3 shows several Help files and their associated contents files in the standard \WINDOWS\HELP folder. Whereas Help files are represented by a closed book icon, the contents file appears as an open book.

Name	Size	Type	Modified
W_over.cnt	2KB	Help Contents File	3/2/95 12:00 PM
W_tour.cnt	1KB	Help Contents File	7/11/95 9:50 AM
Windows.cnt	14KB	Help Contents File	7/11/95 9:50 AM
Windows.hlp	508...	Help File	7/11/95 9:50 AM
Winfile.cnt	3KB	Help Contents File	7/11/95 9:50 AM
Winfile.hlp	43KB	Help File	7/11/95 9:50 AM
Winhlp32.cnt	1KB	Help Contents File	7/11/95 9:50 AM

Contents of 'Help'

Figure 17.3. *A list of Help files and their associated contents files.*

The contents file is an ASCII text file. It is not saved in rich-text format like your topic file, nor is it processed by the compiler. You can construct the contents file in your word processor and save it as "Text Only," or simply use a text editor like Notepad or WordPad. Or you can use the editor included with Help Workshop.

> **TIP** *Since the contents file is just a text file you can easily open files that were produced by other developers. This is a good way to analyze what others have done. Just be careful not to make adjustments to those files.*

While the name "contents" file suggest only an association with the table of contents page of the browser, it also controls the display of the Index, Find, and custom pages.

The .GID file

Technically the contents file is read by WinHelp only the first time it is launched on a user's computer. Unless your computer is exceptionally fast the following message appears when a Help file is first launched: "Preparing Help file for first use." At that time, a hidden file with a .GID extension is created and that becomes the file that WinHelp references for information on displaying the Help Topics browser. For example, in the folder containing WINDOWS.HLP, you would also find WINDOWS.CNT and a hidden file, WINDOWS.GID. (To display this file in Explorer, select Show All Files from the View/Options box.) The primary purpose of the .GID file is to reduce distribution costs. Whereas the WINDOWS.CNT file is 14K in size, the WINDOWS.GID is a whopping 240K.

> **NOTE** *If you are shipping a Help file on a CD and expect the user to launch it from there, you must ship the .GID file as well.*
>
> **NOTE** *If you wanted to keep users out of the .CNT file you might be tempted to ship just a .GID file. This option would also eliminate the initial delay in using the Help system. But you should almost certainly reconsider. When the .GID file is generated it saves its location in a complete path including drive letter. Therefore it will probably not work properly when installed on another computer.*

The Contents page

The table of contents in an effective Help system provides quick access to multiple levels in a hierarchical listing of information. With small Help systems (Figure 17.4), multiple-level topic access is not a problem. The hotspot jumps to topics can all be easily displayed and are accessible from the contents topic without the user having to scroll. However, in larger systems Help authors have had to struggle. Numerous nested organization topics are frustrating to users, as are lengthy ones that require extensive scrolling. The illusion method which was popular in WinHelp 3.1 (a sample was provided with the first edition of this book) is difficult to maintain and only practical for two or three levels of depth.

In answer to this design dilemma, Help authors now have the ability to create an expandable/collapsible table of contents similar to that shown in Figure 17.1. This table of contents, called the Contents page, appears as a tabbed item in the Help Topics browser. For those developers with large, hierarchical Help systems the Contents page provides significant design improvements. It is relatively easy to implement, although not as flexible as many Help authors had hoped. The pros and cons of the Contents page are described in Chapter 8.

The entries displayed in the Contents page are of two types: heading items or topic items. You can display up to nine levels of headings and topics. Heading items are represented by "book" icons. Topic items are represented by "page" icons. See Figure 17.5. Clicking on a heading item "opens the book" and displays subordinate heading items or topic items. Topic items, when clicked, display the associated topic in a Help window.

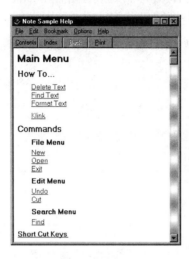

Figure 17.4. *A WinHelp 3.1 style Contents topic.*

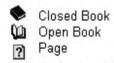

Figure 17.5. *Book and page icons.*

The Contents page greatly simplifies the process of printing a series of topics. If the user clicks a heading item and then clicks Print, all of the topics subordinate to that heading will print. The drawbacks are that each topic will print on a separate sheet of paper and that any subordinate heading items will not print.

Because the contents file consists of numerous text statements, you can construct it in a text editor. However, this process can be tedious and error-prone and it is recommended to create a contents file with Help Workshop or other authoring tool. The *Help Author's Guide* provides good step-by-step procedures for using the contents editor. Therefore, the following section provides a brief overview of creating a contents file with Help Workshop but focuses in more detail on how to create a contents file with statements in a text file.

Creating a contents file with Help Workshop

Help Workshop provides an editor that can assist you in creating the contents file. You begin a contents file by using the File/New/Help Contents command. The contents editor, shown in Figure 17.6, is a WYSIWYG display which simulates the appearance of the actual contents file.

Figure 17.6. *Creating the contents file with Help Workshop.*

You create heading and topic items by adding information through dialog boxes. The Edit Contents Tab Entry box shown in Figure 17.7 contains entry boxes for the topic title, topic ID, the name of the Help file, and the window name.

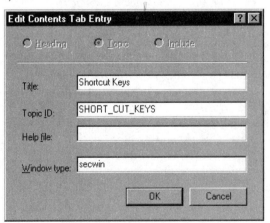

Figure 17.7. *Adding a topic item with Help Workshop.*

There are button controls which can promote or demote item levels. However, a deficiency of the Help Workshop contents editor is that you cannot move items up or down in the list. You must cut and paste items in a text editor in order to change their position. Another deficiency that critically impacts development is that the editor does not immediately check to make sure you have added valid topic IDs for the topic items. A testing function, described in "Testing the Help Browser Components" in Chapter 20, must be used. Look to the major WinHelp authoring tools for better editors.

Creating a Contents page with a text editor

If you are constructing the contents file manually, you type statements into a text editor. You will use one or more command statements to control some of the behaviors of the Contents page. These are followed by heading and topic statements.

To add command statements:

The basic commands used in forming a typical contents file are Base and Title. These commands, as well as others, are detailed in the *Help Author's Guide*. All command statements are preceded by a colon.

1. Open a new file in a text editor.

2. On the first line type :BASE, a space, followed by the name of your Help file. The command can use upper or lower case characters.

3. On the second line type :TITLE, a space, followed by the title you would like to appear in the title bar of the Help Topics browser. If you elect to leave out the title, the title of the Help file specified in your project file will be used.

4. Save the file as Text Only with a .CNT extension.

Figure 17.9 shows the contents file NOTES.CNT. The Base command specifies the associated Help file NOTE.HLP. The Title statement specifies the name of the Help system.

Generally the contents file is given the same name as the Help file, but with a different extension. However, you can name the contents file anything you choose as long as you specify the name in the project file. See the following procedure.

To specify the contents file name:

If you have given your contents file a name that is different from the Help file (except for the extension), you must specify the contents file name in your project file.

1. In Help Workshop, open your project file.

2. Click Options, then Files.

3. In the Contents file box, type the name of the contents file.

4. Save the project file.

Creating heading statements

Heading statements establish a hierarchy of topics for the Contents page. If you want to use a simple single-level hierarchy, you may elect to use no heading items, but rather just add topic statements. However, in this case, you would be better off using the WinHelp 3.1 style Contents topic. The only advantage the Contents page would give you is the ability to facilitate the printing of the entire Help system. Most Help systems will have multiple-level hierarchies; for those you must create heading statements. You can have up to eight levels of heading statements.

To create a heading statement:

1. After the command statements, start a new line and type the number "1" followed by the first heading as you would like it to appear to the user. Insert a space between the number and the heading.

2. Start another line. If you want to have a subhead, type the number "2" and then the heading title. If you want to follow the heading with a topic, follow the instructions in the next section, "Creating topic statements."

The Contents page partially represented in Figure 17.8 has three levels of depth: two levels of headings and one level of topics. The How To heading is a level one heading. The Run Programs text is a subheading of How To. Figure 17.9 shows the associated statements in the contents file.

Figure 17.8. *Sample heading and topic items in a Contents page.*

Creating topic statements

Topic statements are the actual links to topics in your Help system. In a multiple-level hierarchy, topic statements appear in the contents file under the heading statements with which they are associated.

To create a topic statement:

1. Start a new line where you would like to place the topic statement. If the topic text should appear under a certain heading, start the new line after that heading statement.

2. Type a number that is one greater than the number of the preceding heading statement. If the heading is level 1, the topic statement should start with "2."

3. After the level number, type a space then the topic title as you want it to appear to the user.

4. After the title, type an equal (=) sign followed by the topic ID of the topic to be displayed. Spaces can be used around the = sign for readability.

5. Continue to add the rest of your topic items in the same way.

In Figures 17.8 and 17.9, the topics "New," "Open," and "Exit" are level 3 topics which appear under the level 2 heading "File Menu."

Notice there is no physical link between the topic title and IDs in the contents file and the titles and topic IDs used in your topic file. If you modify the title or ID in your topic file you must make a corresponding change in the contents file. If a topic ID in the contents file is not typed as an exact match to the corresponding topic ID footnote there will be an error when the user selects that item. Testing procedures for the contents file are described in Chapter 20, *Compiling, Debugging, and Testing*.

Filling out the Contents page

Continue to add heading and topic statements as described in the above procedures. When you are done, the statements should resemble an outline of your topics. The order of the heading statements in the contents file determines their positioning in the Contents page.

In the Notepad example, there is a three-level hierarchy. (See Figure 17.9.) The first level consists of the section headings "How To..." and "Commands." Since they are NOT followed by equal signs, they are interpreted as heading items. They are simply labels denoting some relationship between the subordinate topic titles. The How To and Commands items are preceded by a "1," indicating first level status.

The How To statement is followed by the topic titles that will appear under it. They are each preceded by a "2" indicating they are second level items. The title text is followed by the appropriate topic ID. The Commands section contains an additional level. There are three submenus, each with its own topic items. The submenus are preceded by "2" and have no topic IDs. The topic items use a level of "3" and have topic IDs appended to them.

You can have heading and topic items at the same level. One of the topics in Note Help is "Shortcut Keys." This is a single topic that doesn't belong to either the How To or Commands sections. Therefore, it is added after the Commands section as a topic item preceded by a "1" indicating first level status.

```
:Base NOTE.HLP
:Title Note Contents
1 Main Menu = MAIN_MENU
1 How To...
2 Delete Text = DELETE_TEXT
2 Find Text = FIND_TEXT
2 Format Text = FORMAT_TEXT
1 Commands
2 File Menu
3 New = COM_NEW
3 Open = COM_OPEN
3 Exit = COM_EXIT
2 Edit Menu
3 Undo = COM_UNDO
3 Cut = COM_CUT
2 Search Menu
3 Find = COM_FIND
1 Shortcut Keys = SHORT_CUT_KEYS
```

Figure 17.9. *The statements in the NOTE.CNT contents file.*

Fine-tuning the topic statements

The command, heading, and topic statements form the basic structure of the contents file. But, you can also direct the display of topics in specific windows and create jumps to topics in other Help files. You can enable these features either though Help Workshop or by adding information to the basic topic statement.

In Help Workshop, the Edit Contents Tab Entry box provides entry fields for a Help file name and window type in addition to the title and topic ID.

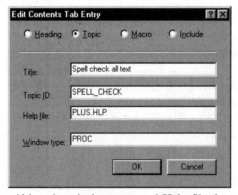

Figure 17.10. *Specifying the window type and Help file through Help Workshop.*

In a text editor you append text to the basic topic statements. The complete syntax for topic statements is shown below (Figure 17.11a) followed by the statement (Figure 17.11b) to match the Help Workshop entry from Figure 17.10.

```
topic title = topic ID[@help_file][>window_name]
```

Figure 17.11a.

```
3 Spell check all text=SPELL_CHECK@PLUS.HLP>PROC
```

Figure 17.11b.

Using a contents topic with a Contents page

If you decide to provide a Contents page in your Help system you may still want to include a contents topic as well. In the event that your contents file becomes corrupted or deleted, the user would still have access to a table of contents. Another reason to use a contents topic would be to offer a graphical menu as an alternative form of topic access.

The Note Help system illustrates this technique. In normal operation the Contents page of the browser would provide topic access. In the event that the file NOTE.CNT file is not found or is corrupted, the "Note Help Main Menu" topic would appear as shown in Figure 17.12. This topic is specified in the Contents setting of the project file. The user can also display the contents topic by clicking a custom button in the button bar named Main Menu. The following procedure describes this technique.

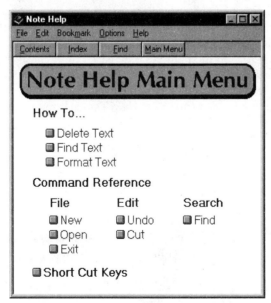

Figure 17.12. *Using a contents (Main Menu) topic.*

To use both a contents topic and contents file:

1. Create a contents topic in the usual manner in your topic file. Include any desired jumps, macros, or graphics. You might use "Main Menu" as the topic heading to differentiate it from the Contents page. Make sure any keyword or title footnotes also use the same heading.

2. Set the CONTENTS setting in the project file (.HPJ) to specify the topic ID of your Main Menu topic.

3. Create a contents (.CNT) file. This will, by default, display the Contents page of the Help Topics browser when the user clicks the Contents button.

4. Add a first level topic item to the beginning of the contents file for the "Main Menu" topic.

5. You may (optionally) want to add a **CreateButton** macro statement in the project file that establishes a jump to your contents topic.

The Index

The search keyword list is probably the most utilized method of topic access in WinHelp systems. While the writing of the keywords themselves plays the biggest role in developing an effective list, the presentation of the keywords to the user is also critical. Microsoft recognized this is in its development of WinHelp 4 and has provided several substantive changes in both the user interface and the coding.

The most obvious change is in the name of the Search function. It is now known as "Index" which more accurately reflects the purpose of the keyword list. The familiar Search button is replaced in Windows 95 with the Index button. Through either the Help Topics or Index buttons, the user can display the Index page in the Help Topics browser.

THE WINHELP 4 INDEX INTERFACE

Besides the Windows 95 look to the Index page itself, there are important functional changes. First of all, the "Select a topic" section is not displayed on the Index page. In WinHelp 3.1 the user selects a keyword from the upper portion of the Search dialog box, an action which results in a display of topics in the lower area. The user then must select a topic title. In WinHelp 4 it is much simpler. If a keyword is associated with only one topic, that topic is immediately displayed when the user double clicks the entry. If a keyword is used by more than one topic, a list of topic titles appears in a pop-up list box. In Figure 17.13 the "deleting text" keyword is associated with three topics. When that entry is clicked, the titles of the associated topics appear in the pop-up Topics Found box.

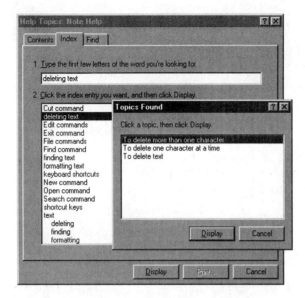

Figure 17.13. *The pop-up Topics Found box.*

DISPLAYING TWO-LEVEL INDEX ENTRIES

Another change is in the presentation of the keywords themselves. Most print indexes use two or three levels of entries to make it easier for the reader to find and process them. In WinHelp 3.1 it is not easy to show two levels of keywords. A common technique is to use a comma or colon after the main entry, followed by the subentry. The resulting effect improves the presentation of the entries but is not as nice as what you see in a print index. For example, the following style of keywords is commonly found in WinHelp 3.1 keyword lists.

```
text, deleting
text, erasing
text, finding
```

In WinHelp 4 any keyword entries using the comma or colon are automatically transformed to produce the effect shown in Figure 17.14. Notice that the long form of the keyword is shown in the text entry box. The K footnotes for these keywords are shown in Figure 17.16.

If you have been using commas and colons all along, you will automatically get the two level index. However, there is a design catch. In order to have the first subentry displayed with an indent you need to use at least one index entry with only the main entry text. Otherwise you would get the effect shown in Figure 17.15. Using the "Text" example, you would need at least one K footnote that contained the entry "text" so that "deleting" appears under the main entry rather than after it on the same line.

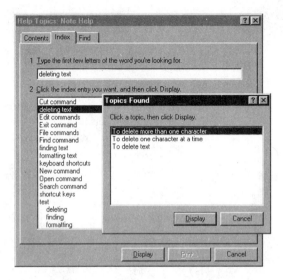

Figure 17.14. *The two-level form is used for the "text" entries.*

Figure 17.15. *A design "catch" with two-level keywords.*

In this particular example there is an overview topic titled "Working with text." This overview topic makes it easy to simply add the single word entry "text" to this topic in a K footnote. You will certainly encounter situations which are not so convenient. Without an overview topic you would probably want to add "text" to the K footnotes of all topics subentries. This method is illustrated in Figure 17.16.

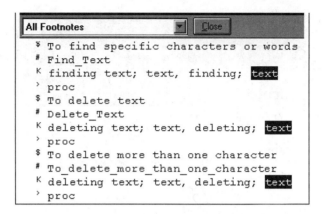

Figure 17.16. *K footnotes in a two-level index.*

You can also specify in the [OPTIONS] section of the project file a character other than the comma or colon to be used as the delimiting character.

To specify an alternate separator character:

- In your text editor, type `:INDEX_SEPARATORS="`*`character`*`"`, filling in the character you want to use.

- In Help Workshop, click Options, then Sorting. In the checkbox labeled

    `Separate index entries using these characters,`

    type the character you want to use.

Moving a WinHelp 3.1 index to Windows 95

If a user opens a WinHelp 3.1 Help file on a Windows 95 system, the Search button is still what will appear. But your Help system will automatically use the new and improved Index page format. This happens automatically with no need to recompile using the WinHelp 4 compiler. The two-level index entries will also appear. A contents file is not required to take advantage of the new Index dialog box.

Figure 17.17 shows the Help file for the Windows 3.1 Paintbrush application as displayed under Windows 95. Notice the Search button in the main window. Also notice the "colors, creating" entry. This problem needs to be resolved as described in the previous section.

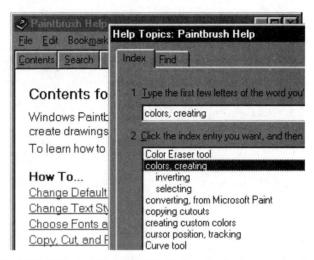

Figure 17.17. *A WinHelp 3.1 Help file displaying the Index page under Windows 95.*

Enabling an Index page in the Help browser

If you have elected to distribute a contents file and have added one or more keywords to your topic file, the Index tab will automatically appear on the Help Topics browser. No additional settings are required. The Index tab will appear regardless of whether you choose to distribute a contents file.

The Index button/macro

You may want to add an Index button to one or more of your Help windows to provide quick access to the Index page. See Chapter 15, *Creating the Help Interface*, for the procedure to add the Index button to a window. There is also a complimentary Index macro described in Chapter 16, *Working with Help Macros*.

The Find (full-text search)

Many developers have longed for full-text search since Windows Help first appeared. It is now available through the Find page of the Help Topics browser. The full-text search (FTS) interface on the Find page makes it easy for intermediate and advanced users to locate topics based on words or phrases contained in the text. While FTS is no substitute for a good index, it does provide a valuable service. First of all, assuming you know a string of text in the topic you are looking for, you can quickly search all topics in the Help file (or family of Help files) for a match. Second, it provides access to topics when the indexing has been done poorly.

Historically the biggest drawback of FTS has been the difficulty the novice user encounters in learning how to perform an effective search. Most FTS engines require the user to type Boolean operators like "AND" and "OR." Another drawback of some FTS engines is that an understanding of the Help file structure is needed in order to narrow the search effectively. A search that results in a list of 30 or 40 topics is of little use.

Fortunately, significant effort has gone into making the new FTS interface easy to work with and it shows. While not necessarily for beginners, the Microsoft FTS is powerful and intuitive. Although some third-party vendors have created FTS engines, the solution provided by Microsoft will certainly become the standard.

The FTS is simple for Help developers to implement as well. No programming is required unless you want to customize the search DLLs. Your work is limited to generating and distributing a full-text search index file. And even that is optional.

How Find works

The Find feature appears as a tab on the Help Topics browser next to the Contents and Index tabs. Similar to the design of the Index page, Find provides an explicit, numbered, three-step process. First you type a word, phrase, or text string. The search engine, by default, automatically performs an evaluation of the entry as you type it. A list of possible word matches appears in the second list box. For example, in WINDOWS.HLP typing the word "note" displays possible matches of "note," "Note," "Notepad," "notes," and "Notes." The number of found topics is displayed in the third list box—in our example, 109. The user can narrow the list by choosing one or more of the items in the matching word list or by typing additional words. For example, selecting the matching word "Notepad" in the example narrows the search to just two topics. (See Figure 17.18.) Double-clicking one of the titles displays the desired topic.

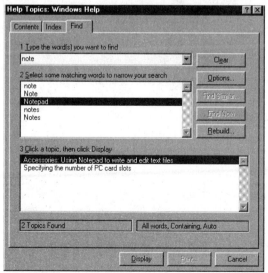

Figure 17.18. *Using the Find page to narrow a search.*

User options

While this process is certainly easy enough for intermediate or advanced users, those unaccustomed to FTS might have difficulty understanding the ramifications of upper and lower case characters, plurals, etc., in the matching list. They also need to know to use CTRL+click to select more than one item.

However for those who are comfortable with FTS it can become even more powerful. The Find Options box, shown in Figure 17.19, allows you to elect to search for all words typed or search for the words in the exact order typed. You can also customize the type of strings that appear in the matching words list. For example, after typing the string "ext" you could choose to either display words starting with that text, like "extension" or ending with it, like "next."

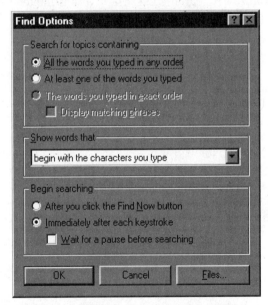

Figure 17.19. *User options for FTS.*

Enabling the Find page

As a Help writer your responsibilities for implementing Find are minimal. By default, the Find tab will automatically appear in the Help Topics browser. However, you need to address the following issues:

- Whether to distribute search index files.

- What level of index files to distribute.

- Whether to include a Find button.

Distributing search index files

The FTS engine is able to perform its quick, sophisticated searches by referencing a search index file. This index file is not to be confused with the regular keyword Index. The search index file has a .FTS extension and must be present on your user's computer along with the Help and contents files. You can choose to have the user generate this index file or you can distribute it along with your Help system. An additional index file with an .FTG extension is generated when you specify multiple Help files in your contents file.

The key element in your decision is related to distribution size of your Help system. The size of the .FTS file can be significant. For example, the Microsoft Paint Help file MSPAINT.HLP is 43K in size. The associated FTS index file is 120K !

If you elect to have the user generate the index file, a wizard is available to make the process simple. The Find Setup Wizard, shown in Figure 17.20, appears the first time the user selects the Find tab from the Help Topics browser. The resulting index file uses the name of the Help file with the .FTS extension. For example, NOTE.HLP would have an index file named NOTE.FTS.

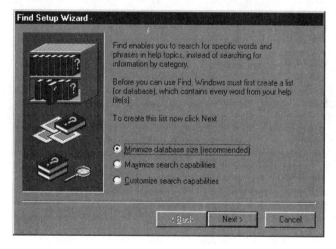

Figure 17.20. *The Find Setup Wizard.*

If you don't want your user to go through the build process, you have to create and distribute the .FTS index file along with your Help file. The FTS index file needs to be regenerated whenever you recompile your Help system.

> **NOTE** *If you are shipping a help file on a CD and expect the user to launch if from there, you must ship the .FTS/.FTG files as well.*

To create an FTS index file:

This procedure assumes you have already constructed a contents file as described in the previous section.

1. Launch your Help file.

2. From the Help Topics browser, click the Find tab. The Find Setup Wizard appears.

3. Use the wizard to select the desired options.

4. Click Finish to generate the .FTS index file.

The .FTS file appears in the folder containing the Help file.

The Find button macro

You may want to add a Find button to one or more of your Help windows to provide quick access to the Find page. See Chapter 15, *Creating the Help Interface* for the procedure to add the Find button to a window. There is also a complementary Find macro described in Chapter 16, *Working with Help Macros.*

Disabling the Find page

For some Help designs it may be inappropriate for the user to have access to the Find feature. Unfortunately there is no working command to remove the Find page. The *Help Author's Guide* references the :NOFIND command which was to inhibit the Find tab from displaying in the Help Topics browser. However, that command is not available in version 4.1 of the Help compiler.

Untitled topics

There are certain topics which you may not want to appear in a full-text search. For example, pop-up definitions, What's This? definitions, flowcharts, pictures, tables, and others. These types of topics may appear out of context when displayed from the Find page. You can elect to keep these types of topics from displaying.

To inhibit the display of topics in Find:

- In the topic file, remove the title ($) footnote from any topic you do not want to appear in the full-text search.

The next time the .FTS file is generated the topics without titles will be excluded.

While you can remove the title footnote from any topic, you have to be careful. The text from the title footnote is used in the Topics Found box of both the Index page and Linking macros when more than one match is found. It is also used in the History list. Without a title the user sees "(untitled #x)" in the list box, where x is the topic number.

If you remove a title footnote from a topic, you should probably also remove the keywords. For example, NOTE.HLP contains a main menu (MAIN_MENU) topic that is unsuitable for full-text search or the Index. Neither the title nor keyword footnotes are used.

To display untitled topics:

The default behavior of the Find page, described above, is to not display topics without titles. If you have untitled topics that you do want to include in the search, you need to make an adjustment in the project file before compiling.

1. In Help Workshop click Options then FTS.

2. Click the box labeled **Include untitled topics in index**.

3. Click Save and Compile.

The next time the .FTS file is generated, the topics without titles will be included.

Be aware that this procedure and the previous one are all or nothing operations. You either include titled topics or you don't. You cannot have some topics without titles appear in the Find and other untitled topics not appear.

Including untitled topics greatly increases the size of the index files. As shown in Figure 17.20, the inclusion of untitled topics can double the size of the .FTG file and triple the size of the .FTS file.

Setting full-text search levels

There are four levels of full-text search indexes that can be generated either by you or the user. The levels, described in Table 17.1, represent increasing sophistication in the search process. These descriptions are displayed when you customize the index files with the Find Setup Wizard. On the first page of the Find Setup Wizard you can select Minimize, Maximize, or Customize. Select Customize to choose phrase or matching phrase searching.

Table 17.1. *Levels of full-text search sophistication*

Search option	Description
Minimum search	Find searches for words only.
Phrase search	Find searches for complete phrases such as a person's first and last name.
Matching phrases	Find displays matching phrases as you type to make it easier to find the phrase you're looking for.
Similarity searches (Maximum)	You can mark topics for later reference. Find can then search for topics that contain information related to the marked topics. This is most useful for very large or modular Help systems.

The user can always rebuild the index file using the Rebuild option of the Find Setup Wizard.

FTS overhead

The overhead of your Help system increases in size significantly, depending on what form of FTS index files you choose to include. Table 17.2 shows the resulting file sizes for the various index options for the Help system WINDOWS.HLP. The .CNT, .HLP, and .FTG file sizes stay constant, but the .FTS ranges from 127K to 404K. Figure 17.21 provides a graphical view of the file size comparison.

Table 17.2. *Comparative index file sizes (WINDOWS.HLP)*

File Type		Min.	Customized p	p+m	Max. p+m+s
FTG		240	240	240	240
FTS		127	172	276	404
CNT		14	14	14	14
HLP		508	508	508	508
	Total	889	934	1038	1166
with untitled topics					
FTG		405	405	405	405
FTS		415	558	908	1171
	Total	1342	1485	1835	2098

p-phrases, m-matching phrases, s-similarity

It may be useful to note that the difference in file size between shipping the WINDOWS.HLP Help file with no index files and one with maximum full-text search would be a difference of 644K. Include untitled topics and the difference goes up to 1.56 MB. If cost of goods is an issue you will want to carefully examine which components you elect to distribute.

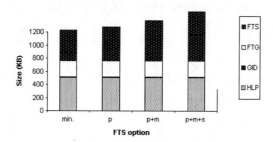

Figure 17.21. *Comparative index file sizes (WINDOWS.HLP).*

Extending FTS

The FTS engine used with WinHelp can also be extended for your own purposes. This is enabled through the full-text search API. You can program the API calls into your application to build a full-text search index for any set of words in a file, including a text file or a Word document (or some other proprietary format). The FTS API is fully documented in the *Help Author's Guide*. From the Contents page, select WinHelp Reference/Full-Text Search API.

Modular Help systems

In WinHelp 4, the coordination of multiple Help files into one system has been improved tremendously—and the contents file provides the gateway. First of all, you can combine the table of contents entries from several contents files into one master Contents page. Second, you can combine the index entries from several Help files into one alphabetized list on the Index page. Finally, full-text searches can address all of the text in several Help files. This section describes how to enable each of these features.

Combining table of contents entries

If you have multiple Help files, you can take a large step toward integrating them by combining the entries from the various contents files into one master Contents page. For your users, this option provides seamless access to the various component Help files. When the Contents page is designed properly users do not even realize they are working with topics in different Help systems.

In designing a modular Help system, you choose one contents file to be the master contents file. When the Help file is launched, WinHelp looks in the master contents file for the names of other contents files. The entries from these files are then merged into the Contents page displayed in the Help Topics browser.

For example, in Windows 95, the operating system Help file is WINDOWS.HLP. The associated contents file, WINDOWS.CNT is the master contents file. It contains references to eleven other Help files. Links to topics in those eleven Help files are displayed in the Contents page when WINDOWS.HLP is launched.

You can combine contents entries in two ways: through topic statements or through include statements.

- Use topic statements when you want to insert links in the master contents file to individual topics in other Help files.

- Use include statements when you want to insert all of the items from a contents file into one location in the master contents file.

Include statements are easier to use than topic statements, however, they may not be as flexible as needed with some contents page designs.

Using topic statements

If you want to insert a link in a contents file to a topic in another Help file, you can use a topic statement that specifies the target file. If the specified file is found on the user's computer by WinHelp, the link appears in the master Contents page. If the Help file is not present, the link is not displayed in the Contents page.

For example, in the Note Help system there are two Help files. Each Help file contains How To and Command topics. If a user has both Help files, the desired effect is to have all the entries appear in the Note Contents page. However, the links to PLUS.HLP have to be interspersed among the NOTE.HLP entries. The left portion of Figure 17.22 shows the original Note Contents page. By adding statements linking to topics in PLUS.HLP you end up with the extended Note Contents page shown in the right portion of the figure. If PLUS.HLP is not available on a user's computer, the Note Contents page reverts to its original form.

```
1 Main Menu=MAIN_MENU>main
1 How To...
2 Delete text=DELETE_TEXT>proc
2 Find text=FIND_TEXT>proc
2 Format text=FORMAT_TEXT>proc
2 Print all text=Print_Text@PLUS.HLP>proc
2 Spell check all text=Spell_Check@PLUS.HLP>proc
2 Spell check portions of text=Spell_Portions@PLUS.HLP>proc
1 Commands
```

Figure 17.22. *The Note contents page with and without the presence of PLUS.HLP.*

The contents file statements for NOTE.CNT are shown in Figure 17.23. The name of the Help file containing the target topic is appended to the appropriate topic ID. In the Help Workshop contents editor, you can add the Help file name in the Edit Contents Tab Entry box. The complete procedure and syntax is described above in "Fine-tuning the Topic Statements."

```
1 Main Menu=MAIN_MENU>main
1 How To...
2 Delete text=DELETE_TEXT>proc
2 Find text=FIND_TEXT>proc
2 Format text=FORMAT_TEXT>proc
2 Print all text=Print_Text@PLUS.HLP>proc
2 Spell check all text=Spell_Check@PLUS.HLP>proc
2 Spell check portions of text=Spell_Portions@PLUS.HLP>proc
1 Commands
```

Figure 17.23. *Statements added to NOTE.CNT linking to topics in PLUS.HLP.*

Using include files

While specifying the name of a Help file in topic statements is very flexible, it is also very time-consuming. Depending on the design of your Help system, you may be able to use an include statement in your contents file instead. A single include statement allows you to automatically combine all of the entries from one contents file into a master contents file.

A good illustration of this type of design is the WINDOWS.HLP Help system. The master contents file, WINHELP.CNT, contains topic and heading statements related to general information about the Windows 95 environment. There are also several smaller Help files that provide more specific Help information, like ACCESS.HLP. These smaller files are referenced in the master contents file with an include statement. The include statement is prefaced by a semicolon and followed by the name of the contents file to include. The position at which you place the include statement determines where the included statements will appear. In Figure 17.24, the include statement for W_OVER.CNT appears between the level 2 heading "Welcome" and the level 2 heading "Using Windows Accessories." The resulting contents page is shown in Figure 17.25.

```
:Base windows.hlp>proc4
:Title Windows Help
. . . . . . . . . . . . . . . . . . . . . . . . . . . . .
:include w_tour.cnt
1 Introducing Windows
2 Welcome
. . . . . . . . . . . . . . . . . . . . . . . . . . . . .
:include w_over.cnt
2 Using Windows Accessories
3 For General Use
. . . . . . . . . . . . . . . . . . . . . . . . . . . . .
:include a_sched.cnt
:include a_plus.cnt
1 How To...
2 Run Programs
. . . . . . . . . . . . . . . . . . . . . . . . . . . . .
:include a_prog.cnt
3 Starting an MS-DOS window =WINDOWS_DOS_START_DOS
3 Optimizing MS-DOS programs=WINDOWS_DOS_CONFIGURE
. . . . . . . . . . . . . . . . . . . . . . . . . . . . .
. . . . . . . . . . . . . . . . . . . . . . .
. . . . . . . . . . . . . .
. . . . . . . . .
```

Figure 17.24. *Portions of the WINDOWS.CNT contents file.*

Figure 17.25. *Portions of the WINDOWS.HLP Contents page.*

If a Help file and associated contents file is not installed on the user's computer, its entries simply will not appear in the master Contents page. There will be no error message. Figure 17.26 shows what the WINDOWS.HLP Contents page would look like without the presence of ACCESS.HLP.

Figure 17.26. *The Contents page of WINDOWS.HLP without ACCESS.HLP.*

To include a contents file using Help Workshop:

1. In Help Workshop open the contents file.

2. Click on an existing item below which you want to insert the items from another contents file.

3. Click Add Below, then Include.

4. Type the title of the contents file to include.

5. Click OK and save the contents file.

To include a contents file using a text editor:

1. In a text editor, open the contents file.

2. Start a new line at the point where you want to insert the items from another contents file.

3. Type :INCLUDE *filename*, where filename is the name of the other contents file.

4. Save the contents file.

Using titles with combined Help files

The title displayed in the title bar of the Help Topics browser is, by default, the same name as the Help file. However, you can elicit different behaviors for the title; review the section, "Sorting out Help's titling," in Chapter 15.

Combining multiple indexes

With WinHelp 4, it is possible to combine the keyword lists of two or more independent Help files. This offers powerful improvements for modular Help systems. When a user clicks the Index tab of the Help Topics browser, the standard Index box appears with index entries from multiple Help files seamlessly displayed in one alphabetized list. As with combining contents entries, if one or more Help files are missing, no errors display to the user. If those missing Help files are installed later, the index is automatically updated with the new keywords.

> **NOTE** *A pre-release feature for the Index of WinHelp 4 has been removed. It is not possible for the user to elect to display the keyword list of just one of the combined Help files.*

Enabling the combined index

To enable the combined index you need to create and distribute a contents file. If you already have a contents file, enabling the combined index feature is simply a matter of adding command statements to it. You choose the Help files that you would like to be represented in the Index and add their names to the contents file using the INDEX command. No adjustments are required in the topic or project files.

To combine indexes using Help Workshop:

1. Open the master contents file.

2. Click the Index Files button, then Add.

3. In the Help filename box, type the name of the Help file you want to combine with the master.

4. Continue to add additional Help file names as necessary.

5. Save the master contents file.

To combine indexes using a text editor:

1. Open the master contents file.

2. Start a new line before the first heading statement.

3. Type :INDEX followed by a space, then the name of the Help file whose index you want to combine with the master.

4. Continue to add additional Index statements as necessary.

5. Save the master contents file.

Using the Note Help example, assume there is an optional add-on product called Note Plus. The add-on contains two new features which are documented in a separate Help file named PLUS.HLP. There is an associated contents file NOTE.CNT. Since the two products are sold separately, two Help files are being used. However, we want to combine them through the contents file.

The master Help system file will be NOTE.HLP since that is distributed with the program that all users will have. The Index statement is added to NOTE.CNT, as shown in Figure 17.27, specifying the name of the associated Help file (PLUS.HLP).

```
        :Base Note.hlp
        :Title Note Help
    ➡  :Index Note Help=PLUS.HLP
        1 Main Menu=MAIN_MENU>main
        1 How To...
        ...
        ..
        .
```

Figure 17.27. *The Index statement in NOTE.CNT.*

The resulting Index page now appears as shown in Figure 17.28. The Plus keywords (spell checking text, printing text) are combined into the Note index list.

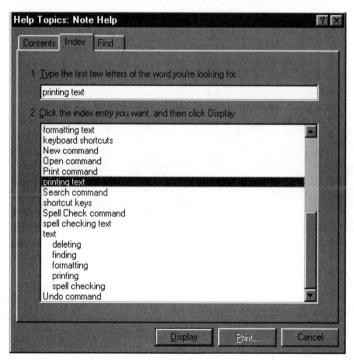

Figure 17.28. *The Index tab for NOTE.HLP.*

Making it a two-way street

You should note that the combined index described above will appear only when you open the Help file NOTE.HLP. If you open PLUS.HLP, the Index page will not include the entries from NOTE.HLP. However, you can fix this problem by providing complementary index statements in each of the Help files in your modular system. Adding NOTE.HLP to PLUS.CNT through an Index statement will produce the desired effect.

This technique is most useful when you can't be sure which Help files will be installed.

Excluding the Contents page

If you want to use the Index page, but not the Contents page, you need to ship a contents file that doesn't include any heading or topic items. The contents file will contain just the Base, Title, and Index statements.

Combining Help file text for searching

In rounding out topic access in your modular Help system, you can also provide full-text searching across all your Help files. The Find files that are searched are the ones specified by the Index statements described in the previous section. Either you or the user can then select the Help files from the Find Setup Wizard. If you have already added the Index statements there is nothing left to do. In the example in Figure 17.29, five of the eleven Help files associated with WINDOWS.HLP have been selected in the Find Setup Wizard. Only the text from those five files will be available through the Find page.

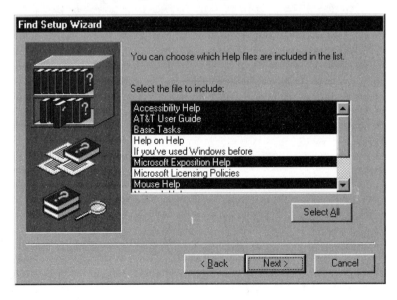

Figure 17.29. *Only Help files selected in the Find Setup Wizard are included in the Find page.*

The browser and WinHelp 3.1

As described in Chapter 20, a Help file compiled with WinHelp 3.1 will operate just fine in Windows 95. You can also use a contents file with a WinHelp 3.1 file running under Windows 95. This is useful for those developers wishing to take advantage of the many benefits of the Help Topics browser but who are not ready to move to the WinHelp 4 compiler. With this solution you can install both the contents file and Help file on Windows 95 systems and install only the Help file on Windows 3.1 systems.

You create your contents file in the same manner described earlier in this chapter. WinHelp will automatically change the appearance and operation of the button bar as shown in Figure 17.30.

When the Help file is launched under Windows 3.1 the Contents button displays the topic specified in the Contents setting. The keywords are displayed in the Search box. Under Windows 95 the Contents button displays the Contents page of the Help Topics browser. The Search button is still present but clicking it displays the Index tab of the browser. The Find tab appears on the browser as well.

> **NOTE** *The contents file will work under Windows 3.1 with the installation of Win32s on the user's computer. Win32s is described in Appendix A.*

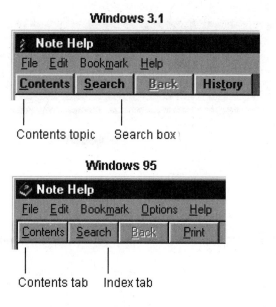

Figure 17.30. *WinHelp automatically changes the appearance and operation of the button bar.*

Using custom pages in the Help Topics browser

In addition to the three standard browser pages described in this chapter, you can add your own tabs for the display of custom pages. This lets you provide topic access of your own design, but requires the creation of a custom DLL. You could, for example, write a DLL to provide glossary functionality similar to the contents tab, or you could write your own FTS interface. In Microsoft Office 95, the Answer Wizard is accessed through a custom tab shown in Figure 17.31.

To add a custom tab:

1. Create a custom tab DLL as described in the Windows 95 Software Development Kit.

2. In Help Workshop, open the contents file.

3. Click Tabs, then Add.

4. Type the name you want to appear on the tab.

5. Type the .DLL filename.

6. Save the contents file.

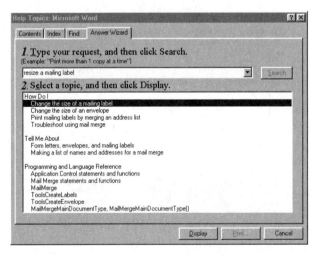

Figure 17.31. *The Microsoft Office Answer Wizard displayed in a custom page.*

Testing the Help Topics browser pages

The Contents, Index, and Find pages bring their own unique testing issues to Help development. These are described in Chapter 20, *Compiling, Debugging, and Testing.*

If you are using a text editor, add the TAB command statement followed by the tab name and .DLL name. See the WINWORD.CNT example in Figure 17.32.

```
:Base WINWORD.HLP>REF
:Title Microsoft Word
:Tab Answer Wizard=MSO95 DLL
:Index Microsoft Word Help=WINWORD.HLP
:Index Microsoft Word Quick Tips-QWINWORD
:Index WordBasic Help=WRDBASIC.HLP
```

Figure 17.32. *Specifying a custom tab in the contents file.*

You can have up to nine tabs in the Help Topics browser. You could have the three default tabs and six custom tabs, or remove the default tabs and use nine custom tabs, or any combination in between.

18

Creating the Project File

Every Windows Help system requires two types of files and they couldn't be more different. The topic file described in Chapter 10 is a robust file which contains descriptive text, graphics, footnote and character attribute codes and often takes countless hours to create. In contrast, the project file is very small, often no more than 10K in size. Yet it is just as important to the success of the Help system as the topic file. The project file provides instructions to the compiler on what topic files to use, where they are located, and how you want the finished Help system to look. It specifies window sizing, position, buttons, and colors. File compression, character sets, and build tags are also managed there. The project file is the Help author's control panel.

This chapter explains:

- How to choose a project file editor.

- How to create and edit a basic project file.

- How to upgrade a 3.1 Help file to 4.0.

- How to use file management options.

- Where to find information on advanced project tasks.

Choosing a project file editor

Every Help file must have its own project file. The project file is an ASCII text file that contains one or more sections of settings. Each setting controls a different aspect of the compiled Help system.

This file can be created in any of three ways: with Help Workshop, with third party authoring tools, or with a text editor. Help Workshop will be used to demonstrate the tasks in this chapter. After you've created the project file, you process it using the Help compiler as described in Chapter 20, *Compiling, Debugging, and Testing.*

Help Workshop

Help Workshop (HCW.EXE) is a utility created by Microsoft and supplied with the WinHelp 4 Help compiler. This utility, shown in Figure 18.1, provides a graphical interface for creating and maintaining a project file. It supports all of the WinHelp 4 project file settings. Help Workshop is described in detail in Chapter 22, *Authoring Tools.*

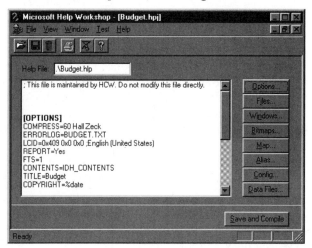

Figure 18.1. *The project file window of Help Workshop.*

Authoring tools

Most of the third party Help authoring tools described in Chapter 22 provide their own methods for creating and maintaining the project file. Many authoring tools provide capabilities that exceed that of Help Workshop and others fall short of what Help Workshop can do.. It is best to make sure the authoring tool you choose provides support for WinHelp 4 project file features. If you aren't satisfied with the project file capabilities of your authoring tool, you can always perform additional functions with Help Workshop.

Text editors

Since the project file format is ASCII text, it can be assembled by typing command statements in any text editor. (See the example in Figure 18.2.) With WinHelp 3.1 this is a pretty simple process. Even the most complicated project files rarely require more than fifty lines of text. The first edition of *Developing Online Help for Windows* describes the creation of a 3.1 project file in a text editor. However with WinHelp 4 the syntax for the Language and Windows statements is extremely difficult to construct. The *Help Author's Guide* describes the syntax for the individual project file settings. (In the Contents page see "WinHelp Reference/Project File Commands/Project file")

Figure 18.2. *Creating a project file in NotePad.*

Creating a basic project file

A project file must be created before you begin to compile a Help file. A basic project file may have just a few settings; for a large Help system, the project file may have several dozen settings. The project file shown in Figure 18.3 is somewhere in between. The complexity of *your* project file depends on the design of your Help system.

Regardless of the size of your Help system, it's often convenient to start with just a basic project file to perform some preliminary builds with the compiler, and then to expand the file as your Help project progresses.

This section describes the contents of a basic project file. The two broad steps are to:

- Start a new project file.

- Specify the location of your topic file(s).

```
[OPTIONS]
REPLACE=New Folder
ERRORLOG=Errors.doc
LCID=0x409 0x0 0x0 ;English (United States)
REPORT=Yes
CONTENTS=Contents
TITLE=Budget Worksheet Help
COPYRIGHT=Copyright © 1995 WinWriters. All rights reserved.
CITATION=Copyright © 1995 WinWriters. All rights reserved.
BMROOT=Bitmaps
ROOT=Topic Files

[FILES]
.\Budget.rtf
#include .\Files.txt
```

Figure 18.3. *Project file statements as displayed in Help Workshop.*

NOTE *A sample project file named BASIC.HPJ is located on the disc in the back of this book.*

To start a new project file:

1. From the Help Workshop File menu, click New.

2. Select "Help project," then click OK. The Project File Name dialog box appears.

   NOTE: If you use an extension other than .HPJ, Help Workshop will regard the extension as part of the file name. It recognizes only .HPJ as a valid extension.

3. Select or create a folder to in which to store your project file.

4. Type the name of your project file, then click Save. An extension of .HPJ is assumed.

   The project editor window appears and displays several statements. These statements are described in detail below in the section "Converting 3.1 Help Files to 4.0."

   Now you need to specify your topic file(s). The minimum requirement for any project file is to specify the topic files.

To specify the location of topic files:

1. From Help Workshop, click the Files button, then Add. The Topic Files box appears.

2. Select your topic file. Click Open, then OK.

   A [FILES] section appears in the project editor followed by the name of your topic file. Every project file must contain a [FILES] section.

   If you are using more than one topic file, continue to select and add each file, one at a time.

3. From the File Menu, click Save. This action saves your file for future work.

   If you're ready to compile your Help file, see the compiling procedure described in Chapter 20.

   Figure 18.4 shows the project editor as it appears after you have started your new project file and specified the topic file(s).

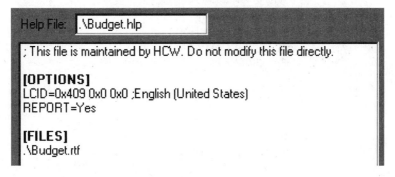

Figure 18.4. *The basic project file settings as displayed in the project editor.*

AN ALTERNATE METHOD FOR SPECIFYING TOPIC FILES

Help Workshop provides an alternate method of specifying the location of project files.

1. In Help Workshop, click Options; then Files.

2. Click the Change button next to the **Rich Text Format (RTF) files** box. The Topic Files box appears.

3. Select your topic files.

To specify file locations with an include file:

Some projects consist of many topic files which are created by several different authors. Rather than having each author make additions to the [FILES] section of the project file, you can use an include file and include statement to point to those topic files.

1. Type the topic file names in a new document and save the file as Text Only. The include file must be an ASCII text file. Also, you may need to add a path to the topic file names in the include file.

2. In Help Workshop, click Files, then Include.

3. Select or type the name of the include file you have just created.

In Figure 18.5, the include file TOPFILE.TXT contains references to several topic files. The include file name is specified in the [FILES] section of the project file as shown in Figure 18.6.

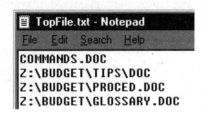

Figure 18.5. *The include file statement in TOPFILE.TXT.*

```
[FILES]
#include .\TopFile.txt
```

Figure 18.6. *The [FILES] section of the project file.*

Expanding the basic project file

The previous section demonstrated the minimum requirements for the project file in order to begin compiling. However, there are two other basic settings which you will likely want to add to your project file: a title and copyright information.

Specifying the Help file's title

By default, the Help compiler uses the text "Microsoft Help" as the title for your Help file. This title appears in the Help file's title bar, and in the taskbar. Since this feature aids users in identifying your Help file, you should replace the default text with your own descriptive title. Figure 18.7 shows how the title "Cardfile Help" is displayed for that Help system.

Help window title   **Taskbar title**   **Help browser title**

Figure 18.7. *The display of the Help file title.*

> **NOTE** *If you are using a contents file in your Help system you can specify the title in either the contents file, the project file or both. The same title then appears in the title bar of the Help window or of the Help browser. However, if the contents file title and project file title are different, the contents file title takes precedence and will also be used in the window definition or contents file. A complete description of title options is provided in the section "Sorting out Help's titling" in Chapter 15.*

To specify the Help file's title:

1. In Help Workshop, click Options, then General.

2. In the **Help title** box, type the desired title of your Help file.

Specifying copyright notices and citations

You can display the copyright to your Help file by adding a copyright notice of up to 255 characters into Help's Version Information box. The Version Information box is shown in Figure 18.8 and automatically appears with every compiled Help file.

You can also enable a citation of up to 2000 characters to appear with any topics that are copied or printed by the user. The citation will NOT appear in text copied from a pop-up window.

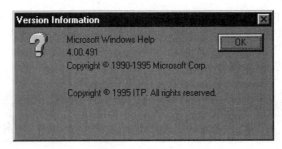

Figure 18.8. *A copyright notation in Help's Version box.*

To specify a copyright and/or citation:

1. In Help Workshop, click Options, then General.

2. In the **Copyright information** section, type the desired text as shown in Figure 18.9.

   To create the copyright symbol (©), hold down Alt, type 0169 on your numeric keypad (with the NumLock on), and then release the Alt key. Or copy it from the Character Map accessory of Windows.

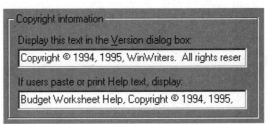

Figure 18.9. *Adding copyright/citation to the Help file.*

TIP *If you are using any sizable amount of text for your copyright or citation, you may want to type and proof them directly in the project file with a text editor. Use the COPYRIGHT and CITATION commands as shown in Figure 18.10.*

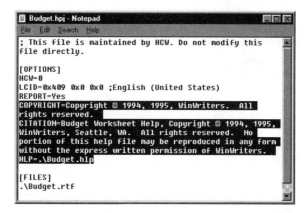

Figure 18.10. *Adding the copyright/citation in a text editor.*

Converting 3.1 project files to 4.0

If you have an existing project file from a WinHelp 3.1 system, you need to make certain modifications to it. First of all, there are several new commands that are required by the new compiler: HCW, HLP, and LCID. Second, certain project file commands have been revised or deleted from WinHelp 4.0. You may need to make adjustments to your project file to accommodate these changes.

To upgrade your project file:

1. In Help Workshop, from the File menu, choose Open.

2. Select the 3.1 project file (.HPJ) that you want to convert.

   The project editor appears as the compiler adds the commands shown in Figure 18.11. Other pre-existing 3.1 settings appear as well.

3. From the File menu click Save to complete the conversion.

> **NOTE** *The HCW and HLP command lines are hidden from view. However, they will appear if you open the project file in a text editor as shown in Figure 18.12.*

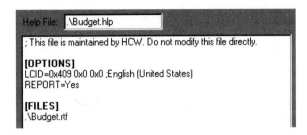

Figure 18.11. *Default project file as displayed in Help Workshop.*

```
; This file is maintained by HCW. Do not modify this
file directly.

[OPTIONS]
HCW=1
REPORT=Yes
HLP=BUDGET.HLP
LCID=0x409 0x0 0x0 ;English (United States)
```

Figure 18.12. *Default project file commands displayed in a text editor.*

WInHelp 4 project file adjustments

The HCW setting provides information to the compiler and should not be edited. The HLP setting specifies the name of the Help file that will be created when the project file is compiled. By default, it uses the project file name and the .HLP extension. The LCID setting is used for sorting keywords and should be edited only if you are authoring a Help file in a non-English language.

You will notice some other adjustments:

- The REPORT setting is automatically enabled whether you included it in your 3.1 project file or not. This setting directs the compiler to display messages during compiling.

- The WARNING setting from 3.1 is not supported in version 4 project files and is automatically deleted.

- If you have specified more than one directory in a single BMROOT statement, Help Workshop creates a separate BMROOT statement for each.

- If you have turned on the COMPRESS setting, the statement is modified to COMPRESS=60 Hall Zeck. This is one of several new compression options. You can modify this as needed.

- Window definitions in the [WINDOWS] sections are automatically converted by Help Workshop to a new format.

- The 3.1 Build Tag format is supported without changes, but any changes made in Help Workshop will use the new format, which has [INCLUDE] and [EXCLUDE] sections.

- MAPFONTSIZE and FORCEFONT parameters are supported, but Help Workshop places the font information in a new [FONTS] section.

- Help Workshop does not add the ERRORLOG setting. The default is for messages to be displayed in a separate window of Help Workshop. If you would like to save these messages, use the ERRORLOG setting to trap any error messages from the compiler and store them in a text file. See Chapter 20, *Compiling, Debugging, and Testing.*

- The OPTCDROM setting is not supported by Help Workshop. The compiler will ignore it. The .GID file, which WinHelp generates for each Help file, now provides the same performance improvements.

- The ICON setting is not supported by Help Workshop. The compiler will ignore it. ICON used an unsupported API in Windows 3.1 that is no longer in existence in Windows 95.

Project File Problems? In some rare instances you may find that Help Workshop will not properly accept your existing project file. Certain options may be omitted or you might encounter an error message during compiling. The solution is to start a *new* project file with Help Workshop. Then you can cut and paste commands from your old project file into the new one or add them using Help Workshop. Most project files can be reproduced in well under an hour.

File management and the project file

As with almost any kind of project, there are certain housekeeping tasks which assist in managing your WinHelp development. This section describes three settings which organize your production files and prevent errors.

Specifying multiple topic file locations

The Help compiler needs to be able to find your topic file in order to compile it. By default, the compiler looks for your topic file in the project file folder and this is where most developers keep it. However, as your Help project increases in size and number of authors, it may prove difficult to maintain all your topic files in the project file folder. If you choose to maintain topic files in other folders, you need to add the name and location of these folders to the project file.

To specify a topic file folder:

1. In Help Workshop, click the Files button. The Topic Files box displays any topic files or folders you have already added to the project.

2. Click Folders, then Add.

3. Select a folder that contains your topic files, then click OK to return to the project editor window. The folder name appears in the [OPTIONS] section. Help Workshop automatically stores the path relative to the project file folder.

   Repeat this procedure for any additional topic file locations. Each folder name will appear as a separate line in the project file as shown in the following example.

   ```
   ROOT=..\DEFINIT
   ROOT=..\COMMANDS
   ```

   Use the Remove button to eliminate any unneeded folders.

> **NOTE** *This setting replaces the WinHelp 3.1 ROOT statement.*

Specifying paths to files

When specifying folder locations for graphics, topic files, and other elements of your Help system, it is best to specify relative paths. This ensures that the compiler can still find the various files if you move your production files to another drive or network location. Relative paths use standard conventions for describing the position of one folder relative to another. Help Workshop, as well as most authoring tools, automatically use relative paths. Figure 18.13 shows the paths displayed in Help Workshop for a variety of file locations.

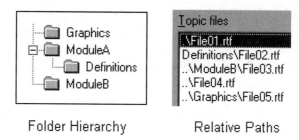

Folder Hierarchy   Relative Paths

Figure 18.13. *Specifying relative paths to files.*

Specifying the location of graphics files

As the number of graphics files in a project increases so does the difficulty in managing those files. Maintaining all of your graphic files in the project file folder can be unwieldy and impractical. Unwieldy, because your project file folder can quickly become crowded with file names. Impractical, because you would have to duplicate graphics that are used in more than one project, like icons and symbols. By default, the compiler searches for any referenced graphic file in the project file folder and any folders defined in the [FILES] section.

The BMROOT setting lets you specify the names and locations of other folders containing graphics associated with your project. This setting makes it possible to create a folder that serves as a graphics "library" that can be used by any number of projects.

To specify a graphics file folder:

1. In Help Workshop, click the Bitmaps button. The Bitmap Folders box displays any folders you have already added to the project.

2. Click Add.

3. Select a folder that contains graphics files, then OK. The folder name appears as a BMROOT setting in the OPTIONS section as shown below.

   ```
   BMROOT=..\Bitmaps
   ```

   Repeat this procedure for any additional graphics file locations. Each folder name will appear as a separate line in the project file. Use the Remove button to eliminate any unneeded folders.

NOTE *Help Workshop does not support the use of the [BITMAPS] section from WinHelp 3.1. However, if you have this section in an existing project file, the compiler will still process it.*

Specifying a substitute path

If you have not been specifying relative paths and you move your project folder to a different drive or network location you may want to specify a substitute path. This saves you the effort of manually changing all the file paths in your project file.

To specify a substitute path:

1. In Help Workshop, click Options, then Files.

2. Click the Edit button next to the **Substitute path prefix** box.

3. Fill in the Substitute Path Prefix box.

   The **Current prefix** is the original path to the project file folder. The **Substitute prefix** is the path to the new location of the project file folder. The pathname in either prefix can be a UNC path, a drive letter, or a relative path.

   Adding comments to the **Comments** box can be useful for recording notes explaining why and when a substitute path was used.

   Specifying a substitute path is the equivalent of adding the REPLACE= setting to the [OPTIONS] section of the project file.

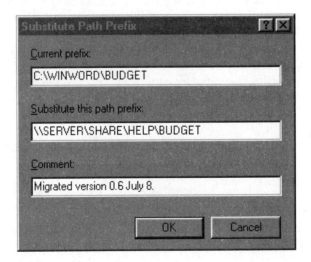

Figure 18.14. *Specifying a substitute path to/from the project file folder.*

Specifying the name of the Help file

By default, the Help compiler uses the name of the project file as the name of the Help file. You can change the name of the compiled Help file at any time with an adjustment in Help Workshop as shown in the following procedure. If you have specified the orginal Help file name in jumps or macros within the Help file, that name will automatically be translated into the new name during compiling.

You can always change the name of the compiled Help file by renaming it in Explorer. However, in that case you would have to rename the file each time it was compiled. Also, errors will result if your Help system contains references to the original file name through macros or jumps.

To specify the Help file name:

1. In Help Workshop, the Help file name is displayed at the top of the project editor window. This default name is automatcially assigned by the compiler based on the name of the project file.

2. To change the name, type the new name in the **Help File** box. You need to type the .HLP extension. It will not be automatically appended, and the compiled Help file will not open without the proper extension.

    This procedures modifies the HLP setting in the [OPTIONS] section of the project file. This setting does not appear in the Help Workshop project editor window.

    You can also make this setting in Help Workshop through Options/File/Help File.

References to project file tasks

Although the basic project file enables you to quickly get up and running with a compiled Help file, it doesn't provide much control over the final product. Fortunately, a full palette of other interesting and useful settings are available for enhancing your Help file.

More advanced project file settings include customizing the appearance of Help with window color and sizing, optimizing Help file size with compression, and creating context-sensitive links between Help and a Windows application. There are over thirty project file settings and sections which you can use. Help Workshop makes it easy to access these. Table 18.1 lists each Help Workshop tab and describes the settings to be found in each. The settings are cross-referenced with the chapter and page references in which they are discussed in this book.

> **NOTE** *A sample project file called ADVANCED.HPJ is located on the disc in the back of this book. This sample file includes examples of all of the project file settings.*

Table 18.1. *Project File Settings*

Workshop Buttons/Tabs	Description	Setting/ [Section]	Discussed in...
Options			
General	"Contents" or default topic$	CONTENTS	Chapter 17
	Help file title	TITLE	This chapter
	message options	NOTES	Chapter 20
	copyright information	COPYRIGHT, CITATION	This chapter & Chapter 21
Compression	compression options	COMPRESS	Chapter 20
Sorting	language options	LCID	Chapter 21
	keyword sorting options	LCID	Chapter 11 & Chapter 21
	keyword separation character	INDEX_ SEPARATORS	Chapter 17
Files	Help file name	HLP	This chapter
	log file name	ERRORLOG	Chapter 20
	topic file name/location	[FILES]	This chapter
	Contents file name/ location	CNT	This chapter & Chapter 17
	temporary file folder	TMPDIR	Chapter 20
	substitute path prefix	REPLACE	This chapter
FTS	full text search options	FTS	Chapter 17
Fonts	character set options	CHARSET	Chapter 21
	font selection	DEFFONT	Chapter 21
	font substitution	[FONTS]	Chapter 21
Build Tags	build tag specifications	[EXCLUDE], [INCLUDE]	Chapter 10 & Chapter 20
Macros	keyword macros	[MACROS]	Chapter 15 & Chapter 16

Table 18.1. *(continued)*

Workshop *Buttons*/Tabs	Description	Setting/ [Section]	Discussed in...
Files	topic file name/location	[FILES]	This chapter
	revision mark acceptance	REVISIONS$	Chapter 23
	double-byte character	DBCS set switch	Chapter 21
Windows	window properties	[WINDOWS]	Chapter 15
Bitmaps	graphic file location	BMROOT, [BITMAPS]	This chapter
Map	context sensitive Help section and ID prefix	[MAP], PREFIX	Chapter 19
Config	startup macros	[CONFIG], [CONFIG-window name]	Chapter 16 & Chapter 17
Data Files	multimedia storage	[BAGGAGE]	Chapter 14 & Chapter 16

19

Programming Calls to Help

The original purpose for the creation of WinHelp within the Windows operating system was to provide a standard for online hypertext documentation in support of software applications. While the non-traditional uses of WinHelp—policy manuals, newsletters, database lists—have grown enormously, the most common use is still to create Help.

If your goal is to develop a Help system in support of a software application, you will need to work in concert with those who are programming the application. A standalone WinHelp system, like a policy manual, can be created solely through the efforts of the Help author. Linking Help to an application, though, involves specialized planning, programming skills, modifications to the project file, and additional testing routines.

This chapter is divided into the following areas:

- How Help is called from an application program.

- Planning your calls to Help.

- Programming your calls to Help.

- Building the Map section of the project file.

- Testing and debugging the calls to Help.

The chapter concludes with information concerning application programs that contain built-in calls to Help.

How Help is called from an application program

More than any other aspect of Help development, programming calls to the Help file from an application program requires close interaction between the application programmer and the Help author. The application programmer adds code to the application which will recognize a "Help event." The Help author writes the topic that appears in response to the event. At points during the development process, the two parties collaborate to link the Help event code and the Help topics. This section provides a "layman's" introduction to the process; the details are expanded in a later section of the chapter.

Help events can take many forms, depending on how the user interacts with the application. However, in every case, a Help event consists of two parts. One, the user has focused on a specific part of the application. Two, the user makes a keypress or mouse click to request Help.

In Figure 19.1, the focus of the Word 6 application was on the Indents and Spacing tab when the user clicked the Help button. This Help event triggered the display of the appropriate Help topic. In Word 6, all of the dialog-box tabs have Help events associated with them. The F1 key is also supported as an alternate way for the user to request Help.

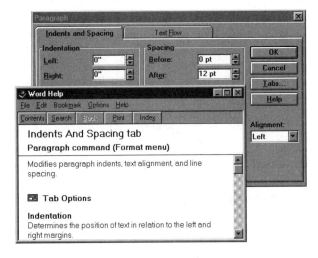

Figure 19.1. *A Help event triggered by the clicking the Help button while the focus is on the Indents and Spacing tab.*

A type of Help event frequently used by Microsoft in their Windows 95 products is called "What's This?" In Figure 19.2, the user first clicked the question mark button, then pointed to an area of the application that required clarification—in this case the Power status section of the Power tab—and then right clicked the mouse. The result is a definition topic displayed in a pop-up window.

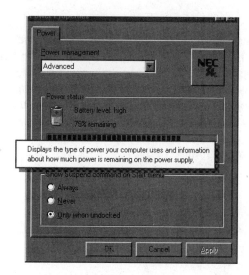

Figure 19.2. *A "What's This?" pop-up definition.*

For each Help event that you want to support in your application, the programmer must add a code segment to the program. Since it is good design to be consistent with your use of context-sensitive help, numerous code segments will need to be added to your application. In the Word 6 Help file, every tab has a Help event code associated with it. The NEC Help file goes a step further, and has a Help event code segment associated with *each section* of each tab.

When a Help code segment intercepts a Help request from the user, it sends a message to WinHelp to launch a specific help file and to display a specific topic or the Help Topics browser. The structure of the Help event code varies among applications and programmers. However, at the heart of the code are calls to the WinHelp API function and context identifiers (IDs).

The WinHelp API (Application Programming Interface) function consists of a variety of commands which control the way topics in the Help file are displayed. The context ID is a number that corresponds to a topic in the topic file. Figure 19.3 shows a typical call to WinHelp as programmed in Visual C++. The context ID is expressed as "22" and the particular command being used is HELP_CONTEXTPOPUP. This code sends a message to WinHelp to display the topic associated with context ID value 22 in a pop-up window.

```
AfxGetApp()->WinHelp(22,HELP_CONTEXTPOPUP)
```

Figure 19.3. *A typical code segment for processing a Help request.*

This particular code segment is located in file MISC.CPP in the Chapter 19 section of your book disc. Other WinHelp commands are described later in this chapter.

In order for the appropriate Help topic to be displayed, WinHelp must translate the context ID into a topic ID. As described in Chapter 10, *Creating Help Topics*, the topic ID is how topics are uniquely identified in the Help file. A translation table called the "Map" associates each context ID with the corresponding topic ID. It is a two-column table which consists of the topic ID in the first column and the context ID in the second separated by a tab or space. The Map is built in the [MAP] section of the project file and is embedded into the Help file during compiling. Figure 19.4 shows a sample [MAP] section. The context ID of 20 is associated with the topic ID of COM_FILE. The topic ID is used in the # footnote in the topic file; in this case the "File commands" topic shown in Figure 19.5.

```
[MAP]
COM_FILE 20
COM_SAVE 22
```

Figure 19.4. *The 'MAP' section of the project file contains topic IDs followed by corresponding context IDs.*

Figure 19.5. *The topic "File commands" is "mapped" through the topic ID "COM_FILE."*

The Map thus becomes the linchpin between the Help file and the application. As long as the programmer and Help author agree on the content of the Map, they can pursue their tasks more or less independently. When the application and Help file are tested together, the links should work. The majority of errors encountered when testing links to Help from the application can be traced to inaccurate or obsolete entries in the Map.

Planning calls to Help

Programming Help into an application is a collaboration between the application programmer and the Help author. The two work together to devise the optimum solution based on available resources and the nature of the product. Even if you're not directly involved in the design and programming of your software product, it helps to understand the options that are available in displaying Help. The proper development of Help topics depends largely on how they will be used in concert with the application. In some organizations, a designer will be in charge of planning the type of topic access to be provided.

Before developing a plan, consider performing usability studies or questioning users at your product's alpha and beta test sites; this can provide valuable feedback about what kinds of calls to Help you should include.

While you can devise your own forms of interaction between the Help file and the application, the following are a few models that have been shown to be very effective.

THE HELP MENU

The most common (and often, the only) link to Help found in Windows applications is for the user to select the Contents command from the Help menu. The Help menu is a standard feature of almost every Windows application, and one which users have come to expect. The Contents command displays either the Contents tab of the Help Topics browser or the default contents topic.

Although many Help menus offer only a Contents command, the user can benefit from other choices. Figure 19.6 shows the Help menu for the CompuServe WinCim application. In addition to Contents, the Help menu includes a Search command. This typically displays the Index of the Help system. The CompuServe Help menu also includes calls to the Help file, "How to Use Help," and a supplementary Help file named CompuServe Directory.

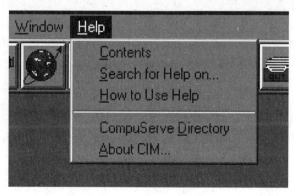

Figure 19.6. *Several commands are available on the WinCim Help menu.*

A HELP BUTTON

Many applications include Help buttons in their dialog boxes or tabs. When the user clicks Help, the Help topic corresponding to that dialog box or tab appears. In Figure 19.7, the Text Flow tab of the Paragraph dialog box contains a Help button which displays the Text Flow reference topic. The F1 key is a standard often used to complement the Help button. Using either F1 or the Help button in the Text Flow tab would display the same topic.

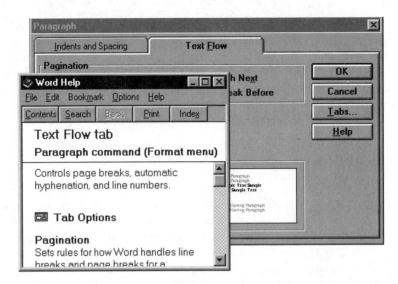

Figure 19.7. *A dialog box tab with a Help button.*

"WHAT'S THIS?"

A form of Help calls used liberally in Microsoft's Windows 95 Help systems is called "What's This?". This call displays a short definition topic in a pop-up window. The design of What's This? topics is introduced in Chapter 1 and described in detail in Chapter 6, *Writing Other Standard Help Topics.*

To activate this Help event, the user selects an element in a dialog box or tab and makes a keypress or mouse click. The standard keypress is F1. If the user right-clicks the mouse, a What's This? floating menu appears. A click on the menu displays the appropriate definition topic. Figure 19.8 shows the Taskbar Properties box of Windows 95. Pressing F1 with the input focus on the Show Clock option displays a definition of it.

What's This? topics are resident in a standard Help file. You construct these topics in the same way that you would construct any pop-up definition topic. Generally, keyword and browse sequence codes are not associated with such a topic. The definition topic shown in Figure 19.8 exists as topic #1113 of WINDOWS.HLP.

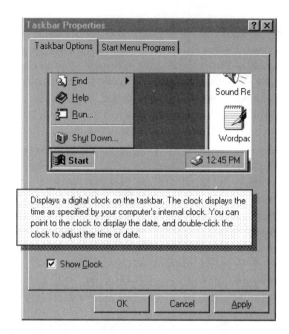

Figure 19.8. *A What's This? pop-up definition topic.*

TIP *It is useful to examine the What's This? topics displayed in Windows 95 for design ideas. The Control Panel applets provide numerous example topics which are resident in WINDOWS.HLP. To examine these topics in a standard Help window, rebuild the full-text search index using the "Include untitled topics" option. Then, in the Find page, type a portion of the text from the What's This? topic you want to display to find the topic.*

An alternate method of requesting What's This? Help is to click a question mark button in the upper right corner of the window. The application program is temporarily disabled and the mouse pointer appears as the one shown in Figure 19.9. The user positions the pointer over an element and clicks once to display the What's This? definition.

Figure 19.9. *The What's This? pointer.*

COMMAND DESCRIPTIONS

Users can also benefit by Help topics which describe the function of menu items. The general behavior is for the user to highlight a command on a menu and press F1. The topic might be displayed in either a standard or a pop-up window. In Microsoft Word 7, the command description is displayed in a pop-up window. As shown in the top portion of Figure 19.10, the user highlights the Break command on the Insert menu. Pressing F1 displays the Break command topic as a pop-up, shown in the lower portion of the figure.

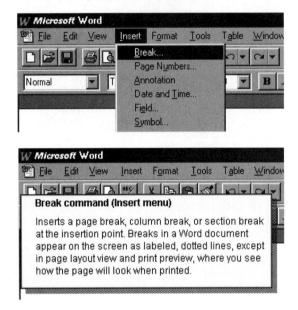

Figure 19.10. *Displaying command descriptions with F1.*

INTERFACE ELEMENT DESCRIPTIONS

Descriptions of tool buttons, status bars, and regions on the interface can also benefit the user. Typically the user presses SHIFT+F1 or clicks a Help (question mark) button. Similar to What's This?, a special pointer appears which the user can position over an element of the window. A click then displays a descriptive topic. In the top portion of Figure 19.11, the user has clicked the Word 7 Help button and then the Numbering tool. The result is the descriptive pop-up shown in the lower portion of the figure.

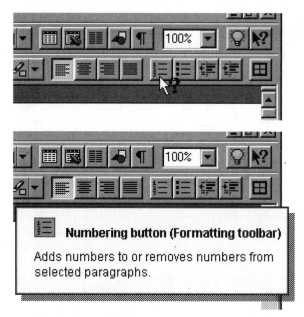

Figure 19.11. *Displaying Help for an interface element.*

This form of support requires more extensive work on the part of the programmer and requires more meticulous testing.

OTHER METHODS

Context-sensitive Help topics can be accessed in other creative ways.

- Some applications provide built-in facilities for attaching your Help file directly to forms and screens. For example, Microsoft Excel can call the WinHelp function from a Help command. With Microsoft Access, you attach Help through Form properties. No programming is required. Help implementation with Excel and Access is described at the end of this chapter.

- An application might be programmed to watch for a certain sequence of events: if the sequence occurs, a particular Help topic can be displayed. For example, a home finance application might track a user's credit card finance charges. If the amount exceeds a certain threshold, a tip might appear instructing the user to shop around for lower interest rates. The tips can reside in a Help file.

Programming calls to Help

The reason that your Help file can run on any installed copy of Windows is that the Windows Help facility is present there. The executable program installed with every version of Windows 95 is WINHLP32.EXE. This replaces the old executable of WINHELP.EXE. In the same way that you need Word to display a word processing document, you need WinHelp to display a Help file. When a user double clicks a Help icon, WinHelp recognizes it and launches the Help file. When an application launches a Help file, the program code calls the WinHelp function of the Application Program Interface (API). The WinHelp function can be used to display Help topics in many different ways, depending on the creativity of the programmer and designer, and the needs of the application.

The WinHelp function calls occur behind the scenes and require programming skills to implement them. However, understanding the basics of the WinHelp function certainly improves communication between the Help author and the programmer, and facilitates testing of Help. Help authors can become a more integral part of the design process by understanding how Help is programmed.

This section presents the calls to the WinHelp function in three forms. The first is the most utilized (and complicated) application: context-sensitive help. This is followed by typical calls to the WinHelp function from a Help menu. Finally, a select group of miscellaneous calls to WinHelp are also presented.

The following is the general syntax for a call to the WinHelp function:

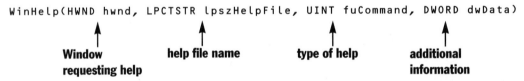

```
WinHelp(HWND hwnd, LPCTSTR lpszHelpFile, UINT fuCommand, DWORD dwData)
```

Window requesting help — help file name — type of help — additional information

You will find it documented this way in the online *Help Author's Guide,* and you may also find it coded this way in an application. However, in the Microsoft Foundations Class (MFC) library, the syntax is simplified:

```
AfxGetApp()->WinHelp(DWORD dwData, UINT fuCommand)
```

In the MFC form, the first parameter is the data, and the second parameter is the command. A limitation of this form is that it requires the Help file to have the same name as the application. If you want to send a command to a secondary window or a different Help file, you will have to use the general form so you can specify the Help file path yourself.

CONTEXT-SENSITIVE HELP

Context-sensitive help is the ability of the Windows software application to display a Help topic that is directly relevant to, or in the context of, the task the user is trying to accomplish. For example, if a user is confused about the options related to a particular dialog box, clicking a Help button in that box could display a relevant Help topic. Or if the user is unsure of the purpose of an item on the application's interface, a pop-up definition could appear.

This "intelligent" response to the needs of the user has enormous value. The need for the user to wade through other methods of topic access (the Contents, Index, Find, etc.), is significantly reduced when context-sensitive Help is enabled by the developer. Despite its value, however, the additional programming labor required to implement context-sensitive Help, in most cases, prevents developers from building much of it into their products.

While context-sensitive Help has always been available to the developer, it is with Windows 95 that there is a greater sense of urgency to implement it. The reason is that Microsoft has chosen to use context-sensitive help liberally throughout the Windows 95 operating system in a form called "What's This? Help." As users become accustomed to the What's This? standard in the operating system (and in other Microsoft products) they expect it in other applications, as well. Unfortunately, there is no magic wand to enable this functionality. While the WinHelp function in Windows 95 supports the display of topics through the What's This? context menu and the question mark button, it is still up to the programmer to add the appropriate code to the application. There are also other forms of context-sensitive Help besides What's This? It can be used with a Help button, with the toolbar, and with the various menus and menu commands. These methods are each described below in the context of using Visual C++ via the Microsoft Foundation Class. The sample application and source files are included on your book disc. General notes on Visual C++, Delphi, and Visual Basic 4 are described at the end of this section.

What's This? Help

The What's This? form of context-sensitive Help is typically used in a tab of a property sheet or in a conventional dialog box. The standard behavior is that the user places the input focus on a control such as a radio button or list box. A right mouse click displays the What's This? context menu which, when clicked, displays a definition topic. Alternatively the user can press SHIFT+F1 or use the question mark button.

The implementation of this feature is demonstrated in the sample application HELPDEMO.EXE. The "What's This?" tab appears as soon as you launch the sample application. There are several locations of What's This? Help: each of the three radio buttons, the furniture preview area, the furniture list box, and the four active buttons (OK, Cancel, Browse, Help). (See Figure 19.12.) What's This? definition is available for each, as shown in Figure 19.12.

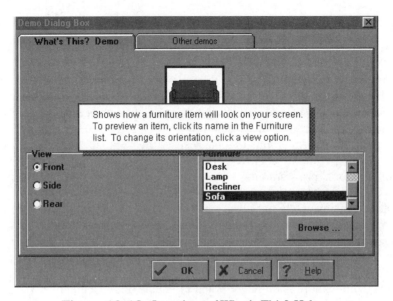

Figure 19.12. *Locations of What's This? Help.*

The size of the What's This? hotspot is governed by the size of the control object. The location of the What's This? pop-up window is normally dependent on the location of the mouse. The size of the pop-up window depends upon the paragraph formatting of the text in the Help topic.

The programming of What's This? functionality consists of several portions of code in the .CPP file for each dialog box. This includes: calls to the WinHelp function, statements in the message Map, and an array of control and topic statements.

> **NOTE** *In C++ programming, a separate .CPP file is created to control the operation of each dialog box. The .CPP extension literally stands for "C Plus Plus."*

First, calls to two WinHelp commands are added to the .CPP file for each page of the dialog box: HELP_CONTEXTMENU and HELP_WM_HELP. The former handles a right mouse click. The latter handles the F1 key and the question mark button. Here is the code in file DEMODLG.CPP:

```
LONG CRoomProp::OnContextMenu( UINT wParam, LONG lParam )
{
    HWND hwnd = (HWND)wParam;
    ::WinHelp(hwnd,
                  AfxGetApp()->m_pszHelpFilePath,
                  HELP_CONTEXTMENU,
                  (DWORD)(LPVOID)aMenuHelpIDs);
    return 0;
```

```
}

LONG CRoomProp::OnHelp( UINT wParam, LONG lParam )
{
   LPHELPINFO pHelpInfo = (LPHELPINFO)lParam;
   HWND hwnd = (HWND)pHelpInfo->hItemHandle;
   ::WinHelp(hwnd,
                   AfxGetApp()->m_pszHelpFilePath,
                   HELP_WM_HELP,
                   (DWORD)(LPVOID)aMenuHelpIDs);
   return 0;
}
```

Next, two lines are added to the message Map: ON_MESSAGE(WM_HELP,OnHelp) and ON_MESSAGE(WM_CONTEXTMENU,OnContextMenu). This handles the Help request from the user and calls the associated WinHelp function commands described above.

```
BEGIN_MESSAGE_MAP(CRoomProp, CPropertySheet)
...
        ON_MESSAGE(WM_HELP,OnHelp)
        ON_MESSAGE(WM_CONTEXTMENU,OnContextMenu)
...
END_MESSAGE_MAP()
```

Last, you have to add the array aMenuHelpIDs that the WinHelp function commands refer to. The first portion of the array consists of #define statements. There is one define statement for each control that offers context-sensitive Help. Each define statement consists of a unique descriptive label and an integer that is arbitrarily assigned by the developer. These statements are referenced in the Map section of the project file as described later in this chapter. The first statement in the following listing deals with the Front radio button. It associates the label "HELPID_FURNITURE_FRONT" with the Front radio button and assigns the integer 13. The integer is used to access the appropriate definition topic in the Help file.

```
#define HELPID_FURNITURE_FRONT 13
#define HELPID_FURNITURE_SIDE 14
#define HELPID_FURNITURE_REAR 15
#define HELPID_FURNITURE_PICTURE 17
#define HELPID_FURNITURE_LISTBOX 16
#define HELPID_FURNITURE_BROWSE 19

static const DWORD aMenuHelpIDs[] =
{
   IDC_RB_FRONT,    HELPID_FURNITURE_FRONT,
   IDC_RB_SIDE,     HELPID_FURNITURE_SIDE,
   IDC_RB_REAR,     HELPID_FURNITURE_REAR,
   IDC_PICTURE,     HELPID_FURNITURE_PICTURE,
   IDC_LISTFURNITURE,  HELPID_FURNITURE_LISTBOX,
   IDC_BTNBROWSE,   HELPID_FURNITURE_BROWSE,
   0, 0
};
```

The second portion of the array associates the #define statements with the IDs of each of the dialog box controls. The radio button labeled "Front" is known to the program by the control ID of IDC_RB_FRONT. That control ID is associated with the #define label of HELPID_FURNITURE_FRONT. The array is terminated with a pair of zeroes.

The Ok, Cancel, Apply, and Help buttons in the dialog box are not referenced in the array. These controls are assigned to standard definitions which are part of the Microsoft Foundations Class. No definition topics are required in the Help topic files for these controls.

The Help button

It is a common practice to place a Help button in each dialog box. Usually clicking such a button will display a topic that describes the overall features of the dialog box or that provides a list of related procedure topics.

A typical implementation of this feature is to code a Help button into a dialog box. Associated with the button is a HELP_CONTEXT call to WinHelp that specifies a certain context ID. This ID is included in the project Map and associated with the appropriate topic ID. The HELP_CONTEXT call displays the topics in the main window. The HELP_CONTEXTPOPUP call displays the topic in a pop-up window. The following is a sample of typical code:

```
AfxGetApp()->WinHelp(22,HELP_CONTEXTPOPUP);
```

If the application is using a tabbed property sheet, the App Wizard of Visual C++ automatically adds a Help button to the lower portion of the sheet. The Help button is automatically assigned a unique context ID for each tab in the sheet. These IDs are referenced in the Map section of the project file. For example, in the sample application, MFC assigned context IDs to the What's This? and Other Demos tabs of the Help Demo property sheet. These numbers appear in HELPDEMO.HPJ.

> **TIP** *An easy way to locate these IDs is to run the application in Visual C++. Click each Help button, monitor the Output window, and record the ID numbers that appear.*

Menu and command descriptions

Another area of context-sensitive Help support is for menu commands. The standard behavior is to display a topic describing the command in response to an F1 keypress while the command is highlighted. An alternate method is for the user to press SHIFT+F1 (or click the Help button) and then point to the item. While this resembles What's This? Help, it is technically different in terms of programming. It also appears slightly different to the user, since a right mouse click will not work.

As with the Help button described above, MFC automatically assigns a unique context ID to each menu command. These context IDs are included in the [MAP] section of the project file.

No additional programming is required. The following is the portion of the [MAP] section of HELPDEMO.HPJ that contains the menu command IDs.

```
[MAP]
..
...
ref_Open_Demo_command 98316
ref_Exit_command 98317
ref_Contents_command 98318
ref_Search_for_Help_command 98309
...
..
```

> **NOTE** *The Help tool button is generated automatically by App Wizard and placed on the main application window.*

Help menu commands

The Help menu is used to provide broad forms of access to Help, as opposed to the specific form of context-sensitive Help. Commands to access the Contents, Index, and Help on Help file are the most common applications.

If you are using Visual C++, the Contents and Search items are automatically added to the Help menu. By default the Contents command uses the HELP_CONTENTS call and the Search uses the HELP_SEARCH call. You can customize the operation of these menu commands by editing their ID fields. However, you then need to put in your own prompts and implement the functions through Class Wizard.

Contents command

Providing access to the contents of your Help system is a necessity for virtually any application. Users expect this form of access to Help. The command text of "Contents" is most commonly used. This works well whether or not you are shipping a contents file. In Windows 95 products, Microsoft uses "Help Topics" as the label. A typical WinHelp function call is:

```
AfxGetApp()->WinHelp(0,HELP_CONTENTS);
```

Search command

If you want to give your user direct access to the Index, a "Search" or "Index" command can be added to the Help menu. Microsoft uses "Search for Help on..." as the command text. A typical WinHelp function call is:

```
AfxGetApp()->WinHelp(0,HELP_INDEX);
```

Help on Help command

Microsoft provides a Help file which describes how to use Help. If you feel your audience may benefit from this, you can distribute it along with your own Help system. In Windows 95 the Help file is called WINHLP32.HLP; in Windows 3.x, it is WINHELP.HLP.

A typical function call is:

```
AfxGetApp()->WinHelp(0,HELP_HELPONHELP);
```

OTHER HELP COMMANDS

There are a number of other commands available with the WinHelp function which you may choose to use to customize control of your Help system from the application. A complete technical description is available in the *Help Author's Guide* (keyword="API,WinHelp").

The sample application includes three of these commands on the Other tab. They are described below.

Keyword search

The keyword search command provides a way to bypass the mapping of context IDs. The application code specifies a keyword when sending a call to WinHelp. The result is the display of the topic with which that keyword is associated. For example, a user wants to get Help on using the Print dialog box. The user clicks the Help button which sends the HELP_KEY call to WinHelp specifying the word "print." The topic with a K footnote containing "print" appears.

This method works well only if the specified keyword is assigned to only one topic. Otherwise the Index appears displaying two or more titles in the Topics Found box. Here is a typical function call:

```
AfxGetApp()->WinHelp((DWORD)"Print",HELP_KEY);
```

Help Topics browser

If you are using Help menu commands to display the Contents and Index tabs of the Help Topics browser, the calls that are used specifically address each tab so as to place the proper one on top. However you can elect to use the more general case of displaying on top whatever the last tab was that the user selected.

For example, you may have just a single menu command titled "Help Topics" which calls HELP_FINDER. The first time the user selects the command the Contents tab appears. Assume the user then works with the Index and return to the application. The next time the user select Help Topics, the Index tab appears on top in the browser rather than Contents. Here is a typical function call:

```
AfxGetApp()->WinHelp(0,HELP_FINDER);
```

Forcing a Help file

The Windows environment encourages the user to switch between several applications during a particular work session. However, if the user is requesting Help from various applications, it is possible that the WinHelp function may display the wrong Help file. This also may occur if you create a modular Help system consisting of multiple Help files. A solution is to use the HELP_FORCEFILE command which more specifically addresses a certain Help file.

The following call to a Help file passes the path, drive, directory, filename, and extension:

```
void CMisc::OnBtnHelpForceFile()
{
        char szHelpFile[_MAX_PATH];
        char drive[_MAX_DRIVE];
        char dir[_MAX_DIR];
        char fname[_MAX_FNAME];
        char ext[_MAX_EXT];

        _splitpath( AfxGetApp()->m_pszHelpFilePath, drive, dir,
fname, ext );
        strcpy(szHelpFile,drive);
        strcat(szHelpFile,dir);
        strcat(szHelpFile,"FORCE.HLP");
        ::WinHelp(GetSafeHwnd(),szHelpFile,HELP_FORCEFILE,0);
}
```

PROGRAMMING TOOLS AND HELP

The Microsoft Foundations Class provides some support for context-sensitive Help; strictly-menu items, toolbars and a single topic for each dialog. Programmers will have to add additional code to properly implement What's This? Help. But the choice of development tool makes the big difference in how easily it is enabled. Visual C++, Delphi, and VB4 all provide different methods of implementing calls to the WinHelp function. Whereas Visual C++ is the most popular development platform, it requires the addition of functions to manage the calling of What's This? Help for objects on a tabbed dialog. The program examples in the HELPDEMO application on your book disc are a useful guide.

Delphi provides much simpler access to Help and performance comparable to Visual C++. However, it remains to be seen whether it becomes widely accepted. Visual Basic also provides fairly easy access to Help calls. Visual Basic is often used for "in-house" application development or for applications that don't require the performance that is delivered by Visual C++ and Delphi. Additional notes on each of these tools is provided at the end of this chapter.

Using Visual C++

With Visual C++, the App Wizard supports the creation of the associated code. It also generates an ample Help file including the .RTF and .HPJ files. This Help file is very rudimentary, but it does provide a starting point for the programmer who works with the product. When you use App Wizard to generate an application with context-sensitive Help, it generates a simple Help project. The following two files are in the same folder as the project: AFXCORE.RTF and application name: .HPJ. It places these files in a subfolder off the main application folder called \HLP.

To match the context IDs defined in the .RTF file with the IDs in the RESOURCE.H file a program called MAKEHM.EXE is called from the MAKEHELP.BAT batch file. It takes the labels defined in the RESOURCE.H file and it puts matching labels with a "H" at the front of the new labels in a new file called *filename*.HM in the HLP folder.

Details and specific syntax are available in the Visual C++ Help file topics concerning context-sensitive Help: "MFC 2.5 Technical Note 28: Context-Sensitive Help Support."

Using Visual Basic 4

Adding context-sensitive Help to forms generated with Visual Basic 4 is accomplished through property sheets. The first step is to determine whether to support Windows 3.x or Windows 95 context-sensitive Help. Windows 3.x Help displays a Help topic when the user selects a control and presses F1. With Windows 95, the topic is displayed in a pop-up window and can be accessed by F1 or by clicking the question mark (What's This?) button. You specify which model you want to use by changing the setting in the WhatsThisHelp property. After selecting the model, you specify the Help file you want use through the HelpFile property, which is a global project option.

Next you assign context IDs to the various controls. The properties to which you assign the context IDs depend on which model you selected. The Windows 3.x model uses the HelpContextID property. The Windows 95 model uses the WhatsThisHelpID property. The context IDs are referenced in the [MAP] section of the project file as they normally would. The WhatsThisButton property adds the What's This? button to the title bar of a Form. See Figure 19.13.

Figure 19.13. *A control properties sheet in Visual Basic.*

Using Delphi

The Borland Delphi development platform provides easy implementation of context-sensitive Help relative to Visual C++. There are two different properties for context-sensitive Help: either HelpContextID (WinHelp 3.x) or What'sThisHelpID. See Figure 19.13.

Building and managing the Map

As described in the first section of this chapter, the Map is a two-column table which resides or is referenced in the project file. It links the context IDs, which a programmer has assigned to the various Help events, to the topic IDs, which the Help author has assigned to the various topics in the topic file. The context ID is a number and the topic ID is a label.

  While the planning and programming of links to Help tends to require considerable labor, working with the Map is fairly easy. The key is for the programmer and Help author to agree on the topic and context ID entries. The system you use for building and managing the Map will depend on how your project team is organized. However in all cases this will require changes to the [MAP] section of the project file. This section describes the various procedures for building and managing the Map.

Modifying the Project File

Any Help system that will be linked to an application program must include a Map section in the project file. Like the [FILES] and [OPTIONS] sections described in other chapters of this book, the Map section begins with a bracketed section name: [MAP]. The section name is followed by a series of statements that consist of a topic ID followed by the associated context ID number. The context ID number can be expressed in decimal or hexadecimal notation. The following sample shows a portion of a typical Map:

```
[MAP]
/* Menu command definition topics */
OPEN_COMMAND 22
SAVE_COMMAND 24
EXIT_COMMAND 0x0017
...
..
```

At least one space or a tab is required between the topic and context IDs. In the sample, OPEN_COMMAND is the topic ID associated with the context ID of 22. The context ID for the EXIT_COMMAND is expressed in hexadecimal notation. The entries in the Map do not have to be in any particular order . You can include comments (/* */) between lines or on the same line as an entry.

> **TIP** *The Map only needs to contain the topic IDs for the topics which will be called by the application. Some authoring tools automatically add all of the topic IDs from the topic file into the Map. While this does not hurt, it clutters up the Map and can cause confusion during maintenance and debugging.*

While many Help authors type the Map entries directly into the project file with a text editor, Help Workshop provides a dialog box for this task.

To add individual entries to the Map:

1. In Help Workshop, click the Map button.

2. In the Map box, click Add.

3. In the **Topic ID** box, type a Topic ID for a topic that will be called by the application. The topic ID cannot contain any spaces and must exist in the topic file. See Figure 19.14.

4. In the **Mapped numeric value** box, type the context ID from the application. Context IDs can be formatted in either decimal or hexadecimal format.

   The topic ID and context ID are required. You can also add a comment for your own reference. This might be the Help topic title or a description of the Help event.

5. Return to the View window. The [MAP] section appears containing the topic and context IDs.

Continue to repeat this procedure for all topics to be accessed from the application program. Use the Edit button to change the topic or context IDs as necessary.

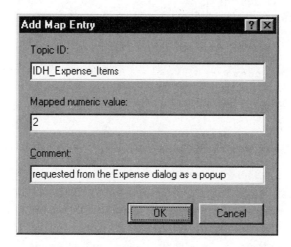

Figure 19.14. *Adding items to the Map with Help Workshop.*

The greatest source of errors in calls from an application program to a Help file can be traced to inaccurate or out-of-date entries in the Map. It is well worthwhile to arrange a good communication scheme between the programmer and Help author under which the the context IDs can be transferred to the Map. The following section provides a method which can streamline the process.

Referencing Map entries

Adding the numeric values directly in the project file as described above is the most common method of assembling the Map. However, while it is fairly straightforward, it can also be problematic. First, the programmer may have developed context-sensitive code and assigned context IDs before the Help author even gets started on the Help file. While you could transfer the context IDs manually into your project file by retyping them, this is tedious and error-prone. In a large application there can be hundreds of context IDs. Second, the context IDs may very well change during application development. This means that the Help author needs to continuously modify the entries in the project file. These problems occur regardless of whether you are editing the project file manually or with an authoring tool like Help Workshop. Fortunately there is an easier method which lets you reference the programmer's context IDs.

In programming languages like C/C++, the programmer assembles the context IDs in what is called a "header file." These header files are simply text files which contain topic IDs and the associated context ID number. C/C++ language header files use .H or .HH extensions. As a Help author all you need to do is reference the header file in the [MAP] section of the project file by adding an #include statement. The advantage is that the header file can be maintained independently of the Help file. No additional information needs to be added to the Map. Typically the programmer delivers updated versions of the header file to the Help author who then recompiles the Help file. The following sample shows an include statement which references a C++ header file:

```
[MAP]
#include .\Helpdemo.hh
```

Help Workshop provides an option for including a header file.

To include a header file

1. In Help Workshop, click the Map button.

2. In the Map box, click Include.

3. Type the name of the header file to include.

The include statement appears in the [MAP] section of the project file.

If you examine the contents of a header file you will find the topic IDs and associate context ID numbers. You will also find each line preceded by a #define keyword. The presence of this keyword is so that the contents of the header file is included in the C/C++ program when the application is compiled. The following is the contents of a sample header file:

```
[MAP]
/* Menu command definition topics */
#define OPEN_COMMAND 22
#define SAVE_COMMAND 24
#define EXIT_COMMAND 0x0017
. . .
. .
```

Also, it is possible to have a combination of include statements and directly typed Map entries in the [MAP] section of the project file. Many of the Help authoring tools provide special support which make it easier to work with the Map and header files.

> **TIP** *You can benefit from using an include statement with your Help project even if you are not working directly with an application programmer. For example, if you have a team of Help authors all contributing entries to the Map, a text file can be assembled in a shared location. This shared file can then be referenced in the [MAP] section of the project file and the Map will always be up-to-date.*

Testing and debugging

When Help calls are programmed into an application, the testing of those links must become part of the formal testing process. The testing of the Help file itself is described in Chapter 20, *Compiling, Debugging, and Testing.* However, the testing of programmed links to Help is covered here as a special case since it brings its own challenges.

The biggest challenge is that this portion of development is a joint effort between the programmer and Help author. First of all, communication is often difficult because they are usually part of different work groups. Second, the application group is likely be on a schedule very different from that of the documentation team. Both of these problems make it difficult to properly test and debug the application and the Help together.

A useful strategy is to break the testing into two parts: preliminary and formal testing. In preliminary testing, the programmer and Help author can each independently test a portion of the project. The programmer reviews the Help event code and the Help author reviews the topic ID assignments and mapping. In formal testing, the application and Help system are brought together and evaluated by testers.

PRELIMINARY TESTING

One of the nicest elements about developing Windows Help is that the programmer and the Help author can work on their respective portions of development and be able to test their work independently. The Help author does not need to rely on the application to be able to test jumps, pop-ups, etc., within the Help file.

With WinHelp 4, Help Workshop provides features which make it possible to do preliminary testing of links between the application and Help file. This includes checking during compiling and testing of the API calls.

Checking compiler messages for inconsistencies

As described in Chapter 10, a topic ID can consist of any unique arrangement of characters. However, for topics that will be addressed by the application, a common standard is to use "IDH_" as the prefix for context IDs. If you use this form for your topic IDs, Help Workshop automatically performs some error checking. During compiling, Help Workshop scans the topic IDs in the topic file for the IDH_ prefix. The IDH_ topic IDs are then compared to the topic IDs specified in the [MAP] section of the project file. If there are any inconsistencies, messages are displayed during compiling.

For example, the warning message in Figure 19.15 indicates that a topic ID found in the topic file is not specified in the project file. Figure 19.16 shows a note message indicating that a topic ID specified in the project file is not in the topic file.

```
HC3038: Warning:
The following Topic IDs are not defined in the [MAP] section of
the Project file:
        IDH_Expense_Items    Topic 5 of BUDGET.RTF
        IDH_Income_Items     Topic 4 of BUDGET.RTF
```

Figure 19.15.

```
HC1010: Note:
The following mapped Topic IDs were not used in any topic:
Income_Items
Expense_Items
```

Figure 19.16.

Based on this information you can examine your Map and topic files and determine where to make an adjustment. The message in Figure 19.15 could be telling you that two items had been mistakenly omitted from the Map. The message in Figure 19.16 might alert you to two topics that had not been added to the topic file. You would have to check the topic and project files and your design notes to find the problem.

Often it is typing errors that are the culprits. If this is the case, you will see complementary items in the warning and note messages. The messages in Figure 19.15 and 19.16 are actually caused by the same inconsistency. The standard IDH_ prefix which was used in the Map was not used in the topic file. You could correct the problem either by adding the IDH_ prefix to the two items in the Map or by removing IDH_ from the topic IDs in the topic file. This will eliminate the inconsistency and neither message will appear in the next build.

The IDH_ prefix is optional; you do not have to use it. It is simply a common standard. You can uses prefixes other than IDH_. This choice is useful if your programmers use a different standard. Or if you use more than one prefix for context-sensitive topic IDs. Often topic prefixes are used to Help manage topics and create reports sorted alphabetically by topic ID.

> **NOTE** *If you are using the compiler setting which excludes notes (NOTES=0) you will not see message HC1010. (Shown in Figure 19.16.)*

To specify alternate prefixes:

1. In Help Workshop, click the Map button.

2. In the text box below the topic IDs, type your prefixes. Separate your prefixes with spaces.

Note that the label above the text box is inaccurate as the specified prefixes are checked *in addition* to IDH_. In Figure 19.17 three additional prefixes are specified in addition to IDH_.

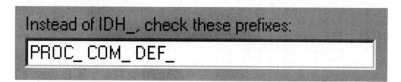

Figure 19.17. *Additional topic ID prefixes.*

The prefixes appear in the [OPTIONS] section of the project file after the PREFIX= command.

Displaying mapped Help topics

Once you have eliminated the inconsistencies during compiling, you can test that each mapped topic displays properly. You can elect to display a topic in a standard window or as a pop-up. The pop-up option is useful for displaying topics that will appear in pop-up windows like What's This?. While you could display a definition topic in a standard window, you wouldn't get a true sense of how it will look as a pop-up.

To display mapped Help topics:

1. In Help Workshop, select Run WinHelp from the File menu. The View Help file box appears. (This box is also discussed in Chapter 18, Creating the Project File.)

2. From the Mapped Topic IDs box, select the topic you wish to display.

3. In the "Open Help file..." section specify whether to display the topic in a standard window ("Invoked by a program") or as a pop-up.

4. Select View Help to display the topic.

If a topic appears, you have received confirmation that it has been mapped to a context ID. Check the topic that appears. Is it the one you expected? If not, you may have assigned the wrong topic ID in the topic file. Does the topic look right, with correct font, spacing, alignment etc.? If not, you need to adjust the topic in the topic file.

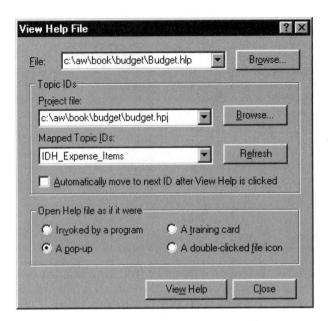

Figure 19.18. *Testing that topics are properly mapped.*

To automate the display test:

- If you are testing numerous topics, select the checkbox under the mapped topic IDs list. Now you can simply click View Help to display the next topic in the topic ID list.

Verifying topic ID assignments

While the previous section provides a quick procedure for making sure that the necessary topics have each been successfully mapped to a context ID, it does not prove that a topic is mapped to the *correct* ID. In order to test that, you need to display a topic by specifying the context ID.

To display a topic by context ID:

This procedure requires Help Author mode to be turned on or the SeqTopicKeys setting to be enabled. See Chapter 20, "Using Help Author mode." You also need a list of context IDs and the topics associated with each.

1. Launch your Help file and display any topic.

2. On the keyboard, press CTRL+SHIFT+J. The Jump box appears.

3. In the Enter topic identifier box, type a context ID you want to test.

4. Click Map Number, then OK.

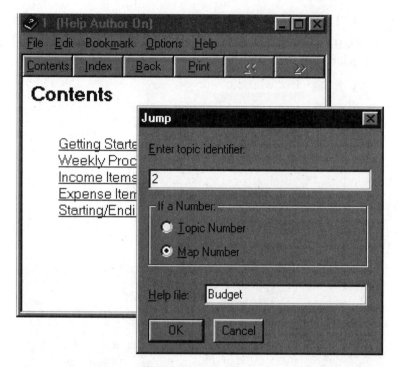

Figure 19.19. *Displaying a Help topic by context ID.*

When the topic appears, determine whether it is the one you expected. If not, you need to perform some analysis. At this point, a change is required either to the context ID or to the topic ID. Be aware that a change to the context ID in the Map may necessitate a similar change in the application code. A discussion between the programmer and Help author is usually required. If you elect to change the topic ID you will have to do so in the topic ID footnote of the topic file and in the Map. A change to a topic ID in the topic file may require adjustments to hotspots that reference that topic ID.

Verifying API calls

If you have properly mapped your context and topic IDs, the problems you encounter when testing the application should be minimal. A final level of testing is available through Help Workshop, which provides more precise testing of the calls to a topic. As explained earlier in this chapter, the application program makes calls to the WinHelp function with specific instructions on how to present the requested Help topic. If you know what calls are being used, you can reproduce them through Help Workshop.

To test WinHelp API calls:

1. Get a list of WinHelp API calls from the programmer for the Help events you want to test. This should include any necessary parameters.

2. From the Test menu, select WinHelp API.

3. Select the appropriate command from the Command list. For most calls to display a topic in a standard window, you would probably choose HELP_CONTEXT and specify a context ID. For pop-up definitions, the typical call is HELP_CONTEXTPOPUP.

4. Type the context ID as shown in Figure 19.20. Note that although the text box label is "Topic ID Number," that is an error. You are actually specifying the context ID.

5. Click Call. Verify that the appropriate topic appears.

Unless subsequent changes are made to the context or topic IDs, you can now be confident that the tested topic will display properly in formal tests with the actual application.

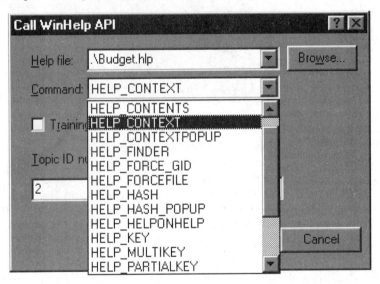

Figure 19.20. *Testing an API call in Help Workshop.*

FORMAL TESTING FROM THE APPLICATION

If you choose to perform the preliminary testing described in the previous sections, you should expect fewer problems during formal testing with the application. Once the application and Help file are bound together you need to test each Help call to ensure it works as expected. Formal testing is the key test, because it simulates how your user will be requesting the Help.

At a minimum, you need to test each of the Help events for which code segments were added to the application. Often a master test script lists the various windows and dialog boxes of the application and lists the Help events associated with each. This may include F1 key presses, SHIFT+F1, Help buttons, and What's This? definitions.

For example, if you've implemented F1 support, you need to press F1 from each dialog box in the application to make sure that the right topic is displayed. This is fairly straightforward. The same pattern would be used for Help buttons in the dialog boxes. If you are using field level Help calls, you will have to press F1 from each field.

Depending on your design, you may have to access Help in several different ways from the same screen element: a Help button, the question mark button, SHIFT+F1, F1, etc. With What's This? and SHIFT +F1, you may need to supply a sketch of the hotspot areas to the tester. Otherwise the tester may miss some areas.

For example, in Figure 19.21, the dotted lines indicate the boundaries of the three What's This? areas. Without a guide, the tester might miss testing some of the sections and waste time testing areas without hotspots. One solution is to draw hotspot outlines on a screen print of each dialog box.

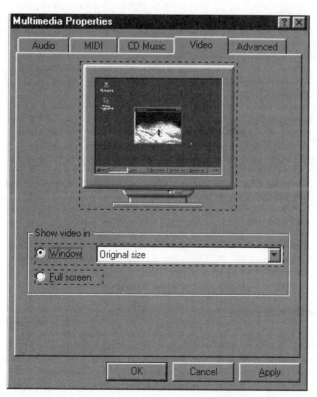

Figure 19.21. *Outlining What's This? hotspot areas.*

View messages to the WinHelp API

If you receive bug reports that incorrect topics appeared during testing, you can use the procedures detailed in the section "Preliminary testing" to track down the problem. However, once the application and the Help file are bound together, it can be more efficient to "spy" on the calls being made from the application to WinHelp. Help Workshop offers a message window that allows you to view the actual WinHelp call.

To view messages:

1. In Help Workshop, select WinHelp Messages from the View Menu. A window appears in which all calls to the WinHelp API will appear.

2. Start the application program and trigger the Help event you want to test.

3. Close the Messages window when you are finished testing.

For example, you receive a bug report that a "Topic Not Found" message appears when the user requests Help from the Expense Item dialog box of the application. You learn from the programmer that the Help event uses the HELP_CONTEXT call and that the context ID is 2. By inspecting the project file, you quickly see that an incorrect context ID value is being used. Through Help Workshop you make the change, then recompile. The WinHelp API test and Messages window confirms that the correction works.

The View Messages window is also useful for reviewing API calls when you do not have access to the Help event code. If you request Help from an application while View Messages is on in Help Workshop, it will report the calls made by the application.

Other common problems

The following are common sources of problems in programming Help:

- **Lack of Map control:** As described earlier, most problems in programming Help into the application can be traced to an inconsistency in the Map. Make sure that both programmers and Help authors communicate changes in topic IDs and context IDs.

- **Failure to include a header (.h) file:** If you encounter a series of errors messages "topic does not exist," check to make sure that you have included all the header files in the Map. A header file typically contains references to several context IDs which will not be compiled into Help if not specified in the Map.

- **Using spaces in topic IDs:** In WinHelp 4.0, a compiler bug affects topic IDs that are specified in include files. The compiler will not recognize topic IDs in the project file that use spaces. Although spaces are valid in WinHelp 4 topic IDs, they are not supported through include files.

Applications with built-in links to Help

Companies commonly distribute specially-designed Excel worksheets to employees for a variety of purposes, such as budgeting, time-keeping, and expense tracking. But these worksheets rarely come with documentation. Similarly, database forms created in tools like Access are custom designed for proprietary uses, but again, documentation is often scarce. A simple and elegant solution is to create a Help system that explains what the worksheet or database form is for and how to apply it to a particular job.

Since the developers of worksheets and databases may not have the programming resources necessary to create calls to WinHelp, Microsoft has built the necessary coding into the Excel and Access products. With either application, you do little more than reference the name of your Help system and then map the number of the topic you want to display.

To link to an Excel worksheet:

The link in an Excel worksheet to a Help file is formed using a module and a button.

1. Open the worksheet.

2. From the Insert menu click Macro, then Module. A blank module sheet appears.

3. In the module sheet type the following lines:

```
Sub buttonname()
      Application.Help "filename.hlp", context-id
End sub
```

   where *buttonname* is a unique name for the Help button, *filename* is the name of the Help file and *context-id* is the map number of the topic you wish to appear.

4. From the Edit menu click Sheet, then Hide. This hides the module from users.

Now you need to add a button to the worksheet to launch the Help file.

5. Click the button tool that is on the Drawing toolbar.

6. Outline a button shape.

7. When the Assign Macros box appears, select the button name from the list.

8. Highlight the default text of the button and type Help, or whatever label you want it to have.

9. Click on another cell and the Help button will immediately become hot, meaning that if you position the pointer over it, a hand will appear.

10. When you click the button, your Help file appears.

11. If you want more than one link to Help, you can repeat the three module statements, changing the button name and the context ID for each additional button.

To link Help to an Access form:

Linking a Help file to an Access form is even easier than working with an Excel worksheet. The coding is internal to Access, you just supply the name of the Help file and the context ID.

1. Open the form in Access.

2. From the View menu, select Properties. The last two properties listed are for linking to a Help system.

3. In the Help File box, type the name of your Help file.

4. In the Context ID box, type the Map number.

   When a user displays the form and presses F1, your Help topic appears.

   You may find other applications that provide this simple procedure for linking to Help files. PowerBuilder and x, two Windows application development tools, link to Help files in this way.

20

Compiling, Debugging, and Testing

During the final stages of Help production, you must perform three important tasks: compiling, debugging, and testing.

Compiling is building your topic and project files into the Help file that you distribute. It also builds your full-text search index file if you are using that feature.

Debugging is identifying and correcting errors that occur during the compilation.

Testing is reviewing the jumps, pop-ups, and other hypertext elements of the Help. It also may include proofreading the text.

Compiling the Help File

The Windows Help compiler uses the information from your topic file(s) and project file to form a binary file that can be read by the Windows Help application (WINHLP32.EXE). The process of compiling your Help is often referred to as a "build."

This section describes how to:

- Choose a Help compiler.

- Compile your Help project and display it.

- Reduce the size of your compiled Help file.

- Compile more than one project at once.

- Speed up compiling and correct memory problems.

> NOTE If you are using a contents file in your Help system, you simply distribute it along with your Help file. It is not part of the compiling process.

CHOOSING A HELP COMPILER

The Help compiler is included with many commercial software development products, including the Microsoft Win32 Software Development Kit (SDK), Microsoft C/C++, Microsoft Visual Basic, and various product offerings from Borland and others. It is also on the Microsoft Developer's Network CD (Level 2). Including previous versions of Windows, there are four compilers available.

Your decision on which compiler to use can be a tough one. While the WinHelp 4 compiler offers numerous improvements to Help system design, it also raises difficult compatibility questions. If you compile with the WinHelp 4 compiler, it means that your Help file will not run under WinHelp 3.1. The At a Glance table introduces the compatibility issue with descriptions of each compiler. Chapter 21, *Development Tasks and Strategies*, provides a detailed exploration of the various development and distribution options.

At a Glance Help Compilers

Compiler Name	Description
HCRTF.EXE	**WinHelp 4 compiler.** This compiler supports all the new Help features available for Windows 95 and Windows NT 3.51. Help files built with this compiler will not run under Windows 3.1 unless you also ship the version 1.3 Win32s files (See "Migrating to WinHelp 4" in Chapter 21).
HC31.EXE	**Windows 3.1 Help compiler.** Help files built with this compiler will run under Windows 95/NT but cannot provide any WinHelp 4 features. The exception is the use of the Contents/Index/Find features which do not require compiling.
HCP.EXE	**Windows 3.1 protected mode Help compiler.** This compiler is identical to the 3.1 compiler in functionality and compatibility, but makes better use of system memory.
HC30.EXE	**Windows 3.0 Help compiler.** This is the original compiler released with version 3.0 and is rarely used.

The compilers are occasionally modified by Microsoft for bug fixes. You can locate the version number of the WinHelp 4 compiler by selecting the Version command on the Help menu of Help Workshop. To display the version number of an earlier compiler, type the executable name (for example, HCP.EXE) at the DOS prompt.

COMPILING YOUR HELP PROJECT

For those familiar with the operation of the WinHelp 3.x compilers, using the WinHelp 4 compiler may be confusing. The three compilers available prior to HCRTF require you to execute a command at a DOS prompt consisting of the compiler name and the name of the project file. For example, the command HCP.EXE BUDGET.HPJ would launch the protected mode version of the WinHelp 3.1 compiler to work with the BUDGET project file. The result would be a Help file named BUDGET.HLP. However, the WinHelp 4 compiler is intertwined with Help Workshop. The procedure is to first launch Help Workshop and then use either menu or button commands to start the compiler. This may not apply if you are using third-party authoring tools, many of which have integrated the compiler into their products.

For a more detailed review of Help Workshop, see Chapter 22, *Authoring Tools.*

To compile from Help Workshop:

1. Run HCW.EXE. You can do so by using the Run command or by double-clicking on the program icon in Explorer. The program icon for Help Workshop is shown in Figure 20.1.

Figure 20.1. *Help Workshop program icon.*

2. From the File menu, click Open and select your project file. The contents of your project file appears.

3. From the File menu, click Compile.

4. In the Compile a Help File box, click Compile.

   A Compilation window appears displaying messages. The file size message, along with a count of topics, appears when compiling is complete.

NOTE *With the WinHelp 4 compiler it is not necessary to close your topic file as it was with previous versions.*

The Compile button on the toolbar can also be used to start compiling. The Compile button symbol is also referred to as the "grinder."

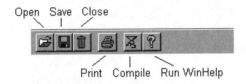

Figure 20.2. *Help Workshop tool buttons.*

One other option is the Save and Compile button in the lower portion of the project editor. Clicking this button saves the most recent changes to the project file before compiling.

To discontinue compiling:

Occasionally you may begin compiling and realize you forgot to make a certain adjustment. You can discontinue at any time by closing the small grinder window (Figure 20.3) which appears during compiling.

Figure 20.3. *Close the grinder window to discontinue compiling.*

COMPILING FROM THE COMMAND LINE

If you want to bypass Help Workshop, you can direct the compiler from the command line. This is useful if you want to link the compiler to an authoring tool such as the Help authoring template provided on your book disc. In order to do so you need to specify one or more command line switches in addition to the compiler name and the name of the project file.

The /C switch is required to start compiling. The optional /M and /E switches are useful for minimizing Help Workshop during compiling and then closing it. For an unknown reason, Help Workshop is launched whenever you execute HCW from the command line. See the *Help Author's Guide* for the complete HCW command reference. (Search under the index entry ="HCW command.")

To compile from the command line:

1. From the Windows Start button, click Run.

2. Type \WINDOWS\HELP\HCW /C /M /E *filename*

3. Click OK to start compiling.

   For example, the following command directs the compiler to work with the project file BUDGET.HPJ. The switches start the compiler, minimize the Help Workshop interface, and close Help Workshop when compiling is done:

   ```
   \WINDOWS\HELP\HCW /C /M /E \BUDGET\BUDGET.HPJ
   ```

> **TIP** *The Run box stores your previous commands. You can select and/or edit existing lines without having to retype them.*

You can also use a DOS command prompt to run the WinHelp 4 compiler similar to what has been the procedure for the WinHelp 3.x compilers. However, since HCRTF is a true, 32-bit Windows program, that method is not necessary.

REVIEWING THE COMPILED HELP FILE

Once the build is complete, you're ready to examine your new Help file. By default, the Help file is given the same name as the project file, but with the .HLP extension. For example, if your project file is named BUDGET.HPJ, the compiler builds a Help file named BUDGET.HLP.

To launch the Help file from Help Workshop:

In Help Workshop you run your Help file by clicking on the Run WinHelp (question mark) icon (see Figure 20.2) or by selecting Run WinHelp from the File menu.

1. From the File menu, select Compile or click the Run WinHelp button on the toolbar. This displays the Compile a Help File box.

2. Check the box **Automatically display Help file in WinHelp when done**. See Figure 20.4.

   If you want to see the compiler messages during the build you should also clear **Minimize window while compiling**. By default, Help Workshop is minimized during compiling since that increases compiler speed.

3. Click Compile. When compiling is complete, your Help file is automatically launched.

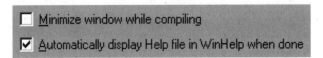

Figure 20.4. *Display options for compiling.*

Now, on successive builds you can start compiling by simply clicking the Save and Compile button. This saves you one click each time. Unfortunately, there is no way to save the settings described in Step 2. Each time you start Help Workshop you must repeat this procedure.

An alternate way to launch Help is select Run WinHelp from the File menu. However, this method is tedious and more particularly suited for testing context sensitive Help topics. This method is described in detail "To display mapped Help Topics" in Chapter 19.

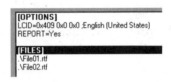

To launch Help from an icon:

You can launch your Help file from Explorer or the desktop just as with any other type of document. Simply double click the WinHelp icon associated with your Help file.If you are compiling Help from the command line, the /R switch directs WinHelp to display the Help file as soon as it is compiled.
The WinHelp 3.1 custom icon feature is no longer available when running a Help file under Windows 95. The default icon is always used.

To create shortcuts to Help files:

1. Click a Help file in Explorer.

2. From the File menu, click Create Shortcut. A shortcut icon appears in Explorer.

3. Drag the shortcut icon to the folder or desktop where you would like to locate it. Figure 20.5 shows several shortcut icons for Help files arranged on the desktop.

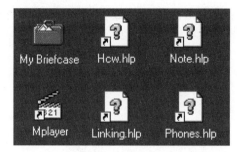

Figure 20.5. *Several shortcuts to Help files on the desktop.*

Another way to locate your Help file is to use the Documents command on the Start menu. The Documents menu displays the last fifteen documents you've worked with, including Help files.

REDUCING THE SIZE OF YOUR COMPILED HELP FILE

One of the most important considerations in the development of a Help file is its physical size. To address that factor, the WinHelp compiler has the ability to reduce the size of your compiled Help file through an on/off compression setting. By using compression you save your user disk space and reduce the cost of goods required to deliver your Help file. Using compression has no effect on the operation of the Help file. All of your jumps, pop-ups, buttons, etc., will work in the same manner and with the same performance.

The file size reductions are significant and have been increased over WinHelp 3.1 compression. Figure 20.6 shows the uncompressed and compressed file sizes for a range of topic file sizes. A 900K file when compressed is reduced to 115K, a savings of almost 800K.

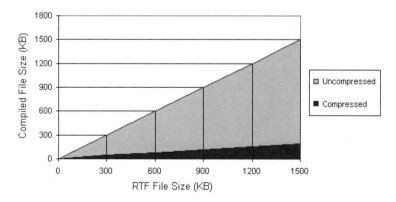

Figure 20.6. *Compiled help file size with and without compression.*

The actual compression ratio you achieve depends on several factors, including the size and number of topic and graphic files in your project. Graphics tend to compress much more than text.

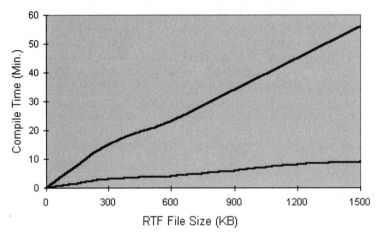

Figure 20.7. *Compile times with and without compression.*

By default, compression is turned off because it takes significantly longer to compile with compression on than with it off. Figure 20.7 shows the effect on compiling times with and without the compression setting turned on. A 900K file only takes 6 seconds to compile without compression as opposed to 34 seconds with compression turned on.

Generally you need to use compression only when you are ready to distribute the Help file. You may also want to try compression during Stage 2 of development (described in Chapter 21) to get an idea of the compressed size of your file.

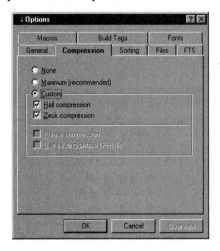

Figure 20.8. *Help Workshop compression options.*

The compression "levels" of WinHelp 3.1 have been replaced with more specific options. These are described in detail in the *Help Author's Guide* (Use the index entry "COMPRESS option"). If you want to get your Help file as small as possible, use the Maximum compression option. Figure 20.8 shows the compression options in Help Workshop. The What's This? topics for each option provide good definitions of each.

To enable compression:

1. In Help Workshop click Options, then Compression.

2. Click Maximum, then OK.

To disable compression:

You can temporarily disable compression before compiling.

1. In Help Workshop, click Files, then Compile.

2. Check **Turn off compression**, then click Compile.

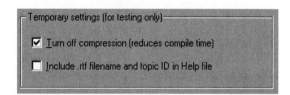

Figure 20.9. *You can temporarily disable compression during compiling.*

If you are compiling from the command line, the /N switch turns off compression when compiling the specified file, no matter what value is specified for the COMPRESS option in the project file(s).

CONTROLLING WHICH TOPICS ARE COMPILED

In a large Help project with an aggressive development schedule, it can be difficult to keep track of the completion status of individual topics. For example, going into a beta test cycle, some topics may be completely finished and approved, others may be complete but dependent on the results of the beta test, and yet others may not yet be suitable for a beta test. Rather than deleting topics or having a build with incomplete topics, you can use the WinHelp build tags.

To use this option you first add build tag footnotes to the topics in your topic file. (See "Adding conditional build tags" in Chapter 10 for this procedure.) Once build tags are assigned to your topics, you can specify which topics to include or exclude from a build by making a project file setting.

For example, assume you have assigned a build tag of "FINAL" to all topics that have been approved, a tag of "BETA" to those that are ready to be tested in the current build, and a tag of "INCOMPLETE" to those not yet ready for evaluation. In your project file you then make a setting that *includes* topics with the FINAL and BETA tags and *excludes* topics with INCOMPLETE tags.

To specify build tags:

1. In Help Workshop, click Options, then Build Tags.

   In the upper portion of the Build Tags tab you add tags of topics you want to include in the build. The lower portion specifies tags to exclude from the build. See Figure 20.10.

2. Click Add to add tags to either the upper or lower portion. The text you type must exactly match the text in the build tag footnotes used in your topic file.

   The project file editor will display the build tags in the [EXCLUDE] and [INCLUDE] sections. See Figure 20.11.

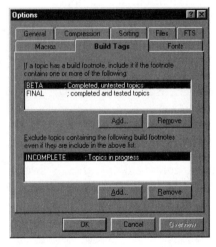

Figure 20.10. *Making the INCLUDE/EXCLUDE settings in Help Workshop.*

```
[EXCLUDE]
INCOMPLETE          ; Topics in progress

[INCLUDE]
BETA          ; Completed, untested topics
FINAL          ; completed and tested topics
```

Figure 20.11. *The appearance of the INCLUDE/EXCLUDE sections in the project editor.*

The Boolean operators used in WinHelp 3.1 are still supported by the compiler, however they are not supported in Help Workshop. You need to form your BUILD option and BUILD TAGS section in a text editor instead. See the "BUILD" topic in the online Help Author's Guide for details.

> **NOTE** *The presence of an [INCLUDE] or [EXCLUDE] section supersedes any BUILD option you may have specified.*

COMPILING MULTIPLE PROJECT FILES

If you are developing a Help system that consists of two or more Help files, you can automate the build process by using a *makefile*. A Help makefile is a simple text file that contains the names of all of the project files included in the system. Instead of specifying a single project file when you're ready to compile, you specify the name of the makefile. The compiler reads the makefile and compiles each of the projects in the order in which they are listed. The Help makefile must include an .HMK extension.

Figure 20.12 shows the contents of a makefile called DOUBLE.HMK which specifies two project files.

```
MODULE-A.HPJ
MODULE-B.HPJ
```

Figure 20.12. *Makefile DOUBLE.HMK.*

You cannot compile a makefile from within Help Workshop, you must use the command line as described in "Compiling from the command line" earlier in this chapter. Figure 20.13 shows the command to compile the makefile DOUBLE.HMK. The /C switch starts the compiler.

```
HCW /C C:\DOUBLE.HMK
```

Figure 20.13. *Command line to compile the makefile.*

The help files are compiled one at a time and messages for each build appear in the compilation window of Help Workshop.

SPEEDING UP THE BUILD

The WinHelp 4 compiler is much faster than previous versions. However, large topic files can still take a significant amount of time to compile. As time grows tight at the end of a project, build performance becomes critical. Consider the following suggestions to speed up the build:

Defer compression until necessary

Compiling a Help file with compression enabled can take ten to twenty times longer than compiling Help without compression. Therefore, avoid compressing your Help file until you really need a compressed version. See "Reducing the size of your compiled Help file" earlier in this chapter.

Use a faster computer

Your computer processor obviously plays a large role in how fast you can compile a Help file. You should consider buying the fastest computer you can afford for your Help development machine.

Divide the Help content into separate topic files

One technique which doesn't require hardware upgrades is to divide your topic file into separate smaller files. You can then debug and test these sections independently. Although this doesn't change the speed of compiling the final version of your Help file, it can make it easier to edit your topic files and debug your Help system. See the section "Organizing your Topic Files" in Chapter 10."

You can do a partial build by clicking the Files button in Help Workshop and removing the topic file(s) you don't want to compile. You can always add them back later. Or open the project file in a text editor, display the [FILES] section, and enter a semicolon at the beginning of the line listing for each topic file you don't want to compile. A different approach is to use build tags in your topic file. See Chapter 12, *Formatting Topics*," for more information about build tags. With either approach you may receive warning messages during compiling if the compiler encounters jumps or pop-ups to topics contained in the excluded files. These messages will not prevent the Help file from compiling.

CORRECTING MEMORY PROBLEMS

The "out of memory" errors common with WinHelp 3.1 compiling have been largely eliminated in WinHelp 4. As a 32-bit Windows application, the WinHelp 4 compiler benefits from Windows 95's improved memory management. However, in the event you encounter memory errors, consider the following suggestions:

Add more system memory

Windows 95 requires more system memory for optimum performance than does Windows 3.1. Although Microsoft claims 4 MB of random access memory (physical RAM) is sufficient to run Windows 95, consider 8 MB as the bare minimum for a machine used to develop Help, with 16 MB recommended.

Close any applications that you are not using

Depending on the amount of system memory available, you may want to close the Windows applications you are not using before starting the build.

Reserve sufficient disk space

The compiler can run out of memory if there's not enough disk space on your system, especially when you're compressing a Help file. If you're building a large Help file with compression on, you may need up to five times as much disk space as the combined size of your topic files. The actual amount of space required depends on the size of your Help file. The TMPDIR option in the project file allows you to specify a folder the compiler should use when creating temporary files for the build. By default, it uses the folder specified by the TEMP environment variable. Help Workshop usually does not create temporary files unless your Help file exceeds 8 MB in size.

To specify a temporary folder:

1. In Help Workshop, click Options, then Files.

2. Click the Browse button next to the **TMP folder** box.

3. Select the folder you want, then click OK.

   You can specify other drives, including network drives (logical or UNC pathnames).

Debugging the Help file

During the compiling phase of Help development you may receive messages which indicate some problem with the build. These "bugs" are usually caused by incorrect topic file formatting, erroneous topic IDs in the topic file, or invalid statements in the project file. It is not uncommon to make coding mistakes due to typing errors or incorrect syntax.

In order to correct these bugs you first need to evaluate the compiler messages for the source of the problem. Then you need to locate that source. Finally make the appropriate correction.

This section includes:

- A description of how the Help compiler displays messages.

- A discussion of how to minimize problems in your builds.

- A list of common messages, what they mean, and how to deal with them.

UNDERSTANDING COMPILER MESSAGES

When compiling begins, a Compilation window opens in Help Workshop. A series of diagnostic messages appears during the compiling process.

If the Help compiler doesn't encounter any problems, the final compiler message indicates: "0 notes, 0 warnings, 0 errors." Often, however, the compiler encounters problems and displays messages, such as those shown in Figure 20.14.

Each diagnostic message consists of a message number, a message type, and the diagnostic description. Many messages also reference a topic number and topic file. See Figure 20.15.

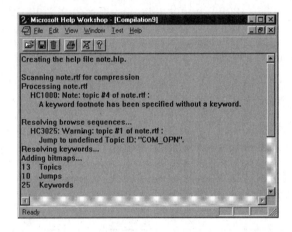

Figure 20.14. *Sample compiling messages.*

Figure 20.15. *Components of a diagnostic compiler message.*

Types of diagnostic messages

The compiler displays three types of diagnostic messages: errors, warnings, and notes.

Errors typically occur when the compiler can't find a topic file or the project file. Errors completely stop the compiling process. Most messages are technically not errors.

Warnings are less serious than errors: they don't stop the build, and usually indicate that the compiler encountered a formatting error or can't find a topic ID. Although you can view a Help file that contains compiler warnings, certain parts of the Help system won't work until you. have performed the debugging routines described later in this section.

Notes are displayed when the compiler encounters something in your topic or project files that is not consistent or is not typically found in Help systems. One example would be if you had added a K-footnote to a topic but neglected to place any keywords in it. The following note would appear: "A keyword footnote or command is specified without a keyword." Notes do not halt compiling nor do they affect the functioning of any elements. Notes are new with WinHelp 4.

The topic number

In messages related to a problem in a topic file, a *topic number* is specified after the message type. During compiling, each topic is assigned a unique topic number. This is not the same as the topic ID. The topic number that the Help compiler displays is based on that topic's position in the topic file. Starting with the beginning of the first topic file, each hard page break is interpreted as a new topic and is assigned the next consecutive topic number.

Figure 20.16 shows the first portion of a topic file COMMANDS.RTF. The compiler recognizes the first topic "New command" as topic #1, "Open command" as topic #2, and "Save command" as topic #3.

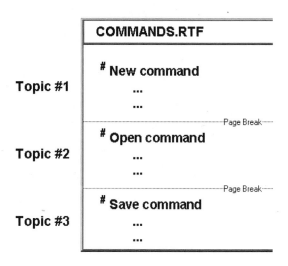

Figure 20.16. *The compiler references topics by their position in the topic file.*

If more than one topic file is specified in the project file, the topic numbering follows the order in which they are listed in the [FILES] section. For example, if the last topic in COMMANDS.RTF is numbered 87, the first topic in PROCED.RTF is numbered 88 and so on.

```
[FILES]
COMMANDS.RTF
PROCED.RTF
GLOSSARY.RTF
```

Depending on the document's page format and the length of the topics, there may be a discrepancy between the number of printed pages and the number of hard page breaks. The compiler doesn't count the actual number of *pages* in the topic file as displayed in your word processor; it counts *hard page breaks.*

The **GoToTopic** macro (in the WinHelp4 template on your book disc) prompts you for a topic number, and searches for it by counting page breaks. In WinHelp 4, you can enable Help Author mode which provides special features for finding topics by topic number. Help Author mode is discussed later in this chapter.

The message number

Each message used by Help Workshop is identified by a specific number. These identifying numbers help in your debugging task, as described in the section "Common compiler messages" later in this chapter.

MESSAGE VIEWING OPTIONS

Viewing your compiler messages is a critical part of the debugging process. You have several options for fine-tuning their display. These include deleting. saving, and hiding messages.

To delete messages:

The compiler messages are displayed by default in the Compilation window in Help Workshop.

To delete the contents of the Compilation window:

- Click the Close (trash can) button or click Close from the File menu.

    If you recompile without deleting the contents of the Compilation window, the window contents are replaced automatically.

To save messages:

You may want to save your messages into a log file which you can open using any ASCII text editor. This process is especially helpful if you have numerous messages. The Compilation window is limited to 64K of information, but, there is no limit to the amount of information that Help Workshop can write to a log file.

1. In Help Workshop, click Options, then Files.

2. Type the name of your errorfile in the **Log file** box.

    You can specify an absolute or a relative pathname if you want the errorfile to be saved in a location other than the project folder. The log file appears as the "ERRORLOG" setting in the [OPTIONS] section of the project editor window.

> **TIP** *If you like to use your word processor to review log files instead of a text editor, use the appropriate default extension for your documents. For example in Word, type ERRORLOG.DOC.*

To hide messages during compiling:

If you don't care to view any messages at all during compiling, you can minimize Help Workshop at that time.

1. In Help Workshop, click the Compile button.

2. In the Compile box, check the box **Minimize Windows while compiling**. Help Workshop and the grinder icon disappear during compiling and reappear when the Help file is complete.

   If you are compiling from the command line, use the /M switch to minimize Help Workshop.

To hide notes:

Many of the notes can be distracting if you are not concerned about the information they contain. For example, you may already know that "Table cell borders are not supported," which is a notes message. You can elect to turn off notes completely for your builds.

1. In Help Workshop, click Options, then General.

2. In the **While Compiling Display** box, clear the **Notes** box.

   This is the equivalent of adding the NOTES=0 statement to the [OPTIONS[section of the project file.

   Notes are supported only in WinHelp 4.

To hide selected messages:

The disadvantage of the previous procedure is that it inhibits the display of all Notes, including ones that may possibly be of interest to you. Also, it doesn't hide error or warning messages. However, you can elect to inhibit the display of any individual diagnostic messages.

1. In Help Workshop, click Options, then General.

2. Click the Errors button to display the Error messages box.

3. Click Add and type the number of the specific message you want to hide.

   This is the equivalent of adding the IGNORE=*number* statement to the [OPTIONS] section of the project file.

For example, if the "Table cell borders are not supported" message is starting to irritate you, just specify its number, "1012."

To hide processing messages:

An additional option of marginal value is available in controlling the display of messages. Disabling the "Progress" setting in Help Workshop eliminates some of the repetitive processing messages of the compiler. The diagnostic and summary messages are not affected.

1. In Help Workshop, click Options, then General.

2. In the **While Compiling Display** box, clear the **Progress** box.

   This is the equivalent of adding the REPORTS=NO statement to the [OPTIONS] section of the project file.

TROUBLESHOOTING COMMON PROBLEMS

This section presents a troubleshooting guide for the most common messages you may encounter while compiling Help. The messages described here probably account for at least 80 percent of all the messages encountered by Help authors during compiling. Advanced users, as well as novices, will frequently encounter them.

Most compiler messages from WinHelp 3.1 have been revised and renumbered in WinHelp 4. The corresponding 3.1 error messages are provided here as a cross-reference.

The Help Author's Guide contains a description for every diagnostic message. You can find them by their message numbers. Each message displayed by the compiler has its own number preceded by "HC."

To locate a message definition:

1. In Help Workshop, select Help, then Help Topics.

2. In the Index, type "HC *message number.*"

A single mistake in a topic file can often lead to several warnings from the Help compiler. For example, if a topic ID contains a typographical error, the compiler will display a warning message each time it tries to reference that topic ID from a jump or pop-up. Correcting the topic ID footnote will correct all warnings related to it.

HC1003: Note: A paragraph marker is formatted as a hidden character.

3.1 ➡ 4753 Hidden Paragraph

There is a paragraph mark in the specified topic which is formatted as hidden text. Although this does not prevent compiling, it merges consecutive sentences in the Help file. To fix the problem, find the hidden paragraph mark and deselect the "hidden" attribute. The **ReplaceHiddenParagraphs** macro in the WinHelp 4 template automates the process of replacing hidden paragraph markers.

Figure 20.17 shows the effect of a hidden paragraph mark. The labels a "Income Items" and "Expense Items" are positioned on the same line.

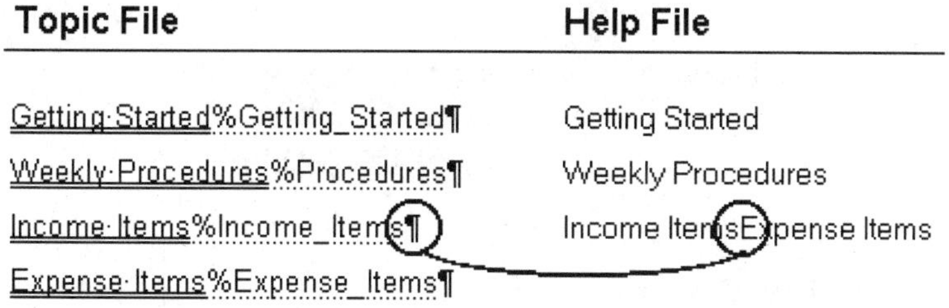

Figure 20.17. *The effect of a hidden paragraph marker in Help.*

HC1010: Note: The following mapped Topic IDs were not used in any topic: topic_ID.

3.1 ➡ 4098 Context String(s) in [MAP] Section Not Defined in any Topic

This message is related to context-sensitive topics. A topic ID you've listed in the [MAP] section of the project file is not specified in your topic files. Check the project file for misspelled topic IDs. Remove from the [MAP] section any topic IDs that are not associated with context-sensitive links. This message can be related to message HC3026.

HC3025: Warning: Jump to undefined Topic ID: "topic_ID."

3.1 ➡ 4113 Unresolved Jump or Pop-up *Contextname*

The most common warning message encountered during the build process is associated with erroneous topic IDs. If the compiler can't find the topic ID specified as the destination for a jump or pop-up, it generates a warning.

When coding your topic file manually (as opposed to using an authoring tool), the problem often results from a typographical error. The following example shows the message displayed when compiling the BUDGET.RTF topic file.

```
HC3025: Warning: topic #1 of .\Budget.rtf :
        Jump to undefined Topic ID: "Getting_Stated".
```

The offending topic is shown in Figure 20.18. The hotspot reference in the See Also section is directing a jump to the "Getting Started topic." However, the target topic ID used in the jump was misspelled as "Getting_Stated," omitting the "r." Because the compiler can't find "Getting_Stated" the warning message appears.

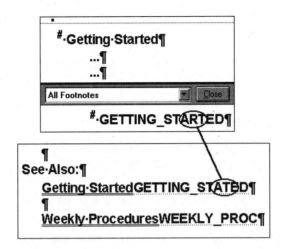

Figure 20.18. *A topic with a misspelled topic ID reference.*

This message can also be caused by a formatting error. You can avoid this error by making sure the hidden attribute is properly applied to each topic ID. Another source for this warning message is a change in a # footnote or deletion of a topic. If jumps or pop-ups in the topic file address the modified or deleted topic, message #3025 appears. This message flags only problems with standard jumps or pop-ups. It does not work with hotspots established with KLinks, ALinks, or the Jump macros. Those need to be tested separately. (See the Testing section later in this chapter.)

> **TIP** *After you've started developing your Help system, you should avoid changing the name of an existing topic ID unless you carefully locate all references to that ID. Otherwise you will invite a host of errors. If you must change a topic ID, carefully use the search and replace feature of your word processor to make the necessary adjustments throughout the topic file.*

HC3026: Warning: topic #k of filename.rtf : The Topic ID "test" has already been defined in topic j in file Test.rtf.

3.1 ➡ 4011 Context string *contextname* already used

Each topic ID footnote must be unique. The message gives you the topic numbers for the first and subsequent occurrences of the topic ID. One of them must be modified. Change any jump references to the topic ID you revise.

HC3029: Warning: The file format of the bitmap file C:*filename* is unrecognized or unsupported.

3.1 ➡ 4692 Unrecognized Graphic Format

You can use only Windows bitmaps and metafiles in the topic file. If you use some other graphic format, the Help file still compiles, but an "Unable to display graphic" message box appears in place of the specified graphic.

HC3046: Warning: The xxx.rtf file is not an RTF (Rich Text Format) file. It appears to have been saved as a Microsoft Word document.

3.1 ➡ 4616 File *filename* Is Not a Valid .RTF Topic File

You probably saved your topic file in your word processor's native format rather than in the required rich-text format.

HC3048: Warning: Nonscrolling region defined after scrolling region.

3.1 ➡ 4792 Nonscrolling region defined after scrolling region.

The non-scrolling region must be the very first paragraph in a topic OR a continuous series of paragraphs starting with the first paragraph. This warning usually occurs when there are two paragraphs formatted with the "Keep With Next" attribute separated by a paragraph without that attribute. In such a case, only the paragraphs before the paragraph without the "Keep With Next" attribute will appear in the nonscrolling region. This often happens unexpectedly when one style tag is based on another style tag that happens to specify "Keep With Next."

HC3107: Warning: A browse sequence has already been defined for this topic.

3.1 ➡ 4312 Browse Sequence Already Defined

Each topic can have only one browse sequence footnote. Also, each browse sequence label must be unique. Check for duplicates.

HC5011: Error: file*name*.hpj : Cannot open the file "filename.rtf."

3.1 ➡ 1230 File *filename* Not Found

You probably changed the name of the topic file, changed the name of the folder in which the topic file is located, or you moved the topic file. The topic file should be in the folder specified in your project file.

Note that with WinHelp 4, your .RTF file can be open in your word processor during compiling. This was not possible in 3.1; message 1230 would appear.

TARGETING THE PROBLEM AREA

A handful of diagnostic messages, described in the previous section, account for the majority of problems flagged during compiling. However, as you spend more and more time with WinHelp development, you will continue to experience new (for you) diagnostic messages. In order to work through these obstacles you can rely partly on the troubleshooting message topics in the *Help Author's Guide*. These topics are fairly comprehensive. You can make even better use of them by understanding that all of the diagnostic messages you encounter can be traced to one of three categories of problems: your computer system, the project file, or the topic file.

System problems are generally related to file management and system resources rather than problems with your actual Help content. System problem messages are often error messages and therefore halt the build. Unlike warnings and notes, errors cannot be ignored, even temporarily. System problems are at once the easiest and hardest to solve. Easy, because the diagnostic messages tend to very clear; hard, because the solution may be beyond your capabilities. These problems are highly dependent on your individual computer and software setup. For example, the message *HC5011: Error: Cannot open the file "Budget.rtf."* indicates a problem the compiler is having physically finding or opening the topic file. A more problematic message is *HC6000: Error: Help Workshop is out of memory*. In this case you may have to close applications or even add more memory to your system! There are no easy answers and you may need to get technical assistance.

Project file problems are generally easy to diagnose and easy to fix. These messages can usually be identified by references in the message description to the project file, or to "sections," or the description may include brackets [ ]. Project file messages are usually warnings or notes. You can temporarily ignore them but often something of major importance will not work properly in your compiled Help file. Explore the project file settings explained in Chapter 18, *Creating the Project File.* Also, in the *Help Author's Guide* a useful series of topics is listed in the WinHelp Reference under "Project File Commands."

The message *HC3014: Warning: Window name "desc" has already been used* provides a clue if you recognize that Window names are defined in the project file. Likewise the reference to "mapped" in *HC1010: Note: The following mapped topic IDs are not used in any topic: [ ]* provides a similar lead. Corrections to the project file are quick and easy to make once you know the problem. However, the best course of action is to use Help Workshop or another authoring tool, since this dramatically reduces the chances of project file problems and makes changes very easy to make.

Topic file problems are the Help author's constant companion. One of the reasons for this is that the topic file is the area where we spend the vast majority of our development time. As we code our topics, jumps, pop-ups and other Help components, typographical and syntax errors are almost inevitable. Topic file problems arise even when you use authoring tools. Since Help is so extensible, developers are always coming up with techniques that aren't explicitly supported by their authoring tools. If your authoring tool does not support a feature you want to use, manual coding is required.

As is true with the project file, becoming familiar with topic file terms can point you in the direction of the solution. For example, in the message *HC1003: Note: Topic #1: A paragraph mark is formatted as a hidden character* the reference to "formatting" is a tip toward the topic file. It is helpful to study the chapters in this book related to topic file coding. Also in the WinHelp Reference, review "Topic File Commands."

The topic file is often directly indicated by the presence of a topic number in the message description as in message *HC3025: Warning: topic #1 of .\Budget.rtf : Jump to undefined Topic ID: "topicID."* While this clearly indicates a problem in the topic file, the more difficult task is finding the offending topic. The topic number is a unique number assigned to each topic during compiling and is unrelated to the topic ID. In order to search for that number, you need to rely on assistance from your authoring tool or to use Help Author mode as described in the next section.

Topic or project file? There are a few messages that are applied to both project and topic file problems. The messages regarding macros are typical of this. Consider the pair of messages below. The descriptions are the same. However if you examine the messages closely, you will see that in the first case the .HPJ file is referenced and in the second the .RTF file is referenced, along with a topic number.

```
HC3005: Warning: Budget.hpj : The macro variable "Browse()" is
undefined.
HC3005: Warning: topic #1 of .\Budget.rtf : The macro variable
"Browse()" is undefined.
```

Testing the Help file

After you've compiled and debugged the Help file, you'll want to test the finished product to make sure it doesn't contain any errors. If you do encounter some problems, you will have to enter the compiling and debugging phases again. This is a constant cycle in Help development.

Unfortunately, there is no automated way to test a compiled Help file: it usually involves examining the Help file topic by topic. Therefore, a formal testing strategy is needed to review even basic Help files.

It is useful to break down the testing of a Help system into several components. This breakdown helps you to concentrate on the unique challenges of each, and to split the testing among different members of your Help team.

Step-by-step strategies are provided for:

- Testing or proofreading the content.

- Testing the hypertext components.

- Testing the Help Browser components.

- Testing graphics, context-sensitive Help, and localized Help.

Also included is a section of testing techniques that apply to all areas.

TESTING (PROOFREADING) THE CONTENT

Although included here under the banner of "testing," the process of reviewing text for spelling, formatting, and grammar is known more commonly as proofreading. The amount of time you'll need to spend proofreading the compiled Help content will usually depend on whether or not the Help text came from a print manual and how much it was modified.

If it is based upon existing print material, much of the grammar- and spell- checking may be complete. If the Help material is new or substantially modified from the print, proofreading must be employed throughout the Help development process, starting with the first draft.

Other publications provide in-depth coverage of many aspects of proofreading. This section highlights the areas that require special attention with online Help.

Proofread from paper

Proofreading online documents can be problematic for several reasons, including the limited resolution of computer displays, the difficulty in making extensive editing marks and comments, and the challenge of getting a global perspective on material divided into small topics. Therefore, you should always print the Help text and perform your review on paper. Since opening the Help file and printing individual topics is so time-consuming, the easiest approach is usually just to print the topic files themselves.

> **TIP** *Before printing the topic files, use the search and replace feature of your word processor to remove the hard page breaks between topics. This significantly reduces the amount of paper used. As soon as printing is complete, close the topic file WITH-OUT SAVING it. The **PrintHelpTopics** macro in the WinHelp 4 template assists with this task.*

Formatting errors

Examine the fonts you used for your Help text on various systems to make sure there is no font substitution occurring. Look for missing bold and color attributes in hotspots. It's a good idea to check the text colors on a variety of systems. Examine the alignment of hanging indents and tables, particularly on different monitor resolutions. Look for uniform spacing before and after paragraphs. Make sure the text is wrapping properly beside graphic images. For tips on ensuring that these kinds of items are formatted properly before testing, see Chapter 12, *Formatting Topics*. Using a style sheet will improve the consistency of your Help content and make it easy to quickly modify specific attributes.

Spelling errors

There's no excuse for spelling errors in any professional document, including Help text. If you are converting from a print document, you'll probably have already spell-checked and proof-read the material. If you are creating your Help text from scratch, it is wise to carefully proof-read all the Help content from printed drafts.

> **TIP** *The full-text search Find feature can be an excellent tool for final spell-checking, even if you don't use the feature in your distributed Help system. The Find page is enabled by default when a contents file is used. You can scroll through the list of words and catch misspellings more easily than when looking at the words in the con-text of a topic. You can also flag inappropriate terms and old product names and ver-sion numbers.*

Inappropriate "print" terms

Watch for text that is inappropriate for online use, such as "at the bottom of the page" or "as shown below." Although these references are difficult to catch when you're reviewing the topic file from print-outs, they become painfully obvious when you see them online. As you begin locating inappropriate phrases, you can use your word processor's search and replace feature to remove the phrases from the topic file wherever they occur. The full-text search feature can again provide assistance in rooting out these terms.

TESTING THE HYPERTEXT COMPONENTS

While proofreading is common to both print and online materials, testing hypertext elements is unique to Help. Online Help contains a number of features which need to be individually tested, including jumps and popups, browse sequences, macros, keywords, and window attributes. The key is to develop a testing plan. While it is tempting to just start clicking away in the Help file, that method is prone to mistakes. The following testing methodology can maximize your testing effort and minimize any omissions.

1. Launch the compiled Help file and, beginning with the Contents page of the Help Topics browser look for any spelling or typographical errors in the book and topic items. A separate section below provides special recommendations for testing the contents file. If you are using a contents topic, check the spelling of the text or hotspots.

2. Click each jump to verify that the right topic appears. If not, make a note of the error. If there is an error, it may prevent you from continuing to test that branch of the Help file. If so, make an additional note to check the complete branch when you receive the next build. Another alternative is to use the Ask on Hotspots command (described below) which allows you to move past broken jumps.

   If another person will be making corrections in the topic file, your notes need to be very precise. See "Flagging errors with bookmarks," later in this chapter for a technique that will help you document errors.

   If there is more than one jump or link in a topic, be careful to test each one. Make sure you follow each branch of the Help file, testing the hotspots in each.

> **TIP** *If you are using invisible hotspots, it may be difficult to find them. To highlight all hotspots in a topic, press ctrl+tab.*

3. Click each **KLink/ALink** hotspot. If the Found Topics box appears, test each title in the list.

   There are numerous options for the display of a linking hotspot. Make sure you know which ones are being used.

4. In the testing of any jumps or links, you need to be aware of the forms of secondary windows that are being employed. Check to make sure that a topic appears in the appropriate window and that the window appears with the proper size, position, and color.

5. Click each pop-up hotspot to verify that the right topic appears. Make a note of the title and notice that you only have to review the content once for a given pop-up topic: for each subsequent occurrence you can simply verify that the hotspot displays the correct topic.

6. Test the browse sequences next. If your browse sequences don't follow the linear order of the topic file, you must know how each browse sequence should behave, including its first and last topic.

> **TIP** *The ForeHelp authoring tool is excellent for managing, creating and maintaining browse sequences in a way that eliminates virtually all errors.*

7. Test the keyword list to make sure the entries are accurate and comprehensive. Display each topic in order to verify that the jumps from each keyword are accurate. If you are using the Help Browser, see the section about the Index page later in this chapter.

8. Finally, if the Help system is using any custom buttons, menu items, or other Help macros, make sure to include these in the testing plan. The Ask on Hotspots feature also works with macros.

> **TIP** *One of the most difficult parts of testing is keeping track of what you have checked. It would be nice if you could automatically generate a schematic of your Help system, but Help Workshop has no such tool. An authoring tool which has attempted to fill this gap is ForeHelp. This tool, which is described in Chapter 22, provides a comprehensive reporting facility. You can generate a list of all topics showing the destinations of jumps and pop-ups. You can also list browse sequences, keywords, and topic IDs. Even if you use another authoring tool, ForeHelp can be used to generate reports for your project. With the reports in hand you can check off the various jumps as you test them.*

Example

In Figure 20.19, the tester starts with the Contents page. The first book is "How To" and it contains two topic items. The first topic item is a jump to a procedure named "Topic A." Topic A in turn contains an Alink hotspot button to Topic B and Topic C. The tester follows the Topic B path—the first jump in the Topics Found list. Topic B has no jumps, just text. Now the tester returns to Topic A using the Back button and clicks the Alink hotspot again. This time the tester selects Topic C and examines that branch and any sub-branches it contains. When all of the How To branches are reviewed, the tester returns to the Contents page. This method is repeated until all the sections have been reviewed.

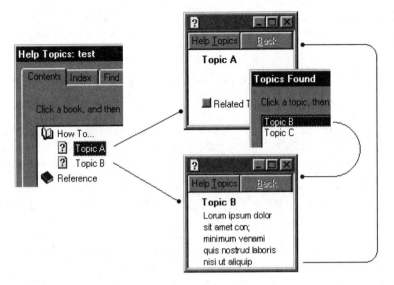

Figure 20.19. *Using a testing pattern.*

TESTING THE HELP BROWSER COMPONENTS

If you are using the Help Browser dialog in your Help system, your testing plan must take on additional responsibilities. This section describes problems and solutions specific to the Contents, Index, and Find pages.

The Contents page

The centerpiece of most Windows 95 Help systems is the Contents page of the Help browser. It is also one of the most error-prone components of WinHelp development. A major problem is that there is no direct link between the topic ID specified in the contents file and the associated topic in the topic file. If the topic ID is typed incorrectly in the contents file or changed in the topic file, there will be an error when a user attempts to use that jump.

To prevent this you must test the integrity of the contents file items and test the links to the Help file. Help Workshop provides a command, described below, for accomplishing this. You may find a better solution with a third party authoring tool.

To test the contents file:

1. Open the contents file in Help Workshop.

2. Click each of the books to make sure the subordinate books and topics appear. Spell-check each of the items.

3. From the Test menu, select contents file, then click Test.

Help Workshop examines each of the statements in the contents file to make sure the syntax is correct. The Compilation window appears to display messages from the test. If there are no problems with syntax, you receive a count of the number of books and topics in your contents file. If there are problems, a diagnostic message appears. These diagnostic messages are not covered in the *Help Author's Guide.*

> **NOTE** *The syntax test assumes that you have used Help Workshop to create your contents file. If you typed the command statements (Base, Index, etc.) manually and there is a syntax error, the message displayed by the syntax test may be incorrect.*

4. Click Yes to test your jumps.

The Help file specified in the contents file is launched and each jump is tested. A topic will be displayed in a secondary window if such a window was referenced in the topic item or a secondary window identifier was used in the topic file. If the test encounters an error, a message appears with information about the offending topic. See Figure 20.20. Unfortunately this message does not appear in the Compilation window and you can't save it to a file. You need to write down the reference.

5. Click OK to continue the test. When it is concluded your Help file is closed.

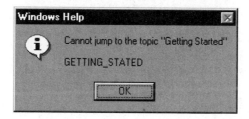

Figure 20.20. *An error message displayed while testing the contents file.*

6. In Explorer, double click the icon for the associated Help file. Make sure the Help Topics browser appears.

The Index page

Whereas the Contents page is highly susceptible to broken jumps, those kind of errors are rare with the Index page. You still need to test each item, but the likelihood of errors is very small, because the keywords which appear in the Index are associated directly with each topic. Even if a keyword is misspelled, it will still bring up the proper topic. Of most importance is to test keywords for writing errors.

1. Launch the Help file and display the Index tab of the Help browser.

2. Proofread each entry for spelling, punctuation, capitalization, and grammatical structure.

> **TIP** *Use the "K keywords" report to generate a list of all the keywords in your Help file. You can then run your word processor's spell checker on the output file. Unfortunately, the topic titles, also included in the report, get in the way.*

3. If you are using two-level indexing, check to make sure the various keywords are aligned at the appropriate first or second level position.

4. Click each index entry to see if the expected topic appears. If you have coded topics to appear in secondary windows make sure the desired window is used. Use the Help Topics or Index button in the button bar of your Help window to return to the Help browser. The Index remembers your place.

   Also check any topics which are supposed to contain a topic entry macro.

5. If there is more than one found topic for a keyword, check the link to each. Check the spelling of the topic titles.

> **TIP** *You can quickly reveal the topic ID of any topic in your help system by using the procedure described later in this chapter in the section "Displaying topic information with Help Author."*

6. Once you've located the errors, return to the topic file to make corrections.

If you are supporting the same keyword footnotes for Windows 3.1 and 95, there are subtle differences in the operation of the Index. See, "Migrating to WinHelp 4" in Chapter 21.

The Find page

Testing the Find full-text search (FTS) feature is much easier than testing either the Contents or Index pages, primarily because it is not practical or necessary to test each word in the FTS index. Because the words in the FTS list are not hotspots or index entries, there is no coding involved. You can be certain that selecting any word in the list will display the appropriate topic.

- If you are shipping the .FTS and .GID files with your software, install the software and make sure the Help file appears properly.

- Check the size of the .FTS file and make sure it is of acceptable size for distribution.

- Make sure the final .FTS file is generated and tested AFTER the final build of the Help file.

- If you are not shipping the .FTS and .GID files, install your software and test the Find Setup wizard. Try the various options to see if you get the anticipated results.

- As stated at the start of this section, the Find can be a useful tool for proofreading your text.

Modular Help systems

If you are combining several help files to work together as a unit, you need to perform additional testing to the system as a whole and for the individual components.

- Assemble the entire Help system in a single folder including all contents and help files. Then test the Contents, Index, and Find pages as described above.

- Make sure the Contents tab contains all of the combined entries and that the items appear in the appropriate places.

- Make sure the Index page displays the keywords in a combined alphabetical list.

- Remove the contents and help files of any supplemental components and test the master help file and contents file again. If the supplemental components are can be used independently you will have to test each of them as well.

- If your Help system will be installed by an installation program, test the modules again after installing them from the master distribution disks.

NOTE *If you are including an uninstall program you may want to alert the programmer that the hidden .GID, .FTS, and .FTG files should also be removed.*

TESTING GRAPHICS

Given the time and expense typically put into creating graphics it makes sense to add them to your formal testing procedure. The following are some key areas:

- **Display testing.** Do graphics look good at various screen resolutions (640x480, 1024x768, etc.) and color depths (monochrome, 16-color, 256-color, etc.)? Do graphics stretch on displays using Large Fonts video drivers?

- **SHG file testing.** Are hotspots correctly coded? Is the tabbing order correct?

- **Aesthetics.** Check the effects on line spacing if graphics appear within text. Also check their effect on appearance and readability within the topic.

- **Visual consistency.** Make sure the style of the graphic matches that of other graphics in the Help file.
- **Transparent bitmaps.** Make sure the background color is visible on any transparent bitmaps.

TESTING CONTEXT-SENSITIVE HELP

Context-sensitive Help offers its own set of testing challenges to the Help Author. Testing techniques for this area of development are covered in detail in Chapter 19, *Programming Calls to Help.*

TESTING WITH HELP AUTHOR MODE

WinHelp 4 provides a facility, called Help Author mode, specifically designed to assist Help developers in debugging topic files. This mode enables you to:

- Browse Help files topic by topic.

- Locate topics by topic number.

- Display information about a topic.

- Test and debug hotspots.

Each of these features is described below and requires enabling Help Author. The latter two items also require a setting in the project file.

Help Author mode can be enabled on any computer whether or not Help Workshop or the compiler are installed. This mode will temporarily alter the behavior of your Help file.

To enable Help Author with Help Workshop:

1. If you have any Help files open, click Close All Help from the Test menu of Help Workshop.

2. From the File menu, click Help Author.

Now Help Author is enabled and you can perform the tasks of locating a Help topic described below.

To enable Help Author manually:

1. Start a text editor such as Notepad or Sysedit and open your WIN.INI file.

2. Use the Find command to search for the [Windows Help] section. There may already be statements in this section.

3. Add the following statement to the Windows Help section:

```
Help Author = 1
```

4. Close WIN.INI and save your changes.

Browsing a Help file with Help Author

One of the difficulties in proofreading a compiled Help file is methodically displaying each topic: it's very easy to miss a topic when you're navigating with jumps, pop-ups, keywords, and so forth. With Help Author mode enabled, you can view each topic in the order it appears in the topic file. While this isn't an effective technique for *testing*, it makes it easier to view and proofread each topic. It simplifies changes since topics are displayed in the same order they are stored within the topic files.

You can also view any of the topics in other developers' Help files without having to follow their patterns of jumps. This is a great way to spy on Help designs.

This feature displays all topics in the current window, even if the > footnote was used, or if certain topics were designed to display only in pop-up windows.

To browse a Help file:

1. Enable Help Author mode as described in this section.

2. Launch the Help file you want to review.

   • Press CTRL+SHIFT+HOME to display the first topic in the Help file.

   • Press CTRL+SHIFT+END to display the last topic in the Help file.

   • Press CTRL+SHIFT+RIGHT ARROW to display each successive topic in the Help file.

   • Press CTRL+SHIFT+LEFT ARROW to go back one topic at a time.

One of the limitations of this form of browsing is that all topics appear in the same window, regardless of any secondary window coding. The topics appear in the same order in which they reside in the topic file. When you reach the last topic, the message: "The topic does not exist" appears.

> **NOTE** *You cannot browse into another help file. If you have a modular Help system, you will have to first open a topic in each of the other Help files in order to browse them.*

TIP *WinHelp 3.1 uses the SeqTopicKeys statement in WIN.INI to enable this testing function. That statement still works with WinHelp 4 and is useful for browsing a Help file without turning on Help Author mode. It also enables you to locate a topic by topic number as described in the next section. Add the following line to the [WINDOWS HELP] section of WIN.INI:* `SeqTopicKeys=1`

To disable Help Author:

- In Help Workshop select Help Author from the File menu.

  -OR-

- Remove the Help Author setting from WIN.INI.

Locating a topic with Help Author

As described earlier, the compiler assigns a unique topic number to each topic as it is processed. When the compiler references these topic numbers in compiler diagnostic messages, you can use the numbers to find a specific topic. Help Author can quickly find a topic based on its topic number.

1. Enable Help Author as described above.

2. Launch your Help file and display any topic.

3. Hold down CTRL+SHIFT and press J. The Jump dialog box appears.

4. In the **Enter topic identifier** box, type the topic number, then click OK.

   The topic assigned to the topic number appears. The text in the titlebar of the Help window is replaced with the topic number of the currently displayed topic, followed by "(Help Author On)." Figure 20.21 shows a sample topic.

NOTE *Help Author is a system setting. Therefore, if you navigate to other topics in the current Help file or in any Help file while Help Author is on, you will see the topic number in the title bar. To return the title text you must turn off Help Author.*

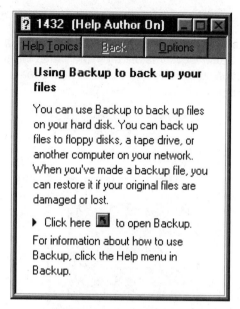

Figure 20.21. *A Help window with the topic number displayed in the title bar.*

Displaying topic information with Help Author

When testing a Help file you will find topics in which there are some problems: formatting, hotspot, or other. At this point you need to identify those topics in the topic file so you can make the appropriate repairs. Help Author mode provides a facility for displaying the topic ID for a topic as you view it in the compiled Help file.

Displaying topic information requires Help Author to be enabled. It also requires you to make a special setting in the project file prior to compiling the Help file.

To display topic information:

1. Enable Help Author mode.

2. In Help Workshop, open the project file.

3. From the File menu, click Compile.

4. Select **Include .rtf filename and topic ID in Help file**. If you are compiling from the command line you can use the /A switch.

5. Compile and run your Help file.

6. Find the topic you want information about, then right click on it.

   The pop-up context menu appears. In addition to the normal items there are two new commands: Topic Information and Ask on Hotspots. See Figure 20.22.

7. Click Topic Information.

The Topic Information box appears. See Figure 20.23. In the lower portion is the topic ID for the displayed topic. Just above it is the topic file which is very useful for finding topics in a project with multiple topic files. You also see information on the topic title, entry macros, and default window.

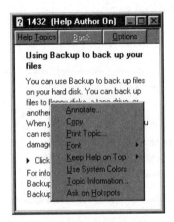

Figure 20.22. *Help Author adds two debugging items to Help's context menu.*

This option increases your Help file size by about one percent, and you may want to compile your final build after turning it off in Help Workshop.

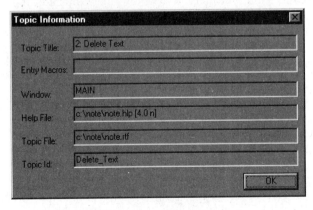

Figure 20.23. *The Topic Information box.*

Displaying hotspot information

When testing a Help file, you may encounter hotspots which are broken. In the past this would disrupt your testing of that path until the hotspot was fixed. With Help Author mode you can bypass broken hotspots during testing. You can also get information on the topic IDs specified in jumps and pop-ups and the syntax associated with a macro.

To display hotspot information:

1. Follow the first six steps "To display topic information" described above.

2. From the context pop-up menu select Ask on Hotspots.

3. Click the hotspot that you want to examine. Either the topic ID or macro syntax appears before the hotspot is executed. In Figure 20.24 the shortcut button image is associated with the **ExecFile** (EF) macro.

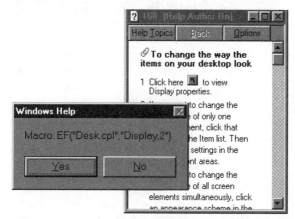

Figure 20.24. *After enabling the Ask on Hotspots command, macro syntax can be displayed.*

Flagging errors with Bookmarks

As you review the Help file, you will usually find a significant number of coding errors, formatting errors, and other discrepancies. Typically you document these items by writing them on paper or in a word processing file. This list is then given to the person who makes the corrections. The person making the corrections must search for each item in the Help file to see what it looks like, then make the appropriate change in the topic file.

Help's Bookmark feature can provide a way to streamline the process of marking errors. The Bookmark command is primarily for Help users to mark a place in a Help file. For example, a user who frequently refers to a topic on printing can create a bookmark and quickly access the topic by selecting it from the Bookmark menu.

Bookmarks can also prove valuable to the Help tester. When you identify a topic error, you can assign a bookmark to that topic. You then give a copy of the Help file along with its bookmark file to the person making the corrections, who can quickly find all of the errors just by selecting them from the Bookmark menu.

Bookmarks are stored in a file named WINHLP32.BMK that is kept in the \WINDOWS folder. Since all Help applications share a common bookmark file, the person making the corrections should make sure to rename their current WINHLP32.BMK file before copying the tester's bookmark file to their Windows directory.

Figure 20.25 demonstrates the use of the Bookmark feature. The Help tester discovered a jump error in the topic and created a bookmark called Jump001. (Since each bookmark must be unique, adopting such a numbering system usually works well.)

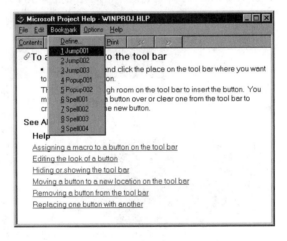

Figure 20.25. *A Help file with bookmarks assigned to errors.*

Annotating topics with test information

WinHelp's annotation feature lets users attach a detailed note to a particular topic. For example, if a workgroup is connected to three different types of printers, the network administrator might annotate Help's printing topic to explain the uses for each printer.

You can use the Annotation feature to document the changes required in a specific topic. Each annotation may contain up to 2,048 characters. In Figure 20.26, an annotation is used to describe a jump that does not work properly.

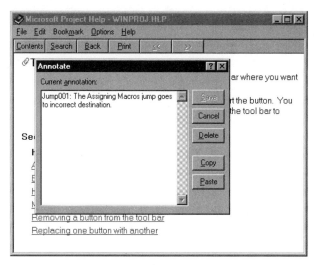

Figure 20.26. *An annotation used to explain an error.*

Annotations are saved in a separate text file that uses the name of the Help file and a .ANN file extension. For example, annotations for Program Manager's Help file are saved in a file named PROGMAN.ANN. The annotation files are saved in the \WINDOWS\HELP directory. You should send the .ANN file to the person making the topic file corrections.

> **NOTE** *Bookmarks and annotations affect only the current copy of the Help file. When you compile a new Help file, you lose all your bookmarks and annotations. To keep a permanent record of those edits, place the .BMK and .ANN files in a separate folder before you compile the new version.*

Generating topic file reports

Some authoring tools provide the ability to generate reports about your Help project. Microsoft Help Workshop can print reports listing each topic title along with its topic number. Such a list is useful for debugging. You can also display an alphabetical list of index keywords, which is useful for spell-checking.

The ForeHelp authoring tool offers more robust reporting which includes topic IDs, topic titles, the number of jumps and keywords per topic and the destination topic. You can also display useful statistics on file size and total keyword and topic counts.

These and other reports are described in detail in the section "Controlling Your Production Files" section of Chapter 23.

21

Development Tasks and Strategies

The type of Help methodology that is right for you depends in large part on the nature of the work you are doing. The previous chapters of this book present extensive information on how to design and implement the various elements of a Help system. This chapter attempts to tie all that information together into a complete and comprehensive methodology for developing Windows Help—from writing through duplicating disks. The first section of this chapter, "The Help Development Cycle," presents a methodology that is appropriate for all kinds of Help developers. The advantages of a complete methodology include greater consistency and accuracy in the creation of Help systems and a less stressful development cycle. Although certain specific tips and techniques may not apply to you, the general system presented here should allow you to devise your own Help development process.

Other issues that directly affect your Help development methodology are discussed in this chapter, including:

- The migration of users to Windows 95/NT.

- The coordination of Help and print documentation.

- The effects of your budget, schedule, and Help team.

- The localization of Help to other languages.

- The porting of WinHelp systems to UNIX and Macintosh.

The Help development cycle

The creation of a Help system consists of many tasks. Some are common to both Help and print publishing; others are specific to Help. The process of creating a Help system is something like the planning and building of a house. Building a house is a complex project, and it is carried out in stages: preliminary and then detailed plans are made, a frame is erected, the frame is filled out, and the finishing touches are added.

The quality of the end product represents the care and skill that goes into each of the stages. To ensure quality, the plans are evaluated in the design stages and the structure is inspected at the conclusion of the various stages of construction.

Following the house analogy, this section presents the activities that make up each stage of Help development and details the typical tasks you will complete during each period. You can modify this task list to fit your particular situation. These tasks will also help you estimate costs and schedule your project as described in Chapter 23, *Managing Help Projects*.

STAGE 1: EARLY DESIGN AND PLANNING

> *The goal of Stage 1 is to take a very broad view of the new Help system, conduct the early planning, create some sample topics and get some early feedback. If you get a "go ahead" at this stage, the detailed planning can begin.*

If a family wants to build a new house, they will begin with the broadest issues, such as their lifestyles and tastes. They will look at existing houses and at pictures, and perhaps draw rough sketches. A great deal of early planning precedes a detailed architectural plan. In Help development the early planning precedes and guides the specific design. The tasks that make up the early design and planning are listed below:

Task list—Stage 1

- ☐ Analyze the design context: the product, the users, the complete documentation set, and the constraints.

- ☐ Determine what kinds of topics you are going to write: procedure topics, command topics, and so forth.

- ☐ Determine whether you need to use the WinHelp 4 compiler or can continue development with WinHelp 3.1. See "Migrating to WinHelp 4" later in this chapter.

- [ ] Determine what, if any, advanced Help features you will use. These include secondary windows, macros, and multimedia elements, and may complicate your development.

- [ ] Prepare an early publications plan and some sample topics. Conduct an internal review of your sample topics.

- [ ] Identify the job skills needed for the project.

- [ ] Prepare a "ballpark" cost estimate and a schedule for your project.

- [ ] Get preliminary approval.

Approval of your preliminary plan marks the conclusion of the first stage.

STAGE 2: DETAILED DESIGN AND PLANNING

The goal of Stage 2 is to fully design your Help system, plan the development process, test a prototype, and get final approval from the relevant people.

Considerable effort goes into building a house before a single board is nailed down. Detailed architectural drawings and plans for the construction effort are necessary. If this is a custom house, the architect may use the detailed design to build a miniature model so that the owners and others can effectively evaluate the house before construction begins.

Along the same lines, a Help system must be designed in detail before a single topic is written. Although Help systems cannot be built in miniature, the Help writer can complete a small subset of the Help system and treat it as a prototype for usability testing and other forms of evaluation. Ideally, flaws in the design can be detected and corrected before the main writing effort begins. The tasks that make up the planning of a Help system are listed below.

Task list—Stage 2

- [ ] Assemble any available information which can contribute to the content of the Help file. Interview programmers, collect programming and design notes, and work with the software.

- [ ] Conduct or otherwise acquire a task analysis and use this to prepare an outline of your topics. Be prepared to revise this outline as the developers change the software product's interface and functionality.

- [ ] Design the layout for each kind of Help topic you will use and plan the appearance of tables, lists, and other elements within your topics. A Word for Windows template is provided on your sample disc.

- [ ] Plan the structure of your browse sequences. Will they be single or multiple level? What is the natural order of the sequences?

☐ Plan context-sensitive access with the programmers. What components will have context-sensitive Help? Through what means—the F1 key, the SHIFT+F1 keys, or special Help buttons on dialog boxes—will context sensitivity be enabled?

☐ Plan the formats for your graphics: monochrome or color, single or multiple hotspot, 16- or 256-color resolution.

☐ Identify which components of your Help system are enabled through the project file versus the topic file.

☐ Determine how the development team will coordinate their efforts, especially in the areas of version control and integration of Help system components.

☐ Select a word processor and/or authoring tool with which to do your Help construction.

☐ Experiment with special design components, like inter-file jumps, custom buttons and menus, and multimedia elements to make sure they operate the way you envision.

☐ If you are distributing full-text search index files, identify what options you want to provide.

☐ If possible, build a prototype, conduct usability tests and other forms of evaluation, and incorporate the results of the testing into your design.

☐ Identify the expected compressed size of the Help file. File size can affect the number of disks required for distribution of a software product or stand-alone Help system. It's usually easier to plan around a size limitation than it is to eliminate pieces of a Help system to meet one.

☐ Distribute the outline and design plans to the appropriate people for approval. Include a "firm" cost estimate and schedule.

☐ Get final approval, having made any necessary changes.

☐ Choose the development team and assign tasks.

A fully planned and approved design marks the conclusion of the second stage.

STAGE 3: FRAMING

> *The goal of Stage 3 is to make progress toward the completion of your Help system while maintaining a broad perspective and the ability to make necessary ongoing changes in the writing of the Help topics.*

Stone fortresses were built block by block from the ground up. Today, houses are built with a framework of 2x4s and other members, and this framework is subsequently filled out.

Likewise, in Help you do not usually write complete and perfect Help topics one after another. Rather, you normally write in drafts. In the first draft you implement jumps, pop-ups, and all forms of navigation. Regarding the writing, it is enough to gather the necessary information. This information can be more carefully structured and filled out with more complete text later—in Stage 4 of the Help Development Cycle.

This approach has several advantages. First, because the writer is moving from topic to topic, he or she retains a good perspective on the whole project. Next, just as a house should be inspected at the framing stage, we can arrange for a Help review before the Help authors have invested enormous amounts of time writing and polishing Help topics. If prototype Help topics have been written, they should be fully linked to the new skeleton topics and be included in the review.

The tasks performed in Stage 3 are listed below:

Task list—Stage 3

- [ ] Begin writing the necessary procedure topics, command topics, and other kinds of Help information. If there is any existing print text, cut and paste useful material into your Help document.

- [ ] Begin generating search keywords; keep a log of search keywords handy so you can add to it throughout the development process.

- [ ] Print a hard copy of your topic files. Review it for organization. Correct any errors. You may choose to use a proofreader, depending on how complete the text is.

- [ ] Add the appropriate footnotes and character formatting to the topic file. Specify topics, topic titles, jumps, pop-ups, and browse sequences. You may choose to automate this work with the aid of one of the Help tools described in Chapter 22, *Help Authoring Tools*. You may also choose to add your current list of search keywords.

- [ ] Identify any processes that may require a graphic or multimedia element to improve comprehension.

- [ ] Create organization topics and/or a contents file to provide access to your Help topics. If you are using a contents file add the desired buttons to the appropriate windows, i.e., Help Topics, Contents, Index, Find.

- [ ] Conduct usability testing whenever possible to check the effectiveness of your Help system.

- [ ] Create a basic project file. You may want to use Title and Copyright settings for version control as described in Chapter 18, *Creating the Project File*. Determine preliminary settings for window position, size, and color.

- [ ] Create a working folder on your computer for your various Help production files. You may want to have separate folders for graphics and archived files.

☐ Start new documents for your Help content with your word processor and/or authoring tool.

☐ Prepare a style sheet and/or template. A sample Word for Windows template is provided on your book disc.

☐ Compile a first draft of your Help system. Use build tags to exclude those topics from your Help system which are not ready for review.

☐ Test the first draft. Make the necessary changes, then recompile and test again.

☐ Distribute the compiled first draft to the appropriate people for review. These people include the manager, writer, editor, designer, and tester.

The formal review of the prototype or skeletal Help in a compiled first draft form usually signals the end of the third stage. Stage 4 is the time to fill out your structure.

STAGE 4: FILLING OUT

> *The goal of Stage 4 is to get the Help system completely written and coded.*

When the framing of a house is complete and has been shown to be sound, you now can perform the many tasks that transform this framework into a solid, substantial structure. Plywood, wallboard, a roof, plumbing, and ductwork are all added. This is the largest part of the job.

So too with a Help system. Once the framework for your Help system is complete and has passed inspection, you can begin building the Help system in earnest. The structure is strengthened by writing pertinent explanations, procedures, and definitions, and all this material must be revised and polished; preferably by an editor who can bring a fresh pair of eyes to the writing.

At this point the Help text represents the writer's best attempt at documenting the software as it currently exists. The technical review is now conducted to ensure that the text properly describes the software—much like building inspections make sure the construction matches the blueprints and conforms to code. Programmers and system designers take their shots at pointing out errors and areas requiring additional explanation.

If you developed a skeleton in Stage 3, much of your coding is complete and you can concentrate on completing the text. If the Help text originated as print material, it should be edited for online use. Graphics are now created and customized. The project file is enhanced to reflect the required features of the end product. The topic file is also modified with respect to fonts and paragraph attributes. Context-sensitive access is enabled so the Help can work with the associated Windows-based application. Jumps and pop-ups are added where necessary to link associated topics.

The compiled Help file is now fully functional and can be used and reviewed by anyone working on the project. Often, this draft Help system accompanies the beta release (the final test release) of the software application.

Task list—Stage 4

☐ Implement any changes from the first-stage review. Research and write any new topics that have been implemented in the application since the first stage.

☐ Complete writing of all explanations, procedures, and definitions.

☐ Print the Help topics and distribute for a technical review and substantive content review. Include an exceptions list which identifies issues that require comment or await software revisions.

☐ Proofread and copy edit the Help document. If substantial portions of the document were copied from an existing print manual, the proofreading and editing required may be substantially reduced. The copy editor can concentrate on the *changes* made to the Help text.

☐ If you are using a contents file, proofread, copy edit, and test the book and topic items.

☐ Make the changes to the content requested by the reviewers.

☐ Create any needed graphics. This includes any conceptual graphics, which are usually diagrams rather than screen captures. Review completed graphics and convert to a format supported by Windows Help.

☐ Begin designing any hypergraphic files. Be aware that for any screen captures, recapturing may be necessary if and when related portions of the software change.

☐ Add the appropriate codes to the topic file for any additional jumps or pop-ups, if this has not already been done.

☐ Update the contents file to include any added topics or linked files.

☐ Create macros for custom menus and buttons.

☐ If you wish to use multiple browse sequences, make the necessary changes to the topic file. Add special accelerated browse-sequence buttons to the project file, if desired.

☐ Identify context-sensitive topics and assign context IDs. Build the Map of context IDs in the project file.

☐ Make final formatting adjustments to the topic file. Make sure all of the fonts and paragraph attributes look the way you want them to look in the finished Help system. Check for hidden paragraph markers and proper table alignment. Remove or replace characters that are not supported by Windows Help.

☐ Modify the project file to incorporate any advanced features such as window size and position, or macros. You may want to use the Title option to identify the Help version, for example "2nd Draft."

☐ If you are distributing full-text search index files, generate them and test them with your system.

☐ Compile a final draft of your Help system.

☐ Test the compression options to determine the best compression method for your Help file. Compare the compressed size of the Help file against your design specifications.

☐ Test the final draft. Make the necessary changes, then recompile and test again. Use the Help file browsing procedure described in Chapter 20, *Compiling, Debugging, and Testing*, to review the appearance of each Help topic.

☐ If you are linking more than one Help file, make sure you test the inter-file links.

☐ If you are using context-sensitive topics, complete the Map in the project file. Test any context-sensitive topics with Help Workshop or other tool. See Chapter 19, *Programming Calls to Help*.

☐ Have your software programmer code the associated application to call the Help. Add the appropriate code to the application to enable context sensitivity.

☐ If you intend to have references in the print text to the Help, communicate those references to the print developer.

☐ Distribute the Help system to anyone working on the project for final comments.

The fourth milestone is reached when the Help file is complete, in terms of content and coding. The review of this final draft and the feedback comments from beta testing push the development process right into Stage 5.

STAGE 5: FINISH WORK

The goal of Stage 5 is to finalize the Help system for actual use.

After Stage 4, someone could live in this house and be sheltered from the elements. But to really meet the needs of the occupants, finish work must be performed. Rough edges are removed, walls are painted, floors are carpeted, and amenities are added. In the case of Help, Stage 5 is the transition from a rough but functional Help system to a fine-tuned, polished piece of work that users will truly appreciate.

Changes to window position, colors, graphics, and browse sequences are common at this stage. The writing may also be given its last polish. Contents topics, jumps, and keywords are given their last tweaks and context sensitivity is fully enabled. Some organizations freeze the interface and halt the addition of new features, which enables the author to complete the documentation of the product. Often Help authors try to delay screen captures until the interface freeze to avoid having to redo screen captures. In Stage 5, the key personnel get a last look at the content before it is committed to distribution. Significant changes at this point can delay the release of a product. Your project is now complete and ready to be used by its intended audience. Generally, the Help file is in distribution within days of the conclusion of this stage.

Task list—Stage 5

☐ Implement any changes from the beta test and final draft review. Write any last topics. Edit the text to match the latest version of the software.

☐ Solicit a review and approval of the Help content from key personnel such as the programmer and project manager.

☐ Make any final adjustments to the project file. Window size, color, the title, and so forth are often tweaked at this point.

☐ Make final screen captures and edit them as needed. Complete any hypergraphic files and specify the hotspot attributes.

☐ Fine-tune the browse sequence(s) to display in the best order.

☐ Review the search keyword list and add any new keywords you have written.

☐ Perform a complete, final proofreading of the text. Spell-check the topic files. Make sure their are no "untitled topics."

☐ Compile the Help and test the hypertext elements. Also test the context-sensitive topics through the Windows-based application. Check the Title and Copyright.

☐ Make the final changes.

☐ Compile and review the final Help.

☐ If you are shipping full-text search index files with your system, generate a final set.

☐ Send the compiled Help and software application out for duplication and distribution, if applicable.

☐ Test the Help system after installing it from the final distribution disks.

☐ Archive all project files.

☐ Perform summative evaluations and begin planning for the next project.

The final milestone in your project is the completion of the compressed, fully tested Help application. During the course of your project you will surely run into tasks which are unique to your own organization. Add those tasks to the lists in this section and fine-tune your personal Help methodology.

Migrating to WinHelp 4

The decision to move your Help development from WinHelp 3.1 to WinHelp 4 is not an easy one. The good news is that your files compiled under Windows 3.1 will run under Windows 95 with features intact. The bad news is that a Help file compiled with the WinHelp 4 compiler won't run under Windows 3.1. The exception is if you also ship the Win32s (version 1.3) files described later in this section. Until a substantial percentage of Windows users have upgraded to Windows 95 (or Windows NT 3.51), you may have to make some tough decisions.

The changes to Windows Help that come with the introduction of Windows 95 are enormous in terms of the their potential to expand Help and increase its effectiveness. However the benefits of the new features have to be measured against the challenges that acquiring them presents to your current Help development scheme. In order to measure the cost/benefit, it may be helpful to break down Windows Help into the following six basic components:

- The topic file.

- The project file.

- The contents file.

- The compiler.

- The Help viewer.

- The user interface.

As shown is Figure 21.1, these six components compose all aspects of Help development and Help presentation. The next section analyzes the effects of WinHelp 4 on each of the six components.

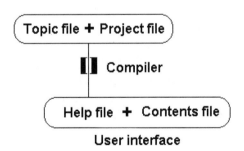

Figure 21.1. *The six basic components of Windows Help.*

THE TOPIC FILE

By far the majority of Help development labor goes into the topic file. As described in Chapter 23, *Managing Help Projects*, over 50 per cent of the labor in a typical Help project can be attributed to writing and coding the information in the topic file. With WinHelp 4 this isn't likely to change. A summary chart of coding changes is presented in Table 21.1.

Certain codes have not undergone any changes at all. The title, browse sequence, and build tag footnotes retain the same functionality and syntax as with WinHelp 3.1. Those codes will have no impact on moving to WinHelp 4. Also, the editor for multiple hotspot graphics (SHED) is unchanged and the topic file syntax for SHED graphics remains the same. (See Chapter 13, *Creating Help Graphics*, for more information.)

Some codes have acquired new capabilities, but they don't need to be modified to work with the WinHelp 4 compiler. For example the context string is now called the "topic ID" and spaces can be used in the string. However you don't have to modify existing topic IDs. "Bitmap by reference" coding retains the same bracketed syntax but the bitmaps which are referenced can now be higher resolution graphic files. You can even use inline graphics.

Other features, like secondary windows, can move to WinHelp 4 without any coding changes. But to access impressive new capabilities, you must make coding changes. For example, the secondary window identifier footnote (>) makes it possible to display topics in a secondary window when requested from the Index, the Find, or the linking macros.

Finally there are a number of features unique to WinHelp 4 that are not available at all with earlier compilers. Authorable buttons, transparent bitmaps, and 29 new macros all require coding that is not compatible with WinHelp 3.1 compilers to be added to the topic file.

> **Bottom Line.** The WinHelp 4 features enabled through topic file codes are numerous and will require substantial adjustments to your existing topic files if you decide to convert. However, few of the features requiring WinHelp 4 topic file codes provide earth-shaking capabilities. With the exception of the allure of the linking macros you probably won't make your decision on whether to move to WinHelp 4 based on the topic file alone.

Table 21.1. *Topic file coding summary*

	Codes	WinHelp 4.0 Changes
#	Context String	now called "Topic ID," spaces allowed in string
$	Title	no change
+	Browse Sequence	no change
K	Keyword	selectable separator character, second level indented index entries
A	Associative Keyword	new
>	Secondary Window Identifier	new
*	Build Tags	no changes
	Bitmaps by Reference	supports 256- and 16-bit color
	Inline Graphics	now possible
	Transparent Bitmap	new
	Authorable Button	new
	Multimedia	supports AVI, WAV formats
	Macros	29 new macros
	Font	WingDings now supported
	SHED graphics	no changes

THE PROJECT FILE

A number of major feature changes are enabled through the project file in WinHelp 4. Some of the most dramatic revolve around the customization of Help windows through buttons, auto-sizing, macros, and pixel measurements.

In order to work with the WinHelp 4 compiler your project file needs to be slightly modified. Help Workshop can provide this service smoothly, however once updated, your project file will no longer work with the WinHelp 3.1 compiler. In addition to the new command statements required to enable new features through the project file, many 3.1 sections and statements have been changed. See Table 21.2. These items are described in detail in other chapters in this book.

Table 21.2. *Project file changes in WinHelp 4*

.HPJ setting	Description
HCW	provides information to the compiler and should not be edited.
HLP	specifies the name of the Help file that will be created when the project file is compiled.
LCID	is used for sorting keywords.
REPORT	is automatically enabled whether you included it in your 3.1 project file or not.
WARNING	is not supported in version 4 project files and is automatically deleted.
[BITMAPS]	is replaced with separate BMROOT statements for each directory.
COMPRESS	is modified to COMPRESS=60 Hall Zeck.
[WINDOWS]	definitions are automatically converted by Help Workshop to the new format.
Build Tags	The 3.1 format is supported without changes. Help Workshop uses new format.
MAPFONTSIZE FORCEFONT	These parameters are replaced with a [FONTS] section.
ERRORLOG	The default is for messages to be displayed in a Compilation window of Help Workshop. This option can still be used to store messages in a text file.

Bottom Line. Any Help file to be moved to WinHelp 4 will require a brand new project file; one which won't be backwardly compatible with WinHelp 3.1. However, the updating is easy and quick with the assistance of Help Workshop; and maintaining two separate project files should not be a problem. The project file is no impediment to your migration plans.

THE CONTENTS FILE

The most dramatic and visible change to WinHelp 4 in Windows 95 is the contents file which forms the Help Topics browser. This comprehensive host for the contents, index, and full-text search pages provides better topic access for users, and offers significant advantages to developers of modular Help systems.

In terms of physical construction, the contents file presents few problems. This file must be distributed in addition to the Help file, but that is unlikely to be a problem. Enabling the Index and Find pages is trivial. And the contents file can be created with almost no impact on the coding of the topic or project files. Constructing the Contents page is a tedious and error-prone process, but that is easily resolved with the use of a Help authoring tool. The biggest challenge to developers who want to embrace the Help Topics browser features is that they will have to significantly redesign their existing WinHelp 3.1 Help systems.

> **Bottom Line.** If you elect to use the Help Topics browser you should plan on making fundamental changes to the presentation of your Help topics. Although the browser can work with WinHelp 3.1 files running under Windows 95, it is hard to envision how the same Help system can be constructed to be effective with and without a contents file.

The compiler

The new addition to the family of Help compilers, HCRTF.EXE, is a true 32-bit windows application (no DOS needed). If you are using this compiler for Help development you will enjoy blazing speed compared to previous versions. Most of the memory problems common to WinHelp 3.x have also been eliminated. In short, it is a pleasure to use HCRTF. The only negative point is that the compiler is always linked to Help Workshop, an authoring tool that may not be part of your development plans.

> **Bottom Line.** While you probably won't move to WinHelp 4 just to gain the performance advantages of the compiler, its speed and memory handling will certainly make it attractive to start using the new technology as soon as possible.

THE HELP VIEWER AND WIN32S

The Windows Help viewer is at once the most important Help component and the most insignificant. While Window Help would not be possible at all without the presence of the Help viewer on the user's computer, it is a passive component that rarely affects Help development methodology. The most important issue is that Help files compiled with HCRTF will work only with the Windows 95 viewer WINHLP32.EXE. A similar problem occurred in 1992 when WinHelp 3.1 replaced 3.0. However, in that case it was possible to provide backward compatibility by installing the 3.1 viewer on 3.0 systems. That is not possible with WinHelp 4. The WINHLP32.EXE viewer will not run on Windows 3.1 without the presence of the Win32s extensions.

A special set of files called Win32s (version 1.3),makes it possible to run 32-bit applications in the Windows 3.1 operating system. This includes Help files compiled with the new HCRTF compiler. However, this compatibility comes at a price. Approximately 3 MB of files need to be installed on the user's computer. The large size of these files means that this option is probably not viable for enabling stand-alone HLPs to run under Windows 3.1. If you are, however, providing Help for a 32-bit application, those Win32s files must be installed for the application anyway. A limitation of Win32s is that it does not provide support for context-sensitive Help. Also the version number, 1.3, is important, as the WinHelp 4 compatibility is not available in earlier releases of Win32s. The files for Win32s are available on your book disc.

Although the name of the viewer has been changed to WINHLP32.EXE, the file WINHELP.EXE is still installed on Windows 95 in the form of a "stub" program. This is used to support API calls from applications programmed for Windows 3.x.

> **Bottom Line** The viewer neither helps nor hinders your move to WinHelp 4. The exception is if your organization installs the Win32s extensions on Windows 3.1 operating systems.

THE USER INTERFACE

In addition to the Help system enhancements available to developers, Windows Help has become easier to work with and more customizable for the user. Ease of use has been improved through a better arrangement of standard buttons and menu items as well as the pop-up context menu. And the ability to quickly copy text from the Help file (including drag and drop) should be a big hit with users. User customization features, including font sizing and a system colors command, fill out the package.

> **Bottom Line.** When evaluating your move to WinHelp 4 it is important to consider how the user controls will affect your Help design. You may want to change previously used arrangement of custom buttons, including Copy, and also reevaluate font size. Your use of colors will also require some planning.

ADDING IT ALL UP

After examining the six components you should have a good idea of where the major impacts will occur in your move to WinHelp 4. Table 21.3 provides a summary. Now take that knowledge and apply it to the strategies described in the next section.

Table 21.3. *Impact Summary*

Component	Development Considerations
Topic File	Numerous coding changes, any of which require using the WinHelp 4 compiler. Only one "killer" feature (linking).
Project File	New project file required. Easily upgradable but not backwardly compatible with WinHelp 3.1.
Contents File	A major improvement in Help. Easily constructed. Requires fundamental changes in design.
Compiler	Significant productivity gains.
Help Viewer	No significant impact.
User Interface	No significant impact.

Strategies for moving to WinHelp 4

Once you absorb the impacts described in the previous section you can begin to evaluate various development strategies. Each individual project comes with its own needs and business challenges, but the following are general models which Help authors are using in their move to WinHelp 4.

1. Use only the WinHelp 4 compiler

One end of the spectrum of development strategies is to completely abandon the WinHelp 3.x compilers and begin working solely with HCRTF. This greatly simplifies your design choices and implementation procedures. With this option you can enjoy all of the features that WinHelp 4 offers.

These great benefits need to be weighed against the disadvantage that you are then supporting only users who have Windows 95/NT and effectively leaving the Windows 3.1 users behind. The exception is if your organization is installing Win32s along with its software application.

The estimates on how fast users will move to Windows 95 range from six months to two years. Novice and casual users will follow the trail of available software products and to a large extent use whatever comes pre-installed on their computers. Large corporations are traditionally slow to embrace new operating systems and may have future versions of Windows NT targeted as an upgrade path.

2. Continue to use only the WinHelp 3.x compilers

The other end of the development strategy spectrum is to ignore WinHelp 4 (for now) and use only HCP/HC31. Because Help files compiled with those compilers are forwardly compatible with Windows 95, you can support all users. This means that, except for evaluating the impact on design, you can continue your Help development exactly as it is right now.

The downside of this strategy is that you don't have access to many of the exciting new features of WinHelp 4. If users come to expect the look and feel of a WinHelp 4 Help file, yours may suffer from the appearance of being out of date. You can use the Help Topics browser with your 3.1 compiled files under Windows 95, but that opens the door to some big design questions.

Sticking with WinHelp 3.1 means your life will be simplified considerably and it provides you the flexibility to slowly find your way into WinHelp 4 development as you see how the market accepts Windows 95.

3. Duplicate topic files

Between the two extremes of development strategies is the murky middle ground which most of us inhabit. Significant numbers of users will likely move to Windows 95 within a year, and

WinHelp 4 offers many features that are too difficult to ignore. You and legions of other Help developers may find yourselves needing to supply two versions of your Help system: one for Windows 3.1 users and one for Windows 95/NT users.

Given the dramatic design changes that will be required for an effective Windows 95 Help system, it appears that the best approach may be to have a diverging development path. In this scenario, you would hold off your coding tasks until as much of the writing is done as possible. Then you would begin coding separate topic and project files. Figure 21.2 shows this production model.

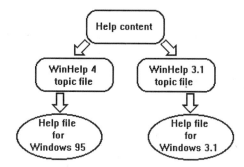

Figure 21.2. *Diverging Help production paths.*

From the point of divergence, any changes to the content would have to be made in two places. This will almost certainly cause confusion during day-to-day development and presents tricky management issues.

The install routine of your application program may have to change to be able to install the correct Help system. Also, if your authoring tool does not support WinHelp 4 you will have to perform that coding manually.

But in the end, you will have built two solid Help systems each tailored to the limits and available design capabilities of their respective compilers.

4. Single source topic files

There are some organizations whose limited resources, both in terms of time and money make it difficult to support two separate development tracks. While somewhat involved, it is possible to create a single topic file that can be manipulated into two different forms; one suitable for the WinHelp 3.1 compiler and another for WinHelp 4.

The first phase is to review your WinHelp 3.1 Help system and identify features that can be enhanced with WinHelp 4. Jumps can be replaced by KLink macros, authorable buttons can take the place of hotspot text, etc. Then, add in the appropriate codes to enable the WinHelp 4 features in addition to the WinHelp 3.1 codes.

Next comes the tricky part. You need to create a system by which you can selectively hide and reveal different codes. When you are compiling the Windows 3.1 version of your Help file you would hide the codes that work only with Window 95 and use the WinHelp 3.1 compiler. When compiling for Windows 95 you would hide the 3.1 codes and reveal the WinHelp 4 codes. If you are using Microsoft Word, WordBasic macros can perform this task.

For example, in the sample file SINGLE.RTF, each topic contains a Related Topics section. There are two forms of codes in each section: a **KLink** macro associated with a an authorable button formatted with a "Link" style tag, and a jump hotspot code formatted with a "Jump" style tag. Two WordBasic macros do the manipulation. One macro, **SwitchToWin40**, changes the Jump style to "hidden" and the Link style to "not hidden." The topic IDs that were already in hidden text are formatted with "strikethrough" so they can be identified on the switch back. After the macro is finished, SINGLE.RTF file is saved and the HCRTF compiler generates the WinHelp 4 Help file. Figure 21.3 shows the topic file prepared for WinHelp 4.

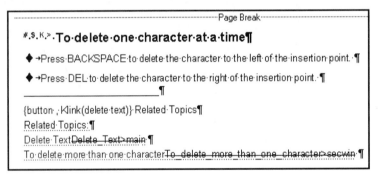

Figure 21.3. *Topic file formatted for WinHelp 4 compiling.*

The other macro **SwitchToWin31** reverses the coding: the Link style is hidden and the Jump style revealed. Again the .RTF file is saved but now the HCP compiler is used to generate the WinHelp 3.1 version. Figure 2.14 shows the modified topic file.

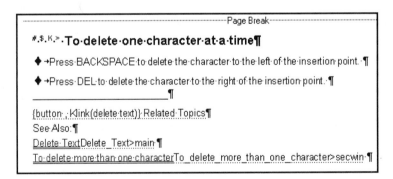

Figure 21.4. *Topic file formatted for WinHelp 3.1 compiling.*

Although two separate project files, WIN31.HPJ and WIN40.HPJ, are required, the same topic file, SINGLE.RTF, is specified in the [FILES] section of each.

At a Glance Migration Strategies

Option	Advantages	Disadvantages
Use WinHelp 4 only	Complete access to all WinHelp 4 features.	Supports only users with Windows 95, Windows NT 3.51, or Win32s on Windows 3.1. Requires modifying topic and project files.
Use WinHelp 3.1 only	No coding changes required. Continue to use current authoring tools. Existing Help files run under Windows 95/NT.	Limited access to WinHelp 4 features. The Help Topics browser can be used when running under Windows 95/NT.
Duplicate topic files	Enjoy all WinHelp 4 features. Continue to support Windows 3.1. Maximizes design flexibility.	Difficult to manage. Significant increase in development labor.
Single source topic files	Enjoy all WinHelp 4 features. Continue to support Windows 3.1. Reduces duplication of effort.	Difficult to manage. Complicated to set up. Limits design flexibility.

How available resources affect methodology

In the development of online Help, as with print documentation, there may be distinct production differences depending on the resources you have to allocate to the project. These production differences include hypergraphics, customized buttons on the Help button bar, the use of the contents file, and advanced .HPJ project file options. These production differences stem from the practical realities of budget constraints, tight deadlines, and possibly a lack of qualified personnel. However, even with limited resources there is no reason that your Help system cannot be effective for your users. With a clean, user-centered design and careful writing, your Help system can be highly effective, even though it lacks some of the bells and whistles.

On the other hand, really large Help systems, those consisting of, say, 500 or more topics, tend to require more elaborate production features in order to serve the needs of the users. For example, a larger Help system may require inter-file linking, multiple browse sequences, and a highly detailed contents file.

Table 21.4 identifies how the extent of your resources can affect the handling of important Help development tasks. This list can help you anticipate your development effort based on realistic expected resources.

Table 21.4. *Comparison of options with your available resources*

Help Tasks	Limited Resources	Expanded Resources
Research, write, and edit the Help content.	Cutting corners in writing the text is never a good idea. However the writer often performs the editing and validation or the Help topics.	A team of Help professionals write the contents, perform the various editing functions, and validate the procedures. Technical edits are performed by subject matter experts.
Code the topic file including topics, keywords, jumps, pop-ups, and KLinks/ALinks.	The entire process of coding topics can often be handled through Help authoring tools.	Help Authoring tools may limit the flexibility in coding the topic file. Certain techniques may be easier to create and debug with an understanding of the underlying coding. This knowledge is acquired through experience and education.
Design efficient topic access and effective screen layout. Conduct usability testing.	Basic design principles are relevant to any size project but can be scaled down. i.e., usability testing can be as simple as having coworkers work with drafts of your Help system.	Screen design, system structure, and usability testing become major aspects of the Help development process. Larger Help systems make topic access more difficult. Specialists in design are often part of the Help team.
Create and code Windows Help macros.	Macros generally aren't required.The basic footnote and character attribute codes provide acceptable functionality.	Macros are often used to accomplish tasks such as enabling custom buttons, linking one or more topics or Help files, and executing other programs. Staff with extensive experience with WinHelp is often required.

Table 21.4. *(continued)*

Help Tasks	Limited Resources	Expanded Resources
Render graphic images to support the Help text and improve navigation.	Simple screen captures can sufficiently support most of your graphic needs. More advanced graphics can significantly tax your budget.	The most effective Help systems routinely employ not only screen captures, but also hypergraphics and high resolution bitmaps. Projects with large budgets can support more creative conceptual illustrations and multimedia elements.
Create and manage the project file.	The basic components of the project file are generally sufficient for constructing a solid Help file.	Larger and more elaborate Help systems nearly always require the use of advanced project file options such as window sizing, macro calls, build tags and context sensitive mapping.
Test the compiled Help file.	The testing of jumps, pop-ups, and links can be completed by the Help author, quickly and without a formal checklist or procedure.	Testing the Help file definitely requires a formal, distinct review strategy that proceeds in a complete organized fashion. Often a person other than the Help author performs the test.

Coordination with print documentation

As Help becomes a more dominant part of the documentation set, the role of print documentation will gradually change. In many cases, print manuals will become much smaller in scope or will take on different roles, such as emphasizing conceptual and strategic information rather than procedures. The print manual for the Windows 95 operating system is only 85 pages! This changing relationship between print and online documentation is discussed in Chapter 1, *Help and the Documentation Set.*

At the present time, however, software products regularly ship with both a Help system and a user's guide, and there is significant overlap between the two components. First, the printed user's guide and Help system include relatively similar content. Second, the two components are broadly similar in presentation: the procedures include a heading or topic title to introduce the procedure, a conceptual element to explain how this procedure relates to the user's task world, and numbered steps to explain how to execute the procedure.

Because of this overlap, Help systems are frequently derived from user's guides. In some instances, the print manual was written and distributed before anyone thought to add a Help system to the documentation set. In other instances, a manual and Help are created as part of a coordinated effort. Some software companies employ largely independent print and Help teams, but if the Help system and the user's guide overlap to a large degree, this approach is unnecessarily expensive. Consequently, in situations in which the finished products significantly overlap, the coordinated development of print and Help documentation is more prevalent than using two teams.

There are, of course, important differences as well. The printed user's guide will typically contain more detailed information, more graphics, a more elaborate layout, and a style of writing that is not strictly modular in the way that Help topics must be. When a print manual and Help are developed in a coordinated effort, there is a choice to make: focus on Help and choose a time to derive the print manual from the Help topic files, or focus on the print manual and then derive the Help from the manual draft. Our experience shows that when the decision is not driven by administrative or scheduling concerns, documentation specialists usually prefer the latter approach. They prefer to trim down the print documentation and adapt it to a modular style of presentation rather than to beef up Help topics into sections of a user's guide.

Furthermore, the second approach may better suit the production requirements of print documentation. Because printing and binding a manual require several weeks, it is acceptable to let Help development lag behind the print effort. This is because the latter stages of Help development, those described in the Stage 4 and Stage 5 task lists, can be performed while the print manual is in production. For these reasons, therefore, the focus of this section is how to derive Help from print.

ADAPTING PRINT DOCUMENTATION TO HELP

When you're adapting print documentation to Help, the key issue is timing the movement of the text and graphics from the word processing or electronic publishing file into the Help topic file. Once the print material is ported into a Help topic file, you have two separate documents, and any revisions caused by changes in the software product must be made in both documents.

A sound plan is to port the print material into your Help topic file after the approval of the final print draft or at some stage when the content of the documentation has stabilized and when the print material has been well edited.

Figure 21.5 illustrates a production timeline that includes both a print and Help component. Print production often begins with an early test version of the software (called an alpha release) and concludes two or three weeks before the release of the application. As described above, the Help production team will require the final draft of the print material before significant work can be done. In Figure 21.5, the first draft of Help is timed to coincide with the final draft of Help.

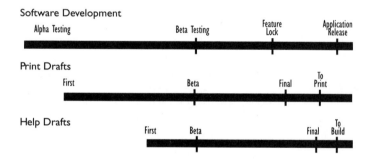

Figure 21.5. *A timeline for development of both print documentation and online Help.*

During the time that the print manual is being planned, written, and edited, significant work on the Help system can take place. Many of the various planning activities listed as Stage 1 tasks can be performed. Also, you may want to port a rough draft of the print manual into your Help topic file so you can plan the appearance and hypertext linking of your Help system. For example, you can use the poorly written Help topics derived from the rough draft sections of the user's guide to plan out your browse sequences, jumps, and so forth. This Help file, however, is a throw-away draft that is distributed only among the Help developers.

REMOVING UNNECESSARY PRINT TEXT

If you are preparing Help based on a print document, you will want to remove text that is relevant only to print. For example, you will certainly need to delete the table of contents and the index. You may also identify certain graphics and topics that are not appropriate for Help.

In addition, a good Help topic generally does not use as much supporting text as does the corresponding print document. Extended explanations can get in the way. This extra text should, in some cases, be edited out. If detailed information must be included in the online Help, it should be relegated to special topics of the Help system and accessed through jumps or pop-ups.

Often it is a difficult process to remove portions of the print text because writers have an attachment to their work. The long hours spent in crafting passages of text for the print manual may inhibit writers from properly editing that text for Help. It is also a lot less work to just use all of the print text for the Help system. Use someone other than the print author to edit and evaluate the text in the context of the Help file you develop. The online Help user likely wants a different presentation of information than the reader of the print document and it is to your benefit to make the extra effort.

Print documents may also have references to "pages" and "figures" which probably don't make sense when read online. One of the tasks in the editing process is to review the print document for these kinds of references. Use the Search and Replace feature of your word processor to root them out. The Doc-To-Help tool, described in Chapter 22 and below, automatically replaces Word for Windows page references with jumps.

Often, the final print draft is dropped into the lap of the Help author late in development, compromising the Help author's ability to properly edit the text. It is useful if, during production of the print manual, the Help author can review the text for its appropriateness to Help. A useful strategy is to mark the text that is not suitable for inclusion in the Help. Most of the major word processors have a color attribute that you can apply to the text. For example, you might choose to mark all of the print text that will be deleted with a red color. When the print draft is complete, it is easy to identify and remove that expendable material. Unless you are working with a color printer, the text prints as black, even though it is colored.

USING SINGLE SOURCE DEVELOPMENT

Adapting print documentation to Help will inevitably lead to management headaches and extensive ongoing maintenance. This is true even when the documentation production paths diverge very late in development. A popular solution is to use a product like Doc-To-Help, described in Chapter 22, which specializes in "single sourcing." Single sourcing is the process of transforming a single copy of your documentation into both a print manual and a Help file. This offers substantial reductions in duplicated labor. If a change is made in a documentation procedure, you make that change in a single word processing file. The authoring tool manipulates that file to produce a printed manual and a compiled Help file. There is no duplication of effort. Figure 21.6 shows a section of the print manual that also contains a hidden hypertext link that will be used in the online Help file.

.To·find·specific·characters·or·words¶

You·can·start·a·search·for·specific·text·at·any·point·in·a·Note·document.·¶

1 →·Move·the·insertion·point·to·where·you·want·the·search·to·begin.·¶

2 →·From·the·Search·menu,·choose·Find.·¶

3 →·Type·the·characters·or·words·you·want·to·find.·¶

4 →·If·you·want·to·match·capitalization·exactly,·select·the·Match·Case·check·box.·¶

5 →·To·specify·the·search·direction,·select·the·Up·or·Down·option.·¶

6 →·Choose·the·Find·Next·button.·¶

7 →·To·find·the·next·occurrence·of·the·text,·choose·the·Find·Next·button·again.·¶

See·Also:¶

Find·command¶

Figure 21.6. *A section of a print manual containing a hidden hypertext link.*

The danger with single sourcing is that it can lead to "dumping" text into Help. The print manual is transformed into an online version which offers relatively poor topic access and display. However taking that path is strictly up to the developer. A good designer will be aware of the problem and use it effectively. Tools like Doc-To-Help let you selectively mark portions of the document for print or for Help, or for both. For example, a conceptual statement may be appropriate for inclusion in the print manual but not needed when a procedure is accessed for context-sensitive Help. The tool then automatically hides specific portions appropriate for printing the manual or compiling the Help file.

You may encounter some authoring tools which provide a conversion facility to transform the Help file into a print document. However, as mentioned earlier, this approach is less appealing to most technical writers. It is much more difficult to expand a Help system into a robust print manual than it is to edit down the print manual into Help topics. Also, many writers generate and distribute early drafts of their Help content in print form before they start coding it into topics.

USING PAGE LAYOUT SOFTWARE

Many companies use page layout (desktop publishing) software, such as PageMaker, Ventura Publisher, and FrameMaker to create manuals. Although these tools are excellent for developing print materials, their use creates problems when developing a corresponding Help system. When the size of the print text is more than about 100 pages, it becomes an economic necessity to transfer that content electronically into a form suitable for Help. This content then can be modified as needed. However, it is the transfer that is the problem. Windows Help requires all text to be in one or more files saved in .RTF format. Although some page layout software packages can save to this format, they may leave behind certain important formatting information. This section describes two of the major page layout software applications and the problems you might encounter with them.

Ventura Publisher

Ventura Publisher uses text, graphic, and style files as separate resources and pulls them all together when you assemble a publication. Any changes to the original files are automatically reflected in the Ventura publication file. While that is a benefit in producing your print material, it means that you do not have formatted text which you can save in rich-text format for your Help. Ventura cannot export a formatted publication into an .RTF file.

One option is to do the bulk of your documentation development within a word processor. If you use a Help style sheet you can format your text as you write it. You can then import the text for the printed manual into Ventura when appropriate, and still be able to save the formatted file in rich-text format for use with Help. For those who do most of their text development in Ventura, there are two options. One is to duplicate much of your efforts in formatting text and embedding graphics in the text. The other is to use the MasterHelp product, described in Chapter 22. This product provides an excellent process for converting a Ventura file into WinHelp. The product was designed expressly for this purpose and is the only one of its type at this writing.

PageMaker

PageMaker is easier to use with Windows Help than Ventura because it supports the rich-text format. You can cleanly export formatted text and graphics directly to an .RTF file. The one difficulty you may encounter is in employing the Story feature. Most publishing departments using PageMaker employ the Story feature to make it easier to work with chapters and discrete sections. Because these stories become separate files, you have to select and export each story individually. Only then can you combine the .RTF files into one file or prepare them as separate topic files.

Because PageMaker recognizes all of the formatting in Word documents, you can easily support most of your writing development in the word processor. You can then import the formatted text into PageMaker when finalizing the print materials and save the text file as .RTF for your Help file.

WinHelp localization

WinHelp can display Help files compiled in any of 29 different languages. However, if you are translating your Help documentation for distribution in other countries you need to pay attention to a number of issues; some of them are unique to Windows Help and others are common to other forms of documentation.

Selecting a translator

Selecting the person or organization to perform the translation of your Help file is the key to success. There are increasing levels of competence to consider in choosing the appropriate translator:

- The proper translation of the words is as important as the crafting of the words in the original language. Experienced translators are adept at maintaining the meaning of the word in the proper context.

- • Experience in the software industry or with your particular subject matter ensure that technical terms and jargon are properly translated.

- • • Experience with online Help means the translator is aware of the nuances of topic-based presentation of information, including limited screen real estate, translation growth, and topic access.

- • • • Experience with Windows Help means the translator is aware of what kind of modifications need to be made and how they affect the compiled Help file. The translator not only knows what not to disturb in the topic and project file coding, but—more important—how to properly and most efficiently make the appropriate coding adjustments.

While experience with a particular authoring tool can be a plus in selecting a translator, it is not required. All Help files share the common .RTF topic file standard; translation can be accomplished in any full-featured word processor.

One source for assistance in translating your Help files is Berlitz Translation Services, 257 Park Ave S, 17th Fl. New York, NY 10010, 212-598-2487.

Alphabetical lists

A common component of many Help systems is alphabetical lists. These may be listings of commands, fields, or even procedures. If you present information in an alphabetized list make sure you let the translator know that that is your intent. Otherwise the items may be translated but not re-sorted. Whereas a glossary topic clearly contains items in an alphabetical order, a short list of fields may not be so obvious. Entries in the contents file may also require alphabetizing.

A related problem occurs if you have topics arranged in alphabetical order through a browse sequence. The translator not only has to translate the topic headings but also to re-sort the browse sequences. For example, you might have topics with headings Beep, Bold, Bookmark, and so on. It is more than likely that those headings will not even end up starting with the same letter, much less be in the same order. The translator then needs to either reorder the topics in the topic file or adjust the browse sequence numbering in the browse (+) footnotes.

Considering the difficulty of coding, you may want to reconsider your use of browse sequences at all.

Contents file entries

In translating contents file entries the work is fairly straightforward. The main task is to translate the visible text of the heading and topic items. In doing so you need to be careful not to modify the coding associated with the topic items.

If you are using Help Workshop, the Translate command protects information that should not be translated. The translator will be able to modify only the hotspot text, as shown in Figure 21.7. The Topic ID, Help file, and Window type fields are grayed out and protected.

If you are editing the contents file in a text editor or an authoring tool that doesn't support the Translation feature you need to use caution in editing.

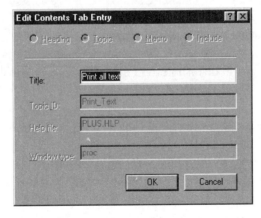

Figure 21.7. *Protected contents file information in Help Workshop.*

To protect the contents file for translation

1. In Help Workshop, open the Contents file.

2. From the File menu, click Translation.

3. Select a heading or topic you want to translate, and then click Edit.

You will also need to re-sort any contents items in an alphabetical list. Make sure the translator is aware of which lists should be alphabetized. Unfortunately, the contents editor of Help Workshop does not provide a facility for moving items up and down in the hierarchy. To sort the items you need to open the contents file in a text editor. If you are using Microsoft Word you can use the Table/Sort Text command to sort a block of items.

Index entries

- When generating your keyword list, be aware of words that may be synonyms but have different meanings in the context in which you are using them. If the translator is not aware of this situation, the two keywords may be translated into the same word and you will lose some of the discrimination you had intended in the index. For example, the words "setup" and "configuration" may mean very different things in your software application, but in a translation to Spanish both words might be changed to "configuración." Flag these types of entries as you become aware of them. If two words are truly synonyms, then there is no problem.

- Translating keywords is almost always accomplished by editing the K footnotes in a word processor. Generally this is the most efficient way of working through a long list of topics. You may want to add leading spaces before each keyword to make it easier to edit them. The leading spaces do not appear in the index.

- You may encounter a technical issue if a topic (or topics) uses a very large number of keywords. The keyword (K) footnote has a limit of 255 characters. If you are pushing this limit in English, translation growth may trigger a warning message during compiling. The solution is to use a second K footnote in the topic to handle the overflow keywords.

Index sorting

When your keyword list is complete and you are ready for compiling you need to make an adjustment to the project file so that the keywords are properly sorted. The character sets of languages have varying rules about how to sort accent and diacritical marks with respect to the standard letters. For example, in Swedish, words starting with vowels with diacritical marks are placed at the end of the alphabet; **z** is followed by **ä**.

To specify a language for index sorting:

1. In Help Workshop, click Options, then Sorting.

2. Scroll down to select the language you want, then click OK.

The language setting is embedded in the LCID statement of the project file. Help Workshop must be used to form the proper syntax for the setting you want to use. The language name is displayed as a comment in the LCID statement.

If you use alphabetized lists in the topic or contents files, the translator will have to make the sorting adjustments manually based on knowledge of the language's rules.

Help file name

Generally, program filenames, including the name of the Help file, are kept the same in both the domestic and foreign versions of a product. However, if you must change the name of the Help file, realize that this will affect any elements of the Help file that reference the filename. If you are using inter-file jumps in the topic or contents file or in custom buttons or menus, you will have to modify that code.

ALinks/KLinks

The linking macros are used prominently in the Microsoft Help model and provide excellent improvements in Help system navigation and efficiency in coding. Both forms of the linking macros make it easier to code references to related topics. On one level, it is a plus for translation because it minimizes the errors that may occur from editing the jump text. However it can also cause problems if you are using **KLink** macros. Since keywords are translated, you must also translate the keywords specified in **KLink** macros. For this reason it is advisable to use **ALink** macros as much as possible in Help files that are to be translated. For more information on the choice between **ALink** and **KLink** macros, see the section "Dynamic links: The **ALink** and **KLink** macros," in Chapter 11.

Custom buttons and menus

If you are using the **CreateButton** or **InsertItem** macros to display custom buttons or menu items you will need to translate the text that appears to the user. You can edit these items in Help Workshop or in a text editor. You can also include accent and diacritical marks in your macro definitions. However, macro syntax is very detailed and care must be taken when modifying these strings.

Authorable buttons need to be translated as well. The translator adjusts the text following the "button" portion of the syntax.

The WinHelp viewer automatically translates the standard buttons, like Contents and Index, when the Help file is displayed by the user. No adjustments need to be made in your production files or during compiling.

Copyright/Citation settings

If you are translating the copyright and/or citation settings of the project file, be aware of their character limits. Translation growth can easily exceed them. The copyright can contain 255 characters and the citation, 2000 characters.

Title bar text

An obscure, but very visible, translation problem is associated with the title of the Help file which appears in the title bar of the Help window. If you have any accent or diacritical marks in your Help file title, you need to make a special adjustment when compiling with the WinHelp 3.1 compilers. The text that is used in the Title setting of the project file must use MS-DOS text characters. It is not enough to just use Windows characters. Figure 21.8 illustrates this. The top portion shows the effect of inserting the "á" character (Alt+0225) into the project file using Windows text.

To properly use special characters, type the title in your word processor and save it in a temporary document as MS-DOS text. Open the temporary document in Notepad (or another text editor) and cut and paste it into the Title= setting in the project file. The result is the proper display of the title as shown in the lower portion of Figure 21.8.

The WinHelp 4 compiler has corrected this problem and the previous procedure is not necessary. The special characters are accepted without a problem in Help Workshop or in a text editor.

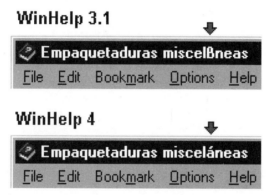

Figure 21.8. *Potential title error during localization with the 3.1 compiler.*

Writing topic headings

When crafting topic headings, use phrases that make them clearly distinct from one another. Be wary of fine distinctions which may not be translated correctly. For example, the topic headings "To delete text" and "To cut text" may be translated to the same phrase unless the translator is aware of the distinction.

Translating topic headings requires changes to the title ($) footnote, since it is used with the Index, **KLink/ALink** macros, Find, and the History box. If a topic title footnote is duplicated, a warning message appears during compiling.

The Compare macro

The WinHelp 4 specification includes the **Compare** macro which is intended for comparing original and translated versions of a Help file. However, at the time of this writing, this macro was not functioning, and no plans had been announced to fix it.

When functioning, the **Compare** macro titles the original and translated versions of a Help file side-by-side. Clicking a jump in one of the Help files executes the same jump in the other Help file. This simplifies the process of reviewing complimentary topics.

Character support in fonts

Some fonts may not support all the characters with diacritical marks in a particular language. This is most likely to occur with non-Western European languages that use the Roman alphabet, such as Polish, Czech, or Croatian.

Japanese/Chinese topic files

If you are creating a Japanese or Chinese version of your Help system, the topic files will be translated using a double-byte character set. You need to make an additional project file setting when specifying the topic file.

To specify a double-byte character set:

1. In Help Workshop, add your topic files as described in Chapter 18.

2. In the Topic File box, select a topic file name.

3. Check the box **Topic files use a double-byte character set**. Repeat for all the topic files.

Cross platform strategies

While Windows is the dominant operating system right now, there are other strong players as well. UNIX and Macintosh have long histories with substantial numbers of users dedicated to those platforms. If you are providing online Help support for your UNIX and/or Mac version of your product, it makes sense to leverage the work you have invested in your Windows Help.

Most of the labor associated with a WinHelp system is in the construction of the topic file. The universal rich-text format makes it easy to move that information across platforms. However, the lack of a standard viewer and the differences in the user interfaces present considerable challenges in moving to UNIX/Macintosh. This section describes those challenges and provides useful conversion tips.

WINHELP AND UNIX

The widespread use of UNIX in certain sectors of industry, education, and government makes it a ripe market for porting your application software. However, there are several fundamental differences between the Windows and UNIX environments. These differences affect not only the application, but the cross-platform development of your Help system.

The UNIX Help viewer

The main hurdle to overcome is that the UNIX environment does not offer a system-wide Help standard like Windows Help. There is no UNIX Help viewer like WINHELP.EXE that is present on every user's computer. However, it is possible to overcome this hurdle with the HyperHelp product described in Chapter 22. HyperHelp supplies a viewer, which when installed on the user's computer, can emulate the display of a Windows Help system. Your existing WinHelp topic and project files can be processed with a conversion utility and compiler that is also available through HyperHelp. At the time of this writing, HyperHelp is the only product which provides this service.

However, there are some features and functions which do not relate to UNIX workstations, X Window/Motif, or OpenVMS environments. Some features are not available from the UNIX operating systems, while others are simply not "practiced" as a style or methodology. Just as Windows has a "Style Guide" for developers to use when developing Windows programs, so too UNIX has a "Style Guide" for UNIX developers to follow. Some commonly accepted functions like making "Help Always On Top" is just not practiced (and does pose some technical challenges) to implement in the UNIX environment due to its network-driven shared processes nature. Here are some examples:

- **Macros**: The following list of macros are not supported in UNIX either because there is no Motif equivalent or because HyperHelp offers a better method of accomplishing the macro function. The macros do not have to be removed from your topic files; they will be ignored or substituted for by HyperHelp.

BookmarkMore, ControlPanel, EndMPrint, ExtInsertMenu, Flush, Generate, HelpOnTop, InitMPrint, JumpHash, MPrintHash, MPrintID, NoShow, PopupHash, ShellExecute, ShortCut, Test

- **Project File Options**: HyperHelp also ignores the following project file commands:

CHARSET, DBCS, DEFONT, FORCEFONT, LANGUAGE, LCID, NOTES, OLDKEYPHRASE, REPLACE, REPORT, MACROS

General Compatibility Issues

There are also four general areas that affect compatibility when you're developing on-line Help for UNIX and for WinHelp:

- **Case-Sensitivity**: In DOS/Windows environments, filenames are not case-sensitive, but in UNIX, they are. This can cause problems when referencing graphic files, text files, Help project files and any others. Try to use filenames that are all lower case to accommodate this difference. One wrong filename can mean that a graphic file is not compiled into a Help file, or that the file used is an incorrect one.

- **TrueType Fonts:** Since TrueType fonts are based on Windows technology, scaleable for both the printer and display, they are not available on UNIX operating systems. If you are designing cross-platform Help files that utilize any of these fonts that do not relate to the standard UNIX fonts, then you may experience problems. However, if you own the rights to distribute a particular TrueType font, you may be able to convert it to an Adobe Type 1 font which can be used with UNIX.

- **Metafile (.WMF) Graphic File Support**: Windows metafiles are not supported by native UNIX operating systems. Metafiles are actually like small executable files that perform GDI calls to the Windows APIs to draw a graphic image. Since these APIs are not available to UNIX, metafiles cannot be read and displayed. Therefore, when authoring for cross-platform Help, use bitmap files instead.

- **DLL Support**: You cannot use Windows DLLs for the same reasons as above. The UNIX operating systems do not have the APIs which are needed to support Windows DLLs. Equivalent functionality can usually be obtained from public domain DLLs for UNIX or a specific DLL can be written by a UNIX developer.

The information in this section was developed with the assistance of Bristol Technology, makers of the HyperHelp authoring tool reviewed in Chapter 22.

WINHELP AND THE MACINTOSH

Windows users have fairly fixed expectations about what online Help should look like, and it's virtually unthinkable that any Windows product would ship without it. On the Macintosh side, however, system-level support for online Help arrived a decade after the first Macs appeared in 1984. The Apple Guide extension, released in late 1994 with the Mac System 7.5, is the Apple-approved standard for online Help, but it has been slow to catch on because its not compatible with System versions before 7.5 (many Mac developers try to support at least System 7.1). Before Apple Guide, Macintosh users were confronted with a variety of Help systems created with HyperCard or proprietary technologies, and it was not uncommon—and this is still true today—for major applications to ship without online Help. Thus, it is still fair to say that many Macintosh users have no fixed expectations of what online Help looks like.

Thus, companies developing cross-platform products were faced with two facts of marketing life: Windows users clearly expect online in WinHelp, while Mac users' expectations are less well defined. Third-party providers MultiDoc Technologies (makers of EHelp) and Altura Software (makers of QuickHelp) saw an opportunity and marketed Macintosh Help compilers that accept your WinHelp .HPJ, .RTF, and graphics files and produce a Help system with many of the features of WinHelp. At the moment, these two products provide your easiest, cleanest path to cross-platform Help development. However, Help writers will inevitably feel pressure to provide Apple Guide on the Mac as OS 7.5 arrives on more desktops and competitors provide Guide systems to their customers. Thus, we begin by examining Apple Guide, and we'll then shift our attention to methods more suited to EHelp and QuickHelp.

Apple Guide

Apple uses the term "assistance" to describe what Apple Guide provides. Avoiding the term "online Help" is more than just a marketing ploy. Apple Guide assistance is fundamentally different from Windows Help, having more in common with Windows cue cards and wizards.

Apple includes Guide assistance for the Mac OS 7.5 itself, and that provides the best example of how Apple feels Guide systems should look. You can choose Macintosh Guide from the Guide menu (a question mark located on the right side of the menu bar), and you'll see the Access window, where you can look for information by topic or use an index or full-text search. (See Figure 21.9.)

Once you've located a topic, Apple Guide displays a series of panels, each containing just a single step. If you've already done a few steps in the task, those beginning steps are omitted, and you pick up the task at exactly the right spot. "Coach marks" help guide you through the steps, highlighting menu commands that you need to choose and drawing red circles around dialog box controls and other items you need to select. The Guide system checks to make sure you've completed the step before proceeding to the next step, and either prompts you when you don't follow along or does the step for you.

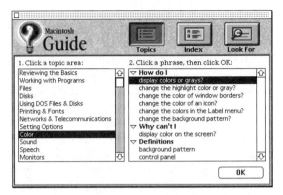

Figure 21.9. *Selecting a topic in Apple Guide.*

In WinHelp, the essential unit of information is a topic that contains the steps in a task. In Apple Guide, the smallest unit of information is a panel that might contain only a paragraph of text or a single step. (See Figure 21.10.) A Guide "sequence" defines a series of panels for a task, and the sequence name is what users see in the Access window. These sequences, however, are not analogous to WinHelp browse sequences because a single panel can appear in any number of Guide sequences, and sequences can be embedded in sequences.

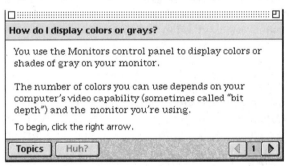

Figure 21.10. *A single step panel in Apple Guide.*

All of this—interactive coach marks, checking to see if tasks are completed, and definitions of panels and sequences—is created using a scripting language unique to Apple Guide. In addition, there are differences in the way indexing is handled, and it is rare for Guide assistance to be available from a dialog box the way context-sensitive WinHelp might be. The Guide authoring tools provide a limited RTF-to-Guide converter, which creates a one-panel sequence for each of your WinHelp topics. It retains text formatting, jumps, and pop-ups, and creates index entries for each keyword. But it discards the rest—browse sequences, macros, A footnotes, and the like. At best, you get a basic shell that requires lots of work to flesh out. At this writing, a Guide-to-RTF converter is not available.

Thus, as you can see, you face many obstacles to easy re-use of your WinHelp text and graphics in Apple Guide. Still, the technological world does not stand still. If your competitor comes out with an Apple Guide system, you may be forced to do so, as well. Perhaps the best solution is to punt—instead of using Apple Guide for online Help, use it to create a short tutorial to appease your marketing department's desire for this checklist item. Otherwise, you can try converting your WinHelp browse sequences into Guide sequences, and your WinHelp topics into Guide panels. This approach will not take advantage of the strengths of either WinHelp or Apple Guide, but it may be better than writing completely unique Help for each. In the meantime, we can only hope that Apple or third parties will provide additional conversion tools.

Making the cross-platform decision

Given the present difficulties in developing truly cross-platform Help between WinHelp and Apple Guide, the best route remains the third-party tools EHelp and QuickHelp. These products let you easily re-use text and graphics between platforms, but there is often a catch. "Reusing text and graphics" sounds like a logical strategy that should be easy to sell to upper management—that is, of course, until upper management realizes their Macintosh Help will wind up looking suspiciously like something first created on Windows. Thus, be prepared to negotiate some additional obstacles:

✔ Many companies developing cross-platform versions of their software began in the Macintosh market and still have a Macintosh mindset. Getting other managers to accept a Windows Help paradigm involves a cultural change. Marketing managers, especially, will lobby for "Maclike" Help without wanting to fund the effort it would take to produce it. And writers used to the Macintosh may find themselves working on Windows authoring tools such as RoboHELP (even to produce the Mac topics).

✔ Many companies with cross-platform versions release the Macintosh version first and follow up with the Windows version later—sometimes much later. Maintaining a pool of shared resources becomes harder when you don't know how subsequent development decisions will affect the re-usability of your materials.

✔ Windows programs have a long tradition of providing context-sensitive Help, and Windows 95 pushes that expectation further with pop-up Help on every control in a dialog box, a time-consuming feature for Help writers. Enabling context-sensitive Help on the Macintosh requires the "buy-in" of engineers who must learn a third-party API to provide the necessary hooks. And competing technologies such as balloon Help for dialog box controls complicate the writing team's ability to re-use text easily.

On the issues of negotiation and diplomacy, we can only offer general advice: Be prepared to offer arguments based on economics and time-to-market considerations. It may be appealing to produce a unique Help system for your Macintosh product, but can you justify the added expense and time? If, as is increasingly true in most companies today, your Windows product generates the lion's share of revenue, how many concessions can you justify in modifying your strategy to fit the Mac development side?

As for maneuvering the technical challenges of cross-platform Help, we have the standard sage advice: plan early, test often. The rest of this chapter is devoted to giving you a head start on planning, testing, and implementation.

Benefits of EHelp and QuickHelp

Both EHelp and QuickHelp provide you with three essential components on the Mac:

✔ A compiler that accepts your .HPJ file, your .RTF files, and your graphics (possibly after some conversion), and produces a Help file with all the major features of Windows Help.

✔ A viewer program needed to display and navigate the compiled Help.

✔ An API that Mac developers use to control the Help system and to implement context-sensitive hooks.

The licensing fees include the right to distribute the viewer with your program. For a more complete description of EHelp and QuickHelp, see Chapter 22, *Help Authoring Tools*.

With proper planning, there should be no reason for you to have to extensively "massage" your WinHelp materials for compiling on EHelp and QuickHelp. In many cases, the process is as simple as transferring your files to the Macintosh, opening the project file in EHelp or QuickHelp, setting some options, and compiling. The following sections help you understand how to ensure that the right topics are included on both platforms, and how to deal with a few inconsistencies in the way text and graphics transfer from one platform to another.

Sorting out the topic outline

It pays to keep in mind that the very definition of "cross-platform Help" implies a strategy of using identical text and graphics wherever possible. This thrifty mindset will guide your planning from the earliest stages.

To begin your Help outline, concentrate on identifying only the topics that are common to both platforms and those that are unique to both platforms. You may want to set up a spreadsheet with columns for your topic ID and the platform:

Topic	Platform
About slide shows	Cross-platform
Setting up a background	Cross-platform
Adding text and graphics	Cross-platform
Adding OLE objects	Windows only
Adding objects with Publish and Subscribe	Macintosh only

Note that you have five topics, but each platform has only four topics each. In an ideal world, this is all you need. But as you write, you'll probably find that some topics must contain small differences between platforms. For example, the "Adding text and graphics" topic might contain a procedure that can only be completed using the ALT key on Windows but uses the Option key on the Macintosh. So, you must create "mirrored" versions of this topic, one each for Windows and the Macintosh. Now the platform category in your spreadsheet contains a fourth type of topic.

Topic	Platform
About slide shows	Cross-platform
Setting up a background	Cross-platform
Adding text and graphics	Mirrored
Adding OLE objects	Windows only
Adding objects with Publish and Subscribe	Macintosh only

By sorting your spreadsheet, you can see that your outline for each platform has grown considerably more complicated:

Windows Outline	Mac Outline	Category
About slide shows	About slide shows	Cross-platform
Setting up a background	Setting up a background	Cross-platform
Adding text and graphics	Adding text and graphics	Mirrored
Adding OLE objects		Windows only
	Adding objects with Publish and Subscribe	Macintosh only

Although each platform still requires only four topics, you now have six topics to keep track of: two cross-platform topics, two versions of a single mirrored topic, one Windows-only topic, and one Mac-only topic. Your biggest challenge will be ensuring that the proper topics are compiled on each platform. We can boil down the essential planning strategy by considering the cross-platform "About slide shows" topic. Let's say this overview topic contains a jump to the mirrored topic "Adding text and graphics." As long as you ensure that both versions of this mirrored topic contain the same topic ID (# footnote) and browse sequence (+ footnote), you need not worry. When you need to compile on Windows, you use the Windows version of "Adding text and graphics," and likewise you use the Macintosh version when compiling on the Macintosh. Because the topic ID is the same, the jump resolves without problem, and the browse sequences work as they should. The actual text of the "Adding text and graphics" topic will be different on each platform, and you can add unique keywords for each platform as well. However, let's say you want your cross-platform topic "About slide shows" to contain jumps to the topics on OLE and Publish and Subscribe. You can't do this and retain "About slide shows" as a cross-platform topic. To do so would require "About slide shows" to become a mirrored topic, with the Windows version containing a jump to "Adding OLE objects" and the Mac version containing a jump to "Adding objects with Publish and Subscribe." It's up to you to decide whether the advantage of splitting a cross-platform topic into mirrored versions is worth the additional time it takes to create, track, and update two topics instead of one. Just remember that, for greatest efficiency, your pool of shared cross-platform topics must be as large as possible.

When it's time to compile, on each platform you need:

✔ A copy of the cross-platform topics.

✔ The appropriate versions of your mirrored topics.

✔ Your platform-specific topics.

Many of us are used to keeping all topics on a single subject in one file. You can use build tags to continue this practice (both EHelp and QuickHelp support build tags). However, as you move files from one platform to another, you often have to change fonts and possibly make other adjustments (discussed in greater detail later). The more you "thrash" topics back and forth between platforms, the greater your opportunities for introducing errors. Therefore, you might want to consider organizing topics into five separate files: a cross-platform file; a file for each version of your mirrored topics: and a file for each set of platform-specific topics. The choice is largely a matter of personal preference. Editing keywords and browse sequence is especially difficult when the topics on a related subject are scattered throughout several files. On the other hand, you may value the security of knowing that topics can't possibly slip onto the wrong platform because you've segregated them into separate files.

To maintain consistency among mirrored topics, you can consider setting up a sort of conditional text feature using Word character styles. Tag all Macintosh text with one character tag and all Windows text with another. When you compile on the Macintosh, change the Windows character tag to hidden text. You then see only the Mac text. You can do the opposite on

Windows. In this way, you can maintain only one version of a mirrored topic instead of two. This method works reasonably well for short pieces of text (swapping "Alt" for "Option," for example), but becomes harder to implement when several paragraphs are involved. And, of course, tagging must be done perfectly, or you get unwanted text or no text at all.

As your deadline looms, you'll need to have a rigorous methodology in place for moving files around and compiling. To simplify matters, you may want to consider doing all writing (even for Mac-only topics) on Windows to take advantage of Windows authoring tools. Moving a copy of the files over to the Macintosh only to compile, while keeping the "golden set of files" only on Windows, also makes it easier to troubleshoot problems. It's especially helpful for one person to coordinate the builds on both platforms, to prevent situations where one team keeps introducing changes into the shared topics that "break" the build on the other platform.

Text appearance

On Windows, the safe font choices are the TrueType fonts Arial and Times New Roman, plus the onscreen font MS Sans Serif. On the Macintosh, these are roughly equivalent to the PostScript fonts Helvetica and Times, with Geneva as the onscreen font. As you move topics—especially shared topics—across platforms, you have two dependable ways to ensure you get the right fonts:

✔ If you're using EHelp or QuickHelp, take advantage of their font-mapping features. You can map each instance of a Windows font type and size to a specific Mac font type and size—for example, 10-pt. Arial to 12-pt. Helvetica. Using this method, you never have to change fonts in the source files; the Mac compiler makes the substitution when it's building your Help file. (The same font size on Windows is noticeably smaller on the Macintosh. For textual material, increase the font sizes a couple of points, from 10-pt on Windows to 12-pt. on the Mac, or 8-pt. on Windows to 10-pt. on the Mac.)

✔ Make sure all your text has been tagged using a consistently named set of paragraph and character styles in a Microsoft Word template. Create mirrored versions of this template on both Windows and the Mac. The style names must be identical on both platforms, but you can choose different fonts and sizes. When you move a file from one platform to another, remember to attach the appropriate stylesheet.

Given these two clean alternatives, be wary of relying heavily on Word's global search-and-replace feature to switch fonts, a messy and often time-consuming alternative that invites oversight. If, for some reason, you must manually change fonts, create macros to minimize the chances of overlooking a critical step.

Once you've got the right fonts, also check for special characters that may display incorrectly, or disappear altogether, as files move across platforms. The problem occurs when a character (for example, a mathematical symbol) has one ASCII value in the Windows font and a different value in your Mac font. Even fonts of the same name are not immune to this problem. For example, ASCII character 240 in the Macintosh Symbol font is an apple, while in the

Windows Symbol font it is a hollow box. Create a topic with all the special characters you plan to use, in the fonts and sizes required, and run a test build on both platforms. (Be sure to share this test file early with your translators, who face additional font problems.) Here are some solid strategies for avoiding character problems:

✔ Despite some differences, the characters in the Symbol font are largely the same on both platforms, and this is usually a dependable way to use characters such as the trademark symbol.

✔ Avoid special characters altogether. For example, use the WinHelp compiler's internal bullet.bmp graphic for bullets, and create a complementary graphic for the Mac. Or, instead of a special character, spell out the name—for example, use Pi instead of the mathematical character.

Graphics

Even if you're using a product such as QuickHelp, which lets you use your bitmap files on the Mac without "retouching," it pays to be aware of two fundamental differences between Mac and PC graphics: resolution and color palettes.

The typical Macintosh monitor has a resolution of 72 pixels per inch (ppi), while most PC monitors are 96-ppi. When fed an unconverted graphic, the Mac or PC will try to display it at the correct size. Let's say you have a screenshot that's one inch wide. The Mac throws out pixels to squeeze 96-ppi of information into a one-inch, 72-ppi space; Windows adds pixels to fill out a one-inch, 96-ppi with just the 72 that it was given. In both cases, the resulting graphic looks distorted. Small graphics, especially screenshots of buttons and tools, suffer the most, as do any graphics with bitmapped text. For larger pictorial graphics, the effects can be less noticeable.

For this reason, you usually need a conversion program that changes the graphic's internal ppi setting. This means the same graphic will appear larger on Windows than it does on the Mac, but that is better than the alternative. Except for large graphics without text, avoid methods that convert from the Mac to Windows aspect ratio, which just produce the same distortion. On Windows, you can use the popular shareware program ShgRez to change the ppi setting of segmented hypergraphics (.SHG files). The powerful scripting capability of the Macintosh program DeBabelizer makes it a popular choice for converting large batches of graphics.

An even thornier issue is the difference between the standard Mac and Windows color systems, a topic that would take an entire chapter to cover in sufficient detail. Now that the Windows Help compiler can display 256-color images, your options are not quite as limited as they once were, but you must still carefully test graphics before re-using them on one platform from the other. In brief, here are some ways to avoid frustration:

✔ To take screenshots of isolated UI elements (buttons, toolbars, and the like) on either platform, set your monitor to display only 16 colors. Most cross-platform applications are designed to look reasonably well at this color setting, and this limited palette transfers with fewer problems from platform to platform.

✔ Use 256-color graphics only when you genuinely need the additional colors to make a point or represent something accurately. You'll need to test and refine these graphics carefully on each platform, so be sure the benefit is worth the effort. Some Macintosh colors, such as the light gray used in many UI elements, have no direct Windows equivalent, and Windows substitutes the color with the closest RGB values—a neutral "doctor's office green" that has had many an art director seeing red. You'll need a graphics conversion tool (again, DeBabelizer is widely respected for the accuracy of its palette conversions), and you'll need to do some trial-and-error experiments with the many dithering options.

The information in this section was developed by Frank Elley, BTC Productions • P.O. Box 390531, Mountain View, CA 94039-0531, Voice: (415) 988-1860 • E-mail: BTCPrdtn@aol.com.

22

Authoring Tools

Chapter 10, *Creating Help Topics,* describes the time-consuming, tedious procedure of manually coding a topic file. Much of the tedium can be avoided with the help of third party authoring tools. These tools not only save you the time of adding the appropriate codes, they also eliminate many errors.

The fast growth of Windows Help has greatly increased the number of authoring tools available to you. In 1992, there were just a handful of tools available. Now, there are at least two dozen. In the first edition of this book, four authoring tools were reviewed: Doc-To-Help, RoboHELP, Help Magician, and Microsoft's WHPE/WHAT. Each of these tools has been significantly enhanced since that time. However, there has been one constant. The individual tools continue to present widely different approaches to creating Help. Each has built a tool based on assumptions about the role of Help and how Help should be constructed. In choosing an authoring tool, it is extremely important to be aware of these disparate assumptions.

This chapter provides an introduction to authoring tools by describing three freely-distributed basic tools. This introduction is followed by a detailed review of three of the most prominent full-featured products. It concludes with descriptions of other popular authoring tools.

Introduction to authoring tools

WinHelp authoring tools are products that automate the creation of project and topic files. For newcomers to Windows Help, these aids translate into a significant reduction in the learning curve. While manually coding Help files is not beyond the abilities of most developers, it takes a substantial amount of time to learn and become comfortable with the coding rules and idiosyncrasies. Both experienced and novice Help developers benefit from the substantial labor savings in coding time and debugging that authoring tools provide. As the size of your Help system increases, the value derived from a Help tool grows dramatically. For almost any project, the reduction in labor costs alone can quickly cover the cost of even the most expensive authoring tool.

This section introduces three authoring tools which are good starting points. The first is the topic coding template included on your book disc. The second is a topic coding template from Microsoft. The third is a project and contents editor from Microsoft.

WINHELP4 AUTHORING TEMPLATE

The large majority of the coding time in any Help project is associated with the topic file. As described in earlier chapters, topic coding consists of specifying topics, jumps, keywords, and other hypertext elements with the use of footnotes and formatting attributes in a word processing document. Since the large majority of Help development work takes place in the topic file, authoring tools that are built around a word processor provide the most efficiency. Several tools are available that take this approach.

One of them is WINHELP4.DOT. This file, available on your book disc, is a Word for Windows template with custom menu commands that assist you in creating a topic file and compiling a Help file. The template is accompanied by a Help file, WINHELP4.HLP, which details its use. Place the template in your \WINWORD\TEMPLATES folder and select it when you are ready to begin a new topic file in Word. WINHELP4 is provided as an introductory tool that assists in creating your first Help systems, and gives you an idea of how other authoring tools work.

As with any Word document, you can import your Help text from an existing document or type it from scratch. Once your text is in place you can begin adding codes to define topics and hotspots. When a new document is opened in Word with the WINHELP4 template, several new commands appear on the standard Word menus. These WINHELP4 commands provide convenient dialog boxes for coding your topics.

You can choose commands from the Insert menu to add topics, jumps, and graphics. Figure 22.1 shows the dialog box for adding a new topic. The dialog box provides an entry form for keying in the topic ID, the title, keywords, and a browse sequence number. Optional items include a topic entry macro, build tag, A-keyword or window type. After you type all of the desired information into the dialog box, WINHELP4 automatically creates all of the necessary footnotes in one quick step. Without the aid of WINHELP4, you would have to manually choose the Footnote command, type a footnote mark (such as # or $), type the appropriate information, and then repeat the process for each additional control code.

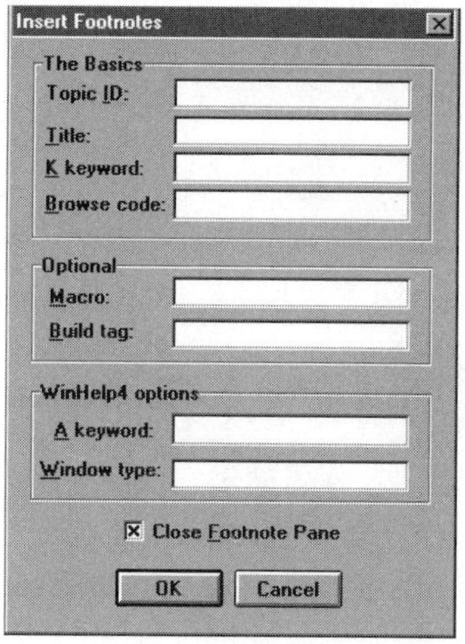

Figure 22.1. *Inserting footnote codes with WINHELP4.*

WINHELP4 also provides a dialog box for adding jumps and pop-ups. The dialog box prompts you for the topic ID of the topic you want to jump to or have pop up. You also type in the text which you want to appear in green as hotspot text in your Help system. WINHELP4 inserts this information into your topic file and formats it, using the appropriate underlining and hidden character attributes.

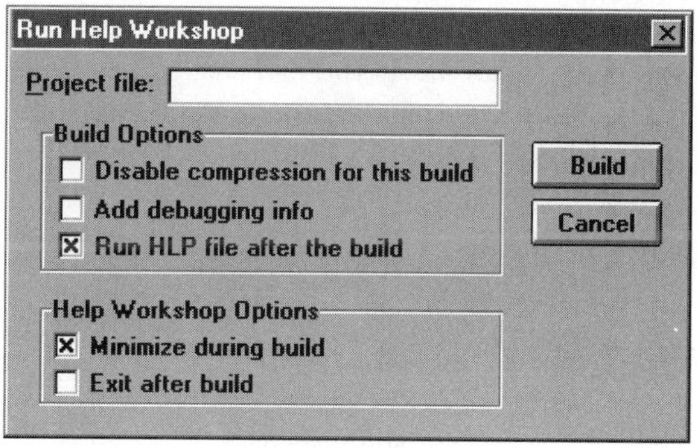

Figure 22.2. *Launching the Help compiler.*

Additional dialog boxes are available to assist with launching the Help compiler, assembling a contents file, and inserting graphics (see Figures 22.2 and 22.3). The main limitation of WIN-HELP4 is that it does not assist in the construction of the project file. You need to use another tool, such as Help Workshop, described below, to fill that gap. Also, you will find that the full-featured products described later in this chapter provide more robust support in implementing the various features of your Help system.

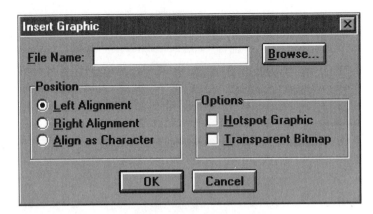

Figure 22.3. *Inserting Graphics.*

WINDOWS HELP AUTHORING TEMPLATE (WHAT)

A template similar to WINHELP4 is available through Microsoft. The Windows Help Authoring Template (WHAT) is an unsupported Word template. This template provides much the same functionality as WINHELP4.DOT. There are two versions: WHAT6 works with Word for Windows 6 and the 3.x compilers; WHAT7 supports Word 7 and the WinHelp 4 compiler. The WHAT templates are available with the Microsoft Developers Network CD.

The WHAT template provides you with the ability to insert all the footnote codes for a topic through a single dialog box. See Figure 22.4. You can also select a single topic or block of text, or even an entire file, and instantly create a fully functional Help application out of your selection. This feature makes it a snap to test small portions of your Help system and is especially handy for experimenting with new Help techniques.

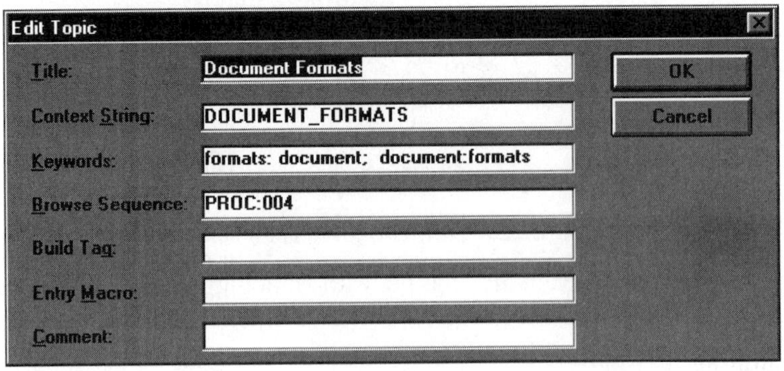

Figure 22.4.

Another feature of WHAT is the ability to place macro commands into your topic file. By choosing the Macro Hotspot command from the Insert menu of Word, a dialog box appears with a comprehensive list of Help macros. Figure 22.5 shows the selection box for adding a macro hotspot. You can choose a macro from the list and specify the Help text that the user clicks on to activate the macro. Both the text and the macro are added to your topic file and are properly formatted. Unfortunately, this feature falls short by not allowing you to specify the associated macro syntax. Chapter 16, "Working with Help Macros" provides specific information on employing Help macros.

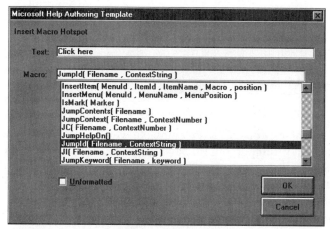

Figure 22.5. *Adding a macro hotspot with WHAT.*

MICROSOFT HELP WORKSHOP

For WinHelp 3.x, Microsoft provides a utility called the Windows Help Project Editor (WHPE) to assist with project file creation. This tool is a complement to the WinHelp Authoring Template (WHAT) described above. In WinHelp 4, WHPE has been replaced with Help Workshop. This tool, HCW.EXE, helps you to create the project and contents files, and to compile, test, and report on a Help file. It does not provide any facilities for adding codes to the topic file. Help Workshop and its documentation Help file are included on your book disc.

You begin by double-clicking HCW.EXE, which launches Help Workshop. Then you can choose to open an existing project file or to start a new one. Starting a new project file is described in Chapter 18 and converting a WinHelp 3.x project file to WinHelp 4 is described in Chapter 21. When you open a project file, the section headings and settings are displayed in a project editor window. Buttons to the right of the window open dialog boxes for adding project file settings such as topic filenames, window size values, and startup macros. All of the WinHelp 4 project file settings are supported in Help Workshop. (See Figure 22.6.) You can quickly access a specific setting's dialog box by double-clicking on a setting in the project editor window.

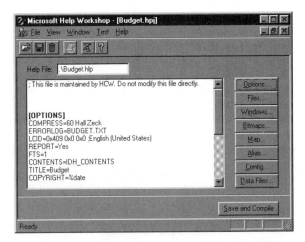

Figure 22.6. *The project editor in Help Workshop.*

When your project file and topic files are complete, you can launch the compiler from Help Workshop. The Save and Compile button saves your settings and launches the WinHelp 4 Help compiler HCRTF.EXE. During compiling, another window appears to display messages. In addition to reporting errors and warnings like the 3.1 compiler does, the WinHelp 4 compiler provides information on compile time and the number of topics, jumps, keywords, and bitmaps, as shown in Figure 22.7. It also provides the compiled size of the Help file. You can delete the compilation window at any time. A toolbar button launches the compiled Help file.

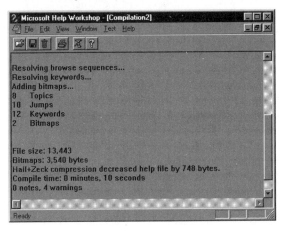

Figure 22.7. *Compiler messages displayed in Help Workshop.*

Another Help Workshop feature is an excellent interactive editor for adjusting window size and position. When you click the Auto-Size button (Windows/Position/Auto-Size) a sample window appears on the desktop. (See Figure 22.8.) You simply move and size that window as needed. You can overlay the sample window onto a compiled Help window to experiment with size and position.

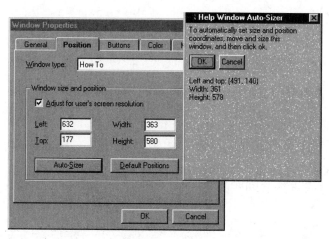

Figure 22.8. *Specifying Help window size and position with Help Workshop.*

Help Workshop also provides an editor for creating a contents file. It displays the heading and topic items as they would appear to the user. However, there is no link between the topic items and the topic IDs in the topic file. You must manually type the destination topic IDs, carefully, for each jump.

You can also perform reporting and testing from Help Workshop. The testing facility, which includes Help Author mode, is described in Chapter 20, *Compiling, Debugging, and Testing.* The reporting facility, also described in Chapter 20, can print a list of topic titles, keywords, topic text, or hash numbers.

The biggest limitation of Help Workshop is that it isn't integrated with the topic file. It is also only loosely supported by Microsoft. However, the documentation that accompanies it is an excellent technical reference on WinHelp and it provides adequate, not great, procedural information about Help Workshop. The documentation Help file is HCW.HLP and the associated contents file is HCW.CNT.

Help Workshop is available on the disc that comes with this book.

Full-Featured authoring tools

Most of the authoring tools described in this section provide a comprehensive solution for Help authoring, including support for macros, hypergraphics, and secondary windows. However, many of the tools still offer only sparse support for acceptable development of keywords and browse sequences. Developers should also be aware that the tools focus primarily on the coding portion of Help development. They tend to ignore the much larger and important portion of your Help development: proper design and effective writing. In short, Help tools are a definite benefit, but they affect only a narrow slice of the Help development pie.

Although a comparison chart of authoring tools appeared in the first edition of this book, due to the widely different approaches the Help tools now offer, such an attempt at present would be deceptive. Most of the authoring tools now support most, if not all, of the WinHelp compiler capabilities. A more useful approach to comparison is to ask yourself two questions: first, "What type of Help system am I trying to build?", and second, "How do I like to work?".

The applications of WinHelp can be quite varied. Answers to the first question might be: to support a Windows software application, to create an online policy and procedures manual, to display database information. Your answer to the second question takes into account the different approaches of the tools: Do you like to write your Help content first and code topics later, or do you like to write a topic, code it; write another topic, code it, etc? Do you want to have a single-source print manual and Help system? Are you interested in the "behind the scenes" coding of your Help system or do you want to be shielded from that process? As you read the descriptions of the various authoring tools, keep in mind your answers to these two questions.

The following products are reviewed in this section:

- RoboHELP

- Doc-To-Help

- ForeHelp

They have been chosen because they are exemplary models of three different approaches to Help authoring and all have substantial followings.

Two of the tools reviewed in the first edition, Doc-To-Help and RoboHELP, are still in a commanding position in terms of installed user base. While the two products have significantly evolved in speed and features support, they still adhere to their basic approaches to Help development. The third tool, ForeHelp, is a relative newcomer which has quickly risen to the top with innovative features.

The reviews of the three tools are followed by descriptions of other authoring tools. Those other authoring tools may very well provide a better solution to *your* Help authoring needs, and they should be considered as strongly as the first three profiled here. Since a new tool appears approximately every month, you may want to consult periodicals such as *The WinHelp Journal* and the STC *Hyperviews* newsletter.

ROBOHELP

RoboHELP, like WINHELP4 and WHAT, customizes Word for Windows with a template that adds commands to Word menus. Like those templates, RoboHELP presents you with dialog boxes that make adding control codes to your topic file quick and easy. Like Help Workshop, RoboHELP provides dialog boxes for setting the various project file options. That is where the comparison with Help Workshop ends, however. RoboHELP is far more robust and automated in the way that it handles these chores. The project-file generation and compiling functions are controlled from within the topic file rather than through a separate project editor. In short, RoboHELP provides a full-featured Help authoring platform that is smoothly integrated into Word. There are two versions of RoboHELP: Version 3.0 supports Word 2 and 6 and works with the WinHelp 3.x compilers. Version 95 supports Word 6 (32-bit), Word 7, and the WinHelp 4 compiler.

To use RoboHELP you begin in Word: start a new Word document by selecting a RoboHELP template. An opening dialog box prompts you for a title, filename, and working folder. RoboHELP opens a new Word document and, behind the scenes, creates a project file. Appearing with Word is a floating toolbar, shown in Figure 22.9. The toolbar includes buttons for adding topics, jumps, pop-ups, graphics, editing the project file, creating a contents file, compiling, launching the Help file, and more.

You add your Help text either by typing the text or by inserting existing files, using the standard word-processing functions. As you add the topic text, you can begin applying control codes. To create a new topic, you click the Topic button from the floating tool bar. A dialog box appears, prompting you for the topic title and an optional search keyword. RoboHELP automatically inserts the appropriate footnotes, including the one for the topic ID. The coding for a browse sequence, build tag, and topic macro can also be automatically generated with entries in the same box.

Once you have specified two or more topics, creating jumps between them is a snap. Position the Word insertion mark where you would like the hotspot text to appear. Then click the Jump button. A dialog box presents you with a list of the topics that you have created. Figure 22.10 shows the Create Hypertext Jump to Help Topic dialog box. The box contains all of the topic IDs in the current topic file. Select the topic ID of the destination topic and click OK. The hotspot text and all of the appropriate jump coding automatically appear in the topic file. Pop-ups are added in similar fashion. You can create new topics on the fly as you add jumps or pop-ups.

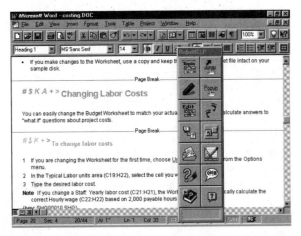

Figure 22.9. *RoboHELP integrates a custom toolbar in Word.*

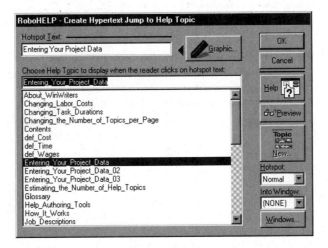

Figure 22.10. *Adding a jump in RoboHELP*

Once you have specified your topics and jumps, you can prompt RoboHELP to compile the finished Help file. Toolbar buttons save the latest changes to the document and update the topic file. Another button launches the Help compiler. An error handler assists in debugging any errors in your project.

As you begin to fine-tune the look of your Help system, you'll have to make adjustments to the project file. The Setup Project button is the gateway to all of the options that can be set in the project file. This includes quick access to window sizing and coloring, macros, context-sensitive links, and more.

In RoboHELP 95 there is full support for customizing secondary windows with toolbar buttons, auto-sizing and absolute coordinates. Also included are style tags and options that support the fonts, font sizes, and window definitions used by Microsoft in their operating system Help files.

RoboHELP's management of graphics and multiple topic files is outstanding. A graphics "gallery" makes it easy to view bitmaps and metafiles, and to integrate them into your topic file with a single click. (See Figure 22.11.) The graphics tools also include screen capture and paint-box utilities. RoboHELP provides an enhanced hotspot editor (SHED) which makes it a snap to connect topics to multiple hotspots.

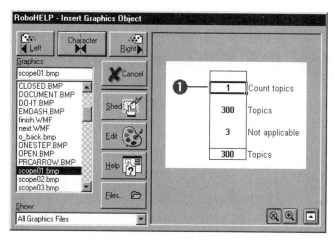

Figure 22.11. *A graphics gallery for previewing and selecting graphics.*

With RoboHELP you can also painlessly divide your text into multiple topic files, which can then be combined into one Help system. The Goto Topic button can instantly display any topic in any topic file that is associated with the current project. If you are using multiple topic files in the creation of your Help system, you can display the topic IDs from any of the topic files. If you are working with multiple documents compiled into one Help file, you can easily add or remove documents from the current project. This organizes production and makes it easy to compile select portions of the document for testing.

One of the most prominent features of RoboHELP 95 is the Contents Tab Composer. This tool greatly simplifies the creation of contents files. It displays all the available topics in the left portion of the window. You form your contents file hierarchy in the right portion. The composer, shown in Figure 22.12, looks similar to the contents editor of Help Workshop, but provides much more functionality. You can automatically add all of the topics in a topic file into your contents hierarchy, or select and add them, one at a time. The composer provides the capability to drag and drop topic items in a way similar to the operation of the outliner in Word for Windows. And you can move items up and down in the list, an important feature missing from Help Workshop.

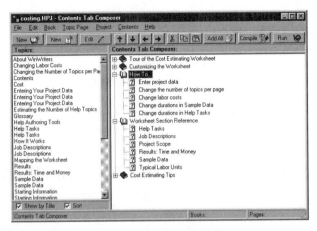

Figure 22.12. *The Contents Tab composer.*

WinHelp 4 **KLink/ALink** macros and authorable buttons are supported as well. You elect to use either a **KLink** or **ALink** hotspot and then choose the appropriate keywords from a list. Various button options are available to activate the macro, including an authorable button. The dialog box for these options is shown in Figure 22.13.

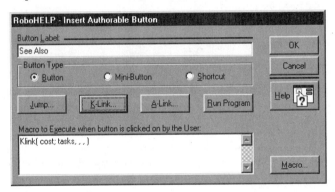

Figure 22.13. *Selecting* **KLink/ALink** *macros and authorable buttons.*

The new SmartHelp OLE Control included in RoboHELP 95 eliminates the need to program context-sensitive Help into any application developed with Visual Basic 4.0, Visual C++ 4.0, Access 95, and Visual FoxPro 3.0, or any other environment supporting the OLE control standard. RoboHELP users can drag and drop the SmartHelp OLE Control to add context-sensitive Help to their applications.

For those developers not using the WinHelp 4 compiler, RoboHELP supports the use of special characters such as curly quotes and em dashes. The RoboHELP postprocessor can recognize these characters in your topic file and automatically convert them to an acceptable RTF code. The postprocessor will also handle Word bullets.

A package called "WinHelp Office" bundles the RoboHELP software with a number of useful items. The WinHelp Video Kit provides support in WinHelp 3.1 for 256-color graphics and Video for Windows files, and provides the Software Video Camera. The HyperViewer allows you to create an expandable/collapsible table of contents. These options require you to ship additional DLLs with your Help system. Also included is the WinHelp Tool Kit which contains utilities for converting Help files into coded topic files, identifying bugs in context-sensitive Help calls, and a comprehensive graphics library from which you can select icons to include in your Help system. WinHelp Office contains a training video tape and a book summarizing WinHelp 4 features and conversion procedures. The Contents Tab Composer is provided as part of the Porting Tool.

RoboHELP is marketed by Blue Sky Software Corporation, the developer of other Windows products, including WindowsMaker. RoboHELP has been available since 1991.

RoboHELP, version 3.0/95
Blue Sky Software Corporation
7777 Fay Avenue, Suite 201, La Jolla, CA 92037
(800) 459-2356, (619) 551-2485, Fax: (619) 551-2486.
http://www.blue-sky.com - Internet:sales@blue-sky.com.
Price: RoboHELP 3.0/95 $499, upgrade from 3.0 to 95 $149,
WinHelp Office $599, upgrade to WinHelp Office 95 $149.

DOC-TO-HELP

Doc-To-Help is a tool designed to work specifically with Word for Windows. However, Doc-To-Help takes a widely different approach by linking Help to the development of print documentation. First, Doc-To-Help assists you in creating an appealing manual, and later it automatically converts that manual into a Help system. It semi-intelligently determines where topics are required and what relationships to establish between topics. Developers working from existing documentation will enjoy substantial savings in converting that documentation into a finished Help file.

There are two versions of the product: version 1.7 is for Word for Windows 2 and 6 users who work in Windows 95 or Windows 3.x. Version 2.0 is a 32-bit application that works with Word 7 and allows users to create WinHelp 4 and 3.x Help files from a single source.

When you start a new project, the Project Wizard guides you through the initial creation of the project. This includes specifying the elements you want in your print manual, like a table of contents, an index, and a glossary. You complete this step regardless of whether you are planning to use Doc-To-Help in creating a print manual.

The next step is to either type in your text or import it. Doc-To-Help includes a variety of templates which offer different page layouts and comprehensive style sheets. Doc-To-Help requires you to apply styles to paragraphs in your document because style tags are used in creating the topic file. You can use the Doc-To-Help default styles attributes or customize them for your own needs. After you format your text, you choose from customized Word menus to add cross references, index entries, and glossary items to your text. Figure 22.14 shows a page of text prepared with a Doc-To-Help project template.

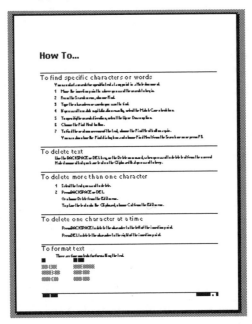

Figure 22.14. *A page of the print manual formed by Doc-To-Help.*

In Doc-To-Help you can also tag a topic as being a certain "topic type." This feature adds the appropriate coding to the topic file so that a topic will appear in a specific pre-defined window. The topic types include conceptual, procedural and context-sensitive topics.

When you are ready to convert your document into a topic file, Doc-To-Help begins working through your entire document file. Cross-references are converted to jumps, glossary items become pop-up definitions, and index entries become keywords. Your use of heading styles in Word determines how the text is separated into topics. The hierarchy of topics is used to determine browse sequences. Organization topics with hotspot jumps are created based on the document heading hierarchy. When this automated process is complete, you have a fully-coded, ready-to-compile topic file. The original print manual text is maintained as a separate Word for Windows document.

The speed with which Doc-To-Help creates the topic file depends in large part upon your computer hardware and the size of your document. The product has made significant improvements in processing time over the previous version. While Doc-To-Help may seem slow, it provides you with a *fully-coded* topic file in less time than any of the other tools reviewed.

Doc-To-Help keeps the source document and .INI file in one folder and the platform-specific files (.RTF, .HPJ, .HLP, .CNT) in child folders. A separate folder is made for each platform you specify.

The final step in producing your Help is to create a project file and compile the topic file. When you choose Compile from the Format menu, Doc-To-Help provides you with several choices for automatically generating a basic project file. The project file supports all the WinHelp settings. Figure 22.15 shows the dialog box which is the gateway to the project file.

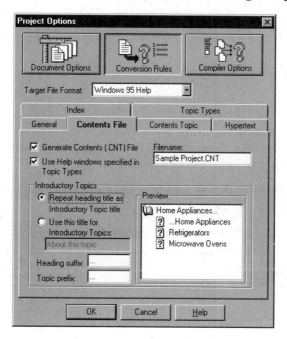

Figure 22.15. *Selecting project file options, including automatic handling of .CNT file generation.*

As with all other authoring tools, the compiling phase consists of launching the Microsoft compiler. If there are any errors in compiling, Doc-To-Help alerts you and can display the messages that occurred. Doc-To-Help also produces a context string map of all topics and places this map in the [CONFIG] section of the project file. This is useful for implementing context-sensitive Help. A map report is also generated, as shown in Figure 22.16.

Topic Title	Context String	Map Number
Help Contents	HelpContents1	1
To find specific characters or words	Tofindspecificcharactersorwords.2	2
To delete text	Todeletetext.3	3
To delete more than one character	Todeletemorethanonecharacter.4	4
To delete one character at a time	Todeleteonecharacteratatime.5	5
To format text	Toformattext.6	6
New	New.7	7
Open	Open.8	8
Cut	Cut.9	9
Exit	Exit.10	10
Find	Find.11	11
Undo	Undo.12	12
Short Cut Keys	ShortCutKeys.13	13

Figure 22.16. *Report of mapped topic IDs.*

If you need to make further links in your topic file, you can specify them by selecting topic names from a list. Figure 22.17 displays the Insert Hypertext Link box which supports the selection of jumps and pop-ups.

Doc-To-Help's single-source/Make Into Help process does not lend itself to quick, minor revisions. If you find you need to make minor modifications (such as minor formatting or fixing a typo), you will probably find it easier to work in parallel and edit both the source document(s) and the topic file(s), rather than change the source document and run the Make Into Help process again.. If, however, your methodology calls for more substantive changes between builds of the Help file, this single-source approach will guarantee that the printed and online documents are in sync and it will be a tremendous time saver.

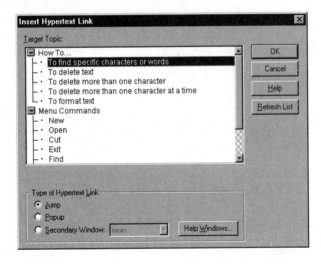

Figure 22.17. *Selecting a target topic for a hypertext jump.*

The Doc-To-Help support for developing a manual extends into other features, like the powerful index editor shown in Figure 22.18. This feature makes it easy to semi-automatically generate a comprehensive index, which is then used to build the keywords in Help. Doc-To-Help will automatically generate a **KLink** Related Topics button based on shared keywords if you select this option.

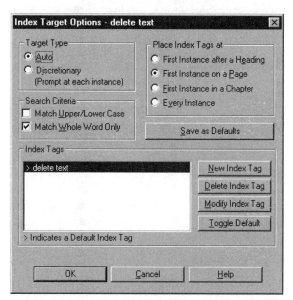

Figure 22.18. *Fine-tuning the index/keyword list.*

The Doc-To-Help package is supplemented with the Hyperformance tools. These tools add useful functions to your basic Help system. The Navigator, shown in Figure 22.19, automatically creates a WinHelp-4-style expanding and collapsing contents window, similar to the contents tab of the Help Topics browser. The Doc-To-Help version is, in many ways, superior to the Microsoft .CNT format. However, the Navigator requires you to ship files in addition to your Help files. In order to stay compatible with Windows 95 Help standards, you can elect to have the Navigator appear in the Help Topics browser in place of the Contents tab.

The other tools include support for 256-color graphics; a utility for adding textured patterns, called watermarks; and a very easy-to-use installation utility for distributing your Help system.

Doc-To-Help is marketed by WexTech Systems which also makes the Smooth Scaling and Quicture products listed in the Utilities section of this chapter. Doc-To-Help has been available since 1991.

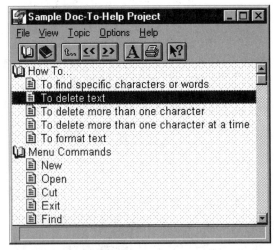

Figure 22.19. *The Navigator is accessed from a custom button in the Help file button bar.*

Doc-To-Help, version 1.7/2.0
WexTech Systems, Inc.
310 Madison Avenue, Suite 905
New York, NY 10017
(212) 949-9595, (800)-WEXTECH
Fax: (212)-949-4007
Price: $395.00. To upgrade from 1.x to 2.0, $129; To upgrade
from 1.6 or earlier to 1.7, $29.

FOREHELP

ForeHelp represents a completely different development format from the other tools so far discussed. Instead of being tied to Word for Windows, ForeHelp offers a completely self-contained product dedicated to Help development. The entire Help development process is controlled from the ForeHelp editor. The editor, shown in Figure 22.20, is similar to Word in both appearance and functionality. Menus and tool buttons are arranged at the top of the screen. You add the text and graphics in the space below. As with the other tools, you can either type in your text or import an existing topic file. Formatting tools are included to specify the characteristics of the text.

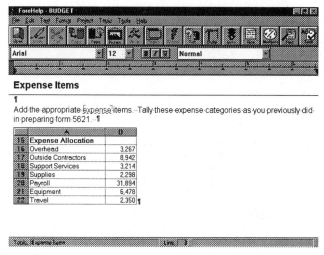

Figure 22.20. *The ForeHelp workspace.*

However, the similarities to other tools quickly ends. In ForeHelp each topic is represented as a separate "page." The controls to move between topics are the same ones that are found in a WinHelp file: Contents, Search, Next, Previous, Back, etc. As a Help writer, you author in a mode that constantly reminds you of the way the user will be working with your system.

A major plus for ForeHelp is that it offers true WYSIWYG development. All of the Help coding is hidden from view. To form a jump or pop-up, click the appropriate button in the button bar and select the destination topic title from a list. To add images, use the Insert Picture button. No coding is displayed in the topic. Graphics are displayed intertwined with the text. Everything is much as it would look in the compiled Help file.

One of the most frustrating aspects of designing Help is the debugging and testing process: you inevitably end up compiling over and over again to review your changes. This becomes an especially important issue when you are fine-tuning Help and time is critical. ForeHelp addresses this problem by making it possible to immediately test your Help file without compiling. The Test button launches a perfect emulation of the compiled Help file as shown in Figure 22.21. Everything works including jumps, pop-ups, and macros. No matter what the size of your topic file, the test mode appears in just a few seconds. There is no need to compile until you are ready to distribute the actual Help file. This is important enough to repeat. NO COMPILING NEEDED UNTIL YOU DISTRIBUTE THE HELP FILE. This capability alone saves countless hours of development time. To return to the editor, simply exit the test Help system.

When you are ready to distribute the Help file for review or actual use, you need to use the Build command. This generates the topic, project, bitmap, and hypergraphics files; then launches the compiler.

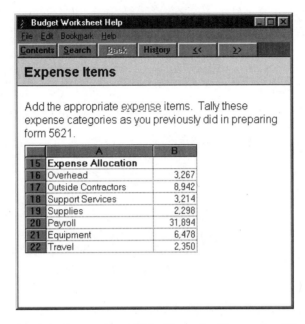

Figure 22.21. *An emulated Help file in the Test mode of ForeHelp.*

Another outstanding ForeHelp feature is its common-sense approach to assembling keyword lists and browse sequences. Keywords are added to each topic through a list box. All keywords become part of an alphabetized master list which can be a boon during proofreading. You can quickly add or remove keywords from their association with a particular topic. As shown in Figure 22.22, the "Expense Items" topic has the "expense" and "items, expense" keywords associated with it.

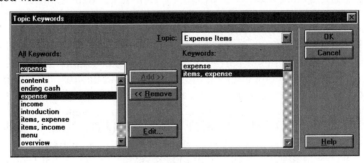

Figure 22.22. *Specifying keywords with ForeHelp.*

Browse sequences are formed in a similar fashion, as shown in Figure 22.23. You create a sequence name and then add topics to it from a master list. Topics that have been assigned to a sequence are grayed out so that they cannot be selected more than once. Up/Down buttons make it easy to change the arrangement of topics within a sequence. There is no need to create browse (+) footnotes; ForeHelp does that for you.

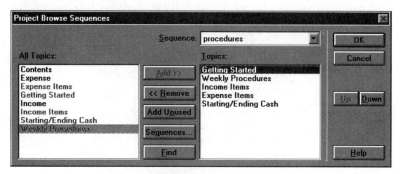

Figure 22.23. *Specifying browse sequences with ForeHelp.*

The support for multiple hotspot graphics is another shining jewel in ForeHelp. All of the other authoring tools require the use of a separate editor (SHED). With ForeHelp you simply double click on a graphic, (already displayed WYSIWYG in the topic file) an action which puts the graphic in what they call "SHEG mode." You can immediately start forming hotspots and linking those hotspots to topics. In Figure 22.24, the hotspot region is drawn right on the graphic image. The destination for the jump is displayed in the status bar.

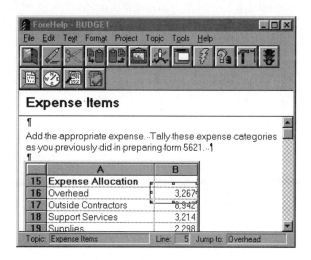

Figure 22.24. *The SHEG mode in ForeHelp.*

ForeHelp is supplemented with other valuable development tools. The Navigator, shown in Figure 22.25, creates a graphical chart of your Help system so you can visualize the flow of your topics. The Reporter (also described in Chapter 20) produces custom reports describing context strings, topic titles, the number of keywords per topic, and many more pieces of topic information. Version 2.0 includes an editor for building a contents file. You can select existing topic titles from a list or create new topics on the fly as you create the contents file.

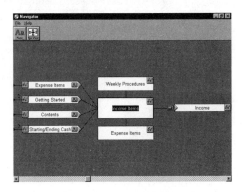

Figure 22.25. *The Navigator provides a visual display of topic links.*

The only downside to ForeHelp is that it requires you to learn a new word processor. If you use Word or another word processor regularly for letters, print manuals, etc., it becomes tedious to brain-switch between the two word processors.

Of all the authoring tools available, ForeHelp is the easiest to learn and to use, yet it still supports all advanced compiler features. It is also a fast product with which you can generate a quick, basic Help system.

ForeHelp, version 2.0
ForeFront
4710 Table Mesa Drive, Suite B
Boulder, CO 80303
(303) 499-9181
Price: $395, $89 upgrade to version 2.95 from version 2, $199 competitive upgrade.

Other authoring tools

The three tools described in the previous section are not the only ones available, nor should they be the only ones you consider. There has been a steady introduction of authoring tools which fill various developer niches. This section describes other authoring tools you may want to evaluate. All of the entries are worthy of your consideration.

CREATEHELP

CHC Software
5 Dartmouth Row
London SE10 8AW
England
CIS: 100111,3452

CreateHelp is an authoring tool that operates within Word for Windows using WordBasic, adding menu options to its standard interface as shown in Figure 22.26. CreateHelp includes additional options for creating hypertext links, adding graphics and other standard Help functions.

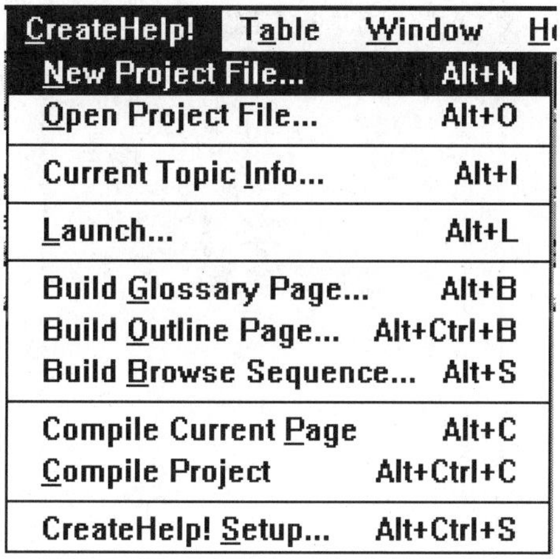

CreateHelp!	Table	Window	H(
New Project File...		Alt+N	
Open Project File...		Alt+O	
Current Topic Info...		Alt+I	
Launch...		Alt+L	
Build Glossary Page...		Alt+B	
Build Outline Page...		Alt+Ctrl+B	
Build Browse Sequence...		Alt+S	
Compile Current Page		Alt+C	
Compile Project		Alt+Ctrl+C	
CreateHelp! Setup...		Alt+Ctrl+S	

Figure 22.26. *A customized Word menu with CreateHelp.*

CreateHelp offers the following features: AutoLink, (a feature similar to Word's AutoText that allows you to format commonly used hypertext links); browse sequence building, collapsible/expandable outline support; easy Glossary page build with custom A-Z buttons; current page compiling for testing links; and SHED and multiple resolution bitmap support.

CreateHelp is shareware and can be downloaded from the WINSDK forum on CompuServe.

HDK

DEK Software International
1843 The Woods II
Cherry Hill, NJ 02825
(609) 424-6565

Help Development Kit (HDK) is an authoring tool that offers many of the features of WinHelp 4 in a 3.1 environment, such as full-text search, an expandable/collapsible table of contents window, 256-color graphic support, push-button toolbars, animation, group link support (similar to ALinks) and more.

You can customize templates, or add your own to the template list, to change the look and feel of your Help systems. Using the Insert Link dialog box, you can create a link, designate its type, indicate the window it should go into, change its color, type in its text, and designate the topic title it should go below. You can also use the same dialog box to attach a macro and modify other attributes.

One of HDK's strongest features includes a Topic Outliner that allows you to see the structure at a glance so you can easily view and modify the structure of the Help file. You can click and drag topics to new locations, add links while in outline view, copy topics, insert new topics, change topic names, and view the hierarchy of the Help file all at the same time.

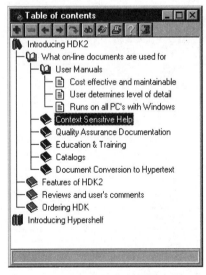

Figure 22.27.

Another powerful feature in HDK is its ability to import existing Word documents into HDK and convert them into online Help. HDK automatically converts many standard Word text formatting: the table of contents becomes the Table of Contents window; headings become topics; glossaries become glossary pop-ups; index terms become keywords; footnotes become pop-ups; bookmarks become jumps to other topics; Wingdings and other symbols become bitmaps; and embedded graphics become linked graphics.

Groups are made up of all the topics beneath a topic in the topic outliner hierarchy. The main topic is called the *parent* and subordinate topics within the parent's group are called *children*. You can use an optional Group button in your Help window to navigate easily among all children within a group. You can also create a nonrelated (KLink-like) list of topics by clicking on your topic choices in the Topic Outliner.

HELPBREEZE

Solutionsoft
999 Evelyn Terrace West, Suite 86
Sunnyvale, CA 94086
(408) 736-1431

HelpBreeze offers a Word for Windows Help-authoring environment that operates on a paradigm similar to that of ForeHelp. It allows you to add animation, slide shows, and 256-color support using a royalty-free slide show .DLL. Instead of using full multimedia implementation [including audio (.WAV), midi (.MID), video (.AVI), and movie (.MMM) file support] you can use this DLL to create smaller-sized presentations that will run on Windows systems without requiring additional hardware or video drivers. Thus HelpBreeze offers more compatibility with end users' equipment. HelpBreeze also offers hypertext emulation which allows you to test your links in the Word document without first compiling, in a manner similar to ForeHelp.

You can use the Edit Group/Browse Sequence command to manipulate groups of Help topics on a global basis, as you can in ForeHelp. This means that you can renumber or regroup topics within browse sequences by automatically creating parent (ordinate) topics that contain jumps to subordinate topics within a group. Undo commands allow you to reverse hotspot and topic actions. HelpBreeze automatically generates context IDs for C/C++, Pascal, and Basic applications and also offers reporting features that list all topic parameters and hypertext links in the Help file sorted by topic, similar to the reporting features offered in ForeHelp.

HelpBreeze also offers a work group edition for $379 and allows you to upgrade from the standard version for $99. Using the work group edition, you can divide large Help projects into manageable modules which you can compile and test individually. You can test links between modules without compiling the entire Help system, and you can create links between modules by selecting the target topic from a list.

HelpBreeze is simple, yet powerful. The interface is easy to use, and offers a floating Help palette, providing easy access to online Help commands.

> **NOTE** *SolutionSoft offers another tool, ViewerBreeze that turns Word for Windows into a complete, integrated system for creating Multimedia and MediaView titles. In order to use this product, you must already have Viewer/MediaView.*

HELP MAGICIAN PRO

Software Interphase, Inc.
82 Cucumber Hill Road
Foster, RI 02825
(401) 397-2340

Help Magician Pro 3.0 (HMP) is one of the older authoring tools on the market; they pioneered the model that ForeHelp uses. It does not use the Word for Windows interface for entering text, and that can take getting used to. HMP's interface is easy to understand and it allows you to use Word, Word Perfect, and Ami Pro files.

Help Magician Pro includes a simultaneous test mode, allowing you to test jumps and pop-ups to other Help files by double-clicking on the word or phrase you want to test. It also includes an emulation of the standard WinHelp buttons so you can test the Search, Contents, Back, History, and Browse functions. It allows WYSIWYG Help viewing, displaying jumps and pop-ups in green text with the appropriate underlining.

Other features include: A Visual Basic Help Wizard that scans VB source code (saved as text) and builds a Help-file shell, complete with context sensitivity, based on the design of your forms; a Glossary Wizard that generates a glossary shell complete with an A-Z Shed file, a non-scrolling region, a Close button, and headings, with mid-topic context strings, for every letter; a context string reference utility that is a separate executable that extracts and displays the context strings from any Help Magician source file. A "Preview" button displays any topic in the file. This utility is particularly useful when working with the Shed Editor.

Inserting jumps is easy with the helpful dialog box shown in Figure 22.28.

Some other Help Magician features include 256-color graphic support with a royalty-free DLL that you must ship with your Help file. It also includes multiple-file project support, and audio (.WAV), midi (.MID), video (.AVI), and movie (.MMM) file support.

Their technical support is friendly, knowledgeable and over all excellent. They have a BBS line and offer fixes free within 48 hours on the BBS for user-reported problems.

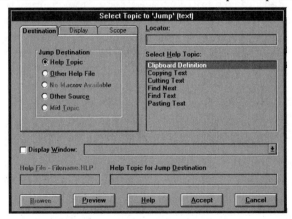

Figure 22.28. *Inserting jumps with Help Magician Pro.*

HELP PERFECT

Niceware
P.O. Box 2264
3500GG Utrecht
The Netherlands
(913) 832-8787

Help Perfect converts WordPerfect files to the Windows Help format. You must first build your Help project in WordPerfect before using Help Perfect to convert it to a WinHelp-formatted file for the compiler. Then Help Perfect compiles the document for you, and lets you test the file. It automatically generates keywords based on topic titles, references and targets for cross references, entries in WordPerfect lists, and hotspots. It also generates an Index using the index codes you enter in WordPerfect.

The perfect job for this application is a document created in WordPerfect (such as a policy and procedures manual) that you want to use to create an online document. Or, if you want full-text-search capabilities in your document, this is a good tool for the job. However, if you want to build a new Help file, you may need a different tool.

HELP WRITER'S ASSISTANT

Olson Software
4 Anaru Place
Palmerston North
New Zealand
+64 6 359 1408
CIS 100352,1315

This is a spiffy shareware authoring tool for Help developers looking for a WYSIWYG interface that hides topic file codes from view. It also releases you from the need to code a project file; it creates it for you through its New Project Wizard. Its text editor is not a powerful word processor, but does offer formatting and does the job.

When adding topics, it offers up a Topic Properties dialog box that lets you check options such as "Duplicate in Nonscrolling Region," "Copy Title to Context String," "In Browse Sequence," and "Include in Contents Tree." These make adding topics quick and easy. You can also add keywords, macros, and create build tags using other properties dialog boxes. You can also create keyword sets, defining a group of keywords by one name instead of retyping each word in the group every time you want to use them.

This tool comes bundled with SHED Graphics Editor and Microsoft Windows Screen Capture utility, version 3.10.

You can obtain evaluation copies of this tool and Olson Software Help Tools from CompuServe or the Internet:

CompuServe: In the WINSDK forum, Section 16 [WinHelp/Tools} as HWA11.ZIP.
Internet: Via ftp from ftp.cica.indiana.edu.HWA11.ZIP is in the pub/pc/win.3/util directory.

An evaluation copy of this tool is available on the disc that comes with this book.

HLPDK/PA

Hyperact, Inc.
P.O. Box 5517
Coralville, IA 52241
(319) 351-8413

HLPDK/PA is a cross-platform hypertext/hypermedia Help development tool that allows you to write and compile your applications in one of three environments: Windows, OS/2, or DOS. It allows you to write one Help file and compile it to many platforms. You can use your favorite text editor to create Help text, save it as an .RTF or .TXT file and then compile it in the HLPDK/PA editor, or use the HLPDK/PA's Help editor to mark up and compile your project. You can compile the Help for any supported target Help platform with one mouse click; the compiler performs inside the editor.

HLPDK/PA supports writing Help files to the following platforms: Viewer, DESQview, QuickHelp, PopHelp, Multimedia Viewer 2.0, World-Wide-Web (WWW) HTML (supporting WWW readers in Windows, Macintosh, UNIX-Motif, and VMS platforms), OS/2, THELP, TVHC, Native Paradox 4.x and text, Native Memory HDX and text, and word processing files via .RTF and text files. You can view the results immediately without needing extra files (HLPDK/PA includes the appropriate viewers to let you do this) or view them on the appropriate platform. With the exception of DOS platforms (THELP, TVHC, and Native Memory HDX), Multimedia Viewer, and WWW HTML, viewer files are not required when the files are transported to the appropriate platforms.

HLPDK/PA can also read and convert HTML files to WinHelp and OS/2 platforms. You can also convert WinHelp and other Help files into HTML files that can be read by the viewer supplied with the software or by any HTML viewer. It also includes an image editor that allows you to manipulate, scan, and edit images.

HLPDK/PA lets you create DOS Help files that can be read with one of two royalty-free viewers included in this product. The source code for the viewers can be purchased separately. Keep in mind that if you are distributing DOS Help files created with HLPDK/PA, you must ship one of the viewers with your Help file for it to be usable. There is no cost for distributing their DOS viewers, but it will occupy disk space, so this could be a concern for some.

This is not the product for beginners. The interface is different from that of other authoring tools and could take you a little bit of time to become accustomed to. But this is a powerful tool and its online Help support is both plentiful and good.

INTERACTIVE HELP

HyperAct, Inc.
P.O. Box 5517
Coralville, IA 52241
(319) 351-8413
CIS 76350,333

Interactive Help for Windows (IH) is a WinHelp DLL extension language that allows you to extend the power of your WinHelp documents without writing your own DLLs. You can transform a WinHelp project from a passive document viewer into a dynamic application driver by adding forms and dialogs to your WinHelp titles. IH links your titles dynamically to external resources, monitors and controls WinHelp activities, executes standard WinHelp macros, and uses WinHelp's "Callback" internal API function.

IH uses a Pascal-like interpreted language called PASTERP, to add power to your WinHelp application. To use Interactive Help for Windows all you need to do is create a text file that includes your PASTERP routines, list it in the [BAGGAGE] section of your project (.HPJ) file, and register three routines in the [CONFIG] section of your project file. You do not have to learn DLL programming, maintain macros, or struggle with compilers to use this application.

Interactive Help hooks into your WinHelp document, automatically monitors WinHelp events, activates specially-named procedures (supplied by you) to trap these events and handles them according to your needs. Using IH, you can harness the PASTERP extended library functions to provide support for procedures and functions that are more related to the PC environment. For instance, you can use SETTIME or SETDATE to set the time and date of your PC environment from within a Help application.

Some of the significant tasks you can perform using this tool are trapping and handling WinHelp events, breaking the 255-character WinHelp macro limit, and exposing and using the WinHelp internal extension functions from within your WinHelp documents.

MASTERHELP

Performance Software, Inc.
575 Southlake Blvd.
Richmond, VA 23236
(804) 794-1012

MasterHelp has probably the most colorful online Help files I've seen. Its workplace is quite different from those of the other authoring tools that work with Word for Windows. Its beautifully designed and colorful Help is easy to use after you review the "Understanding the MasterHelp Workplace" topic. You can use MasterHelp to convert a .DOC file or .RTF file from another Help project quickly and easily. MasterHelp comes with a Getting Started document which is short, sweet, and gets right to the point, without a lot of conceptual information.

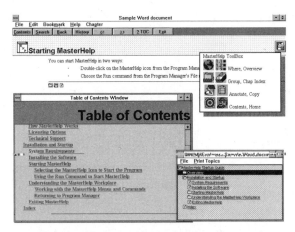

Figure 22.29. *The MasterHelp interface.*

MasterHelp uses your style sheets, and you control the screen appearance using the Options file. It creates pop-ups that display the viewer, chapter indexes, overviews, subsidiary topics, and also offers two options for creating hypertext jumps to "See Also" topics by embedding them in text or at the end of a topic pop-up. See Figure 22.29.

MasterHelp offers extended graphic support that lets you use their graphic calls or create your own. The nice part about their extended support is that, instead of displaying the graphic, MasterHelp displays a pop-up and allows the user to determine whether to view the graphic or not. And MasterHelp lets you use graphic files other than those supported in standard Help tools: bitmaps, metafiles, and segmented graphics. However, when you use their extended support, you have to bundle and ship all the graphics used this way with the Help application. Thus, you need to distribute more disks to support this feature. In addition, you must include the DLL file that enables the extended support option you choose.

MINIHELP PLUS 3.2.1

Paul Arnote
1208 Randolph
Leavenworth, KS 66048

You can use MiniHelp with any ASCII text editor to build a WinHelp-compatible Help project. It will default to NotePad unless the file is too large. In WinHelp 95, it calls WordPad when it views large files. You can click a button and immediately bring up the .RTF or .HPJ file for your current Help project.

The first thing you do is code your source file and then configure your project. When you configure your project, all files (source, compiler, etc.) must be in MiniHelp's directory. After you configure your project, MiniHelp creates an .INI file that contains similar information to that in a project file. MH uses this file for directions on the names of the other files it will create when you compile your Help project. See Figure 22.30.

MiniHelp does not provide syntax error checking when building your .RTF file, so you must be very careful when typing in syntax. You have to type in codes manually, with no assistance like you find in RoboHELP, ForeHelp, or Doc-To-Help. For example, to code for a pop-up named ASCII to appear in a topic you would type the following text:

```
.POP ASCII "The text for the ASCII popup would be typed here."
```

This requirement can be daunting enough to many.

The price is cheap, and the only other tools you need are an ASCII text editor and the Help compiler. It offers support for macros, graphics, and all the other features of the major Help authoring tools; it just takes a little longer to do things.

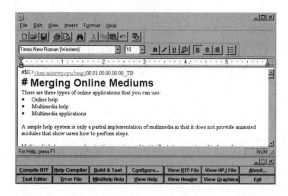

Figure 22.30. *The MiniHelp interface viewing an .RTF file using WordPad.*

SOS HELP! INFO-AUTHOR

Lamaura Development Ltd.
Rabley Park Ridge
Potters Bar
Hertfordshire EN63LX
+44 0 707 643499
(208) 765-9439
CIS: 1000016,1254

SOS Help! is a WYSIWYG Help design system for Windows. It includes its own word processor, so you need no additional software to run it. Its manual is also online, so documentation is easy to find, if a little scattered. It includes a Help tracker for viewing the status of your topics, such as the date they were last updated. It also includes an expandable/collapsible table of contents. This is a shareware application that is available for review in the WINSDK forum on CompuServe.

VB HELPWRITER

Teletech Systems
750 Birch Ridge Drive
Rosewell, GA 30076
CIS 72260,2217

VB HelpWriter is a standalone Help authoring application that operates on a paradigm similar to that of ForeHelp in that it doesn't require an outside text editor and will let you test your Help topics, jumps, and links in its editor. Its specialty is in serving Visual Basic programmers, allowing them to generate a basic Help file framework by automatically linking their program forms, and thus generating a glossary and formatting topics automatically based on the code of the forms.

You can drag and drop to create hypertext links and test without compiling. VB HelpWriter checks for orphaned and bad jumps, offers popups, bordered and shadowed paragraph support, built-in CASE (Computer Aided Software Engineering) functions, generates code that will link to WinHelp API calls, prints detailed topic reports, and much more.

You can use the standalone interface to enter text, add graphics, jumps and topics, and compile. See Figure 22.31.

This tool is of special interest to Visual Basic programmers since it allows them to generate a basic framework Help file without being a knowledgeable Help author. However, this program should also be of interest to any Help author needing to generate context-sensitive Help code without VB programming knowledge.

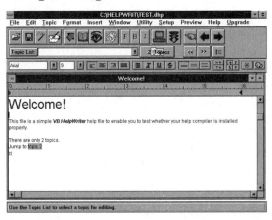

Figure 22.31.*The interface for VB HelpWriter.*

VISUAL HELP

WinWare
P.O. Box 2923
Mission Viejo, CA 92690
(714) 584-4492
CIS 70272,1656

Visual Help is a standalone WYSIWYG graphical authoring environment that also happens to be shareware. It provides its own word processor and a test mode like ForeHelp which lets you test most features of your Help project without the need to compile it first. Its interface is similar in look and feel to Microsoft Visual Basic and it uses object-like technology to provide easy-to-use building blocks for creating Help files. Visual Help supports all the basic WinHelp functions and lets you add advanced options such as multimedia objects and custom buttons. It supports multimedia by embedding sound and video into Help files that will play on a multimedia-equipped PC.

You don't have to type in context strings, footnotes, or some of the more boring aspects of Help development if you use Visual Help. However, if you are a power Help builder, you will suffer because of some of the limitations. You cannot import from existing (non-Visual Help) projects. You can use cut and paste to import from other sources to get around this limitation. There is no exporting to full rich-text format, which means you always have to compile your project inside Visual Help. And finally, no custom browse sequences. Visual Help creates a default browse sequence that runs from the start to the end of your Help file.

VISUAL HELP BUILDER

ProtoView Development Corporation
2540 Route 130
Cranbury, NJ 08512
(609) 655-5000

Visual Help Builder provides a full graphical WYSIWYG interface for building online Help systems and works with Microsoft Word for Windows. You can use the .RTF files created by other authoring tools, but once you convert them to Visual Help Builder you can't go back and edit them in another authoring tool. You can use a project document or a model definition when creating a new project. The project document applies to any new online project file and is most often used. The model definition is used to create a conversion model that will be applied to several .RTF files. It will be unattached to any particular .RTF file, but will act as a guide to apply to an entire system or large project after you've worked out the development bugs.

This product is used mostly to build a Help system based upon a Visual Basic application. It uses Visual Basic forms to use context-sensitive Help support. For most Help developers, this product is too advanced, in that it also requires knowledge of Visual Basic. However, if you are a Visual Basic developer, it is easy to use and comes bundled with well-written and easy-to-fol-low documentation containing lots of graphics and examples.

WP2HELP 2.0

Merc Software
7931 Forest Avenue
Munster, IN 46321
(213) 836-6444

WP2Help is a Windows Help authoring tool used with WordPerfect for Windows files. You can use WP2Help to create and edit Help topic files. WP2Help is easier to use to create Help files in WordPerfect because it provides dialog boxes to add Help features that you would normally create by typing Help coding into the word processor manually. For example, in a normal WP document, you would type in codes for bold, underline, and italic text. You can use the dialog boxes to add these kinds of features to your document without worrying about typing the codes directly into your document.

WP2Help offers functions that are similar to other WordPerfect for Windows functions: a set of specialized commands becomes available on the WP menus when you open your WP application. The result is a version of WordPerfect for Windows that has all the original word processing functionality and yet is optimized for creating Help files.

Adding a hotspot to text or graphics is easy with the dialog box shown in Figure 22.32.

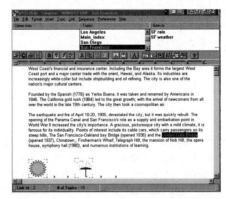

Figure 22.32. *A WP@Help dialog box.*

The interface for WP2 is friendly and its accompanying Help file is straightforward and easy to use. This is the perfect tool for anyone converting a text file written in Word Perfect to a Help file.

WYSI-HELP COMPOSER

UDICO
Four Commercial Blvd. 36
Novato, CA 94949
(415) 382-8840
CIS: 76474,30

WYSI-Help Composer contains its own word processor and, like ForeHelp, offers one environment for writing, testing, and compiling your Help project. You can create your own formats and text styles within WYSI-Help. Its toolbar contains buttons easily recognizable if you are used to the more popular Windows-type word processors. Its dialog boxes assist you in easily creating hypertext and hypergraphic links. You can easily create new links by pointing and clicking. The Comes From box contains higher level topics pointing to the topic currently selected in the Topics box. The Topics list contains a list of all the topics currently in the project. The Goes To box contains the topics associated with the currently selected topic in the Topics box.

WYSI-Help contains a Graphical Topic Navigator to show all your Help file connections, and a Macro Editor to assist you in writing macros. Its word processor contains a spell-checking program, preview mode, and offers point and click link generation.

Preview mode allows you to see the results of your Help coding without requiring you to compile your Help project first. You can test jumps and pop-ups as soon as you create them.

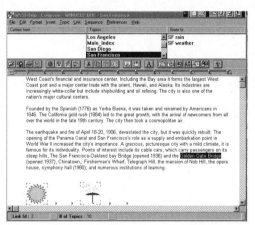

Figure 22.33. *The WYSI-Help Composer interface.*

WYSI-Help's own Help system is very nicely done. The WYSI-Help Composer Learner Guide also provides an excellent tutorial to take beginners from basic to advanced Help authoring tasks.

WYSI-Help contains support for macros, automatic link generation (it scans your Help file for specific text contained in a reference list and automatically creates hypertext links for that text), secondary windows, and external program linking (linking to sound, macros, and other Help files).

The information in this section, "Other Authoring Tools" was written by Lin Laurie • WinPro Online Press • Seattle, WA • 206-784-5821.

Cross-platform tools

The largest of these specialty areas is concerned with converting (or porting) Windows Help systems to file formats for Help in other operating systems, like Macintosh, UNIX, and OS/2. WinHelp files are designed to work under Windows and will not operate in other operating environments in most cases. Other operating systems have their own Help file formats. SPF for OS/2, HGML for Mosaic on the INTERNET, UNIX, and Apple Guide for the Macintosh.

There are two different approaches to this task: using the existing Help file format or an emulated version. Operating systems like OS/2 come with their own fairly robust Help viewers and file formats. There is a compiler and file format. You could assemble Help systems in this environment, manually or with tools.

Under UNIX there is no significant system-wide Help file format. In this case a third party viewer is required to display Help. The Macintosh is a special case. Starting with System 7x in 199x the Macintosh added a Help file format. It is significantly different from Windows Help. A conversion from WinHelp will result in certain features not being transferred. This is a situation where you may need to do a partial port and then fine-tune the Mac Help system.

HYPERHELP

241 Ethan Allen Highway
Ridgefield, CT 06877 USA
203-438-6969 (phone)
203-438-5013 (fax)
info@bristol.com (email)
http://www.bristol.com (web site)

HyperHelp allows software developers to add hypertext Help to their UNIX® or Digital OpenVMS® applications, including context sensitivity. If you are planning to port your WinHelp file to UNIX, HyperHelp lets you quickly convert your Windows system into one that runs under UNIX. HyperHelp accepts the same rich-text format (RTF) files, project files, and bitmap files as does WinHelp. Figure 22.34 shows a Help file generated with HyperHelp.

The HyperHelp development system consists of two separate applications: the *HyperHelp Compiler* and the *HyperHelp Viewer*. The HyperHelp Compiler is used to generate your online Help system. The HyperHelp Viewer is used to display on-line Help from your application.

You can use a Microsoft Windows word processor such as Word™, or WordPerfect® to create .RTF files; FrameMaker® to create .MIF files; a Standard Generalized Markup Language (SGML) editor to create SGML files; or an ASCII text editor to create HyperHelp text (.HHT) files. You may choose to use one of the authoring tool products described earlier in this chapter to generate your topic and project files.

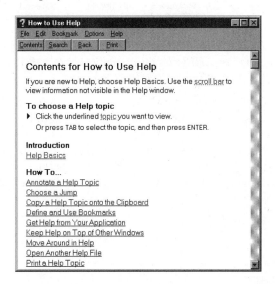

Figure 22.34. *Like Windows 95 Help facility (above left), HyperHelp displays online Help information about an application in a separate, movable window.*

The HyperHelp Viewer is a separate application, installed on the user's computer, that takes the .HLP file as input and displays it in a separate, movable window. The pull-down menus, dialogs, buttons, color scheme, and other properties of the HyperHelp Viewer application can be easily customized.

HyperHelp Bridge™ is an optional component of the HyperHelp product line which allows you to author in FrameMaker or SGML editors, then produce Help files that can be used with the Microsoft Windows, Windows 95 and Windows NT Help facilities. Figure 22.35 shows this process.

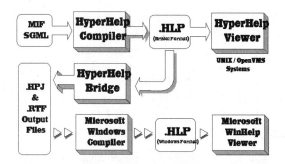

Figure 22.35. *The HyperHelp Bridge can convert compiled HyperHelp Help files back into source .RTF and .HPJ files for use with Windows 3.1, Windows 95, and Windows NT Help compilers.*

HyperHelp Bridge allows you to single source your topic files for all versions. The HyperHelp API allows software developers to add online Help to their applications. There is a compiler and file format.

HyperHelp costs x with no royalties. HyperHelp is available for Sun SPARC SunOS and Solaris, HP700/800 HP-UX, IBM RS/6000 AIX, DEC Alpha Digital UNIX and OpenVMS, DEC VAX OpenVMS, SGI IRIX, SCO ODT, UnixWare, and Solaris for Intel platforms.

QUICKHELP

Altura Software
510 Lighthouse Avenue, Suite 5
Pacific Grove, CA 93950
(408) 655-8005
CIS 70760,376

This tool generates Mac versions of your WinHelp files. It isn't a Help authoring tool; it works with existing Help files only. It consists of two applications: a compiler and a viewer. The compiler converts WinHelp files into Mac files that are viewed with the viewer. This tool is 90-95 percent WinHelp compatible with the following exceptions: Complex paragraph borders, the OEM character set, the international English character set, picture scaling, small caps, underline styles other that those used with jumps and pop-ups, and a 32,767 pixel limit for topics (roughly 68 screens at a 640x480 screen resolution).

QuickHelp converts .BMP, .WMF, PIC, .DIB, and .SHG graphic files. Windows metafile results may be erratic. Mac and PC use different bitmap resolutions [Mac 72 pixels per inch (ppi) and PC 96 ppi] and this could cause a problem with graphics sizing. However, QuickHelp does have a control to adjust the settings and this should alleviate the problem when used properly.

23

Managing Help Projects

Building a Help system, like any other project of substance, absorbs a significant amount of resources in terms of people, time, and money. The careful management of these resources makes it possible to complete your project on schedule, within budget, and according to project specifications. Of course, projects commonly change scope during development, and budgets and schedules often get changed. But that is even more reason to impose controls early on. A good plan can assist you in making the right decisions regarding slipped schedules and unexpected labor charges.

This chapter provides:

- Descriptions of the skills needed to develop a Windows Help system.

- A typical model for a Help development team.

- A model for estimating the cost and amount of labor required to produce your Help system.

- A model for scheduling the tasks and personnel required to produce your Help system.

- Several techniques for controlling versions of Help files during production and through general distribution.

Skills and personnel

The people who develop Help systems possess a variety of skills and come from a wide range of backgrounds. Generally, these people can be divided into two broad groups. The first group consists of managers or writers in existing publications departments. Most companies have one or more dedicated writing professionals. With the advent of Windows Help, these professionals typically have been charged with placing information online. Since many of these individuals are accustomed to working in the print medium, the additional technical requirements entailed in producing Windows Help can be more than they are prepared to handle. However, Windows Help is well within the capabilities of those willing to learn about it.

The other group of Help developers consists of programmers, whose prime responsibility is writing the code for Windows software products. In many corporate software environments the development of Help is a programmer's responsibility because the delivery medium, the Windows Help application, is software. Programmers, however, may not always have the requisite writing skills. Also, some programmers tend to want to avoid this part of the project as much as possible. Part I of this book will be especially useful to programmers, because it deals with communication topics, an area with which they may be relatively unfamiliar.

Whether a person's background is as writer or programmer, certain skills are required for effective Help development. Some of these skills are common to all forms of technical communication, some are specific to online information. The rest of this section defines those skills. For a more complete description of publication management read *Managing Your Documentation Projects*, by JoAnn Hackos.

HELP DEVELOPMENT SKILLS

A variety of skills are required to produce a Windows Help system. In many organizations one person must wear many hats. In others there is a team of documentation specialists. In either case, the skills described here must be provided by someone. The skills include:

- Writing

- Editing

- Designing

- Coding

- Creating graphics

- Testing

- Managing

Writing

Although much attention in Help development is paid to information access and navigation between topics, nothing substitutes for clear, accurate, and pertinent information. The Help writer, in many organizations, is the same person who develops the print materials. In other situations, the programmer who develops the software also writes the Help. More recently, organizations are employing writers specifically for Help development. Whatever the background, it's generally best to leave the development of Help text to those with good writing skills.

The prime responsibility of the writer is to plan and generate the content that is read by the user. Planning may include working with the software being documented and determining what types of topics are required: definitions, procedures, commands, etc. Writing the content is always the biggest portion of the job and includes formulating an outline and crafting the words that appear in the topics.

Another skill often provided by the writer is the generation of index keywords. Keywords are the Help equivalent to the index of a printed document. It is just as important to have a well-designed, meticulously executed index as it is to have a high-quality back-of-book index. Unfortunately, the generation of good keywords is a manual process. None of the Help authoring tools can automatically generate an effective index. Attend an indexing training class and read Chapter 9, *Creating the Index*. Also, review the indexes of other people's Help systems. Look for effective uses of word structure, punctuation, and capitalization that you can use in your Help files.

In addition to writing skills, the Help writer must have a reasonable grasp of Help design—even though the overall architecture of the Help system may be the responsibility of a designer.

Editing

Most Help systems go through a form of basic editing called *copy editing*. This consists of checking grammar, punctuation, spelling, and formatting. Good editing requires a solid grounding in the structure of language, and experience with the presentation of information online. If you are developing your Help system from print documentation, you might be able to assume that if the print text was well edited, the vast majority of your Help text is already correct in terms of grammar, punctuation, and style. However, more and more Help systems are being developed independent of the printed documentation, thus requiring a complete edit of the Help text. Copy editing is a minimal requirement for a professional Help system.

Other forms of editing include the *substantive* edit and the *technical* edit. These are often absent from Help development—and the resulting Help systems usually show the lack.

In the substantive edit, the editor makes sure that the Help system accomplishes the goals described in the document specifications. This is also referred to as a developmental edit, where the editor looks at the "big picture." If several writers are contributing to a Help system, the editor must blend their work into a unified style. This form of editing requires an experienced editor who is involved from start to finish with the development of the Help system.

The purpose of the technical edit is to ensure that the information the writer has developed is accurate. A technical edit is generally performed by someone with an intimate knowledge of the subject matter. In software documentation, it is often the programmer who is asked to review the draft.

Designing

The contribution of the Help designer should not be underestimated. Development of an effective Help system is much more than just putting print text into an electronic form. Many key design principles are expressed in the design chapters of this book. The effectiveness of hypertext tools such as Windows Help is largely reliant on quick access to specific topics. The talented designer balances the depth and breadth of content with the amount of jumping and scrolling required to access information.

An understanding of the differences between print and online documentation is important to good design. A designer develops a proper screen layout, chooses the appropriate writing style, and plans the structure of the material. The designer may also be called upon to adjust the Help system to one or more different audiences. With the emergence of WinHelp 4 and the Microsoft model for Help system design, the designer plays a pivotal role in determining the direction of new Help systems.

The best introduction to design is to review as many Help systems as possible. Use the Windows Explorer to locate all of the Help files (find *.HLP) installed on your system and look through them. Use the "Browsing a Help file" technique described in Chapter 20, *Compiling, Debugging, and Testing*. You don't need to be an expert to see what techniques are effective in Help systems. Local chapters of the Society for Technical Communication hold annual competitions through which you can view emerging Help designs. There is over two decades of research concerning online Help and hypertext development. If you'd like more information, see the bibliography of this book.

A valuable element of design that is rarely employed is usability testing. Usability testing can be as simple as having a few people from your company experiment with your Help system. It also can be as complex as recording and analyzing user actions in a fully equipped observation center. The objective in any case is to find out if the Help system is helping the user.

Coding

Writing, editing, and design are skills common to both online and print documentation. Experience with a word processor usually gives you all the technical skill you need. Help development, on the other hand, requires additional skills. Turning text and graphics from your word processor into a Windows Help system requires an understanding of the Help compiler, the coding of topic and project files, and some general knowledge about the Windows operating system.

Your understanding of this information is what separates you from the multitude of other technical writers who work only with print publications. Chapters 10-20 of this book are dedicated to the coding of Help systems.

Your ultimate success will depend on your knowledge of the underlying Help coding. If you plan to spend a significant amount of your time working with Help systems you need to review the "Step-by-Step Procedures" and "WinHelp Reference" sections of the *Help Author's Guide* (HCW.HLP) on your book disc. Practice building a few sample Help systems without using an authoring tool. Browse the online support forums where much of the discussion deals with raw coding.

This is not to suggest ignoring Help authoring tools. Help development is incredibly inefficient and error-prone without the use of one *or more* authoring tools. However, the many authoring products discussed in Chapter 22 should be regarded as tools to make you more efficient and ease your introduction into Help development, not as magic wands.

Some programming experience is a plus for creating macros and debugging the Help file. If you use graphics in your Help, knowledge of graphic file formats and experience with illustration software is helpful.

Creating Graphics

When it comes to simple screen captures of dialog boxes and icons most Help writers are capable of producing acceptable images. However the creation of quality icons, graphical buttons, descriptive illustration, and splash screens requires experience and/or formal training in graphic arts.

Today's graphic tools are so powerful that they may provide a false sense of adequacy about the graphics we create. Know what is acceptable to your users. Buying a hammer doesn't mean you can make a birdhouse and the purchase of a graphics tool doesn't mean you can render a great illustration.

Figure 23.1 nicely illustrates the value of a skilled graphics professional. Whereas most competent writers could have captured the screen image of the open folder and the icon, a graphic artist is able to add a sense of movement which helps clarify the process for the user.

Figure 23.1. *A quality graphic that simulates motion to demonstrate a process.*

Testing

The testing of compiled Help files is often conducted by everyone involved with the development. The Help writer tests repeatedly during development. But every Help system to be widely distributed should undergo a formal testing process. Testers often come from a quality assurance department, but basic training in the features of the Windows Help system can make virtually any meticulous person a competent tester. Each component of the Help system must be methodically reviewed. The nature of a hypertext system means that more than one path to each topic has to be checked. The topic file(s) must be checked to make sure that no topic has been left out.

The tester does not have to know much about the construction of Help or programming. Essentially, the testing of a Help system is the same as testing any software application. If a formal application test structure exists in your company, you should use it for your Help. Specific testing strategies are described in Chapter 20, *Compiling, Debugging, and Testing*.

Validating, another form of testing, is the exercise of checking every procedure and step against the actual software to ensure that the program actually works the way the documentation says it does. The best validator is a person who is familiar with software in general but has not worked much with the software under review. This lack of experience prevents the validator from making assumptions that could not be made by the typical user. A validator can expose numerous flaws in the effectiveness and accuracy of documentation. One or more validation checks is essential in the development of any Help system.

Managing

In the past the person in charge of Help development had other obligations as well. An existing manager from Publications, Programming, or a related department would likely take on this responsibility. With the trend toward replacing print documentation with online Help, a manager specifically in charge of Help development is increasingly common.

Being a good manager requires a thorough understanding of the Help development process. This does not mean being an expert on every aspect of coding or indexing or the other skills. But the manager does need to know enough to successfully evaluate the work of others on the project. Besides experience with the various skill areas, the manager must be able to form, guide, and motivate the Help team. The ability to produce cost estimates and schedules is also key. Experience with electronic worksheets and project management software is a plus. Those elements are described in this chapter.

The majority of Help development managers have their roots in the technical writing area—with good reason. While Help authoring is intimately tied to software development, the construction of a Help system more closely parallels the development of print documentation than that of a software product. Print publications and Help systems share their most central component: the words. Even if you are not developing a print manual as part of your documentation set, you will find general print management techniques useful. However, the successful Help manager understands how Help differs from print. A good manager is also able to bridge the gap between the Help team and those developing the application software.

These basic concepts, combined with the tried and tested management techniques used for print development, provide a good basis for Help management. Assembling a team of Help professionals should be a first priority for the manager.

At a Glance Help Skills

Skill	Responsibilities	Characteristics
Writing	Write content of the topics Generate keyword list Capture screen images	Solid writing skills Knowledge of indexing Familiarity with design Ability to render basic graphics
Editing	Perform copy and substantive edit Conduct technical edit	Solid language skills Knowledge of online writing principles
Designing	Develop screen layout Choose writing styles Plan Help file structure	Familiarity with online models Knowledge of online design principles Familiarity with usability testing
Coding	Create project file Add footnote and character codes to topic file Compile Help files	Experience with a word processor Understanding of the Help compiler, coding, and the Windows operating system Knowledge of graphic file formats
Creating Graphics	Create icons, buttons, illustrations	Formal training in graphic arts Experience with graphic tools
Testing	Operate all hypertext components Validate all procedures	A meticulous nature Familiarity with general software operation and specific WinHelp operation
Managing	Produce a Help file on time, within budget, and to specification Guide, groom, and support personnel	Understanding of the Help development process Experience with management tools Familiarity with print management Good leadership

Building a Help team

The Windows Help standard developed by Microsoft has been designed so that Help authoring is within the capability of most people. However, even basic Help development has a steep learning curve. And many organizations want more than a basic Help system. One way for you to bridge the knowledge gap is to form a Help team (either on staff or on a contract basis) of professionals with the skills described in the previous section. Professionals typically spend portions of every week keeping up on technical developments in Windows Help as well as in Windows in general. In addition to the technical know-how, a full understanding of Help development techniques and training in the writing and organizing of Help topics are skills that take years to master.

TEAM STRUCTURE

Most Help development teams are centered around a lead writer. Consider a medical analogy: the surgeon is the focus of all the action in an operating room. The surgeon's skills are the ones upon which the success of the operation relies. The surgeon understands the overall plan and can improvise when necessary. Other specialists, like the anesthesiologist, nurses, and technicians, surround the surgeon to provide their expertise as needed. In Help development the lead writer is the surgeon. See Figure 23.2. The writer provides the key skill: the crafting of the words. Usually it is the writer who guides the operation from planning through the final builds.

Surrounding the writer are those specializing in editing, designing, creating graphics, coding, and testing. The editor receives draft documents from the writer and returns them after they have undergone the various edits. When the writer sees the need for an illustration, a graphic artist may be charged with rendering it. The tester is used when needed throughout the development.

While lines of communication are generally open among all team members, the major interaction in terms of the flow of content, reviews, and revisions, all goes through the Lead Writer.

Depending on the organization, a manager may be involved with more than one project, some of them including print manuals as well. While the manager might guide the project and be ultimately responsible for it, the writer is still the key component in its success or failure. Filling the position of the writer should be the highest priority.

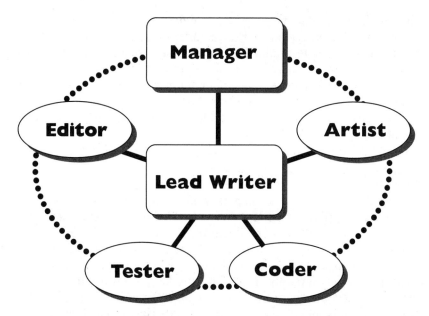

Figure 23.2. *Surgical Structure for a Help Development Team.*

When you choose Help writers, also consider their indexing skills. Although most writers can handle the development of a rudimentary index, you might want to hire an experienced indexing professional to handle your keyword development. This is a skill that cannot be learned overnight and one that requires a certain personality. Make sure that any indexer you engage understands the difference between print and online indexes. Knowledge of WinHelp 4's full-text search feature is an added plus.

The Help designer often is a consultant used only at certain periods during a project. The job of the designer includes keeping up with the latest hypertext and Windows Help techniques. It also includes usability testing. The level at which you perform usability testing depends largely on your resources and the importance of effective Help. A mainstream software release with good online Help reduces technical support costs and creates good will. In such a case, some form of usability testing is essential.

An in-house Help system might not have the same cost benefits, and formal usability testing might not be practical. For formal usability testing, a professional trained in the design and analysis of such a testing program is required. For informal purposes, the Help author can devise a set of key tasks and have several other staff members attempt to access information on those tasks. Their feedback can dramatically improve the Help system.

On very large projects or those that require the highest attention to writing quality, you may want to consider using a technician just for coding. Relieving the writer from those duties provides that person with more time to attend to the words and outline. The technician codes the completed text and graphics, manages the topic and project files, and performs the compiling and debugging. A technician can come from either a programming or publications department. With the prevalence of Help authoring tools most writers have also taken on the coding tasks as well. This makes the writer even more central to the project as the writing and coding often comprise over half of the total labor on a project.

SOURCES FOR CANDIDATES

Universities are an excellent source for experienced and inexperienced workers. Institutions with technical writing programs are good places to find budding writers whom you can train in Help development. New graduates can cut their teeth as Help testers and technicians. Institutions with graduate programs in Education or Technical Communications are good sources for advanced Help professionals. Much of the original research being done with online Help and hypertext is at the university level. Although these graduates might not have specific Windows Help experience, they have the skills and understanding required for a Help designer. The transfer of general online Help skills to Windows Help production is not a problem at all.

Consultants can benefit any organization that is getting involved with Help development for the first time. Setting up the basic structure for your topics is the single biggest barrier to getting started. Consultants can evaluate your specific needs and lay out an appropriate development plan. This might include a topic-file shell with all of the features you might need. The plan also can include custom macros and style templates to control the appearance of your Help content. Then you can begin adding your text to this shell.

Cost estimating

Very few Help projects get far into the planning stage without questions arising about cost. Cost estimating, therefore, is central to the planning of Help projects. Unfortunately, accurate estimates are as difficult to achieve in Help development as in most complex activities. In the following sections, however, we provide some assistance in developing reasonably accurate estimates for your Help projects.

Whether you are doing cost estimates by hand or with a computer, there is one fundamental item you are concerned with: money. Of course there are less quantitative costs that are equally important, like the impact on other projects and on human resources, but that's a different book. This section helps you determine what it's going to cost to get the job done.

The job in this case is a Help system. The central cost component in Help development is human labor. The cost of equipment is negligible compared to the amount of labor it requires to complete a professional Help system. In order to determine labor costs you need to assemble several pieces of information:

- The size of the project.

- The tasks that need to be completed.

- The compensation to be paid to those completing the tasks.

- The rate at which the tasks are completed.

The topic is the basic unit of all Help systems. The size of a Help project is generally determined by the number of topics in the topic file. In the process of creating the topics certain tasks need to be completed. (See Chapter 21 and the task list on the book disc for examples of tasks typical of Help development.) The completion of the various tasks requires individuals with certain skills; their pay rate directly affects the cost of the Help system. Individuals work at different speeds and certain tasks require different amounts of time to complete than others. These pieces of information can be assembled into equations which calculate the costs of the project.

For example, assume that you are creating a Help system of approximately 300 topics. The creation of those topics will require dozens of tasks, of which one might be to "Write a first draft" of the Help text. Someone will be needed to perform that task and that person will receive a wage for performing it. Generally we pay workers on either a salary or hourly basis. Even when dealing with salaried employees, it is best to transform their pay into hourly rates. Let's assume that the writer on this project will be paid $40 per hour. Let's assume that in the past this author has, on the average, completed one topic per hour. This collection of data can then be arranged as follows:

$$\text{Write 300 topics} \quad @ \frac{\$40}{\text{per hour}} @ \frac{1 \text{ hour}}{\text{per topic}} = \$12,000$$

The result is that the cost estimate for writing the topics is $12,000. Notice that the units of hours and topics are arranged in the equation so they cancel each other out leaving just $ dollars. This basic calculation can be applied to every facet of Help development.

There are three variables that play a significant role in accurate Help estimates:

- Whether there is existing text.

- Whether an authoring tool is being used.

- Whether context-sensitive Help is being employed.

The first reflects the fact that the writing of the Help system content is the most time-consuming part of the process. Any existing material you have which can be transformed into Help content significantly reduces the cost of the project. If it takes you one hour to write a topic from scratch, you can probably rework existing text into that same topic in about a third of that time. Although Help topics have different writing requirements than print material, it makes sense to leverage existing information.

The second item concerns Help authoring tools. The various tools offer excellent efficiency in certain areas of Help development, mainly the coding of topic and project files. You will certainly see decreases in your Help development costs if you use a tool. Of course, every tool comes with its own strengths and weaknesses. You need to be aware of where the benefits come from with the tool you choose.

A final item is your use of context-sensitive Help. Microsoft has used context-sensitive Help extensively for years, but it has really roused attention in Windows 95 with What's This? pop-up definitions. This, and any form of context-sensitive Help, significantly increases the time required in the areas of planning, coding, and debugging/testing.

Taken together, the basic labor calculation along with these adjustments, makes cost estimating a bit complicated. To ease the brain pain, we offer a cost estimating model, in the form of a Microsoft Excel worksheet, that is applicable to many different organizations. The WinHelp Cost Estimating Worksheet is included on the sample disc that accompanies this book. It is described in detail in the following sections and a Help file is attached to it.

THE WINHELP COST ESTIMATING WORKSHEET

The basic goal of this worksheet is to calculate the total labor time and the associated costs required for a Help project. These figures reflect the various skills involved in the project and the cost of the individuals providing those skills. The cost is calculated separately for permanent staff and hourly contract employees. Because health benefits vary greatly, they are not included in these calculations. Nor does the worksheet include such fixed costs as equipment and general overhead.

> **NOTE** *In a Microsoft Excel worksheet, columns are identified by letters and rows by numbers. References to a cell or group of cells are put in parentheses. A range of cells in a row or column uses the cell references for each end of the range separated by a colon. A rectangular block of cells uses the cell references of the upper left and lower right corner cells of the array, separated by a colon. For example, a reference to a single cell might look like this: (D14), to part of a row like this: (C76:O76), to part of a column like this: (H4:H18), and to a rectangular block of cells like this: (E35:P92).*

The Help manager uses this worksheet by entering basic information that defines, in an approximate way, the total size of the Help effort. The formulas underlying the worksheet automatically fill in the number of hours for the various skills and the associated cost of those skills. So, for example, in the case of the hypothetical Help project shown in Figure 23.4, the worksheet predicts that 205 hours will be necessary to write and revise the first draft (C34). Also, the worksheet shows that the management time required will cost a total of $7,605 if the manager is brought in on a contract basis (I67) and $3,457 if the manager is on staff (I69). These formulas are based on experience gained from thousands of hours of Help development.

There are many organizational contexts in which Windows Help systems are created; no single worksheet can fit every context. This worksheet can be useful to you on two levels. First, it is an example of the kind of worksheet that you can create for yourself to fit your own particular circumstances. Even if you choose to create your own worksheet, the cost model underlying this one, and many of the formulas used here, should be very helpful.

Second, this worksheet and the formulas it contains reflect the way you create Help and the actual costs you encounter. Alternatively, if you are just beginning to create Windows Help systems, you can use this worksheet, and the various assumptions it embodies, as a guide to your own Help development and your own estimating processes. Keep in mind that the Help development methodology reflected in this worksheet is a summary of the tasks described in detail in Chapter 21, *Development Tasks and Strategies,* and in the "Scheduling" section of this chapter.

Defining the scope of the project

Let us trace the process by which you use this worksheet. The starting place is the top left section of the worksheet, where you define the scope of the project. The first step is to indicate the total size of the Help project. The size of a Help project can be estimated in terms of the total number of Help topics or the page count of a print manual that covers the same functionality as the Help system. You can use either method with this worksheet. If you have an existing print manual that is being converted to Help, you can elect to estimate by page count: enter the number of pages in the manual. The size of the page is assumed to be 7" x 9", formatted in a Microsoft publication style. The worksheet then calculates the expected number of topics by using a multiplier of topics per page. The default ratio is 3:1.

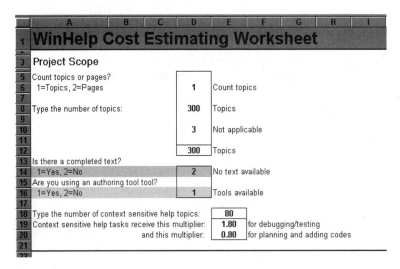

Figure 23.3. *Defining the scope of the project.*

If you are creating a Help system from scratch, you can estimate the scope of your project directly in terms of topics. In order to estimate the number of topics, consider the size and nature of the software and draw upon your experience. Tally the number of definitions, procedures, and other types of topics you expect to use. In this case the number of pages and topics-per-page ratio are not applicable.

TIP *A rule of thumb for estimating the number of Help topics based on the page count of an existing print manual is that a page of print text usually corresponds to two to three Help topics. Therefore, a 100-page document would translate to somewhere between 200 and 300 Help topics. This is a very rough number and you will almost certainly want to adjust this to your own materials. (The worksheet uses the ratio of 3:1.)*

A rule of thumb for estimating topics from scratch is to count the number of commands on the menus of your application software. Then multiply this number by 3 to get the number of Help topics. This rule of thumb assumes that on the average, each command will require a procedure topic, a command topic or conceptual topic, and a definition topic. This rule gives acceptable estimates with a minimum of work. In Figure 23.3 the number of topics is specified as 300.

Microsoft's model for their operating system Help files tends to use more procedures, very few command topics, and more definition (or What's This?) topics. A rough analysis has shown that the 3:1 ratio described above still holds.

Defining the scope of a project also requires answers to three questions:

- Is there any completed text?
- Are you employing any authoring tools?
- How may topics will be context-sensitive?

If you indicate that there is completed text from a print manual or other source, many of the worksheet figures will be considerably lower than if the writing were done from scratch. The total cost for the project, shown at the bottom of the worksheet, will also be lower. The figures affected by the answer to the first question are highlighted in blue in the worksheet and comprise the Writing/Design and Administration sections. See Figure 23.4.

Typical Labor Units for Help Skills

	Writing	Design	Coding	Testing	Editing	Mgr.
Contract Staff	$45.00	$45.00	$35.00	$25.00	$40.00	$55.00
Yearly	40,000	40,000	30,000	25,000	35,000	50,000
Hourly *	$20.00	$20.00	$15.00	$12.50	$17.50	$25.00

* Assumes: 2000 hrs./yr. (not including benefits)

Help Tasks — All values in hours.

	Total	Writing	Design	Coding	Testing	Editing	Mgr.
Writing and Design							
Write/revise 1st draft	205	150	25				30
Compile 1st draft	15			15			
Review 1st draft	60				10	25	25
Create graphics	35	15	15				5
Build keyword list	40	20	5			15	
Write/revise 2nd draft	85	75	10				
Compile 2nd draft	10			10			
Edit 2nd draft	40				10	30	
Write/revise final draft	50	40	10				
Review final draft	35				10	15	10
Compile final draft	10			10			
Total Writing/Design	585	300	65	35	30	85	70
Adminstration							
Planning (CS)	79	24	18			24	12
Version Control	55	15		15	5	15	5
Duplication/Distribution	25			10		5	10
Total Administration	159	39	18	25	5	44	27
Project/Contents Files							
Create Basic HPJ	20		5	10			5
Create Contents file	35		15	15			5
Add HPJ Enhancements	25		10	10			5
Context sensitive map (CS)	17	5	4	5			3
Total Proj./Contents	97	5	34	40	0	0	18
Coding Topic Files							
Add codes (#$K+A>!) (CS)	24			18			6
Code graphics	10			5			5
Debugging/testing (CS*2)	37			15		15	7
Add jumps, popups, links	35	5	10	15			5
Total Coding	106	5	10	53	0	15	23

		Writing	Design	Coding	Testing	Editing	Mgr.
Total Hrs.	947	350	127	153	35	144	138
Contract	$41,065	$15,732	$5,724	$5,367	$875	$5,763	$7,605
Staff	$18,251	$6,992	$2,544	$2,300	$438	$2,521	$3,457
Cost Total							

Figure 23.4. *Calculated hours for skills and tasks.*

Similarly, if you indicate that an authoring tool is being used, some of the figures and the total cost are also reduced. The figures affected by this second question are shown in yellow and make up the Project/Contents File and Coding Topic Files sections. Note that your actual results may vary considerably depending on the quality of your authoring tool. For example, while Help Workshop is an authoring tool, it provides no support in constructing topic files, which is where the majority of coding labor goes.

Finally, the quantity entered for the number of context-sensitive topics affects only certain tasks, but can have a big effect on the summary values. To determine the number of context-sensitive topics, you need to be familiar with your system design. If you are new to context sensitivity read Chapter 19, *Programming Calls to Help*. Some organizations provide context-sensitive Help topics for each dialog box or window. Others use field level Help like What's This?. Depending on your design, you should be able to estimate the number of context-sensitive topics from a programmer's specification.

The "Context sensitive map" task values are included in a cost estimate only if the number of context-sensitive topics is greater than zero. Three other tasks, "Planning," "Add Codes," and "Debugging/Testing" are dependent on the number of context-sensitive topics and two special multipliers. One multiplier is for "Debugging/Testing" (E18) and the other is for "Planning/Adding Codes." (E19) The two multipliers are necessary because the associated tasks can have different impacts on the development of context-sensitive Help. Two multipliers are provided by default which offer typical results, however you can change these values at any time.

Once you finished defining the project scope, the cost estimate is complete. All the worksheet values are automatically and immediately adjusted. The next sections describe how to evaluate and customize the results.

Skills and tasks

There are six columns (D through I) of rates, one for the key Help skills described in the first section of this chapter (with the exception of Creating Graphics, which is more or less peripheral). You can specify rates for both staff members and outside contractors. The rates for each are based on the average price you might expect to pay for such services, not including benefits. Actual rates vary by region and level of experience. You can modify these rates to match those at your organization. Just type the new value into the appropriate cell. For contract workers, use an hourly rate in the Contract row. For staff members, use a yearly salary in the Yearly row, and an effective hourly rate will be calculated for you.

These rates are used to provide the cost summary that appears at the bottom of the worksheet (B65:I69). The summary multiplies the total number of hours for each worker by that worker's rate. If one person wears several hats in your organization, just specify that person's rate in each of the appropriate skill areas.

The labor rates are followed by a list of common Help tasks. These tasks are described in detail in Chapter 21, *Development Tasks and Strategies*. They are divided into four categories:

Writing/Editing, Administration, Project/Contents Files, and Coding Topic Files. Each task is segmented into columns for each of the skills: Writing, Design, Coding, Testing, Editing, and Managing. The values in the table represent the number of hours required for each skill position to complete the various Help tasks. For example, the task "Write/revise final draft" requires 40 hours for writing and 10 hours for design (D42:E42). For the task "Add codes (#$K+A>!)" the allocation of 18 hours for Coding is straightforward (F58). But notice that the Manager is also budgeted for 6 hours (I58). This could be for meetings between the manager and the person doing the coding.

For each category there are subtotals for tasks and each skill position. So from the example you know that generating the project and contents files will take a total of 97 (B56) hours of which 40 are for coding (F56). Totals are provided in range B65:I69. The example project will require 947 hours with a staff cost of $18,251.

> **NOTE** *Worksheet summary values are rounded to the nearest whole number.*

Supporting data

The hours that appear for the various tasks are based not only on the values you defined for the project scope, but also on the values in the Sample Data section of the worksheet. Figure 23.5 shows the section of the worksheet containing the Help data (K24:X62). Each of the values in the data set is expressed in minutes per task only because it provides an easy unit to work with. The Sample Data is derived from records of more than eight thousand work hours of WinHelp development performed by the authors.

The sample data provides two values for each task and skill. The Writing/Design and the Administration tasks are directly related to the condition of whether or not there is existing text. For each skill and task there is one value which is used if the answer to the condition is Yes and a different value if the answer is No. For example, the data for "Write/revise first draft" has two values for Writing (M30:N30). If there is existing text (Yes) the value is 10 minutes per task, if not, the value is 30 minutes per task. The Project/Contents Files and Coding Topic Files categories use values that are based on the second conditionæwhether or not you are using an authoring tool.

Sample Data

This data represents over 8000 hours of developing Help applications for retail distribution.
See Chapter 24, "Managing Help Development" and BUDGET.HLP for detailed explanations.

You can modify this data to match your personal data records.
 n/a=the task is not applicable to the skill.

All values are in minutes per topic.

Writing/editing	Text?:	Writer Yes	No	Designer Yes	No	Technician Yes	No	Tester Yes	No	Editor Yes	No	Manager Yes	No
Write/revise 1st draft		10	30	2	5	n/a	n/a	n/a	n/a	n/a	n/a	3	6
Compile 1st draft		n/a	n/a	n/a	n/a	2	3	n/a	n/a	n/a	n/a	n/a	n/a
Review 1st draft		n/a	n/a	n/a	n/a	n/a	n/a	2	2	2	5	2	5
Create graphics		3	3	3	3	n/a	n/a	n/a	n/a	n/a	n/a	1	1
Build keyword list		3	4	1	1	n/a	n/a	n/a	n/a	2	3	n/a	n/a
Write/edit 2nd draft		5	15	2	2	n/a	n/a	n/a	n/a	n/a	n/a	n/a	n/a
Compile 2nd draft		n/a	n/a	n/a	n/a	2	2	n/a	n/a	n/a	n/a	n/a	n/a
Copyedit		n/a	n/a	n/a	n/a	n/a	n/a	2	2	3	6	n/a	n/a
Write/edit final draft		3	8	2	2	n/a	n/a	n/a	n/a	n/a	n/a	n/a	n/a
Review final draft		n/a	n/a	n/a	n/a	n/a	n/a	2	2	2	3	2	2
Compile final draft		n/a	n/a	n/a	n/a	2	2	n/a	n/a	n/a	n/a	n/a	n/a

Administration	Writer Yes	No	Designer Yes	No	Technician Yes	No	Tester Yes	No	Editor Yes	No	Manager Yes	No
Planning	3	4	2	3	n/a	n/a	n/a	n/a	3	4	2	2
Version Control	2	3	n/a	n/a	2	3	1	1	2	3	1	1
Duplication/Distribution	n/a	n/a	n/a	n/a	2	2	n/a	n/a	1	1	2	2

Project/Contents Files	Tools?:	Writer Yes	No	Designer Yes	No	Technician Yes	No	Tester Yes	No	Proof Yes	No	Manager Yes	No
Create Basic HPJ		n/a	n/a	1	1	2	3	n/a	n/a	n/a	n/a	1	1
Create Contents file		n/a	n/a	3	3	3	5	n/a	n/a	n/a	n/a	1	1
Add HPJ Enhancements		n/a	n/a	2	2	2	3	n/a	n/a	n/a	n/a	1	1
Map Context Sensitive Links		4	7	3	6	4	6	n/a	n/a	n/a	n/a	2	2

Coding Topic Files	Writer Yes	No	Designer Yes	No	Technician Yes	No	Tester Yes	No	Proof Yes	No	Manager Yes	No
Add codes (#$K+)	n/a	n/a	n/a	n/a	3	6	n/a	n/a	n/a	n/a	1	2
Prepare bitmaps	n/a	n/a	n/a	n/a	1	3	n/a	n/a	n/a	n/a	1	1
Debugging	n/a	n/a	n/a	n/a	2	5	n/a	n/a	2	3	1	2
Add jumps, popups	1	2	2	3	3	7	n/a	n/a	n/a	n/a	1	2

Figure 23.5. *Sample data for skills and tasks.*

Customizing the worksheet

It is important to recognize that the data used here and the various multipliers may not fit your circumstances. However, the WinHelp Cost Estimating Worksheet is given in a form that you can easily customize for your individual situation. If the data values do not seem to fit your experience, change them. If the context-sensitive multipliers need tweaking, then adjust those as well. You may find that you want to add additional formulas and assumptions to the worksheet. The more you customize the worksheet, the more accurate your results. If you record actual rate information from your projects, those figures can be used to continuously update your worksheet.

The values here are less realistic for very small (fewer than 50 topics) or very large (more than 800 topics) projects. With very small projects, the amount of time spent on planning may easily be more than the time spent on writing and coding. The economies of scale on large projects would probably require lowering the average values in the data set. The amount of conceptual versus reference information in your Help text will also make a difference in budgeting. Straightforward documentation of procedures and command syntax is less time consuming to develop than conceptual text, which requires examples, analogies, and more creative thinking.

The cells in the worksheet are all initially protected, except for your answers to the introductory questions. To unprotect the document, select Unprotect Sheet from the Tools/Protection menu.

COST ESTIMATING ANALYSIS

If you record actual times for your own completed projects the historical data can provide added insights which will help you attack future projects. Help projects in general share certain characteristics which become very evident when you examine historical data. Here are a few examples based on the 300-topic scenario presented above.

Labor distribution

Figure 23.6 shows the distribution of time required for tasks in a typical Help development effort where all of the text is created from scratch without authoring tools. You can see that writing accounts for 33 percent of the labor. Note that the coding work is only 23 percent of the total. Yet, coding is the area that receives the most focus among many new developers. The size of the "pie" can be significantly reduced by using authoring tools, taking advantage of existing documentation, and strictly planning the writing tasks.

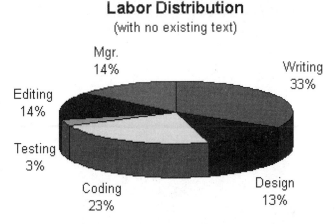

Figure 23.6. *Distribution of Help development hours.*

Using authoring tools

Another significant factor is whether or not you employ a Help authoring tool. Figure 23.7 shows the effects on the various skill areas with and without an authoring tool. Without the use of an authoring tool, the coding of the topic file takes 246 hours. This is cut by 93 hours to 153 hours if an authoring tool is used. Over a third of the coding time is saved. The actual savings you enjoy will depend on the tool you choose and how you use it. The savings due to authoring tools are primarily in the areas of coding your topic and project files. The effect on the other development tasks is relatively small, if any.

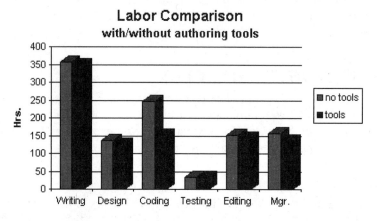

Figure 23.7. *Comparing labor with and without the use of authoring tools.*

The development of Help also requires the purchase of appropriate software and hardware. However, the cost of this equipment is usually amortized over several Help projects and is often only a fraction of your total development cost. If you are just getting started with Help, you will be purchasing, at a minimum, word-processing and graphic tools, Windows, and the Windows Software Development kit. A Help authoring tool is strongly recommended. Your computer should be a fast 486 machine with at least 8 MB of memory and a 300 MB hard drive.

At A Glance Cost Estimating

✔ The central cost component in Help development is human labor.

✔ Generating cost estimates requires knowledge of project size, tasks, compensation, and work rates. The basic equation to calculate the cost to complete a task is:

# of topics x unit of time per topic x wages per unit of time.

✔ Other important variables are the presence of existing text, the use of an authoring tool, and the need for context-sensitive Help.

✔ Use the WinHelp Cost Estimating Worksheet to generate cost estimates, or as a guide for creating your own worksheet.

✔ Recording actual summaries of work times makes estimating future projects more accurate.

✔ The tasks associated with writing and coding typically account for half of the total labor on a Help project.

✔ Authoring tools can significantly reduce costs, depending on the tool and how you use it.

Scheduling

Creating a schedule for your Help project is another important management task. While cost estimating provides you with control over the costs of your project, scheduling allows you to manage your time appropriately. The work rates and skill positions described earlier in this chapter can be used for scheduling as well. This section guides you through the steps of developing a schedule for your Help project and then provides tips on ways to improve your schedule.

BUILDING A SCHEDULE

There are four basic elements to scheduling a project:

- Assemble a list of tasks.

- Estimate the time and resources needed for each of those tasks.

- Establish predecessors for each task.

- Lay out those factors against a calendar.

These elements combined together result in a tool called a Gantt chart. The creation of this chart is relatively simple, but can pay large dividends in controlling your project. If a problem arises you can quickly get an idea of its impact on your schedule. While you can construct this type of chart with pencil and paper, a software application like Microsoft Project can perform the job more efficiently. The book disc contains a Microsoft Project sample file. The data is also available in Excel, dBase, and text file formats.

Assemble a list of tasks

The first step is to create a comprehensive task list for your particular project. Tasks involving writing, editing, and administration are common to all forms of publishing. Broad tasks specific to Help include coding the topic file and project files, compiling, and testing. For best results you should divide these broad tasks into smaller, specific task items. A well-written task item is one that specifies an outcome. It is also one that can be assigned to a single individual on your Help team and can be easily monitored. For example the item "Write 1st draft" is very clear in terms of what is expected of the person doing the task. You can also envision the amount of time it takes to perform this task and be able to assign a due date to it.

The task list for a typical Help project is provided in the sample PROJECT.MPP file and also in TASKS.DOC on the book disc. These tasks are derived from the detailed task list presented in Chapter 21, *Development Tasks and Strategies*. Assemble all of your expected tasks in a single column list. Then sort them by broad categories, like Planning or Writing. Sorting by categories helps to make sure you haven't left out any tasks and makes it possible to summarize your efforts for others.

Assign time estimates and resources

Once you have a list of tasks, you need to assign a quantity of time to each task. The WinHelp Cost Estimating Worksheet can assist you by providing estimates of labor requirements for the various tasks. Even if you aren't sure of the amount of time a task will take, it still helps to try to estimate.

Generally hours are used as the unit of time since pay rates are usually based on hours. However with projects of longer duration you may choose to use days as the unit. While some projects take several months and even years, units of time larger than hours or days are hard to work with. Record the number of estimated hours or days in a second column next to each task on your list.

At this time, you may also want to assign the tasks to various people. One of the benefits of a master schedule is the ability to track the progress of several workers. The first section of this chapter details the different skill positions which you may choose to employ. Add the task assignments in the third column of your schedule.

In Figure 23.8, the task "Write topic outline" is estimated to take 5 days of the Writer's time.

Task	Days	Assigned to:
Prepare document plan	5	Mgr
Write topic outline	5	Writer
Prepare budget/schedule	3	Mgr
Choose team	3	Mgr
Assign tasks	2	Mgr
Design screen layout	5	Writer
Distribute outline	1	Designer

Figure 23.8. *Assigning time estimates and resources to a task.*

Establish predecessors

Whether your project is large or small, the projects tasks will be completed in a certain order. Certain topics need to be completed before other topics can be started. When you add these dependencies to your chart, you are in effect building a schedule and flow chart.

For example, writing a topic outline would have to be completed before you could distribute that outline for review. The task "Write topic outline" would therefore be a "predecessor" of "Distribute outline." In order to add this information to the chart, two new columns are required, one for the predecessors and one for a unique task identifier. This identifier is a shorthand that makes it easy to reference tasks repeatedly on your chart. Generally tasks are numbered as they appear in the task list, but a task's number doesn't matter as long as each number is unique. In Figure 23.9 the "Write topic outline" task (task #4) is shown to be a predecessor of "Distribute outline" (task #9).

ID	Task	Days	Predecessors	Assigned to:
3	Prepare document plan	5	1	Mgr.
4	Write topic outline	5	3	Writer
5	Prepare budget/schedule	3	3	Mgr.
6	Choose team	3	5	Mgr.
7	Assign tasks	2	6	Mgr.
8	Design screen layout	5	7	Writer
9	Distribute outline	1	4	Designer

Figure 23.9. *Assigning predecessors to tasks.*

There are also Help tasks that run concurrently. In Figure 23.10, we see that before the Writer can begin the task "Write topics" the tasks "Assemble information" and "Prepare style sheets" must be completed. However, the Editor can be preparing the style sheets at the same time that the Writer is assembling information.

ID	Task	Days	Predecessors	Assigned to:
16	Revise design	3	14	Designer
17	Assemble information	5	13	Writer
18	Prepare style sheet	3	7	Editor
19	Write topics	20	17,18	Writer
20	Write keywords	3	19	Writer

Figure 23.10. *Assigning multiple predecessors to a single topic.*

Apply a calendar

The final step is to combine the tasks and associated times with a calendar. You already have the tasks, times, predecessors, and assignments in columns on your worksheet. Now, after the assignments column, draw a time scale on the top line of your worksheet, going from left to right. If your project will take only a few months, you may want to add dates to denote the beginning of weeks. However, it's best not to try to display each individual day. This chart is intended to give you a broad view of your Help project.

Every task in your list should have a start and a finish date. For some tasks, the date is explicitly handed to you by someone in your organization. For example, "You will receive software to work with on November 1st," or "The deadline for compiled Help is March 15." Many of the tasks will not have dates yet. Start with the tasks which have dates assigned and mark those dates on your chart. If you know a starting date for a task and the number of hours it takes, you can make a good guess as to a finish date. In Figure 23.11, the task, "Prepare documentation plan" begins on May 14th. Since the estimated time for that task is five working days, the finish date is displayed as May 18th.

Draw lines to indicate the duration of each task. Note that the duration of a task may exceed the time estimated for the actual work. While a task may be estimated for 20 hours, those hours may be distributed over the course of a month. In Figure 23.11 the task "Prepare budget/schedule" is estimated to take three days spread over a seven-day period. The seven-day period is also called a "span time."

Task	Days	14	15	16	17	18	19	20	21	22
Prepare document plan	5									
Write topic outline	5									
Prepare budget/schedule	3									
Choose team	3									

Figure 23.11. *Task hours may be distributed over a span of time.*

A completed chart is shown in Figure 23.12. While this chart was done in Microsoft Project, it could also have been done with a similar project management tool, or by hand. The advantage of using a software tool is that any change you make to the data instantly adjusts the graphical timeline.

Microsoft Project uses some of its own terminology. The "Name" column displays the tasks. "Duration" is the span of time for each task and "Resources" are the workers assigned to the various tasks.

In all but the smallest project, several different paths are followed during development. The writer proceeds along one path of tasks while the editor, manager, tester, and others follow their own path. This is best viewed with the help of a flowchart which can be generated from your scheduling information. Microsoft Project can automatically display a flow chart, called a PERT chart, once you have entered the information described in this section. Figure 23.13 shows a portion of such a chart. Each tasks is represented by a square box. The arrowed lines indicate the relationships between tasks and the flow of work.

ID	Name	Duration	Resource	May 5/14	5/21	5/28	June 6/4	6/11	6/18	6/25	7/2
1	Project Assigned	1d	Other								
2	**Planning**	**22d**									
3	Prepare documentation plan	5d	Mgr.								
4	Write topic outline	5d	Writer								
5	Prepare budget/schedule	3d	Mgr.								
6	Choose team	3d	Mgr.								
7	Assign tasks	2d	Mgr.								
8	Design screen layout	5d	Writer								
9	Distribute outline	1d	Designer								
10	Distribute design	1d	Designer								
11	Review outline	2d	Mgr.								
12	Review design	2d	Mgr.								
13	Approve outline	1d	Mgr.								
14	Approve design	1d	Mgr.								
15	**Framing**	**51d**									
16	Revise design	3d	Designer								
17	Assemble existing information	5d	Writer								
18	Prepare style sheet	3d	Editor								
19	Write topics	20d	Writer								
20	Write keywords	3d	Writer								
21	Review/edit hard copy	1d	Writer								
22	Code topic file: first draft	10d	Technicia								

Figure 23.12. *Sample project schedule.*

Most project management tools automatically determine what is called the "critical path" of the project. The critical path is the one that takes the longest to complete. A delay to any item on the critical path results in a delay in the completion date of the project. By paying special attention to items on the critical path you can avoid missing deadlines or minimize the effect of delays. In Figure 23.13, Microsoft Project displays the critical path in bold lines; the tasks outlined in bold are on the critical path. Using this example we can see that a delay in the "Create macros" task will cause a delay in the completion of the project. This might, therefore, be a task to monitor more closely than "Final formatting" which is not on the critical path.

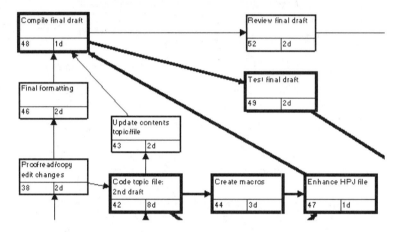

Figure 23.13. *Sample project flow chart (PERT).*

At A Glance Scheduling

✔   Basic schedule elements include a task list, time estimates, resources, and a timeline.

✔   Use the WinHelp Project template as a guide for creating your own schedule.

✔   Write tasks with specific outcomes that can be assigned to a single individual.

✔   Use the WinHelp Cost Estimating Worksheet to estimate task times.

✔   Assign tasks to team members and determine predecesessors to each task.

✔   Apply the task durations to a timeline. Use a scale suitable for the length of the project.

✔   Monitor the critical path to control completion dates

Controlling your production files

Almost every complex project requires orderly work habits and some kind of system for keeping track of the many files that are created before the final product is complete. This section suggests some procedures that are specific to managing a Windows Help development project.

As your Help development project grows in size, the number of files collecting in your project folder will increase. Unlike print material, which often consists of one document file, Help projects consist of a project file, one or more topic files, a contents file, a compiled Help file, and numerous graphic files. Furthermore, these files change frequently during production: text is added and modified; topics, jumps, pop-ups, and hypergraphics are coded; and context-sensitive links are defined. Consequently the same file may exist in several versions. Keeping track of these many files in their respective versions is a significant chore. There is potential for an editor to be working hard on an obsolete draft of a topic file or for an incorrect graphic to be added to the Help system. Without systematic work habits and a well thought-out system for version control, the problem of multiple files can plunge you into chaos.

This section focuses on:

- Tracking changes in content.

- Tracking changes in topic file elements.

- Tracking compiled Help files.

- Archiving files and backups.

At a Glance Controlling Production Files

> ✔ Use the Revision Marks feature of Microsoft Word and Help Workshop to assist in managing changes to your Help system content.
>
> ✔ Use Help Workshop, HULK, or a Help authoring tool to create a table of topic IDs, titles, keywords, and browse sequences.
>
> ✔ Use the title and copyright settings to label builds. Add a date stamp to the Help Version box.
>
> ✔ Estimate the value of your various files' production and replacement costs and devise a backup strategy to protect your investment.

Tracking changes in content

As the size of your Help project grows, so does the difficulty managing the changes in content. Each review and editing cycle generates numerous modifications to the text. If you have two or more writers working on one Help system, the pain of resolving changes becomes even more acute. If you are using Microsoft Word and the WinHelp 4 compiler, a good solution is to use "Revisions Marks."

The Revision Marks feature of Word places formatting attributes in your topic file when you enter changes. Text that you delete is displayed in strike-out text, new text is underlined. Different colors can be applied to tag changes from different authors. Figure 23.14 shows a topic which has been edited in Word with Revision Marks turned on. With Revision Marks, you can review the prospective changes without losing the sense of the original text.

Once the changes are approved, the Help compiler can automatically process the revision marks: strike-out text is deleted and underlined text is added. There is no trace of revision marks in the compiled Help file. Previous to WinHelp 4, developers would have to accept the marked changes in Word before compiling. To use the Revision Marks feature you need to enable settings in your topic and project files.

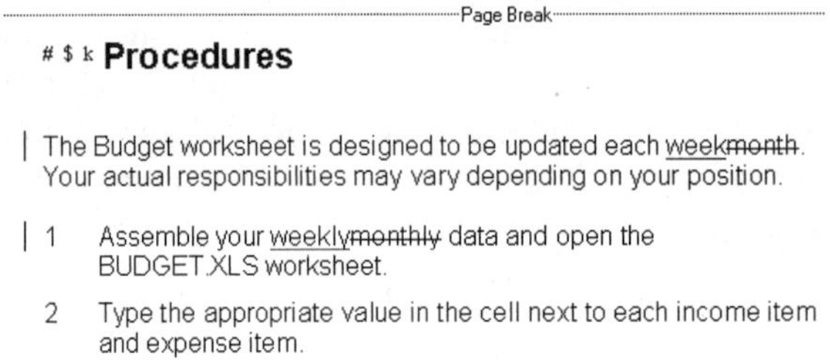

---Page Break--

$ k **Procedures**

| The Budget worksheet is designed to be updated each week~~month~~.
Your actual responsibilities may vary depending on your position.

| 1   Assemble your weekly~~monthly~~ data and open the
       BUDGET.XLS worksheet.

  2   Type the appropriate value in the cell next to each income item
       and expense item.

Figure 23.14. *Edits in a Word topic file with Revision Marks turned on.*

To apply revision marks in Word:

1. From the Tools menu, click Revisions. In the Revisions dialog box, select Mark Revisions. This turns on the revision-mark feature. It will stay in effect until you turn it off.

2. Make the changes to your topic file. By default, deleted text is lined out, and added text is underlined. All revisions are displayed in colored text.

To compile with revision marks:

1. Save the changes to your topic file in rich-text format (RTF).

2. Open the project file in Help Workshop.

3. Click the Files button, then click **Accept revision marks in topic files**. This is the equivalent of adding REVISIONS = YES to the [FILES] section of the project file.

4. Compile your project.

Tracking topic file elements

While the revision-marks procedure described in the previous section works well with the general content of your Help file, it is not appropriate for tracking changes to the hypertext elements of your topic file. These include jumps, pop-ups, macros, keywords, and other codes embedded in your topic file through footnotes or formatting. As your Help file grows in size, the management of these codes becomes just as difficult as that of the content.

For one thing, a typical Help file includes a number of elements that require references to each other: jumps, pop-ups, macros, and hotspot graphics all use references to topic IDs. When you're working with your topic file, it is often inconvenient to search for a topic in order to find the topic ID you want to refer to. Also, as your project grows in size or uses multiple authors, errors can occur due to duplicate topic IDs. Remember, topic IDs must be unique.

To remedy this problem, most authoring tools provide a facility for displaying existing topic IDs. If your authoring tool doesn't provide satisfactory results you can produce your own table of topic IDs as you develop your topic file. In its simplest form, such a table lists the topic titles and topic IDs. When you need to refer to a topic, you can look it up in this table by its topic title. You can also add keywords, browse sequences, and context-sensitive mappings to the table.

Here are some useful sources for generating various kinds of reports.

HULK reports

A free utility called HULK can generate a report from your topic file. HULK (Help UniversaL Kit), is a potpourri of tools for editing, testing, and compiling Help files. One of the features is a trio of reports that display the keywords, topic titles, or context strings (old terminology) residing in the topic files of a selected project. See Figure 23.15. These reports can be exported for use in a word processor or spreadsheet. Unfortunately HULK is an unsupported utility and the reporting is not very flexible or powerful. HULK was available on the Microsoft Developer's Network CD up through the July 95 issue. A new release will not be available until HULK has been updated to be compatible with Windows 95.

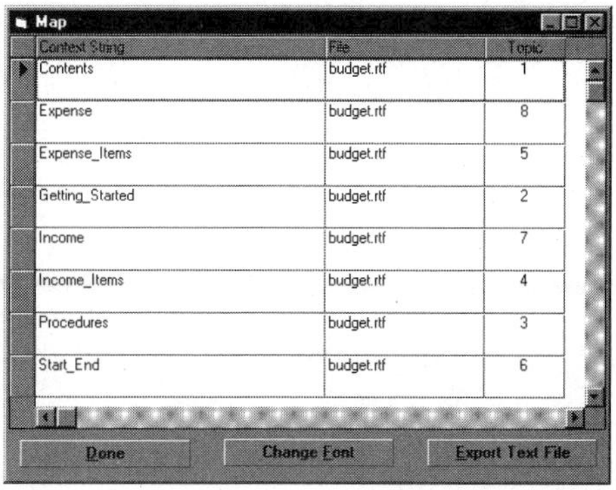

Figure 23.15. *A report of context strings generated by HULK.*

ForeHelp reports

A better solution is provided in the ForeHelp authoring tool, one of the tools reviewed in Chapter 22, *Help Authoring Tools*. Figure 23.16 shows a report, generated by ForeHelp, that includes the topic title, context string (topic ID), jumps available from each topic, and keywords associated with each topic. Many other report items are available. You select items to include in your report and the report is instantly generated.

Title	Context Strings	Jumps To	Keywords
Contents	Contents	Getting_Started Procedures Income_Items Expense_Items Start_End	contents menu
Expense	expense		
Expense Items	Expense_Items		expense items, expense
Getting Started	Getting_Started	Income_Items Expense_Items Start_End	overview introduction
IDH_CONTENTS	IDH_CONTENTS		
Income	income		
Income Items	Income_Items		income items, income
Starting/Ending Cash	Start_End		starting cash ending cash
Weekly Procedures	Procedures		procedures weekly procedures

Figure 23.16. *A ForeHelp project report.*

Help Workshop reports

Help Workshop provides six reporting options including lists of topic titles, keywords, and topic text. The report information is extracted by Help Workshop from a compiled Help file. The results are displayed in the Compilation window and saved to a text file. Unfortunately you can't generate a comprehensive report containing all of the option items. You need to combine the results of each report in a word processor or spreadsheet. Completely absent is a report that generates topic IDs.

To generate a report in Help Workshop:

1. From the File menu of Help Workshop, click Report. The Report box appears.

2. Specify the Help file you want a report for.

3. Specify a filename for the report.

4. Click a report option.

5. Click Report. The report appears in a compilation window and is saved as a text file.

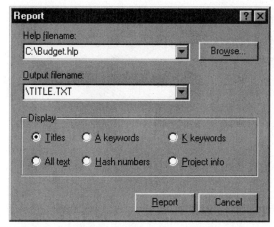

Figure 23.17. *Generating a report of topic titles with Help Workshop.*

Context-sensitive Help reports

If you are using context-sensitive Help, tracking context IDs is vital. Chapter 19, *Programming Calls to Help*, describes the process of "mapping." Briefly, mapping consists of assigning unique numbers, called context IDs, to the various topic IDs so that the application program can request specific Help topics. When mapping, the Help author must coordinate with the application programmer to establish the context IDs. A topic table is an excellent way to communicate with the programmer. The HULK and many other authoring tools can assist in creating topic tables.

Tracking compiled Help files

During the development of your Help application, you will compile numerous builds. Most of these builds will be made to fix various bugs that you encountered during testing. These interim builds have a short life span because you generally compile a new version that takes the place of the previous one. However, you will distribute certain builds of your Help to managers, reviewers, testers, proofreaders, and others involved with the Help project. These distributions are usually made at important milestones in the project, such as a beta test candidate. Because of these distributions, it is necessary to identify these builds so that you and others can quickly know what you are working with. You could always look at the date of the file, but that can be inconvenient, and the reviewer may not know what date to look for. A more handy way is to modify the Help title or the copyright for various drafts, or to modify both.

Figure 23.18 shows two separate Help builds, one overlaid on the other. One of the files is identified as version 0.3 and the other as 0.5. Chapter 18, *Creating the Project File*, describes how to modify the Help title. You can remove that version number and replace the actual Help file title in the final build.

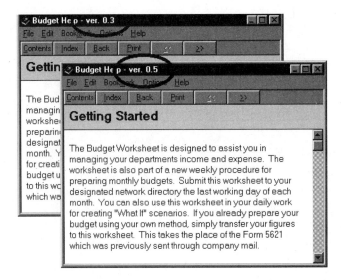

Figure 23.18. *Using titles for version control.*

The Copyright setting, also described in Chapter 18, allows you to identify the draft in the Version Information dialog box of the Help file. See Figure 23.19.

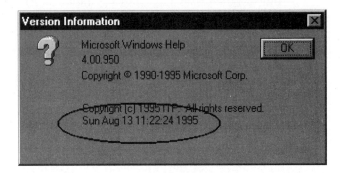

Figure 23.19. *A date stamp displayed in the Help/Version box .*

To date a build:

1. Open your project file in Help Workshop.

2. Click the Options button, then General.

3. In the **Display this text in the Version dialog box** box, type `%date` after any existing text. See Figure 23.20.

4. Compile the Help file. The date appears in the Version box on a separate line after any copyright text.

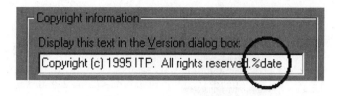

Figure 23.20. *Adding a date stamp to the Copyright setting.*

Archiving files and backups

An important aspect of version control is archiving and backing up files. As you produce subsequent drafts of your Help, the number of files will increase rapidly. Text documents, topic and project files, compiled Help files, bitmaps, hypergraphics, and other miscellaneous files—all parts of a Help project—will accumulate. The amount of time invested in developing most Help applications would suggest saving everything associated with the project. However, it may be a practical necessity to purge files that are of no further use on the project.

During the course of your Help development you will probably perform several, if not dozens, of builds. As you modify your Help system there will be changes to numerous files. To avoid errors and to protect your work, it is a good idea to devise a logical and workable system for naming and deleting files and folders.

Since there are so many different kinds of files in Help development, there are various considerations for forming a comprehensive backup plan. Table 23.1 shows some general principles:

Table 23.1. *Archiving and backing up your files*

File type	Considerations
Project file (.HPJ)	Required by the compiler. Generally, this file does not undergo frequent changes. Changes to the project file are often made by a single individual and therefore easy to track. In even the largest projects, this is a very small file which is easy to back up. Since it is a simple text file, the project file could be completely reconstructed in well under an hour. A print copy, often no more than one sheet, can be kept for quick reference.
Topic file(s) (.RTF)	Required by the compiler. These are the heart and soul of Help development and represent very great time and expense. Often over 50 percent of the labor in a Help project is reflected in the rich-text format topic files. The content frequently changes and those changes can be critical to the success of the Help file. Topic files most often reside in the project folder. However, it is common for topic files to be maintained by separate Help authors in various locations. In such cases, version control becomes very important. Extreme care needs to be taken to create a regular and frequent backup strategy.

Table 23.1. *(continued)*

File type	Considerations
Contents file(s) (.CNT)	An optional Help system element. The contents file, when used, must be distributed along with the compiled Help file. This file can be tedious to construct without a Help authoring tool. It may undergo frequent revisions due to the heavy inclusion of topic IDs, and should be backed up regularly. The contents file is often under the control of one person, but in the case of modular Help systems there may be several contents files maintained by separate individuals.
Full-text search file (.FTS, .FTG)	An optional Help system element. An extremely large file which may exceed the size of the Help file. Only the distributed version of the full-text search file is of any value and it can be easily reconstructed at any time. Old versions are of no use and can be freely deleted (if not already overwritten by new versions). Of more importance is to record the settings (on paper or in a note file) you use in creating the full-text search file, as those settings are easily forgotten. Note: you can provide full-text search functionality without shipping the full-text search file as described in Chapter 17, *Help Topic Access.*
Graphics files (.BMP, .WMF)	These files change infrequently, but the final versions should be zealously guarded. They often require significant time and expense to develop. Graphics are usually maintained in a folder separate from the project folder. Old versions of graphics are often discarded. However, be careful: it is not uncommon for a complicated graphic to be built in stages. The interim graphic files can be useful when updating or correcting graphics. **TIP** *While graphics files take up enormous amounts of storage space relative to text, they also compress significantly. Use a compression tool like WinZip to archive old or currently unused graphic files.*
Multimedia files (.WAV, .AVI)	The huge size of these files (10 MB for a 30-second video or 200K for a 10-second sound bite) almost requires their archival as soon as a project has been completed. Once rendered, these files rarely change and a single backup copy is usually sufficient. If custom-generated for a project, multimedia files can be expensive to replace. However, certain forms of multimedia, like sound clips, are accessed from a purchased CD-ROM and are readily available if replacement is necessary.

Table 23.1. *(continued)*

File type	Considerations
Help authoring files	Various Help authoring tools create files for their own use when working with your Help project. Generally these files are maintained by the authoring tool in the project folder. Their value varies depending on how often they are updated and the role they play in streamlining your Help development. You will usually want to make them part of a regular backup routine, but their loss is not generally critical. All the authoring tools create project and topic files, which should be preserved as described above.

At a Glance File Protection Value

File Type	Size	Replacement Cost	Changes
Project	Small	Low	Often
Topic	Small to very large	Extremely high	Continual
Contents	Small	Medium	Frequent
Full-text search	Large to very large	None	Not Applicable
Graphics	Large	Extremely high	Seldom
Multimedia	Very large	Depends on source	Seldom
Help authoring	Small to medium	Usually low	Continual

TIP *For easy, yet adequate protection of your production files, make copies of all the files used during compiling at each of the major milestone builds in your project. For example, after the first draft of your Help system you will have, at a minimum, a topic file and a project file. You may also have graphics and authoring tool files. Copy all of these files into a separate folder. Continue to copy important files into separate folders until your project is complete. Figure 23.21 shows a sample folder structure for the BUDGET Help project. The latest topic and project files reside in the BUDGET folder. Copies of those files as they existed at the time of version 0.3 and version 0.5 are saved in separate folders. If you encounter a build with a significant number of errors, you may want to refer to the files from a previous build.*

Figure 23.21. *Using folders to store copies of production file for interim builds.*

Glossary

action statement   The main part of a step. Consists of a command verb plus its object, for example: "Drag the icon." Often action statements include a modifier.

A-keyword   A type of keyword that enables you to create topic links using the **ALink** macro. A-keywords are added to a topic file using an uppercase A (A) footnote. Unlike K-keywords, A-keywords don't appear in the Index.

alpha software   A version of the software product which is not ready for release outside the company but which Help authors and others within the company can work with.

authorable button   A three-dimensional push button displayed in a Help topic. Authorable buttons are created using the **{button}** statement.

authoring tool   Software that automates the process of creating Help files. Most authoring tools either work with a word processor (such as Microsoft Word) or are standalone programs with built-in word processing capabilities (such as ForeHelp).

auto-sizing	The process by which a secondary Help window's height is automatically adjusted based on the length of the topic it displays.
baggage	Help's internal file system, used to store multimedia files. With the aid of a DLL, you can use baggage to store and retrieve any kind of file (which simplifies distribution and prevents the user from accidentally deleting a file).
base file	The master contents file in a family of Help files.
beta test	Rigorous testing of a software product which is close to completion. Beta testers are usually selected from people who currently own one or more of your products, based upon the hardware and software they use.
bitmap graphic	A file format that stores a graphic image as a collection of pixels. Bitmaps are usually created in a paint program and constitute one of the three main file formats used in Help (the other two are metafiles and hypergraphic files).
book icon	A symbol used in the Contents page of the Help Topics browser to represent a group of Help topics. Also used in Windows 95 to represent Help files and contents files.
branches of a hierarchy	The groups and subgroups that make up a hierarchy. Because hierarchies are often envisioned as trees, we say that a hierarchy is made up of branches. Large branches are divided into smaller branches. The trunk of this tree is called the "root."
browse sequences	Groups of Help topics that users can view in a sequence determined by the Help author. For example, a Help author might make a browse sequence for all the printing topics. When browse sequences have been implemented, users navigate through each sequence using the Next and Previous buttons on the button bar.
build	The process of compiling a help file; Help authors often use the term to refer to a compiled help file.
build tag	A topic footnote used to determine which topics are included when the compiler builds the Help file. Build tags use an asterisk (*) footnote marker.

coaches

A form of performance support Help (along with wizards). A coach consists of a series of Help topics that guide the user in performing tasks using the software product's regular interface. Cue cards are a form of coach Help used by Microsoft.

color depth

The number of colors in a graphic image. Color depth is often referred to as the number of bits per pixel; for example, a 256-color bitmap has a color depth of 8 bits.

command reference

Print documentation that describes the commands in a software product. A command reference is akin to the command topics in a Help system.

command topic

An explanation of a command and, when present, the elements of the command's dialog box. The function of command topics overlaps the function of What's This? Help topics.

compiler

A development tool used to build a binary file. Microsoft's Help compiler processes the project file to convert topic files, graphics, and other source files into a Help file that can be read by the WinHelp program.

compression

A method used to decrease the size of a file. The Help compiler provides several compression settings that can significantly reduce the size of the Help file. The greater the compression, the longer it takes to compile your file.

conceptual element

The component of procedure topics that directly follows the topic heading. The conceptual element explains the purpose of the procedure and any other important conceptual information. May be omitted when not needed.

condition

Conditions are special circumstances or problems that apply to some of the users of the software product and, if they apply, call for some action. For example: "If the edges of the scanned graphic are blurry, choose Sharpen Edges."

construction

The process of creating a compiled Help system that is ready to ship with a software product. Construction (or "implementation") includes coding a topic file, creating an .HPJ file, and compiling. Construction contrasts with design.

contents	The online table of contents, formatted as an expanding and collapsing list of Help topics. The contents appears on the Contents page of the Help Topics browser. The information displayed in the contents is specified in the contents file.
contents file	A text file with a .CNT file extension that provides the instructions for the Contents tab in the Help Topics browser. It can also be used to instruct WinHelp to merge the keywords of specified Help files on the Index and Find tabs.
contents topic	In a Help file without a contents file, the contents topic serves as the table of contents. The CONTENTS setting in the project file enables this feature.
context ID	A unique integer that is "mapped" to a topic ID in order to provide context-sensitive links between a Help file and a software program. Context IDs can be assigned by the software developer or the Help author, but they must be mutually agreed upon.
context sensitivity	The integration of the Help system and the software product. With context sensitivity the user can display a Help topic keyed to the particular part of the interface the user is currently working with.
control codes	Footnote markers (such as # $ K +), special statements (such as **{bmc sample.bmp}**), and text formatting (such as underline and hidden text) that appear in a topic file. Control codes are used by the Help compiler to build a Help file.
Cue Cards	A form of coach Help used by Microsoft.
debugging	The process of removing errors (or "bugs") from a Help system. Debugging involves analyzing compiler messages, modifying the project source files, and recompiling the project until there are no errors.
deep level reference	Detailed print documentation containing theory, technical notes, and other little used content.
demo (or tour)	A form of interactive computer documentation that teaches the user the main features of a product and, often, the basics of using it. Demos or tours resemble tutorials, but they are not interactive. The user simple watches them.

design	The process of planning the content, structure, and appearance of a Help system and then writing the content and creating the graphics. Design contrasts with construction.
diagnostic topic	One kind of troubleshooting Help topic. Diagnostic topics consist of lists of problems or symptoms encoded as hotspot text. Users navigate through one or more diagnostic topics in order to find the appropriate recommendation topic, the topic with the desired information.
direct object	A noun that follows the action verb and "receives" the action. For example, the sentence "Drag the icon" consists of an action verb followed by a direct object.
DLL	Dynamic Link Library, a type of Windows program. Functions stored in DLLs can be accessed by a Help file to perform special operations and extend the capabilities of WinHelp. DLLs have a .DLL file extension.
error message	A loose term for system message.
error message topic	A Help topic that is associated with a particular system message. An error message explains a problem or issue and makes clear either the corrective action that is required or the user's choices. Often, users click a Help button in the system message box to display the error message Help topic.
feedback statement	Feedback is information that lets the user know he or she has acted correctly and that the system has responded properly. Feedback statements provide feedback information and are sometimes used along with action statements in steps.
Find	The form of access to Help information that uses full-text search. Find appears on the Find page of the Help Topics browser.
full-text search	A form of information access in which a user can type in a word or phrase and find Help topics that contain that word or phrase.

gerund

A verb used as a noun. Always ends in "ing." Gerunds often have objects. The topic heading "Deleting files" consists of a gerund and its object. Gerunds are the traditional way of phrasing topic headings, entries in the contents, and many index entries. Now root forms and even infinitive forms are being used for topic headings and in the contents.

.GID file

An index file which provides the link between the Contents page of the Help Topics browser and a Help file. The index file is created the first time a Help file is launched and is marked with the hidden file attribute. The index file has a .GID file extension.

glossary topic

A single lengthy topic with an alphabetical list of all the pop-up definition topics in the Help system. Users can click entries on this list to display desired pop-up definitions.

graphic by reference

An alternative to pasting a graphic in a topic file. To place a graphic by reference, you type a statement such as **{bmc sample.bmp}** in a topic file. Placing a graphic by reference has several advantages; for example, only one copy of the image is stored in the Help file, regardless of the number of topics in which it appears.

graphics

Any picture or diagram that appears in a Help system. Many graphics are pictures ("screen captures") of the software product's interface. Graphics are often bitmaps. Graphics can be static (just ordinary pictures) or hotspot graphics—graphics that exhibit some special behavior when clicked. Video and animation are special multimedia graphics.

hard page break

Formatting used in a topic file to separate Help topics.

Help Author mode

A Help Workshop setting which allows a Help author to determine how a Help file is coded. This capability is useful for debugging a Help file.

Help Author's Guide

An online Help file published by Microsoft to document the Help compiler and Help Workshop. The *Help Author's Guide* contains two files: HCW.HLP and HCW.CNT.

Help button

A command button on a dialog box or system message box that, using context sensitivity, displays an associated Help topic.

Help file	A hypertext file created by processing topic files, graphics, and the project file using the Help compiler. Help files have an .HLP extension and are read by the WINHLP32.EXE application.
Help statement	Any of several statements included in a topic file. The main statements are: **{bmc}**, **{bml}**, and **{bmr}** to place a graphic image by reference; **{button}** to add an authorable button; and **{mci}** to play a multimedia file.
Help system	Online computer documentation optimized to support the user's ongoing work. A Help system includes all files distributed to the user (.HLP files, .CNT files, DLLs, and so forth).
Help topic	The basic unit of Help information. The kinds of Help topics in standard Help include procedure topics and command topics. In constructing a Help system, you create a Help topic by adding a hard page break to the topic file.
Help Topics browser	The main dialog box in WinHelp 4.0. It contains a Contents tab, an Index tab, and a Find tab, plus any custom tabs (created with a DLL). Also called the Help Topics dialog box.
Help viewer	A term referring to the software used to read Windows Help files. The WinHelp 4.0 viewer (or "engine") has the filename WINHLP32.EXE and is installed in the Windows directory as part of the Windows 95 or Windows NT 3.51 operating systems. See also *WinHelp*.
Help Workshop	A program from Microsoft used to create and edit project and contents files, and build and test Help files. Help Workshop uses the information in the project file to combine the topic files, graphics, and other sources into a Help file.
hierarchy	A form of organization that consists of groups (or branches) which are divided into subgroups.
Hotspot Editor	A program used to add multiple hotspots to a single graphic image. Also known as Segmented Hypergraphics Editor. The Hotspot Editor saves files using an .SHG file extension. The filename for the Hotspot Editor is SHED.EXE (or SHED2.EXE for version 2.0).

hotspot

An area of a Help topic that, when clicked, jumps to another topic, displays a pop-up topic, or runs one or more Help macros.

hypergraphic

A graphic that contains one or more hyperlinks (or "hotspots"). Hyperlinks can jump to other topics, display pop-ups, or run one or more Help macros. Hypergraphics are usually created in the Hotspot Editor and constitute one of the three main file formats used in Help (the other two are metafiles and bitmaps).

hyperlink

An area within a Help topic that jumps to another topic, displays a pop-up, or runs one or more Help macros. When the user moves the cursor over a hyperlink, it changes shape to represent a pointing hand.

hypertext

The electronic presentation of data—including text, graphics, and multimedia—that is linked together in a web that allows users to browse related topics in any order they choose. Windows Help is a hypertext system.

index

A list of entries (also called keywords) used to provide access to topics in a Help system. The index appears on the Index page in the Help Topics browser. You create index entries by adding K-keywords to the topic files.

index entry (or keyword) A word or phrase in the Help system's online index that the user can choose in order to display a Help topic that was assigned to that word or phrase. We use "index entry" when referring to the words and phrases the user sees in the index. We use "keyword" or "search keyword" to refer to these same words and phrases as they exist as footnotes in the topic file.

index file

A term referring to any of three different file types. Index files are associated with the contents file (.CNT), full-text search (.FTS) and the full-text search group (.FTG).

infinitive

A form of a verb consisting of its root form (the stripped down form) of a verb plus the preposition "to." For example: "To delete."

infinitive subheading

A phrase, usually boldfaced, that begins with the preposition "to" and directly precedes the steps in a procedure topic. Useful when two (or more) different procedures appear in one procedure topic. For example: "To move a picture or drawn object between pages."

information access   The means by which users find the Help information they need. WinHelp 4 has numerous forms of information access: contents, index, full-text search, jumps, browse sequences, back button, history button, bookmarks.

inline graphics   A graphic image that is pasted into a topic file, rather than placed by reference. Inline graphics frequently cause errors in Help files built using the WinHelp 3.1 compiler.

intelligent Help   A Help model that exists more as a concept than in reality. Intelligent Help monitors the user's actions and infers what the user is trying to do and what problems the user is having. Intelligent Help can also engage in a natural language dialog with the user. A natural language Help system functions like a patient human assistant.

interfile jump   A hyperlink that displays a topic contained in another Help file.

jump (hypertext jump)   A form of information access in which the user clicks a hotspot (or hyperlink) in one Help topic and thereby views another Help topic displayed in a main or secondary window.

keyboard shortcut topic   A list of keyboard combinations (and mouse actions) that enable users to work more quickly. (Not to be confused with *shortcut buttons*.)

keyword   A word or phrase associated with a topic, usually for indexing purposes. There are two types of keywords: K-keywords and A-keywords.

K-keyword   A word or phrase that appears as an index entry in a Help system. Keywords are added to a topic file using a K footnote.

layering   A technique in which users can choose different kinds and amounts of information. A jump to an overview topic is a kind of layering. Layering is an effective strategy to use in conjunction with minimalism. If the user wants more than minimalist documentation, layering provides it.

linking macros

One of two Help macros—**ALink** and **KLink**—that enable you to create dynamic hyperlinks to topics in other Help files. Links created using these macros are dynamically updated as Help files are added to or deleted from your Help system.

list topic

A topic consisting solely or primarily of jumps to other Help topics. List topics are an important form of navigation.

macros

Any of over 85 built-in WinHelp functions that enable you to control and customize Help functionality. Macros provide the ability to customize the Help interface, create hyperlinks, run external programs, and much more. If Help macros don't provide the functionality you're looking for, you can create a DLL.

main window

One of two window types used to display Help information. Unlike a secondary window, the main Help window has a menu and cannot be auto-sized.

map

A section of the project file used to link topic IDs to context IDs, which are required for building context-sensitive Help.

marker macros

Any of several Help macros that enable you to conditionally modify the Help interface or perform another action. These macros let you save a text marker, and then test whether or not the marker exists and perform an action depending on the result.

master file

A term used to refer to the main contents file in a family of contents files. The master file contains statements which link multiple Help files.

metafile

A graphics file with a .WMF file extension that stores a graphic image as a collection of geometric points and shapes. Vector graphics are usually created in a drawing program and are one of the three main file formats used in Help.

Microsoft Developer's Network

A subscription CD-ROM service that provides tools, utilities, and support for developing Windows software products.

MIDI file	An audio file composed of musical notes and other information necessary for a synthesizer (such as a sound card) to play a song. MIDI—which stands for "musical instrument digital interface"—controls which notes are played, the duration of each note, and the instrument used for each.
mid-topic jump	A special form of jump that is used in long topics. Mid-topic jumps do not display a new topic; they scroll the current topic so that the user views another part of that topic.
minimalism	A documentation strategy that stresses brevity and letting users exercise their own problem-solving abilities. See *Layering*.
modifier	Modifier of an action statement. A phrase or clause that adds extra meaning to an action statement. The prepositional phrase "From the Insert Menu" is a modifier that explains the location of the Date and Time command: "From the Insert Menu, choose Date and Time."
modular Help	A family of Help files that are linked together, primarily through the contents file and the linking macros. In a modular Help system, jumps created with linking macros and all of the items appearing in the Help Topics dialog box (that is, accessed using the Contents, Index, and Find tabs) create the appearance that all of the Help topics reside in a single Help file.
multimedia	The presentation of video sequences, animation sequences, and sound. Multimedia can be included in Help systems using such file formats as AVI and WAV.
multiple hotspot graphic	A graphics file containing more than one hotspot, each of which can jump to a different topic, display a pop-up, or run one or more Help macros. Sometimes called "segmented hypergraphics," multiple hotspot graphics are created using the Hotspot Editor.
multiple resolution bitmap	A file containing several bitmap images at different resolutions (such as EGA, VGA, and 8514). These files are created with the multiple resolution bitmap compiler and have an .MRB file extension.

nonscrolling region	A special area at the top of a Help topic displayed in WinHelp that remains in place when the rest of the topic scrolls. Often topic headings appear in nonscrolling areas.
note	A component of procedure topics and other topics. Contains information that does not fit comfortably in the rest of the topic. Often notes explain user options and conditions.
object	A word or phrase the completes the action of a verb. In the following example, "text file" is the object of the gerund "saving": Saving a text file. One kind of object is a direct object.
online	A general term referring to the electronic delivery of information on a computer. Online Help refers to information which supports a software application.
online tutorial	See *tutorial documentation*.
overview topic	A topic that provides the conceptual background for a group of related procedure topics—and possibly a related command topic as well. There is a jump from each of these topics to the overview topic. Sometimes, a single Help topic can have its own overview topic.
page icon	A symbol used in the Contents page of the Help Topics browser to represent a Help topic.
palette conflict	A problem that arises in 256-color mode when Windows tries to display two or more 256-color images that use palettes containing different colors. To correct the problem, you should edit the images so they use the same colors.
performance support	A model of Help that maintains a dialog with the user and walks the user step by step through tasks. Performance support Help is somewhat similar to tutorial documentation, except that users accomplish actual work. Performance support Help takes two different forms: wizards and coaches.
pictograph	A small graphic that conveys a specific word or idea. In Help, there may be a pictograph that that means "This is a command topic." The word "icon" is a rough synonym for pictograph.

pop-up definition topic   A brief explanation of an unfamiliar term that appears in a pop-up window.

pop-up window   A small window, without controls, that appears over but does not replace a main or secondary window. Often they are used to define unfamiliar terms. They appear when the user clicks hotspots that have been coded to display a pop-up window.

procedure topic   The most prevalent kind of topic in standard Help. Consists of a procedure or, possibly, several short procedures. A procedure briefly explains the purpose of a task and how to perform it. A procedure contains some or all of these components: topic heading, conceptual element, infinitive subheading, steps, and notes.

production files   See *source files*.

project file   A text file with an .HPJ file extension that directs the Help compiler to the files that should be processed and specifies the features to be added to the Help system.

prototype   A trial model of the finished product that the designer is willing to throw away. In Help, we prototype a small subset of the finished Help system—for example, all the topics that pertain to printing. The prototyped topics should be completely written and linked so that they can be meaningfully tested.

purpose   The main reason the user is performing a task. The goal or intended result of a task. Users need to understand the purpose before they will attempt to carry out a task.

purpose modifier   A modifier of the core sentence of a step that explains the purpose of that particular step.

qualified entry   When an index term is sufficiently broad that it has been assigned to many Help topics, it is desirable to logically divide it. For example, the broad entry "numbering" might be divided into "numbering footnotes," "numbering pages," and so forth. When we make such divisions, we are qualifying the index entry. When we qualify an entry, the qualifiers may appear as subentries or as main entries.

quick reference card   A very brief form of print documentation containing various kinds of shortcut information. Comparable to shortcut topics in Help.

quick start guides   A very brief form of print documentation that provide the absolute minimum amount of information necessary to get aggressive users up and running immediately.

recommendation topic   One kind of troubleshooting Help topic. Recommendation topics resemble procedure topics, but they explain how to solve a problem rather than how to perform a task. Users access recommendation topics by navigating through diagnostic topics.

resolution   A term used to measure the size or quality of an image or hardware device. For Help authors, resolution usually refers to the number of pixels on the screen (for example, a VGA monitor is 640 pixels wide by 480 pixels tall).

rich-text format (RTF)   The format used to create Help topic files. RTF files contain Help information and describe layout characteristics such as character and paragraph formatting, page dimensions, and so forth. Many programs can read and write RTF files as a means of exchanging information with other programs.

root form   The "stripped down" form of a verb. Roots often have objects. The topic heading "Delete files" consists of a root and its object. Root forms can be used as topic headings, as entries in the contents, and in many index entries.

rule (or score line)   A graphic element, a line. A layout device used to organize Help information. For example, tables often use rules.

screen region topic   A Help topic consisting largely of a graphic of a major component of the software product's user interface. Typically this graphic consists of multiple hotspots, each of which, when clicked, pops up an explanation of a particular element on the graphic.

SDK   Software Development Kit, a compiler and a variety of development tools used to build software. The Windows SDK (or WinSDK) is used to create Windows software programs.

search keyword   See *keyword*.

secondary result

A secondary result is a by-product of the main purpose of a procedure. A secondary result usually is routine, but can be harmful.

secondary window

Along with main windows, one of two types of windows used to display Help information. Unlike the main window, secondary windows do not have a menu and can be auto-sized. In WinHelp 3.x, secondary windows cannot include buttons.

Segmented Hypergraphics Editor

See *SHED*.

SHED

Segmented Hypergraphics Editor (more commonly known as the Hotspot Editor), a Microsoft utility that is used to create a multiple hotspot graphic. The filename is SHED.EXE or SHED2.EXE.

shortcut button

A button on a Help topic that a user clicks to perform an action in the software product's interface. Usually the user clicks a shortcut button to open a folder or dialog box where the user is supposed to perform some action. Not to be confused with keyboard shortcut topic.

shortcut topic

See *keyboard shortcut topic*.

single hotspot graphic

A graphic that contains one hotspot region encompassing the entire graphic. Single hotspot graphics are usually created using standard topic formatting. See *multiple hotspot graphic*.

source files

A term used to refer to all or some portion of the files used to create a Help system. Source files include topic files (.RTF), project files (.HPJ), contents files (.CNT), graphics files (.BMP, .SHG, and .WMF), and others.

special issue

An issue in Help that a relatively small number of users will care about. Special issues consist of little-used user options and rarely occurring conditions.

standard Help

The predominant model for Help systems. Standard Help systems serve a reference function and, like print books, contain a contents, index, and jumps (akin to cross references). What's This? Help can now be considered a part of standard Help. See also *performance support Help*.

step

A component of procedure topics. Consists of an action statement and, at times, a feedback statement.

subentry

An indented entry in an index that divides the main index entry into logical parts. Subentries in the online index function much like subentries in a print index.

system message

A message that the system displays to provide useful information, to ask the user to confirm an action, or to inform the user that an error has occurred. Because system messages are brief, system message boxes often include a Help command button that displays the relevant error message Help topic.

task orientation

A key principle in designing and writing Help and other documentation. The idea is that users want to accomplish work with software and do not care about the technology that underlies the software. Thus, we design Help topics around our user's backgrounds and jobs, reaching into their world as much as possible.

tip

A type of note in a Help topic that conveys a faster or more efficient way of doing something.

topic entry macro

A macro that runs when the user displays a Help topic. Topic entry macros are created using an exclamation mark (!) footnote marker.

topic file

A rich-text format file containing the Help content and various codes (such as footnotes or graphic statements) and formatting (such as underline and hidden text) recognized by the Help compiler. Topic files are usually created with a word processor or a standalone Help authoring tool.

topic footnote

Formatting used to define the attributes of a Help topic. The Help compiler recognizes nine footnotes; for example, a topic ID is specified using a pound sign (#) footnote marker, and an index keyword is specified using an uppercase K (K) footnote marker.

topic heading

The heading or title that the user sees at the top of a Help topic. See also *topic title*.

topic ID	A unique identifier that must be assigned to each topic in a Help system. Topic entry macros are created using a pound sign (#) footnote marker. Topic IDs are used throughout the topic file to create jumps, pop-ups, and other hypertext elements.
topic number	A unique number assigned by the Help compiler to each topic. Topic numbers are useful for debugging Help systems and appear in diagnostic messages.
topic title	The way in which the Help topic is identified in the Topics Found dialog box, the Find dialog box, the History List, and the Bookmark menu. The Help author assigns the topic title using the $ footnote. Not the same as the topic heading (a kind of title) that appears at the top of Help topics.
Topics Found dialog box	A list box that lets the user choose the Help topic he or she wishes to view. In the Index, a Topics Found dialog box is displayed when the user has chosen an index entry that is associated with multiple topics. In a Help topic, a Topics Found dialog box is displayed if the user chooses a related topic button coded with the **ALink** or **KLink** macros and if multiple topics have been associated with the macro.
transparent bitmap	A 16-color bitmap in which WinHelp replaces the white pixels with the color of the background of the current Help window. Transparent bitmaps are commonly used for displaying images that aren't rectangular (circles, squares, and so forth) against a colored window background.
troubleshooting topic	Help topics that enable a user to identify and address a problem. Usually these are problems which do not result in system messages but which are nonetheless problems from the user's point of view. There are two kinds of troubleshooting topics: diagnostic topics and recommendation topics.
tutorial documentation	Print or online documentation that enables the user to learn how to use the product but does not normally let the user accomplish actual work. Many users are unwilling to spend time with tutorials. See also *demo*.

untitled topics

Topics which have not been assigned a dollar sign ($) footnote. Titles are often omitted in definition topics which the Help author does not want displayed in a full-text search.

usability testing

The most important means of evaluating how successful your Help system will be. People resembling your intended users work with the software and your Help system and their performance and level of satisfaction are observed and recorded.

user option

A user option is a variation on the main purpose of a procedure. If the procedure deals with opening a file, a user option is opening the file in read only form.

user's guide

The most important piece of print documentation. It consists primarily of procedures.

vector graphic

A file format that stores a graphic image as a collection of geometric points and shapes. Vector graphics are usually created in a drawing program and constitute one of the three main file formats used in Help (the other two are bitmaps and hypergraphic files).

wave file

A waveform audio file containing digitally sampled sound clips. These files tend to be of very high quality, but are very large (even when compressed). Wave files have a .WAV file extension.

What's This? Help

A form of context-sensitive Help used widely in Windows 95 software programs. Similar to balloon Help on the Macintosh, What's This? Help displays a pop-up window when the user clicks the right mouse button over a certain dialog box control.

Win32s

A set of Windows system files that can be installed on a Windows 3.1 system to enable it to run 32-bit applications (including Help files built with the WinHelp 4 compiler).

window type

The name and properties that define a Help window. There are two window types—main and secondary. The main window type must be named "main." Secondary window types can be named by any string of up to eight characters the author chooses.

Windows Help application

The software (WinHlp32.EXE) which is shipped with every copy of Windows (and Windows NT) and displays or "runs" the Windows 95 Help systems we author. It resides in the Windows folder.

WinHelp

A term referring to the software used to read Windows Help files. The WinHelp 4 viewer (or "engine") has the filename WINHLP32.EXE and is installed in the Windows directory as part of the Windows 95 and Windows NT 3.51 operating systems. As a technical term it refers to one of the many Windows programming function calls.

WinSDK

The <u>Win</u>dows <u>S</u>oftware <u>D</u>evelopment <u>K</u>it, a compiler and various tools required to build Windows software programs. The WinSDK includes the Help compiler. Also the name of a CompuServe forum which includes a library of WinHelp files.

wizards

A form of performance support Help. Wizards allow the user to accomplish tasks by making choices in a series of wizard panels. The wizard is a substitute for the software product's regular interface.

Bibliography

Apple Computers. *Multimedia Demystified*. New York: Random House, 1995.

Boggan, Scott, Dave Farkas and Joe Welinske, *Developing Online Help for Windows*. Florence, KY: International Thomson Computer Press, 1993. (ISBN 85032-219-8)

Bonura, Larry. *The Art of Indexing*. New York: Wiley, 1994.

Burger, Jeff. *The Desktop Multimedia Bible*. Reading, MA: Addison-Wesley, 1993.

Carlisle, K. E. *Analyzing Jobs and Tasks*. Englewood Cliffs, NJ: Educational Technology Publications, 1986.

Carroll, John M. *The Nurnberg Funnel: Designing Minimalist Instruction for Practical Computer Skill*. Cambridge, MA: MIT Press, 1990.

Dumas, Joseph S. and Janice C. Redish. *A Practical Guide to Usability Testing*. Norwood, NJ: Ablex Pub. Corp., 1993.

Gery, Gloria, ed. *Performance Improvement Quarterly*, volume 8, no. 1 (1995), a special issue on electronic performance support systems.

Hackos, JoAnn T. *Managing Your Documentation Projects*. New York: Wiley, 1994.

Hoft, Nancy. *International Technical Communication*. New York: Wiley, 1995.

Holtzblatt, K. and H. Beyer. "Making Customer-Centered Design Work for Teams." *Communications of the ACM*, October 1993, 36 (10), pp. 93-103.

Horton, William K. *Designing and Writing Online Documentation: Hypermedia for Self-Supporting Products.* Second edition. New York: Wiley, 1994.

Horton, William K. *Illustrating Computer Documentation: The Art of Presenting Information Graphically on Paper and Online.* New York: Wiley, 1991.

Microsoft. *The Microsoft Publications Style Guide* (Version 1). Redmond, WA, 1991.

Microsoft. *The Windows Interface Guidelines for Software Design.* Redmond, WA, 1995.

Mischel, Jim. *The Developer's Guide to WinHelp.EXE.* New York: Wiley, 1994.

Price, Jonathan and Henry Korman. *How to Communicate Technical Information: A Handbook of Software and Hardware Documentation.* Redwood City, CA: Benjamin/Cummings, 1993.

Pruitt, Stephen. *Viewer How-To CD.* Corte Madera, CA: The Waite Group Press, 1994.

Rubin, Jeffrey. *Handbook of Usability Testing: How to Plan, Design, and Conduct Effective Tests.* New York: Wiley, 1994.

Rubinstein, R. and H. Hersh. *The Human Factor: Designing Computer Systems for People.* Burlington, MA: Digital Equipment Corporation, 1984.

Van der Meij, Hans M. and John M. Carroll, "Principles and Heuristics for Designing Minimalist Instruction," *Technical Communication* 42 (2), May 1995, pp. 243-261.

Wellisch, Hans. *Indexing from A to Z.* New York: H.W. Wilson, 1991.

Index

Working with the book disc

The CD-ROM disc that comes with this book contains over 80 MB of Help authoring software, including the MS Help compiler and Help Workshop. The software is arranged in three categories:

- Demonstrations of commercially available Help authoring products.

- Help authoring tools, including Help Workshop and compiler.

- Sample files associated with chapters of this book.

A master Help file, ROADMAP.HLP, is available to describe the contents of the CD and assist you with installation and launching of the various items. Some software requires using a setup program, some must be copied to your hard disk, and other software can be run from the CD.

To launch the Roadmap:

1. Insert the disc in your CD-ROM drive.

2. Double-click the My Computer icon on your desktop, then click the icon for your CD-ROM drive.

3. Double-click the Roadmap icon.

The Roadmap is a WinHelp 4 file. If you are not running Windows 95, you can view the CD-ROM listing in the PRINTALL.RTF document.

To install Help Workshop and compiler:

Help Workshop and the compiler are located in the \TOOLS\INSTALLED\MSTOOLS folder. We recommend you copy the files: HCW.EXE, HCRTF.EXE, HCW.HLP, HCW.CNT, and HWDLL.DLL to your hard disk. You can place them in any folder.